BREWING BEER IN THE BUCKEYE STATE, VOLUME I

A HISTORY OF THE BREWING INDUSTRY IN EASTERN OHIO

FROM 1808 TO 2004

ROBERT A. MUSSON, M.D.

Brewing Beer In The Buckeye State, Volume I
A History of the Brewing Industry in Eastern Ohio from 1808 to 2004

Copyright 2005, by Robert A. Musson, M.D.

Created by Zepp Publications, Medina, Ohio
Contact at: grossvater@zoominternet.net

All rights reserved. No part of this book or CD/DVD collection may be reproduced or utilized in any form or by any means, except for brief excerpts for the purpose of review, without permission in writing from the author. The information in this book may not be incorporated into any commercial program or other book, without written permission from the author.

ISBN #0-9668954-2-8

Library of Congress Control Number: 2005901032

Cover art created by the author

Printing and binding done by Indiana Publishing Company/Gazette Printers

This work was created in the United States of America.

TABLE OF CONTENTS

Introduction	5
Acknowledgements	7
What is a brewery?	10
Overview of the brewing industry in Ohio	14
The temperance movement in Ohio	22
Summary of eastern Ohio breweries	29
Top ten lists	50
Ashland County breweries	51
Ashtabula County breweries	52
Athens County breweries	56
Belmont County breweries	58
Carroll County breweries	66
Columbiana County breweries	67
Coshocton County breweries	74
Cuyahoga County breweries	76
Erie County breweries	169
Fairfield County breweries	181
Gallia County breweries	184
Guernsey County breweries	185
Hocking County breweries	187
Holmes County breweries	188
Huron County breweries	190
Jackson County breweries	194

Jefferson County breweries	195
Knox County breweries	202
Lake County breweries	204
Lawrence County breweries	207
Licking County breweries	211
Lorain County breweries	217
Mahoning County breweries	221
Medina County breweries	233
Meigs County breweries	234
Monroe County breweries	236
Morgan County breweries	237
Muskingum County breweries	238
Ottawa County breweries	245
Portage County breweries	247
Richland County breweries	249
Stark County breweries	255
Summit County breweries	276
Trumbull County breweries	296
Tuscarawas County breweries	298
Washington County breweries	309
Wayne County breweries	312
Appendix: Ohio U-Permit Numbers	316
Bibliography	318
Index	323
Dedication	342

INTRODUCTION

Welcome to the world of Ohio's brewery history! This book is meant for anyone with an interest in beer, brewing, local history (or history in general), advertising, architecture....or anyone who likes reading about the growth and development of an industry over nearly two centuries, and the people who made that growth happen....especially with some rags-to-riches stories of immigrants who came to America with only dreams and made fortunes through their hard work, innovation, and some luck (both good and bad) as well. In this modern era, it can be refreshing to remember why people have and continue to come to the United States to build new lives.

My interest in the brewing industry began nearly thirty years ago, when in the height of the "disco era", I began collecting beer cans at the age of thirteen, along with many of the other adolescent boys in my neighborhood in Akron, Ohio. At the time, our primary goal was to accumulate as many different cans as possible, although most of us knew or cared little about the companies or people that made the beer. In 1976, there were only four operating breweries in the state, and only one of those was nearby in Cleveland. Needless to say, there wasn't much of a local flavor to collecting at that time, and the focus was on national brand beers like Budweiser, Pabst, Schlitz, Miller, and Falstaff, or some of the small remaining local brands in neighboring Pennsylvania, such as Iron City, Stoney's, Rolling Rock, Koehler, etc.

At the beginning, I was only vaguely aware of the concept that breweries had previously existed in Akron and surrounding communities, mainly because my parents had memories of names like Burkhardt, Renner, Leisy, and Erin Brew. However, because those brands had disappeared from the landscape many years earlier, their cans and advertising were hard to come by, and on the rare occasion when they showed up outside, they were rusted nearly beyond recognition. When they showed up at flea markets, their prices were beyond what my lawn-mowing money could provide, and none of those brands ever showed up in my collection. Until.......

After several years of disinterest in can collecting in the early 1980s, I became interested again after finding a 1950s cone top can from Louisville, Ky. at an antique sale. Cone top cans had always been hard to come by, and were typically unaffordable when they did show up. For $15, however, my budget (now supplied by working as a restaurant busboy at the nearby mall) wasn't stretched too far, and I finally had one of these odd-shaped cans in my collection. That single event in February 1984 sparked a rebirth of my interest in can collecting, although I was now alone in my interest (at least locallly), as all of my friends had long since moved on to more typical hobbies and interests.

I soon passed the thousand can mark, accumulating cans from party stores and while on vacation, as well as at flea markets, etc. Within three years, the accumuating began to slow and I feared that my collecting days might again come to an end. Not wanting that to happen, I decided to invest $24 in a membership in the Beer Can Collectors of America (BCCA), an organization founded in St. Louis in 1970. This was a real turning point for me with the hobby, as I now was able to communicate with collectors all over the country, and even the entire world. The hobby in general was in a period of decline, but it was about to hit a phase of rapid regrowth, as others such as myself began to find their way back to a hobby that they had briefly enjoyed in their youth. The difference now was that they had jobs and more money available to invest in cans and other items that they found. Within a few months, my collection was growing at a rapid rate, eventually climbing to over 8,000 cans by the mid-1990s. Along the way I had found an interest in collecting some of the other items that were used to market beer, such as signs, bottles, matchbooks, can openers, etc. To further those interests, I joined the American Breweriana Association (ABA), the National Association of Breweriana Advertising (NABA), and the East Coast Breweriana Association (ECBA).

Along the way, I found myself collecting more items from defunct breweries, particularly in Ohio and Pennsylvania. One book that I found particularly helpful, *American Breweries*, was at the library and listed all of the known breweries that had existed in the country, going back to the 1600s. I decided to use this during a family vacation in Pennsylvania in 1994, looking for remains of breweries that might still be standing (although the majority were long gone). I had recently found a tray from a small brewery in Kittanning, PA., and was surprised that it did not appear in the book. Although I later found out that this omission had merely been an oversight, I decided to research the brewery at the Kittanning public library, and found quite a bit of information available in the old city directories. After I returned to Akron, I decided to do a bit of a search on the hometown breweries, and in November 1994, my researching officially began. History seemed like a treasure hunt, in the same way that beer cans had once been, and I was beginning to tire of having to keep up with all the new can labels that were appearing in the stores. This provided an alternate interest, and one that was considerably less expensive to pursue (at least at the start).

My focus was initially just on Akron breweries, although I began to find some interesting information on other companies in nearby cities as well. Going through old microfilm of newspapers at the library, I found a huge load of advertising from the region's breweries, beginning around 1900 and continuing into the 1950s. At one point, I found myself going back to the library as often as I could, sometimes spending as much as six hours at a time going through newspapers, making copies, and giving myself severe headaches. At that point, I began to think about writing an entire book on Akron's breweries. To that end, I also began taking photos of items from my collection as well as those of other collectors. All of this came together in 1997 with the self-publishing of my first book, *Brewing Beer In The Rubber City*. Selling a total of 500 copies, it didn't quite make the best-seller list, but it was a start. Looking back, I think of so many things that I could do now to make that book better, but even just seven years ago, computers did not have the abilities they do now, especially with color and graphics.

My interest in local history did not end there, as I soon found myself continuing to chase after the history of breweries in other nearby cities. The appearance of eBay and the overall evolution of the Internet around this time was a tremendous help in allowing me to communicate with other collectors and finding information and items that I would eventually use in the project. The end point of that project is the book/DVD you are reading. It has truly been a decade-long labor of love, but one that I have thoroughly enjoyed. My interest hasn't ended here, however, as I have already begun researching the breweries of western Ohio for a second volume of this project. I can only assume that it will be another several years before *Brewing Beer In The Buckeye State, Volume II* is available, but it will likely be produced in the same format as the current volume. Until that time, I hope you enjoy reading this book as much as I enjoyed writing it.

Cheers!

ACKNOWLEDGEMENTS

A project of this size and scope would never have come together if not for the support and assistance from a large number of people, and I would like to mention as many as possible:

My wife and best friend Jenny, who has slowly gained a greater appreciation of my hobby every year and has been amazingly supportive throughout the past decade. She continues to make me a better person every day.

My parents (see page 342), who were surprisingly supportive of my interest from the age of thirteen on. Trips to the Cleveland Stadium parking lot after Browns games to look for beer cans have not been forgotten, nor have the countless family vacations over the past 25 years that were planned around visiting brewery cities in Ohio, the East Coast, and the Midwest, nor the way they allowed me to hijack the basement of our home to house my ever-enlarging collection.

Jenny's parents, who have been supportive of my interest as well. As her father is a tireless collector of Civil War relics, he in particular understands my obsession.

Carl Miller, who got me interested in historical writing and whose book, *Breweries of Cleveland*, was a critical reference source for my section on that city. Carl gave me a great deal of help and suggestions, and made his huge wealth of research available to me. In addition, he wrote sections in this book on the breweries in Berea, Willoughby, Lorain, and Steubenville.

Bill Carlisle, collector extraordinaire, who never hesitated to allow me to photograph items in his huge collection, and who introduced me to many other collectors in the area through the years. Bill's ongoing enthusiasm for the subject of brewery history is hard to match.

Don Augenstein, who has also acquired an impressive collection of Ohio brewery items, and who has made all of his items available for photos. In addition, his very well-constructed web site, www.ohiobreweriana.com, has given my writings a much wider exposure than they would have had otherwise.

Larry and Amy Moore, who have also been gracious enough to allow me to photograph items in their home. In addition, their work in overseeing the local chapter of the BCCA (the Renner Old Oxford Chapter) has helped to maintain the collecting spirit in eastern Ohio and given many of us a forum to meet and exchange items, ideas, and good times.

Ken Bryson, who has allowed me on several occasions to photograph and scan some very fragile items from his extensive collection, as well as hooking me up with some very nice items for my own collection.

The staff of The Beer Institute in Washington, D.C., particularly Deona Smith, who allowed me full access to their collection of more than a century of brewing industry trade journals for copying and scanning. Much of the information and images contained in these many volumes is not available anywhere else and provides a unique aspect to this project.

Henry Timman, well-known historian of the Norwalk and Sandusky area, who provided me with a tremendous amount of information and some great images of the breweries in that region, including several breweries that had never before been documented.

Glenn Kuebeler, who allowed me to photograph many of the tremendous items in his collection relating to the Kuebeler-Stang and Cleveland & Sandusky Brewing Companies.

Art Distelrath, who wrote the section on the Consumers Brewing Co. of Ashtabula, and who allowed me to use several images of items from his collection.

Karen Davis, librarian of the Sylvester Memorial Wellston Public Library, who actually went to the trouble of taking numerous digital photos of the Wellston Brewing Co. plant prior to its demolition, just for my project. While I worked with many librarians around the state, Karen went above and beyond the "call of duty".

The late Ernie Oest, whose travels around the country in the 1950s allowed him to photograph many of the early breweries prior to their demolition. In a number of cases, Ernie's photos are the only ones known to exist for some of the smaller breweries in the state. In addition, many of the rare pre-Prohibition labels in this book originally passed through his hands. Every brewery historian and collector in the country owes "Uncle Ernie" a debt of gratitude for his having collected this information long before it was a popular or widespread hobby.

Bob Kay, the country's foremost beer label collector and historian, who has provided me with many labels for my collection and numerous scans of pre-Prohibition labels from his own collection for reproduction in this book.

John Phillips, owner of one of the finest collections of Ohio bottle labels, who went to the trouble of scanning and emailing numerous images of labels from his collection. In addition, his remarkable web site, at http://jophison.dynamiknet.com, documents an extensive collection of microbrewery labels from across the country.

Albert Doughty, Jr., who has thoroughly documented the breweries of the Ohio Valley, and whose research has uncovered some great images of the breweries in Belmont County, all of which he has graciously made available to me for this project.

Fred Miller of the Tuscarawas County Historical Society, who has made numerous photos available and who has sent me many clippings about local breweries over the past six years.

Bud Weber of the Stark County Historical Society, who also made numerous illustrations and pieces of information available to me.

Margie Vogt of the Massillon Museum, who also made numerous rare photos and information available to me.

The American Breweriana Association (www.americanbreweriana.org), and in particular Stan Galloway, for allowing me to use photographs from the group's magazine.

The American Truck Historical Society (www.aths.org), which maintains a huge library of truck photographs, many of which are pictured here.

The United States Library of Congress, which has detailed, scanned images of many century–old panoramic lithographs of various Ohio (and other state) cities available at its web site, at http://memory.loc.gov/ammem/pmhtml/panmap.html.

The eBay web site, as well as the Internet in general, for opening up the lines of communication between collectors all over the world. eBay is both loved and hated by various members of this hobby, but it has allowed me access to a lot of the unusual items that are pictured in this book, many of which have been buried for years, out of the hands of collectors.

Other individuals who have helped to provide me with items or information over the years include: Harry Andrist, Susan Appel, Mike Baker and Museum London, George Barone, Gary Bauer, Bob and Jeanette Bendula, Bob Bickford, Tim Botos, Scott Bristol, Timothy R. Brookes, Karen Bujak and all of the staff of the *Great Lakes Brewing News*, Tom Burkhardt, Randy Carlson, Kim Carpenter, Joe Crance, Mike Cunningham, Kami Dolney, marketing coordinator of the Great Lakes Brewing Co., Jeff and Debbie Dowers, Don Dzuro, Carl Thomas Engel, the staff of Enlarging Arts, Jody Farra, Tom Flerlage, Charlotte Frampton, Marvin Gardner, "BeerDave" Gausepohl, Bruce Gregg of the Beer Can Collectors of America, Irv and Greg Grossman, Chuck Henry, Dr. Tim Holian, Tom Hug, Don Johnston, Jack Kern, Chuck Knaack, Tom Leo, Jack and Dianne Linna, James Maitland, Norm Meier, Todd Milano, Robert Miller, Jeff Musser, George Mylander, the late Walt Neal, Glen Nekvasil, Ruth Neiman, Bob Newnham, Jim Nicholson, Janet Peat, Glen C. Phillips, John Phillips, Mark Price of the Akron *Beacon Journal*, Eric Princell, Bob and Mary Ann Renner, Charlie Renner, Phil Rickerd, Matt Russell, the late Bill Salk, Patricia Seitz, Dale E. Shaffer, Emmitt Shaffer, Erman Stapleton, John Steiner, Denver Stufflebeam, Bill Toohey, Andrew Venclauskas, Michael Weiss, Dale Van Wieren, Dr. Don Wild, Kevin Wise, and George Zurava. Also thanks to the National Association of Breweriana Advertising and the East Coast Breweriana Association. I can virtually guarantee that there are others whose names I have forgotten to list, but you know who you are and your assistance has been appreciated!

I would like to thank the staff of The Western Reserve Historical Society in Cleveland, especially Ann Sindelar, for access to their large photograph collection.

In addition, I would like to thank the staff of the Cleveland Public Library and the Cleveland State University Library. I would also like to thank the staff of the Sandusky Library and Follett House Museum in

Sandusky, the Edison Museum in Milan, the Milan-Berlin Public Library, the Lorain Public Library, the Norwalk Public Library, the Mahoning Valley Historical Society, the Public Library of Youngstown and Mahoning County, the Youngstown *Vindicator*, especially Neva Yaist, the Warren–Trumbull County Public Library, the Black River Historical Society, the Lorain Public Library, the Guernsey County District Public Library, the Muskingum County Library System, the Zanesville *Times Recorder*, the Akron-Summit County Public Library, the Summit County Historical Society, the Wayne County Public Library, the Mansfield-Richland County Public Library, the Mansfield *News Journal*, the Massillon Public Library, the Rodman Public Library in Alliance, the Canal Fulton Public Library, the Stark County District Library, the Ashtabula County District Library, the Washington County Public Library, the Briggs Lawrence County Public Library, the Bossard Memorial Library in Gallipolis, the Meigs County District Public Library, the Nelsonville Public Library, the Fairfield County District Library, the Newark Public Library, the Public Library of Mount Vernon and Knox County, the Holmes County District Public Library, the Coshocton Public Library, the Kate Love Simpson Morgan County Library, the Monroe County District Library, the Bellaire Public Library, the Martins Ferry Public Library, the Tuscarawas County Public Library, the Dover Public Library, the Public Library of Steubenville & Jefferson County, Leetonia Community Library, the Columbus Metropolitan Library, the Ohio Historical Society in Columbus and its Museum of Ceramics in East Liverpool, the East Liverpool Historical Society, and the Carnegie Public Library of East Liverpool. I would also like to thank the staff members of the county recorder's offices (where all deed records and transfers are located) in each of the counties I visited.

Thanks also to Michelle N. Barbieri and Shannon McCarthy of The Sanborn Library, LLC. It should be noted that all Sanborn Map© reprints less than seventy-five years old are copyrighted by the Sanborn Map Company, The Sanborn Library, LLC. All Rights Reserved. Sanborn Maps© have been reproduced with written permission from The Sanborn Library, LLC. All further reproductions are prohibited without prior written permission from The Sanborn Library, LLC. However, as of the time of publication of this book, any maps prior to 1930 are considered public domain.

And finally, thanks to you, the reader, for sharing my interest in brewing history.....Enjoy!

# *What Is A Brewery?*

Since a large portion of this book focuses on the individual breweries of eastern Ohio, it is fair to ask at the beginning, "What exactly is a brewery?" While the answer may seem obvious ("A place where beer is made"), a discussion of the subject may cover numerous aspects of a brewery's function. This book attempts to explain each brewery's operations from a personal standpoint (the people who owned the brewery and worked there), a historical standpoint, a commercial standpoint (including how its products were marketed and sold), and a functional (or mechanical) standpoint.

If one looks at the typical architectural layout of a turn-of-the-century brewing plant (and numerous ones remain standing throughout the state today), one quickly notes a consistent theme from one plant to another. With a few exceptions, most of the plants had a central (and often fairly ornate) brewhouse, generally four to six stories in height, with a series of other structures ranging from one to four stories in height making up the remainder of the complex. The consistency in the appearance of these structures was no coincidence, as this layout was used to maximize the efficiency of the brewing process. Earlier, smaller brewing plants were often a hodgepodge of buildings, built at different times as needed, and they gave the early breweries no clear visual identity (and were often very inefficient, with relatively small outputs). The industrial and mechanical revolutions of the late Nineteenth Century, and particularly the advent of mechanical refrigeration, changed all that, allowing the creation of a brewing process that would still be in effect a half-century later. Indeed, many of the breweries that were still doing business into the 1960s were using physical plants that had been built around the turn of the century.

The following are excerpts from an article, written by Fred Baumann, a noted brewery architect of the time, which appeared in *The Western Brewer* in 1879, and these give one a good sense of how the layout of the "modern" brewery came to exist:

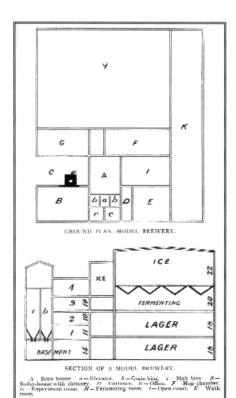

"A brewery is today, properly speaking, a sort of laboratory for the conversion of malt into beer. The process involves, as is well known, the following successive phases: First, the receiving and storing of the materials, malt, hops, and grain; second, the crushing of the malt (and grain, if such is used); third, the extraction of the wort from the crushed malt (and grain); fourth, the boiling of the wort; fifth, the cooling of the hot wort down to the most favorable temperature; sixth, the fermenting of the wort; seventh, the subsiding and storing of the beer, allowing it to continue fermenting.

[Regarding the arrangement] The above plan almost explains itself. Malt and grain are stored in the bins *c* and *b*. It is well to have two bins for each, to have it in hand to empty one bin wholly, and clean it, before touching the other, for it is a fact that the bottom contents of a bin are the last to flow through the spout. The elevator within *a* handles the stuff and puts it through the crushing mill placed on the fourth floor, whence it flows into the mash tub placed on the third floor. Hot and cold water are let into this mash tub from tanks placed on the floor above. The mash juice is let into the sud kettle placed on the second floor, wherein the wort is prepared in whatever manner preferred by the brewer. The boiled wort flows into a large settling tank, placed on the first floor, whence it is let over a Baudelot cooler placed in the basement. This cooler I would divide in two; the upper half to be fed with common water, in order to first reduce the rather hot wort to the ordinary temperature; the lower half to be fed with ice water, to produce the further cooling to the proper temperature.

The basement story further contains the engine, from two to four pumps, an air pump for the discharge of the beer from the lager vats, and a suction fan for ventilating the fermenting room. From the Baudelot the wort is directly pumped into a vessel placed over the fermenting vats and under the ceiling of the room, wherein it is again allowed to settle before being discharged into the fermenting vats.

The arrangement, as above proposed, is most saving in labor. The process is a continual one from the loft down to the basement, where the wort flows forth ready for the fermenting vats. One single lift puts it into these vats whence, again by its gravity, it is discharged into the larger vats. Since during the process each individual apparatus is employed for but three hours (more or less),

"Typical" brewery layout at the turn of the century [from *One Hundred Years of Brewing*]; Specific brewery diagrams are also shown in the sections on the Steuben Brewing Co. (Jefferson County) and Standard Brewing Co. (Cuyahoga County).

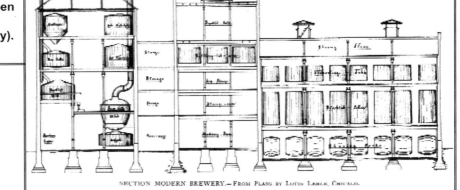

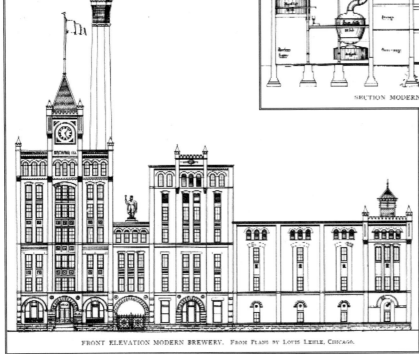

it is very feasible to continue working during day and night, making three suds [brews] in every twenty-four hours. By so doing, each apparatus need only have one-third the capacity of what would otherwise be required. The saving and convenience of this is very evident, though a widespread disbelief in nightwork exists for the present.

[Regarding construction] Filth and rot of any kind are the greatest enemies of the brewer. Cleanliness is his defense. Water flows in streams over floors, and dampness is the result, creating rot in wood. Though wooden floors may be covered with cement, such covering has never been tight: the water oozes through, attacking the boards and floor beams. Vermin and hosts of deleterious fungi are the result, affecting the taste and durability of the beer. Wood, therefore, should not be employed in the construction of a model brewery.

The walls, built of hard common bricks, I propose to line on the inside face with hollow bricks, say three inches thick, and paint with asbestos paint [!!]. This lining, if well done, prevents any wind from blowing through the walls, and affords a perfect insulation, by dint of the confined air within the hollow spaces. The smoothness of the inside face of the walls affords no hold for dirt and fungi, and is most readily kept clean. No other insulation, no wood lining, is needed for the malt and grain bins.

The floors I propose to construct of iron beams with brick arches spanned from beam to beam. This affords the best foundation for a cement floor, which should be of the best Portland cement, even and as smooth as possible, graded and guttered so as to allow washing by means of streams of water. The ceiling should be treated the same as the inside face of side walls. Windows may be made very light, of iron, though pitch pine wood is very acceptable. Stairways I should avoid altogether. Beside a platform elevator, communicating from cellar to garret, I would arrange iron ladders against the walls with rubber lining to their bars."

Aside from the technical aspects of the plant, the construction of a new brewery at the turn of the century was a big deal for most cities, both large and small. Like any factory, the construction of a brewery represented both new jobs and a source of tax income for a community. Most communities took great pride in their breweries, and their grand openings were often significant events with hundreds of people attending and drinking beer into the night. Local newspaper articles often reported the events and gave detailed descriptions of the plants.

In the 1870s and 1880s, the first of the large modern-style breweries began to appear in Ohio, particularly in Cleveland (Schlather, Leisy, Gehring), Cincinnati (Moerlein, Windisch-Muhlhauser, Hauck, and numerous others), and Columbus (Hoster). While the layouts of these plants were impressive enough, their appearance on the outside was even more striking, with architectural features that gave each plant a unique identity that would associate it with the brewer who had paid for it and approved its design. Virtually all of these were German immigrants, many of whom had come to America with nothing and were now celebrating their success with the creation of structures that often reminded one of the ornate buildings seen in Europe.

By 1900, the uniqueness of brewery architecture had begun to give way to more practical concerns, and the appearance of most brewing plants began to have a certain consistency from one city to another. This was also partly due to the fact that new breweries at that time were built by stock companies, consisting of numerous investors who were not immigrants, and who were more interested in making money than spending it on expensive architectural features. As the years passed, this trend accelerated: The few breweries that began operation from scratch after Prohibition's end (Schoenling and Delatron in Cincinnati; Youngstown, Akron, and Canton Brewing Companies; Franklin in Columbus, etc.) generally operated out of converted warehouses or older factories that were remarkable only for their total lack of architectural beauty.

While breweries represented employment for men in the community, they also were dangerous places, like virtually all industrial sites of the late 1800s and early 1900s. While considerably less dangerous than coal mines or steel mills, breweries were still the scenes of numerous injuries and even deaths in the early days. Certainly many of the injuries, especially minor ones, were never mentioned in the news, but the following passages give accounts of some of the various events that took place:

[from *The Western Brewer*, December 15, 1877] The explosion of a large beer hogshead took place at Hoster's brewery Saturday evening, by which Matthias Baumaister, an employee at the brewery, was so seriously injured that he died shortly afterward. He, with another man, was engaged in lining the hogshead with pitch, a process which requires some care on the part of workmen in order that there may no danger result. The pitch was heated as usual in a thin fluid state, when the plugs were inserted and the hogshead rolled about in order to distribute the substance over the interior and in the crevices. After the hogshead has been rolled about for some time the pitch becomes thick and that portion which does not adhere to the inside runs slowly through the bung. In order to expedite matters in this regard, a cone-shaped iron bar is heated to a moderate degree and inserted in the bung, for the purpose of keeping it open that the pitch may be in a condition to run out of it faster.

Contrary to oft-repeated cautions on the part of the proprietors, and with a carelessness which was more the outgrowth of a long experience than anything else, Baumaister thrust the iron bar into the bung after it had become too hot for the purpose. The result was that the pitch was immediately set on fire and the gas generated rapidly. One of the men heard the crackling of the fire, and immediately hastened out of danger, warning Baumaister that an explosion was imminent, but the latter only smiled and muttered something about there being no danger. However, he pulled the bar out and stepped around in front of the hogshead. Scarcely had he done so, when there was a terrific explosion, and he was struck by flying pieces of heavy wood and hurled violently several yards distant.

The terrific force exerted by the explosion was something wonderful. The heavy, strong material of the hogshead was fairly torn into splinters, and exerted itself with considerable damage against different parts of the building. One large piece of wood was thrown about one hundred feet through the window of the brewery.

The injured man was picked up in an unconscious state, and taken to his home on Mohawk Street, where physicians were summoned, and found that his ribs were crushed in over the heart, the left elbow broken, besides serious injuries which appeared on his head. Baumaister only lived a short time, and is supposed to have died from the effects of internal injuries.

[from the *Tuscarawas Advocate*, February 9, 1899] John Seibold, son of Mike Seibold, proprietor of the New Philadelphia Brewery, narrowly escaped suffocation at the brewery last Thursday evening. He had gone into one of the big vats to varnish the sides and bottom and remained too long in the necessarily poison-laden air. The carbonic acid gas combined with the odor of the varnish brought about a depression in the circulation of young Seibold and he was taken from the vat in bad condition. Restoratives were promptly given him and a doctor called. In a few hours he was out of danger and subsequently recovered.

[from *The Western Brewer*, November 15, 1883] A singular accident happened at 9 o'clock on the night of the 14th ult. in Moerlein's brewery, Cincinnati. Through some carelessness of the engineer in charge, a condenser in a huge ice machine containing several hundred gallons of ammonia burst with a great report, doing some damage and causing a fire alarm to be turned in. The fumes, however, rose in a great white cloud, and in a few minutes had permeated the entire neighborhood, driving people out of their rooms for quite a distance in hot haste. One man in the brewery was rendered insensible, but afterward recovered. The white cloud rolled into the street and nearly prostrated car drivers and passengers on the line near. The stables were directly adjoining the building containing the condenser, and all the fine horses in the stalls were killed by the fumes before they could be reached and liberated, it being impossible to enter the stable for some time.

[from *The Western Brewer*, January 15, 1881] Geo. Donnenwirth, Jr., proprietor of the Bucyrus brewery, at Bucyrus, Ohio, while superintending the cutting of ice on December 20, fell, striking on his head and shoulders, and suffered a slight fracture of the skull.

[from *The Western Brewer*] An obituary notice on the death of Jacob Halm, proprietor of the Fountain City Brewery, Bryan, Ohio, who was killed April 7, 1883, by being accidentally caught in the machinery at his plant when it was starting up.

Similar accidents happened in other breweries, some more commonly than others. Ammonia leaks from ice machines were a common problem, and significant leaks also occurred at the Becker brewery in Lancaster and the Union Brewing Co. in Canton. Fires were probably the single greatest threat to a brewery's existence, especially in the 1800s, when roofs and many of the internal structures were still made of wood. Hot cinders could land on the roof from the brewery's own smokestack or a passing train, and within minutes much of the structure would be ablaze. The Renner brewery in Akron was struck by fire on three different occasions: the first, in 1873, leveled the existing wooden structures, after which it was rebuilt with brick. The following two fires damaged the inside of the plant, but repairs were made and the building remains standing to this day. Fires were also reported at Akron's Burkhardt brewery (on two different occasions) and the Union brewery in Canton, and fires destroyed the Younghans brewery in Lancaster, Peter Rich's small brewery in Sterling, both the Kuebeler and Stang breweries in Sandusky, the City Brewery in Tiffin, the large nine-story malt house of the Weber brewery in Cincinnati (which began when a Roman candle flame from a July 4th, 1887 celebration landed on the roof, soon engulfing the entire building in flame and eventually leveling it), the Oppmann brewery in Cleveland (also destroyed by July 4th pyrotechnics just two years later), the Ives brewery in Cleveland (a victim of arson, when the brewery was torched by a Confederate sympathizer near the end of the Civil War), the Renner brewery in Youngstown (destroyed after a boiler exploded, decapitating the plant engineer and sending boiler parts across the river, several hundred feet away, and setting the plant ablaze), and a portion of the Lorain Brewing Co. plant (that and the Stang brewery fires were started by cinders from passing trains).

Other dangers were present as well: the malt house of the Hughes brewery in Cleveland collapsed in 1868 under the weight of 12,000 bushels of grain stored inside; Akron's Burkhardt brewery was severely damaged by a tornado in 1890, and Cleveland's Leisy brewery sustained significant damage from a windstorm some years later; Christian Achauer of Zanesville's Washington brewery was killed when he fell through a trap door in a gangway in the upper floors of his brewery, as he was attempting to close windows to protect against an oncoming storm.

In addition to the physical dangers listed was the risk of financial ruin, especially for smaller brewers who did not incorporate their breweries. In the days before mechanical refrigeration, the only source of ice for a brewery that was not near a river or lake was a man-made ice pond. Ice would be cut from here and used to cool the beer as it was being stored and lagered. If the winter was not cold enough to freeze a significant amount of ice, however, this stored beer might be ruined. This happened in the winter of 1890, the warmest of the past century, when insufficient ice production caused several smaller brewers to go bankrupt, including George Dilger of Louisville (who continued to battle financial problems until committing suicide in 1905) and Frederick Weis of the Wooster brewery. If a brewer had insurance against any of these threats, he could usually recover in a reasonable amount of time. If not, he would likely be forced into bankruptcy.

After the appearance of the brewery workers' unions in the late 1800s, some of the working conditions improved, decreasing the health risks somewhat. Further improvements in technology helped as well, and after the brewing industry fired up again after the end of Prohibition, reports of deaths and serious injuries became dramatically less common. In modern times, the presence of OSHA, the government agency overseeing worker safety, has further forced employers to create safeguards against employee injuries, primarily through education. None of that was likely a century earlier, when many of the brewery employees were immigrants who spoke little or no English and were often illiterate.

The modern brewery is a wonder of technological advancement. While there are far fewer new breweries in the United States now than there were a century earlier, the ones that are still operating are generally very streamlined and monitored by computers, such that millions of barrels of beer can be produced each year with a minimal number of actual employees. This is especially true of the large national brewers such as Anheuser-Busch (whose brewery in Columbus was opened in 1968, and then modernized and enlarged in the 1990s), and Miller (whose brewery in Trenton, north of Cincinnati, opened in 1991 and remains the state's largest). At the other end of the spectrum are the microbreweries and brewpubs, which produce a few hundred or a few thousand barrels per year, using a handful of staff. Both small and large breweries are generally clean, bright facilities which are very safe for workers, in stark contrast to the dark and dangerous plants of the past.

Breweries will likely continue to be an important part of the landscape for a long time into the future, as drinking the unofficial national beverage continues to be a significant aspect of the American way of life.

An Overview of the Brewing Industry in Ohio

The brewing of beer, like other spirits, is well-documented as having begun in the earliest days of recorded civilizations, thousands of years ago, although brewing in some form was likely taking place even earlier than that. Beer in various forms (or similar beverages) was popular in nearly every culture, not just for its inebriating effects, but also because of the nature of its production, which involved the boiling of ingredients prior to fermentation, in which alcohol was created. The combination assured that all potentially harmful bacteria were killed off, making the brew safe for drinking, while the water sources in many areas were not known to be pure. This was especially true for explorers and settlers in new lands, where local water quality was often questionable.

Brewing spread to Europe and continued throughout the Middle Ages, when the gradual colonization of America began. Europeans, from Christopher Columbus to the Pilgrims, crossed the Atlantic to explore and live in the New World, and in many cases, large amounts of beer and/or ale were brought for the long journey across the ocean. Once here, ale and beer appear to have been brewed domestically for consumption in the small individual colonies, as far back as the first English-speaking colony at Roanoke Island, N.C. in 1585. Based on a letter written several years after this by Thomas Hariot, one of the survivors of this original colony, a type of ale was made there using "mayze", or corn: "Wee made of the same in the countrey some mault, whereof was brued as good ale as was to be desired. So, likewise, by the help of hops, thereof may bee made as good beere."

The first commercial brewery in the New World is generally accepted to have been in New Amsterdam (on Manhattan Island, New York City), where Adrian Block and Hans Christiansen established a business in 1612 (this brewery was also the site of the birth two years later of Jean Vigne, the first non-Native American to be born in New York. Vigne grew up to be a brewer himself). As the city enlarged, more breweries followed, and they also began appearing in other large cities such as Boston and especially Philadelphia (where nearly 400 brewing operations are known to have existed throughout its history). The initial colonial brewers generally operated on a fairly small scale, although by the 1700s, several large-scale breweries were already in existence.

At the same time, settlers had begun moving west, beyond the Appalachian mountains, and small settlements began to appear along major rivers such as the Ohio. A small brewery was established around 1765 by the British army near Fort Pitt, at the center of what is now Pittsburgh, and it is certain that many early settlers west of this were brewing ale or beer for themselves or for tavern use soon afterwards. It was several decades later, however, before a commercial brewing operation was established in the territory that would become the state of Ohio in 1803.

Ohio's first brewery is a subject of some debate. Surely many domestic "home brewing" operations [for the purpose of this book, that would be a brewer producing less than 100 barrels annually on average, whether or not the beer was sold commercially] existed among the earliest settlers, but the state's first commercial brewer of any significance remains unclear. The first brewer in the eastern half of the state is thought to be George Painter of Zanesville [see Muskingum County], who commenced brewing in 1807 or 1808, depending on the source of information (and the accuracy of those sources). In Cincinnati, much has been written about the town's early days, although much of the information regarding breweries is conflicting. While one early summary of the town's commercial enterprises states that two unnamed brewers existed there as early as 1805 (and it is unknown whether those were home brewers or commercial), it is stated in *Cincinnati Breweries*, by Robert J. Wimberg, that James Dover started the city's first brewery in 1806. However, according to *Over The Barrel*, by Timothy J. Holian, it was not until 1811 that Davis Embree opened the city's first well-documented brewery. Suffice to say, it was within five years of Ohio's statehood that commercial brewing had commenced. According to *One Hundred Years of Brewing*, the state had thirteen brewers by 1809-1810, but the size and extent of these early enterprises remains a mystery, not to mention their exact locations.

Many more breweries followed, with most of the earliest ones being along major roads or waterways. By 1820, nine breweries had opened in the eastern half of the state [see the Top Ten Lists section], and a total of five had opened in Cincinnati. Ultimately, Cincinnati would have more than any other city in Ohio, with nearly one hundred operating through the years (while nearly five hundred breweries are known to have operated throughout the state in its two centuries of existence). Of the nine breweries in the east, most were relatively small operations which lasted a few years, and only one, the Zoar community brewery in Tuscarawas County, was operated on a relatively large scale, staying in business nearly to the end of the century.

The products of these earliest breweries were generally varieties of beer, ale, porter, and stout, as these were the typical malt beverages of the English-speaking culture that settled Ohio. The word *beer* is actually a generic term which can refer to a wide variety of beverages made from the fermentation of the extract of malted grain [a good visual description of the brewing process can be found on page 147, in the section on the Carling Brewing Co. (Cuyahoga County)]. The grain used for malting is most commonly barley, but others, such as corn, rice, and wheat, can be used as well.

While the terms *beer* and *ale* have often been used interchangeably through the years, ale specifically refers to a brew which is top-fermented and is somewhat heavier and more bitter than beer. *Ale* traditionally did not contain hops for flavoring until the mid-1800s, after which hops were frequently used in varying quantities. English and Canadian ales tend to retain much of their original properties to this day, while many Americanized ales have evolved into brews which are much closer to lager beer in flavor. *Pale, light, brown*, and *amber* ales are so named because of their color, which depends on the type and amount of grains used. *Stock ale* is an older, pre-Prohibition style ale which has a heavier malty flavor, and which is often aged longer for a secondary fermentation, giving it a sort of fine wine taste in some cases. *Cream ale* is more difficult to define, as it can refer to a number of different brews, although it first appeared in North America. In general, it is a light-bodied ale, sometimes a mixture of ale and lager, which is cold aged like lager beer. It has a smooth and mildly hoppy flavor with a fluffy head, and the term "cream" is used to denote good taste. *Strong ale* usually has a stronger taste, and in most cases carries a higher alcohol content. *Porter* is generally darker and heavier than ale due to the use of black or chocolate roasted malts, and its flavor can range from sweet to dry and bitter. *Stout* uses unroasted barley malts, is the darkest brew, black in color, and is generally heavily hopped, giving it a bitter taste, although some variations, such as cream stouts, actually have a somewhat sweet taste. Ireland's Guinness Stout is the world's best known variety of this. *Bitter ale* is a golden draft ale with a strong hoppy flavor, and it is far more popular in England (especially in pubs) than in America.

Among the beers available in America's early days, the variations were generally based on alcohol content. *Strong beer* had the highest alcohol content and the strongest taste, usually due to a longer time of boiling the malt in the brewing process. As a result, it would keep for a much longer period of time, making it ideal for use on ships, or for storage in cellars like wine. *Table beer* and small beer generally had a very low alcohol content and were meant to be consumed almost immediately after being brewed, as they would spoil more quickly. The term *small beer* actually refers to a number of different brews, some of which have almost no alcohol (similar to modern near beers). While not common today, some small beers were made by running water through the mash after the first batch of liquid wort has been extracted for brewing. The second brew is naturally much thinner and weaker, and it produces much less alcohol in the fermentation process. Some early small beers were entirely non-alcoholic and were sold purely as soft drinks. The term *common beer* is a generic term used to describe any of these early beers, often made in a rural or home-brewing setup, with minimal or no aging, and with no unique flavoring ingredients, to be sold immediately on draft at a local tavern. Common beer was seen purely as an alcoholic thirst quencher, while many of the more complex ales and beers were to be appreciated by more refined taste buds, similar to fine wines.

By the 1850s, Ohio (and the rest of the country) was beginning to have progressively larger numbers of German immigrants, mainly due to political instability and wars in Germany. With this came a revolution of sorts in the American brewing industry, as the Germans brought with them the concept of lager beer. Lager beer differed from ale in that it was bottom-fermented, and differed from common beer in that it required aging, usually several months worth (*lagern* means "to store" in German). The end result was worth the trouble, however, as lager beer proved to be far more popular in the long run, and varieties of lager beer continue to dominate the

American beer market to this day. The aging process required that the beer be stored in a cool environment, and in the earliest days, this was usually accomplished through the use of underground caves or stone-lined cellars, which allowed a constant temperature throughout the year. Lager beers were often classified by the styles and recipes that were made popular in different European cities, so that Munchner beer came from Munich, Germany; Wurzburger came from Wurzburg, Germany; Pilsener came from Pilsn, Czechoslavakia; Budweiser (a term used by many brewers prior to Prohibition, it has since been trademarked by Anheuser-Busch) came from Budweis, Czechoslavakia, and so on. Many brewers in the early 1900s brewed several of these varieties, although the Pilsener style had become the most dominant by the 1950s.

As late as the 1870s, most breweries in the region were relatively small, one- or two-story wood frame structures, containing a single brew kettle which could turn out a few thousand (or in many cases, a few hundred) barrels of beer per year. However, by 1874, twenty-three brewers in the state were producing 10,000 barrels or more annually, fourteen of which were in Cincinnati (including the state's largest brewery, that of Christian Moerlein). As breweries enlarged and outputs increased toward the end of the Nineteenth Century, underground caves and cellars became less and less practical, forcing brewers to build larger above-ground buildings to hold beer cellars for the aging process. The invention of mechanical refrigeration and ice production around the same time made this process much more efficient, allowing the cellars to maintain a constant temperature. The influx of immigrants from a wide variety of countries, mostly European, continued in large numbers over the following fifty years, and this was a large source of the increasing demand for lager beer. As a result, ale gradually lost favor, and by 1910 a scant few exclusive ale breweries remained in the state. Many of the lager beer breweries produced ale, but in most cases its sales accounted for a relatively small portion of a company's overall revenue.

Many new breweries began to appear in Ohio from the 1850s on, and most that appeared over the next thirty years were primarily lager beer breweries, operated by first generation German immigrants. Many of these immigrants had come to America at an early age, perhaps in their teens, and had often worked in numerous cities around the country, learning the intricasies of the art of brewing, before settling in one particular town to establish or purchase a long-running brewery of their own. While not all were successful, there were many who, through hard work, dedication, and persistence, saw tremendous success with their beers and as a result became tremendously wealthy. In several cities, large and architecturally impressive mansions still stand today that housed these wealthy brewers and their families at the turn of the century. Many of these brewers, such as Cleveland's Otto Leisy and Leonhard Schlather, were tremendously charitable as well and gave much back to the cities that helped them to gather their wealth. Few examples better illustrate the "rags-to-riches" story so characteristic of the American Dream.

The late 1800s saw a continued increase in German, Irish, and Bohemian (Czechoslavakian) immigrants, all of whom viewed lager beer as a major part of their culture. While this was a boon to the brewers, many of whom expanded their plants frequently to keep up with demand, it also led to many public displays of drunkenness, leading eventually to the Temperance movement, whose ultimate goal was the eradication of alcohol throughout the country (see the section on the Temperance movement in Ohio). Brewery expansions became commonplace, as many of these facilities went from two-story wooden frame structures to four- or five-story brick structures, with architectural features that were nothing short of stunning (for one of the best examples, see the Schlather Brewing Co., Cuyahoga County). By 1894, sixty brewers in Ohio were producing 10,000 barrels annually, with leader Christian Moerlein producing nearly 250,000 barrels alone.

As the market became more congested with brewers, competition naturally became a factor. Many of the early German immigrant brewers maintained friendly com-

Cleveland *Anzeiger* (the German-language newspaper), July 30, 1872, advertising breweries in Cleveland and Cincinnati to an increasing number of German immigrants

petition with each other, as many were good friends who socialized together and even encouraged their sons and daughters to marry into other brewers' families. In fact, a tracing of the family trees of many German brewers in Cleveland were connected by marriages, sometimes multiple ones. In those days, however, the demand far outweighed the supply of beer. By the 1890s, many of the breweries were being operated by the following generation, whose expectations were higher and whose priorities were more business-oriented. At the same time, the supply had caught up with demand, especially in larger cities, and was made worse by an economic downturn in the early part of the decade. As a result, price wars between brewers began to appear, especially in Cleveland and Cincinnati, and large brewers battled each other for control of saloon properties (saloons were a hot issue, as many of them were tied to one particular brewer in a city or region and sold only that brewer's beer on the premises).

In addition, labor unions began to appear in the late 1880s, giving the larger brewers their first challenge from the brewery employees, whose working conditions were often unpleasant, as they were for workers in most industries around the same time. Clashes between labor and brewery management, however, were relatively minor in the state, especially in comparison to battles fought in other industries during the same era. Another challenge that appeared during this era was the increasing presence of competition from national brewers from Milwaukee and St. Louis, such as Anheuser-Busch, Pabst, and Schlitz. These brewers had grown exponentially over the proceeding twenty years and had found ways to transport their beer to cities throughout the Midwest for bottling. Prior to this, local brewers had dominated sales in most areas, although large brewers such as Schlather in Cleveland had developed a strong presence throughout the eastern and southeastern portion of the state, and for a number of years, several brewers in Cincinnati had flourished along the Ohio River from Marietta west. One final insult was the doubling of the federal tax on beer from one dollar to two dollars, instituted in 1898 to help finance the Spanish-American War. Despite the fact that much of this tax increase was passed on to the consumers, business suffered overall. The end result of this turmoil was a significant slowing of growth in the industry throughout Ohio, most notably in Cincinnati, which was congested with large breweries.

The 1890s also saw the rise of a new trend in the industry which would continue through most of the following decade. Prior to this, the typical brewery had begun business as a small concern, often run by immigrants who developed a local reputation for one or several particular styles of beer, before growing into a large and profitable company. In the decades surrounding the turn of the century, however, multitudes of breweries began to appear across the state, operated not by immigrant brewers, but by pure businessmen who saw the potential money in beer sales. Their plan was to form stock companies to build capital for the construction of modern state-of-the-art plants which were to be operated by brewmasters who had experience in the business, most of whom were German or Bohemian. The idea of stock companies was nothing new in the brewing business; many of the established immigrant brewers had incorporated as early as the 1880s, for the purpose of building capital for plant additions. However, these brewers were still in charge of all business operations in their companies, as they had been since the beginning. The new wave of corporate breweries separated the brewing and business into two separate entities, allowing the brewmasters to focus only on the beer.

The first of these corporations in eastern Ohio was the Consumers Brewing Co. of Newark, formed in 1897. This was followed two years later by the Crockery City Brewing & Ice Co. of East Liverpool. Within another ten years, nearly every moderate- to larger-sized city in the state had at least one new corporate brewery. Some of these were established by men with connections in the liquor or bottling industries, such as George Meredith of East Liverpool, who had previously operated a whiskey and beer bottling firm, distributing beer from Cleveland's Schlather brewery. Others were run by men with no brewing connections whatsoever, such as Cleveland's Forest City Brewing Co., run by Michael Albl, a local grocer, and Joseph Troyan, a local clothier. Four of these companies, the Standard Brewing Co. of Cleveland, the Akron Brewing Co., and Canton's Stark Brewing Co. and Home Brewing Co., were founded and operated entirely by local saloon owners, who wanted to establish a consistent supply of beer at a price that they controlled, instead of being at the mercy of the large established brewers who had previously controlled prices entirely on their own.

Another facet of many of these corporate breweries was a focus on bottling beer for home sales, a concept that had been used only on a very small scale by the older established brewers. While the older brewers still tended to focus their marketing on traditional kegged beer for saloons, the newer companies often focused their marketing on home sales of bottled beer, and often targeted women as beer consumers as well. Some advertised prominently that home deliveries were available. This was also a tactic to use against the Temperance forces which were continuing to gain ground in this era, as the saloon was frequently being targeted as a major social problem, being blamed for alcohol-induced family breakups, violence, and other societal ills. Focusing on sales of beer to the home seemingly encouraged men to stay home to drink with the family or friends, taking the saloon out of the argument. Some of the companies were even named with this in mind: The Consumers Brewing Co. name was used in Newark and Ashtabula, and the Home Brewing Co. name was used in Canton, Columbus, Toledo, and Springfield.

Another phenomenon of the era was the appearance of corporate brewery mergers and conglomerations, some on a small scale, others on a huge scale. The phenomenon had begun a decade earlier when British investors had begun purchasing American breweries on a city-by-city basis, forming conglomerates to manage the plants and essentially controlling nearly all beer production in those regions. Despite an intense effort by these investors to purchase breweries in Cleveland and Cincinnati, they were ultimately unsuccessful, and all of the major breweries in the state remained home-owned. However, by the late 1890s, the benefits of locally-owned conglomerates had been recognized, and Ohio's first one appeared in 1898, when the Cleveland-Sandusky Brewing Corporation was formed, joining nine breweries in Cleveland with the Kuebeler-Stang Brewing and Malting Corporation of Sandusky (which had formed two years earlier as a partnership between that city's two largest brewers). Ultimately fourteen breweries were involved with Cleveland & Sandusky, and while it did not include the city's largest brewer (Leisy), the company still managed to dominate beer sales along the Lake Erie coast from Ashtabula to Toledo over the next twenty years.

After the turn of the century, more conglomerations followed, such as the Stark-Tuscarawas Brewing Co., which combined five breweries in Canton, Massillon, Canal Dover, and New Philadelphia; the Columbus Associated Breweries Co., which combined four large breweries in that city, including the huge Hoster Brewing Co., the Huebner-Toledo Breweries Co., combining three breweries in that city; and the Dayton Breweries Co., combining six breweries in that city. Yet another combine was in the works around the same time; this one would have joined five breweries in eastern Ohio with two in western Pennsylvania. However, this one never came to pass. On a smaller scale, other mergers were occurring, where one brewer would acquire a smaller or less efficient plant in the same city, and either operate or close the smaller plant. The Simon Linser Brewing Co. in Zanesville, for example, was operating three plants in that city for several years, although by 1914, only Linser's main plant was still open. Most of these combines operated very profitably and remained in business until the onset of Prohibition.

During this period of industry reorganization and growth, the Prohibitionists continued to wage their battle against alcohol and the saloons (see the following section on the temperance movement). In the elections of 1908, 57 of 88 counties in the state, primarily rural ones, voted in favor of the Rose Law, which forced these counties to go dry from 1909 to the end of 1911. Although the majority of counties went wet again in 1912, the law caused the premature demise of some breweries, such as the Cambridge Brewing Co., Consumers in Ashtabula and Tuscarawas Valley in Canal Dover. In addition, it gave a chilling preview of some of the problems that the entire country would face in attempting to enforce national Prohibition a decade later.

In the last few years leading up to Prohibition, most of the state's breweries were back in business and continuing to grow. Even though the likelihood of national Prohibition became greater with each passing year, numerous breweries in larger cities continued to hope for the best, making significant capital improvements; large new bottling facilities were being built as late as 1916 in Akron and Cleveland, and the Akron Brewing Co. built a huge new brewhouse the following year. Despite the optimism, Ohio voters approved statewide Prohibition in November 1918, making alcohol sales illegal after May 26, 1919.

At this time, brewers had few choices; if they wanted to stay in business, they were forced to utilize their plants in alternate ways, usually involving the production of soft drinks and/or near beer. Numerous brewers acquired local bottling contracts for national soft drink names such as Coca-Cola (made by Crockery City in East Liverpool and the Stark Brewing Co. plant in Canton) and Whistle Orange Soda (made by Burkhardt in Akron and the Star Brewing Co. in Minster), and some had an extensive line of available soft drinks. Most had extensive ice production equipment, allowing them to continue in the ice business, and many became dealers in coal and other fuels as well. While the unique construction and architecture of most breweries was not well-suited to other forms of industry, the buildings were usually good for use as cold storage facilities. The Standard Brewing Co. of Cleveland used its plant to get into the frozen food business as well. Some companies dabbled in all of the above, essentially making money from their investments in any way possible. On the other hand, some brewers, such as George Gund II in Cleveland, walked away from brewing entirely, investing their money in other fields and continuing to make money. Gund invested in decaffeinated coffee, which he later sold to Kellogg's, which renamed it as Sanka. The money that Gund made started him on the way to becoming Cleveland's richest man, being worth $600 million at the time of his death.

Non-alcoholic malt beverages, also known as near beers, were a tricky business. Production of near beer seemed like a natural progression, as its production required much of the same existing equipment that would otherwise sit idle. There were several different methods of producing near beer, most of which involved the production of regular beer, followed by a dealcoholization process. Unfortunately, some of these dealcoholizing processes altered the taste of the beer negatively, rendering it nearly undrinkable. This problem, in combination with the fact that the beer no longer contained alcohol (which for many consumers was more important than the taste), left a painfully small market for most non-alcoholic cereal beverages. In addition, the abundance of beer bootlegged across Lake Erie from Canada, along with illicit back room home brewing operations, shrunk the market for near beers even further.

As a result, by the mid-1920s, the majority of remaining breweries were either closing their doors or at least stopping production of malt beverages. A few survived throughout the Prohibition era, such as Belmont in Martins Ferry, Renner in Akron, Seibold in New Philadelphia, Crystal Rock in Sandusky, and several in Cleveland. Of those that closed their doors, such as Leisy in Cleveland and Burkhardt in Akron, the cessation of brewing did not necessarily spell the end of business. These families had maintained separate real estate holding and management companies to oversee the numerous properties owned by the brewers (this trend had begun more than a decade earlier, as a result of legislative attempts to prevent brewers themselves from directly owning establishments with liquor licenses). Many, but not all, of these properties represented former saloons, and they continued to yield a steady income for many years. In these cases, the companies maintained enough cash reserves to be able to refurbish their breweries and return to brewing after Prohibition ended.

When, at midnight on April 7, 1933, national Prohibition officially ended, the few breweries in Ohio which were prepared, such as Renner in Akron, released a flood of bottled 3.2% beer which was bought up almost instantly. The intense demand after fourteen dry years was much greater than the small initial supply, but as more brewers opened their renovated plants by that summer, the local industry was able to attain a stable balance. In addition to the breweries that opened for business, numerous others were formed as stock companies with the intention to get into the business, but were unable to generate enough investors to move forward. More brewers appeared in 1934, including the huge Brewing Corporation of America in Cleveland, which represented a reorganized Peerless Motor Car Corporation and its renovated plant, formed for the purpose of brewing Canada's Carling Red Cap Ale. While it stumbled several times in its early days, this plant would be the state's largest within thirty years. In Cincinnati, the Schoenling Brewing Co. also appeared in 1934, and seventy years later, its plant has remained as one of the rare survivors in the state's brewing industry, despite its eventual sale to the Boston Beer Co.

Overall, sixty breweries opened for business in Ohio between 1933 and 1948. Other brewers that entered the business in 1934 and after generally had brief but fleeting success for a variety of reasons. Most of them, such as the new Akron Brewing Co., Canton Brewing Co., and Youngstown Brewing Co., were operated in converted warehouses or factory buildings, and they had no established brand name or reputation on which to rely, as opposed to the older brand names that had returned such as Leisy, Burkhardt, Erin Brew, P.O.C., Hudepohl, etc. In addition, they were operated by men with minimal or no experience in the field of brewing. During the Great Depression, operating any business could be a challenge, and many of these companies declared bankruptcy or reorganized as many as six times over the following decade. Aside from Schoenling and Carling, the longest survivor of the new companies was the tiny Matz Brewing Co. of Bellaire, opened in 1936 by men with experience in the brewing business, but which stayed around only until 1953. Experienced brewers were at risk as well: overall, eighteen Ohio brewers had closed by 1942.

As the Depression gave way to World War II, the brewing industry was thriving, but success was being seen by a smaller number of brewers, ones that were growing rapidly and squeezing the smaller ones out of the industry. Advancements in transportation, refrigeration, communication, advertising methods, and overall brewing and packaging technology were allowing the national brewers such as Anheuser-Busch, Schlitz, and Pabst to infiltrate markets throughout the country. These same three companies had a presence in Ohio prior to and immediately after Prohibition, but their presence (and that of numerous medium-sized regional brewers from Pennsylvania, New York, and throughout the Midwest) became an outright threat to the local brewers after the end of WWII. In a six-year period from 1948 to 1954, twenty-four breweries (most relatively small) in Ohio closed their doors.

The ones that survived that era were forced to make huge capital improvements in their plants, spending millions of dollars for new equipment, bottling facilities, trucks, etc. just to stay competitive. However, despite these efforts, they were only buying time, because for most of them, success would soon disappear. In Cleveland, for example, Pilsener's P.O.C. brand and Standard's Erin Brew brand were the city's top two sellers in the early 1950s; ten years later, both were out of the business. After the industry shakeout of the early 1950s, most smaller brewers were gone, forcing the remaining ones to compete with each other and the national companies. Ultimately, the national companies were far better prepared for these battles with large advertising budgets and well-entrenched distribution networks.

The next wave of closings came between 1956 and 1964, when eight large and well-established brewers (such as Cleveland's Leisy, Standard, and Pilsener, Akron's Burkhardt/Burger, and Cincinnati's Red Top) closed their doors or sold their plants to larger regional competitors. At that point, only eight brewers remained in the entire state, and a decade later, that number had dropped to four (including newcomer Anheuser-Busch, which opened its sixth national brewery, a huge state-of-the-art plant on the north side of Columbus, in 1968). Statistically, 63% of the beer consumed in Ohio as of 1949 was made in Ohio, but by 1964, that number had dropped to 43%, demonstrating the increasing dominance of national and regional brewers in the state. Nevertheless, as of 1964, the state's brewing industry still employed 2,500 workers, leading to more than $22 million in payrolls.

Competition aside, another huge factor which decimated Ohio's brewing industry was the state's malt tax structure. Ohio placed a tax of 36 cents on each case of 24 bottles or cans, compared with 24 cents in Pennsylvania, eight cents in New York, and seven cents in both Wisconsin (home to Schlitz, Pabst, Miller, and Blatz) and Missouri (home to Anheuser-Busch, the top selling brewer in the world). Only Michigan had a higher state tax on beer production. This tax cut into brewers' profit margins, allowing them less money to allocate for marketing and plant upgrades, and giving them a significant competitive disadvantage against out-of-state brewers, especially the larger national companies. Eventually, all of Ohio's original brewery companies left the business, the last holdout being Hudepohl-Schoenling in Cincinnati, which sold its plant to the Boston Beer Co., maker of Samuel Adams Beer, in 1997. This, along with Anheuser-Busch in Columbus and the Miller Brewing Company's huge plant that opened in 1991 in Trenton, near Cincinnati, were the state's only large-scale breweries remaining at the Millenium.

Ohio's brewing industry was certainly not alone in its woes. Consolidation in the industry and the continued growth of the America's largest brewers (now Anheuser-Busch, Miller, Coors, and Pabst, the four of which sell more than 80% of the country's beer) had led to the demise of most smaller brewers in the country by the 1990s. Anheuser-Busch alone had sales of more than 100 million barrels of beer in 2002, giving it roughly one-half of all beer sales in the U. S. and revenue of more than $15 billion. Another contributing factor to this growth was a change in marketing and consumer taste preferences over the past thirty years. While many smaller local brewers had attempted to maintain a loyal long-term following in their regions, often among factory workers and other laborers between the ages of 35 and 60, the national brewers had begun to focus on younger professional consumers, under the age of 30, especially those of college age.

The most popular beers were fairly light-bodied and of relatively low alcohol (around 3.5-4.0%), along with their low-calorie counterparts. This was a complete transformation from the pre-Prohibition era, when traditional lager beers were heavy, malty, and filling. After Prohibition, brewers recognized that more beer could be sold if it had a lighter body and was less filling. This concept was noted by Youngstown's Renner Brewing Co. as early as the 1930s by the term *Suffigkeit* on its labels, meaning "one leads to another". By the 1950s, lighter pilsener-style beers had begun to dominate the market in Ohio, and low-calorie "light" beers appeared the following decade. By the Millenium, these styles represented nearly the entire output of the successful national brewers.

After eastern Ohio's last remaining brewery (Christian Schmidt, operating out of the old Carling plant in Cleveland) closed in 1984, and Cincinnati's Hudepohl brewery closed in 1988, any hope of local flavor in the the state's brewing industry appeared to be headed for extinction. However, it was at that time that the modern era of brewpubs and microbreweries first appeared in Ohio. The state's first, the Great Lakes Brewing Co., opened as a brewpub on Cleveland's west side in 1988, in a renovated century-old store building, and quickly developed a loyal following. The concept of the brewpub was to offer carefully crafted and essentially home-brewed beers, with a variety of ingredients (fruit or vegetable extracts, coffee, chocolate, etc.), and in a wide variety of styles, many not seen in Ohio in more than a century. By the mid-1990s, Great Lakes' success led to the construction of a large associated microbrewery, allowing the company to bottle and distribute its various award-winning brands throughout the state and into other states.

Its success led to the opening of more than 70 brewpubs of various sizes across the state over the following fifteen years. The usual clientele for these establishments was an urban, professional crowd that desired a unique taste to its beer, along with an upscale menu, often of specialty foods. These patrons generally could afford the difference as well, since most specialty brews were considerably more expensive to make than standard national brands. A change in the state's law regarding allowable alcohol content passed into legislation in 2002, altering the definition of beer in Ohio to include brews up to 12% alcohol by volume, instead of the traditional 6% definition of the past. Great Lakes was one of the proponents of the law change, as it allowed for a wider variety of craft brews similar to those brewed in Europe. These higher-alcohol brews often incurred a higher price, and while several pubs have taken advantage of the new law, the market for these specialty brews remains relatively small.

However, most brewers who entered this inviting field quickly found that the business climate was not as easy to succeed in as they might have hoped. Many who entered had been home brewers as a hobby, and the brewing was their primary focus. However, operating a brewpub also required experience in food service and managing a business, and it was in these areas that some fell flat. The industry was also hurt by the economic downturn just after the Millenium, which led to the loss of many professional jobs. In Cuyahoga County, for example, seventeen brewpubs or microbreweries opened between 1988 and 2000, but as of 2004, only seven remained, and two of these (Rock Bottom and the Cleveland Chophouse and Brewery) were owned by the same national chain which financed their operation. Across the state, 37 brewpubs (approximately 50% of those that had opened) remained in business as of 2004. Quality of brewing was not a problem for most of the casualties: several, such as Akron's Liberty Street Brewing Co. and Cleveland's Diamondback Brewery, won numerous national awards for their beers just prior to closing, purely for business reasons.

The future of Ohio's brewing industry in anyone's guess. The current period seems to be a fairly stable one, as the majority of small brewers that have survived thus far appear to be prepared to stay in the business long-term. Competition is less of a factor in this climate than it had been forty years earlier, although the success of the the brewpubs over the past decade provided a wake-up call of sorts to the big brewers. Anheuser-Busch in particular has responded with a number of darker, full-bodied specialty brews, many under the super-premium Michelob brand name, to compete with the brews being sold on tap in brewpubs. Looking ahead, however, it appears that there will be room for both the macro- and micro-brewers in the industry throughout the foreseeable future. As the unofficial national beverage, beer is seen in many different ways by Americans, but providing a wide variety of available brews satisfies both the unrefined drinker who is looking for a thirst-quencher with alcohol, as well as the beer connoisseur who is looking at the beverage as if it is a fine wine. It would appear that beer is being viewed now by an increasing number of Americans much as it is viewed by Europeans, which after four centuries brings this story full circle.

THE TEMPERANCE MOVEMENT IN OHIO

Americans have been enjoying beer and other alcoholic beverages since the discovery of this continent several hundred years ago. In fact, it is thought that the pilgrims landed at Plymouth Rock, Massachusetts in 1620 because their shipboard supply of beer was running dangerously low. Beer, wine, and harder liquor were a vital part of society for many people, both for their inebriating effects as well as the fact that the purity of these beverages could usually be assured, at least relative to local water supplies.

For nearly as long as Americans have been enjoying alcohol, there have been those who saw the darker side of drinking, especially its potential to cause physical, social, and moral decay. As early as the 1670s, preachers would speak of the ill effects of alcohol on Christianity (while they continued to drink in private). This argument would continue for another 250 years, although another century would pass before the purely medical effects of alcohol use and abuse were discussed in detail. By the early 1800s, however, the average American was drinking the equivalent of several gallons of hard liquor each year.

The majority of alcohol consumed was in cities, especially in the east. While alcohol consumption crossed most social, economic, and religious lines, the largest amounts of alcohol were had by laborers, who often had little education. With time, these people were increasingly of immigrant status, mostly German, Irish, and later other European nationalities. Most of the alcohol consumed by these groups was distributed through saloons, the center of the social world for many people.

The sight of drunken "rowdiness" in and around saloons, an increase in a wide variety of alcohol related crimes (ranging from petty thefts to murder), and a fear that religion was increasingly taking a back seat to drinking for many saloon patrons, gave rise to the establishment of a large number of temperance societies along the east coast between 1800 and 1830. These societies were often initiated by local religious leaders and were aimed at reducing the amount and strength of alcohol consumed. However, by the 1840s, the idea of making alcohol illegal altogether was becoming increasingly popular, until 1851, when Maine became the first state to make all alcohol sales illegal.

Ohio (with the exception of Cincinnati) remained sparsely populated until the 1830s and 1840s, at which time the growth of cities and industries brought with them some of the problems commonly associated with "demon alcohol". Around this same time, there was a gradual development of local temperance groups throughout the state, some more vocal and some less so. The activity of the individual local groups was largely dependent on the strength of the

This Currier & Ives print, first published in 1846, shows "The Drunkard's Progress, From The First Glass To The Grave". Step 1: A glass with a friend; Step 2: A glass to keep the cold out; Step 3: A glass too much; Step 4: Drunk and riotous; Step 5: The summit attained/Jolly companions/A confirmed drunkard; Step 6: Poverty and Disease; Step 7: Forsaken by friends; Step 8: Desperation and crime; Step 9: Death by suicide. Meanwhile, the wife is left crying at home with the child.

personalities of their leaders, since there was not yet a strong national network linking these groups together.

In Summit County, as an example, the first temperance newspaper appeared in 1844. Known as the *Buzzard*, it was renamed the *Cascade Roarer* when Sam Lane became editor later that year. Lane was a staunch Prohibitionist who wielded a great deal of power and respect in Akron, serving as sheriff, mayor, and newspaper editor at different times. The *Cascade Roarer* was developed in response to the Washingtonian temperance reform movement, popular on the East Coast at the time, and the newspaper quickly achieved a weekly circulation of 2,500, impressive in that Akron was not yet a heavily populated town. Similar local newspapers were started in towns across the state around the same time.

As the temperance movement gained popularity, a sense of fanaticism and extremism overtook many of its followers. One such group in Cuyahoga Falls took matters into its own hands (as described in 1892 by Sam Lane in his *Fifty Years and Over of Akron and Summit County*):

"To the good women of Cuyahoga Falls is due the credit of being the original Anti-Whisky Crusaders—not, indeed, with the spiritual weapons employed in later years, by Mother Stuart and her contemporaries—prayer and praise—but with such carnal weapons as axes, hatchets, hammers, etc., wielded by their own good right arms.

The Washingtonian reformation of the early and middle forties, followed by the efficient operations of the Sons of Temperance for several years, made Cuyahoga Falls, Akron, and many other villages on the Western Reserve, practical Prohibition towns. In the early and middle fifties, however, the encroachments of the beer and whisky traffic were such as to produce serious alarm among the good women of Cuyahoga Falls for the safety of their husbands, sons, and brothers, and a vigorous revival of the temperance cause was inaugurated. Committees were appointed to visit the various dealers and plead with them to abandon the traffic, but with only partial success.

It was at length determined to resort to sterner measures than 'soft persuasion and mild eloquence,' and on Saturday morning, March 6, 1858, a large volunteer force of women, in solid phalanx, armed with hammers, hatchets, axes, etc., started out to make an assault on King Alcohol, in his entrenchments. The first place visited was the room of Captain Isaac Lewis, over the post office. On reaching the top of the stairs, finding the door locked against them, they battered it down and proceeded to demolish sundry jugs, bottles, etc., removing a barrel of ale to the street below and emptying its foaming contents into the gutter. Next the grocery and liquor store of Joshua L'Hommedieu, on the lower floor of the same building, was invested. Having heard of the intended raid, "Josh" had removed his liquors from the cellar to a smoke-house in the rear. But the crusaders were equal to the emergency, and soon whisky, Otard brandy, and other liquors, were flowing in miniature torrents towards the Cuyahoga River.

The next point visited was the place of Mr. John Tifft, who received his callers with great courtesy, placing before them a collation of doughnuts, pies, etc., pleasantly turning over to them all the liquors that he had left—part of a barrel of beer—which they also poured into the street gutter. At Rockwell's place nothing was found. Jones' variety store on the south side of Broad Street, near the covered bridge, had been "cleaned and garnished" for their reception, by the removal of all liquors to the rear of his store and covering them with rubbish. But the women were too keen-scented and sharp-sighted for the success of this ruse, and Jones' two barrels of whisky, and other liquors, were soon mixing with the pellucid waters of the Cuyahoga. The saloon of "Hen" Lindsey, across the way, was next visited, a few bottles only—said to have been filled with water—being demolished, his main stock in trade having been previously "spirited" away.

At the American House, the proprietor refused to give his visitors access to his liquor cellar and they became so demonstrative that Justice Charles W. Wetmore was called in to read the Riot Act, and admonish them to "disperse and depart to their several homes and lawful employments." But they didn't disperse "worth a cent," and were proceeding to batter down the cellar door, when an armistice was brought about by the landlord pledging himself not to furnish any more liquors to the people of the town.

The last place visited was Heath's drug store, the door of which was barred against them, and forcible entrance prevented, by similar assurances from the proprietors, as those made by the landlord of the American, though it was stated that such arrangements had been made, that had entrance to the store been effected, the discharge of certain chemicals would have made the visit anything but agreeable.

Though these proceeding were irregular and illegal in their nature, it is but just to say that the great majority of the law-abiding people of the village sympathized in the movement, the more so because of the proneness of dealers themselves to disregard the laws regulating the traffic, by furnishing liquors to minors and otherwise. Among the ladies participating in the crusade was Mrs. Elizabeth W. Wait, wife of Mr. George A. Wait, a dealer in millinery and fancy goods. Against Mr. and Mrs. Wait, Mr. Joshua L'Hommedieu brought suit before Justice Wetmore for one hundred dollars damages for the destruction of one barrel of brandy, the justice giving him a judgement for $60. The defendants appealed the case to the Court of Common Pleas. The trial of the case was postponed from time to time, until June 1859, when it was marked, "Settled at Plaintiff's Costs," said costs being collected from "Josh" on execution some two or three months later by the writer, then serving his second term as sheriff."

This extreme vigilantism predated by many years the similar raids on saloons throughout the country carried out by Carry Amelia Moore, aka Carry Nation, whose antics with hatchet in hand made for popular reading in newspapers around the turn of the century. In reading the above passage, one can sense in the editorial tone of the writer a great deal of sympathy for these women and their cause despite the blatant illegality of their acts.

By 1860, the temperance movement had quieted somewhat, as more important issues took precedence when the country readied itself for the Civil War. Despite the fact that President Lincoln was a teetotaler and believed in the prohibition cause, he did not make it into a political issue. Temperance as a nationwide and statewide issue would rise again, however, in the mid-1870s, when times were more stable.

In 1873, a new army of "crusaders" evolved, again on a largely regional or local level. This time, however, the violence and destruction had been replaced by simple prayer. Following the example of "Mother" Elizabeth Thompson, a 60-year-old housewife from Hillsboro, Ohio, groups of respected "society women" would walk through their towns, stopping in front of each saloon, hotel, brewery, or any establishment that was thought to contribute to the alcohol problem. On occasion they would attempt to enter a saloon, but more often, they would just stop on the sidewalk in front of it, kneel, and begin to pray, in full view of the public on the street. While some were greeted with ridicule or intimidation (one Canton brewer and saloonkeeper's wife splashed water on praying crusaders while supposedly washing the sidewalk, and a Cleveland saloon owner's wife attempted to chase crusaders away with dogs), the women often achieved their goal of having the saloon closed, at least for the day (although in some cases the establishment would close permanently).

These crusaders had their greatest effect in small, primarily rural towns, and several brewers ceased operation around this time for that very reason (John Bechtel, near Mount Vernon, closed his 40-year-old brewery in 1876 due to the crusaders). Another brewer, Jonathon Burkholder, from Wayne County, ceased brewing around 1882 due to the teachings of the local church, which had adopted the temperance theme despite the overwhelming German heritage of the congregation. Some brewers, however, stopped or limited their brewing only for a few months or so before resuming. Mother Thompson's movement only lasted for two years, and ultimately had no significant long term impact.

1874 saw the formation of the Women's Christian Temperance Union (WCTU) in Cleveland, as an outgrowth of the local Presbyterian churches. Led by Frances Willard, the WCTU was the first strong national political group lobbying in favor of the temperance cause, and it would continue to be a strong force for the next 50 years.

Despite the activities of the WCTU and various local groups, few national or state politicians were yet willing to make prohibition a strong political issue. Rutherford B. Hayes, who served as Ohio's governor between 1867 and 1876 prior to being elected President (serving one term from 1877 to 1881), believed strongly in the temperance cause. His wife was known as "Lemonade Lucy" for her strong beliefs and unwillingness to serve alcohol in the White House. Despite this, Hayes chose not to pursue the controversial issue in Washington.

The Prohibition Party was formed in 1869 in an attempt to provide a presidential candidate who would further the temperance cause on a national basis. Despite the backing of a number of respected liberal thinkers of the day and a great deal of media attention, this third party never received a significant number of votes in any election.

The small scale temperance activists of this era were being countered by lobbying from the United States Brewers Association. Founded in 1862, the USBA was formed in response to the imposition of heavy taxes on brewers by the federal government, in order to help pay the high costs of the Civil War. By the 1870s, and for the next forty years, its focus had shifted toward lobbying against the temperance cause.

In this ongoing war between the "drys" (temperance or prohibition activists) and the "wets" (those who were against prohibition), the balance shifted

Wood engraved print from *Harper's Weekly*, March 14, 1874. This scene, showing crusaders praying in a saloon, appears to be fairly accurate for the time. The caption, as written with the German accent of the saloonkeeper's wife (standing at the right) is "You shust git out".

significantly after 1893, with the formation of the Anti-Saloon League (ASL). As was the case with the WCTU twenty years earlier, Ohio would play a pivotal role in the formation and growth of this powerful group.

The Ohio branch of the ASL was headed by Wayne Wheeler, a graduate of Oberlin College, a small liberal arts school in Lorain County, and who later received a law degree from Western Reserve University in Cleveland. Wheeler was a brilliant political manipulator who was able to convince numerous state politicians to vote in favor of dry issues. Those who remained on the "wet" side became his political enemies, and more than one career was ruined by Wheeler's ability to assassinate the character of an opponent.

Wheeler worked throughout the state over the next decade, encouraging local politicians to vote in favor of dry issues. The city of East Liverpool became the first large industrial city to vote itself dry, in 1907. At this point, the political power of the ASL was becoming increasingly evident. The Aiken Bill was passed in the Ohio legislature that year as well, raising annual saloon license fees from $350 to $1,000. For small saloon owners, this was crippling, and many were either forced to close or lay off staff.

By this time, the state had three local option laws: a township law had been passed in 1888, and approximately 1,200 townships in the state had since abolished saloons; a municipal law had been passed in 1902 for entire villages and cities; and in 1906 came a local option law for residence districts within larger cities. Each of these had been effective in reducing the number of saloons in the state, primarily in more rural areas. In 1908 came a bigger blow—passage of the Rose Law, allowing entire counties to vote themselves dry (in other words, making all alcohol sales illegal, and closing many saloons completely as a result.) In the Fall elections that year, 57 of 88 counties in Ohio voted themselves dry, beginning January 1, 1909. Most of these were rural counties, and the majority were in the southern half of the state. The larger industrial cities—Cleveland, Akron, Youngstown, Canton, Columbus, Cincinnati—all remained wet, as they had much greater proportions of alcohol-drinking industrial workers, and also a greater number of recent European immigrants, who were less likely to support the temperance cause.

Over the next year, some brewers in dry counties attempted to stay in business producing ice and non-alcoholic "temperance" beers. Others continued to produce real beer and sell it in areas which had remained wet. Breweries along the Ohio River had an easier time, as West Virginia remained wet during this period and continued to provide a market for alcoholic beverages. Some breweries, faced with a steep decline in revenue, closed altogether. Several of these plants (in Canal Dover, Cambridge, Ashtabula, and Wellston) were less than ten years old and had new state-of-the-art equipment. The closing of these plants led to personal financial ruin for some of their investors.

Between 1909 to 1911, much of the state received a taste of what was to come a decade later with national Prohibition. Bootlegging and speakeasies appeared in several areas despite frequent raids by local authorities and penalties to offenders. John Buehler, a brewer from Steubenville, was repeatedly accused of providing illegal beer in town (Jefferson County having gone dry), until he closed his plant entirely in 1910. By 1911, the voters in many of these counties recognized the failure of this local option legislature, and most of the counties became wet again beginning on January 1, 1912. Many idle breweries in these areas reopened at this time.

Despite the problems associated with local option, and voters' reversal of local Prohibition laws, the ASL considered its activities to be a success. By 1913, the political power of both the ASL and the WCTU was continuing to grow, and their sights were now set on spreading the movement to the entire country. Typical propaganda consisted of articles, brochures, postcards, and other advertising discussing the many supposed evils of alcohol, including alcoholism, all types of crime, breakups of families, loss of jobs, and danger to children. After the United States entered World War I in April 1917, a new argument was raised: grains used in the production of beer and other liquors was hindering the war effort, suggesting that U. S. troops in Europe might starve or otherwise be harmed due to the "waste" of grain to produce liquor at home.

Gradually, the concept of national Prohibition became increasingly likely. A few individual states had already voted in favor of statewide Prohibition, including West Virginia in 1914. The brewers, and their political action group, the USBA, were no match for Wheeler and the ASL when it came to propaganda and lobbying. Many brewers had naively continued to assume that the country would never actually allow Prohibition to take effect, even as late as 1918. Their token efforts to fight back were far too little and too late.

After the United States entered WWI, several factors combined to give the ASL its ultimate victory. The new argument that grains should be used for the war effort strengthened public opinion against alcohol, an opinion which the ASL had been cultivating for twenty years. In addition, there had been an increasing anti-German sentiment in the country since the war had begun in 1914. Once the United States entered the war, these feelings intensified significantly. Since the vast majority of breweries (especially those in Ohio) were still owned by 1st, 2nd, or 3rd generation German-Americans, beer and the brewing industry suffered by association. While national paranoia toward German-Americans never reached the extent that existed in WWII toward Japanese-Americans, the end result was a further strengthening of the Prohibition cause.

Wayne Wheeler

Each year, Ohioans were asked to vote on the issue of statewide Prohibition, and in 1914, the issue lost by 84,000 votes. Three years later, however, the issue lost by only 1,100 votes (while the vast number of individual counties were voting dry, the largest and most industrial counties were voting wet by large majorities, skewing the overall total). In the elections of November 1918, however, residents finally voted in favor of statewide Prohibition. Production of alcoholic beverages ceased in December of that year, and all sales of remaining alcoholic beverages ended on May 26, 1919. After this, a few breweries closed their doors permanently, though most attempted to remain solvent through sales of near beer (also known as cereal beverage or malt tonic), soft drinks, and ice. Most of these companies eventually failed, however, and by Prohibition's end in 1933, only a handful of breweries in eastern Ohio were still operating.

By the end of the war in November 1918, national Prohibition had become inevitable. The death knell for brewers was the 18th Amendment to the Constitution, known as the Volstead Act. Named for Minnesota congressman Andrew Volstead, the amendment was actually largely written by Wayne Wheeler, and it outlawed the production and sale of beverages containing more than 0.5% alcohol, with few exceptions. After being passed by Congress in the Fall of 1919, the bill was vetoed by President Wilson, although this veto was quickly overridden by Congress. After ratification by 36 of the 48 states, the amendment went into effect January 17, 1920, after which time the entire country was officially dry.

Nationwide and in Ohio, Prohibition was a colossal failure on nearly every level. Bootlegging flourished, as there were millions of dollars to be made by anyone bringing illegal liquor from Canada, Mexico, the Caribbean, etc. Speakeasies existed in virtually every city, with liquor coming in unabated from both international and domestic sources. Many back-room stills and small-time brewing operations existed, although records of their existence were not usually kept. The quality and purity of these illicit beverages were questionable at best (in fact, the cocktail as we know it developed in the 1920s, as fruit and various juices were added to the illicit liquor to cover its inferior taste), and at worst they were downright poisonous, but the desire to drink kept customers coming.

Enforcement of Prohibition laws was attempted, but most federal agents were poorly paid and therefore were easily bribed to look the other way. Some agents became very wealthy merely by not enforcing the law. Political corruption and scandals were the order of the day, both on a national and local level. President Warren Harding and his associates, known as the "Ohio Gang", were among the most corrupt leaders the country has ever seen, and similar corruption was seen among the leaders of many of the larger cities in the country. The combination of potential financial gain from bootlegging and other vices, and a lack of law enforcement led to a dramatic increase in organized crime, which became well established during the 1920s in most large cities, including New York, Chicago, and Cleveland.

Much of the enforcement of Prohibition laws was aimed at small-time brewers and moonshiners (who couldn't afford to bribe their way out), while many of the large-scale bootlegging operations went undisturbed. An Akron woman appeared in court in June 1927 to defend her husband, who was accused of illegal home brewing (as reported in the Akron *Beacon Journal*). She testified that the husband was acting on her behalf, since Akron's city water made her sick. The judge disagreed, calling the city's water "the best in the country". Asked why she couldn't drink coffee instead, she claimed that made her sick as well. The judge still found her husband guilty and fined him $100 plus court costs.

After the onset of the Great Depression, illicit alcohol sales took on a greater importance for some. One

Medical prescription form for alcohol, or "medicinal liquor", from the Prohibition era. The laws were enforced and overseen by the U. S. Treasury Department.

minor incident in Canton in the early 1930s, as described by Bud Weber of the Stark County Historical Society, was typical of the late Prohibition era in Ohio and the rest of the country. During that era, Weber's father, Otto, began brewing beer in the basement at home. He and his wife would work late into the night, brewing beer and cleaning and filling bottles. He would often make 100 cases of beer at a time, and then take them around to various local speakeasies and social clubs (which would be frequented by public officials, policemen, etc.) in the family car.

One night, he was involved in a minor accident while making his deliveries. When the police arrived, they noticed the illegal cargo, but chose not to say anything about it. "Can you drive the car?" asked a policeman. When Weber said yes, they told him to get out of there. The police knew that if he was turned over to Prohibition agents, it would mean the end of their beer supply! As Bud Weber states, "It was part of life. We didn't think too much about it being illegal. At $2.00 a case, each batch of beer brewed meant $200 in pocket, and that really came in handy during the Depression, when food stamps and welfare were the alternatives." Otto Weber put his experience to good use: he became the brewmaster for the Canton Brewing Company shortly after the end of Prohibition.

Even the Volstead Act itself was filled with provisions that allowed legal loopholes for those looking to make money in the business of providing liquor. Physicians were allowed to prescribe alcoholic spirits if they felt there was a medical reason, and needless to say, many "medical" reasons to drink alcohol developed after 1919. Similarly, the law allowed sales of alcohol for religious ceremonies, and also in industry for a variety of chemical processes. Falsified documents led to phenomenal abuses of the law through these two provisions alone.

Despite the many problems associated with Prohibition, it seemed that nobody wanted the "Roaring Twenties" to end. In the 1928 election, Herbert Hoover easily won the presidency, campaigning for a continuation of Prohibition, which he referred to as "a great social and economic experiment, noble in motive and far-reaching in purpose." One year later, however, the Roaring Twenties came to an abrupt halt with the crash of the stock market, plunging the United States and the rest of the world into the Great Depression. This would ultimately lead to Prohibition's end, although it would take another three years. By 1931, there were signs that the country was further tiring of Prohibition, when in October President Hoover attended Game 4 of the World Series in Philadelphia and was roundly booed by the crowd, who chanted "We Want Beer! We Want Beer!"

By 1932, the Depression had only deepened, despite Hoover's repeated assertions that recovery was imminent. Economic recovery became the primary political issue of that year's elections; Prohibition as an issue was increasingly ignored. Franklin Roosevelt, Hoover's Democratic challenger, boldly proposed bringing back beer, which would be taxed heavily to bring hundreds of millions of dollars into the federal treasury. In the past, this proposal would have been attacked by the dry forces. However, the ASL had become a much weaker organization after Wheeler's death in 1927. In addition, farmers in rural America, who had traditionally been supporters of the dry movement, saw the return of beer and liquor as a potential salvation, providing a large market for their grains. In the end, economic concerns outweighed the moral concerns associated with alcohol's return, and Roosevelt won the election that November.

Within three months of Roosevelt's inauguration, he had succeeded in having Congress modify the Volstead Act, allowing the sale of 3.2% beer. On April 7, 1933, the George J. Renner Brewing Company of Akron (which had stayed in business throughout Prohibition selling de-alcoholized beer) was the only brewery in eastern Ohio which was ready with the real thing, which went on sale to a crowd of 2,000 at the brewery just after midnight. The relatively small brewery was not able to keep up with the demand, however, and within a few days, beer from breweries throughout the Midwest was flooding into Ohio.

By the end of the year, the 21st Amendment (often referred to as just "Repeal") had been passed by Congress and ratified by 36 states, allowing the sale of full strength beer and hard liquor as of December 5, 1933.

The token protests by the WCTU and other dry activists were largely ignored, and the Prohibition era was officially over.

In the aftermath of Prohibition, local option again became the rule, allowing a wide variety of "blue laws" regulating alcohol sales to evolve, and these differed by state, county, township, and town. Some areas remained totally dry, while others banned Sunday sales or restricted the size or number of containers (cans or bottles) that could be sold.

For many years, 3.2% beer continued to be sold in Ohio, for sales to those between the ages of 18 and 21. (While 3.2% represented the maximum percentage of alcohol for this class of beer, the actual percentage was often between 2.0 and 2.8%.) Full strength beer, which could be anywhere from 3.2% to 7.0%, could only be sold to those over the age of 21. In the 1980s, 3.2% beer was eliminated, and the age for legal consumption of all beer became 19. Still later, the age limit in Ohio was raised to 21, which remains the current limit at this time.

The ASL eventually faded away, and while the WCTU still operates to this day (with more information available at its web site: www.wctu.org), its political clout is nowhere near the level it achieved in the early part of the century. In fact, since Repeal, alcoholic beverages have never again been seriously challenged, at least not on a national or statewide basis.

In more recent years, the focus of government has shifted toward control and eradication of a wide variety of drugs, creating scenarios eerily reminiscent of the 1920s. The government's attempts to fight the massive influx of illegal drugs from around the world are usually one step behind the smugglers, who have huge financial payoffs awaiting them if they are successful. The futility of the government's current efforts were effectively illustrated in the 2000 movie *Traffic*, which could easily have been written about the Prohibition era if it were taking place 75 years earlier. Organized crime, which became well entrenched during that era and which has been glorified countless times by Hollywood, continues to operate, only now with more international connections and an interest in drugs and weapons, in addition to the old favorites—gambling and prostitution. If there is a lesson to be learned, it may be that morality can only be enforced to a limited extent by passing laws, and that people will ultimately find a way to get the vices they want, one way or another.

Eastern Ohio Breweries

Ashland County

Ashland

1.	Gerhard Lepper	c.1849-mid-1860s

Loudonville

1.	Union Brewery, Graf & Roth	c.1873-c.1877

Ashtabula County

Ashtabula

1.	Consumers Brewing Co	1906-1909
2.	Independent Brewing Co.	1905-1907
3.	Lift Bridge Brewing Co.	1994-1998

Athens County

Athens

1.	O'Hooley's Pub and Brewery	1996-operating

Nelsonville

1. a.	Hocking Valley Brewing Co.	1905-1919
b.	Hocking Valley Cereal Beverage Co.	1919-c.1924
c.	Hocking Valley Brewery, Inc.	1947-1950

Belmont County

Bellaire

1. a.	Charles Hankey	mid-1860s-early 1870s
b.	John E. Vogel	early 1870s-c.1876
2. a.	Bellaire Brewing Co	1905-1919
b.	Bellaire Beverage Co.	1919-1924
c.	Matz Brewing Co.	1936-1953

Martins Ferry

1. a.	Belmont Brewing Co.	1890-1919
b.	Belmont Products Co.	1919-1933
c.	Belmont Brewing Co.	1933-1940

Carroll County

Sherrodsville

1.   Atwood Lake Yacht Club   1995-operating

Columbiana County

East Liverpool

1. a.	Henry Greenwood, Spring Water Brewery	1888-1912
b.	Greenwood Brewery, Martha Greenwood	1912-1915
2. a.	Crockery City Brewing and Ice Co.	1900-1919
b.	Crockery City Ice and Products Co.	1919-1946
c.	Webb Corporation	1946-1952

East Palestine

1. a.	J. Anderton & Co.	1879-1884
b.	William Arnold	1895-1900
c.	John Schilpp	1902-c.1904

Leetonia

1. a.	Jacob Garlach & Seegar	1873-1874
b.	Haller & Seegar	1874-1877
c.	Benjamin F. Haller & Bro.	1877-1881
d.	Dominick Zanini & Co.	1881-1884
e.	Zanini & Siegle	1884-1887
f.	Louis T. Siegle & Co.	1887-1888
g.	Leetonia Brewery (Louis F. Siegle)	1888-1906
h.	Leetonia Brewing Co.	1906-1913

North Georgetown

1. a.	Samuel Biery	mid-1860s-1873
b.	Daniel Biery, Kasper Newarth (& Kickenbaugh)	1873-1876

Salem

1. a.	William Moff	1866-1890
b.	Gustav Zelle	1890

Coshocton County

Coshocton

1.	L. Mayer/George Sleigh	c.1852-late 1850s
2. a.	Frederick Mayer	late 1850s-c.1869
b.	Lewis Bieber	c.1869-c.1874
c.	Charles Boes	c.1874-c.1877

Roscoe

1. a.	Conrad Mayer	c.1866-1880
b.	Frederick Bohn	1880-1884

Cuyahoga County

Beachwood

1.   Captain Tony's Pizza and Pasta Emporium   1993-1996

Bedford Heights

1. Buckeye Brewing Co./The Brew Keeper   1997-operating

Berea

1. a. Edward Davis   1870-1878
   b. E. Davis & Son   1878-1880
   c. Edward Davis, Jr.   1880-1884
   d. George Neubrand   1884-1893
   e. Frederick Bullinger   1893
   f. Pannonia Brewing Co.   1893-1894
   g. North Shore Export Brewing Co.   1896-1897

2. a. Quarryman Taverne and Church Street Brewery   2001-2003
   b. Cornerstone Brewing Co.   2004-operating

Brooklyn (aka Brighton)

1. George Henninger   c. 1861-1874

Chagrin Falls

1. a. William H. Sykes & Lysander B. Wilkinson   c. mid-1850s-1869
   b. Albert A. Goodwin & Lysander B. Wilkinson   1869-1870
   c. Albert A. Goodwin & Emory Sheffield   1870-1877
   d. Albert A. Goodwin   1877-1880

Cleveland

1. a. Bennett & Weldon, Cleveland Brewery   1832-1832
   b. Robert Bennett, Cleveland Brewery   1832-1834
   c. Joseph & Richard Hawley   1834-1837
   d. Hawley & Childs   1837-1840
   e. Herrick Childs   1840-1847
   f. Samuel C. Ives   1847-1856
   g. Ives Cleveland Brewery   1856-1865

2. Reverend Elijah F. Willey   c.1835

3. a. Charles C. Rogers, Forest City Brewery   1839-1871
   b. Beggs & Rogers   1871-1873
   c. Rogers & Hughes   1873-1878
   d. J. P Haley   1878-1880
   e. Carling & Co.   1880-1884

4. a. Blackwell, Lloyd, & Co., City Brewery   1841-1842
   b. Ives & Lloyd, City Brewery   1842-1847

5. a. George W. Hamilton, Eagle Brewery   early 1840s-1848
   b. Hamilton & Tutbury   1848-1856
   c. John Tutbury & Co.   1856-1857
   d. John Quinn   1857-1863
   e. Quinn & Spear   1863-1864
   f. John Quinn   1864-c.1869

6. a. Truman Downer, Spring Street Brewery   1846-1848
   b. Downer & Wyman   1848-1850
   c. John M. Hughes   1850-1857

7. a. M. Stumpf & Co.   c.1846-1850
   b. Michael Stumpf   1850-1886

8.	a.	Thomas Newman, Forest City Brewery	1850-1864
	b.	Newman & Rogers	1864-1869
	c.	Newman & Fovargue	1869-1872
	d.	Fovargue & Dangerfield	1872-1874
	e.	Daniel Fovargue	1874-1881
	f.	Fovargue & Newman	1881-1883
9.	a.	John A. Bishop	1852-1882
	b.	Lezius & Kaenzig	1882-1882
	c.	Christian Kaenzig	1882-1884
	d.	Mrs. Elizabeth Kaenzig	1884-1888
	e.	Louis Lezius	1888-1890
10.	a.	Martin Stumpf	1852-1859
	b.	Kindsvater & Mall, Lion Brewery	1859-1871
	c.	Jacob Mall, Lion Brewery	1871-1889
	d.	Jacob Mall Brewing Co.	1889-1900
	e.	Gund Brewing Co.	1900-1919
	f.	Sunset Brewing Co.	1933-1933
	g.	The Sunrise Brewing Co.	1933-1939
	h.	The Tip Top Brewing Co.	1939-1944
11.	a.	Matthias Mack	c.1852-1857
	b.	Mack Brothers	1857-1873
12.	a.	Schmidt & Hoffman	1852-1887
	b.	Cleveland Brewing Co.	1887-1898
	c.	Cleveland & Sandusky Brewing Co.	1898-1919
13.	a.	John Dangeleisen	c.1856-c.1870
	b.	Henry Rochotte	c.1870-c.1874
	c.	Frank Payer	c.1874
14.	a.	Jones & Co.	c.1856
	b.	Jones & Lloyd, Star Brewery	1856-1857
	c.	James Lloyd	1857-1858
	d.	Lloyd & Keenan	1858- ?
	e.	J. Gromlich	1868-1868
	f.	Charles Yahraus	1868-1874
	g.	Carl Seyler	1874-1880
	h.	Louis Chormann	1880-1885
	i.	Lezius & Uehlein	1885-1888
	j.	Diebolt & Uehlein	1888-1889
	k.	Diebolt & Ruble	1889-1891
	l.	Diebolt Brewing Co.	1891-1919
	m.	The Diebolt Co.	1919-1923
15.	a.	Charles E. Gehring	1857-1891
	b.	C. E. Gehring Brewing Co.	1891-1898
	c.	Cleveland & Sandusky Brewing Co.	1898-1919
16.	a.	Leonhard Schlather	1857-1884
	b.	L. Schlather Brewing Co.	1884-1902
	c.	Cleveland & Sandusky Brewing Co.	1902-1919
	d.	Cleveland-Sandusky Co.	1919-1933
17.	a.	John M. Hughes	1858-1884
	b.	Hughes Brewery, Mrs. Cornelia Bowlsby	1884-1887
	c.	Hughes Brewing Co.	1887-1895
	d.	Spencer Brewing Co.	1899-1900
18.	a.	Jacob Mueller	1858-1864
	b.	Frederick Haltnorth	1864-1873
	c.	Isaac Leisy & Co.	1873-1882
	d.	Isaac Leisy	1882-1893

	e.	I. Leisy Brewing Co.	1893-1919
	f.	Isaac Leisy Co.	1919-1923
	g.	The Leisy Brewing Co.	1934-1959
19.		Michael Lucas	late 1850s-1874
20.	**a.**	Frederick Weidenkopf	c.1858-1859
	b.	Hamilton & Weidenkopf	1859-1859
	c.	George W. Hamilton	1859-1864
	d.	John Whitlock & Co.	1864-1864
	e.	Whitlock & Lowrie	1864-1868
	f.	John Whitlock, Cleveland Brewery	1868-1874
21.	**a.**	J. Stoppel & Co.	1858-1868
	b.	Brown & Brothers	1868-1869
	c.	Stoppel's Actien Brewery	1869-1870
	d.	Stoppel & Fox	1870-1872
	e.	J. Kraus & Co.	1872-1878
	f.	Joseph Stoppel	1878-1882
	g.	Stoppel's Sons & Co.	1882-1887
	h.	Stoppel's Co-operative Brewing Co.	1887-1891
	i.	Columbia Brewing Co.	1891-1898
	j.	Cleveland & Sandusky Brewing Co.	1898-1918
22.	**a.**	H. Lloyd & Co., Cleveland City Brewery	1859-1870
	b.	Lloyd & Keys	1870-1895
	c.	Daniel H. Keys	1895-1909
23.	**a.**	Stumpf & Kestla	1863-1865
	b.	Martin Stumpf	1865-1866
	c.	John Davies	1866-1872
	d.	Davies & Hammond	1872-1875
	e.	V. D. Hammond, Briggs Street Brewery	1875-1876
	f.	Davies & Weisgerber	1876-1877
	g.	John Davies	1877-1878
	h.	Clark R. Hodge	1878-1880
	i.	Gavagan & Sterling, Lakeside Brewery	1880-1882
	j.	Patrick Gavagan	1882-1914
	k.	Gavagan & Oppmann	1914-1914
	l.	Segal & Oppmann	1914-1916
24.		Jacob Wagner	1864-1872
25.	**a.**	Jacob Baehr	1866-1873
	b.	Mrs. Magdalena Baehr	1873-1898
	c.	Cleveland & Sandusky Brewing Co.	1898-1901
26.	**a.**	Wittlinger & Weber	1866-1867
	b.	Wittlinger & Fahle	1867-1868
	c.	George Wittlinger	1868-1871
	d.	John Fox (Fuchs)	1871-1873
	e.	Alexander Charters	1873-1874
	f.	Crump, Porter, & Bro.	1874-1876
	g.	A. Porter & Co.	1876-1877
27.	**a.**	J. Koestle & Co.	1867-1870
	b.	Joseph Koestle	1870-1877
	c.	Mrs. J. Koestle	1877-1879
	d.	Mrs. Elizabeth Koestle	1879-1881
28.	**a.**	Gottfried Reindl	1867-1868
	b.	Muth & Brothers	1868-1871
	c.	George Muth & Son	1871-1882
	d.	Geo. V. Muth, Star Brewery	1882-1896

	e.	The Star Brewing Co.	1896-1898
	f.	Cleveland & Sandusky Brewing Co.	1898-1913
29.	a.	Adam Schumann	1867-1869
	b.	Andrew W. Oppmann	1872-1874
	c.	Oppmann & Lehr	1874-1876
	d.	Andrew W. Oppmann	1876-1882
	e.	Oppmann Brewing Co.	1882-1891
	f.	Phoenix Brewing Co.	1891-1898
	g.	Cleveland & Sandusky Brewing Co.	1898-1908
30.	a.	Philip Griebel	1868-1878
	b.	Allen & Co.	1878-1879
	c.	Philip Griebel	1879-1882
31.	a.	August Burckhardt	1868-1876
	b.	Anton Kopp & Co.	1876-1877
	c.	Kopp & Mueller	1877-1878
	d.	Rudolph Mueller	1878-1879
	e.	William Schneider & Co.	1879-1880
32.	a.	Joseph Zika	1870-1872
	b.	Braun & Dietz	1872-1872
	c.	Braun & Schneider	1872-1878
	d.	Christian Schneider	1878-1880
	e.	Christian Schneider & Son	1880-1888
	f.	John H. Schneider	1888-1895
	g.	Union Brewing Co.	1895-1898
	h.	Cleveland & Sandusky Brewing Co.	1898-1899
33.	a.	Hoffman & Paschen	1871-1873
	b.	Hoffmann & Vollkopf	1873-1874
	c.	Henry Hoffmann	1874-1881
34.	a.	Mrs. Matilda Mack	1874-1876
	b.	J. M. Mack	1876-1882
35.	a.	Joseph Beltz	1876-1878
	b.	Beltz & Mueller	1878-1881
	c.	Joseph Beltz	1881-1897
	d.	Jos. Beltz & Sons	1897-1901
	e.	Beltz Brewing Co.	1901-1906
	f.	Cleveland Home Brewing Co.	1906-1919
	g.	The Cleveland Home Brewing Co., Inc.	1933-1952
36.	a.	Aenis & Metzger	1877-1879
	b.	Aenis & Froelich	1879-1880
37.	a.	William Aenis & Co.	1880-1881
	b.	Aenis & Haller	1881-1884
	c.	Mrs. Mary Angel	1884-1886
	d.	Wenzl Medlin, Bohemian Brewery	1886-1889
	e.	Bohemian Brewing Co.	1889-1898
	f.	Cleveland & Sandusky Brewing Co.	1898-1898
38.	a.	Carling & Co.	1884-1890
	b.	Carling Brewing Co.	1890-1891
	c.	Barrett Brewing Co.	1891-1898
	d.	Cleveland & Sandusky Brewing Co.	1898-1911
39.	a.	Mrs. Jacob Voelker	1887-1891
	b.	Mrs. Catherine Voelker	1891-1895
40.		Hermann H. Imbrey	1887-1888

41.	a.	Medlin Pilsener Brewing Co.	1893-1894
	b.	Pilsener Brewing Co.	1894-1919
	c.	Pilsener Ice, Fuel, & Beverage Co.	1919-1933
	d.	The Pilsener Brewing Co., Inc.	1933-1962
42.		Buckeye Weiss Beer Brewing Co.	1899-1899
43.		Wenzl Medlin Weiss Beer Brewery	1899-1904
44.	a.	Kress Weiss Beer Co.	1902-1904
	b.	Standard Brewing Co.	1904-1905
	c.	Excelsior Brewing Co.	1905-1919
	d.	Eilert Beverage Co., Inc.	1919-1933
	e.	Eilert Brewing Co.	1933-1940
	f.	Kings Brewery, Inc.	1940-1941
45.	a.	Forest City Brewing Co.	1904-1919
	b.	Forest City New Process Co.	1919-1924
	c.	Forest City Brewery, Inc.	1933-1944
	d.	Carling's, Inc.	1944-1946
	e.	Brewing Corp. of America, Plant 2	1946-1948
46.		Carl E. Beltz Weiss Beer Brewery	1905-1914
47.	a.	Standard Brewing Co.	1905-1923
	b.	Standard Food Products Co.	1923-1933
	c.	The Standard Brewing Co., Inc.	1933-1961
	d.	Schaefer Brewing Co. of Ohio, Inc.	1961-1964
	e.	C. Schmidt & Sons, Inc.	1964-1971
48.	a.	Fishel Brewing Co.	1904-1907
	b.	Cleveland & Sandusky Brewing Co.	1907-1919
	c.	Cleveland-Sandusky Co., Inc.	1919-1922
	d.	Cleveland-Sandusky Brewing Co.	1934-1936
	e.	Cleveland-Sandusky Brewing Corporation	1936-1962
49.	a.	Brewing Corporation of America	1934-1953
	b.	Carling Brewing Co.	1953-1971
	c.	C. Schmidt & Sons, Inc.	1971-1981
	d.	Christian Schmidt Brewing Co.	1981-1984
50.		Real Brewery, Inc.	1934-1935
51.		Great Lakes Brewing Co.	1988-operating
52.		Crooked River Brewing Co.	1994-2001
53.		Rock Bottom Brewery	1995-operating
54.	a.	Diamondback Brewery	1996-2000
	b.	Barons of Cleveland	2000-2000
55.		Western Reserve Brewing Co.	1997-2002
56.	a.	John Harvard's Brewhouse	1997-1999
	b.	House of Brews	1999-2000
57.		Cleveland Chophouse and Brewery	1998-operating
58.		Alyce On The East Bank	1998-2000
59.		Wallaby's Grille & Brewpub	1998-2000

Cleveland Heights

1. The Firehouse Brewery and Restaurant — 1995-1997

Rocky River

1. Rocky River Brewing Co. — 1998-operating

Strongsville

1. a. Melbourne's/Strongsville Brewing Co. — 1989-1995
   b. Mad Crab Restaurant and Brewery — 1996-2003

2. Ringneck Brewing Co./The Brew Kettle — 1995-operating

Westlake

1. Wallaby's Grille & Brewpub — 1995-2000

2. Local Brewing Co., dba Wallaby's Brewing Co. — 1997-2000

Erie County

Huron

1. Morrison & Wheeler — 1812-c.1820

Kelley's Island

1. Island Café and Brewpub — 1999-operating

Milan

1. a. John Scholl — 1850-1863
   b. Francis & Gottlieb Humbel — 1863-1869
   c. Anton Herb — 1869-1892
   d. Mary Herb — 1892-1897
   e. Herb Bros. — 1897-1899
   f. Joseph Herb — 1899-1904
   g. Joseph Herb Brewing Co. — 1904-1919
   h. The Milan Brewing Corp. — 1933-1951

Sandusky

1. J. Lea — c.1844

2. Charles S. Higgins, Phoenix Brewery — 1848-c.early 1860s

3. a. Philip Dauch & Andrew Fischer — 1852-1853
   b. Philip Dauch — 1853-1862
   c. Windisch, Bright & Cable — 1862-1868
   d. Fox & Windisch — 1868-1872
   e. Fox, Stang, & Homegardner — 1872-1875
   f. John Bender & Co. — 1875-1878
   g. Lena Bender — 1878-1880
   h. Frank Stang — 1880-1892
   i. Stang Brewing Co. — 1892-1896
   j. Kuebeler-Stang Brewing and Malting Co. — 1896-1898
   k. Cleveland & Sandusky Brewing Co. — 1898-1919
   l. The Crystal Rock Products Co. — 1919-1933
   m. The Cleveland-Sandusky Brewing Co. — 1933-1935

4. a. Vincenz (Winsen) Fox — 1854-1866
   b. Soergel, Dorn, & Raible — 1866-1871
   c. Soergel, Strobel & Ilg — 1871-1874

	d.	Strobel & Ilg	1874-1879
	e.	A. Ilg & Co., Sandusky City Brewery	1879-1890
	f.	Sandusky Brewing Co.	1890-1890
5.	a.	Bavarian Brewery, George Baier	1857-1859
	b.	George Baier & Charles Pusch	1859-1866
	c.	George Baier	1866-1873
	d.	Nicholas Wagner	1873-1874
6.	a.	E. G. P. Mittleburger, Bay City Brewery	1859-c.1867
	b.	Alder & Co., Bay City Brewery	c.1867-c.1868
7.	a.	Jacob Kuebeler & Co.	1867-1892
	b.	Jacob Kuebeler Brewing & Malting Co.	1892-1896
	c.	Kuebeler-Stang Brewing & Malting Co.	1896-1898
	d.	Cleveland & Sandusky Brewing Co.	1898-1918

Fairfield County

Lancaster

1.		Justus Younghans (aka Zink & Younghans)	c.1840-c.late 1860s
2.	a.	Ochs & Co.	1867-1868
	b.	Becker, Ochs, & Co.	1868-1877
	c.	Becker & Co.	1877-1884
	d.	E. Becker Brewing Co.	1884-1916
	e.	The Lancaster Brewing Co.	1934-1942

Gallia County

Gallipolis

1.	a.	Xavier Brandstetter	c.1865-1876
	b.	Frederick Henkel	1876-c.1888

Geauga County

No known breweries

Guernsey County

Cambridge

1.		Hermann Berns	1870-c.1877
2.	a.	Cambridge Brewing Co.	1901-1905
	b.	The Brewery Co.	1905-1906
	c.	Cambridge Brewing Co.	1906-1909

Harrison County

No known breweries

Hocking County

Hide-A-Way Hills

1.	The Lodge At Hide-A-Way Hills (aka Blueberry Hill, Rush Creek Brewery)	1993-operating

Holmes County

Millersburg

1.	Pierre Maillard, Millersburg Brewery	c.1866-c.1877

Winesburg

1.	Leo Wiegand	c.1868-1884
2.	Godfrey Schmidt	c.mid-1880s-1890s

Huron County

Monroeville

1.	a.	John & Henry Roby, Monroeville Brewery	1848-1866
	b.	Charles P. Prentiss	1866-1877
	c.	Urlau, Rupp & Co.	1877-c.1884

Norwalk

1.	a.	Pickett Latimer (operated as a distillery)	c.1827-1848
	b.	Richard Joslin (converted to a brewery in 1859)	1848-1862
	c.	Frank Humbel	1864-1866
	d.	John Beardsley & Joseph Farr	1866-1869
	e.	Patrick & James Brady	1869-1870
	f.	Anthony Lais, Star Brewery	1870-1884
	g.	Estate of Anthony Lais	1884-1889
	h.	Henry Lais	1889-1906
	i.	Lais Brewing Co.	1906-1912
2.	a.	George A. Merkle	1837-1841
	b.	James Pearse, Norwalk Brewery	1841-c.1844
3.		Zechariah Standish	c.1849-c. mid-1850s
4.	a.	Peter & Augustus Ott and Veith Bishop	1859-1866
	b.	Peter and Augustus Ott	1866-1876
	c.	Levi Fletcher & Joseph Miller	1876-1878
	d.	Fletcher, Miller & Ott	1878-1881
	e.	Ott & Miller	1879-1881
	f.	Theresa Ott (operated by Peter Ott until 1890)	1881-1906

Peru

1.	William Taggart, Peru Brewery	c. 1828

Jackson County

Wellston

1.	Wellston Brewing and Ice Co.	1905-1910

Jefferson County

Steubenville

1.	a.	Andrew Dunlap, Steubenville Brewery	1815-1819
	b.	Robert Thompson & William Shiras, Jr.	1819-early 1820s
	c.	Charles F. Laiblin	early 1820s-1840

	d.	Joseph Basler & Francis Zimmerman (lease)	1840-1845
2.		James and John Fife	1817-1818
3.	a.	Alexander Armstrong	early 1820s
	b.	Mr. Woods (lease)	1820s
	c.	Mr. Rolly (lease)	1830s
	d.	Frederick Beter & George Shipler (lease)	1834-1844
	e.	Joseph Basler, Sr.	1845-1852
4.	a.	Joseph Basler, Sr.	1852-1870s
	b.	Basler & Brother	1870s-c.1883
5.		Ernhart H. Schaffer	1859-1877
6.	a.	John C. Butte, City Brewery	1861-1873
	b.	Bernhard Miller	1873-1876
	c.	John C. Butte	1876-1882
	d.	Rall & Klein	1882-1886
	e.	Charles L. Rall	1886-1895
	f.	Mrs. Lucy E. Rall	1895-1896
	g.	John Buehler	1896-1910
	h.	Steuben Brewing Co.	1912-1919
	i.	Steuben Beverage Works	1919-1920
7.		John Scofield	c.1869-c.1873

Knox County

Mount Vernon

1.	a.	John Arentrue	c.1837-1858
	b.	Ann Arentrue	1858-1871
	c.	Keller, Rowley, & Miller	1871-1875
	d.	John Younger	1875-1876

Pleasant Township

1.		Frederick Rohrer	c.1825-1832
2.	a.	Jacob Kurtz	1835-1837
	b.	George Pfeifer & Jacob Kurtz	1837-1850
	c.	John Bechtel	1850-c.1876

Lake County

Painesville

1.	a.	Schram, Garfield, & Co.	1866-1867
	b.	Alexander H. Garfield	1867-1868
	c.	Garfield & Warner	1868-1879
	d.	Harmon Carroll	1879-1889

Willoughby

1.	Oscar F. White	1879-1884
2.	Willoughby Brewing Co.	1998-operating

Lawrence County

Ironton

1.	**a.**	Joseph Hochgesang & Jacob Blessig	1859-early 1870s
	b.	Geiger & Loeb, East Ironton Brewery	early 1870s
	c.	Joseph Hochgesang, East Ironton Brewery	early 1870s-1875
	d.	Meyer & Rothenberg	1875-1876
	e.	Jacob Meyer	1876-1880
2.		Leo Ebert	1862-1863
3.	**a.**	Leo Ebert, Eagle Brewery	1863-1880
	b.	Leo Ebert & Co., Eagle Brewery	1880-1897
	c.	Leo Ebert Brewing Co., Eagle Brewery	1897-1909
	d.	The Ebert Brewing Co.	1912-1917
	e.	Ironton Brewing Co.	1917-1918
	f.	Court Products Co. (vinegar production)	1918-1919

Licking County

Newark

1.		Michael Morath	early 1840s-1858
2.	**a.**	John Kneule	late 1840s-1865
	b.	Hager & Knosman	1865-1869
	c.	Charles Korzenborn & Otto Bingmann	1869-1891
	d.	Korzenborn Brewery, Charles Bingmann	1891-1897
	e.	Charles Korzenborn Brewing Co.	1897-1915
	f.	Home Brewery	1915-1916
3.	**a.**	Jacob Graff	late 1840s-c.1859
	b.	Jacob Graff & William Rickrich	c.1859-1865
	c.	Rickrich & Co.	1865-c.1870
4.		Michael Morath, City Brewery	1858-c.1871
5.		Augustus Morath, Rock Hill Brewery	early 1860s-c.1869
6.	**a.**	Adolph Bentlich, White Top Brewery	c.1864-1870
	b.	Benner, Bentlich & Eichhorn	1870-1879
	c.	William Bentlich & Peter Eichhorn	1879-1884
7.		Philip Rickrich, Spring Hill Brewery	1866-c.1884
		(also known as Rickrich & Brother, Rickrich & Senger)	
8.	**a.**	Consumers Brewing Co.	1897-1919
	b.	Consumers Products Co.	1919-c.1930
	c.	The Consumers Brewing Co.	1933-1954
9.		Bunky's Brewpub/Legends Brewing Co.	1998-2001

Lorain County

Amherst

1.	William Braun	1868-1884

Avon

1.	Creekside Brewhouse and Tavern	2000-2003

Elyria

1.	**a.**	John Bishop	1864-1877

    b.   Andrew Plocher   1877-1879

Lorain

1. Lorain Brewing Co., branch of   1905-1918
Cleveland & Sandusky Brewing Co.

Wellington

1. John M. Crabtree   1871-c.1876

Mahoning County

Austintown

1. Meander Brewing Co.   1991-1993

Green Township/New Albany

1. William Moff   late 1850s-1862

New Springfield

1. John Seeger   c.1870-1879

Youngstown

1.
    a. John Smith, Youngstown Brewery   1846-1870
    b. John Smith's Sons   1870-1901
    c. John Smith's Sons Brewing Co.   1901-1904
    d. Smith Brewing Co.   1904-1919
    e. Smith Products Co.   1919-1925

2. American Brewery, Enoch Smith   early 1850s-1873

3.
    a. Philip Schuh & John Bayer   1865
    b. Philip Schuh   1865-1869
    c. Mathias Seeger, City Brewery   1869-1880
    d. Christian Seeger   1880-1881
    e. John Bayer   1881-1883
    f. George J. Renner, Jr., City Brewery   1885-1913
    g. Renner Brewing Co.   1913-1919
    h. The Renner Co.   1919-1921
    i. The Renner Co. (offices only, no brewing)   1921-1933
    j. The Renner Co., Inc. (aka Renner Brewing Co.)   1933-1962

4.
    a. Christian Haid   late 1860s-1873
    b. Mary Haid   1873-1876
    c. Jacob Knott (aka Knott & Klahs)   1876-1890

5.
    a. Youngstown Brewing Co.   1936-1947
    b. Crystal Top Brewery, Inc.   1947-1948

6. B & O Station Brewery & Restaurant   2002-2004

Medina County

Medina Township

1. The Burkhardt Brewing Co.   1999-2001

2.
    a. Wallaby's Grille & Brewpub   1999-2000

    b.   Brown Derby Roadhouse   2001-operating

Meigs County

Pomeroy

1.	a.	Frederick Schaffer	1849-1865
	b.	Gottlieb Wildermuth	1865-1898
	c.	Gottlieb Wildermuth Brewing Co.	1898-1919

Monroe County

Miltonsburg

1.		Frederick Stauzel	c.1842-c. mid-1860s

Woodsfield

1.	a.	Michael Lang	mid-1860s-1882
	b.	John H. Lang	1882-1884

Morgan County

McConnellsville

1.	a.	Theabold D. Young	c.1862-1875
	b.	Burckholter & Reed	1875-1880

Morrow County

No known breweries

Muskingum County

Zanesville

1.	a.	George Painter	c.1808-1811
	b.	Jacob Young	1811-c.1814
2.		William Marshall & James Boyd	1813-1815
3.	a.	Joseph Lattimore & Caleb Johnson	1816-1829
	b.	David Ballentine	1829-1835
	c.	operated as a flour mill	1835-1849
	d.	operated as a white lead manufacturing plant	1849-1859
	e.	Jarvis Wainwright, Muskingum Steam Brewery	1859-1871
4.	a.	C. F. Haas, America House Tavern & Brewery	1835-1848
	b.	John Clossman, Market Brewery	1848-1868
5.	a.	Christian F. Achauer	c.1848-1881
	b.	Herman Achauer	1881-1884
	c.	Zinsmeister & Linser	1884-1891
	d.	Simon Linser, Washington Brewery	1891-1901
	e.	Simon Linser Brewing Co.	1901-1919
	f.	Hill Top Beverage Co.	1919-1928
	g.	Simon Linser Co. (beer distributor only)	1933-1958
6.	a.	City Brewery & Malt House, Goebel & Fisher	1854-1861
	b.	Horn & Kirsner	1861-1865
	c.	John A. Brenner & Co.	1865-1885

	d.	Brenner & Co. malting plant only	1885-1893
	e.	Zanesville Star Bottling Works, soda only	1893-1898
	f.	Frank L. Normann	1898-1900
7.	a.	Conrad Fisher	1856-1875
	b.	Fisher Brothers	1875-1885
	c.	John A. Brenner & Co., Red Star Brewery	1885-1893
	d.	Star Brewing Co.	1893
	e.	Armbruster & Schmitt	1894-1900
	f.	Simon Linser Brewing Co., plant 2	1900-1905
8.	a.	Sebastian Bohn	c.1865-1892
	b.	August Bohn	1892-1919
9.	a.	Horn & Co.	1865-1869
	b.	Merkle Brothers	1869-1880
	c.	Adolph Merkle	1880-1891
	d.	The Riverside Brewing Co.	1891-1900
	e.	The Bavarian Brewing Co. (aka Simon Linser Brewing Co., plant No. 3)	1900-1914

Noble County

No known breweries

Ottawa County

Marblehead

1. Frontwaters Restaurant & Brewing Co. — 1996-2003

Middle Bass Island

1. J. F. Walleyes Eatery & Brewery — 1998-operating
2. Hazards Microbrewery and Restaurant — 1999-operating

Put-In-Bay/South Bass Island

1. Put-In-Bay Brewing Co./Brewery at the Bay — 1996-operating

Perry County

No known breweries

Portage County

Brimfield

1. Blimp City Brewery — 1998-2003

Garrettsville

1. Garretts Mill Brewing Co. — 1995-2002

Kent

1. Mugs Brewpub — 2000-2003

Ravenna

1.	a.	Adam Grohe	1865-1866
	b.	Philip Balser (& Anthony Wolf, briefly)	1866-1868
	c.	Nicholas Englehart	1868-1872

d.	Philip Balser	1872-1876

Richland County

Mansfield

1.	a.	Harvey & Long	1857-1859
	b.	Long & Aberle	1859-1864
	c.	Frank & Aberle	1864-1866
	d.	Reiman & Aberle	1866-1883
	e.	Reiman & Weber	1883-1884
	f.	Renner & Weber, Eagle Brewery	1884-1900
	g.	Renner-Weber Brewing Co.	1900-1919
	h.	The Renner & Weber Brewing Co.	1934-1951
2.	a.	Joseph Leuthner	c.1859-c.1864
	b.	Leuthner & Schmutzler	c.1864-1871
	c.	Schmutzler & Co.	1871-c.1876
3.	a.	Frank & Weber	1866-1883
	b.	Martin Frank	1883-1899
	c.	Martin Frank & Son	1899-1919
	d.	M. Frank & Son Brewery	1933-1940
4.	a.	Wooden Pony Brewing Co.	1996-1998
	b.	Wooden Pony Brewing Co.	2001-2002

Stark County

Alliance

1.	a.	Henry Klingler & Florian Knam	mid-1860s-c.1873
	b.	Florian Knam	c.1873-1879
	c.	Mary Knam	1879-1880
2.	a.	Alliance Brewing Co	1905-1919
	b.	Alliance Beverage Co.	1919-1924

Canal Fulton (aka Fulton)

1.	a.	Michael Ruch	1840s-1860s
	b.	Christian Ruch, Fulton Brewery	1860s-1888
	c.	Ernest Schneider/Schneider Bros.	1888-1891
	d.	Christian Ruch	1891-1894
	e.	Jacob Babst	1894

Canton

1.		Canton Brewery	1817-c.1823
2.	a.	George Nighman	1830-1833
	b.	Lydia Nighman	1833-c.1840
	c.	Bicking & Melchior	c.1840-1847
	d.	Bicking & Thaddeus Nighman	1847-1852
	e.	Thaddeus C. Nighman	1852-1860
	f.	Kasper Balser, City Brewery	1865-1876
	g.	Mrs. Louisa Balser, City Brewery	1876-1890
3.	a.	Jacob Hahn	early 1830s-1835
	b.	John & Henry Scholder	1835-1852
	c.	Christian Graff	1852-late 1850s
4.		Peter Melchior	1848-1864

5.	**a.**	John D. Graber	1865-1873
	b.	Otto Giessen & Joseph Klopfenstein	1873-1875
	c.	Giessen & Baker	1875-1877
	d.	Otto Giessen	1877-1883
6.	**a.**	Joseph Klopfenstein	1874-1875
	b.	Knobloch & Hermann	1875-1880
	c.	Adam W. Knobloch, Union Brewery	1880-1888
	d.	Edel & Seiferth, Union Brewing Co.	1888-1891
	e.	Canton Brewing Co.	1891-1891
7.	**a.**	Otto Giessen	1884-1887
	b.	Rommel & Kraft, Canton Brewing Co.	1887-1888
	c.	William Rommel, Canton Brewing Co.	1888-1891
	d.	Edel & Rommel, Canton Brewing Co.	1891-1905
	e.	Stark-Tuscarawas Brewing Co.	1905-1919
8.	**a.**	Stark Brewing Co.	1902-1905
	b.	Stark-Tuscarawas Brewing Co.	1905-1919
	c.	Stark-Tuscarawas Co.	1919-1927
	d.	Tuscora Brewing Co. (non-producing)	1933-1934
9.		Home Brewing Co	1906-1923
10.	**a.**	Graber Brewing Co.	1933-1933
	b.	Canton Brewing Co, Inc.	1933-1937
	c.	The Canton Brewing Co.	1939-1941

Jackson Township (aka New Berlin)

1.	**a.**	Christian Kropf	c.1868-c.1879
	b.	Henry C. Kropf	c.1879-c.1884
2.	**a.**	The Brewhouse	1996-2000
	b.	New Berlin Brewing Co.	2000-2001
	c.	Gridiron Brewpub and Grille	2001-2003
3.		Thirsty Dog Brewing Co.	1997-2004

Louisville

1.	**a.**	Peter B. Moinet	1865-c.1869
	b.	Joseph Moinet	c.1869-1873
	c.	Moinet, Roth, & Graber	1873-1876
	d.	Graber & Dilger	1876-1878
	e.	Dilger & Menegay	1878-1881
	f.	George Dilger	1881-1894
	g.	Kropf Ale Co.	1897-1899
	h.	The Louisville Brewing Co.	1899-1901
	I.	Louisville Brewing Co.	1901-1906

Massillon

1.	**a.**	Charles J. Bammerlin, Forest City Brewery	1842-1862
	b.	Leonard Bammerlin, Forest City Brewery	1862-1881
2.	**a.**	Frederick Haag	1845-1871
	b.	Stoolmiller & Seippel, City Brewery	1871-1877
	c.	Emma Holbyson	1877-1879
	d.	M. Webber	1879-1881
	e.	Leonard Bammerlin	1881-1883
	f.	Julius Wittman, Empire Brewery	1883-1884
3.	**a.**	James H. McLain & Co.	1883-1885

	b.	Massillon Brewing Co.	1885-1887
	c.	Erhard & Schimke	1887-1891
	d.	Robert Schimke	1891-1893
	e.	Paulina C. Schimke	1893-1894
	f.	Anton Kopp	1894-1898
	g.	John W. Schuster	1898-1900
	h.	Schuster Brewing Co.	1900-1901
4.	a.	Schuster Brewing Co.	1901-1905
	b.	Stark-Tuscarawas Brewing Co.	1905-1919
	c.	Schuster & Co.	1919-1924
	d.	Massillon Brewing Co. (non-producing)	1933-1935

Navarre

1.	a.	Daniel Groff & Isaac Rudy	c.1850-1853
	b.	Thomas McCullogh & Jacob Zinsmaster	1853-1856
	c.	Jacob & Christian Snyder & Jacob Zinsmaster	1856-1859
	d.	Christian Snyder & George Eberhard	1859-1860
	e.	Christian Snyder & Frederick Hess	1860-1862
	f.	Peter Dommy & Frederick Hess	1862-1863
	g.	Peter Dommy & Barnhard Klein	1863-1864
	h.	James Leeper & Barnhard Klein	1864-1865
	i.	William Hanson	1865
	j.	Christian Ruch	1865-1866
	k.	Garver, Grossklaus, & Ricksaker	1866-1867
	l.	Grossklaus, Hug, & Ricksaker	1867-1868
	m.	Grossklaus & Hug	1868-c.1874
	n.	Edward J. Hug	c.1874-c.1876

Nimishillen Township (aka Rome)

1.	a.	Christian/John Sommer	c.1868-1872
	b.	Christian Kropf	1872-1884

Perry Township (also listed as Canton)

1.	a.	Christian Sommer	c.1850-1877
	b.	John Sommer & Co.	1877-1878
	c.	Cristian Kropf & Co.	1878-1904
	d.	Kropf Cream Ale Co.	1904-1912

Uniontown

1.	a.	Philip Seesdorf	1851-1855
	b.	Frederick Housholter	1855-1860
	c.	Peter Follmer	1860-1862
	d.	Jonathan Hubler	1862-c.1865

Waynesburg

1.	a.	Roger Morledge	c.1840-1848
	b.	Henry Scholder	1848-1857
	c.	James Ross	1857
	d.	Madison Mays	1857-1862
	e.	Henry Gruber	1862-1877
	f.	Christian Gruber	1877-c.1888

Summit County

Akron

1.	a.	John T. Good & Michael Bittman	1845-1850
	b.	John T. Good	1850-1855

	c.	John & Jacob Good	1855-1861
2.		Marshall Viall	c.1846-c.1855
3.	a.	George Harmann & John Brodt	1848-1855
	b.	George Kempel	1855-1866
	c.	Christopher Oberholtz	1866-1869
	d.	Frederick Oberholtz & Co.	1869-1874
	e.	John A. Kolp	1876-1879
	f.	Frederick Horix	1879-1888
	g.	Renner Brewing Co.	1888-1901
	h.	George J. Renner Brewing Co.	1901-1919
	i.	Renner Products Co.	1919-1933
	j.	George J. Renner Brewing Co.	1933-1953
4.	a.	John and Jacob Good	1861
	b.	Jacob Good	1861-late 1860s
	c.	Jacob R. Guth	late 1860s-c.1873
5.	a.	Conrad Fink, John Fink, Frederick Haushalter	1863-1864
	b.	John & William Fink	1864-1866
	c.	Jacques Lockert & Theodore Schell	1866-1868
	d.	Louis Lockert & Theodore Schell	1868-1869
	e.	Louis Lockert, South Akron Brewery	1869-1870
	f.	Joseph C. Wirth	1870-1872
6.	a.	Frederick Gaessler	c.1865-1877
	b.	Gaessler & Burkhardt, Wolf Ledge Brewery	1877-1879
	c.	Wilhelm Burkhardt, Wolf Ledge Brewery	1880-1882
	d.	Margaretha Burkhardt, Wolf Ledge Brewery	1882-1886
	e.	Mrs. Margaretha Burkhardt	1886-1902
	f.	M. Burkhardt Brewing Co.	1902-1919
	g.	Burkhardt Products Co./Burkhardt Co.	1919-1923
	h.	Burkhardt Consolidated Co.	1923-1930
	i.	The Burkhardt Brewing Co.	1933-1956
	j.	The Burger Brewing Co.	1956-1964
7.	a.	Fred Horix & John Kirn	1870-1873
	b.	Fred Horix	1873-1879
8.	a.	The Akron Brewing Co.	1903-1919
	b.	The Akron Beverage & Cold Storage Co.	1919-1924
9.		Akron Brewing Co.	1934-1943
10.	a.	Liberty Brewing Co.	1994-1996
	b.	Liberty Street Brewing Co.	1996-2001

Barberton

1.	a.	Charles W. Specht	1896-1898
	b.	Christina Specht	1898-1901

Boston Township

1.	Boston Mills Brewery, proprietor unknown	c.1820s

Copley Township

1.	Thirsty Dog Brewing Co.	1998-2005

Cuyahoga Falls

1.	Joseph Clarkson, Cuyahoga Falls Brewery	1856-1873

Green

1. a. Burkhardt's Brewpub — 1991-1993
   b. Burkhardt Brewing Co. — 1993-2000
   c. Mugsy's Brewpub (brewing done by Burkhardt) — 2000-2000

Hudson

1. Four Fellows Brewpub — 1999-2000

Northfield

1. Northfield Park Microbrewery — 1997-operating

Trumbull County

Niles

1. Ohio Brewing Co. — 1997-2002 (restaurant closed in 1999)

Warren

1. a. George Clement — c.1858-early 1870s
   b. George Clement, Jr. — early 1870s-1880

2. a. Augustus Graeter — c.1838-late 1850s
   b. Herman Graeter — late 1850s-1867
   c. Jacob Waldeck & William Mack — 1867-1868
   d. Jacob Waldeck — 1868-c.1877

Tuscarawas County

Canal Dover (aka Dover)

1. a. Frederick Crater — c.1848-1862
   b. George Diehl & Basil Downey — 1862-1869
   c. Philip Miller & Co., Dover Steam Brewery — 1869-1873

2. a. Nicholas Montag — c.1856-1865
   b. Andy Dangleisen — 1865-1870
   c. Frederick Bernhardt — 1873-1896
   d. Dover Brewing Co., Frederick Bernhardt — 1896-1899
   e. Dover Brewing Co., Christian Bernhardt — 1899-1905
   f. Stark-Tuscarawas Brewing Co. — 1905-1908

3. a. Tuscarawas Valley Brewing Co — 1906-1911
   b. Martin Brewery — 1912
   c. Consumers Brewing & Ice Co. — 1912-1914

New Philadelphia (aka Blackfield)

1. a. Michael Berger — 1864-1871
   b. Rudolph Kapizky — 1871-1876
   c. Seibold & Hafenbrak — 1876-1884
   d. New Philadelphia Brewing Co. — 1884-1905
   e. Stark-Tuscarawas Brewing Co. — 1905-1919
   f. Stark-Tuscarawas Co. — 1919-1927
   g. Seibold Products Co. — 1927-1933
   h. New Philadelphia Brewery, Inc. — 1933-1945
   i. The New Philadelphia Brewery Co. — 1945-1949

Strasburg

1.	a.	Klopfenstein & Harberdier	1875-1877
	b.	Jacob Seikel	1877-1890

Zoar

1.	a.	Zoar Community Brewery	c.1820s-1898
	b.	Alexander Gunn	1898 (possibly longer)

Vinton County

No known breweries

Washington County

Marietta

1.	a.	John Smith	mid-1840s-1850
	b.	Jacob Gaddel	1850-mid-1850s
	c.	Caroline Gaddel	mid-1850s-1860
	d.	Bernhard E. Stohr & Jacob Hennemann	1860-1865
	e.	Gaddel, Maser, & Co.	1865-c.1873
2.		Frederick Grohs	c.1858-c.1862
3.	a.	Christian Held	1866-1868
	b.	Martin Seamon	1868
	c.	George M. Kestel, Union Brewery	1868-1876
	d.	Fidel & William Rapp	1876-1877
	e.	John Schneider	1877-1884
	f.	Elizabeth Schneider	1884-1890
	g.	William Feller & Co., Marietta Brewery	1898-1903
	h.	Marietta Brewing Co.	1903-c.1924
	i.	Marietta Brewing Co. (non-producing)	1933-1934
	j.	American Brewery Co. (non-producing)	1934-1935
4.		Marietta Brewing Co.	1997-operating

Wayne County

Smithville (aka Green)

1.	a.	John Burkholder, Smithville Brewery	1830-1875
	b.	Jonathon S. Burkholder, Smithville Brewery	1875-1882

Sterling (aka Amwell, Milton)

1.	Peter & Christian P. Rich	c.1873-1888

Wooster

1.	a.	Joseph J. Ramseyer, Apple Creek Brewery	c.1860-1870
	b.	Rich & Roth	1870-1874
	c.	Rich & Mougey	1874-1879
	d.	Mougey & Graber	1879-1882
	e.	Graber & Renner	1882-1884
	f.	John Graber	1884-1888
	g.	Frederick Weis	1888-1890
	h.	Wooster Brewing Co.	1890-1903
	i.	Wooster Artificial Ice & Brewing Co.	1903-1916
2.		Wendel Young	1864-1878

243 Total Breweries

Top Ten Lists

Ten earliest known breweries in eastern Ohio

1. George Painter brewery, Zanesville-1808
2. Morrison & Wheeler brewery, Huron-1812
3. Marshall & Boyd brewery, Zanesville-1813
4. Steubenville Brewery-1815
5. Lattimore brewery, Zanesville-1816
6. James & John Fife, Steubenville-1817
7. Canton Brewery-1817
8. Zoar Society brewery-between 1817 and mid-1820s
9. Armstrong brewery, Steubenville-1820
10. Frederick Rohrer tavern & brewery, near Mount Vernon-1825

Ten longest lasting breweries in eastern Ohio

1. George J. Renner Brewing Co., Akron-105 years (1848-1953)
2. Leisy Brewing Co., Cleveland-101 years (1858-1959)
3. Herb/Milan Brewing Co.-101 years (1850-1951)
4. Burkhardt Brewing Co., Akron-99 years (1865-1964)
5. Renner Co., Youngstown-97 years (1865-1962)
6. Renner & Weber Brewing Co., Mansfield-94 years (1857-1951)
7. Mall/Gund/Sunrise brewery, Cleveland-92 years (1852-1944)
8. Seibold/New Philadelphia Brewing Co.-85 years (1864-1949)
9. Stang/Cleveland-Sandusky Brewing Co., Sandusky-83 years (1852-1935)
10. Smith Brewing Co., Youngstown-79 years (1846-1925)

Ten largest breweries in eastern Ohio (peak annual capacity)

1. Brewing Corp. of America/Carling/Schmidt-3,000,000 barrels (Cleveland plant only)
2. Leisy Brewing Co., Cleveland-565,000 barrels (1918)
3. Standard Brewing Co., Cleveland-550,000 barrels (after WWII)
4. Pilsener Brewing Co., Cleveland-500,000 barrels (1950s)
5. Burkhardt/Burger Brewing Co., Akron-300,000 barrels (1950s)
6. Cleveland-Sandusky Brewing Corp., Cleveland-200,000 barrels (Fishel plant)
7. George J. Renner Brewing Co., Akron-200,000 barrels (prior to WWII only)
8. Forest City Brewing Co., Cleveland-200,000 barrels
9. Renner Co., Youngstown-175,000 barrels
10. Cleveland Home Brewing Co.-175,000 barrels

ASHLAND COUNTY

Ashland

1. Gerhart Lepper brewery

Gerhart (also spelled Gearhart, Gierhard) Lepper was a German immigrant, born in 1810, who purchased land on the west side of the town of Ashland in the spring of 1849. Soon after this, he established the county's first brewery, although its exact location is uncertain. He owned property on both sides of Town Run, as well as a large tract of land west of town, but it seems likely that the brewery would have been along the small creek. Lepper was assisted by two younger German immigrants, Lewis Fisher (b. 1822) and Frederick Miller (b. 1825).

The small brewery appears to have operated until the mid-1860s, after which Lepper continued to work as a farmer and fruit grower. He remained in Ashland until 1884, when he died of old age.

Loudonville

1. Union Brewery

The origin of Loudonville's only brewery is somewhat obscure. It is known to have been in existence by 1873, when it was being operated by Graf and Roth. Charles Roth was a local butcher, born in Germany in 1838, and John Graf was a blacksmith who had just arrived from Germany. Graf had been born in Renchen, Baden, in 1818, and had later served as a lieutenant in the German army. He had five sons, one of whom, William, was also a blacksmith. It remains unknown which members of the Graf family were involved with the brewery, although it appears that much of the actual brewing was performed by Fred W. Krause, a Prussian immigrant and farmer, born in 1820.

The brewery was located on the east side of Mount Vernon Road, along the Black Fork of the Mohican River. Annual production of lager beer was between 100 and 200 barrels. The brewery appears to have ceased operation by 1877, although it was still listed in the 1880 Loudonville business directory. There is no evidence of it operating after this, however, and there is no trace of it today. Krause remained in the area until his death in 1887. Roth remained in the area until his death in 1890. John Graf died in 1897.

Ashtabula County

Ashtabula

1. Consumers Brewing Company

(Edited from an article by Art Distelrath, originally published in the American Breweriana Journal, September/October 1994, Issue #70)

At the turn of the century, Ashtabula, Ohio was a busy port town on the great shore of Lake Erie, located about 60 miles east of Cleveland. Its inhabitants were rugged sailors, railroad men, and mill workers who enjoyed Ashtabula's reputation as one of the toughest ports in the country.

Many regional brewers saw Ashtabula as a prime spot to market their brews, and opened branch offices there. Among them were Jackson Koehler's Erie Brewing Co., Leisy, Schlather, and Cleveland & Sandusky Breweries of Cleveland, the Finlay Brewing Co. of Toledo, and the huge Windisch-Muhlhauser Lion Brewery of Cincinnati. In December 1904, a group from Ashtabula met with investors from Cleveland and decided to build a brewery in the city. By the next month, the Consumers Brewing Co. was formed with Dr. O. Mueller as president and Thomas A. Dillon as secretary. The brewery had a capital stock of $200,000 and shares were offered at a price of $100 each.

The contract for the brewery was awarded to the Joseph Schneible Co. of New York. Schneible was in the process of constructing similar breweries in Indianapolis and Cincinnati, and was well known for its architecture. Work was scheduled to begin as soon as weather permitted and to be completed by September 1, 1905. Plans called for a "strictly up-to-date outfit" and a model brewing facility following the Schneible Pneumatic System, with an annual capacity of 45,000 barrels. The building itself was to be of massive construction with a glazed brick interior to make it as fireproof as possible.

After an initial attempt to secure a water supply failed, a tract of land was purchased next to the Crystal Spring, at

Brewery photo courtesy of Art Distelrath

the foot of Topper Avenue, and was said to have "living water in abundance". The water from the Crystal Spring had been sold on various railroads for its mineral characteristics. The New York Central, Nickel Plate, and other railroads that ran in the vicinity raved that Crystal Spring's water was "delicious and wholesome".

In September 1905, the Windisch-Muhlhauser/Lion Brewery of Cincinnati and the Consumers Brewery locked horns in a beer price war. The Consumers Brewery was able to lure Windisch-Muhlhauser's local agent, John Finn, to distribute its beer for between $7.00 and $7.50 per barrel. The Consumers ally in the war was the newly built Ohio Union Brewing Co. in Cincinnati, which used the same Schneible system and was nearly identical to the Consumers plant. Ohio Union brewed Consumers' beer while the Ashtabula brewery was being built. The Lion Brewery responded by lowering its price to $5.00 per barrel and said that it would meet the price of the Consumers brewery even if it meant giving beer to the dealers for free. The local saloon owners took advantage of this and enjoyed large profits during the beer war because the standard price of five cents per glass was not affected. The price war was only between the Lion and Consumers breweries, so other breweries watched with great interest as their products were not affected either. It is unknown how low the price of beer went that September, but Lion eventually withdrew from the Ashtabula market.

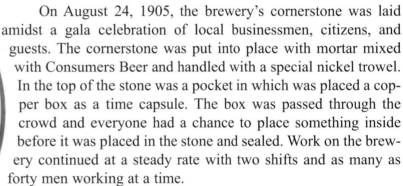

On August 24, 1905, the brewery's cornerstone was laid amidst a gala celebration of local businessmen, citizens, and guests. The cornerstone was put into place with mortar mixed with Consumers Beer and handled with a special nickel trowel. In the top of the stone was a pocket in which was placed a copper box as a time capsule. The box was passed through the crowd and everyone had a chance to place something inside before it was placed in the stone and sealed. Work on the brewery continued at a steady rate with two shifts and as many as forty men working at a time.

In October 1905, an investment group of capitalists from Cleveland attempted to buy out the stockholders of the Consumers Brewing Co. and seven other independent breweries in Northeast Ohio and Northwestern Pennsylvania in an effort to form a brewery syndicate and control the beer output and cost over that area. The other companies involved were the Smith and Renner breweries in Youngstown, the Alliance Brewing Co., the Crockery City Brewing and Ice Co. in East Liverpool, the Standard Brewing Co. of New Castle, PA., the Meadville Brewing Co. of Meadville, PA., and the Union Brewing Co. of Sharon, PA.

Stock advertising tray [Art Distelrath collection]

The Consumers stockholders met on October 24th and held a heated discussion concerning the proposed buyout. The stockholders from the Cleveland area were in favor of the buyout and saw an opportunity to make a profit on their brief investment. On the other hand, the Ashtabula stockholders were united and fought against the buyout. They saw the buyout as a loss of permanent income for themselves and the city. The Ashtabula stockholders were outvoted by their Cleveland counterparts and a price of $150 per $100 share was set.

The Ashtabula stockholders were not pleased with the outcome, but they had one opportunity left to prevent the plant from being taken over by the syndicate. Their strategy was to find local investors to purchased enough of the remaining stock to block the Cleveland contingent. At the time of the buyout, only $80,000 of the $200,000 total had been sold and the locals saw ample opportunity to save their interest and brewery. Surprisingly in the end, the syndicate was not able to raise the money needed, and all the breweries remained independent.

The Ashtabula brewery continued to move forward and plans were made to start brewing operations in the summer of 1906. New officers elected for that year were George J. Lowe as president, Charles Zeile as vice-president, Albert Eisele as treasurer, and John C. Topper as secretary. On October 31, 1906, the Consumers Brewing Co. opened for business, and a demand for its beer filled the city. The first barrel of beer was delivered to John Goggin's saloon in the Ashtabula harbor. Mr. Goggin won the honor of receiving the first barrel by bidding the sum of $60 a year earlier. The following day, Consumers Beer was flowing in nearly every saloon and restaurant in the city. It was a great day for the city of Ashtabula and it was the realization of the hopes of many people.

The plant's brewmaster was Henry P. Harr, a graduate of brewing schools in both Berlin and Copenhagen. Production was limited to lager beer, and at the time of opening, only kegs were available, as the bottling works was not yet finshed. When this department finally began operation, it had the capacity of filling 200 cases per day. On February 6, 1907, "Bula Beer" went on sale, and it rapidly became very popular among the local beer drinkers in town.

Local rumors had it that the water used by the brewery had an off-flavor, and that this contributed to the company's demise. However, tests had shown this rumor to be false when the Crystal Spring water was tested by chemists from the Wahl & Henius Institute of Chicago. The water was declared to be among the best they had ever tested for brewing, and the brewery spared no expense in advertising and ensuring that the water they used was pure.

The Consumers brewery had great success initially, brewing over 3,600 barrels monthly, and quickly establishing itself as one of Ashtabula's most successful businesses. This success was short-lived, however, as the Prohibition movement was gaining ground in the city and surrounding region by the Fall of 1908. Passage of the Rose Law had paved the way for local option on this issue. In that year, the brewery had begun producing a temperance beer, known as "Non-Alcoholic Bula Beer", although it met with little success.

By early 1909, the first "dry law" was passed, prohibiting the sale of alcohol on Sundays. This was known as "the lid" and was strictly enforced in town. Prohibitionists were not yet satisfied, so another law was passed preventing the brewery from making or selling beer within the city limits. For a while, the brewery got around that law by making beer and transporting it a few hundred feet away to the township line, where they then sold it to township saloonkeepers. Later that year, however, the entire county went dry, putting an end to that practice, and the brewery's business.

On October 7, 1909, the county common pleas court ordered the corporation dissolved and the brewery was placed into a receivership. John Topper, the company's former secretary, was named receiver and gave a bond of $25,000 for the plant. He attempted to continue the business until the property could be sold for profit. Bootleggers briefly brewed small batches of beer there, but soon they disappeared and the plant stood idle.

In 1912, the plant was sold at auction to the Tonawanda Brewing Co. of New York. The Tonawanda Co. had purchased the Consumers brewery only for its equipment, as it was intending to build a new brewery of its own. When the equipment was removed from the building, huge sections of walls were knocked out, leaving the deserted building an eyesore. The property was purchased in 1914 by John Masino, but the buildings stood quietly for the next decade.

In the 1920s, the deserted brewery attracted the attention of the Ku Klux Klan, which had become quite powerful in the city and other parts of the county. The brewery, with its high tower and location in Osborn Heights, on high ground east of the city, was easily visible from some distance. The Klansmen used the roof of the plant to burn crosses, while setting off loud dynamite charges in a nearby gravel pit to draw attention to the crosses. These could easily be seen in the downtown area of Ashtabula, as well as for long distances in all directions. This continued for several years until Masino took his own dynamite charges and blew the top two stories off the tower, thus ending the Klan's use of the building.

Several years later, the city council decided to do away with the remaining structures altogether, and they were subsequently dynamited to their doom. In the 1930s, the Civilian Conservation Corps crushed the remaining chunks of brick and concrete for use as a roadbed in the Gulf Park area of Ashtabula. Today, all that remains of the Consumers brewery is a rusted water pipe sticking out of the hillside near the former Crystal Spring. The spring itself has all but disappeared, leaving behind a small overgrown pool. The Riverview apartment complex occupies the site of the former brewery on what is now East 51st Street, overlooking the steep bank of the Ashtabula River.

2. Independent Brewing Company

Little is known about Ashtabula's other pre-Prohibition attempt at brewing. Andrew Dalin was a local bottler of Leisy Beer from Cleveland. With capital from Otto Leisy himself, the Independent Brewing Co. was formed in 1905, to operate out of Dalin's bottling works at 141 Bridge St. Other initial investors included William Downs, W. W. Kunkle, and L. A. Saules. Exactly how much was brewed is not known for sure, but it appears that it must have been a very small operation. The fledgling company was gone after 1907, leaving no advertising to remember it by. The bottling works is no longer standing.

3. Lift Bridge Brewing Company

The roots of Ashtabula's first brewery in 85 years go back to 1992, when local attorney Dan Madden and friend Ken Frisbie, both of whom had dabbled in home brewing as a hobby, decided to create an entirely new local source for beer. Their project, costing over $200,000, was partially funded by a loan from the city, and The Lift Bridge Brewing Co. was put together over the next two years. The name was a reference to the large Bascule type drawbridge over Ashtabula Harbor, one of only two such bridges in the United States. The plant was located at 1119 Lake Avenue, and operated as a microbrewery, with the first brew sold to the public on December 9, 1994.

Dan Madden was the brewmaster, overseeing the plant's 15-barrel brewhouse, which allowed an annual capacity of up to 15,000 barrels. Traditional German recipes and styles were used and numerous brands were produced, including Amber Lager (a Vienna-style lager which won a silver medal at the 1997 BTI World Championship), India Pale Ale, Oktoberfest beer, Winter Gale Ale, Oatmeal Stout, Eisbock, Alt-Bier, and Continental Pilsener Beer. There was a great initial demand for Lift Bridge's brews, and the facility was expanded somewhat to keep up. An aggressive distribution strategy placed these beers throughout eastern Ohio, and even as far south as Cincinnati, as well as into western Pennsylvania. Despite this, all brewing operations ceased on February 1, 1998, and the equipment was sold off.

Also Note:

1. In 1903, the Ashtabula Brewing & Cold Storage Co. was incorporated with $10,000 capital stock. Incorporators were C. S. Smith, H. M. Reynolds, J. I. DeWitt, John Masino, and M. I. Manning. Likely due to an inability to raise capital, no actual brewing ever took place.

2. In August 1905, the Erie Brewing Co. of Erie, PA. purchased land at Lake, Railroad, and Second Streets, with the intention of building a branch brewery at that location. Perhaps influenced by the growing local Prohibition movement, the parent company never built the new brewery. It also operated a large beer garden at Lake, Railroad, and Depot Streets until the dry movement forced its closing.

ATHENS COUNTY

Athens

1. O'Hooley's Pub and Brewery

O'Hooley's Pub was established in September 1981, and in 1985 moved to its current location at 24 West Union St., on the outskirts of the Ohio University campus. In 1995, the decision was made to convert the restaurant into a brewpub, and over the next year the brewing equipment was brought in. The official opening of the new brewpub was on Halloween weekend, 1996.

Jim Prouty, a former Ohio University student, is the founder and owner of O'Hooley's. The name is taken from an Irish Gaelic term meaning "party". The original brewmaster was Terry Hawbaker, with Kelly Sauber as the assistant brewer. They were later succeeded by Brian Hoyle, Doug Brooks, and most recently by Floyd Beattie.

Through the brewpub's first eight years, many different brands and styles of beer have been produced, including Ohio Pale Ale (which took the "Best of Show" award at the 1998 Bluegrass Micro Festival in Kentucky), Raspberry Wheat, Raspberry Brown Ale, Golden Ale, Scottish Ale, Old Athens Barley Wine, Anniversary Porter, Indian Summer Wheat, O'Hooley's ESB, J. S. Bock, Spinning Hippie, Irish Stout, Bong Water Hemp Ale, and Winter Season Ale. Many of these are seasonal and are only available on a limited basis. Each batch from the 7-barrel system may vary somewhat as various ingredients are tinkered with.

Although the pub does not offer a full menu, it retains a true pub "feel" and remains a popular local spot.

Nelsonville

1. Hocking Valley Brewing Company

The Hocking Valley Brewing Company was formed by a group of Nelsonville area saloon owners in April 1905, with a capital stock of $100,000. The company's president was James Dew, with Frank Patton as vice-president, G. D. Ridenour as secretary, and Gothold Kuebler as brewmaster (the latter was later replaced by Eugene Hohenadel). Other initial directors of the company included E. J. Rosser, Frank Emish, J. P. Reynolds, Harry F. Ambrose, Joe B. Winefordner, and John V. Morgan. All of these men, as well as the other thirty or so saloonists in the town, would sell the new brewery's beer in their saloons almost exclusively.

Groundbreaking for the brewery took place later that month, in a ceremony attended by all of the stockholders. The spade used to break ground was adorned by bells and flowers, and later would hang from the wall of the president's office. Construction began immediately on a new state-of-the-art brewery, designed by the Huetteman & Cramer Co. of Detroit. With a central four-story brewhouse, the plant cost approximately $58,000 to build.

Located at 693 Jackson Street, the brewery officially opened to the public on January 17, 1906. A large celebration took place, complete with an orchestra and a large number of guests who sampled the first batch of "Hock Hocking" Beer. The name was a term used by the local Delaware Indians, meaning "shaped like a bottle". The Delaware had used this term to describe the nearby river (later named the Hocking River), which rushed through a narrow gorge, over a falls, and into a wide channel, like a bottle. The company again saluted the area's earliest inhabitants on the bottle label, which featured an image of Chief Logan, the leader of the Mingo Indians.

The plant's original annual capacity was 12,500 barrels, although within one year of opening, the company's success led to an expansion of the facility, increasing the capacity to 20,000 barrels, while the capital stock increased to $150,000. When at full operation, the plant employed twenty men.

Production continued uneventfully until the Rose Law of 1908 allowed Athens County to vote itself dry beginning the next year. Hock Hocking sales were hit hard, but sales to surrounding wet counties allowed the company to remain solvent until the county went wet again in 1912. By 1913, the company's president was Ira Blackstone, while Patton remained vice-president.

Brewing resumed until statewide Prohibition began in 1919. At that time, the company reorganized as the Hocking Valley Cereal Beverage Company, and began producing HV Near Beer, Root Beer, and Hock-Ola (a questionably named cola). The company's ice plant continued to produce "Crystal Ice" during this time as well. Production of beverages appears to have stopped around 1924, after which the plant was used only for ice production. Two brief attempts were made to start brewing operations again after Repeal in 1933, but these were both unsuccessful.

After more than a decade passed, a new company was formed in 1946 to revive brewing operations at the now 40-year-old facility. Known as the Hocking Valley Brewery, Inc., the new organization employed forty men and was run by 32-year-old Reinhold J. Asbeck as president and master brewer, Edward Paas as vice-president and sales manager, Edward Alban as secretary, treasurer, and chief engineer, and Oral Daugherty as plant manager. Although some of the original brewing equipment remained, the plant was modernized to increase the annual capacity to 40,000 barrels, and a new bottling facility was installed. Battling financial difficulties during the first year, it was not until December 1947 that the brewery actually began to operate, with the first beer available to the public by the following February.

Again, Hock Hocking Beer was the anchor brand of the plant. It was sold throughout Ohio and into West Virginia, while Edelbrau Beer was sold mainly in Kentucky, and the Forest Rose brand was revived for sale in the Lancaster, Ohio area (previously having been made by the brewery there until it closed in 1942).

Unfortunately, competition from larger breweries in the state and nation made survival nearly impossible for a small, low budget brewery like this. Also complicating the situation were problems with packaging the beer. Some batches of beer were contaminated by improper cleaning of bottles, while other bottles were sealed improperly, allowing the beer to go flat.

The company had incurred a large debt from the purchase of new equipment, but was having difficulty paying this off by 1950, when many of the shareholders grew restless and began selling off their stock. By April of that year, brewing operations had ceased, and the remaining beer was eventually sold off. Asbeck, who had worked in the brewing industry since the age of sixteen, then moved to Newark, where he joined the staff of the Consumers Brewing Co. until its demise four years later.

The brewery building has housed several different businesses through the years, including an egg hatchery and a warehouse. The entire plant remains basically intact today, and as of 2004, new owners were attempting to renovate the plant for shops, restaurants, and condominiums.

Bellaire

1. Hankey/Vogel brewery

Belmont County's earliest known brewing establishment appears to have begun operation in the mid-1860s. Located at 220 Hamilton Street, between 32nd and 33rd Streets (house numbers were changed completely in later years), the small brewery was initially operated by Charles Hankey (also spelled Henkey, Hanky, Henke), a native of the Brunswick province of Germany, born in 1832. Over the next decade, it appears that the brewery may have only operated intermittently, and may have been leased by a number of different parties for brewing, with annual production generally between 100 and 200 barrels. By the early 1870s, Hankey was operating a cigar store elsewhere in town, and the brewery, which essentially consisted of a residence facing the street and brewing equipment in a small rear building, was being operated by John E. Vogel.

Vogel appears to have ceased brewing operations around 1876, at which time he converted the structure into a grocery, which he operated for a number of years. The building has since been razed. Interestingly, the city's only other brewery would later appear less than a block to the south on Hamilton Street.

2. Bellaire/Matz Brewing Company

William (Wilhelm) Feller came to the city of Bellaire in 1903. A native German, he had come to the United States at the age of seventeen, living first in Cincinnati, then in Zanesville. There he first entered the brewing field before moving south to become a major force behind the creation of the Marietta Brewing Company in 1898. Several years later, he had his eye on the beer drinkers of another industrial Ohio River town, in a larger metropolitan area which would allow much more growth potential for a new company. Thus the Bellaire Brewing Company was born in late 1903, with an initial capital stock of $85,000.

Feller became the company's first and only president, with Conrad Rumbach as vice-president, and Charles W. Rodewig as secretary and treasurer. Other directors included Charles R. Powell, Sebastian Wimmer, John B. Watt, and Emil Schmidt. Rumbach was a native of Switzerland, born in 1849, and was proprietor of the Germania Saloon (which also offered its patrons a billiard parlor, ten-pin alley, and beer garden), as well as being vice-president of the local Dollar Savings Bank. Watt and Schmidt were proprietors of hotels in the city.

Construction soon began on a new state-of-the-art brewery, located at the southwest corner of Hamilton and 32nd Streets, on a hillside and along a main line of railroad tracks. The company's first brew was sold to the public in 1904, and soon after this the directors' optimism led to an increase of the company's capital stock to $110,000. Various additions to the plant would occur over the next fifteen years, including an enlargement of the ice house, which increased its daily capacity to sixty tons.

The company's directors remained largely unchanged over the years, with

William Feller

three notable exceptions: Rumbach died in 1912 after slipping on icy pavement, fracturing a hip, and subsequently developing pneumonia. Wimmer became the company's new vice-president after this. In 1914, William Schneider became the new brewmaster, having formerly been associated with the Portsmouth Brewing & Ice Co. in Portsmouth, Ohio. In June 1918, Feller and his wife were killed instantly in an auto accident just west of town.

Beer production continued through November 1918, when postwar Prohibition brought an end to all brewing operations.

View of the brewery in the early 1950s, as photographed by the late Ernie Oest. Note the billboard for 1884 Beer at the right.

Remaining beer continued to be sold until May 1919, when all sales in the state of Ohio came to a halt. After this, the company reorganized as the Bellaire Beverage Co., for the production of cereal beverages and eight different flavors of soda pop. This continued until 1924, when the doors closed, the equipment was liquidated, and the building was sold for $20,000 to the First National Bank of Bellaire.

The plant remained essentially empty until March 1936, nearly three years after the end of Prohibition. At that time it was purchased for $1.00 by a new group, incorporated two months earlier as The Matz Brewing Company, with the stipulation that the company would pay all real estate taxes due on the building. William Matz had previously been the brewmaster of the nearby Belmont Brewing Co. and Belmont Products Co., and he now became the new company's president, treasurer, and brewmaster. Vice-president was Albert W. Eick, who had been the president of the Belmont Products Company. Charles F. Neugart was the secretary, and P. A. Bower was the plant's chief engineer.

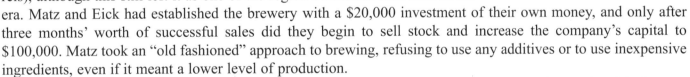

New brewing and bottling equipment was installed, giving the plant an annual capacity of 35,000 barrels (later increased to 40,000 barrels), although this still left it as one of the region's smallest breweries of the era. Matz and Eick had established the brewery with a $20,000 investment of their own money, and only after three months' worth of successful sales did they begin to sell stock and increase the company's capital to $100,000. Matz took an "old fashioned" approach to brewing, refusing to use any additives or to use inexpensive ingredients, even if it meant a lower level of production.

Brewing began on July 15, 1936, and when the first brew officially went on sale October 3rd, the new anchor brand was Matz Olden Time Beer, selling at $1.41 per case. Later would come the introduction of '84 Pilsener Beer, Matz Urbrau (renamed in 1947 as Directors' Reserve Beer), 1884 Golden Ale (originally made several miles north in Martins Ferry, the brand name was continued by Matz after the Belmont Brewing Co. closed in 1940), and a number of seasonal beers as well, including Matz Bock Beer, released each year on St. Patrick's Day. To advertise the release of the bock beer in 1939, a float was driven around the area throughout the entire week, topped with a small beer wagon and two live goats.

At its peak, the brewery employed more than 100 men, all of whom were welcome to drink as much Matz Beer as they liked while on the job (something unheard of today). Free beer for the employees, as

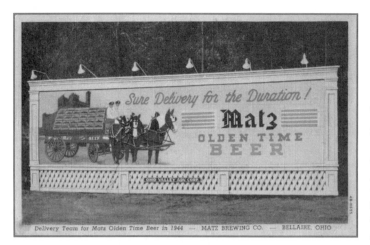

Promotional postcard showing the Matz Olden Time Team, used for deliveries in Bellaire and Wheeling during World War II due to rationing of gasoline and tires [courtesy of Albert Doughty & Bill Carlisle]

well as visitors, was dispensed from a vending machine on the loading dock.

Despite temporary grain rationing during World War II, sales in 1946 were more than $1.1 million, with more than 13 million bottles being filled and sold. The following year saw an expansion of the bottling works, doubling its capacity. Production continued through 1953, after which the brewery closed for good, another victim of industry competition. In fact, at the time of its closing, the Matz Brewing Co. was the last operating brewery in the upper Ohio River Valley, out of nearly thirty that had operated through the years between Marietta and Pittsburgh. The company's small size and relatively low overhead had allowed it to survive the Depression and the war, but competition in the 1950s was the final straw.

The equipment was auctioned off the following year. The plant was later used as a warehouse, and was razed completely in 1960. An apartment complex stands at the site today. William Matz later moved to Cleveland, where he died in 1961 at the age of 88. Albert Eick lived the remainder of his life in Pittsburgh, where he died in 1980.

Martins Ferry (aka Martinsburg, Martinsville)

1. Belmont Brewing Company

The origin of Martins Ferry's only brewery was five years prior to its first actual brew. In 1885, The Ohio Wine Company was founded with $50,000 capital by three men from Cincinnati, all native Germans: William Lipphardt, Ferdinand H. Eick, and John C. Wagner. Lipphardt was formerly the owner of a saddlery and leather goods store and Wagner owned a pharmacy. Eick was a native of Recklinghausen, Westphalia, born in 1845, who had come to America in 1857. He worked for many years as a bookkeeper before moving to Martins Ferry to begin a career in the winemaking business.

The Ohio Wine Co. plant was located on the old County Road, later known as Washing-

Belmont Brewery, circa 1905 [courtesy of Albert Doughty]

(left) Ferdinand H. Eick [courtesy of Albert Doughty]; (below) William Lipphardt [courtesy of George Lipphardt and Albert Doughty]

ton Street, although as the plant expanded through the years, the address became 208-240 Jefferson Street, which was at the rear of the original buildings. The plant consisted of a primary four-story building which contained large grape presses and fermenting vats, with a long, two-story building behind that for wine storage and bottling. The plant was capable of producing 150,000 gallons annually, with several different types of wine being produced. Immediately adjacent to the rear of the plant was the Wheeling Terminal Railway (later the Wheeling & Lake Erie R.R.) trestle, which would soon prove to be a serious problem for the winemakers.

After several years of producing wine, it was discovered that the frequent and sometimes severe vibrations from the passing trains were disturbing the wine during the all-important fermentation process, which was having a detrimental effect on the finished product. A successful lawsuit for $1,000 was filed against the Wheeling Terminal Railway for damages in 1889, but the problem still remained, due to the location of the plant. Faced with the prospect of moving elsewhere, the proprietors opted to convert the plant into a brewing establishment, in which beer production would be relatively unaffected by the vibrations.

And so it was that the entire plant, already valued at $16,000, was converted into a brewery in 1890, with an initial annual capacity of 10,000 barrels, and the Belmont Brewing Company was born. Lipphardt was its initial president, with Wagner as vice-president, and Eick as secretary and treasurer. Also involved with the formation of the company were August Kraatz, a former blacksmith, William Happy, a former millwright, and Jacob Kern, Albert Lipphardt, and William H. Helfenbein. The capital stock was eventually raised to $200,000 by 1896.

Belmont Lager Beer was popular enough to necessitate a gradual expansion of the plant over the next fifteen years. This culminated in 1905 with the erection of an ornate and completely modern five-story brewhouse. Costing around $100,000 to build, it stood atop some of the original wine cellars. This addition increased the plant's annual capacity to 40,000 barrels, while employing up to 120 men. Three brews were made each day, six days a week. Two on-site wells provided water for brewing, and it was said by some that the quality of the well water was nearly identical to that used by Bass & Co., a famous English brewer. In addition to Belmont Lager, Belmont Bock Beer was brewed each December, then released each year on March 15, and was a very popular late winter treat.

Sold in most of the saloons in the region, Belmont Beer would typically cost $5.00 for a draft barrel, $1.00 for a four-gallon keg, 25 cents for three quarts at a saloon, or five cents for a fourteen-ounce mug (or a bottle, if one preferred to drink at home). In some saloons, the beer was sold on charge accounts, with a collector from the brewery coming around every two weeks. On collection days, the collector might offer free beer to everyone in the saloon. Certain "bar flies" would follow the collector from saloon to saloon, getting free drinks at each stop.

Early in 1902, William Lipphardt resigned to take ownership of a factory in Chattanooga, TN. He was replaced by a newer member of the company, Henry Bieberson of nearby Wheeling, WV., who remained president until Prohibition. Bieberson had been born in Germany in 1848, and subsequently came to America at the age of sixteen. Living in Wheeling for the remainder of his life, he operated a popular restaurant there for nearly thirty years, while serving as director of two area banks, prior to joining the Belmont Brewing Co.

Brewmaster at this time was 29-year-old German native William Matz, although he was forced into temporary retirement due to an illness and was briefly replaced by Henry Bieberson, Jr. Matz returned to the position some time later, when Bieberson, Jr.

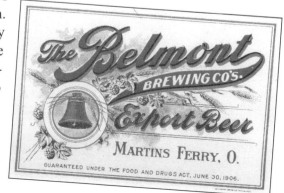

moved to Delaware, Ohio, to enter the relatively new field of movie theater ownership. Also, in May 1915, Ferdinand Eick died, with his post as a director and secretary being filled by his 26-year-old son, Albert W. Eick.

The company's sales improved after 1914, when the state of West Virginia went dry, putting all of the competing breweries in Wheeling, just across the Ohio River, out of business. Although this was a dark omen of things to come, much of the demand from the thousands of thirsty steelworkers who lived in the region was now supplied by the Belmont Brewery and the nearby Bellaire Brewing Co.

Wheeling Island is in the middle of the Ohio River, but is considered part of West Virginia. It is said by those who lived on the island at the time that some men would wear custom-made trousers, seven or eight sizes too large, put on a top coat, and walk across the bridge to Bridgeport, Ohio. After drinking for a time in the local bar, they would hang as many bottles as possible inside the oversized trousers, then carefully walk back across the bridge, and store the beer in their basements. If time permitted, they would make several of these trips in a day, giving them enough beer to last for several weeks.

These activities lasted only until statewide Prohibition closed all of Ohio's saloons in 1919. After this, the Belmont Brewing Co. temporarily closed its doors. Meanwhile, a new company was formed with a capital stock of $400,000, to be known as the Belmont Products Company, which purchased the entire plant. A prospectus for potential investors in the new company gives a great deal of information about its functions, as well as the state of the physical plant at that time. Several excerpts follow:

"The properties in question include the entire plant, machinery, and equipment formerly owned by The Belmont Brewing Co. and occupying two blocks on the north side of Jefferson St., from Second to Fourth Streets—in all approximately 58,000 square feet of ground. The buildings, with the exception of the stables, are all of substantial stone and brick construction, the interior being composed of concrete and steel. The total floor space occupied is approximately 60,000 square feet. There are four steam boilers, having a total of 700 horse power, two water wells, supplying pure water, two electric dynamos which provide power and light for all purposes, and two Frick Refrigerating machines which, in addition to caring for the necessary refrigeration throughout the plant, are used to make ice, part of which is needed in shipping the product to, and storing it at outlying stations, and the remainder is sold to ice distributors. The daily capacity of the ice making plant is 25 tons.

The massive brewing kettle is of solid wrought copper and has a capacity of 335 barrels. This gives the plant an easy production capacity of 100,000 barrels per year. All other machinery and equipment in the brewhouse is installed in proportion and is arranged to provide maximum efficiency in the various operations necessary in the process of manufacture.

In the bottling department the equipment and arrangement are of the best and most practical known to modern practice. The soaker (which thoroughly washes and sterilizes the bottles), filler, corker, Pasteurizer and labeler are of the latest automatic type. These make possible a daily output (8-hour day) of 120 barrels, or 36,000 pint bottles.

The properties, plant, and equipment—everything—are being purchased for $250,000. The present day value of the building alone, exclusive of machinery and equipment, is estimated to be not less than $650,000. Add to this the excluded items and you have a value that comfortably exceeds a million dollars.

The management will be of the best. At the head of each vital department stands a man fitted by training to manage it in a manner that will ensure maximum results. A. W. Eick, President and General Manager, was secretary-treasurer of the Belmont Brewing Co., having served that company in various capacities for twelve years. He is president of The Fenray Photoplay Co., the Wheeling Milling and Grain Co., The LaCroft Land Co., and vice-president of the Standard Motor Sales Co., Wheeling. His father was one of the founders of the Belmont Brewing Co. and it is his ambition to make the record of the new company a credit, in every way, to the history of its brilliant predecessor.

J. C. Jung, the secretary-treasurer, was with the Belmont Brewing Co. eighteen years. He has a wide and favorable acquaintance among distributors in the district and possesses rare integrity and ability that make his choice for this important office a wise one. [In addition, the new company's vice-president was Marshall Cropper, who was later succeeded by J. V. Haid.] William J. Matz, as brewmaster, means that the same efficiency in production and the same high standard of quality, that has made the products of the Belmont Brewing Co. famous during the past sixteen years of his service, will prevail."

Following this was a lengthy statement on the salability of cereal beverages (near beer), which were to be the primary product of the new company under the names Bel-Brew and Johnnie Ale, as well as a discussion about the possibility of manufacturing dairy products in the old brewery, and then another lengthy but optimistic statement about the likelihood of beer being legalized again, and why investment in this new company would be wise.

The company operated uneventfully until May 1923, when Eick and Haid were indicted with several other local men for conspiracy to violate the national Prohibition laws. Specifically, a significant amount of real beer was appearing in the Wheeling area, and its origin was traced to the Belmont brewery, after which the plant was temporarily closed

(above) Albert Eick [courtesy of Albert Doughty]; (below) Serving trays, 1935.

down during the investigation. The bigger issue, however, was that Eick was found to be involved in the transport of a train car carrying 5,000 gallons of grain alcohol (purchased for $50,000) from Tennessee, which was then distributed throughout the area. Raw alcohol was frequently used during the era to make cheap whiskey, which was colored with burnt sugar. Although this was a small local aspect of a much larger bootlegging scheme (nearly 200,000 gallons of grain alcohol was to be purchased from a government storage facility in Tennessee, at 30 cents per gallon, and resold throughout Ohio and other areas for $10 per gallon), Eick was found guilty and fined.

Aside from this episode, Eick ran the Belmont Products Company effectively, as it survived in a very difficult era, lasting until Repeal in 1933. Most of the original investors came and went, but by 1929, Matz had become the president of the company. A small associated ginger ale bottling works, known as the Spark-Lin-Ale Co., occupied a portion of the plant for several years during the 1920s, making both Cup Top and Bagdad Ginger Ales.

Upon the repeal of Prohibition, it took little time for the brewing of real beer to begin, as the equipment had remained intact throughout the prior fourteen years. At 8:00 A.M. on May 12, 1933, the first new batch of Belmont Beer was released to the public, among much fanfare. Cars and trucks were lined up for three blocks outside the brewery, starting the previous night, and continuing throughout the day. Matz and Eick remained in charge of the company until October 1935, when they sold the entire enterprise to a new group, headed by Samuel Ungerleider. They then moved several miles south to Bellaire, where they took over the former Bellaire Brewing Co. plant and operated it as the Matz Brewing Company. After their departure, Belmont reorganized entirely and the plant was enlarged and modernized to allow for an annual capacity of 120,000 barrels, while employing between 100 and 150 men. A relatively large distribution network allowed its beer to be sold in seven states.

Samuel Ungerleider was born in Budapest, Austria-Hungary in 1885, came to Wheeling in 1900, and soon became involved in the local distilling business, culminating in his ownership of the Ungerleider Distilling Co. of Columbus, OH. Put out of business by Prohibition, he moved to Cleveland, where he became an investment banker and stockbroker, and later moved to New York City. After Repeal, he formed the Distillers & Brewers Corporation of America (with headquarters in Jersey City, N.J.), which oversaw the operation of the Belmont brewery. Ungerleider served as president, with R. T. Norment as vice-president, W. D. Singer as secretary, treasurer, and plant manager, and Glenn Eckert as assistant treasurer. Replacing Matz as brewmaster was Rudolph A. Bender, a veteran of breweries in Milwaukee and Rochester, N.Y.

Bender reformulated the company's beers, and many new brands subsequently entered the market, including Black Crown Lager and Bock Beer, Bender's Pilsener Beer and Porter, 1884 Golden Ale, 18 Kt. Golden Ale, John L. Ale (named after John L. Sullivan, the famous boxer from the turn of the century), Johnnie Ale (the non-alcoholic version

to be sold in areas that had remained dry), Old German Style Beer, Old Stock Ale, and Old South Ale ("manufactured under the supervision of Old South Brewing Co., Inc., of Statesville, NC."—this was a company organized around 1934, but which never actually brewed any beer itself; it was, in a sense, similar to modern-day contract brewers. By 1935, however, it was gone.) Also returning was the Belmont name, now attached to a wide variety of brews: "Pink Elephant Ale," bock, pilsener, lager and premium draught lager beers. Even Bel-Brew non-alcoholic beverage returned for a time.

Like many other breweries in the 1930s, Belmont quickly saw the potential advantage of compact, disposable packages, and in December 1935, it unveiled the "Stubby" bottle. Holding twelve ounces like the traditional long-necked bottles, the Stubby had a very short neck, making it easier to stack. A news release at the time stated, *"Women in particular like it because it is handy to store, makes a beautiful addition to any table setting, and can be discarded when empty. Like all glass bottles for beer, the new Stubby is socially acceptable."* In addition, advertisements at the time stated, *"Keeping abreast with the times, the Belmont Brewing Co. is thoroughly investigating the subject of canned beer, and as soon as the practicability of dispensing beer in this kind of a container has been proven, the Belmont Brewing Co. will be one of the first to adopt this method."* Beer had first been sold in cans in 1935, so the concept was still very new and somewhat unproven, although it was not long before it became widely used in the industry. However, for unknown reasons, Belmont never moved forward into the canning of its beer.

Another short-lived facet of the new company was an attempt at expansion into Pennsylvania. In 1934, it purchased the plant of the defunct Rockwood Brewing Corporation in Rockwood, PA., a small town in the south central part of the state. Located at 204 West Main Street, it was originally built in 1908 and operated until Prohibition. After Repeal, brewing operations briefly started again before the plant was purchased by the Belmont Co., specifically for the production of ale, with this division of the company to be known as the Belmont Ale Brewery Corporation. In addition to Belmont Pink Elephant Ale, Pennsylvania Dutch and Pennsbury Beers were also made there. After the first year, however, its operation was not felt to be profitable, and the brewery was closed for good, with all production being transferred back to Ohio. The brewery building is no longer standing.

Despite the fact that only three breweries were operating in the upper Ohio River Valley after Prohibition (compared to more than twenty before Prohibition), competition from larger regional and national breweries was much more intense in the 1930s and 40s. The combination of competition and general business conditions of the era led to the company declaring bankruptcy

(above) Belmont made this plea to local residents in an attempt to stay solvent [from the Martins Ferry *The Daily Times*, August 19, 1937];

(below) Belmont Brewing Company bottling house as it appeared in 1995, at the corner of Jefferson and 4th Streets. Built half a block west of the main plant, this is the only remnant of Belmont County's brewing history. Since this photo was taken, the semicircular stone at the top of the building, in which the company name was carved, has been removed.

in 1937. Ungerleider's group then sold its stock in the company to a local group, and a subsequent reorganization allowed the company to continue functioning under new president H. Mendel Taylor, vice-president Charles J. Michel, secretary Charles Lopeman, and treasurer Glenn Eckert. However, the end came in 1940 when the Belmont Brewing Co. closed its doors for good. It was felt by some that the quality of the company's beer had declined significantly after William Matz left in 1935, and this likely was another strong contributing factor in the brewery's demise.

Samuel Ungerleider continued his career as a stockbroker, living in New York City for the remainder of his life, until he died in 1973 at the age of 87. The brewery was purchased in 1942 by a group that intended to raze the structure for any salvageable materials for the war effort, but this deal fell through, and beginning the following year, the plant was used as the Arctic Foods Company storage warehouse, until that company closed in 1954. The structure, Martins Ferry's tallest, was razed in March 1958, although the bottling house, built in 1916 (at a cost of $100,000), is still standing today. It is located on the other side of the railroad trestle from the main brewery site, at the corner of Jefferson and South 4th Street. The Ohio Valley Chemical Co. occupies most of the old brewery's site today. The railway trestle which caused all of the problems for the original winemakers still stands next to the site, although all of its rails have long since been removed.

Also Note:

1. Dillonvale Brewing Company

In the summer of 1902, there was an announcement of the formation of the Dillonvale Brewing Company, with plans for a brewery to be built in the town of Bellaire. With a capital stock of $50,000, this new company was incorporated by R. Shively Neel, William A. Gerke, Plummer G. Haynes, Ross W. Parkhurst, and George C. Neel. For unknown reasons, the plans to build a new brewery never materialized, and the company quickly disappeared into history.

2. GlaCo Products Company

The Bellaire Bottling Works began operation at 3601 Franklin Street in Bellaire around 1910. Managed by John P. Glaser, the works bottled a variety of carbonated soft drinks. Around 1924, it was renamed as the GlaCo Products Company, most likely due to the addition of cereal beverage production. While not technically a brewery, the company had an "L" permit number, indicating that it was licensed to produce non-alcoholic cereal beverages. Old Tavern Brew, made in the early 1930s, is the company's only known product. Although the label does not specifically state that it is a malt product, its appearance is very similar to a post-Prohibition beer label from Clarksburg, WV. Production of Old Tavern Brew appears to have been brief, and although the company remained in business into the late 1930s (operated by Glaser's son Joseph), it never moved into the production of real beer after Repeal in 1933.

3. Bellaire Brewing Company

Soon after William Matz purchased the old Bellaire Brewing Co. plant in 1936 to begin operations as the Matz Brewing Co., a new company was formed with the old name. Led by Columbus investors Howard J. Heilman, G. M. Rowe, and R. Grouche, the new Bellaire Brewing Co. was to construct a new modern plant in the city and have its beer available by the end of the year. Like many other business plans of the era, however, this one never came to pass.

CARROLL COUNTY

Sherrodsville

1. Atwood Yacht Club brewpub

Carroll County's only brewery began operation in April 1995. Located at 2637 Lodge Drive SW, on the east shore of Atwood Lake, the Atwood Yacht Club is a private organization that was founded in 1948. Although its mailing address is Sherrodsville, it is actually much closer to the village of Dellroy. Atwood Lake, which was formed as part of a flood control project in the 1930s, is a popular attraction for fishing, boating, camping, golfing, and hiking.

Monroe Township, in which the clubhouse stands, has been a dry territory for many years, as voted by local residents. As a result, getting a liquor license for the restaurant and bar was difficult. However, a quirk in Ohio's liquor laws allowed the club to serve alcohol if beer was brewed on the premises (even in a dry territory). For this reason, in early 1995 a small 9-barrel brewery was set up in a room to the side of the bar, and the restaurant was completely renovated. Liquor could then be served along with the freshly brewed beer. No beer is bottled or sold outside of the club, and the brewpub is limited to club members. Overall, only a few hundred barrels at most are brewed per year, with most being made in the summer.

Coaster courtesy of George Barone

The head brewer is Rich Marks of Alliance, and he produces one brand: Main Sail Ale, which comes in both dark and pale varieties, brewed in batches as needed. There are no current plans to expand operations.

Columbiana County

East Liverpool

1. Henry Greenwood/Spring Water Brewery

Henry Greenwood was born in Oldham, Lancashire, England, in May 1837. At the age of ten, he began working in the local cotton mill, where he remained for fifteen years before coming to America in 1862. He initially came to Beaver Falls, PA., where he worked in the brewery of his brother-in-law, James Anderton. By 1880, he had moved on to work at the Beaver Falls Brewing Co., of which he was a part owner. In 1885, he sold his interest in that operation and moved to East Liverpool with his wife and thirteen children, to establish the first brewery in this Ohio River city.

His small plant would operate for nearly 30 years, situated along the bank of Carpenters Run in California hollow, on the outskirts of town. The brewery used only spring water which bubbled up out of solid rock in the nearby hollow. Its primary products were pale ale, cream ale, and porter, for distribution in the city and along the Ohio River. Initially these were distributed in barrels only, but later a small bottling house was added. The brewery consistently used the name "East Liverpool Spring Water Brewery" throughout its life.

The brewhouse was a two-story building, 24 feet square, with a brew kettle, mash tub, and malt cooler. The only other buildings were a small icehouse, two sheds, a hog pen, and the bottling house. The aging cellars were adjacent to the brewhouse, two feet underground. This complex was behind the Greenwood residence at 401 Ridgeway Avenue, but was also listed as being on the south side of Sheridan Avenue (the next street over).

In July 1903, Greenwood retired from actively running the brewery, turning it over to his sons Thomas and Joseph. Henry would die just one year later. At this point the plant became known as the Greenwood Brothers Brewery, and it remained a small family operation over the next decade.

The growing temperance movement in the early part of the twentieth century led to East Liverpool going dry in 1907. Passage of the Rose Law the next year allowed Columbiana County to vote itself dry from 1909 through 1912. (For more information on this, see the following section on The Crockery City Brewing Company.) During this time the brewery stopped all beer production, although it resumed in 1912 for an additional three years.

By then, Joseph had left to work in the pottery industry, which was thriving in

Greenwood brewery [courtesy of Ohio Historical Society Museum of Ceramics]

East Liverpool. Martha Greenwood, Henry's widow, became the proprietor, while Thomas remained the brewmaster. Over the last two years, the plant was only in partial operation, and Martha had closed it down for good by late 1915. Nothing remains of the site today, as U. S. Route 30 (the Lincoln Highway) runs through California Hollow.

2. Crockery City/Webb Brewing Company

In April 1899, the Crockery City Brewing & Ice Company was organized by parties from both Pittsburgh and East Liverpool, with capital stock of $200,000. The city's second brewery would initially operate in conjunction with the existing East Liverpool Ice & Coal Co. on West 8th Street, run by George W. Meredith and Joseph Turnbull.

Meredith had been born in 1850 in Utica, N.Y., and had worked in the pottery industry for many years before entering the bottling business. He operated a large liquor bottling and distributing company along with the ice and coal business, and was simultaneously a local bottler and distributor for the Schlather Brewing Co. of Cleveland prior to entering the brewing business himself. Turnbull had been born in 1856 in McKeesport, PA., but grew up in nearby Salineville, OH. He had worked as a coal miner until 1885, when he moved to East Liverpool and entered the retail coal business, to which he later added ice production.

View of the new brewhouse soon after its opening; the wooden buildings at the right of the complex were part of the existing East Liverpool Ice & Coal Co. and were soon replaced with modern buildings which still stand today
[courtesy of the Ohio Historical Society Museum of Ceramics]

Meredith became the new company's initial president, with John J. O'Reilly as vice-president, John Pfeiffer (of Rochester, PA.) as treasurer, Turnbull as secretary, and Philip Morley as general manager. Also a major player in the new venture was Samuel J. Wainright, of the Wainright branch of the huge Pittsburgh Brewing Co. consortium, and he would soon become the company's president. Soon after incorporation, construction began on the new $75,000 plant, the center of which was a five-story brewhouse, the tallest building in the county.

The plant was located in a narrow ravine on the north side of the city, just east of the ice plant on the north side of West 8th Street, near the intersection of Jefferson Avenue (later renamed Franklin Avenue). The streets surrounding the brewery complex were renamed and rerouted several times over the years, and in fact three different streets were called West 8th Street at different times. One of these, the main road along which the brewery stands today, was renamed Webber Way in the 1940s. It ran along the course of what had previously been one of the main railroad branches through the city, known as "Horn Switch". This was originally the primary route of shipping beer from the plant. In later years, the plant's address became 242–250 W. 8th St.

The company's name was a referral to East Liverpool being the pottery and crockery capital of the world, due to a large number of natural clay deposits in the area. The plant's formal opening was on September 29, 1900. Both lager beer ("Blue Label" brand) and ale were produced, at an annual capacity of 30,000 barrels, and the large ice plant had a daily capacity of 50 tons. Two on-site artesian wells provided all of the plant's water needs. Advertising its production of "spirits that lull that tired feeling", the company also pointed out that "Our beer is pure…because we do not use filthy river water…we take no chance of contagion…" Thirty men were employed by the plant at its outset, although as many as forty-five were employed during the busy summer season.

Early in 1906, a rumor was swirling through the region that suggested an impending consolidation of

Horse-drawn delivery wagon making its rounds; some saloons served both Schlather and Crockery City Beer for a time after the local brewery's opening [courtesy of the East Liverpool Historical Society/Museum of Ceramics]

eight area breweries: the Crockery City Brewing Co., Alliance and Consumers (Ashtabula) Brewing Companies, Smith and Renner Brewing Companies of Youngstown, Meadville (PA.) Brewing Co., Standard Brewing Co. of New Castle, PA., and the Union Brewing Co. of Sharon, PA. As it turned out, the rumor was just that; the deal was never finalized, and each of the companies continued to operate independently.

In 1907, the brewhouse was enlarged to seven stories, and with additions to the ice plant, the improvements cost over $10,000. However, the ice business was sold off to a local competitor one year later, as it was not felt to be profitable at that time. The company would return to the ice business in 1915, when $75,000 was spent on the erection of a new plant with a daily ice production of 75 tons.

Of greater concern to the brewery was the growing temperance movement. As in many cities, this movement had begun prior to 1900, but in East Liverpool it had a larger and more vocal backing. At the turn of the century, the most common crimes in the city were intoxication and disorderly conduct, and this had become a significant concern to the common citizen. The Anti-Saloon League had been attempting to pressure the local government to limit the operation of local saloons starting in 1893, but it was not until 1900 that the issue was first put to a vote. Although the voters that year chose to keep saloons open by a 3:2 margin, the issue was put to a vote again in 1903 and 1907.

In the latter election, the city of 20,000 people was voted dry for the first time in its history, making it one of the state's largest cities to do so. Beginning in July 1907, the city's eighty-nine saloons closed down, eighteen months prior to Columbiana County going dry due to the Rose "local option" Law of 1908. (Ironically, during the same election in which Columbiana County voted itself dry by local option, the issue had come up again for a vote in the city of East Liverpool. This time, the city voted itself wet by a large majority, but because of the countywide Prohibition vote, the city's saloons remained closed for another three years.) [For an excellent discussion of the events leading up to both local and national Prohibition, as well as the effects thereof, see *The City of Hills and Kilns (Life and Work in East Liverpool, Ohio)*, Chapter 6, by William C. Gates, Jr.]

Unlike the much smaller Greenwood Brothers brewery nearby, which depended on local sales, the Crockery City brewery was not crippled by local Prohibition. It had sales eastward into Pennsylvania, northward into Mahoning County, and all along the Ohio River, areas which remained wet, and the plant was able to remain in production until Columbiana County went wet again, beginning in 1912. Expanding the company's influence northward was the leasing in 1914 of the small Leetonia Brewing Co. plant in northern Columbiana County, recently closed, for storage and distribution purposes.

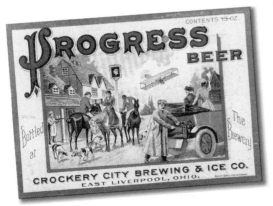

The company's officers remained essentially the same throughout the pre-Prohibition era, with the exception of Turnbull, who died in January 1913. Personnel additions over the

Serving tray, circa 1935

next few years included William Stoffel as superintendent of bottling operations, Anton Zix, formerly of the Wellston (Ohio) Brewing & Ice Co., as brewmaster, and Ambrose E. Webber as general manager. Webber was born locally in 1876, and had been the manager of Meredith's earlier bottling plant prior to becoming the new brewery's foreman at its inception. New brands around this time included C. C. (Crockery City) Beer (introduced in 1910), and Progress Beer.

The brewery had survived the first wave of Prohibition, between 1907 and 1911, but in 1919 it would be put to a more severe test. When all sales of alcohol became illegal in the state of Ohio in May of that year, the company was renamed as The Crockery City Ice and Products Company, and the production of soft drinks and near beer commenced. Later that year, the company purchased the local plant of the Tatgenhorst Brothers dairy, renaming this division as the City Pure Milk and Ice Cream Co. Such diversity would allow the company to continue functioning as a profitable enterprise for the next fourteen years.

By 1923, Wainwright and Meredith had left the company, and Webber moved into the position of president. His 23-year-old son Leonard C. Webber, who had joined the company some ten years earlier, was appointed vice-president. The two men remained at the top of the company for the next twenty years. Ambrose Webber was also the proprietor of the local Diamond Drug Store at the same time.

With the repeal of Prohibition on April 7, 1933, the company would move quickly to return to brewing. 3.2% beer was available for sale on April 15, and was greeted with much enthusiasm from East Liverpudlians. Full-strength beer would not return until the end of the year, however. Modern brewing equipment was installed, increasing the plant's annual capacity to 65,000 barrels. Within two years the plant had become the city's second largest employer, with 135 men working in the company's various divisions. By that time, Louis H. Nichols was the plant's chief engineer, and Alfred A. Mueller was the master brewer, although he would later be replaced by Thomas J. Keane.

Several changes took place around 1939. The company sold off its dairy operation to the Golden Star Dairy Co., which continued to run the plant next door to the brewery until the 1970s. The Crockery City Co. also became the new local bottler of Coca-Cola around this time, doing business as the Coca-Cola Bottling Co. of East Liverpool, and utilizing the brewery's bottling works. In addition, a new division of the company was established for the dealing of livestock. This was known as Crockery City Farms, with the livestock all located on a farm along U. S. Route 30 near Lisbon, several miles north of East Liverpool.

On June 1, 1946, the brewing division was purchased for $500,000 by a new group of investors from Akron, to be known as the Webb Corporation. Chairman of the board of the new group was George Bachmann, the owner of a bar in Akron. George A. DeLuca, of the DeLuca Distributing Co. in Akron, was the president, with café owner Anthony C. DeLuca as vice-president, attorney Dominic Olivo as secretary, and bar owner Boris Mitseff as treasurer. The new master brewer was William F. Obert, assisted by Henry Paczek, although he was soon replaced by Henry Bossert. By 1950, more modernization had increased the plant's annual capacity to 80,000 barrels, and by then, Olivo had become the company's president and plant manager, with William Bamer as secretary and treasurer. One year later, Bamer had risen to the company's presidency. During this time, the Webbers continued to operate the Crockery City Farms and Coca-Cola Bottling Co. out of the same complex.

Several new brands of beer and ale had hit the market after Prohibition, and even more were released after World War II. Webber's Old Lager and Bulldog Ale were the standard brands used throughout the era, even after the plant's purchase by

Photo taken in the early 1950s, soon after the brewery's closing, by the late Ernie Oest [provided by the American Breweriana Association]

the Webb Corporation. Most of these were bottled or kegged, although in the Spring of 1949 the company began to use cap-sealed cans made by the Continental Can Co., but only for the packaging of Webber's Old Lager Beer. Advertising these brands was mainly via point-of-sale signs, newspapers, and the brewery's monthly brochure, the *Valley Echo*, but in 1949, the company also began using radio with Webb's *Parade Of Sports* on local station WLIO.

In addition, White Label Pilsener Beer was released in early 1948, with a name that was thought to be competition for Carling Black Label Beer from Cleveland. In fact, the name actually was chosen in a slogan contest among employees, and the slogan "Get That White Label On Your Table" won second prize in a later contest held by the national Small Brewers Association. Nevertheless, the company was sued in 1949 by New Jersey's John F. Trommer Brewing Co. for infringement against its White Label brand, although when put to the test, no registration for Trommer's brand could be found. The issue was raised again two years later when Trommer was purchased by Brooklyn's Piel Bros. Brewing Co., which filed another suit against Webb for brand infringement. By that time, Webb was on its last legs and the point was moot.

By 1951, national competition had taken its toll, and financial difficulties led to the company declaring bankruptcy in September. Several attempts were made to refinance the company to pay off outstanding debts, including the issuing of 99,000 shares of additional stock, at $1 per share, to the 125 stockholders. When this and other attempts failed, brewing operations officially ended on February 9, 1952. Federal agents then arrived to pour the remaining 700 barrels of untaxed beer down the drain (leading to newspaper articles joking about drunken fish in the Ohio River), and the brewery's remaining contents were liquidated. One year later, the large brewhouse was vacant, although the Coca-Cola Bottling Co. continued to operate, with Leonard Webber in charge after his father's death in 1954. Leonard continued to manage the company until his death in 1965, and several years after that the buildings were vacated. The plant remains standing and nearly completely intact to this day, occupied by several small businesses. However, the brewhouse has undergone significant decay in the past few years, and unless a large-scale renovation of the building takes place, it may soon fall prey to the wrecker's ball.

East Palestine

1. Anderton/Arnold/Schilpp Brewery

East Palestine's only brewery began operations around 1879, apparently as a branch of the J. Anderton & Co. brewery of Beaver Falls, PA. Originally built as an ale brewery, it was operated by Jonathan Anderton, a native of Streetbridge, Lancashire, England, born in the 1850s. He had come to America with his father James, who operated the much larger plant in Beaver Falls, and the rest of their family. The smaller Ohio branch consisted only of a small two-story brewhouse, with an associated feed mill and stable at the site. Located on the south side of Lake Run, on the east side of South Walnut Street, the plant produced only a few hundred barrels of ale annually until 1884, after which it was abandoned.

The brewery sat unused until 1895, when it was purchased by William Arnold, who operated it for five years until he died around 1900. Two years later, it was leased by John Schillp, who had formerly worked for the Crockery City Brewing Co. in East Liverpool. It appears that he renovated the plant and operated it for the production of lager beer only for one or two years before abandoning it altogether. Nothing remains of the brewery today, as the site is occupied by a parking lot.

Leetonia (aka Laetonia, Sutonia)

1. Louis Siegle/Leetonia Brewing Company

Louis T. Siegle

Established around 1873 by (Jacob) Garlach & Seegar, this small brewery was located at the southwest corner of Stoey (now Stoy) and Mill Streets, on the south side of town. Garlach died the following year at the age of 39, and his share was then purchased by Benjamin Haller, who had taken full control of the plant by 1877. In 1881, Haller sold it to Dominick Zanini, who was one of very few Italian immigrants to operate a brewery in the state. Zanini was then joined in 1884 by Louis T. Siegle, who was a native of New Castle, PA., born in 1860. Siegle took over full operation of the plant after Zanini's death in 1887, at the age of 42. After this, the plant was known as the Leetonia Brewery. Consisting of several one- and two-story buildings, the plant was producing only 200-300 barrels of lager beer per year, although Siegle increased the plant's annual output to around 700-800 barrels over the next decade.

In 1907, the brewery was incorporated as the Leetonia Brewing Company, with a capital stock of $50,000. Louis Siegle was the president of the new company, and other incorporators included George J. Neidmayer, Simon Schram, James Degnan, and Michael Hughes. With more improvements, the plant's annual capacity reached 4,000 barrels, and porter was now being produced in addition to lager.

After passage of the Rose Law in 1908, Columbiana County voted itself dry by local option, although the brewery was able to stay functional during the next three years by selling Leetonia Beer to the nearby counties to the north and west, all of which remained wet. By 1912, Columbiana County's voters had changed their minds and voted the county wet again.

Production, however, only continued through 1913. After this, the small plant was purchased by the Crockery City Brewing Co. of East Liverpool, to be used for storage and distribution. Siegle remained in the area, however, until his death in 1941. The brewery had closed completely by the onset of Prohibition, and was gradually razed over the next few years. A portion of the west wall of the foundation remained intact until 1999, with the surrounding area littered with bricks and stones that were part of Leetonia's only brewery. In that year, however, the lot was finally graded for construction of a new residence.

North Georgetown

1. Moff/Biery/Newarth brewery

George Moff was a native of Wurtemburg, Baden, Germany, born in 1793, who had come to the United States in the early 1850s. In 1855 he purchased property in the village of North Georgetown and established a small brewery, assisted by his son John, born in 1844, and Samuel Burgerer, a young brewer's apprentice, born in Switzerland, also in 1844. An older son, William, simultaneously operated his own brewery in the Salem area. The site was located in the northwest section of the tiny village (today little more than a crossroads), several hundred feet north of Main Street (also known as Bowman Road or County Road 400) and one block west of North Street.

Moff died in 1863, and the property soon came into the hands of Samuel Biery (also spelled Beiry), who appears to have continued brewing operations, perhaps only intermittently. A small operation, it generally produced only 100 barrels or less of beer annually.

Biery sold the property to his son Daniel and Kasper Newarth for $1,800 in March 1873. Newarth is listed in the 1874 industry directory as being the brewer, assisted by a man named Kickenbaugh, who does not appear in any local records. The property was sold again in 1876, at which time it appears that all brewing operations ceased. Samuel Biery died in that same year, at the age of 76. Nothing remains of the brewery today.

Salem

1. Salem Brewery

William Moff was a native of Wurtemburg, Baden, Germany, born in 1833. He was the son of George Moff, the brewer in North Georgetown, and he came to America with his parents in the early 1850s. He then moved to the Salem area in the late 1850s. Initially living in Green Township of Mahoning County, immediately north of the town of Salem, he had established a small home-brewing operation by 1860. In 1866 he purchased land on the south side of Salem, at 79 Franklin Avenue (today 448 Franklin St.).

Salem Brewery, circa 1880s [provided by Dale E. Shaffer, Salem, OH.]

Soon after this he moved into town and established its only brewery. Brewing both ale and lager, he turned out between 300 and 800 barrels per year. The plant consisted of a two-story brewhouse, with a small icehouse and storage cellar built into a hillside.

Salem, Ohio was a somewhat difficult town in which to operate a brewing establishment, however. Having been founded by Quakers, the town leaders had little tolerance for excessive drinking. Local abstinence societies began to evolve in the 1840s, and gained strength in the following years, although it was not until 1901 that Salem and all of Perry Township voted itself dry. Due to social pressures, therefore, much of the Salem Brewery's products were sold outside of town.

The brewery was sold around 1890 to Gustav Zelle, another German immigrant, born in 1855. Leaving his homeland in 1878, he worked in New York and Pittsburgh before moving to Salem. While it is possible that he may have briefly continued brewing operations at the small plant, it is known that brewing ceased in 1890. Zelle then converted the plant into a local distribution center and bottling house for the L. Schlather Brewery of Cleveland. Later, beer from other Ohio companies was distributed here as well. This operation continued until approximately 1910, after which the brewery was converted into a residence. It remains standing to this day, still used as a private home.

Also Note:

The Wallaby's brewpub chain of Westlake, Ohio opened a Wallaby's Grille in downtown Salem in 2000, at 544 East Pershing Street. While the Wallaby's beer brands were sold at the restaurant, no beer was brewed on-site. Despite the demise of the Wallabys chain later that year, the restaurant remained open as of mid-2004.

COSHOCTON COUNTY

Coshocton

1. L. Mayer/George Sleigh brewery

Coshocton's two breweries were somewhat difficult to research, as many local records from this era are incomplete, conflicting, or inconclusive. It does appear that the two breweries were loosely connected, although one can only speculate over the exact links between them.

According to *History of Coshocton County, Ohio: Its Past & Present* (from 1882), "…the first brewery in Coshocton was started in a building on the west side of Second Street, between Locust and Sycamore, about 1852, by L. Mayer." Based on census and deed records, however, there is no record of an L. Mayer at the time. However, one name is mentioned in several references and appears to have been involved with the brewery's operation, at least in the early days: George Sleigh. (Amazingly, his name is spelled variously as Sleigh, Schleigh, Schlee, Slea, and Slay, making the research a bit more confusing, to say the least.)

Sleigh was a German immigrant, born in 1821, who owned several pieces of property on the north side of Coshocton at this time, including a large piece of land along the Tuscarawas River. Although no details are really known, it appears that brewing operations on Second Street came to a halt in the late 1850s, and a new brewery was established on the larger tract of land three blocks away soon after this. Nothing remains of Coshocton's first brewery today.

2. Frederick Mayer/Lewis Bieber/Charles Boes brewery

After the small brewery on Second Street ceased operations in the late 1850s, a second brewery was established on the west side of the north end of North Fourth Street, along the Tuscarawas River, on land owned by George Sleigh. In the 1860 census, the brewery is shown as being operated by Frederick Mayer, a German immigrant, born in 1820, while Sleigh lived next door and is listed as a wagon maker. Assisting Mayer at this time was Michael Bruh, another German immigrant, born in 1810.

History of Coshocton County, Ohio: Its Past & Present, however, states that Lewis Bieber established this brewery in 1866, although records indicate that he actually purchased the site in 1869. Bieber was a native Bavarian, born in 1830, who came to America in the 1850s. He lived in Newark, Ohio for several years, where he worked at Michael Morath's City Brewery, then came to Coshocton around 1864. It is very possible that he worked at the Mayer brewery for several years before purchasing it. According to the 1870 census, Bieber was assisted by sixteen-year-old George Sleigh, Jr., who still lived next door.

It appears that Bieber continued to own the brewery over the next decade, although by 1874, its actual operation had been transferred to Charles Boes. Little is known about Boes, but he continued brewing operations, producing only around 200 barrels of ale and lager beer annually, until approximately 1877. There are no remains of the small brewery today, and the site is occupied by the Stone Container Corporation mill. Bieber moved back to Newark after the brewery closed, and he remained there until his death in 1892.

Roscoe

1. Conrad Mayer Brewery

Conrad Mayer purchased land on the north side of Main Street (now W. Chestnut Street, or state route 541), in the south end of the small village of Roscoe, in October 1865. Soon after this he established the village's only brewery. It was another small plant, with annual production of ale and beer between 200 and 400 barrels. By the spring of 1881, brewing operations had been transferred to Frederick Bohn, who continued until approximately 1884. Unfortunately, neither deed nor census records give much information on either Mayer or Bohn.

Today, thanks to historic preservation, most of the village of Roscoe (including the brewery) has remained as it was in the mid-1800s, when it was a port along the Ohio and Erie Canal. The area has become a major regional tourist attraction, and the brewery (which was not much more than a brick house with an attached building in the back, where most of the brewing likely took place) was occupied by an antique store in recent years, located at 460 W. Chestnut St. The stone beer cellar, which was built into a steep hillside at the rear of the property, has also survived intact.

CUYAHOGA COUNTY

Beachwood

1. Captain Tony's Pizza and Pasta Emporium

Captain Tony's chain of Italian restaurants was originally founded in 1972. Located at 5 Commerce Park Blvd., just off of Chagrin Blvd., the Beachwood franchise began brewing beer on a limited basis on-site in 1993, although brewing operations had ceased by 1996. The restaurant remained open for several years after that before closing.

Bedford Heights

1. Buckeye Brewing Company/The Brew Keeper

The Cleveland area's second BOP, or "brewed-on-premises" facility, The Brew Keeper opened on April 29, 1997, at 25200 Miles Road. Like The Brew Kettle in Strongsville, the site consists of personal brewing facilities for customers, as well as a small microbrewery, known as the Buckeye Brewing Company. Novice brewers can brew nearly any type of beer, brewing just over twelve gallons at a time in one of the six kettles. The staff provides all the ingredients, recipes, equipment, and instruction. This is also Ohio's first site that allows customers to make a wide variety of their own wines. A beer bar was added later at the site, with several craft beers from the area on tap.

The microbrewery uses a 3-barrel brewing system which yields an annual capacity around 300 barrels, much of which is packaged in 22-ounce bottles for sale at area stores. Garin Wright has been the brewer of this family-owned establishment since the beginning, and seven standard brews are made at this time: Hippie India Pale Ale, Seventy-Six IPA, Czech Pilsner, Wheat Cloud Hefe-Weizen, Cleveland Lager, Vanilla Bean Porter, Sierra Blanca Belgian Wit, and Martian Marzen Oktoberfest Lager. Other specialty brews that have been available include Downtown Brown Ale, Buckeye Blue Lager, Buckeye Red Amber Ale, Yuppie ESB Ale, Sasquatch Pale Ale, Old Mammoth Stout, Buckeye Kolsch, Fuggle Ale, and Miles Lager, as well as Little Jerk Root Beer. Wright won two bronze medals at the 2000 national Real Ale Festival in Chicago, for Sasquatch Pale Ale and Old Mammoth Stout. He also won a gold medal at the 2002 Festival for the Belgian style Ho Ho Ho Magic Tincture.

Wright is currently looking for a new location to build a larger 10-barrel brewing system. More information can be found on Buckeye's web site at www.buckeyebrewing.com .

Berea

1. Davis/Neubrand/Pannonia Brewing Company
(by Carl Miller)

In December 1870, advertisements began appearing in Berea's *Grindstone City Advertiser* for Edward Davis' new brewery on River Street (now Rocky River Drive), opposite Depot Street. Although the brewery actually sat in what was then Middleburg Township just outside Berea Village, Davis nevertheless advertised his enterprise as the "Berea Brewery" (in later years the area was annexed into the city of Berea).

The initial products of the brewery included a wide variety of brews: present use ale, stock ale, pale ale, amber ale, champagne ale, kennett ale, cream ale, porter, and brown stout. Prices ranged from nine dollars for a keg of present use ale up to fourteen dollars for a keg of kennett ale, including delivery to any household in the village. Interestingly, Davis' prices appear to have been slightly high compared to prices of ale brewed in nearby Cleveland. However, it is likely that shipments of ale from Cleveland were not as regular or substantial as demand might have required, thus allowing Davis to build a local trade regardless of his higher prices. Indeed, by 1874 the Berea Brewery was producing about 2,000 barrels of ale per year, although production appears to have dropped off during the remainder of the decade.

By 1878, Davis' son, Edward, Jr. had become a partner in the brewery, and it was the young Davis who took over operation of the plant when his father died in June 1880. However, Edward Jr. did not remain with the brewery for long. By 1884 he had left Berea for Camden, Michigan, where he spent the rest of his years engaged in farming.

The Berea Brewery was then sold to German immigrant George Neubrand, who had already made a small fortune in the local shoe making industry. The brewery was one of a handful of area businesses in which Neubrand had invested over the years, and his various holdings characterized him as "one of the richest men in town" upon his death in 1893.

Local resident Frederick Bullinger was next in possession of the brewery, having purchased it from Neubrand's heirs. The new proprietor was occupied primarily as a stone mason contractor, but he also owned one of Berea's few saloons. Frequented mainly by the village's many quarry workers, Bullinger's saloon did not enjoy a highly favorable reputation, it often being the origin of a variety of "ruckuses". Bullinger apparently did little to improve the situation himself. On the contrary, he was frequently caught in flagrant violation of Sunday closing ordinances and liquor license requirements. One observer noted that "the sight of the marshal with Bullinger in tow and a deputy wheeling a keg of beer confiscated at Bullinger's" was something witnessed by villagers on more than one occasion. Be that as it may, Bullinger was apparently interested in the brewery only for investment purposes, having sold the works for a healthy profit soon after buying it.

The Berea Brewery was attractive to investors because of its particularly strategic location for the shipment of beer into the Ohio interior. In fact, the brewery was located in a section of town known by the locals as "The Depot", named for the busy freight depot which dominated the area. The brewery's proximity to the depot provided quick access to a number of rail lines which sprawled throughout the southwestern portions of the state.

Among those who recognized the benefits of the brewery's location was a group of local investors who organized the Pannonia Brewing Company. Purchasing the Berea Brewery from Frederick Bullinger, the new company began operations late in 1893. Among the incorporators of the venture was Joseph Schimkola, an experienced brewer from Cleveland who undoubtedly filled the position of brewmaster for the new firm. Through the years, the plant had begun brewing lager beer in addition to the various ales, but was still producing just under 1,500 barrels annually. Physically, the plant still consisted only of a primary two-story brick brewhouse, in an era dominated by ever-enlarging breweries of great pomp and style

The Pannonia Brewing Co. was short-lived, passing into receivership early in 1894. However, that fact did not dissuade new investors from approaching the brewery. In 1896, the newly formed North Shore Export Brewing Co. purchased the old plant for $35,000 and commenced production of beer. The new company's operation of the plant was brief, however, as on January 16, 1897 a fire destroyed much of the plant. Beginning early in the morning, it was raging out of control by the time help arrived. A bucket brigade was begun in an attempt to stop the destruction, but it quickly became obvious that the building would be lost, and the attention of those present turned to saving the vats full of beer in storage. As a result, a three-day gala of drinking ensued, which was remembered by many people on Berea's north side for many years.

The estimated loss was valued at $60,000, and no attempt was ever made to rebuild the small plant. Only an empty lot is left at the site today, with a few remnants of the brewery's foundation. Interestingly, the fire was a relief to the local "dry" factions in Berea, who had been outnumbered since the area near the brewery had been annexed into the town some years earlier. The loss of the town's only brewery meant one less source of demon alcohol.

2. Quarryman Taverne and Church Street Brewery/Cornerstone Brewing Co.

"Dare Mighty Things"...with that motto, Berea's first brewing operation in over a century, the Quarryman Taverne and Church Street Brewery, opened August 7, 2001. Located at 58 Front Street, it was situated in a former storefront that had been occupied for two years by the Quarry Ridge Brewpub, a restaurant that had never actually opened. Dave Sutula, a veteran of the Ohio brewpub scene, was the brewmaster, although other staff brewers included Mark Ward, formerly of the Crooked River Brewing Co., and Doug Beedy, formerly of the Liberty Street Brewing Co. in Akron.

At the outset, the pub offered six brews: Yellow Jacket Lager, Grindstone Pale Ale, Harvest Moon Pumpkin Ale, Berea's Best Bitter, an amber ale, and Railway Razz, similar to Sutula's offering at the Willoughby Brewing Co., but brewed in Berea with a slightly different recipe. Other brews were added over the next two years, including Marzen Lager, Tangle-Foot English style pale ale, Wild Irish Red Ale, Sodog IPA, Invictus Barley Wine style ale and Saison Etrange Belgian style ale (both packaged in 25-oz. wine bottles), Frambozen raspberry ale, Brillin Donne honey brown ale, Smooth Sail Summer Ale, Maple Leaf Porter, and Brewbaker's Percolator Stout, made with coffee from the coffee shop next door. By the end of 2003, the brewpub had closed its doors, but on October 11, 2004, the site reopened as the Cornerstone Brewing Co., again with Doug Beedy as brewer. New brews included Grindstone Gold, Sandstone Lager, Esoteric Ale, Berea Brown, Breakfast Stout, and Autumnal Equinox, a spiced ale made with apple cider.

Brooklyn (Brighton)

1. George Henninger brewery

In operation by 1861, this small brewery was located in the village of Brighton, in Brooklyn Township, at a site just east of Pearl Road (U. S. Route 42) near the current line between Brooklyn and Cleveland. It appears to have been owned throughout its existence by George Henninger, a German immigrant, although he leased the brewery between 1864 and 1868 to Joseph Huber, and later to John Ditton, both of whom were also German natives. The brewery appears to have been sold and closed around 1874. Its only trace today is Henninger Road, which crosses Pearl Road near the brewery's site.

Chagrin Falls

1. Sykes/Goodwin brewery

Chagrin Falls' only brewing operation appears to have been established by William H. Sykes in the mid-1850s, although by 1863, the operation was listed in the local business directory as "Sikes and Sessions". Located on the side of a hill just west of town, at approximately 553 Chagrin Blvd., the brewery remained small, apparently not turning out more than 100 barrels of beer annually during its existence. Also involved in the operation during the early years was Lysander B. Wilkinson, a native of Connecticut.

In January 1869, Sykes sold the brewery for $1500 to Albert A. Goodwin, a native Ohioan who was born in 1833. The following year, Wilkinson sold his share of the operation to Emory Sheffield, who remained in the partnership through 1877. Production dwindled through the following decade, with a mere 18 barrels of beer being produced in 1878. Production appears to have ended in 1880, after which the small plant disappeared without a trace.

Cleveland

1. Cleveland Brewery

The first well-documented commercial brewing operation in Cleveland and Cuyahoga County appears to have begun operation in the spring of 1832. It was located in the city's Flats district along the Cuyahoga River and the Ohio and Erie Canal (later taking the address of 109 Canal Street, near Champlain). The Ohio and Erie Canal (usually referred to as the Ohio Canal) was completed in the same year, connecting Cleveland and Lake Erie with Portsmouth, Ohio and the Ohio River. More importantly, it established a route of trade connecting the Mississippi River and the Gulf of Mexico with Canada, New York, and all of New England. This was a critical point in Cleveland's development, after which its growth exploded. Many of the city's earliest businesses began along the canal, allowing easy transport of both raw materials and finished goods.

(left) Samuel C. Ives [from *Breweries of Cleveland*]; (above) Drawing of the brewery showing the addition of 1852 on the right side, from an advertisement in the Cleveland *Plain Dealer*, August 12, 1863.

The Cleveland Brewery was established by Robert Bennett and local physician Dr. Samuel J. Weldon. Weldon was one of the nine members of the fledgling Cleveland Board of Health, and it can be assumed that the brewery's beer, ale, porter, & stout may have been put to at least some medicinal use, as was common practice at the time. This would especially have been true during a cholera outbreak in the city which occurred shortly after the brewery's establishment. While early water sources in many areas were tainted, it could reasonably be assumed that beer and other alcoholic beverages were relatively free of harmful bacteria, partly due to the alcohol content, and also from the boiling that took place in the brewing or distilling process.

Weldon's association with the brewery appears to have ended after one year, and although a malting operation was added around the same time, Bennett had sold the brewery by 1834 to Joseph and Richard Hawley. Three years later, Herrick Childs purchased Joseph Hawley's share, and by 1839 had purchased Richard's as well. While brewing 1,600 barrels per year, Childs leased the brewery one year later to Thomas Hawley and his son-in-law John Hawley Cooke. They brewed ale and porter for the following three years before Childs took charge of the plant again through 1847. Though confusing to follow, such a succession of owners was not unusual for a brewery in this era. In fact, several other breweries in Ohio had operations similarly leased out for between several months and several years while actual ownership of the plant remained constant.

In 1847, the entire Cleveland Brewery was rebuilt with brick, and upon completion was sold to Samuel C. Ives, formerly a brewer for Childs and more recently an owner of the City Brewery (see entry #4). Ives quickly built the business into a thriving enterprise, such that in 1852, a large four-story addition was built, increasing the annual output to more than 7,000 barrels of ale (pale, amber, cream, and the popular "Old Beeswing"), porter, and stout. These were brewed under the watchful eye of brewmaster John C. Brewer, a well-respected name in the industry.

The brewery continued to grow through the 1850s, until Ives died in 1856 at the age of 45, due to liver disease (and likely hastened by stress caused by a long-standing illicit affair with an East Indian woman; see *Breweries of Cleveland* for the full story.) The brewery was left in his will to his fourteen-year-old daughter Eliza. On her behalf, the plant was leased to H. G. Lucas & Co., consisting of maltster Henry G. Lucas and his partners, Francis Rowe and George Newman. One year later, Lucas took over sole operation of the plant and continued in that position through August 1862.

At that time, the brewery's management transferred to Eliza Ives' new husband Frank D. Stone, who had recently returned from service for the Union Army in the Civil War. He continued to operate the plant successfully until January 1, 1865, when it was torched by a Confederate sympathizer, as the war's end and inevitable Union victory grew near. The ensuing fire was a spectacular sight, but was a fatal blow to the brewery, which burned to the ground. Instead of rebuilding the business, Eliza and Frank Stone moved to Iowa for a fresh start as sheep farmers.

2. Reverend Elijah F. Willey brewery

Elijah F. Willey was a Baptist Clergyman who purchased property in Cleveland's Flats district along the Cuyahoga River in 1835. At a site near Willey Street and along Walworth Run, a small creek, he established a brewery around the same time. While specific information about the operation has not surfaced, it was likely a very small and short-lived venture.

3. Rogers/Forest City/Carling & Co. brewery

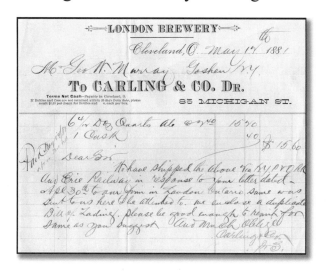

1881 bill of sale for Carling Ale made in Cleveland, to be sent by railway to Goshen, N.Y.

Located in the Flats district at the northwest corner of Seneca (West 3rd) Street and Canal (its later address being 85 Michigan Street), the Forest City Brewery began operation in 1839 for the production of ale. Irish immigrant Charles C. Rogers was its founder and owner for more than thirty years. His business grew slowly over the years, and by 1858 this had necessitated the erection of a three-story addition to the plant. Rogers produced mostly Stock Ale, brewed using water from a nearby spring on Seneca Street, and sold at one to two years of age. Rogers retired in 1871, and operations were assumed by his younger brother, William H. Rogers, and Robert Beggs. Two years later, Beggs' share of the plant was taken by Hazen Hughes, and in 1878, former policeman John P. Haley took full ownership of the brewery. During this forty-year period, the popular trend toward lager beer was ignored in favor of the continued production of ale. Annual production of over 6,000 barrels made it one of the larger breweries in the city, although by the late 1870s, this number had declined to around 2,500 barrels.

In 1880, Haley sold the aging plant to Carling & Company of London, Ontario. Founded in 1840, Carling was already a well-known name in Canada. The large parent brewery was operated by founder Thomas Carling's son, Sir John Carling, who was also a member of the Canadian Parliament. Seeing the potential for expansion of his brewing success into the United States, Carling sent John S. MacBeth and Hugh Spencer to Cleveland to secure a brewing site for Carling Ale, as well as porter and stout. The Forest City Brewery was ideal in that it had exclusively produced ale throughout its existence, and it was thus renamed as the London Brewery of Carling & Co., with Spencer as brewmaster and MacBeth as plant manager. From the beginning, the company sought a wide distribution of its products in the United States, and it hired the Chicago-based firm of Barrett & Barrett to distribute Carling products via distribution centers in several cities in the east and midwest.

After only four years, Carling sold the Cleveland branch and the rights to produce Carling Ales to MacBeth. At that time, brewing operations were moved from the original site to a former malt house and distillery along the bank of the Cuyahoga River (see entry #38). The original plant is no longer standing.

4. City Brewery

Around 1841, the City Brewery was established on Canal Street in the Flats district, near the Ohio Canal.

Originally operated by Blackwell, Lloyd, & Co., the brewery was under new management by 1843, as noted in the Cleveland *Herald*: "The undersigned would respectfully inform the lovers of Good Ale and Strong Beer, that the City Brewery has a plenty on board, and is now under full sail, with S. C. Ives, Master." Brewing operations continued under the direction of Samuel C. Ives and Henry Lloyd until the plant closed in 1847. Ives later operated the Cleveland Brewery on Canal Road, while Lloyd later established the Cleveland City Brewery on St. Clair Avenue.

5. Eagle Brewery

The Eagle Brewery, located at 32 Michigan Street near Seneca (W. 3rd) Street, was originally established in the early 1840s by George W. Hamilton. After just a few years in operation, the brewery was completely leveled by fire in December 1845. The Cleveland *Herald* reported the brewery's value as being about $2,000, representing Hamilton's life savings. The loss was uninsured, but a collection was organized for Hamilton's benefit, and the brewery was quickly rebuilt.

Englishman John Tutbury joined the business as a partner around 1848. However, by 1856 Hamilton had left the partnership, and the plant was doing business under the name of J. Tutbury & Company. When Tutbury died in 1857, management was taken over by John Quinn, a brewer who had been employed at the plant. Under Quinn's direction (and briefly joined in partnership by Hannibal E. Spear in 1863), the Eagle Brewery continued to brew beer until 1869, when it closed for good.

6. John M. Hughes, Spring Street Brewery

Established in 1846, exclusively as an ale brewery, the Spring Street Brewery was located on Spring (W. 10th) Street between Main Street and St. Clair Avenue on the east side of the Flats district. Original proprietor Truman Downer was joined after two years by a new partner, Thomas F. Wyman. However, in 1850 the partners sold their growing business to John M. Hughes, a brewer from New York who had worked for them since his arrival in town three years earlier. While Hughes purchased the brewing aspect of the business for $3,200, the adjacent malting facility was sold separately to John B. Smith.

Six months after Hughes' purchase, the brewery burned to the ground one night. Despite the total loss, the company was rebuilt and re-established within several months, and its business and reputation both continued to flourish. This success was due in part to the work of brewmaster Carl Gehring, who had been with the firm since 1849.

In 1857, seeing a need for expansion, Hughes began work on an entirely new plant several blocks away, which was finished and ready to occupy by early 1858 (see entry #17). In the process, however, he lost Gehring, who went on to found his own brewery (see entry #15), and more recent employee Leonhard Schlather, who also left to found his own brewery (see entry #16). The latter two men saw the tremendous potential for the relatively new concept of lager beer, and their future successes would greatly surpass those of John M. Hughes.

7. Michael Stumpf brewery

What appears to have been the first brewery in Cleveland to brew lager beer was established in 1846 by brothers Michael and Martin Stumpf, both recent immigrants from Darmstadt, Hesse, Germany. Located at 242-246 Lake Street (later Lakeside Avenue), between Muirson (E. 12th) and Canfield (E. 13th) Streets, the brewery remained small throughout its existence, selling lager to local German saloons. Martin Stumpf left the partnership in 1850 to found his own brewery one block away (see entry #10), and Michael continued to operate the plant on his own, with the assistance of three hired hands, all German immigrants. After a fire in 1857, the plant was fully rebuilt three years later and brewing continued as before.

Stumpf's sons William and Louis had joined him in the brewery by the 1870s, although business was in slow decline through the decade. Producing over 1,100 barrels in 1875, the brewery turned out less than 300 barrels just four years later. In 1882, brewing at the plant ceased for good, after which the main building was converted into the family home. Stumpf then became a tax assessor for the city, although he died in 1886.

8. Newman/Fovargue, Forest City Brewery

Located at 32-38 Irving (later E. 25th) Street, near Pittsburgh Avenue, Cleveland's *other* Forest City Brewery (as opposed to entry #3) was established around 1850 by Thomas Newman. As with the other Forest City Brewery, this was exclusively an ale brewery, at least until its last ten years of existence. In 1864, Newman was joined in the firm by William H. Rogers, the brother of Charles Rogers, who operated the older Forest City Brewery. While it is possible that there was a business link between the two plants, there is no actual evidence of this. However, soon after Rogers left the partnership in 1869 to manage his brother's older brewery, the Forest City name was dropped from the Irving Street plant.

After Rogers left the firm, his position was taken by Daniel Fovargue, a twenty-three-year-old native of Cambridge, England, who worked as an apprentice until taking over the brewery in 1872 upon Newman's retirement. He was joined in the business for three years by James Dangerfield, but had sole ownership by 1875. By this time, the brewery's annual capacity was around 9,000 barrels, although actual production ranged between 2,500 and 3,500 barrels through the end of the decade. It was also around this time that Fovargue added production of lager beer to the plant, and this accounted for two-thirds of the plant's production by 1878. In 1881, operation of the brewery was assumed by Creasey Fovargue, Jr. (Daniel's brother) and Thomas Newman, Jr., as Daniel Fovargue was operating a saloon in town. Within two years, however, brewing ceased at the plant for good. The Fovargue brothers remained in Ohio, with Creasey moving to Sandusky, where he died in 1915, and Daniel remaining in Cleveland until his death in 1927.

Forest City Brewery as it appeared around 1870

9. John A. Bishop brewery

Established by Bavarian immigrant John A. Bishop (nee Bischof) in 1852, this small brewery was located at 371 Broadway Avenue (later renumbered as 522 Broadway), near Pittsburgh Avenue. Initially producing lager beer, the plant later began brewing ale as well, and in an unusual twist, had phased out lager production by the early 1880s. The plant grew very slightly over its nearly forty-year existence, and as late as 1879, it was turning out a mere 1,200 barrels annually. It was sold to the firm of Louis Lezius & Christian Kaenzig in 1882, but one year later, Lezius left the partnership to become involved in a brewery two blocks away (see entry #14). Kaenzig's wife Elizabeth was managing the plant by 1887, but two years later Lezius had returned to oversee operations. In 1891, production ceased for good.

10. Jacob Mall/Gund/Sunrise Brewing Company

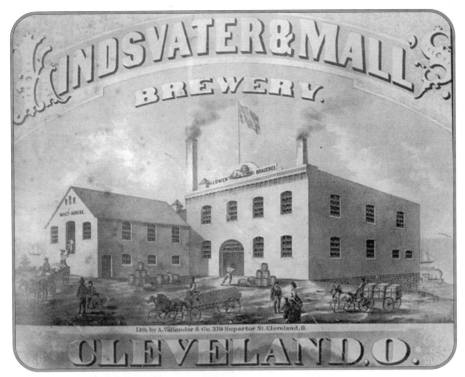

(above) Lithographed advertisement for the Lion Brewery, circa late 1860s, showing Lake Erie in the background [Bob and Jeanette Bendula collection]; (below) George F. Gund [from *The Western Brewer*].

Cleveland's second longest-lasting brewing operation was established in 1850 by Martin Stumpf. After four years of working in partnership with his brother Michael at their brewery on Lake Street (thought to be the city's first to brew lager beer—see entry #7), Stumpf, a German immigrant, left to operate his own brewery one block away at 141 Hamilton Street, between Muirson (E. 12th) and Canfield (E. 13th) Streets. Once Martin was in business at his new plant, he continued production of lager beer until 1859, when he sold the plant for $5,000 to Jacob Mall and Paul Kindsvater. Stumpf founded yet another small brewery in the area four years later (see entry #22).

Under the new owners, the plant became known as the Lion Brewery, and its business continued to grow through the following decade. Kindsvater was the owner of a popular saloon nearby, while Mall was a German-trained brewmaster, and this combination was a success. So much so, in fact, that the brewery had expanded to its limit at the site by 1870, after which the plant was relocated to the north side of Davenport (formerly Wilson) Avenue, two blocks to the north, and along the bluff overlooking Lake Erie (the site later took the address of 1417-1476 Davenport Avenue). This site had been purchased years earlier by Martin Stumpf for building underground lagering cellars, and probably for easy access to the lake for ice in the winter. Despite this growth, Kindsvater left the partnership one year later, leaving Mall as the sole owner.

Jacob Mall was a native of Gebrichen, Baden, Germany, who had come to Cleveland in 1853, at the relatively old age of thirty-six, working initially as the brewmaster at the Schmidt & Hoffman brewery on the city's far east side. After he took full ownership of the Lion Brewery, it grew slowly, from production of around 5,000 barrels of Mall's Crystal Lager annually through the 1870s, to over 10,000 barrels by the time of Mall's death in 1891. Just two years prior to this, the company had been incorporated as the Jacob Mall Brewing Company, with capital stock of $100,000. Soon after this began the process of gradually replacing the original buildings, culminating in 1896 with the erection of a new, four-story brewhouse. These changes increased the plant's annual production dramatically, to 30,000 barrels. After Mall's death, the plant's management was assumed by his son-in-law, Gustav Kaercher.

The brewery continued to grow despite an economic downturn in 1893, and increasingly competitive and even hostile conditions in the local brewing industry, but in 1897 the entire plant was sold to George F. Gund, who would take its success to new heights (Kaercher stayed on as the company's vice-president for more than a decade, with Joseph Ranft and later Jacob Fickel as secretary). Gund was the son of John Gund, owner of the large John Gund Brewing Company of LaCrosse, WI. George had worked for his father, and later moved west where he became the president of the Seattle Brewing & Malting Co., but now, at the age of forty-

The Jacob Mall brewery, built in 1889, as it appeared around the time of its takeover by George F. Gund [Bill Carlisle collection]

two, he was returning to the midwest. His initial priority was to break away somewhat from the tradition of exclusively selling beer to saloons, as he recognized the potential for home beer sales in bottles. This required the construction of a new bottling plant, and when it was completed in early 1898, Gund's Crystal Bottled Beer made its first appearance in the Cleveland market, with production overseen by long-time brewmaster Fred Kiefer. This would later be joined by Ye Old Lager, Gund's Finest, Gund's Special, and Gund's Bock Beers. As the Gund name became more widely known in the area, the brewery was renamed as the Gund Brewing Company on January 1, 1900.

The brewery itself was a marvel of modern brewing technology, being among the first in the area to incorporate electric lighting and smoke eliminators in the plant. Also utilized were automated bottle fillers and the new "Cork Crown" bottle cap. Other innovations appeared as well in later years, such as selling bottles in cardboard cases of twenty-four, as opposed to the traditional wooden crates. In addition, Gund was one of several brewers in the area to offer a "Profit-Sharing Plan" for consumers, in which coupons were offered with every case of beer sold. These coupons could be redeemed for items out of a catalog, and included a wide range of household items.

George F. Gund was an entrepreneur in the truest sense of the word. Using money generated by the brewery, he invested in other ventures, such as mining companies, realty, and banking. He had been on the boards of two banks when in Seattle, and was associated with two in Cleveland as well. He was also involved with the United States and Ohio Brewers Associations. When he died in March 1916 at the age of sixty, his son, George F. Gund II, came from Seattle to take over management of the brewery.

George II quickly introduced a new brand of beer, Gund's Clevelander, which was met with good local sales. However, sales were short-lived, as statewide Prohibition stopped all beer production at the plant in November 1918. Over the next six months, all remaining beer in the plant was sold off through an arrangement with the Pilsener Brewing Company across town. As the Gund family had invested in other ventures, they closed the brewery completely at this time, and unlike most of the other brewers in the city, did not move into the production of cereal beverages or soft drinks.

Wooden sign with decal, made by the Meyercord Company shortly after the turn of the century.

While the brewery sat quietly, Gund continued to find ways to make money, to a far greater extent than ever before. The Gund Realty Company was established in the brewery's former office building across the street from the brewery, and this managed numerous properties owned by the brewery, many of them former saloons. Soon after the production of beer stopped, Gund also purchased the Kaffee Hag Corporation for $130,000. A small coffee-making company, it had one asset that appealed to Gund: a process for removing caffeine from the coffee without destroying the taste. The Kaffee Hag Corporation moved into the old brewery complex, and began to grow quickly, being capitalized at $1,000,000 within two years of Gund's purchase. In 1927, Gund sold the company to Battle Creek, Michigan's Kellogg Company, known largely for the cereals and other foods that it produces to this day. The purchase price: $10,000,000. In eight years, Gund had seen his investment grow by eighty times! Much of this was paid in Kellogg stock, and this stock eventually became the basis for the family fortune. Kaffee Hag continued to flourish, especially after its sale to General Foods, when the coffee product was renamed as Sanka.

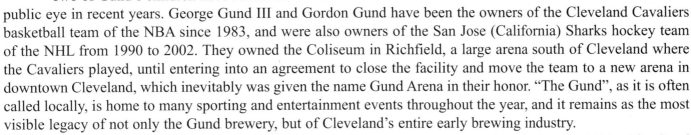

(left) George F. Gund II [Cleveland State University Library]; (below) Gund Arena today

Gund invested his wealth in numerous Cleveland businesses, and eventually became the largest shareholder in the Cleveland Trust Company, the state's largest bank, of which he later served as president. He was considered to be the wealthiest man in the city for many years, until his death in 1966. His estate at the time was estimated at $600,000,000, much of which was left to the George Gund Foundation, founded in 1951, which still supports many social, educational, and artistic causes to this day. Gund's six children share a family fortune most recently estimated at $1.6 billion by *Forbes Magazine*.

Two of Gund's children have remained in the public eye in recent years. George Gund III and Gordon Gund have been the owners of the Cleveland Cavaliers basketball team of the NBA since 1983, and were also owners of the San Jose (California) Sharks hockey team of the NHL from 1990 to 2002. They owned the Coliseum in Richfield, a large arena south of Cleveland where the Cavaliers played, until entering into an agreement to close the facility and move the team to a new arena in downtown Cleveland, which inevitably was given the name Gund Arena in their honor. "The Gund", as it is often called locally, is home to many sporting and entertainment events throughout the year, and it remains as the most visible legacy of not only the Gund brewery, but of Cleveland's entire early brewing industry.

Back at the old brewery, the Kaffee Hag Company was operating for a time during the 1920s. The Gund Realty Company still owned the plant, and another portion of it was leased in 1927 to Abraham Miller and Joseph Hecht, doing business as the Erie Sales Company for the manufacture of malt syrup. As soon as Prohibition ended in early 1933, the pair organized the Sunrise Brewing Company to operate out of the facility. As it had not produced any beer in more than fourteen years, the brewery needed a total overhaul, but once the new equipment was installed, the plant's annual capacity reached 75,000 barrels (later improvements would bring that number to 120,000 barrels). The new company's choice for brewmaster and vice-president was Jaro Pavlik, a veteran of the local brewing industry since 1897, working at both the Pilsener and Standard Breweries prior to Prohibition. Sunrise Beer and Ale arrived on the scene in August of that year, and were later followed by the Golden Dawn and Old German brands. Beer was sold initially in kegs, but the bottled variety was available by the following year.

After less than two years of business, the new company came under investigation by the government, being charged with several crimes, including the recycling of tax stamps on sold beer kegs for reuse, and falsified records of beer production to

Jaro H. "Jerry" Pavlik

Sunrise delivery truck from the mid-1930s

reflect a smaller output than was actually produced (all done for the purpose of paying less Federal tax on the beer sold). As a result of the inquiry, the company was ordered by the Federal court to be sold to pay heavy fines, its operating license was forfeited, and brewing operations ceased at the end of 1934.

This, however, was not the end of the line for the brewery. By March 1935 the plant had been purchased by local businessmen David and Harry Frankel, for $125,000. Just one year later, another management shakeup brought in Abraham Miller as president. Pavlik, who had survived the problems of the prior owners, remained with the new company as brewmaster and vice-president, and both Sunrise and Golden Dawn Beers returned to the local marketplace. These were

A Virtual Tour of the Sunrise Brewery

The November 15, 1933 issue of *Modern Brewery* magazine contained a fairly detailed description of the inner workings of the Sunrise plant. Some of the highlights follow:

"The Sunrise Brewing Company of Cleveland is one of the first of the new type of modern brewing establishments to be erected. Following the current trend toward modernization and economy in operating costs, this company has installed complete new equipment throughout. One of the unique features of this installation is that the plant has been laid out so that every square foot of available working space has been utilized. Because of the ingenious arrangement of equipment, there is no lost motion in the plant's operation.

The capacity of the Sunrise Brewery is three 165-barrel brews per day. There is a 150-barrel mash tun and a 170-barrel brew kettle. The portion of the building in which the engine room is located is two stories in height. The engine room is on the first floor, while on the roof has been placed a 400 gpm cooling tower made of California redwood. This tower has been located in such a position that full advantage may be taken of the cool winds that blow off Lake Erie, and which serve as a natural cooling medium.

The fermentation room is 47 x 58 ft. and 12 ft. high, and is on the second floor. Here are located two 160-barrel square settling tanks, two 192-barrel round closed fermenters, and ten 150-barrel square open fermenting tanks. The closed fermenter tanks are used for the reclamation of carbon dioxide gas. Directly below the fermentation room, on the first floor, is the chip cask cellar, which is of the same dimensions, and is 14 ft. high. In this room are located eight 170-barrel tanks and five 322-barrel tanks. Beneath the chip cask cellar is the stock cellar of the same width and length as the other two rooms, and 15 ft. high. This room contains five 398-barrel tanks and four 322-barrel tanks. The total holding capacity of all tanks in these three rooms amounts to 8,552 barrels. All tanks are constructed of steel, and were assembled and welded in their respective locations.

On the first floor, adjacent to the long wall of the chip cask cellar, and between it and the engine room, is the racking room, 50 x 31 x 10 ft. high. Here are located the carbonator, the beer filter apparatus, and a double-pipe beer racking cooler. On the second floor, directly over the racking room are located the double-pipe water sections of the wort cooler, and also a "sweet water" tank, from which water at 35 degrees F. is passed to the attemperator coils, and also to the water section of the wort cooler. The mash and brew kettles, and the steam boiler, are located on the first floor, next to the engine room, and the malt and hop storage areas are on the second floor directly above them. The keg wash room is also on the first floor, against the short wall of the racking room. Though at the present time the Sunrise Brewing Company makes keg beer only, ample space is provided for the installation of bottling machinery should it be decided at some later date to sell the product in bottles.

The beer producing cycle in this brewing establishment is of unusual interest in that it combines the older methods and arts of brewing with the newer methods, developed within the past fifteen years as a result of modern refrigerating and cooling equipment, which greatly accelerates plant operation at points where speed is essential, and assures a uniform quality in the plant's finished product. In the initial stages, the wort goes from mash tub to brew kettle, following the usual practices of brewing. The brew kettle is fitted with a filter, which strains the wort as it is pumped from the brew kettle to the large square, uninsulated steel tank on the second floor. It remains in this tank some time, losing a portion of its heat. From this tank it is pumped directly to the modern wort coolers.

The wort then passes to the fermentation cellar, which is kept at a room temperature of 40-42 degrees F., and remains here for 24 hours. It is then pumped to the fermentation tanks, where the beer is allowed to work for six days, until its temperature rises to 50 or 52 degrees. The attemperator coils are then turned on and the beer is cooled in two days to 42 degrees, and is then run through the double-pipe cooler, where the beer temperature is further reduced to 38 degrees. The beer is then carried to the basement stockroom, which is kept at 32 degrees, and in this room it is stored for at least a month. The beer is next pumped to the racking room, where it is carbonated and filtered, and then goes to the chip cellar, which is also kept at 32 degrees, and there it rests for two or three weeks longer. At the end of this period it passes through the beer cooler located in the racking room, where more carbon dioxide is added and the beer refiltered if necessary, and so on to the racking room."

joined three years later by the arrival of Cheerio Ale and Tip Top Beer. Tip Top was supposedly brewed according to an old Bohemian recipe used in Europe by Pavlik's family, and by 1939, its successful sales led to a change of the company's name to the Tip Top Brewing Company.

In 1940, a large portion of the company's stock was purchased by Alfred "Big Al" Polizzi. Polizzi had previously been involved with the establishment of the Lubeck Brewing Company in Toledo, brewing Lubeck Beer which was distributed in the Cleveland area. When that brewery closed in 1939, Polizzi purchased enough stock to take control of the Tip Top company, which then added the Lubeck brand to its production. Despite Polizzi's reputed underworld ties, his four years as president and treasurer of the brewery were relatively uneventful.

Polizzi sold the entire plant to the Brewing Corporation of America in June 1944 for $400,000 (at the same time that Brewing Corporation of America was also purchasing the Forest City Brewery elsewhere in town). The purchase was for the Tip Top Company's war-time grain rations (which were used to brew more Carling Red Cap Ale and Black Label Beer at the main plant on Quincy Avenue), not to utilize the Tip Top facility; in fact it was permanently closed at the time. Polizzi retired at the same time and moved to Florida, where he spent his remaining years involved in real estate.

The Davenport Avenue brewery continued to house the Tip Top Distributing Company, local distributors of Pabst Blue Ribbon Beer from Milwaukee, until the 1960s, when most of the plant was razed. On the south side of the street, the office building housing the Gund Realty Company, as well as the original Gund stables and garage next door, remained standing until 1999, when both were razed for the construction of both the new studios for WKYC-TV, Channel 3, Cleveland's NBC television affiliate, and the new local headquarters for the FBI. These two complexes cover the entire former brewery site, in an area known today as the "Davenport Bluffs," and during their construction, some of the brewery's original foundations were uncovered one last time before disappearing into history forever.

(top left) Serving tray, circa 1934; (above) Label for a quart bottle; (left) Giant outdoor billboard with neon lights, shown in *Modern Brewer*, June 1938.

11. Mack Brothers brewery

Matthias Mack was an Irish immigrant who began brewing lager beer around 1852 at a site between Vermont and Washington Streets. This was in an area known as "the Angle", an Irish neighborhood just north of Detroit Avenue on the city's near west side. By 1857 he had been joined in partnership by his brother John M. Mack, and they operated the small brewery as the "Mack Brothers". The plant remained a small neighborhood concern throughout its existence, producing between 300 and 700 barrels annually. It also was entirely a family operation, with at least five Macks taking part in the business at different times. Around 1874, the small plant ceased operation, while the family business moved to the city's southeast side (see entry #34).

12. Schmidt & Hoffman/Cleveland/Cleveland & Sandusky Brewing Co.

After numerous additions, the Cleveland Brewing Co. plant was one of the city's largest breweries, as shown in this image taken after its consolidation into the Cleveland & Sandusky Brewing Co. in 1898. [Carl Miller collection]

Cleveland's first large-scale and long-lasting lager beer brewery began operations in 1852, in East Cleveland Township at the intersection of Hough and Ansel Avenues (9807 Hough Ave. in later years). Despite being in a rural area several miles east of downtown Cleveland, the site was ideal for brewing beer, in that it was adjacent to both a brook which provided a source of pure water and a pond which could be used to cut ice in the winter, and it sat atop a hillside which allowed underground lagering cellars to be constructed easily. (The site is no longer rural by any means—it is one block from the former Mount Sinai Hospital complex, and the hillside overlooks Rockefeller Park and Martin Luther King Drive, just north of Euclid Avenue and University Circle, which with Severance Hall and numerous museums is the center of Cleveland's cultural community.)

The brewery was established by Robert Hoffman and C. W. Schmidt. The latter was a recent immigrant from Germany, having been born in Gruenstadt and having played a role in the country's political uprisings of 1848. After serving in the revolutionary parliament until it was overthrown, he then fled to France (and was sentenced to death in absentia in Germany for his role in the uprising.) He then headed to America, and directly to Cleveland, where he immediately began organizing the new brewing establishment, although he would sell his share of the plant to his son Charles just nine years later (the elder Schmidt outlived his son, continuing to live in the area until his death in 1887, at the age of 82.) The brewery turned out 700 barrels in its first year, but as lager beer became increasingly popular, the plant and its output gradually grew, reaching over 7,000 barrels by the mid-1870s. By 1878, the plant included four ice houses with a capacity of three thousand tons of ice, nine aging cellars, and one fermenting cellar containing fourteen vats.

Robert Hoffman died in 1882, after which his position as president of the company was taken over by his son Louis. Two years later, Charles Schmidt died as well, with his son Carl taking over his position as vice-president. In 1887, the company was joined by Ernst W. Mueller, who purchased a large share of its stock while serving as secretary and treasurer. Mueller, born in Alsenz, Bavaria in 1851, had come to America as a child and for many years had worked in his father's malting business, Peter Mueller & Co., which was one of the largest in Cleveland. It was at this time that the brewery began to grow at a rapid pace. Renaming itself as the Cleveland Brewing Co. in 1887, the company was producing around 10,000 barrels annually. Expansion of the plant, capped by the completion of a large new brewhouse in 1895, allowed this number to pass 40,000 barrels by 1894, making it the city's fifth-largest brewery. It was probably no coincidence that during this rapid growth phase, the company's management had been taken over by the Mueller family: Hermann Mueller as president, Rudolph Mueller (cousin of Ernst) as vice-president, Ernst Mueller as secretary, and Julius Mueller as treasurer.

In June 1898, the Cleveland Brewing Company was one of nine in the city that joined together to form the Cleveland & Sandusky Brewing Co. as a way to counter a highly competitive environment that had developed in the city over the previous decade. Ernst Mueller eventually became the new company's president, but was later removed from the position due to internal politics (see entry #45), moving on to run the Cleveland Home Brewing Co. (see entry #35) for many years. Even without Mueller, The Cleveland Brewing Co. plant continued to undergo additional expansion over the years and remained as one of the new combine's primary beer-making facilities.

Brewing ceased in September 1919 after the onset of statewide Prohibition, and the plant was vacated. The stable building across the street was converted into a boxing arena for a few years before being converted back into a stable for horses to be rented for rides in nearby Rockefeller Park. While the cellar building was razed in 1938, much of the remains stood through the 1940s. According to an article in the Cleveland *Press* from 1941, visitors to the Brewery Restaurant, operating in a former saloon next door, often heard stories from former brewery wagon driver Jugend Blaett, of ghosts in the upper floors that could be heard late at night rolling barrels and pounding bungs in place. The viability of this claim was questioned only by the fact that Blaett could barely hear the interviewer's questions, having to cup his hand over his ear. Ghosts or not, the remaining buildings and stables were razed a few years later, leaving no remains at the site today.

13. John Dangeleisen brewery

John Dangeleisen opened a beer garden with a small associated lager beer brewery and malt house on Forest (East 37th) Street near Broadway around 1856. Never a large operation, it was nevertheless the site of at least one reported skirmish (and probably several more unreported ones) as told in the Cleveland *Leader* on June 8, 1858:

"A fight took place at Daegleison's on Sunday afternoon last, which had its origin in long and frequent draughts of that enticing and highly-respectable beverage called 'lager beer.' The combatants, some six or eight in number, were mostly Germans, and pitched into each other, it is said, with great earnestness. Two or three were thrown into the canal, and the consequent dunking considerably cooled their ardor and restored quiet. Lager beer on Sunday afternoons is *not* a very desirable institution."

Somewhere around 1870, Dangeleisen moved on to other commercial ventures, and ownership of the brewery passed into the hands of Henry Rochotte. During its final year of business (1874), it was briefly operated by Frank Payer. At the time of its founding and greatest popularity, the beer garden was in a remote and quiet area south of the city, but by the time of its closing, it was rapidly becoming surrounded by local industry.

14. Diebolt Brewing Company

Situated at the top of a steep bluff overlooking a main railroad line into the city, the Star Brewery was established around 1856 on Pittsburgh Street, opposite Jackson (later East 27th) Street. The address of the site changed through the years, and was listed variously as 39 Broadway, 70 Jackson & Broadway Extension, 37-39 Pittsburgh, 54-62 Pittsburgh, and finally, after the turn of the century, 2702 Pittsburgh Street, but all referred to the same plant. Brewing pale and amber ales and porter, it was originally operated by Jno H. Jones & James Lloyd, although by 1858 Jones' share had been taken by Robert Keenan. Frequent changes in ownership followed through the years, and by 1868, it was being operated by J. Gromlich, who soon sold to Charles Yahraus. Yahraus sold the plant to Carl Seyler in 1874, at which time the plant was yielding less than 2,000 barrels per year. Seyler increased annual production to nearly 6,000 barrels, a large portion of which likely

**Turn-of-the-century lithograph featuring the newly enlarged Diebolt Brewery
[Carl Miller collection]**

Delivery trucks filled with crates of bottles, ready to leave the Diebolt brewery, circa 1914 [courtesy of Carl Miller].

being lager, although by 1878 he had sold the plant to Louis Chormann (also spelled Schauerman).

Chormann continued to operate the brewery until 1885 when it was sold to Louis Lezius and August Uehlein, both former employees of the Oppmann brewery on the city's west side. Just three years later, Lezius left the partnership, selling his share to Anthony J. Diebolt for $3,300. One year after this, Uehlein sold his share to Edward A. Ruble, although the latter died in 1891, after which Diebolt purchased his share to gain full control of the brewery.

Diebolt was a native of Buffalo, NY, where he had worked in the brewery of Gerhard Lang before coming to Cleveland in 1887 at the age of twenty-one. He first worked at Wenzl Medlin's Bohemian Brewing Co. on the city's west side for a year, before purchasing a share of the Pittsburgh Avenue brewery. After he took full control of the company in 1891, it was reorganized as the Diebolt Brewing Company. Diebolt was joined in his new venture by brothers Joseph and Mathias, who came from Buffalo in 1893. Anthony served as company president throughout its existence, with Joseph as vice-president and Mathias as secretary and treasurer. Another brother, Frank, also worked for the company as a brewer, while a brother-in-law, Joseph Irr, served as the company's collector in the 1890s.

At the time of Diebolt's purchase of a share in the brewery, its growth had stagnated, with annual sales around 4,000 barrels. Within ten years, however, that number had grown to 20,000 barrels, and by 1907 the plant's annual capacity had grown to 80,000 barrels. Diebolt's White Seal Beer was the company's flagship brand, advertised as "The Triumph of Brewing," and was sold along with Diebolt's Standard Beer, Bohemian Export, Malt Tonic, and of course, bock beer in the spring. All were brewed under the supervision of brewmaster Paul Hohman.

By 1912, the plant consisted of six large, castle-like buildings covering four acres. At the rear of a central courtyard was the four-story stockhouse, which gave the plant an impressive, if imposing, appearance. Across Pittsburgh Avenue was the large stable building, which far outlasted all of the other structures at the plant, standing until 1979. An entirely new bottling plant was built in 1915, as bottled beer for home sales continued to grow in importance. Typical of many structures in the brewing industry that were built in the last years before Prohibition, this new facility did not share the ornate architecture of the rest of the plant.

Beginning in 1908, the brewery opened a subsidiary business, the Cleveland Hygeia Ice Company, using the plant's ice making machinery. Large quantities of

Another view of the Diebolt brewery in 1923, looking west on Broadway [Cleveland State University collection]

(right) Nearly a decade after Prohibition took effect, the Diebolt aging tanks were still in place. Here they are being removed during the plant's razing in September 1928 for enlargement of the railroad right-of-way [Cleveland State University Library].

artificial ice were produced for wholesale purposes, and shipped via the railroad lines that ran just behind the brewery site. Within a few years, one-third of the plant was being utilized for ice storage.

In May 1919, as statewide Prohibition took effect, the company (now known as just the Diebolt Co.) continued in the ice business while introducing non-alcoholic Perlex Beverage. Like many of the city's other near beer offerings, sales of this were poor, however, and all beverage production ceased in 1923. The Diebolt brothers, like most other brewers of the era, had previously entered the real estate business to manage their saloon properties in the city, and this proved to be far more profitable in the long run. The brewery and ice plant, however, would ultimately be taken from them after a five-year court battle with real estate developers Oris and Mantis Van Sweringen. The Van Sweringens, who had built the Terminal Tower, the city's tallest building at the time, successfully attempted to take the brewery property by eminent domain so that the land could be cleared for the railroad approach to the main terminal. The entire brewery was razed in 1928. Despite this, the brothers' real estate business continued to flourish, making each of them millionaires. Mathias Diebolt died in 1934, and soon after this, the Great Depression brought an end to the company's real estate successes. Anthony Diebolt died in 1940, and when Joseph died in 1946, his assets (representing those of all three brothers, none of whom had married) were valued at only $20,000.

The Diebolt stable building stood on the north side of Pittsburgh Avenue, across the street from the rest of the brewery complex, and remained standing until 1979. The structure was even more imposing in appearance than the rest of the brewery, resembling a large fortress more than a stable. A large concrete horse head stood out above the main doorway until the end. A large branch of the U.S. Postal Service stands at the site today.

15. C. E. Gehring Brewing Co./Cleveland & Sandusky Co.

Established in 1857, the brewery of Carl Ernst Gehring on Cleveland's near west side would eventually grow into the city's third-largest of the late 1800s. Gehring was a native of Goeppingen, Wurttemburg, Germany, born in 1830, who came to America at the age of eighteen after a four-year apprenticeship at a brewery in his homeland. After working at the Eagle Brewery on Michigan Street, he became the brewmaster of the Spring Street Brewery, first under Truman Downer and later for John M. Hughes. Although Gehring had likely been trained in the brewing of lager beer in Germany, he brewed only ale at the Hughes plant, as that was still the most well-known and popular malt beverage in the city in the 1850s.

In 1857, Hughes rebuilt his successful ale brewery, and it was at this time, after eight years as brewmaster there, that Gehring took his $600 of savings and established his own brewery in a small building at Pearl (W. 25th) Street & Brainard Avenue (Gehring's friend Leonhard Schlather, also a German immigrant, worked for Hughes as well and left at the same time as Gehring to found his own successful brewery—see entry #16.) It was here that Gehring began brewing lager beer, along with the still-popular ale and porter. Gehring was a one-man show at the beginning, functioning as brewer, salesman, deliveryman, and collector while producing 1,800 barrels during his first year in business. The plant grew rapidly as lager beer became increasingly popular with the

(left) Cleveland City Atlas, 1874;
(below) Carl Gehring
[from *The Western Brewer*]

city's many German immigrants. In 1874, the brewery produced just under 12,000 barrels, as it passed former employer John M. Hughes in production (Hughes was still the largest ale brewer in the city, but his production was in slow decline, as was the market for ale in general.)

Around 1876, Gehring's large plant was replaced by an entirely new and larger one which filled the block between Pearl and Brainard Avenues, along Freeman Street. The new plant consisted of a 155-barrel brew kettle (the city's largest), thirty-six fermenting tanks, a malt house capable of malting 12,000 bushels of barley per year, two ice houses, and six lagering cellars. It employed twenty-five men and six delivery teams, while sending beer as far away as New York, Pennsylvania, West Virginia, and Virginia. By 1879, production was just shy of 20,000 barrels.

Throughout this time, Gehring and his family continued to live in a house adjacent to the brewery. His four sons all worked for the company as well: C. E. Gehring, Jr. worked as assistant brewmaster under William Dertinger, who was Gehring's son-in-law; Frederick "F. W." Gehring was the company's bookkeeper; John A. Gehring was originally the brewery's collector but eventually succeeded his father as its president; and Albert Gehring, the youngest son, who was also a company director.

By 1885, business was continuing to grow at a furious pace, necessitating the construction of yet another new and larger brewhouse, costing $150,000 to build. The plant now exclusively produced lager beer, as ale and porter continued to decline in popularity. The size of each brew was nearly doubled to 280 barrels, allowing production in the new facility to reach 68,000 barrels in 1888, just under 80,000 barrels in 1894, and 90,000 barrels by 1901, leaving it as the city's third-largest brewery behind the Leisy Brewing Co. and old friend Leonard Schlather's plant.

Gehring himself had become politically active over the years, serving on the Cleveland City Council, serving as the city's police commissioner in 1875, and serving as president of the Forest City Bank. He also was president of the Local Association of Brewers of Cleveland, and had always been a strong advocate for advances in brewing technology and the industry in general. He died on March 5, 1893 of liver disease, after which most of his estate of $1,000,000 was left to his wife and children.

The brewery was incorporated in 1892 as the C. E. Gehring Brewing Company, with shares held entirely by family members. After Gehring's death, the remaining family members came to disagreements regarding the management of and the future direction of the brewery. In 1898, however, the decision was

**C. E. Gehring and his employees, circa 1875
[Carl Miller collection].**

Gehring Brewery complex as it appeared at the turn of the century, when it joined the new Cleveland & Sandusky Brewing Co.

made to sell the company to the newly organized Cleveland & Sandusky Brewing Co. combine for $1,250,000 and stock in the new company. F. W. Gehring was one of the main proponents and organizers of the new combine, and became its first president. The Gehring plant was the largest to join the combine at the beginning (Leonhard Schlather did not join the group until 1902), and this was a critical factor in the new company's early success. In fact, its ninety-five employees accounted for nearly one-third of all workers in the new company's eleven breweries (as of 1898). The plant remained one of the main breweries in the combine until it closed in 1918 at the onset of statewide Prohibition. The entire complex was in the process of being razed when it was destroyed by an arsonist's fire in 1927. Brainard Avenue was renamed as Gehring Avenue, and this serves as the only physical reminder at the site (just off the west end of the Lorain—Carnegie Bridge and within a block of the city's West Side Market) today.

16. Leonhard Schlather/Cleveland & Sandusky Co.

Similar to the Gehring brewery several blocks away, Cleveland's second-largest pre-Prohibition brewery was established in 1857. Its founder, Leonhard Schlather, was a native of Jebenhausen, Wurttemburg, Germany who had come to America in 1853, at the age of nineteen, with his brother Frederick. After working with family members in a brewery in Altoona, PA. for three years, he came to Cleveland and found work at the Hughes ale brewery, where he worked with his old friend from Germany, Carl Gehring. One year later, when Hughes built an entirely new plant several blocks away, both Gehring (see entry #15) and Schlather took the opportunity to establish themselves as independent brewers.

Schlather's new plant included a four-barrel brew kettle and was located in a two-story frame building on York (W. 28th) Street near Bridge Avenue. Within four years, rapid growth necessitated the purchase of land a half-block away, at the northeast corner of York and Carroll, where the brewery was expanded significantly (in later years the site's address became 1903 W. 28th Street, although during Prohibition, the plant used the address of the bottling house, which was 2600 Carroll Avenue). Growth continued over the next decade, and by 1874 the brewery was turning out nearly 18,000 barrels of lager beer per year.

By 1878, Schlather had out-

(above) Leonhard Schlather in later years; (left) Schlather posing with his employees outside of his original brewery, circa 1875

(below) Ornate new Schlather brewery, built in 1879; the brewhouse was in the far left portion of the building, while offices were at the street corner, fermenting took place to the right of that, and the beer cellars were at the far right. While in most breweries these areas were all in visibly separate structures, architect Andrew Mitermiler incorporated them all into one grand and massive building [Don Augenstein collection]; (right) Artist's rendering of the new plant as it appeared in 1880 in *The Western Brewer*

grown his facility, and intent on continuing to grow, he had the entire plant replaced with a huge new one, designed in an impressively ornate fashion by local architect and Bohemiam immigrant Andrew Mitermiler, who was responsible for designing most of the city's other large brewery plants which were built between the 1870s and the 1890s. All wooden frame construction that was present in the original brewery was now replaced with brick and stone, and the end result was one of the city's most impressive brewing facilities ever seen. Massive and castle-like in appearance, the plant's image was used in much of the brewery's advertising for the next twenty years. It also allowed Schlather to increase his output dramatically, to 27,000 barrels in 1879 (making it the city's largest brewery at the time), while employing fifty men.

While the vast majority of Schlather's beer was sold in the city of Cleveland, a significant portion of it was sent to other areas of Ohio and other states for distribution. Schlather beer was distributed out of the defunct Salem, Ohio brewery by Gustav Zelle beginning in 1890, and Schlather beer was sold in East Liverpool, Ohio by George Meredith, who later was one of the founders of the Crockery City Brewing Co. there. Schlather also owned numerous saloons in other cities along the Ohio River, giving it a large presence throughout southeastern Ohio. Other more distant cities had distributors for Schlather beer as well, including Pittsburgh.

The brewery was incorporated in 1884 as the L. Schlather Brewing Company, with capital stock of $500,000. By this time, annual production had reached 50,000 barrels, and within a decade this number had passed 70,000 barrels. Available types consisted mainly of Standard Lager, Select Export, Pilsener, Kulmbacher, and Munich Beers, all brewed under the supervision of brewmaster John Schneider. Additions to the plant through this period included a separate stable building and in later years a bottling house on the south side of Carroll Avenue. By the turn of the century, the plant had an annual capacity of 150,000 barrels, with actual production around 90,000 barrels, still leaving it as the city's second largest brewery, behind only the Leisy Brewing Company.

Leonhard Schlather was in his mid-sixties by this time, but had no sons to inherit his brewing legacy. And so it was that in 1902,

Serving tray made of brass and porcelain, circa 1890s

he sold his plant to the Cleveland & Sandusky Brewing Co., reportedly for the sum of $1,500,000. This now became the new combine's largest plant and gave the company a huge boost in its attempt to dominate the Cleveland market. Also boosting the new company was the acquisition of Schlather's sixty-plus saloons in the Cleveland area, as well as its two main bottled beer brands, Schlather Pilsener and Starlight. Schlather himself became a member of the company's board of directors. In addition, he continued to serve on the boards of several banks as well as charitable and other local organizations. He divided his time between his large and lavish summer estate in Rocky River, several miles west of Cleveland, and his home across the street from the brewery. It was there that he died of kidney failure in 1918, at the age of 83.

The brewery continued to operate successfully under the management of the Cleveland & Sandusky Brewing Co. for the next seventeen years. In 1919, with the enactment of statewide Prohibition, beer production came to a halt for good. The plant continued to operate in the production of non-alcoholic beverages such as Bola and Gold Bond, and soda, although the bottling plant across the street was the main point of activity by the mid-1920s. By Prohibition's end in 1933, the entire brewery had been razed, and the bottling plant was then vacated in favor of the more modern Fishel brewery (see entry #45) across town, which became the primary plant for the Cleveland-Sandusky Corp.

The brewery site today is occupied by Dave's Supermarket. Three concrete plaques were saved from the old brewery's exterior prior to its demolition, one of which is on display at the Great Lakes Brewing Co., while the other two are at a house in Zoar, Ohio, where Leonhard Schlather once had a residence. The bottling house was purchased in 1997 by the Great Lakes Brewing Company (see entry #51) as part of its expansion, and the building serves as the brewhouse and bottling works for all of Great Lakes' bottled beers to this day.

17. John M. Hughes brewery

John M. Hughes had successfully operated the Spring Street Brewery since taking it over from founder Truman Downer in 1850 (see entry #6). By 1857, growth of his business necessitated the construction of an entirely new plant several blocks away. Costing $15,000 to build, the new brewery and four-story brick malt house were located at 15 West Street, along the Ohio Canal, between Merwin and Vineyard Streets, and were occupied by early 1858. Employing twenty men and with an annual capacity of 10,000 barrels of ale (exclusively), it was the city's largest brewery complex at the time.

Hughes had already established a reputation for producing high quality ales (as compared to other ale brewers in the city), largely due to the skill of his former brewmaster C. E. Gehring, who had left the firm at the time of the move to found his own brewery elsewhere (see entry #15). Despite the loss, Hughes' reputation for quality continued with all of the varieties of ale he produced, and business flourished at the new site.

One major setback occurred early one morning in December 1868, when the entire malt house spontaneously collapsed under the weight of 12,000 bushels of barley and malt inside. Although the four employees inside escaped without injury, the loss of building and grain was nearly $15,000. Hughes quickly had the structure rebuilt (more substantially, one would assume), and business continued as before.

Hughes died of heart disease in June 1871, at the age of seventy-six. His passing was noted by a special mention in the Cleveland *Leader*, written by his employees. As he had been loved and well-respected by all twenty of them, his passing was viewed as a personal loss, something that would not typically have been said about other brewers in that era. It was also a loss for the city, as he and his wife Eliza had been active in the Cleveland Protestant Orphan Asylum, actively courting financial contributions for many years. After Hughes' death, Eliza maintained ownership of the brewery, while active management of the plant was under nephew Levi F. Ives. By 1884, ownership had passed to

Notice to customers in 1870 regarding a change in prices [Bill Carlisle collection]

Eliza's sister, Miss Cornelia A. Bowlsby, most likely in a type of trusteeship.

The firm was incorporated in 1888 as The Hughes Brewing Company, at which time Arthur Hughes (brother of John) became its president. Upon Hughes' death two years later, he was succeeded by John H. Kirkwood. Levi Ives continued throughout this time as the brewery's secretary, treasurer, and general manager. However, as the brewery had never added lager beer to its production, its days were numbered, a victim of the dramatic decrease in the popularity of ale in the latter years of the nineteenth century. As late as the 1870s, the brewery had turned out between 7,000 and 11,000 barrels annually (maximizing the plant's capacity). Output dwindled through the 1880s until 1894, its final year of production, when only 1,500 barrels were brewed.

Over the next four years, the plant was used as a distribution site for the J. & A. McKechnie Brewing Company of Canandaigua, N.Y. In 1899, one last attempt to use the plant for brewing came from Hugh Spencer (formerly the brewer for Carling & Co.—see entry #3), who organized the Spencer Brewing Company. Again brewing only ale, the new venture had failed by 1901, and the brewery closed for good. Times were changing in the Flats; the Ohio Canal behind the brewery would cease operation in 1913 and was later filled in. While West and Merwin Streets still exist today in the shadows of the Detroit-Superior Bridge, the brewery and surrounding buildings are all a distant memory.

18. Isaac Leisy Brewing Co.

The story of Cleveland's longest-lasting brewing concern (and largest as well, at least prior to Prohibition) begins in the year 1858, when the first lager beer was brewed at the site by Jacob Mueller. Located at 135-139 Vega Street, at the northeast corner of Vega and Fulton Road, the plant was originally in Brooklyn Township, several miles southwest of downtown Cleveland. After this area was incorporated into the city, the brewery's address eventually became 3400 Vega Avenue.

Mueller operated the plant until 1864, when he sold it to Frederick Haltnorth, the proprietor of one of Cleveland's largest and most popular beer gardens, located on the city's east side. Haltnorth built the plant into a thriving enterprise, turning out as much as 12,000 barrels annually in the early 1870s. By 1873, Haltnorth had begun to seek a buyer for the company, and on July 2, he completed a deal in which the brewery was sold for $120,000 to brothers Isaac, August, and Henry Leisy. On that day, a new era in Cleveland's brewing history began.

(above) Frederick Haltnorth's brewery in the early 1870s; (above right) Isaac Leisy [both images courtesy of Carl Miller].

The Leisy brothers were natives of Friedelsheim, Bavaria (although the family was Swiss by ancestry), who had come to America in 1855 with their family of fourteen, including parents and siblings. They joined many other fellow Mennonites in traveling to rural Iowa, where they established a large farm. Like several other members of the family before him, however, 17-year-old Isaac soon began training as a brewer, working at breweries in Warsaw, IL, St. Louis, and Germany before returning to Iowa in 1862. At that time, he moved to Keokuk, where he joined brothers John and Rudolph (and Jacob Baehr, who later established his own brewery in Cleveland—see entry #25) in purchasing what soon became the Leisy & Bros. Union Brewery.

After several years of success in the Keokuk brewery, Isaac began looking for other opportunities in a larger city. In June 1873 he came to Cleveland with other brewers from around the country for the Thirteenth Annual Brewers Congress, and it was here that he met Frederick Haltnorth. Cleveland had much to offer that

Staff of the Leisy brewery, with Isaac sitting front and center, circa 1875 [The Western Reserve Historical Society, Cleveland, Ohio]

Keokuk did not. It was growing rapidly and had large numbers of European immigrants, helping to make the city's existing breweries thrive. Cleveland obviously appealed to now 35-year-old Isaac Leisy, as he had finalized a deal to purchase Haltnorth's brewery within a few weeks of the meeting. While Isaac held the largest share of the company, he also enlisted brothers Henry, also a brewer, and August, a furniture dealer, to come to Cleveland to join him in this new enterprise, which was named Isaac Leisy & Company.

Upon assuming control of the brewery, the Leisys worked aggressively to grow their business. Distribution of Leisy Beer throughout Cleveland was relatively easy, but establishing a distribution network through Ohio and elsewhere became a top priority for the brothers. Due largely to the large number of railroad lines leaving Cleveland, however, Leisy Beer soon found its way into other states. By 1878, for example, a depot was established in Pittsburgh for distribution of Leisy Beer there (Henry Leisy subsequently moved there to maintain this facility). In addition to wide distribution, the Leisys were some of the state's earliest brewers to recognize the potential for sales of bottled beer, and by 1878 they had established their own bottling plant across the street from the brewery. Annual output from the brewery ranged between 18,000 and 24,000 barrels throughout the 1870s, consistently making Leisy one of the city's top two breweries.

Despite the success of nine years in the brewing business, Henry and August Leisy left the partnership in 1882 to operate a farm in Nebraska. Isaac was left in total control of the business, and would soon put his own, highly visible mark on the company. In 1883, he hired architect Andrew Mitermiler to design and build a new stock house on the premises. This was followed by a new malt house and brew house, such that by the end of 1884, the brewery had been nearly entirely rebuilt. The end result was a vision in Victorian architectural splendor. The new plant, which remained largely unchanged until its closing in 1959, was not only huge (especially for 1883), but was adorned with many architectural features which caught one's eye. Most notable of these was a large statue along the roofline portraying King Gambrinus (also known as King John I of Flanders), the patron saint of beer.

In addition to the spectacular brewery buildings, the premises also included a large greenhouse, pond, walkways, and gardens. Across Vega Avenue was a large stable building where the nearly 250 horses lived to pull the brewery's delivery wagons. The complex also included a blacksmith shop, woodworking shop, harness shop, and a cooperage for making wooden barrels. There was a large Victorian mansion next to the brewery, which was occupied by

Ornate lithograph showing the brewery and grounds, circa 1900 [Carl Miller collection]

(left) Isaac Leisy's mansion, completed shortly before his death in 1892, two doors east of the brewery [Western Reserve Historical Society]; (below) Otto Leisy.

Isaac's son Otto, and which had originally belonged to Frederick Haltnorth when he had owned the brewery. Finally, on the east end of the complex, was Isaac's own home, completed in 1892. A large three-story brownstone mansion, it had several gables and copper-plated towers which were typical of the era, and it served as the crowning touch to a brewery which was characterized by style just as much as it was known for the high quality of beer produced within. The Leisys were well-known throughout the neighborhood, partly for the beer they produced, partly for the many jobs they provided, and partly for the generosity and sense of community displayed by Isaac through the years.

Despite all of Isaac Leisy's accomplishments, he was not blessed with good health, and in fact he died of heart disease in July 1892, at the young age of fifty-four. Responsibility for managing the brewery subsequently fell on the shoulders of his 29-year-old son Otto, who inherited part of his father's million-dollar estate. Otto had grown up watching his father's brewery grow and thrive, and he had come to know the industry well. He was therefore well suited to manage what had become the city's largest brewery (with over 80,000 barrels produced annually by 1894) through the economic panic of 1893 and through the intense competition among the city's breweries, which increased dramatically in the 1890s.

Otto's first major challenge was dealing with the newly-formed Cleveland & Sandusky Brewing Co. in 1898. This combine was created as a way to avoid some of the costly competition between rival brewers in the city and operate in a more cost-effective manner. The concept was first raised a decade earlier, when British investors, looking to create a similar combine, had offered Isaac Leisy $1.5 million for his plant, which he refused. A local effort to create a combine was begun in the early 1890s, but this too was thwarted by Leisy's refusal to participate. Even after Cleveland & Sandusky's founding in 1898, rumors circulated for years about the possibility of Leisy joining it, especially after Leonhard Schlather sold his brewery, the city's second largest, to the combine in 1902. However, Leisy remained independent throughout its existence.

As the city's largest brewer, Leisy was in a more favorable position than some of the city's other independent brewers to compete with Cleveland & Sandusky. Owning and operating over 200 saloons in the Cleveland area, Leisy was able to control the beer sold in each, thus guaranteeing a large business from these sites. Due to continued expansion of the plant, the brewery's sales continued to grow rapidly throughout the pre-Prohibition era: 100,000 barrels sold in 1898; 300,000 barrels in 1913, and over 565,000 barrels in 1918 (representing nearly full capacity for the facility). Home sales of bottled beer continued to grow, representing thirty percent of the plant's output by 1917. Accordingly, a large bottling plant was built in 1915 across Fulton Avenue from the main complex, and an additional facility was built two years later.

Like his father before him, Otto Leisy began to suffer from poor health and died of a stroke at the young age of fifty-one in March 1914. He had been a large investor in other local industries and was a director of two local banks. He and his family became very wealthy, and had given away large sums of money to

(left) Ornate serving tray, circa 1905; (below) Newspaper advertisement for Bevera Beverage, the company's only hope during Prohibition.

local charities. After his death, the position of company president remained vacant. His sister, Amanda Corlett, became the company's vice-president, while a cousin, Hugo Leisy (son of August) moved from Nebraska to become the company's secretary and treasurer. During this time of transition, the brewery continued its successes as in the past, despite the rise of the temperance movement and the approach of Prohibition.

As Prohibition drew near in 1917, the company released a non-alcoholic malt beverage called Bevera, hoping to maintain sales in dry territories and protect its share of the beer market, if in fact Prohibition were to occur. Advertised heavily, the brand was available virtually everywhere that soda and other non-alcoholic beverages were sold. When Prohibition did take effect in May 1919, only Bevera and a similar cereal beverage, Leisy Premium, were available for sale.

As was the case with most of the other cereal beverages made during the early 1920s, Leisy's two main brands were met with very poor sales. This was felt by some to have been the result of Cleveland's proximity to Canada, allowing easy access to bootlegged Canadian beer. To offset this, the company released a line of soft drinks, but combined sales were still disappointing, and the brewery closed its doors in 1923. The remaining stock of Bevera, 6,000 barrels in all, was poured down the sewer, after which the brewing equipment was sold to plants in other countries, and the huge old Leisy brewery remained quiet for the next decade. During that time, the family continued to operate the Pontiac Improvement Company, formed in 1914 with capital stock of $4,500,000 to oversee the management of the brewery's real estate holdings, many of which were former saloons.

Ten long, dry years later came the end of Prohibition, and with it a frenzy by the public to buy their beloved brew. Beer sales were tremendous in and after April 1933, even though the beer contained only 3.2% alcohol until the following November. Several breweries in Cleveland opened quickly and took advantage of the initial rush to buy beer, but the Leisy name was not part of that rush. As the family had been out of the brewing business for some time, the plant had no brewing equipment and would need to start completely from scratch. New president Herbert F. Leisy, son of Otto, was born in 1900 and was too young to be involved with the running of the company before Prohibition. However, at the age of thirty-three and with degrees from Yale University and the Harvard University School of Business, he was now in charge of the entire operation and oversaw the plant's resurrection, along with brewmaster Carl Faller, who had been with the company since 1900. Other officers of the company included Earle Johnson as vice-president and Daniel Ford (who was married to Otto Leisy's niece) as secretary. The Pontiac Improvement Co. served as the brewery's parent company and provided the capital needed to start brewing again.

Several months of rebuilding with all-new equipment were followed by the first brew in the spring of 1934. Initially, the same three brands were available as before Prohibition: Leisy's Premium (draught beer, sold only in taverns), Leisy's Special

Herbert F. Leisy [Western Reserve Historical Society]

Celebrating the return of Leisy's Beer are (L to R) Herbert Leisy, Carl Faller, brewery employee Phillip Bernauer, Earle Johnson, and Daniel Ford [courtesy of Bill Carlisle].

Brew (sold in clear bottles), and Leisy's Extra Pale (sold in brown bottles), [and a fourth, seasonal brew, Leisy's Bock]. These were delivered throughout the area via a new fleet of thirty-six trucks (of three different types) made by the International Harvester Co. Each truck had a special musical horn which sounded the first few notes of the popular Prohibition song "How Dry I Am". A huge planned celebration ensued when the finished products were first made available for sale on May 14th. Local celebrities were present and there were live radio broadcasts from the plant, as the festivities went on well into the night.

The family's name had obviously been remembered by many Clevelanders: the plant's initial annual capacity was 120,000 barrels, but this was not nearly enough to supply the tremendous demand for Leisy's Beer. By later that summer, the capacity had been raised to 240,000 barrels, and the company stated that it was the city's leader in beer sales once again. Continued improvements in plant operation would elevate that total to 500,000 barrels by 1940. However, actual sales never reached that level: the company's best year after this was 1949, when over 330,000 barrels were sold. This was only sixty percent of the total sold in 1918, when competition from national breweries was much less of a concern.

Grain rationing during World War II limited growth to some extent, as the government alloted the grain available to each brewery based on pre-war sales. To alleviate the shortage, Leisy purchased the grain allotment of the Akron Brewing Company, thirty miles to the south, in July 1943, essentially putting the small Akron brewery out of business. This was a common practice by large brewers at the time, taking advantage of smaller brewers that were struggling to survive.

The business of packaging beer had changed somewhat in the aftermath of Prohibition. While Leisy had been an early champion of bottled beer in the late 1800s, bottles still represented less than one-third of the brewery's output in the years leading up to Prohibition. Most brewers still sold the vast majority of their beer in barrels, and this trend still continued in the immediate post-Prohibition era. However, bottles (and after 1935, steel cans) quickly took over as the preferred packages for consumers, such that by 1950, seventy percent of beer was sold in those formats.

While long-necked returnable bottles remained the most common type, Leisy introduced its squat, throwaway "Schooner" bottle (also known as a "Stubby) in 1935, and this was a hit with local beer drinkers. Also a minor hit was the short-lived Leisy Growler, a large vessel which held one-eighth of a barrel, and which utilized a bicycle pump to pressurize the vessel for tapping (similar, though smaller, cans are used frequently in Europe to this day, but use a small carbon dioxide canister to pressurize the can). Leisy Beer did not appear in steel cans until the late 1940s, when its Dortmunder brand was sold in cap-sealed,

Original artwork for a bus sign, circa 1952 [Bill Carlisle collection].

cone-topped cans. Shortly thereafter, Leisy's Light Beer appeared in similar cans. By 1953, however, the company had switched to the more popular flat-topped cans, and sales in these packages continued throughout the 1950s, although bottles continued to represent a much larger proportion of beer sold in packages.

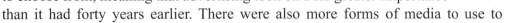

In the post-Prohibition era, and especially after World War II, as national and regional brewers began to distribute their beers over a wider area, there was an increasingly large number of brands for the consumer to choose from, meaning that advertising took on a far greater importance than it had forty years earlier. There were also more forms of media to use to advertise one's products. Leisy advertised heavily on local radio stations from the 1930s on, sponsoring the daily "Leisy Sports Review". Once television became established in the late 1940s, Leisy sponsored telecasts of Cleveland Indians baseball games, as well as a Saturday night television movie known as Leisy Premier Theatre, starring movie star Basil Rathbone. In addition, signs, billboards, and displays in stores and bars increased in number to make consumers think about Leisy's Beer. All of this advertising took its toll on profitability, however, as the cost of advertising per barrel of bottled beer rose from $1.08 in 1945 to $4.55 in 1955.

The brewery had introduced a new brand of beer in 1939. Known as Leisy's Dortmunder Style Beer, it was typical of a trend in the industry to offer "premium" beers, using higher quality ingredients (and theoretically tasting better), to be sold at higher prices than the brewery's standard beers. Premium beers generally competed price-wise with popular national brands such as Budweiser and Schlitz. Leisy's Dortmunder was formulated by brewmaster Carl Faller, who by this time was eighty-three years old (he died just a few months after the new brand's release, to be succeeded briefly by Arvid Luehman, and later by Herbert Noll). The side of the can read: *"The old walled town of Dortmund in the Ruhr Valley was founded by Charlemagne. Dortmund is the famous brewing center from which this beer derives its name. A genuine Dormunder brand premium beer brewed and lagered in the old world tradition. The hallmark for this beer is a replica of the Dortmund town hall, oldest in Europe."* While the brand was not heavily advertised until after World War II, Leisy's Dortmunder remained one of the company's most popular for the next twenty years. Ironically, the company was sued in 1959 by the Association of Dortmund Brewers for use of the name, which was felt to be an infringement on the brewers of that city. As Leisy was soon to go out of business, the suit was eventually dropped.

The year 1952 marked the Leisy family's 90th year in the brewing business, and this fact was celebrated throughout the year, along with a celebration of the company's 300 millionth gallon of beer produced. In the same year came the repackaging of Leisy's Light Beer, a brand which had already been around for more than a decade, targeted at the increasing number of consumers who were seeking a beer with lighter body than the older brands. The number of consumers was increasing so much that Leisy's Light became the brewery's most popular brand through the 1950s. The

**(above) One of thirty-six Leisy delivery trucks from the local White Motor Company, circa 1947;
(right) Inside the new bottling plant, part of the $1.5 million spent on improvements after World War II [both photos from The Western Reserve Historical Society].**

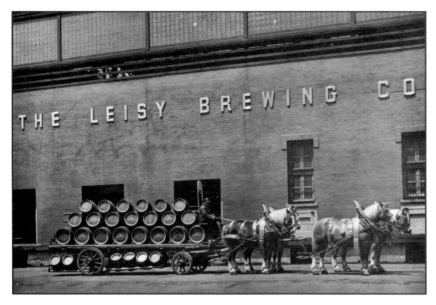

Leisy's horse-drawn beer wagons evoked a sense of nostalgia and were used for promotional activities in the 1950s. The view at left shows another contrast of eras, as the team marches past the new bottling plant [Western Reserve Historical Society].

anniversary year was the company's last profitable one, after which came a seven-year slide into oblivion.

Despite remaining popular in Cleveland, Leisy's sales gradually declined as national and other local brands slowly gained larger shares of the local market. By the early 1950s, Leisy was not even the city's biggest selling local brand. Sales dropped from over 330,000 barrels in 1949 to less than 150,000 barrels by 1955. In addition, Ohio's tax of thirty-six cents per case of beer sold made it harder to turn a profit from the beer that was sold (only Michigan had a higher state tax on beer). As a result, Leisy raised the price of a can or bottle of beer from twenty cents to twenty-five cents in 1956 (at the same time that both the Standard and Pilsener breweries nearby did the same thing).

One of the brewery's attempts to regain some of the lost market was the introduction of Leisy's Mellow-Gold Beer in 1955. Marketed more toward female and younger beer drinkers, it was said to have less bitterness than most beers, due to its expensive "vacuum aging" process. This process required the beer to be sold at a higher price than any of the company's other products, and this single factor likely spelled doom for the brand, which was only in production for three years. In 1956 came the introduction of Black Dallas Malt Liquor, a high-priced premium beer that contained more alcohol than normal beer. Malt liquor was just becoming established in the brewing industry at the time, and

Leisy's Mellow-Gold Beer was available between 1955 and 1958 [Billboard photo from The Western Reserve Historical Society].

while it would become much more popular twenty years later, the addition of malt liquor did not jump-start Leisy's sales as hoped.

Another attempt to increase sales volume took place in 1958, when Leisy purchased the George F. Stein Brewery of Buffalo, N.Y. The Buffalo plant was immediately closed, after which its brands were produced in Cleveland and sent to New York for distribution. This was becoming an increasingly common practice in the industry in the 1950s and 60s, as competition continued to weed out most of the

For several months in the summer of 1950, Leisy rented a 154-foot long blimp, formerly used during WWII for coastal patrol, for advertising. Stationed in Akron, it flew all over northern Ohio, visiting cities where Leisy had distributorships [from the Sandusky *Register*].

Five varieties of canned beer from the Leisy brewery between 1949 and 1959 [Dortmunder can courtesy of Bill Carlisle]

country's smaller brewers, while allowing the larger companies to increase their sales volume further.

In the same year, George S. Carter rejoined the Leisy company as its new president. He had served as the plant's general manager before joining the Pilsener Brewing Co. nearby in 1951. His return was seen as one last attempt to bring the company back to a profitable position, although it was not to be. His first effort resulted in the production of Leisy Pilsner Beer, released in December 1958. As its advertisements indicated, it was specially brewed under the watchful eyes of current brewmasters Carl Fromm and Otto Kalsen, using a particular yeast strain that was brought from Munich, Germany, to give the beer a European-style flavor.

Despite the company's high hopes, Leisy Pilsner was not the cure for the brewery's financial woes. Ten months later, in October 1959, the brewery shut down all production, and 101 years of brewing history at the site came to an end. Within two years, its equipment was dismantled and was on its way to Athens, Greece, for use in the Karlos Fix brewery, within sight of the Parthenon. Under a special contract, the primary Leisy brands (Leisy's Light, Pilsner, and Dortmunder) continued to be brewed until 1964 by the Canadian Ace Brewing Co. of Chicago. The beer was then shipped back to Cleveland for distribution (similar to the contract Leisy had with the Stein brewery two years earlier), and the Leisy company received royalties for the beer sold. The rights to brew Black Dallas Malt Liquor were taken over by the Atlantic Brewing Co., also of Chicago, which made the brand until it closed in 1965. It was then brewed by the Walter Brewing Co. of Pueblo, CO. into the late 1960s.

Herbert Leisy remained in the Cleveland area for the remainder of his life, working as a securities analyst for the Boyd-Watterson Co. until his death in December 1977, at the age of seventy-seven. Cousin Hugo Leisy had continued to operate the Pontiac Improvement Co. until his retirement in 1958, and he also remained in the area until his death in 1967, at the age of ninety-eight.

The brewery buildings housed a series of small businesses until the complex was sold to the Packaging Corporation of America. In March 1974, much of the historic complex was razed, along with Frederick Haltnorth's original Victorian frame home on the property (Isaac Leisy's larger home having met its end nearly thirty years earlier). The family's Hochwald estate in Cleveland Heights, with its splendid view of the city, had been

Dismantling the plant had begun by 1961 [Western Reserve Historical Society]

converted into the Shawnee Club, an exclusive speakeasy operated by gambler Al Wertheimer, during Prohibition. It was later converted into a sanitarium, and briefly was used as a retreat for alcoholics, before being converted into Saint Ann's Maternity Hospital in 1950. Being too large and expensive to maintain, it was razed in 1970. Surviving, however, were two limestone polar bears and two limestone goats which stood outside of the brewery. Commissioned by Herbert Leisy thirty years earlier, they each stood ten feet high and weighed four tons, and upon the plant's demise were donated to the Cleveland Metroparks Zoo, where they remain today. Also surviving today are the bottling plant at the northwest corner of Vega and Fulton, the newer bottling plant and warehouse on the northeast corner, and a few foundation segments of the original plant. Also remaining is the plant's smokestack, where at the top remains a faded, six-pointed brewer's star with an "L" in the center, the company's trademark. That remains the only visible evidence of what was once a huge, thriving family enterprise. To this day, however, "Good Old Leisy's" remains well-remembered by many Clevelanders as being synonymous with top-quality beer.

19. Michael Lucas brewery

Michael Lucas was a native of Hesse-Darmstadt, Germany, born in 1830, who established a small brewery in the late 1850s at 5 King Street, overlooking the Lake Erie shoreline just east of downtown. While specific information has not surfaced, it was likely a lager beer brewery, although it does not appear that Lucas ever reached a substantial level of output. Production appears to have ceased in 1874, and the small plant disappeared into history without a trace.

20. Weidenkopf/Whitlock brewery

Frederick Weidenkopf was a tavern owner in the Flats district who established a small lager beer brewery at 119 Canal Street in approximately 1858. While the original purpose of establishing the brewery was likely to provide beer for his own tavern, Weidenkopf reportedly had developed outside sales of $15,000—$20,000 within two years, such that he soon was looking for a partner in his thriving business. While he was joined for a few months by George W. Hamilton, formerly with the nearby Eagle Brewery (see entry #5), Hamilton was operating the brewery on his own by the end of 1859.

Despite the brewery's early success, it was up for sale just two years later at public auction, due to an unpaid debt by Hamilton to a local malt dealer. The brewery's contents as listed at the time included 328 lager beer kegs, 64 wooden casks, 8 tubs, 1 copper kettle, 1 pump, 1 wash tub and cooler, 1 malt mill, and 1 delivery wagon. By 1864, the plant was being managed by John Whitlock and partner William Lowrie. Lowrie left the partnership in 1868, after which Whitlock continued to operate the plant until his death in 1874, at which time the brewery closed for good.

21. Stoppel/Columbia/Cleveland & Sandusky Co.

Joseph Stoppel was a German immigrant who had come to Cleveland in 1848 and since that time had operated a very successful saloon and distillery. In 1859 he decided to add production of the increasingly popular lager beer to his business, and thus opened "J. Stoppel & Company's Belle View Brewery" at the southeast corner of Canal and Ohio Streets in the Flats district. The company grew quickly, and by 1869 had incorporated as Stoppel's Actien Brewery ("actien" is a German term meaning joint ownership by stockholders; it is still used in the name of several breweries in Germany to this day). In 1872, Stoppel chose to return to Europe, selling his thriving establishment to J. Kraus & Company for $50,000. Despite brewing nearly 7,000 barrels of beer annually through the mid-1870s, the new owners were unable to match Stoppel's success, and their mortgage with him went into default. This forced his return from Europe in 1877 to file suit against the brewery's investors, including his own mother-in-law. This action led to a public auction the following year, and when Stoppel's bid was the highest, he again became the brewery's owner.

Only known photograph of the Stoppel/Columbia brewery, at the time of its takeover by the Cleveland & Sandusky Co. in 1898.

Production had continued in the range of 5,000-7,000 barrels annually during this time, and with Stoppel back in charge, the brewery's finances were once again stabilized. In 1882, he returned to Europe for the remainder of his life, turning over operation of the plant to his sons Alphonso and Omar, who went by the name of Stoppel's Sons & Co. They met with similar success as their father, and by 1887 had reorganized the company as the Stoppel Co-Operative Brewing Co., with capital stock of $200,000. This money was used to construct a huge and entirely new facility two blocks south at 43-51 Commercial Street (later renumbered to 2740 Commercial Street). It was here that the Stoppels first employed the new vacuum fermentation technology, which shortened the length of the fermentation process and reduced the chance of bacterial contamination of the beer. By 1894, the new plant was producing more than 20,000 barrels annually.

Alphonso Stoppel died in 1891, after which the plant was sold to a group of investors, led by Joseph Erlanger, and was renamed as the Columbia Brewing Company, although the Stoppel family remained as partial owners. Three years later, the company's president was Isaac Joseph, with Andrew Squire as vice-president, Emil Joseph as secretary, and W. C. Pollner as general manager. By 1898, the general manager was F. A. Sarstedt and the general agent was Henry F. Eilert, who would later own his own brewery on the city's west side after Prohibition. It was in this year that the plant was sold to the Cleveland & Sandusky Brewing Co. combine. Over the next twenty years, the plant continued to operate uneventfully, producing 35,000 barrels annually, until the advent of Prohibition in November 1918. At that time the brewery closed for good and was later razed, leaving no remains today.

22. Lloyd & Keys, Cleveland City Brewery

Beginning in 1859, the Cleveland City Brewery stood overlooking the east side of the Flats district, at 19-23 St. Clair Street (later 952-954 St. Clair). Founded by Henry Lloyd, a Welsh immigrant who had previously worked at the City Brewery (see entry #4), it operated exclusively as an ale brewery, and remained so throughout its fifty-year existence. Soon after beginning operation, Lloyd was joined in the business by Daniel H. Keys, formerly a clerk with the Ives Cleveland Brewery.

The partnership was a successful one, and the plant's initial output of 1,500

Illustration from *100 Years of Brewing*

barrels per year had increased to over 6,000 barrels by the mid-1870s. After Henry Lloyd died in 1875 and was succeeded by his son William, the company's output saw a slow decline until the end of the decade, when the annual output leveled off between 3,000 and 4,000 barrels per year, a number which continued for the next thirty years. After William Lloyd died in 1895, Keys continued to manage the plant and its fifteen employees.

Despite the plant's small size and the intense competition between the city's larger breweries, the Cleveland City Brewery had carved out a niche for itself, especially after the turn of the century, when it was one of the city's last two remaining ale breweries. Its line of ales, porter, and stout were sold in three states and remained popular enough for the company to remain in operation.

In early 1909, Keys retired after more than sixty years in the field of brewing, after which production at the site ceased and the plant was sold off. Keys died in March of that year, at the age of eighty-six. The building was soon razed and within two years, the huge William Edwards Co. wholesale grocery warehouse was built on the site. This building still stands and has recently been converted into luxury apartments.

23. Stumpf/Davies/Gavagan brewery

After Martin Stumpf sold his brewery on Hamilton Street to Kindsvater & Mall in 1859 (see entry #10), he was back in the brewing business just four years later. With partner Joseph Koestle, he founded the Briggs Street Brewery (later known as the Lakeside Brewery) in 1863 at the southeast corner of Briggs (later E. 22nd St.) and Davenport Ave., sitting atop the hill overlooking the lakeshore railroad lines. This small yet long-lasting brewery had the address of 7-11 Briggs St., and later 1181 E. 22nd St. after the turn of the century. Despite being one of the city's earliest lager beer brewers, it appears that Stumpf established this brewery solely for the production of ale.

The brewery changed hands on a frequent basis in its early years. After co-founder Joseph Koestle left the partnership in 1865, Stumpf operated the brewery alone for one more year before selling it to John Davies, who ran it until 1878 (intermittently with partners Venewel Hammond and Ernst Weisgerber). The plant was then operated for two years by Clark R. Hodge before being sold to Patrick Gavagan and John Sterling. Sterling left the new partnership in 1882, after which Gavagan continued to operate the plant continuously through 1914. At that time, he was joined by Andrew Oppmann (a descendent of the Andrew Oppmann who had previously operated a large brewery on the city's west side). Gavagan relinquished his share of the brewery soon after this, selling it to Joseph Segal. Two years later, the plant closed its doors for good.

Despite being in business for fifty-three years, the brewery had its greatest success in its early years, turning out nearly 4,000 barrels of ale and porter as late as 1874. Soon after this, annual production decreased to a range of between 500 and 1,500 barrels, a level it would maintain for the remainder of its existence. In addition, in its early years, the brewery complex included a malting works. This was sold in the 1890s to the Pabst Brewing Co. of Milwaukee, which used the building as a bottling and distribution plant for a few years before moving elsewhere.

24. Jacob Wagner brewery

This small lager beer brewery, located at 332 St. Clair Street, was established by Jacob Wagner around 1864, in conjunction with his saloon next door. Seven years later, when Wagner attempted to sell the brewery at a public auction, it was valued at $9,500. His attempt was unsuccessful, and the brewery appears to have ceased operation soon after this.

25. Jacob/Magdalena Baehr/Cleveland & Sandusky Co.

Jacob Baehr, a native of Heidelberg, Germany, emigrated to America in 1850 and came to Cleveland by way of New York City. After working as a cooper for several years, he moved to Keokuk, Iowa, where he was a part owner of the Leisy & Bros. Union Brewery there from 1862 to 1866. He then returned to Cleveland to estab-

(left) Baehr brewery building in 1898; the front of the building was occupied by the family's saloon and living quarters, while brewing operations took place in the back of the building; (right) Jacob and Magdalena Baehr; [both from *Cleveland und Sein Deutschthum, 1897-98*].

lish his own brewery at 325-329 Pearl Street (today the building's address is 1526 W. 25th Street). Soon his small plant was producing 3,000 barrels annually, while wife Magdalena operated a saloon in the front of the building and their eight children lived upstairs. Baehr's Mennonite background led him to establish several strict rules in his brewery, such as employing only men who attended church regularly and selling beer only to customers who drank in moderation.

Baehr's death in 1873 was not the end of the brewery, as its operation was assumed by his widow Magdalena. In fact, she proved to be a shrewd businesswoman, increasing the output of the brewery to 15,000 barrels annually by 1894 and 25,000 barrels four years later. Sales consisted of six types of beer: Vienna, Kulmbacher, Pilsener, Franciscaner, Lager, and Extra Export (which was merely a premium variety that was sold only in the city). The increase in production was partially a result of physical improvements to the plant in 1892, including the construction of a new brew house, stock house, wash house, kegging facilities, and enlarged grain storage. During this time, Mrs. Baehr continued to operate the saloon while raising her children. Two of her children gradually took over much of the plant's operation: Emil as brewmaster, and Herman as manager.

Magdalena Baehr sold the plant in 1898 to the new Cleveland & Sandusky Brewing Company combine, and Herman joined the new company's board of directors. However, in 1901 the plant was closed and its production and name were transferred to the Phoenix Brewery, which was renamed as the Baehr-Phoenix Brewery. Mrs. Baehr lived the remainder of her life in the area, while son Herman C. Baehr became involved in local business and politics, serving as president of the Forest City Savings and Trust Co., and later as a director of the Cleveland Trust Co. He also was elected and served as the city's mayor from 1910 to 1912. The brewery building was remodeled over the years and still stands intact to this day (occupied by the Exhibit Builders Co., which produces exhibits for trade shows), with even its original smokestack still standing.

26. Wittlinger/Porter brewery

Located at 366 Lorain Avenue, at the corner of Harbor Street, this brewery was established in 1866 by George Wittlinger and William Weber. After one year, the latter had sold his share to Franz Fahle, who then sold his share to Wittlinger one year later. In 1871, John Fox (nee Fuchs) had taken ownership of the brewery, selling it two years later to Alexander Charters. The following year it was being operated by Crump, Porter, & Brother, at which time production was just under 1,000 barrels annually. By 1876, A. Porter & Co. was listed as the proprietor, although the brewery closed for good one year after this.

27. Joseph Koestle brewery

Joseph Koestle was a co-founder of the Briggs Street Brewery (see entry #22), although he had left that partnership in 1865. Two years later, he established another small brewery at 38 Freeman Street which was in operation from 1867 to 1881. After Koestle died in 1876, at the age of forty-eight, it was operated by his wife Elizabeth. Production appears to have peaked at around 3,200 barrels in 1874, and had dropped to half that number by the end of the decade, before the plant closed two years later.

28. George Muth/Star Brewery/Cleveland & Sandusky Co.

Established in 1867 by Gottfried Reindl, this lager beer brewery was located at 4125 Buckley Street, near Burton (later West 41st Street). The site was ideal for the brewing of beer, in that it had a nearby source of pure water, a nearby ice pond, and was built on a hillside where cellars for aging could be built. Reindl, however, was not the ideal man to operate the plant. Soon after starting brewing operations, he issued two separate mortgages on the property, and by the following year had defaulted on both. A public auction was held, during which the first mortgage holder, George Muth, purchased sole ownership of the property for $800.

Star Brewery, circa 1890s [from *Breweries of Cleveland*]

Despite Muth's lack of experience in the brewing industry, he proceeded to continue operations with his brother Matthias. This lasted until 1871, when the latter was found to have hung himself in the brewery's attic, blamed at the time on "temporary insanity". After this, Muth brought his son, George V. Muth, into the business. It was at this point that the brewery began to prosper, producing around 3,500 barrels annually by 1874 and 4,500 barrels annually by the end of the decade. When the elder Muth died in 1881, his son George V. took over sole proprietorship of the plant. Four years after this, the original plant was replaced by a modern three-story brick structure, which would ensure the continued growth of the plant, now also known as the Star Brewery.

By the mid-1890s, annual production was over 13,000 barrels. However, in 1895, Muth contracted a case of blood poisoning (sepsis), leading to the amputation of his right foot. He immediately began searching for a buyer for his plant, and by the next year had sold it to Carl A. Strangmann and John M. Leicht, two brewers from Virginia, for $100,000. They renamed the plant as the Star Brewing Company, named for the brewer's star which had appeared on Muth's beer kegs. Muth continued to live across the street from the brewery until his death in 1899.

In 1898, the Star Brewery was one of the original companies to join the new Cleveland & Sandusky combine. At that time, Strangmann left the area altogether, while Leicht joined the new company, becoming a vice-president. Brewing operations continued at the plant until 1913, when it was closed permanently. The plant was later razed, leaving no remnants.

29. Andrew W. Oppmann/Phoenix/Cleveland & Sandusky Co.

Located at Columbus and Willey Streets (its later address was 2240 Columbus Street), this small lager beer brewery was originally established in 1867 by Adam Schumann. By 1871, however, Schumann had lost ownership of the plant due to unpaid debts. Soon after this, it was purchased by Andrew W. Oppmann, a Bavarian native who had come to America in 1863 at the age of nineteen. Oppmann had already

Andrew Oppmann [Harvey G. Oppmann collection]

(left) Oppmann's original frame brewery; (below) Oppmann brewery workers in October 1880 [both from Harvey G. Oppmann collection]; (bottom left) Rebuilt Oppmann brewery, circa 1898 [Carl Miller collection].

lived life to the fullest by the age of twenty-eight, having briefly joined the United States Army Cavalry, crossing the country by horseback, traveling to the Orient, and working in breweries in New York, St. Louis, and Chicago. The Great Chicago Fire of 1871 caused him to leave that city and come to work in a Cincinnati brewery, and it was there that he met Frederick Haltnorth of Cleveland, who enticed Oppmann to join his west-side brewery as brewmaster. This arrangement lasted for only a few months before he left the position and acquired the Schumann plant to begin his own brewing business.

By the mid-1870s, the plant still remained one of the smallest in the city, producing only around 2,500 barrels annually. Oppmann's hard work and determination, however, had caused this number to double by the end of the decade. He was a tireless worker and problem solver, and held several patents for new processes and mechanisms that he had invented for use in the brewing process. The brewery continued to see more success each year, until 1887 when it was incorporated as the Oppman Brewing Company. Oppmann himself was the company's largest shareholder, holding forty percent of the company's stock, while many employees also held stock.

In early 1889, an independent bottling works, known as the Anhaeusser Co-Operative Bottling Company, was established across the street from the brewery. Operated by Herman Anhaeusser (Oppmann's bill collector), Gottlieb Kuebler (the brewmaster), and Henry Boehmke (Oppmann's vice-president), this new concern would purchase Oppmann beer and subsequently bottle it and market it as "The Anhaeusser Malt Tonic," for home sales as a health beverage. These sales did not compete with Oppmann's, as the brewery exclusively sold its beer in barrels to saloons. The large market for home sales in bottles had not yet been fully recognized, especially by many of the traditional German brewers.

As Oppmann's brewery continued to grow and prosper, on July 4, 1889, it was struck by a devastating fire which was felt by some to have been started as a result of nearby fireworks gone astray. Despite a loss of nearly $35,000, work quickly began on rebuilding the brewery. This time, the plant would be a large and ornate structure, with many of the fancy architectural features which were typical of the era. This new structure allowed the plant to produce as much as 50,000 barrels annually, a number which was realized in less than a decade.

Just two years after the erection of this new plant, Oppmann retired from the local brewing business to focus on real estate development (a residential area at West Boulevard and Madison Avenue would later be known as Oppmann Terrace; Oppmann himself continued to travel and dabble in real estate and other businesses until his death in 1910 at the age of sixty-six.) After Oppmann sold his share in the brewery to the remaining stockholders, the company was renamed as the Phoenix Brewing Company, the new name symbolizing the company's rising from the ashes just like the mythological bird of the same name.

The new company's president, Philip Gaennsler, was a prominent member of the German society in Cleveland and a successful business owner. A long-time stockholder in the brewery, he guided the company successfully for the next several years. The Phoenix Brewing Company was one of the original breweries to join the new Cleveland & Sandusky combine in 1898, and in fact was the second-largest brewery in the group at the time. After 1902, when the nearby Baehr brewery branch was closed and production was shifted to the Phoenix branch, the latter was known as the Baehr-Phoenix Brewery. The large plant was permanently closed in 1908, however, when the combine attempted to reorganize and consolidate its operations. It was later razed, leaving no remains.

30. Philip Griebel brewery

Philip Griebel operated a small lager beer brewery beginning in 1868 at the intersection of Columbus Street and Barber Avenue on the city's southwest side (the site was originally in Brooklyn Township, but was later annexed into the city of Cleveland; after Columbus St. was renamed, the brewery's address became 987-1005 Pearl Street). Production peaked in the mid-1870s at around 1,700 barrels annually, but this number had dropped below 1,000 barrels by the end of the decade. The brewery closed in 1882.

31. August Burckhardt brewery

August Burckhardt established a small lager beer brewery at 483 Pearl (West 25th) Street, at the corner of Monroe Avenue, in 1868. In 1876, the facility was sold to Bavarian immigrant Anton Kopp, who was joined in the business the next year by Rudolph Mueller, the cousin of Cleveland brewer Ernst Mueller. The brewery was producing around 2,500 barrels annually at this time, and Mueller became the sole proprietor in 1878, when Kopp left the partnership. When the brewery closed two years later, it was under the management of William Schneider & Company.

1874 Cleveland City Atlas

Kopp would later operate his own brewery near Massillon, sixty miles to the south.

32. Schneider/Union/Cleveland & Sandusky Co.

Located on the southeast corner of Train Avenue and Ash (W. 47th) Street, this lager beer brewery was established in 1870 by Bohemian immigrant Joseph Zika. Within two years, the plant had been sold to the partnership of Frank Braun & George Dietz, and then quickly resold to Christian Schneider. Schneider was a cooper and maltster by trade, born in Bavaria in 1824 and residing in Cleveland since 1840, and he entered the field of brewing in September 1872. For a time he employed Anton Kopp (formerly of George Muth's brewery, and later several others) as his brewer, and although the brewery's capacity was 11,000 barrels, it actually produced around

Union Brewing Co. plant as it appeared at the time of its purchase by the Cleveland & Sandusky Brewing Co. in 1898

4,000 barrels annually throughout the decade. The plant itself was a two-story structure with three underground cellars and an ice house.

In 1880, Schneider was joined by his son John, who was a lawyer by profession. He learned the brewing trade as well, and when the elder Schneider retired in 1889, John Schneider became the brewery's sole proprietor. Just two years later, in May 1891, the plant was completely destroyed during a thunderstorm, when lightning struck the elevator shaft, setting off a massive fire. The loss was valued at $125,000 and was only partially covered by insurance. Although the plant was quickly rebuilt, the company's business never fully recovered, and by the end of 1893 the property was seized for a Sheriff's sale.

The brewery was sold in 1895 to a group of investors, including James Storer and George Myers, both sons-in-law of Christian Schneider, and Emil Joseph of the Columbia Brewing Co. This new group incorporated as the Union Brewing Co. with capital stock of $100,000, although at an annual production level of 5,000 barrels, the new company was among the city's smallest breweries. In 1898, the owners sold the plant to the new Cleveland & Sandusky combine, which then closed it in 1902. The plant was later enlarged significantly and housed a warehouse and the Bowman Ice Cream company at different times. It still stands today, although one must look closely to see any evidence of the original brewery's lines.

33. Henry Hoffmann brewery

Henry Hoffman, born in Germany in 1827, and William Paschen established this small lager beer brewery on the city's southwest side in 1871. Located at the corner of Rhodes and Walton Avenues (formal address 153 Walton, and later 789 Walton), the plant occupied a former clock factory. Paschen left the partnership just two years later, after which Hoffman was briefly joined by a new partner, Conrad Volkopf. One year later, Volkopf had left and Hoffman was operating the brewery with his son William. By 1878, the plant's annual capacity had reached 8,000 barrels, although actual production appears to have

1874 Cleveland City Atlas

never been above 3,000 barrels in any year. Brewing operations ceased soon after Henry Hoffman's death in 1881.

34. J. M. Mack brewery

John M. Mack had been a part operator of the Mack Brothers brewery on the city's near west side for fifteen years when the small plant closed in 1874 (see entry #11). At that time, the operation was moved to 2390 Broadway, on the city's southeast side, where the brewing of lager beer began again. Briefly operated by Mrs.

Matilda Mack (widow of William Mack), as well as Morris and Charles Mack, it was back in the hands of John M. Mack two years later, and the brewing of around 500 barrels per year continued until the small plant closed in 1882.

35. Joseph Beltz/Cleveland Home Brewing Company

One of the city's largest and longest-lasting breweries, the Cleveland Home Brewing Company had humble beginnings when it was established in 1876. Located at the corner of Slater (E. 61st St.) and Outhwaite Avenue (its later address being 2501-2515 E. 61st St.), the site was originally used by Joseph Beltz as a cooperage, after which a saloon and wine shop were added prior to the establishment of brewing operations. Beltz was a native of Germany's Rhine Valley who had come to America in 1867 at the age of twenty-seven. His specialty being Weiss Beer (a light, top-fermented, wheat-based beer which had a limited but loyal following among some German immigrants in the late 1800s and early 1900s), his brewery started out slowly, turning out a mere three barrels in 1878. It was at this time that he was briefly joined in his venture by Michael Mueller, although this lasted for only three years. Output had risen to nearly 500 barrels by 1884, and just over 1,000 barrels in 1894, still leaving it as the city's smallest brewing operation.

After an unimpressive first twenty years in the brewing business, Beltz was joined by sons Lawrence and John in 1897, and one year later began producing ale and porter in addition to weiss beer. As the business began to expand, the brewery's further growth potential was envisioned, and in 1901 it was incorporated as the Beltz Brewing Co., with $100,000 of capital stock. Joseph Beltz held the titles of president and treasurer, while Valentine Koenig was vice-president, Lawrence C. Beltz was secretary, and John J. Beltz was brewmaster. At the same time, lager beer was finally produced at the plant, leading to a dramatic increase in sales, which numbered 10,000 barrels that year. As the plant was enlarged further, its annual capacity had reached 75,000 barrels by 1906, and later improvements would push that number to 100,000 barrels. By this time, the production of weiss beer had ceased, with its small and dwindling market not worth the effort by comparison to the far more popular lager beer. However, one of Beltz's sons, Carl, would continue the weiss beer tradition at his own small brewery for another nine years (see entry #47).

In May 1907, a controlling interest in the brewery was taken by Ernst W.

German-language advertisement for the new Beltz Brewing Company from 1902 [Bill Carlisle collection]

(right) Cleveland Home Brewing Co. plant in the 1930s [Cleveland State University Library collection]; (above) Delivery wagon, circa 1907 [courtesy of the Great Lakes Brewing Company].

Mueller, a veteran of the Cleveland brewing industry. Having previously operated the Cleveland Brewing Co. on the city's far east side, he more recently had served as president of the large Cleveland & Sandusky Brewing Co. combine until internal politics led to his removal earlier in the year (see entries #12 and #45). Upon joining the Beltz brewery, he reincorporated it as the Cleveland Home Brewing Co., with capital stock increased to $500,000. Mueller served as president while Joseph Beltz remained as vice-president, Carl F. Schroeder (who had also left Cleveland & Sandusky at the same time due to internal politics) served as secretary and treasurer, and Rudolph Mueller (Ernst's cousin) served as sales manager.

The new company's philosophy was to focus on the home consumer of bottled beer (as suggested by the name) as opposed to just saloon sales. Its main products were "The Home Beer", Meister Brau, Yako (a near beer introduced in 1917, its name represented "okay" spelled backwards), and low alcohol Malt Liquid. The beers were bottled by an independent bottler next door (A. Weber), until 1914 when the brewery opened its own bottling department. The company's philosophy proved to be a successful one, as the other breweries in the city gradually followed suit in focusing increasingly on the home beer drinker in the years leading up to Prohibition.

Upon the enactment of Prohibition in 1919, the company's focus changed to production of ice and liquid malt, in addition to Yako (although production of the latter did not survive the Prohibition era, as the market for near beer was dismally small). The following fourteen years were lean, but the company survived the era intact. Ernst Mueller remained as president until his death in 1931, at the age of 79. He was succeeded by Herman Schmidt, one of the company's investors, and later by Otto W. Beltz (one of Joseph's sons, he had also served as an officer of the Alliance Brewing Co. in Stark County prior to Prohibition).

Less than two months after the Repeal of the Volstead Act in April 1933, the Cleveland Home Brewing Co. was back in the beer business with production of Clevelander Beer (the same brand having previously been made by the Gund Brewing Co. prior to Prohibition), and one week later, the return of Meister Brau. In October of that year came what would become the company's flagship brand for the next eighteen years, Black Forest Beer, which supposedly was brewed from an eleventh century Bavarian recipe. This was brewed under the supervision of brewmaster George Lezius, a veteran of the Cleveland brewing industry. Soon after this, Omar E. Mueller, son of Ernst Mueller, succeeded Otto Beltz as president of the company.

**Sonny DeMaioribus sitting in his office in 1941
[Cleveland State University Library].**

By the end of the decade, an increasing portion of the brewery's day-to-day operations were being overseen by long-time employee Alessandro "Sonny" DeMaioribus. Sonny had begun working in the brewery's office several years prior to Prohibition, and he continued there throughout the next thirty years, becoming the company's vice-president, secretary, and general manager by 1939. It was Sonny who was behind the introduction that year of Sonny's Premium Beer, a higher-priced brand using higher quality ingredients than the usual beer brands. Although its sales were not especially good, the brand continued in production for many years. Sonny also was well-known in local politics as a member of City Council, serving two terms as council president, and as chairman of the Cuyahoga County Republican party.

After World War II, the company's success began to drop off quickly, marked by the deaths of Omar Mueller in 1946 and George Lezius in 1947. Sonny DeMaioribus purchased the remaining stock in the company and appointed his brother, Dr. Anthony D. DeMaioribus, as brewmaster, the latter giving up his dental practice in the process. It was felt that the quality of the company's brands declined considerably after this, and sales followed.

The only two cans produced by the brewery, circa 1950

Post-Prohibition improvements in the brewing facility had increased the plant's annual capacity to 175,000 barrels, although the company's peak production was only 111,000 barrels in 1945. This had dwindled to 35,000 barrels in 1951, despite the addition of a new brand, Dee Light Beer and Ale, and the addition of a canning line for packaging of Black Forest and Dee Light Beers in cap-sealed cans. Seeing no improvements ahead, the company stopped beer production in January 1952, and the equipment was auctioned off. With assets of more than $2,000,000, however, the company continued to operate for a time in real estate management. The abandoned plant became a local eyesore over the next few years and was razed by the end of the decade; today the site is occupied by an urban housing project. Sonny DeMaioribus continued in local politics until his death in 1968, at the age of 70. The Black Forest name returned for several years in the mid-1990s, when it was used by the Crooked River Brewing Co. as a brand name for its lager beer.

36. William Aenis brewery

Around 1877, William Aenis began brewing beer at 557-559 Columbus Street, in partnership with Charles Metzger. The facility grew quickly, producing more than 4,000 barrels by the following year. Metzger left the partnership in 1879, to be replaced by John F. Froelich. The following year, Aenis moved his brewing works to Pearl St., where it continued operation for another eighteen years (see the following listing).

37. Bohemian Brewing Company

William Aenis moved his successful brewing operation (see the previous listing) from Columbus Street to 1033 Pearl (W. 25th) Street, near the southwest corner of Vega Avenue (it also went by the address of 121 Vega Avenue), in 1880. Doing business initially as William Aenis & Company, he then formed a three-year partnership with Martin Haller before ownership of the brewery was transferred to George Denbert in 1884. It briefly passed into the hands of Mrs. Mary Angel, after which original partner John F. Froelich was back in the business. In 1886, Froelich sold the plant to Bohemian immigrant Wenzl Medlin, who then formed the Medlin Bohemian Brewing Company.

Medlin then sold the brewery in 1889 to a group of employees, headed by Moses Halle, who became president, with J. C. Weideman as vice-president, Jacob Borger as secretary, Leo Mayer as treasurer and plant superintendent, and Simon Fishel, who quickly worked his way up to ownership of the company. Medlin stayed on for another three years, however, as brewmaster. The plant had grown considerably by this time with the addition of a four-story brewhouse, allowing it to produce over 25,000 barrels in 1894. When Fishel joined with the new Cleveland & Sandusky Brewing Company combine in 1898, however, the plant was closed and its production transferred to the Barrett brewery on Riverbed Road, which then took the name of the Bohemian Brewing Co. There is no trace of the original Bohemian brewery today.

38. Carling & Co./Barrett/Cleveland & Sandusky Brewing Co.

Carling & Company, of London, Ontario, had operated a highly successful U. S. branch in Cleveland, beginning in 1880 (see entry #3). After only four years, Carling sold the Cleveland branch and the rights to produce Carling Ale, Porter, and Stout to plant manager John S. MacBeth. At that time, brewing operations were moved from the original site on Michigan Avenue to the former Umbstaetter malt house and distillery, situated

(left) Bottle label, circa 1905 [Bob Bickford collection]; (below) Barrett/Bohemian brewery in 1958, as photographed by Ernie Oest; the portion at left was the original Umbstaetter distillery and was nearly a century old

on a hillside along the west bank of the Cuyahoga River, at 393 West River Street (its later address was 1530 Riverbed Rd.) This site was said to have a spring of the highest quality, providing water for the brewing process. Brewing of Carling products and their distribution over a wide area of the eastern United States continued as before.

In 1891, MacBeth sold his interest in the brewery to the distribution agents, Barrett & Barrett of Chicago. This consisted of brothers Charles and William Barrett, and William subsequently moved to Cleveland to manage the brewery, which was then renamed as the Barrett Brewing Company. Production of Carling Ale, Porter, and Stout continued to be the plant's main focus. At this time, a new six-story brewhouse was built on the north side of the plant, increasing annual capacity to 150,000 barrels (although actual production was closer to 25,000 barrels annually by the mid-1890s).

In 1898, the Barretts sold their brewery and rights to the Carling name to the new Cleveland & Sandusky Brewing Co. combine. The plant was then renamed as the Bohemian Brewery branch, taking the name of another branch of the combine which was closed at the time of its purchase. The Carling brand name continued in production until 1911, when the plant was permanently closed. It was later converted into a warehouse, and continued to stand until being razed in the 1960s. Nothing remains at the site today except an overgrown hillside. The Carling name would be resurrected twenty-three years later by the Brewing Corporation of America (formerly the Peerless Automobile Company—see entry #49), which would again distribute Carling Ale and Beer over a wide area.

39. Mrs. Jacob Voelker's weiss beer brewery

Jacob Voelker had operated a small bottling works at 19-21 Howe Street, at the edge of the Flats, for nearly twenty years prior to his death in 1884. After this, the works continued to operate under the management of Voelker's widow, Catherine, and their son Jacob, Jr. Following a popular trend at the tail end of the century, in 1887 the Voelkers added a small weiss beer brewing operation, producing a few hundred barrels annually. Jacob, Jr. died in 1890, although Catherine continued to operate the brewery through 1895. As with the city's other weiss beer breweries, the demand for the wheat-based beer was not great enough to allow the operation to continue. After this, the bottling works continued to operate until 1904, when Catherine Voelker died at the age of seventy. The brewery's location today is roughly at the site of the Ritz-Carlton Hotel, just west of the Terminal Tower.

40. Herman H. Imbery weiss beer brewery

Hermann Imbery was a west side saloon owner and home brewer for a number of years before opening a small weiss beer brewery at 947 Pearl (W. 25th) Street in 1887. Like most of the city's other weiss beer brewers, it can be assumed that he met with little success, as the brewery was no longer in operation by the end of 1888. Imbery remained in the area, however, working as a teamster.

41. Pilsener Brewing Company

The story of Cleveland's most famous brewing mystery began in 1892, with the opening of the Pilsener Brewing Company. Founded by Bohemian immigrant Wenzl Medlin, this was actually Medlin's second attempt at operating a brewery, soon after selling the Bohemian Brewery (see entry #37) on Pearl Street. Medlin had come to America in 1866 at the age of seventeen, after learning the art of brewing in his homeland, specifically in Plzen (Pilsen), Bohemia (located today in the western portion of the Czech Republic). He came to Cleveland twenty years after that, and after spending six years with the Bohemian Brewery, he set out to establish an entirely new plant at the southwest corner of Clark and Gordon (W. 65th) Streets (later taking the address 6605 Clark Avenue). Incorporated in July 1893, the company was initially known as the Medlin Pilsener Brewing Co., with Medlin as brewmaster and treasurer, and fellow Bohemian Vaclav Humel as president.

It would appear, however, that Medlin's forte was brewing, not business, as the company was bankrupt within two years. As a result, his duties as treasurer were relinquished, and under Humel's supervision the company was able to right itself and continue in business. Medlin continued on as brewmaster, however, and remained with the company until 1899 (after leaving, he started a small weiss beer brewery [see entry #43], which remained in business for just five years). After his departure, he was replaced by a succession of Bohemian brewers over the next twenty years: Joseph Liska, Jaro Pavlik, Vinzenz Spietschka, Zdenek Sobotka, and Frank Knopp.

After 1894, the company had considerable success with its primary brand, Extra Pilsener Beer, with an increase in output from 6,000 barrels in 1894 to 26,000 barrels just four years later. This rapid growth necessitated the expansion of the plant, and in 1901 a new five-story brewhouse (designed, as usual, by Cleveland architect and fellow Bohemian Andrew Mitermiler) was completed, along with a new boiler house and stable building. This addition, which included a 300-barrel brewkettle and increased the plant's annual capacity to 150,000 barrels, gave the complex a layout and appearance that it would retain for the rest of its life as a brewery.

For the company's first twelve years of existence, its officers consisted mostly of local Bohemian merchants, and turnover was frequent. In 1904, however, Vaclav Snajdr took over the company's presidency, with Carl Anders and vice-president, James C. Wolf as treasurer, and Frank Kratochvil as secretary, and it was this stable leadership that would guide the brewery through the following twenty years.

In 1906, a bottling works was added to the plant, and for the first time, Extra Pilsener Beer appeared in bottles, along with a premium version, Extra Pilsener Gold Top, and a third brand, known as "Zunt Heit". Soon after this came the first appearance of the mysterious three letters that were used as the company's slogan, and which became the company's flagship brand from 1914 until its eventual demise in 1987: "P. O. C."

While the brewery never specifically stated the original meaning of the three letters, it was commonly assumed that they stood for "Pride Of Cleveland". However, various advertisements through the years suggested that the letters may actually have stood for "Pilsener of Cleveland", while an advertisement from 1910 used the letters to state: *"**P**urest is the bottled beer we make. **O**ur Extra Pilsener the best beer obtainable. **C**hoice of imported hops and malts containable."* By the 1950s,

(left) Postcard, circa 1910; the lower three stories of the section to the right of the brewhouse represented the original plant as constructed in 1892; (above) Pilsener Brewing Co. founder Wenzl Medlin [from the *Western Brewer*].

the slogan stood for both "Pilsener On Call" and "Pleasure Of Course". More cynical customers who watched the quality of the brand slip in the 1970s and 80s tended to refer to it by any one of a number of variations of "Piss On Cleveland". At least one contest was promoted by the brewery around 1915, via postcard to the company's customers, in which anyone could guess the meaning of the name. No clear answer was ever revealed, however, keeping the question alive to this day.

Despite the fact that P.O.C. beer was sold only in the Cleveland area, its sales continued to rise in the decade prior to Prohibition. As such, a $300,000 expansion of the brewery was underway by late 1914, mainly consisting of a large new building on Clark Avenue, just north of the brewhouse. This housed the company's offices, a new bottling plant which was capable of filling 5,000 bottles per hour, an assembly hall, a

Horse-drawn wagon, circa 1907 [from the Olstyn Carriage Co. catalog, courtesy of the Western Reserve Historical Society].

rathskeller which could seat 500 guests, and an adjacent garage which housed the company's thirty delivery vehicles. After this, the five-acre complex at the southwest corner of Clark and W. 65th Streets became known as "Pilsener Square".

At the onset of the Prohibition era in 1919, the production of beer gave way to the production of several varieties of de-alcoholized P.O.C. "special brew" and "foaming beverage", as well as several varieties of P.O.C. soft drinks (ginger ale, parfay, etc.), still under the supervision of brewmaster Frank Knopp. The Pilsener Brewing Company survived the era much more successfully than most of its local competition, and in fact was the only brewery in the city still producing near beer when Prohibition ended in 1933. Despite this, the market for non-alcoholic beverages alone was not strong enough to keep the company profitable. Looking for other ways to put the plant and its resources to good use, the firm reorganized in 1928 as the Pilsener Ice, Fuel and Beverage Co., with capital stock of $500,000, specializing in coal and ice delivery along with the variety of beverages. By this time, turnover of the company's officers had left Carl Anders as president and Adolph Humel (son of Vaclav) as vice-president, along with long-time officers Frank Kratochvil and James C. Wolf.

When Prohibition ended in April 1933, Pilsener was the first brewery in Cleveland to put its real beer back on the market. As it had continued to produce near beer throughout the era, it took little work to remove the de-alcoholization from the brewing process. Even so, it was a full month later, on May 4th, when the first P.O.C. Beer in fourteen years was available for sale. The fuel and soft drink businesses were subsequently abandoned, as the beer business was immediately more profitable. By this time, Adolph Humel had taken over the company's presidency, with Fred J. Anders (son of Carl) as vice-president.

In 1935, however, the brewery was purchased by the City Ice and Fuel Company, a locally owned firm specializing in coal and artificial ice sales. Doing business throughout the midwest and in Canada, it was a huge company with annual revenue in the range of $25 million. As both the ice and coal businesses were beginning to slip, the company was attempting to diversify by entering the brewing industry. In addition to Pilsener, the company purchased the American Brewing Company plants in New Orleans, LA. and Miami, FL., and the Wagner Brewing Company of Granite City, IL. (which was

The Pilsener Brewing Co. bottling plant was built in 1906, and remains the only structure in the complex still standing today [Cleveland Public Library photograph collection].

The bottling process was still somewhat labor-intensive in 1933 [Cleveland State University Library]

subsequently closed in 1940). Pilsener was reorganized with new officers, and through the remainder of the decade the company was managed by president Robert C. Suhr, with W. A. Schmid as vice-president, Harry W. Dunkle as treasurer, and John Fetterman as secretary.

While P.O.C. Beer (in Pilsener, Dark, Special, and Bock varieties) remained the company's flagship brand, a new premium brand known as Toby Ale (named after an English folk tale character), hit the market in 1940. Brewed as a true top-fermented ale, with higher quality ingredients and selling at a higher price, the brand remained available through the early 1950s, although it never caught on in a big way with local beer drinkers. By the early 1950s, two additional brands had appeared: Half and Half (a blend of light and dark lager beers), and Regal Lager Beer, which was the specialty of the affiliated breweries in New Orleans and Miami. Frank Knopp, brewmaster from long before Prohibition, continued to oversee all brewing operations until his death in 1947. After this, he was succeeded by Carl Fromm, formerly of the Ohio Brewing Co. in Columbus, OH.

Little expansion of the brewery was undertaken in the first decade after Prohibition ended. The plant's annual capacity by the beginning of WWII was 175,000 barrels, slightly more than it had been thirty years earlier. While grain rations limited production somewhat during the war years, the brewery began a large-scale enlargement of its brewing operation, overseen by new president Frank Sullivan, once the rations were lifted in 1947. Over the next four years, $5 million was spent increasing the plant's annual capacity to 400,000 barrels (later improvements would bring this total to 500,000 barrels). The investment paid off quickly—by 1949, the company was operating at near-capacity with sales of 360,000 barrels.

The expansion included the installation of a canning line for the first time, and P.O.C. beer was first sold in cap-sealed cans in 1949. The brand was available in both cap-sealed and flat-topped cans at different times until 1952, when the cone-topped cans were phased out (in a trend seen throughout the country, as this type of can was nearly gone by 1960). Despite the convenience and disposability of cans, approximately three-fourths of P.O.C. Beer was still packaged in bottles.

As with all of the city's other brewers, Pilsener became increasingly dependent on advertising to remain successful in light of the dramatic increase in competition from regional and national brewers after WWII. While much of this took the form of point-of-sale advertising (signs, etc.), there was a significant increase in the amount of radio and television advertising during this period as well. P.O.C. Beer had sponsored occasional music and sports programs on local radio stations since the 1930s. After the war, Pilsener became the sole sponsor of Cleveland Barons hockey games on radio, and sponsored some of their early television games as well. P.O.C. Beer was associated with the Barons to the extent that it was the only beer sold at the Cleveland Arena downtown, dispensed at the "Pilsener Cellars", a

Local deliveries of beer resumed in 1933

small restaurant in the lobby. The brewery also was a sponsor of boxing and tennis events, and a wide variety of outdoor sports as well.

After the huge post-war enlargement of the plant was completed, Pilsener was still only the city's third largest brewer. In an attempt to become more competitive in the Cleveland market, as well as in other cities, the company hired George S. Carter, sales manager for the nearby Leisy Brewing Company, to take over as brewery president at the beginning of 1951. Within a few months, Carter (along with new vice-presidents Bernard C. Hoag and Paul A. White) had helped to create a total makeover for the P.O.C. brand, with a completely new formula and label. Despite the company's claim that the new "Genuine 51 Flavor", as the formula was known, was based on the brand's original recipe from fifty years earlier, it was actually more consistent with the current national trend toward light-bodied, less filling beers (though this was more than a decade before the appearance of the true "light" beers, with fewer calories, that are commonplace today). Along with a new modern-look-

Celluloid sign for Toby Ale
[Bill Carlisle collection]

ing label and logo, the brand was set to compete with all of the large regional and national brands. The Genuine 51 Flavor campaign was a resounding success—within two years of its appearance, the company's sales had doubled and P.O.C. had become the city's sales leader, a position where it would remain for several years.

Along with enlargement of the brewing facility and an aggressive sales campaign came an expansion of the geographic distribution of P.O.C. Beer. By the early 1950s, the brand was being sold throughout Ohio and into

Pennsylvania, West Virginia, New York, and several other eastern states. As sales and demand continued to increase, the company found itself in need of extra brewing capacity. In 1952, Pilsener's parent company, now renamed as the City Products Corp. and operating out of Chicago, purchased the Franklin Brewing Company plant in Columbus, OH. Opened in 1933 as the Riverside Brewing Co., the plant had been known as the Franklin Brewing Co. since 1934 and had seen good local success with its primary brand, Ben Brew Beer. Located at 117 North Sandusky Street, the plant was still fairly modern and added 150,000 barrels of annual capacity to Pilsener's total. P.O.C. Beer was made in both cities until 1954, when further enlargement of the Cleveland plant made production in Columbus unnecessary, after which that plant was closed (and subsequently razed).

Pilsener's sales increased for five consecutive years (a considerable feat considering the nature of the industry at the time and the difficulties being encountered by the city's other brewers during the same period), peaking in 1955 at 412,000 barrels. Based on this encouraging trend, the company planned to invest another $5 million in purchasing another brewing plant, either in Cleveland or elsewhere, to help satisfy the increased demand. The ultimate goal was to provide an annual brewing capacity of one million barrels (double the existing capacity). However, just as the company seemed poised to enter the realm of the large regional brewers, sales in 1956 dropped unexpectedly. As a result, plans for expansion were put on hold (permanently, as it turned out).

Pilsener was beginning to feel the effects of national competition, although thus far it had weathered the storm far better than its local counterparts. While the company would remain profitable for several more years, its earlier successes began to fade as the larger national breweries continued to become more and more dominant in Cleveland and the surrounding region. Perhaps sensing that the brewing industry was rapidly becoming a difficult place to operate successfully, City Products Corp. had continued to diversify itself, and

(above) P.O.C. first appeared in cans in 1949; the cone-topped cans were phased out just three years later; (right) Half and Half Beer was available in cans and bottles during the 1950s, but never achieved major sales

The P.O.C. label on cans and bottles had been redesigned with new colors by 1953

had invested heavily in the growing mass merchandizing industry. Owning a large number of retail department stores and supplying goods to others, such as the Ben Franklin Department Store chain, City Products was certainly moving in a different, and ultimately more profitable direction.

Just as Pilsener's success was continuing to decline, it suffered a major loss in 1958 with the resignation of George Carter, who returned to the Leisy Brewing Co. (see entry #18), which was making one last attempt to stay in business. In the same year, City Products sold off its Miami brewery to Anheuser-Busch, Inc., maker of national sales leader Budweiser Beer. After four more years of slow decline in sales of P.O.C. Beer, City Products made the fateful decision in 1962 to sell off all businesses which were not related to the mass-merchandizing industry, and as a result, the Pilsener Brewery and the American Brewery in New Orleans were put up for sale. (That same year, Decca Records in England rejected a chance to sign the Beatles; and in a move rivaling that fateful decision, a young man named Sam Walton, who owned a franchise of another retail division of City Products, was rejected by City executives when he proposed a new concept of widespread discount stores in Arkansas. This decision eventually led to Walton's independent formation of his multi-billion-dollar Wal-Mart chain.)

The Pilsener Brewery, which was now one of only three surviving breweries in the city, was purchased in early 1963 by the Duquesne Brewing Co. of Pittsburgh, PA. Duquesne had operated as a large combine known as the Independent Brewing Co., consisting of sixteen breweries in the Pittsburgh area, prior to Prohibition. Since 1933, it had continued to grow and had established itself solidly in Ohio with its Duquesne (later known just as "Duke") brand of beer. Upon the purchase of the rights to P.O.C. Beer, it immediately closed the Cleveland plant for good, transferring all production to its huge Pittsburgh plant. Duquesne then fell victim to competitive pressures in 1972, when it closed and sold its brands to the C. Schmidt & Sons Brewing Co. of Philadelphia and Cleveland. The P.O.C. brand thus returned to its home city, where it continued to be produced at the Schmidt plant on Quincy Avenue until its closing in 1984. For two more years, the brand was produced at the Philadelphia plant until it too closed in 1986, after which the brand quietly disappeared from the market after eighty years of being one of Cleveland's favorite beers. In 1999, the name briefly reappeared as a nostalgic specialty brand brewed at the Local Brewing Co. in Westlake, although production there lasted for only one year. The Pilsener brewery, meanwhile, housed a series of small businesses over the next thirty-five years until a fire gutted the main brewhouse complex in 1998. It was soon razed, leaving only the bottling house and many fond memories in the minds of Clevelanders, some of whom wonder to this day what "P.O.C." originally stood for.

The brewery burned in early 1998, after which it was razed. The faded "Home of P.O.C." sign thus disappeared into history.

42. Buckeye Weiss Beer Brewing Company

Certainly one of the city's shortest-lived breweries appeared in 1899, when Frederick Ehle and John J. Hammer formed the Buckeye Weiss Beer Brewing Co. at Hammer's residence at 390 Denison Avenue, several miles south of downtown. Presumably a very small operation, it did not survive to see the new century, however, and both men had left the area by the following year. A few embossed bottles with the company's name are all that have survived.

43. Wenzl Medlin's International Weiss Beer Brewery

After coming to America from his native Bohemia, Wenzl Medlin operated the Bohemian Brewing Co. (see entry #37) on Pearl Street, and later established the Pilsener Brewing Company (see entry #41) as well. After severing ties with both companies, he established his own small weiss beer brewery in 1899 at his residence at 1417-1419 Pearl Street. Compared to his two previous brewing ventures, the imposingly named International Weiss Beer Brewery met with minimal success, and had closed by 1904. Medlin continued to live at the site until his death in 1912, at the age of sixty-three.

44. Excelsior/Eilert Brewing Company

This small brewery's history began in 1902 with its operation as the Kress Weiss Beer Company. Located at the corner of Sackett Avenue and West 32nd Street on the city's southwest side (later taking the address of 3131-3135 Sackett Avenue), the brewery was owned and operated by Andrew Kress (with Joseph A. Ludwig as vice-president and Stephen S. Green as secretary and treasurer). He made the popular wheat-based beer on a small level for less than two years before the company was reorganized on December 24, 1903 as the Standard Brewing Company. While Kress remained as the plant's general manager, the new corporation was led by Stephen S. Creadon, a long-time west-side saloonkeeper, who had created the city's first saloonkeeper-owned brewery. Less than a year later, the company relocated to a site further west, on Train Avenue (see entry #48).

The brewery on Sackett Avenue did not remain empty for long, as it had reopened by July 1905 as the Excelsior Brewing Company. The new firm was established by forty-six-year-old recent German immigrant Jacob F. Haller, formerly the brewmaster of the Diebolt Brewing Company (see entry #14), and who had previously worked at breweries in Kentucky, Toledo, Chicago, and St. Louis. While Haller became the new company's brewmaster, its president was Louis Kurzenberger, with William C. Glunz as secretary, and Charles Heintel as treasurer. After the new company's founding, it sold an impressive 10,000 barrels in its first year. Within two years the plant was undergoing additions, including a new three-story brewhouse. This brought the annual capacity up to 30,000 barrels, although it still left the plant as one of the smallest in the city. The plant both bottled and kegged its beers, although household sales in bottles were the company's primary focus.

Over the next twelve years, the brewery continued to operate successfully with its two primary brands, the aptly named Excelsior Success Beer and Golden Seal Beer. The plant was enlarged several times, even as late as 1917, when many other brewers had begun to back away from expansion due to the threat of Prohibition. These threats came to pass in 1919 with the advent of statewide Prohibition, at which time beer production at the Excelsior plant came to a halt.

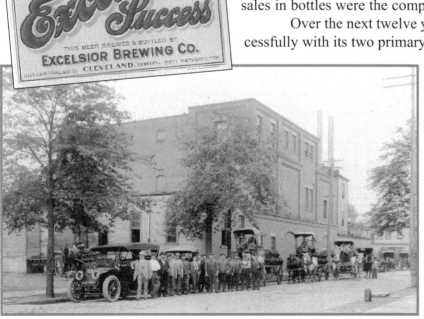

(left) Excelsior Brewing Company plant after several expansions, circa 1910; **(above left)** Bottle label [John Phillips collection]; **(above)** Jacob Haller [from *Cleveland und Sein Deutschthum*, 1907].

(left) Horse-drawn wagon, circa 1905 [from the Olstyn Carriage Co. catalog, courtesy of the Western Reserve Historical Society]; this gave way to the motorized delivery truck, below left, circa 1915 [Carl Miller collection]

At the onset of Prohibition, the company was reorganized as the Eilert Beverage Company, with capital stock of $400,000. Jacob Haller sold the plant to Henry F. Eilert, but remained with the new company as its vice-president. Eilert was a German immigrant who had already worked in several local breweries before Prohibition, as well as operating a wholesale wine and liquor business on Lorain Avenue near the West Side Market. The new company produced several brands of near beer, including Muenchner Double Brew, Eilert's Clev-Ale, and Golden Seal. These were brewed by a process in which almost no alcohol was produced, allowing Eilert to avoid the de-alcoholization process which most other brewers utilized, but which had a tendency to damage the beverage's flavor, if not destroy it completely. A number of soft drinks were made as well, including EBCO Cola, Eilert's Pep, orange soda, birch beer, root beer, ginger ale, grape juice, etc. The company overcame long odds and survived until late in the Prohibition era, when Eilert temporarily retired.

As the end of Prohibition approached, the company reorganized again, this time as the Eilert Brewing Company. Henry Eilert came out of retirement to return to his brewery, being one of only two Cleveland brewers still having a permit to produce near beer. He hoped to have 30,000 cases of his beer available as soon as beer was legalized, and as early as December 1932 (four months before Repeal) was taking orders for beer in case the law was repealed early. While this goal was not met, the new Eilert's Supreme Lager was on the market in June 1933, after which the company continued its pre-Prohibition successes, at least for a time.

Expansion of the brewery after the end of Prohibition increased its annual capacity to 75,000 barrels during the 1930s. New brands which appeared at this time included Eilert's Supreme Lager and Munchner Lager, Eilert's Lind-Ale and Clev-Ale (a brand which first appeared years earlier as a cereal beverage), All-American Beer, and Canada Black Horse Brand Beer. Business continued through the remainder of the decade, with Henry Eilert remaining as vice president and treasurer of the company, with E. B. Sanders as president, Howard R. Hirsch as secretary, and George A. Hartung as master brewer.

Soon after Repeal, a group of Chicago businessmen attempted to create a national brand name of beer, King Kole, which instead of being all produced at one site, like Anheuser-Busch's Budweiser in St. Louis, would be produced by various independent licensee breweries across the country, and subsequently advertised nationally. Eight breweries had become affiliated with this plan by 1934, including Eilert. However, the plan never fully materialized and Eilert was the only brewery to actually brew King Kole Beer, and its sister brand, King Kole Ale. Both brands sold well in the Cleveland area, and represented a significant portion of the brewery's sales in the 1930s. In 1940, the company's name was changed to King's Brewery, Inc., to better reflect what had become the company's anchor brands.

As World War II approached, the government instituted the Defense Tax in July 1940, raising the federal tax on beer from $5 to $6 per barrel. This increase made it very difficult for many of the nation's smaller brewers to make a profit, and King's Brewery was one of these. Due mainly to these increasing taxes, the brewery went into default and was declared bankrupt in January 1941, after which all production ceased and the assets were liquidated. Henry Eilert retired at that time and remained in the area, where he died in 1952 at the age of 81. The brewery complex has remained largely intact since that time, occupied by a bottling works and later by small businesses, although the top floor of the brewhouse section was removed in later years.

45. Fishel/Cleveland & Sandusky Brewing Company

Although the large brewery on E. 55th Street was known for more than fifty years as the headquarters for the Cleveland & Sandusky Brewing Company, it actually housed the Fishel Brewing Company when it was built in 1904. While the chain of events which led to its founding had begun several years earlier, this was the last new brewery plant to be built in the city prior to Prohibition.

The Cleveland & Sandusky Brewing Company came into being on February 8, 1898, when it was incorporated with capital stock of $6,000,000. This came after several attempts had been made over the previous decade to combine various breweries in the city into a single, larger entity. The stated purpose of the merger was to avoid the pitfalls of competition (price wars, advertising, etc.) between rival brewers, allowing the constituent members to pool their resources, save money and share the wealth. Another advantage of the merger, although unstated, was that the large combine would have a dramatic competitive advantage over smaller companies that had not joined it.

The merger was a symbol of the times, as similar mergers were occurring in large cities across the country around the same time. For example, a conglomerate of twenty breweries in western Pennsylvania became the Pittsburgh Brewing Company in 1899, and a rival group of sixteen breweries in the same area became the Independent Brewing Company in 1905. Similar, though smaller, associations appeared elsewhere in Pennsylvania and Ohio over the next few years. A central figure in some of the mergers which had taken place in Pennsylvania was Philadelphia broker John P.

The nine breweries which were operating as the Cleveland & Sandusky Brewing Company as of 1900 [from *One Hundred Years of Brewing*]

Persch, and he was hired to help arrange the financial details for the proposed merger in Cleveland. Upon completion of the deal, Persch (who received a reported $250,000 for his efforts) was not involved with the company to any significant degree. [The formation and early years of the Cleveland & Sandusky Co. are discussed in much greater detail in Carl Miller's *Breweries of Cleveland*.]

At the time of its inception, the new combine consisted of nine breweries in Cleveland and two in Sandusky. The initial members were: Baehr (see entry #25), Barrett (see entry #38), Bohemian (see entry #37), Cleveland (see entry #12), Columbia (see entry #21), Gehring (see entry #15), Phoenix (see entry #29), Star (seen entry #28), and Union (see entry #32), along with the Kuebeler and Stang breweries in Sandusky (see Erie County). Initially, the combine was slated to include the Pilsener, Gund, and Diebolt breweries as well, but for various reasons these did not join the new company. Several years later, the new Standard Brewing Company was courted to join as well, but ultimately a deal could not be finalized.

The Bohemian brewery was closed immediately after Cleveland & Sandusky's formation, with both its production and name transferred to the larger Barrett brewery in the Flats. The Baehr brewery was closed in 1901,

(left) President Ernst Mueller; (below left) General Manager Simon Fishel
[images from *Western Brewer* and *One Hundred Years of Brewing*]

with its production transferred to the Phoenix brewery, and soon after this came the closing of the Union brewery as well. Leonhard Schlather (see entry #16) sold his plant to the combine in 1902 for $1.5 million, adding 90,000 barrels to the combine's annual sales, along with sixty saloon properties. In 1904, the combine built its only new plant, the Lorain Brewing Co. branch, thirty miles to the west (see Lorain County). At this point, the company dominated sales of beer all along the Lake Erie coast, from Ashatabula in the east, almost to Toledo in the west. The company's production comprised seventy-five percent of the beer sold in Cleveland and sixty percent of beer sold in Northeast Ohio. And while various rumors through the years had the combine expanding to include yet more breweries in other cities, forming a potentially statewide monopoly on beer sales, no further expansion took place after 1904.

Once the Cleveland & Sandusky Company had begun to operate as a combine, its initial president was F. W. Gehring of the Gehring Brewing Co. After several months, Gehring left the position and was succeeded by Ernst Mueller of the Cleveland Brewing Co. First vice-president was Jacob Kuebeler of Sandusky, while second vice-president was John M. Leicht of the Star Brewing Co., and William Chapman was the company's secretary and treasurer. Most of the individual companies' owners, who had received cash and stock shares for their breweries, became directors of the combine. Simon Fishel, from the Bohemian Brewing Co., became the combine's general manager. The company's business offices were in the American Trust Building on Public Square.

The tremendous initial success of the combine did not come without its share of controversy, however. Within a year of the company's founding, charges of unfair business practices were being made by rival brewers such as Otto Leisy. Among the accusations was that the combine was charging less than the standard price of $7 per barrel of beer to undercut the competition, forcing other local brewers to enter into a "price war" to maintain their customer base. Other charges suggested that the combine would frequently purchase or lease saloon properties where rival beers were sold. If the saloonkeeper did not agree to switch to combine-brewed brands, he might be evicted.

Beyond the local brewers and their squabbles, the Ohio Attorney General's office investigated the combine in 1899 for possible violation of state antitrust laws. While the case ended up in court, bringing in rivals such as Anthony Diebolt and George Gund to testify, the evidence was not conclusive enough, and the combine was allowed to continue operation for the following twenty years. One result of the price wars, however, was the formation in 1903 of the Cleveland Brewers' Board of Trade, which subsequently helped to stabilize local beer prices at fixed amounts, and limited the "unfair" practices of saloon property manipulation by the brewers.

Still, controversy continued to follow Cleveland & Sandusky's activities. By 1904, Simon Fishel had resigned from the company, due to an ongoing personal dispute with president Ernst Mueller. Fishel was a native of Bohemia, born in 1846, who had come to America as a young adult after learning the brewing trade in Europe. His ascencion in the local brewing industry began when he was involved in the purchase of the Bohemian Brewing Co. from founder Wenzl Medlin in 1889, and his resignation from Cleveland & Sandusky would ultimately lead to his becoming one of the city's most powerful brewers. On his own, Fishel had estab-

Horse-drawn wagon, circa 1905 [from the Olstyn Carriage Co. catalog, courtesy of the Western Reserve Historical Society]

**The new Fishel Brewing Company plant, circa 1905
[Bill Carlisle Collection]**

lished an entirely new brewing concern by the end of the year, to be known as the Fishel Brewing Co.

Construction quickly began on a large new plant, located at 2764-2776 East 55th St. (formerly Wilson Avenue), on the city's southeast side. Five stories in height, the fancy new brewery was modern in every respect, and had yielded its first batch of Fishel $500 Bond Beer by early 1905. The name was a reference to a promise (on the bottle label) by Fishel himself that anyone who could prove that "injurious substitutes" for the finest ingredients were used in the brewing process would be paid $500. The name was later changed to $500 Gold Bond Beer, and still later to Gold Bond Beer, a name which would last for more than sixty years. Fishel's business practices were more aggressive than many of his rivals, especially in establishing a presence for his new brand in local saloons, and within one year of operation, his plant had sold 54,000 barrels, already making it the city's third largest independent brewery.

Recognizing Fishel's potential as a major competitor, Cleveland & Sandusky soon began looking into the possibility of buying the Fishel plant. In March 1907, this became a reality when the Fishel Brewing Co. became the fourteenth brewery (and eleventh active plant) to join the Cleveland & Sandusky combine. Fishel's shrewd negotiating abilities brought him $850,000 for the sale, half of which went to his stockholders, and half to himself. Not only that, but as a part of the deal (which was kept quiet until after the deal had been completed), Fishel had been offered the presidency of the combine, to replace Ernst Mueller. Mueller, who was not previously aware of this detail, was furious and threatened legal action. He felt that a certain group of officers of the company had wanted him out ever since he had opposed the purchase of the Standard Brewing Company several months earlier, and this had been their chance. However, as Mueller himself was shown to have approved the Fishel purchase (despite not knowing that Fishel had been offered the presidency), the decision of the directors was considered final. Despite the threats of Mueller and various other stockholders of the company who were unhappy with the turn of events, no legal action ever took place.

Mueller's departure from the company was not the end of his career in the brewing industry, however. He soon had affiliated himself with the Beltz Brewing Co. on the city's east side (see entry #35), which was then reorganized as the Cleveland Home Brewing Co. With several former officers from Cleveland & Sandusky (who had resigned over the Fishel controversy), and the allegiance of many German saloon owners who maintained their loyalty to him, Mueller built Cleveland Home into a successful company, keeping it open through the Prohibition era until his death in 1931.

With Fishel directing the combine's future direction, attention returned to the business of making beer. The purchase of Fishel's brewery increased the combine's production significantly (now averaging around 500,000 barrels annually, yielding approximately $1 million in sales per year), but at a heavy price. In fact, the high cost of bringing Fishel back to Cleveland & Sandusky nearly pushed the company into bankruptcy, giving it a net loss of nearly $300,000 in 1908. However, by 1910 the situation had stabilized, and the company returned to profitability where it remained for the following decade. The closing of the Baehr-Phoenix plant in 1908, the Barrett plant in 1911, and the Star plant in 1913 helped to streamline production, cutting the total number of plants in the company to eight, and the number in Cleveland to five.

With all of these plants came a wide variety of brands and styles of beer. The company's flagship brands

Advertisements for the new brand appeared in the Cleveland *Plain Dealer* in November and December 1914

remained Fishel's Gold Bond and Kuebeler-Stang's Crystal Rock, but other favorites included Schlather Pilsener and Starlight from the Schlather brewery, and Carling Ale and Porter from the Barrett brewery. New brands which appeared through the years included Kellersaft (meaning "cellar juice," it was introduced in 1905), Clicco-Brew (introduced in 1914), Culmbacher Lager, and a seasonal generic bock beer.

After guiding one of the state's largest brewing organizations for a decade, Simon Fishel died of pneumonia in January 1917. During his career, he had risen to vice-president of the Ohio State Brewers' Association and was a director of the United States Brewers' Association. One of the city's first Jewish brewers, Fishel had been active in the city's Jewish community. He was one of the founders of the Euclid Avenue Temple, of which he was president, and was a director of the city's Montefiore Jewish home. He was succeeded as Cleveland & Sandusky's president by his son Theodore, while a second son, Oscar, served as vice-president.

Fishel's sons assumed management of the company at a difficult time. The future of the brewing industry in 1917 was being challenged by increased war-time taxes and the increasing threat of the Prohibition movement. In November 1918, when Ohioans voted to accept statewide Prohibition and beer production stopped, the combine closed its Gehring, Lorain, and Kuebeler branches. Within a year, the Cleveland and Columbia plants had also closed, leaving only the Fishel and Schlather plants in Cleveland and the Stang plant in Sandusky operating. After all beer sales stopped in May 1919, the combine reorganized as the Cleveland-Sandusky Company, although it also was known as the Gold Bond Beverage Co. and the Bola Products Co., while the Stang plant was also known as the Crystal Rock Products Co.

While the Prohibition era would prove to be disastrous for the brewing industry, Cleveland-Sandusky's management remained optimistic at the outset that sales of cereal beverages could be successful, and that the saloon business might survive without serving alcohol. Along those lines, the company produced several brands of near beer, including old favorites Crystal Rock, Starlight and Gold Bond, as well as new names such as Bola, Fifty-Fifty (made by contract for a national distribution network), New York Special Brew, and Kuebler Malt Tonic. In addition, a number of non-cereal soft drinks appeared, most notably Whistle Orange drink, Brownie Chocolate drink, Crystal Rock Water, Deerfield and Tommy-Green Ginger Ales, and Johnny Bull Ginger Beer.

While the company remained marginally successful through the Prohibition era (although certainly not by comparison to the pre-Prohibition era), sales of near beer were nowhere near those of real beer, especially in competition with the city's many illegitimate sources of alcohol, smuggled across Lake Erie from Canada or made in back room stills and available at the more than 2,000 speakeasies in the city. As a result, the company had closed the Fishel plant by 1922 and consolidated its entire Cleveland operation in the bottling facility of the Schlather plant, where it remained for the following ten years. By the end of the Prohibition era, production of near beer had ceased altogether, and although the company had survived the era intact, its profit margins had been on a continual downward spiral, putting it in perilous financial condition when the Volstead Act was repealed in 1933.

By April 1933, Hascall C. Lang, a well-established area investment banker, had replaced Theodore Fishel as the company's president, and it was Lang's job to convert the aging and nearly bankrupt company back into a powerful brewing concern. Unable to successfully borrow the necessary capital to refurbish the company's plants, Lang was able to lean on the company's stockholders to raise the funds. The Stang plant in Sandusky, which had continued to brew Crystal Rock Beverage through most of the Prohibition era, needed the least amount of work, and by July of that year, it was again producing Gold Bond and Crystal Rock Beers to be shipped to Cleveland for sale.

The Schlather plant and its bottling works, which had maintained most of the company's production for the previous ten years, were permanently closed. The Fishel plant, which was still relatively modern even though it had been vacant for some time, was chosen to be the main plant which would keep the company alive for nearly thirty more years. A tremendous amount of refurbishing was required, however, and it wasn't until early 1934 that the brewery turned out its first batches of Gold Bond and Crystal Rock Beers, along with newcomer Old Timers Ale. New York Special returned briefly as a brand of real beer, although it would reappear in the 1950s as a cereal beverage. All refurbishing and subsequent brewing operations were overseen by brewmaster John Aubele, Jr., although after his death in 1935, he was succeeded by Frank Gollwitzer and Charles Neumann. With the plant's modernization, its annual capacity reached 120,000 barrels, a number which in later years would increase to 200,000 barrels. Interestingly, despite the fact that Cleveland & Sandusky had been the region's largest overall brewer before Prohibition, by the mid-1950s it would be the city's smallest remaining brewer.

Just one year after reopening, the brewery was hit by a major strike in April 1935, which was the result of a long standing dispute between the brewery workers' union and the teamsters' union. The dispute centered around whether brewery truck drivers should be under the control of the teamsters or the brewery workers. Although the brewers themselves were essentially neutral in the dispute, they were losing hundreds of thousands of dollars every month due to plant shutdowns, and Cleveland & Sandusky was particularly hard hit. The strike grew violent when the breweries attempted to use replacement workers, and the violence was worst at the Sandusky plant, where business was interrupted to the extent that the company closed the brewery altogether in May. The plant's equipment was subsequently transferred to the Cleveland branch, which became the only one remaining in the company. The strike was resolved in November of that year, and business was finally able to resume.

By mid-1936, financial difficulties forced the company into a reorganization plan, after which the company reincorporated as the Cleveland-Sandusky Brewing Corporation. In addition, the Cleveland-Sandusky Real Estate Corporation was formed to manage the many remaining saloon and former brewery properties, owned by the company for many years. At the same time, Hascall Lang was replaced as president by Oscar J. Fishel, although Fishel's tenure was relatively brief. His proposal in 1940 to sell the entire company for $93,000 to the Brewing Corporation of America was rejected by the company's stockholders, and Fishel subsequently resigned. He was succeeded by Frank P. van de Westelaken, the company's brewmaster who had just joined Cleveland-Sandusky in 1937. Van de Westelaken was a nationally-known brewer who had worked at breweries in six different cities prior to Prohibition and who had served as president of the Master Brewers' Association of America. In van de Westelaken's honor, the company introduced a new premium brand around this time, known appropriately enough as Brewmaster's Special Beer. Brewed with higher quality ingredients and selling at a higher price, the brand was advertised heavily after WWII, but had been discontinued by 1950.

Van de Westelaken's long history in the brewing industry was a distinct advantage and allowed the company to remain successful throughout the 1940s. In 1944, the company held a centennial celebration, based on information that the Stang brewery had been founded in 1844. In fact, by all available records, that brewery actually began operation in 1852 (although Sandusky's first small brewery appeared in 1844, it was unrelated), and although

Brewmaster Frank P. van de Westelaken and a label for the relatively short-lived Brewmaster brand of premium beer named after him.

(left) Delivery truck (built by Cleveland's White Motor Co.) outside the brewery's loading dock in 1949; (below) Homer Marshman [Cleveland State University Library].

the Crystal Rock brand didn't appear until the early 1890s, it was subsequently dubbed as Ohio's oldest beer (and although some brands in Cincinnati, such as Hudepohl, might have been able to argue that point, none ever did). The fact that the earliest brewery to become a part of Cleveland & Sandusky opened in 1839 (Charles C. Rogers' Forest City Brewery in the Flats, which later evolved into the Barrett Brewery) was never taken into account, but then historical accuracy was not a top priority at the time.

Of far greater importance in this era was dealing with the grain rations brought on by WWII. Both malt and hops had become rationed by the government beginning in early 1943, and the rations became smaller as time went by. The brewery's overall output dropped off as a result, and the Gold Bond brand was discontinued entirely. Nevertheless, the plant was operating near capacity in 1944 and for several years after (gross annual sales peaked in 1946 at $2.7 million). When the grain rations were lifted in 1947, the company put a large portion of its advertising behind the Brewmaster premium brand, in an attempt to make it a household name to compete with large regional and national brands. Two years later, however, the brand had not achieved the widespread acceptance that had been hoped for, and as a result it was discontinued. 1949 saw the reappearance of Gold Bond Special Beer, a name which had long been well-known to Clevelanders, although it was now reformulated to be the company's premium brand. At the same time, the Crystal Rock brand, which had become the company's basic low-cost brand, was discontinued, at least temporarily.

Frank van de Westelaken knew the brewing industry well enough to see that despite the company's war-era success, there were clouds on the horizon, mainly trends of increasing competition and higher costs of brewing materials, which would make it increasingly difficult for the company to remain profitable. In 1949, he left the company to take a brewmaster position in Nashville, TN. He was succeeded briefly as brewmaster by Jaro Pavlik, who was approaching his fiftieth year in the local brewing industry. After Pavlik's retirement the following year, he was succeeded by Harry A. Glantz, and later by Henry Stamberger. Taking van de Westelaken's position as president of the company was chairman of the board Homer Marshman, a local attorney and businessman. Marshman was already known to Clevelanders as one of the founders of the Cleveland Rams NFL football team in 1936, and although the team had moved to Los Angeles in 1946, Marshman became one of the owners of the newer Cleveland Browns NFL franchise in 1954. Despite his experience in the business world, Marshman could not stem the tide of increasing competition, and by 1952, the company found itself operating in the red.

Around 1950, the company added a canning line to its bottling department, and Gold Bond Beer first appeared in flat-topped steel cans. By this time, disposable cans were becoming increasingly popular with the public, and Cleveland-Sandusky became the last of five

Three variations of metal cans used between 1950 and 1962; (far left) The first can appeared around 1950 [Bill Carlisle collection]

(left) Three brands available in cans after the mid-1950s; the Old Timers and Crystal Rock brands continued to be canned by the International Breweries Co. branch in Buffalo, NY. after Cleveland-Sandusky closed; **(below)** Marvin Bilsky.

breweries in the city to add canning lines around the same time. Beer drinkers were becoming less and less loyal to the old brands, due to the onslaught of new names and labels appearing on store shelves from out-of-state brewers. Cans added just another option for the consumer's convenience, and it was this sort of convenience that might make the difference between making a sale and not making it. By the late 1950s, all of the company's brands were available in cans. For the consumers who preferred bottles but wanted a disposable package, there was also the "shorty" bottle, a squat, can-shaped package which was the modern version of the earlier "stubby" and "steinie" bottles.

Advertising was critical to any brewery that wanted to survive the fierce competition of the era. Cleveland-Sandusky had operated with less capital than most of the city's other breweries since Repeal, however, and its budget for advertising was always fairly tight. As early as the 1930s, the company had sponsored local weekly radio programs such as the "Gold Bond Polka Party", and by the early 1950s it was also sponsoring a weekly drama called "State Trooper" on local television. In the mid-1950s, the company began sponsoring Cleveland Browns television broadcasts, largely through Marshman's connection with the team. Advertising through the broadcast media was expensive, however, and the company used that less than many of its local competitors. Point-of-sale advertising such as signs and displays in bars and grocery stores was less expensive and remained somewhat cost-effective.

Despite the company's best efforts, it remained unprofitable. Another effort to bolster sales was marked by the return in 1955 of New York Special Brew, originally seen during Prohibition. As one-third of the state remained dry at this time, the brand allowed the company to still target these territories, even considering marketing it to children.

In the same year, the company was joined by new general manager Marvin Bilsky. At the relatively young age of thirty-four, Bilsky already had much experience in mass merchandising through his involvement with his family's wholesale bakery, and he had forged relationships with numerous local groceries and supermarket chains. He brought a level of enthusiasm that had not previously been seen in the company, and he was felt by some to be the company's last hope to survive. Within months of Bilsky's arrival, Marshman returned to the position of chairman of the board, while Bilsky assumed the position of president. One year later, the latter had purchased a controlling interest in the company, and the responsibility to make the company sink or swim would fall entirely on his shoulders.

Bilsky quickly brought back the dormant Crystal Rock brand, as a low-budget beer to be sold only in supermarkets. Not everyone wanted to pay the higher price for the premium brands, and the revived brand sold well. Gold Bond received a new marketing campaign as well, with the slogan "direct from old Quebec", referring to Laurentian Mountain Spring water that was being used in the brewing process, giving the beer "that lively Canadian flavor" (the similarity to Carling's advertisements which capitalized on their Canadian heritage were probably no coincidence). Soon after this came a complete modernization of the Gold Bond label, with a stylized shield replacing what was left of the original "bond" appearance. Later, the name would be simplified to the catchier "GB" Beer.

Bilsky's marketing techniques quickly translated into improved sales, and by

Cleveland-Sandusky plant as it appeared in 1960. Despite being the city's "newest" brewery (aside from Carling) the plant had seen no significant additions or modernizations and was beginning to show its age, just two years before it closed for good

1958 the brewery's annual production had increased to 111,000 barrels. With sales of $1.8 million yielding a net profit of $32,500, the company turned a profit for the first time since early in the decade. Now looking to further these gains, the company purchased the equipment of the recently closed Star-Peerless Brewery in Belleville, IL., in order to modernize the Cleveland plant for the first time in years. Soon after this, the company welcomed the addition of brewmaster Otto Kalsen, formerly with the Leisy Brewing Co. Within three years, Kalsen had risen to become the company's vice-president. Remaining optimistic about its future, the company began planning to increase distribution to a six-state area. In 1960, the company also entered into a contract to be the exclusive distributor of Italian Swiss Colony Wine, mainly through supermarket chains. Wine had been a previously untapped revenue source by local brewers, and Bilsky's supermarket connections made this seem like a wise choice.

The company's profitable status was short-lived, however. In September 1962, the effects of competition and the increasing cost of doing business led to the plant shutting down all brewing operations for good. While the company would continue to distribute its three remaining brands through the end of the decade, the beers themselves would be brewed by the International Breweries, Inc. Appropriately enough, this was a five-brewery combine similar to what Cleveland-Sandusky had once been, with headquarters in Detroit, MI., although the beers were actually brewed at branches in Findlay, OH. (formerly the Krantz Brewing Co.) and Buffalo, NY. (formerly the Iroquois Beverage Corp.), and shipped to Cleveland for distribution. When that combine folded in 1966, the brands continued to be produced by Toledo's Buckeye Brewery and by the Queen City Brewing Co. in Cumberland, MD. until 1968, when Cleveland-Sandusky's offices closed for good. The old Fishel brewery in Cleveland was razed in the early 1970s, leaving no remains of the city's first and largest corporate brewing enterprise.

46. Forest City Brewing Company

January 1904 saw the organization of the Forest City Brewing Company, with a capital stock of $200,000. Established by local businessmen Michael Albl (who was the new company's president until his death in 1916) and Joseph F. Troyan (a clothier by trade, he became the secretary), the company boasted that it was owned and operated entirely by Bohemians. Albl was born in Stenovic, Plezen province, Bohemia, and had come to America in 1865, working for nearly his entire career as a grocer. Bringing brewing industry experience to the company was treasurer and general

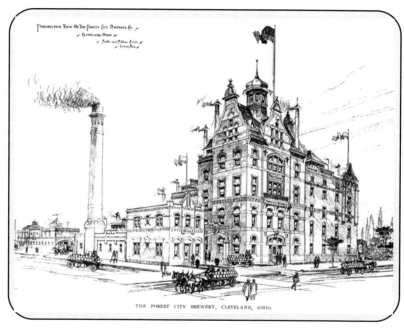

Architect's drawing of the brewery, taken from the *Western Brewer*, 1904

(left) Delivery wagon, circa 1907 [from the Olstyn Carriage Co. catalog, courtesy of the Western Reserve Historical Society]; (below) Bottle label [Bob Bickford collection]

manager Vaclav Humel, formerly of the Pilsener Brewing Co. (also established by Bohemians) on the city's west side.

The new plant was located on Union Avenue at East 69th Street (later taking the address 6900-6922 Union Avenue), near Slavic Village, an area with a high concentration of Eastern Europeans, Designed by the architectural firm Mueller & Mildner of Detroit, the brewery was under construction within a few months of the company's organization. As was typical of large breweries built after the turn of the century, the building's supports and all of the brewery's vessels (fermenting tanks, aging casks, etc.) were of steel construction instead of wood, making the plant far more fire-resistant than earlier breweries. The ornate plant featured a five-story brewhouse with a 225-barrel kettle, two 50-ton refrigerating machines, and two 100-horsepower engines. Its annual capacity would be 50,000 barrels, and the cost of construction was estimated at $220,000.

John Silhavy was the company's original brewmaster, and he oversaw production of the brewery's anchor brand—Select Pilsner Beer. The beer was primarily bottled for home sales, which had become an increasingly large market after the turn of the century, although some was also kegged for sale in local saloons. Silhavy was succeeded in 1909 by Max Hansky, who remained with the company for more than 30 years.

Statewide Prohibition in 1919 spelled the end for beer production at the plant, but the company reorganized as the Forest City New Process Company. While Troyan still remained, the company's president at this time was Joseph V. Chapek, with Albert Panck as plant manager. Forest City stayed in business through the production of X-L-N-T De-Alcoholized Beer, as well as by having the local franchise for Zem-Zem Grape Juice. By 1928, Chapek had been succeeded by Frank E. Albl, son of the brewery's founder. However, poor sales finally caused him to cease operations in 1930.

Three years later, the brewery was acquired by a new group of businessmen, led by former County Commissioner Jack H. Harris. Harris and partner Carl F. Lang invested heavily in the Ohio brewing industry as soon as Repeal appeared likely. They purchased the New Philadelphia brewery (see Tuscarawas County) and renovated it for brewing beer that summer. They also took an interest in Cincinnati's former Windisch-Muhlhauser brewery, which they intended to operate as the Forest City Brewery of Cincinnati, although it was instead incorporated as the Lion Brewery, Inc. (One year later, it became the Burger Brewing Co., remaining open until 1973.) The partners also attempted to purchase the Huebner brewery of Toledo and the former Tuscarawas Valley Brewing Co. in Dover, but both of those ventures failed.

The Cleveland plant was incorporated as the Forest City Brewery, Inc. in March 1933, with Arthur L. Guggenheim as vice-president and treasurer, and Joseph L. Klein as secretary. Although it was one of the city's newest breweries, the plant required an investment of $400,000 in

Two different types of delivery trucks lined up outside the brewery in July 1933 [Bill Carlisle collection]

Jack Harris in later years [Cleveland State University Library]

order to return to operation. By early summer the first beer was on the market and seeing brisk sales, especially with minimal local competition, as most other Cleveland breweries were not yet in full production. According to a later promotional brochure, the brewery led the city in sales for 1934 and accounted for one-fourth of the beer sold in Cleveland. Over the next few years, upgrades in technology and efficiency had increased the brewery's annual capacity to 140,000 barrels, and after $120,000 worth of further improvements in 1937, it was able to produce 200,000 barrels per year.

The company's main product throughout its existence was Waldorf (German for "Forest Village" or "Forest City") Beer and Ale, still brewed under the supervision of Max Hansky, and utilizing the slogan "Champagne of Beers."

Waldorf was available in many different variations, some seasonal. Waldorf Samson Ale and Samson Brau Lager were named for their alcoholic strength, and their labels featured the biblical character Samson. In addition, the company produced Old Bohemian Style Pilsner and Lager Beers, made both in Cleveland and at the New Philadelphia brewery, and around 1936, it also brewed DeWitt Beer and Ale for the DeWitt Hotel chain.

Forest City was the first Cleveland brewery to recognize that non-returnable throwaway packages were the wave of the future. It was the first brewery in the city to can its beer, when in 1935 Waldorf Beer and Ale appeared in flat-topped cans produced by the American Can Company. Retailers were initially skeptical about the new containers, which had recently been invented, but canned beer would continue to be sold by Forest City on a small level until the onset of World War II. Its brands were also sold in squat, disposable "Steinie" bottles as well as the standard returnable long-necked bottles.

Three variations of canned beer produced by Forest City between 1935 and 1941; the woodgrain can actually came in five versions, each with a different slogan in the red band; the bock can is an extremely rare display variety, circa 1935 [Norm Meier collection]; (below left) Tin-over-cardboard sign [Jack Linna collection].

After 1934, once the city's other breweries were all back in business, Forest City's early success became a dim memory, as the Waldorf brand's sales were hit hard by local competition. Harris sold his interest in the company in 1938, after which Carl Lang became the company's president. One year later, however, the firm declared bankruptcy. In 1940, a new group of investors bought the brewery for $135,200, and the Waldorf brand limped along for a little longer. Former State Representative Joseph G. Ehrlich was the leader of this group, serving as the company's new president, with F. W. Drybrough as vice-president and Eugene J. Meyer as treasurer.

Business at the outset of World War II, however, was no better than a few years earlier. By 1944, Ehrlich had acquired all of the company's outstanding stock, and that July he sold the plant to the Brewing Corporation of America (see entry #49) for $477,000. For the next four years, it was known both as Carling's, Inc. and Plant #2 of the B.C. of A., makers of Black Label Beer and Red Cap Ale,

Forest City plant as it appears today, the largest of four standing breweries in the city. Aside from the removal of the brewhouse tower and gables, the plant remains basically intact.

handling production overflow from the main plant on Quincy Avenue.

By 1948, however, tightening federal restrictions on grain forced the permanent closing of the Union Avenue plant (as well as the temporary elimination of the Black Label brand), after which all brewing equipment was removed. The plant later housed a wholesale furniture warehouse and several small businesses, and it continues to stand nearly intact to this day, although the ornate brewhouse architecture and tower have been removed. In 1976, the building was added to the National Register of Historic Places.

47. Carl E. Beltz Weiss Beer Brewery

Weiss beer had always been a beverage that was on the fringe of popularity in America, but it never became an overwhelming favorite like lager beer did. A light-colored, wheat-based beer, it nevertheless had a loyal following among some German immigrants in the late 1800s and early 1900s. Joseph Beltz had operated one of the longest-lasting weiss beer breweries in the city (see entry #35), but when he began brewing lager beer in 1901, the latter's overwhelming popularity was such that the production of weiss beer was stopped altogether just four years later.

At that time, one of his sons, Carl E. Beltz, continued the tradition a few blocks away, at 2654 E. 67th Street. It was here, in a residential neighborhood, that Beltz operated his own weiss beer brewery in his backyard, producing a few hundred barrels annually through 1914, when the operation was shut down. Looking at the seven weiss beer breweries that functioned in Cleveland between 1876 and 1914, all were essentially glorified home-brewing operations, and only the Beltz family was able to operate successfully and for more than a few years. After this time, weiss beer largely disappeared from the market in Cleveland. The building's foundations are all that remain today.

Delivery wagon for Carl Beltz's Weiss Beer
[Bill Carlisle collection]

48. Standard/Schaefer/C. Schmidt Brewing Company

Cleveland's first brewery to be owned and operated entirely by saloonkeepers began operation in December 1903. Working out of a small plant on Sackett Avenue (see entry #44), the Standard Brewing Company was founded by Irishmen Stephen S. Creadon and John T. Feighan, both of whom had grown up on Cleveland's near west side. While Feighan was a banker, Creadon was a saloon owner and was well aware of the plight of the city's other saloon owners who were being financially manipulated by the city's breweries, most of whom had been locked in fierce competition for the past decade and were using the small saloons as pawns in the battle to sell their beers. Following a trend in many other cities in Ohio and the rest of the country, Creadon and Feighan formed a company in which the majority of stock was held by saloon owners. Beer brewed here would be sold in their saloons, allowing them to escape the economic control of the city's larger brewers.

After one year of operation, the Standard Brewing Company relocated further west to the site of a former flour mill at 137-143 Train Avenue (soon renumbered as 5708-5936 Train Avenue, just north of Clark Avenue).

Though this new plant was small, $200,000 was invested into it to build a five-story brewhouse in 1906, a four-story stock house one year later, and a new bottling works on the south side of Train Avenue one year after that. The expansion allowed the company's sales to double from 35,000 barrels in 1906 to 70,000 in 1910.

The company's brewmaster was Jaro Pavlik, who came from a family of Bohemian brewers. His heritage led him to create Standard Old Bohemian Style Beer, although the company's flagship brand for its first fifty years of existence took on an Irish name due to the heritage of the company's founders. Known as Erin Brew, it quickly became one of the city's best-known and popular brands. So as to not alienate the brewery's German customers, the label also carried the name "Ehren Brau". A third brand, known as Full Weight Tonic, was also produced by Standard and was said to improve the appetite and give tone to the nervous system.

As was the case with most of the city's independent brewers after the turn of the century, an offer was made by the dominant Cleveland & Sandusky Brewing Com-pany in 1906 to purchase the Standard plant. The Standard stockholders were offered $650,000, far more than the company was worth, but in the end the deal was called off due to parties on both sides who disapproved of the deal. It can safely be assumed that the many saloon owners who held stock in Standard did not want to be associated with Cleveland & Sandusky, a company which was the very epitome of the competition and manipulation they had sought to avoid. The Standard Company would continue to operate independently throughout its existence.

Stephen S. Creadon

Despite the company's original reason for existing—as a way for saloon owners to create their own source of beer—this purpose slowly faded through the years. Expansion of the plant had required large amounts of money, which had come from $250,000 of stock sales, many of which were purchased by non-saloonkeepers. In addition, as the construction of the large bottling plant illustrated, the company was rapidly becoming more dependent on home sales of bottled beer. Attempting to appeal more to housewives, the company's advertising increasingly used terms such as "liquid food", "pure food tonic", and "choicest home beverage" after 1910. These phrases were also aimed at temperance advocates, as breweries across the country were trying to distance themselves from other, more intoxicating forms of liquor in the years leading up to Prohibition. Two non-alcoholic beverages were produced briefly during this era, Metzz and Mizz, but neither one met with much success and they were discontinued.

(above) Architect's drawing of the new Standard Brewery [taken from *Cleveland und Sein Deutschthum*, 1907]; (below) Delivery wagon, circa 1907 [from the Olstyn Carriage Co. catalog, courtesy of the Western Reserve Historical Society]

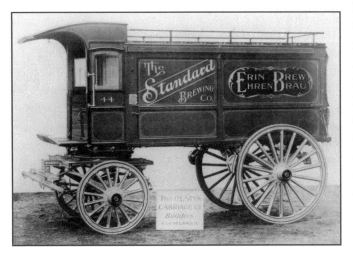

(right) John T. Feighan [Cleveland State University Library];
(below left) Delivery truck, circa 1915 [courtesy of American Truck Historical Society];
(bottom right) Serving tray, circa 1915 [Carl Miller collection].

Ultimately, of course, the temperance forces won, leading to the onset of Prohibition in May 1919. Original founders Stephen Creadon and John Feighan were still the company's chief officers, and they converted the Standard plant to the production of near beer, releasing three brands: Old Bohemia Brew, Standard Special, and Full Weight. Sales of cereal beverages, however, were disappointing, causing the company to look for other ways to put its large plant to use. An affiliated entity, known as the Standard Food Products Company, was formed in 1922 and helped the brewery to survive the Prohibition era by dealing in dairy products, frozen foods, and soft drinks (Creadon had died in 1921 at the age of fifty-five, after which the company began producing Creadon's Ginger Ale in his honor), as well as becoming involved with meat packing. Also, the brewery continued to operate the associated Lake City Ice Company, formed by the company's directors in 1906. The production of near beer did not last through the end of the Prohibition era, ending soon after brewmaster Jaro Pavlik left the company in 1929. John T. Feighan took over the company's presidency after Creadon's death, with Charles Renz as vice-president and Creadon's son George as treasurer.

With the repeal of Prohibition in April 1933, the company quickly returned to the beer business. Although production of near beer had ceased several years earlier, the brewing equipment had remained intact, and in late May, Standard became the city's third brewery to release the real thing to the public. Under new brewmaster Gotthold Kuebler, the Erin Brew and Old Bohemian brands quickly became Cleveland favorites again. In an attempt to take advantage of the initial rush for beer that spring, Standard had hired 150 new employees by the time that the beer was released, to help keep up with the demand. Over the next few years, modern, efficient brewing equipment gradually replaced the older, outdated equipment, and after completion of a five-story addition to the cellar building in 1939, the plant's annual capacity had grown to 250,000 barrels. This number increased to 400,000 barrels soon after the war's end. This made Standard the city's third-largest brewery, even though its beers were only being marketed and sold within a fifty-mile radius in Northeast Ohio.

John T. Feighan continued at the helm of the Standard brewery throughout this period. With James F. Kelley as vice-president, John M. O'Donnell as secretary, and George E. Creadon as treasurer and plant manager, the company continued to grow until wartime grain restrictions curtailed the plant's output. As late as 1946, the brewery's output had been reduced by fifty percent. When the war-related rationing of grain was lifted in 1948, a two-year expansion project began, costing $4.5 million. Consisting of a new four-story brewhouse and stockhouse, and a large modern bottling facility at the west end of

These drawings of the addition to Standard's cellar building appeared in the *Brewers Journal* in May 1939. A decade later, a new modern brewhouse was built to the left of this addition, obscuring the original ornate plant from Train Avenue.

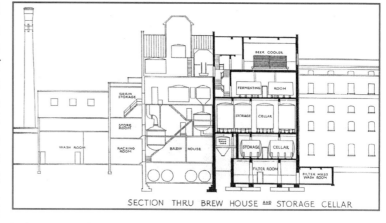

the complex, the expansion, when completed in March 1950, increased the plant's annual capacity even further, to 550,000 barrels. The new bottling facility allowed the company to can its beer for the first time, utilizing flat-topped steel cans, 210 of which could be filled per minute by the new equipment. The expansion project allowed the brewery to extend its sales as well, now throughout Ohio and into parts of Michigan, Pennsylvania, and New York. This was critical for the company's economic success, as Ohio's tax of thirty-six cents per case of beer sold was becoming a huge obstacle for Ohio breweries trying to make a profit. Taxes on beer sold in the other three states were dramatically lower, making sales there much more attractive financially. Standard finished the decade of the 1940s in good shape, however, with Erin Brew Beer being the city's largest selling brand.

As the competition from local, regional, and national brewers became much more intense after the end of the war, advertising began to play an ever-increasing role in the company's success. As a result, advertising gradually took up a larger portion of the company's budget. While advertising in newspapers and on billboards continued, there was more point-of-sale advertising in bars and supermarkets. In addition, radio and television were quickly becoming an integral part of American culture in the late 1940s and early 1950s. Taking advantage of this, the brewery sponsored various programs on both radio and TV, but the biggest coup was the company's sponsorship of the 1948 Cleveland Indians radio broadcasts. Cleveland has always been known for its sports fans, and the fans listened to the radio in record numbers that year when the Indians won the American League Pennant and eventually the World Series. This propelled Erin Brew Beer to be the top seller in the city until 1951. The power of mass-media was just beginning to be tapped.

By 1952, Erin Brew had been replaced by the nearby Pilsener Brewing Company's P.O.C. Beer as the city's top selling brand. In an attempt to bring Erin Brew back to the top, its logo was completely redesigned with a modern look. In the spring of 1953,

(above) Erin Brew was still sponsoring the Cleveland Indians into the mid-1950s; (right) Delivery truck from the late 1940s (note the Standard neons in the window) [Carl Miller collection]

(left) John T. Feighan, Jr. in later years; (right) George E. Creadon [Cleveland State University Library].

the beer was also given a new recipe (under the supervision of new master brewer Richard Edwards, who replaced Gotthold Kuebler after his retirement), known as "Formula Ten-O-Two", which was promoted with a vigorous advertising campaign. Although Erin Brew would never again be the biggest brand in the city, its sales remained respectable for a number of years.

John T. Feighan died in August 1953, at the age of seventy-seven. While he had been a director of the brewery for fifty years, his primary career had remained banking, having started as a teller at the west side Forest City Bank, and eventually rising to become a vice-president of the Cleveland Trust Company. His position as president was taken by George E. Creadon, while Feighan's sons Francis and John, Jr. became vice-president and treasurer. Another vice-president was Benton P. Bohannon, Creadon's son-in-law (and son of James A. Bohannon, the founder of the Brewing Corporation of America). When Creadon died in 1960, John T. Feighan, Jr. succeeded him as president, while Bohannon became Chairman of the Board.

The task at hand for all of these directors was daunting. While the company had been successful in the 1940s and early 50s, the latter portion of that decade saw a gradual dwindling of company sales, due to tremendous competition from national brands that were beginning to dominate the market. Combined with increases in overhead, especially the costs of advertising, the result was a gradual reduction in profits (problems common to virtually all of the city's brewers during the same period). In an effort to change this negative trend, the Erin Brew brand went through another design change before being phased out entirely by 1960, to be replaced by Standard Premium Beer. Sales of the new brand were no better, however, and as a result, 200 of the plant's employees were laid off.

A last-ditch effort to keep the brewery alive resulted in the release of Red Velvet Ale (specially formulated by brewmaster Carl Moeller) in cans and bottles in 1960, followed by Red Label Beer, in bottles only, the following year. Both brands were marketed cleverly: Red Velvet Ale was sold in cases of twenty-four *sixteen*-ounce bottles, for the same price as a case of twelve-ounce bottles. Red Label Beer was sold in cases of twenty-eight, at the same price as a case of twenty-four.

Nevertheless, neither brand provided the needed boost to sales, and in May 1961, the company sold the entire plant for

(above) Two varieties of flat-topped cans used in the early 1950s; (right) Standard brewery, looking east on Train Avenue, after expansion in 1950 [photo taken by employee Ed Kintop]

Tin-over-cardboard sign from 1960, after the retirement of the Erin Brew brand

$2,000,000 to the F. & M. Schaefer Brewing Company of Brooklyn, NY. Schaefer was a well-known name on the East Coast, advertising itself as "America's Oldest Lager Beer", but it was attempting to establish a reputation in the Midwest as well. Formed in 1842 by brothers Frederick and Maximilian Schaefer, both recent immigrants from Prussia, the company had begun operation in midtown Manhattan, but in 1916 had moved across the East River to Brooklyn. In 1950 it purchased Albany's Beverwyck Brewing Company and began brewing Schaefer Beer there. As the brand had "conquered" the east, brewery president Rudolph J. Schaefer II (a part owner of the Cleveland Browns football team) now wanted to begin brewing Schaefer beer for sales throughout Ohio and into neighboring states, through its subsidiary Schaefer Brewing Co. of Ohio, Inc., operated by his son, Rudolph J. Schaefer III.

In addition to brewing Schaefer Beer, part of the agreement with Standard was that the new owners would continue to brew Standard and Red Label Beers and Red Velvet Ale. However, a lawsuit filed by the Carling Brewing Company accused Schaefer of brand infringement, due to the similarities between the latter two brands and its own Red Cap Ale and Black Label Beer. As a result, Red Label and Red Velvet were withdrawn from the market, although Standard Premium Beer continued to be produced throughout Schaefer's tenure on Train Avenue.

In the three years that Schaefer owned the brewery, it spent $1.5 million in improvements to the plant. By 1964, this had paid off by making the company the country's sixth-largest brewer, with nearly 4.5 million barrels of beer sold. However, one year earlier it had purchased the former Gunther/Hamm brewery in Baltimore, MD. for additional production, and in 1964 the decision was made to leave Cleveland and continue to concentrate production in the east. The company continued to grow over the next decade, until a gradual decline in sales led to the closing of most of its breweries and its eventual sale in 1980 to the Stroh Brewing Co. of Detroit.

At the same time that Schaefer was leaving Ohio, another eastern brewer was looking to enter the area to strengthen its presence and extend its sales westward. The C. Schmidt & Sons Brewing Company of Philadelphia had been founded in 1860 and was one of eastern Pennsylvania's strongest brands. In 1954, Schmidt had purchased the Adam Scheidt Brewing Company in nearby Norristown, PA. to increase its production. By 1964, its sales of 2,000,000 barrels made it the country's fourteenth-largest brewer when it purchased the Train Avenue plant in Cleveland, and Schmidt's Beer began a twenty year association with the city. Schmidt's Beer and Ale had been sold sporadically in Ohio since the 1930s, but now a major marketing push was aimed specifically at Northeast Ohio, and to a lesser extent into areas west and south of that. In addition to the Schmidt brand, the Standard Beer brand limped along for a short time before being discontinued in the late 1960s, cutting the last ties to the plant's origin.

While Schmidt was highly successful at the old Standard brewery, which by now was capable of turning out 700,000 barrels annually, it found itself in need of additional brewing capacity by 1971. After the Carling Brewing Company abruptly closed its huge plant on Quincy Avenue across town, Schmidt purchased the plant and moved its entire operation there (see entry #49), with brewing beginning in early 1972. After that, the Train Avenue plant was purchased by the Miller Brewing Company of Milwaukee, which removed all brewing equipment and sent it to the Miller plant in Ft. Worth, TX. The Train Avenue brewery stood empty for a time before being razed in 1974. The original bottling works and garage on the south side of Train Avenue remain today, as well as the newer bottling house built in 1948. This building had fallen into a severe state of disrepair and had become a major neighborhood eyesore by the mid-1970s before being renovated, and today it is a major depot for U-Haul trucks.

49. Brewing Corporation of America/Carling/C. Schmidt & Sons Brewing Co.

(Note: A more extensive and detailed story of the rise and fall of the Carling Brewing Company can be found in Carl Miller's *Breweries of Cleveland*.)

Northeast Ohio's only national brewery company was one of only two entirely new brewing establishments to open in Cleveland after Prohibition's end. The Carling brand had already been familiar to Clevelanders for more than fifty years, having been brewed at the old Rogers Forest City Brewery (see entry #3) beginning in 1880, and later at the Barrett/Bohemian brewery (see entry #38) elsewhere in the Flats from 1884 to 1911, even after its takeover by the Cleveland & Sandusky Brewing Company.

Known primarily for its ales, the Carling Brewing Company's history already went back more than a century, to when Thomas Carling, a native of Yorkshire, England, settled near London, Ontario in 1818. Carling was a farmer and part-time home brewer, whose local reputation grew over the years, until 1840, when he retired from farming to establish a brewery. When he died five years later, his sons William and John continued in the business (by then known as W. & J. Carling's City Brewery), watching it grow in popularity. In 1878, they erected a huge new plant to replace the original one, and although that was destroyed by a fire one year later (after which William Carling caught pneumonia and died), it was rebuilt quickly and business continued to grow. By 1890, the company employed one hundred men and produced 30,000 barrels of ale, porter, and lager annually.

John Carling had gradually moved into politics, leaving the company in 1885 to become Canada's Minister for Agriculture (later becoming knighted as Sir John Carling). Prior to this, he had extended the Carling name into the United States through the Cleveland branch, as mentioned above. After his departure from the company, other Carling family members continued to operate it successfully. In 1927, one particular ale recipe was renamed as Red Cap Ale, which rapidly became one of the best-selling brews in Canada. By this time, Carling's London facility was the country's largest brewery. Three years later, Carling joined several other Canadian brewers to form the Brewing Corporation of Canada, which was then renamed as Canadian Breweries, Ltd. in 1937.

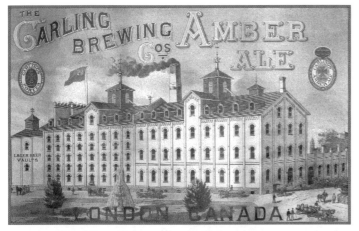

(above) Lithograph, circa 1895 [Museum London collection, London, Ontario, Canada; courtesy of curator Mike Baker and Glen C. Phillips]; (above right) Thomas Carling; (below right) Magazine advertisement from 1929.

The Peerless Motor Company had a long history of success dating back to 1869, when Cincinnati's Peerless Wringer Company merged with Cleveland's Mercantile Manufacturing Company. Initially producing washing machine wringers and machine tools, the company later moved into the production of bicycles, and the Peerless Bicycle enjoyed great success in the 1890s. In 1900, the newly invented automobile afforded the company an opportunity to expand into what would be a profitable venture for the next thirty years. Finding its niche in the production of luxury cars, the company found itself competing with the likes of Packard, Cadillac, and Pierce Arrow. Among the many models that were built through the years was the "Green Dragon", driven by early racer Barney Oldfield, who established

James Alvin Bohannon [Cleveland State University Library]

some of the earliest land speed records. A huge production facility was constructed between 1906 and 1909 (replacing the small original plant on Lisbon Street) on the city's far east side at 9400 Quincy Avenue (on the southeast corner of Quincy and E. 93rd St.) During WWI, the factory was converted for production of trucks that were sent in large numbers to Europe.

Events of history destined Peerless and Carling to cross paths in a very successful way. Peerless remained profitable through the 1920s, until the stock market crash of 1929 sent the national economy into a tailspin. At the onset of the Great Depression, the market for expensive luxury cars dried up quickly, which had severe economic repercussions for the company. In an attempt to improve the company's financial situation, Peerless hired 33-year-old James A. Bohannon away from a rival automobile company to be its new president. Within two years, however, it became obvious that Peerless's market share would not recover any time soon. At the same time, the company was ill-equipped to try to compete with larger companies such as Ford in the manufacture of smaller low-priced cars. As the company's future continued to darken, the decision was made in late 1931 to stop all automobile production.

In the mean time, Bohannon and the company's executive committee set about the task of finding an alternative way to put their huge facility to use. By 1932, it had become increasingly apparent that the Depression would not disappear any time soon, and as a result, it became more likely that Franklin Roosevelt might be elected president. Sensing that this might bring an end to Prohibition, Peerless began looking into the prospect of converting the factory into a huge brewery. However, with no experience in the field and no prior brand name recognition, getting started would be potentially very difficult, especially as a large brewery which would be in more direct competition with the giants: Anheuser-Busch, Pabst, and Schlitz (small local brewers who were also new to the field, such as Sunrise and Eilert, had similar handicaps, but on a small regional basis, advertising new products was somewhat easier. Still, virtually all of these new companies had disappeared from Northeast Ohio by the end of WWII, while Carling just barely survived).

As a result, Bohannon went north of the border, contacting the well-established Brewing Corporation of Canada in an attempt to secure the rights to brew its popular Red Cap Ale and Black Label Beer in the United States. The Canadian company agreed, in return providing the technical assistance needed to convert the car factory into a brewery, while its president, E. P. Taylor, would sit on the Peerless Board of Directors. The new brewing operation was known as the Brewing Corporation of America, operating as a subsidiary of the Peerless Corporation. Wall Street clearly liked the idea; when the announcement of this new venture was made in July 1933, Peerless stock quickly rose from seventy-five cents per share to five dollars per share.

Now came the huge task of converting the factory into a brewery. Nearly one million dollars was spent on the project, which was the city's largest construction project of 1933. Fifty tons of copper were used just to build equipment in the new brewhouse, which required two new floors to be added to the east wing of the front of the plant. The two new brew kettles, each with a 400-barrel capacity, stood in full view of the public through large plate glass windows. Ten miles of piping were installed throughout the

Artist's rendering of the Peerless/Carling plant at the time of its reopening as a brewery in 1934

WHO WAS E. P. TAYLOR?

The Brewing Corporation of America would likely never have come to exist if not for one E. P. Taylor. Far more well-known in Canada than in the United States, Edward Plunket Taylor was the mastermind behind the formation of Canadian Breweries, Ltd., the American brewery's parent.

Born in Ottawa in 1901, Taylor had already established a rabbit breeding business by the age of twelve. After graduating from McGill University in 1923, he was named as a director of Ottawa's Brading Breweries by his grandfather, who had a controlling interest in the company. Taylor was not a brewer, however, but a pure businessman.

In 1930, he formed the Brewing Corporation of Canada as a tool to begin what he called "The Grand Design," purchasing numerous breweries in perilous financial condition to help reduce overall costs and minimize competition. In less than a year he had control of ten breweries, including Carling. Another nine would quickly follow, and by 1939, his renamed Canadian Breweries, Ltd. controlled sixty percent of Ontario's brewing business. Always looking to expand his interests, Taylor was very receptive to James Bohannon's request in 1933 to brew Carling products in the United States. Carling was also brewed in Great Britain after 1952, and Taylor's knack for business mergers led to the formation years later of Bass Charrington, Ltd., which was England's largest brewing company at the time.

At its peak in the 1960s, Canadian Breweries was considered to be the world's largest brewing organization, with thirty-one breweries around the world, selling mostly Black Label Beer in more than fifty countries. After this point, however, there was a general decline in the industry, and in 1968, Tayor sold a large portion of Canadian Breweries stock to Rothmans Pall Mall, Ltd., effectively retiring from the business of brewing. He continued as chairman of his own Argus Corporation, which had interests in paper production, broadcasting, chemicals, mining, food and merchandizing businesses, and farm machinery, in addition to brewing.

Along the way, he had also helped bring about the formation of the country's first planned community, known as Don Mills, in Toronto, in 1952. He also became heavily involved in thoroughbred horse racing after his first horse purchase in 1936. Perhaps based on his rabbit breeding experience, Taylor built up an unprecedented line of champion race horses at his three farms in Ontario and Maryland. Altogether his horses won more than 10,000 races, including Northern Dancer, the first Canadian horse to win the Kentucky Derby and the Preakness.

After an amazing career, E. P. Taylor died in 1989, at the age of eighty-eight.

plant, sending beer to the rear factory portion, which was lined with vats for fermentation and storage. In the depths of the Depression, giving employment to the hundreds of workers who helped transform the plant had a significant effect on the local economy, and once completed, the new facility would initially employ seventy men. It had an annual capacity of 200,000 barrels, which could be expanded if necessary to 1,000,000 barrels, all under the watchful eye of brewing supervisor Otto P. Rindelhardt (who came from Canada to oversee brewing operations) and brewmaster Herbert J. Kresser. When the plant reopened for business in June 1934, 20,000 Clevelanders entered through the tiffany-lined entry way to sample the new brews and tour the sprawling facility. With 165,000 square feet of floor space devoted to brewing, this was easily the city's largest brewery, although this only represented about half of the factory's available space (which would be fully utilized after the many expansions in the future).

From the very start, Bohannon's strategy for the Brewing Corporation of America was different than that of any other brewery in Cleveland, let alone the entire state of Ohio. The concept of a truly national brewer was still just that—a concept—in 1934. While Anheuser-Busch, Schlitz, and Pabst had found ways to distribute their beers over a large geographic portion of the country prior to Prohibition, no beer had yet been consistently sold

Inside the elaborate marble-lined brewhouse in 1934

coast-to-coast. Bohannon, however, saw no reason that complete national distribution of his beer couldn't be achieved in the 1930s with the right business plan, especially with recent improvements in transportation (the U. S. Route system was put in place in the mid-1920s, as a precursor to the Interstate system of the 1950s), refrigeration technology, and marketing (radio, for example, had first appeared during the Prohibition era, and national broadcasts were routinely taking place).

In addition, Bohannon staked his company's early fortunes on the ability to successfully mass-market a brand of ale instead of beer. This was an idea that made good sense on paper, but not necessarily in the real world of Depression-era America. Ale was a product which had been in America since the first Europeans had arrived centuries earlier. However, since the appearance of lager beer in the mid-1800s, ale had dropped drastically in popularity. After the end of Prohibition, many breweries made ale in addition to lager beer, but in most cases ale made up a relatively small portion of the overall sales. In Cleveland, the Sunrise, Forest City, Cleveland-Sandusky, and Eilert breweries sold brands of ale in the 1930s, while Leisy, Standard, Cleveland-Home, and Pilsener did not (Pilsener's Toby Ale first appeared in 1940, but overall sales were disappointing). Nationally, there was no dominant brand of ale to be found; Anheuser-Busch and Schlitz did not brew ale, and Pabst Old Tankard Ale was never a big seller for the company. P. Ballantine & Sons of Newark, N.J. (like Carling, also founded in 1840) had a popular ale which sold well along the East Coast, and in later years, after its purchase by the Falstaff Corporation expanded its production nationwide, it took the title of "America's Largest Selling Ale".

Bohannon sensed a potential niche to be filled if a well-established brand of ale could be properly marketed on a widespread basis. Seeing the popularity of Carling's Red Cap Ale in Canada, a call to the Carling brewery seemed like the best idea. However, Canadians were still largely of English heritage, and ale remained a solid part of their culture. In the United States, the influx of German immigrants years earlier had changed the nation's taste dramatically in favor of lager beer. Still, establishing a national brand of ale seemed like an idea that was worth a try. The pricing of this ale was another matter.

After Repeal, the typical cost of a twelve-ounce bottle of beer was ten cents, or fifteen cents for a premium brand, such as Budweiser or Schlitz. Bohannon's idea was to charge twenty cents per bottle of Red Cap Ale, putting the new brew in a class of its own, cost-wise. This thinking may have been ahead of its time (imported beers today are typically more expensive than domestic beers, and many microbrewed beers are considerably more expensive than their mass-produced counterparts). However, consumers have much more disposable cash today, while in the Depression literally every penny counted. Therefore, despite a heavy advertising campaign which stressed ale's British heritage, and its mention in great literature through the ages, Red Cap Ale's sales were very disappointing through the brewery's first two years. As a result, with the company's finances already in dire straits by 1935, Bohannon backed away from his initial strategy by instead pushing two lower-priced brands, Black Label Beer and Amber Creme Ale

Delivery trucks appeared throughout the region after the brewery's opening in the mid-1930s

along with Red Cap Ale. Both of these brands sold well and allowed the company to show its first profit by 1936. Many years later, one wonders if Red Cap Ale might have met with far greater long-term success if it had been competitively priced from the beginning.

Once a standard lineup of three successful brands was established (along with Black Label Bock Beer, sold briefly each spring into the late 1950s), the company set about the building of a massive distribution network, the end goal being nationwide distribution of Carling products. By 1939, this network covered a large portion of the Midwest and extended to the East Coast, and the plant's output that year rose to more than 400,000 barrels. Expansion continued throughout World War II, as large amounts of Red Cap Ale were sent overseas to American troops. At the same time, Black Label Beer was the company's biggest domestic seller, and by the war's end, it was being sold in nearly half the country.

By this time, the brewery's annual capacity had climbed to 750,000 barrels, making it the largest in the state of Ohio. Otto Rindelhardt had been succeeded as master brewer, first by Dr. Joseph L. Rea, and later by O. F. Steideman, John C. Jahreis, and George J. Wagner. Bohannon served as the company's president and chairman of the board, with vice-presidents E. P. Taylor, Lawrence J. Strickland, Paul L. Creighton, and S. Taylor Creighton.

July 1944 saw the company's purchase of both the Tip Top (see entry #10) and the Forest City (see entry #46) breweries in Cleveland, partly to acquire the war-time grain rations of both, but also for extra brewing capacity. While the smaller Tip Top plant was permanently closed, the Forest City plant on Union Avenue operated under the "Carling's, Inc." subsidiary for four more years, elevating the company's overall production to over one million barrels annually, the first brewery in the city to surpass that number. During its brief operation by Carling, the Union Avenue plant was also known as Plant #2 of the Brewing Corporation of America. It was during the war that Red Cap Ale was first packaged in  cone-topped steel cans, all painted olive drab, for exportation to troops. Even after the war's end, the government further restricted brewers' access to grains, and as a result the company ceased production of Black Label Beer altogether. With this (temporary) decrease in production, the Union Avenue plant closed its doors for good in 1948. Despite the restrictions, Bohannon stated that 1946 was the first year in which Carling products were sold in all forty-eight states, a direct result of the large distribution network that had been established. This good news, however, masked several huge underlying problems which would soon turn Bohannon's company upside-down.

Bohannon's aggressive marketing strategies were ahead of their time in many ways, but ultimately they, in combination with several major blunders, led to disaster in the three years following the end of the war. At the top of the list of problems was the massive distribution network that had been developed prior to and during the war. While more than 200 distributors across the country were carrying Carling products by 1946, many were being allocated so few cases of beer, due to continued post-war grain restrictions, that they and their customers were not developing any particular loyalty to Carling, especially with the rapid increase in competition during the same period from the other "national" brewers. As a result, many of these distributors were close to abandoning Carling products altogether by 1948. Making this problem more acute was the cessation of production of Black Label Beer. This had been the company's best domestic seller dur-

Rare olive drab cone-topped can, sent to troops overseas. These cans were produced at both plants between approximately 1944 and 1946, and there are two versions, one stating "Brewing Corporation of America", and the other stating "Carling's, Inc.", indicating production at the Union Avenue plant; the cans were not subject to the usual federal taxation.

Tin-over-cardboard sign, circa 1950

ing the war, but its lower "popular" price yielded a lower profit margin. Bohannon still remained convinced that Red Cap Ale, with its higher "premium" price, was the company's brand of the future, and it received the company's full attention when grain restrictions took effect. When these restrictions were lifted in 1947, Black Label returned to the market, but at a higher premium price, which alienated customers further. Once again, American tastes had shown that ale <u>alone</u> would not allow Carling to achieve its coveted national market.

Interestingly enough, the Carling distribution network was just as weak in Cleveland as anywhere else. Due largely to the company's refusal between 1944 and 1946 to allocate any more beer to local distributors than to those in other cities, many beer drinkers on the North Coast developed a lasting resentment, feeling that the company seemed disinterested in the consumers in its own home town. While the company's actions were consistent with its overall strategy of establishing a wide geographic network, the results locally were typical in that no particular areas seemed to have become Carling strongholds, not even at home. The overall result was a forty percent drop in sales between 1947 and 1949, as the company went from a two million dollar profit in 1946 to a nearly one million dollar loss in 1948.

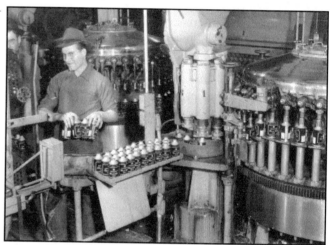

Yet another tactical mistake was Bohannon's belief that the country's beer drinkers were ready for exclusively disposable packages. Disposable bottles and cans had been available since the mid-1930s, and they certainly helped to reduce costs normally associated with shipping returnable bottles back to the brewery, especially from long distances. However, they had not yet achieved the widespread popularity of long-necked returnable bottles, which had been around since the late 1800s. In addition, draft beer in taverns remained popular as it had been for many years. Therefore, when quart bottles disappeared in 1943, draft beer was discontinued in November 1944, and long-necked bottles were phased out in 1945, it was just another roadblock to the successful marketing of Carling beers. Realizing this some time later, the company brought back all three forms of packaging.

The final straw for Bohannon was the commencement in 1946 of

After the war-time restriction of metal use was lifted, Carling beer and ale appeared domestically in both twelve (right) and thirty-two ounce (above) cone-topped cans. Their appearance was not widespread, however, as the plant operated nine bottling lines to just one canning line. In the photo above right, from 1942, Mike Mahlenko works on the canning line, which had a capacity of 153,600 cans per sixteen hour day [Cleveland State University Library].

(left) Ian R. Dowie; (below) George M. Black, Jr.

a five million dollar expansion of the plant. While rapid increases in sales had required several prior expansions of the brewery before and during the war, the unforeseen and dramatic drop in sales after the war made the timing of a huge and costly addition especially poor. The resulting effect of all these factors was near-bankruptcy for the company, and it looked as if the end was near for the giant brewery by the end of 1947.

Salvation came, as it had fifteen years earlier, from north of the border. In 1945, Canadian Breweries, Ltd. had struck a deal in which it took a majority ownership of the Brewing Corporation of America, with Bohannon receiving a large amount of Canadian Breweries stock in exchange. This was part of E. P. Taylor's "Grand Design" which would eventually lead to worldwide distribution of Carling beers over the next twenty years. When Bohannon called his Canadian counterparts in early 1948, they quickly came to Cleveland to evaluate the situation. Quickly realizing the severity of the company's predicament, they soon set in motion a plan to save the brewery. A change in management came first, with Bohannon being "elevated" to Chairman of the Board. In reality, he had essentially been rendered powerless, and he thus remained with the company for only one more year. After retiring in 1949, he remained in the Cleveland area until his death in 1968. Many of the remaining management positions were filled by Canadian executives, giving the company a whole new face by late 1948.

Saving the company was recognized as a formidable task, considering the ominous downward trend in sales. The new management team was made an offer in early 1949 by the Falstaff Brewing Corporation (which was successfully pursuing its own goal of national distribution, and was among the nation's top ten brewers by this time) to purchase the Brewing Corporation of America. Although the offer was attractive to E. P. Taylor, the deal fell through at the last minute.

The actual job of bringing the company back to profitability largely fell on the shoulders of new vice-president George M. Black, Jr., and Canadian Breweries vice-president of sales Ian R. Dowie (Dowie became the American company's president in 1951 when Black returned to Canada as president of Canadian Breweries). Dowie came to Cleveland after helping Canadian Breweries rise to become Canada's top beer seller. Upon beginning his new job, he began a thorough evaluation of the Brewing Corporation of America's entire business plan.

Realizing that Red Cap Ale was not going to be the sales juggernaut that Bohannon had always hoped for, he looked instead to Black Label Beer, always dependable and popular, to be the company's anchor brand. He also realized that Black Label's price would need to drop to a competitive level in order to jump-start sales, and thus the slogan, "Premium Beer at the Popular Price" was used in Black Label advertising beginning in 1950. The brand's price varied geographically, as it was lowered to match the price of the local brands in each area that it was sold. With a far greater advertising budget, Carling brands had a clear advantage over most smaller local breweries. Similar strategies were used by other large regional and national breweries at the time, and this was a major factor leading to a drastic drop in the number of smaller brewers in the country in the 1950s and 1960s.

As more of these smaller local companies closed their doors, companies like the Brewing Corporation of America were able to capitalize on the decline in competition by increasing their market share. Dowie also worked to build many new and stronger relationships with distributors, both local and distant. With no supply shortage to deal with, Carling could now keep these distributors well-stocked and allow customers nationwide to develop new loyalties to Black Label Beer and Red Cap Ale.

Dowie's efforts paid rapid dividends, as business improved dramatically in both 1950 and 1951, and led to a continued rise in sales throughout the following decade. By 1953, the company became Cleveland's first brewery to sell more than one million barrels in a single year. Around the same time, its earlier expansion project was completed, bringing the plant's annual capacity to 1.8 million barrels (future expansions would bring this

Two aerial photos, taken by Robert Runyan in 1951, show the brewery's expansion project finally taking shape after many years of planning [Bruce Young collection]

capacity up to three million barrels). In early 1954, the company was renamed as the Carling Brewing Company, and around the same time came a radical transition in label design. The familiar black label (used since 1934) evolved into a white label with a black square logo (used only for a year or so), before evolving further into a bright red label with black square logo that remained as the company's trademark for more than twenty years and was associated with its greatest international success.

Another reason for the company's dramatic successes in the 1950s was the catchy phrase, "Mabel...Black Label". First appearing in 1949, the phrase showed up in the vast majority of Black Label advertising through the mid-1960s, and to this day it is still remembered by many people who watched television or listened to radio during the era, as the phrase was heard often. On television, Mabel was played by actress Jeanne Goodspeed, who brought out Black Label Beer before giving a trademark wink to the camera. The phrase was one of the earliest and certainly most successful national marketing campaigns for a brand of beer, as it accompanied the company's ascension from near-bankruptcy to the national top five in beer sales.

As Carling's sales continued to climb in the early 1950s, it became clear that repeated expansions of the Cleveland facility would not be enough to achieve and maintain a profitable national market. Transportation costs would continue to cut into profits on sales in more distant areas, especially due to Carling's lack of a large-selling premium-priced beer, along the lines of Budweiser or Miller High Life. Therefore, like most of the other national brewers of the 1950s, Carling opened several branch facilities around the country, beginning in 1954. The first of these was the outright purchase of the large Griesedieck-Western Brewing Company, with branches in Belleville, IL. and St. Louis. Carling continued to brew G-W's very popular Stag Beer, which strengthened its position in the Midwest. Although the older St. Louis plant was closed after just three years, the Belleville plant continued to be one of the company's primary facilities for many years.

At the same time as the Griesedieck-Western purchase, plans were being made for the construction of an entirely new Carling brewery in Natick, MA., near Boston, where the company had seen good sales for many years. This plant opened its doors in 1956, and was followed by new plants in Atlanta (1958), Baltimore (1961) and Fort Worth, TX. (1965). In addition, Carling also purchased the Frankenmuth, MI. plant formerly owned by the Frankenmuth Brewing Co. and the International Breweries, Inc. in 1956, the Tacoma, WA. plant formerly known as the Heidelberg Brewing Co. (with Carling taking ownership of the popular Heidelberg brand of beer) in 1959, and the Phoenix plant of the Arizona Brewing Co., with its popular A-1 Beer, in 1964. For a brief time, Carling operated nine breweries across the country, with a tenth plant in San Francisco being planned.

This massive expansion was a tremendous success in its first few years, as the company's national sales continued to rapidly climb, passing two million barrels in 1956, three million barrels the following year (by which time the company had performed an amazing feat, rising from 62nd in national sales in 1949 to eighth in 1957), and eventually reaching an all-time peak of more than 5.7 million barrels in 1964. At that point, Carling ranked fourth in the country in sales, behind perpetual leader Anheuser-Busch, along with Schlitz and Falstaff, and its directors still maintained their lofty goal of becoming the country's leading beer-producer, as Carling had been in Canada. This goal, of course, would never be reached.

In 1962, Ian Dowie returned to Canada to continue as president of Canadian Breweries, Ltd. For several years he had been president of both the Canadian and U. S. companies, and had split his time between the two countries, but now chose to focus entirely on Canadian operations. In his place, Henry E. Russell, formerly in charge of Carling's New England operations, became president of the U. S. company. Coincidentally or not, it was soon after this that the company's fortunes would begin to turn sour. Several factors came together to lead the company into a gradual decline in sales after the peak year of 1964.

Ultimately, the key problem was that Carling was now being forced into competition against the other national breweries. During the company's fifteen-year climb to the top five, it was primarily competing against smaller local and regional brewers, and the "premium beer at the popular price" concept was well-suited for those battles. By the mid-1960s, however, the majority of those breweries had closed their doors (in Ohio, for example, there were thirty-two operating brewery companies as of 1949, but by 1965, that number had dropped to eight, including Carling itself), and most of the remaining competitors were either on the verge of closing or were larger brewers with huge advertising budgets. In addition, the large brewers that saw long-term success had popular premium-priced brands which allowed much higher profit margins. Carling's only premium-priced brand was Red Cap Ale, and prior attempts to popularize Red Cap had not been especially successful. Further attempts in the early 1960s to reformulate the brand's taste and modernize its image did not improve the situation. Ongoing attempts to establish a premium-priced product led to the introduction of Carling Malt Liquor on a test basis in selected markets, but the public's response was lukewarm. Several years later, a similar fate befell the short-lived Black Label Malt Liquor. A brief attempt to establish Heidelberg Beer (popular in the Northwest, coming from the Tacoma brewery) as a national brand was also unsuccessful. As had been the case since 1949, Carling's success or failure would depend largely on the performance of Black Label Beer, even with its low profit margin (this was a problem shared by the Falstaff Brewing Corp., also in the national top five at the time, which ultimately led to its decline as well).

After switching to flat-topped cans in 1950, Black Label Beer went through a radical change in design in the mid-1950s

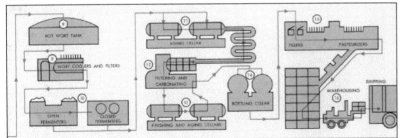

(above) Schematic diagram of the Carling brewing process; (right) Henry E. Russell [both images from a company brochure, courtesy of Bill Carlisle]

Another setback for the company was a tremendous lack of success in its markets in the West and Southwest, where its newest breweries existed. The Texas plant closed after less than a year, largely due to poor regional sales, but also related to skepticism about the new plant's Continuous Brewing Process. The latter was a technical innovation intended to brew beer more efficiently, in a continuous stream. Like most new technologies, it had problems that needed to be worked out, but Carling quickly gave up on the experiment, selling the plant to the Miller Brewing Co. (which still operates it today, without the Continuous Brewing Process) in 1966. In the same year, the Phoenix plant was sold to the National Brewing Co. of Baltimore, as Carling withdrew from the Southwest altogether.

Carling saw a brief return to glory in 1968 and 1969 when sales improved, partly due to labor strikes and work stoppages for Anheuser-Busch and Pabst, but also to new marketing innovations such as the Keg Bottle. This was a unique barrel-shaped package, designed especially for Carling, which was a throwback to the "Steinie" and "Stubby" bottles of thirty years earlier. It was introduced in May 1968 at the Cleveland plant with great fanfare, and it seemed to be an immediate marketing success. Similarly, the introduction of the radically different "Tankard Can", evoking an appearance of pewter from the Middle Ages, showed that Carling, while still in the national top ten in sales, was willing to take chances to maintain its share of the American beer market.

In the same year, E. P. Taylor sold a majority of his stock in Canadian Breweries, Ltd. to Rothmans Pall Mall, a South African tobacco company. To many observers, this transition was the beginning of the end for Carling, as Rothmans had no experience in the brewing industry whatsoever. By 1970, the earlier rebound of sales had stopped, as Carling dropped to eighth nationally, with just under five million barrels sold. On the outside, it was business as usual at the seven operating breweries, and in fact a large modernization project was being planned at the Cleveland plant. On the inside, however, it was quickly becoming obvious that drastic measures were needed to keep the company profitable. With a drop of over one million barrels in sales over the previous two years, the clear answer was to cut overhead by getting rid of the excessive brewing capacity in the company.

The Cleveland plant was the oldest in the group, and while it was not necessarily as outdated as Carling subsequently claimed, it was chosen to be the first one closed, ending Cleveland's 68-year association with Carling. Brewery workers union president Anthony C. Sapienza was the first to find out, when company officials summoned him from the stands of the Cleveland Indians' home opener in April 1971 to give him the bad news. On May 9, when brewing ceased at the plant, it came as a great shock to the community, as more than 600 jobs were to be lost or transferred, including management. While everyone agreed that sales had dropped, most Cleveland workers and union leaders blamed mismanagement and disagreed with the claim that the plant was inefficient. In any case, within a few months, activity had ceased at the plant as existing beer was shipped out, and the plant sat quietly, awaiting further word on its fate.

From Quincy Avenue, the plant was still an impressive sight in the early 1960s [Bill Carlisle collection].

By summer of that year, Carling's headquarters had moved to Waltham, MA., near the Natick plant. Henry Russell resigned as president soon after this, and further shakeups in management would soon take place. The results, however, were no better, as sales continued to drop. The Atlanta plant, only fifteen years old, was the next to close in 1973 (being sold to the Coca-Cola Co.), even though Black Label was still clinging to the national top ten. In the same year, the company acquired the right to brew and market the super-premium Danish brand Tuborg, which finally gave Carling a successful premium-priced product. Despite this, the company lost $10,000,000 in 1975, and the modern Natick plant was closed, as Carling fell out of the national top ten for the first time in nearly twenty years.

By the end of 1975, Canadian Breweries, Ltd. (which had been renamed as Carling O'Keefe Breweries) was also struggling finanancially, and it cut ties with its U. S. operations. To stay alive, Carling soon entered into a merger with the National Brewing Co. of Baltimore, which had also been struggling financially despite its popular Colt 45 Malt Liquor and National Bohemian Beer brands. The new Carling National Brewing Company started out strong initially with combined annual sales of more than four million barrels in 1976. However, within two years, this number had dropped by twenty percent, and another merger was quickly being sought. A proposal to merge with Pabst was blocked by the Justice Department due to anti-trust laws, but in early 1979, Carling National was purchased for more than $35,000,000 by the G. Heileman Brewing Co. of LaCrosse, WI.

Heileman was a company that had slowly grown through acquisitions, primarily of Midwestern breweries, but the Carling National purchase set it on course to become a national powerhouse. By the mid-1980s, it operated eleven breweries across the country, and in 1985, its sales peaked at more than one billion dollars, making it the country's sixth-largest brewer. Black Label continued to be marketed across the country, now in a redesigned white can, specifically noted as being "Canadian Style Beer", with several varieties (Black Label Light Beer, Non-Alcoholic Malt Beverage, Low Alcohol Beer, and even Black Label 11-11 Malt Liquor). Red Cap Ale, however, was not part of the Heileman deal, and its appearance in the United States came to an end (it also disappeared from the Canadian market around the same time). Black Label's reputation and national popularity had largely eroded by this time, however, and it was not one of Heileman's larger sellers.

Heileman soon fell prey to the same forces that had brought Canadian Breweries, Ltd. to its knees, when in 1987 it was purchased by Australian investor Alan Bond. Bond's organization rapidly mismanaged the company into massive losses, leading to a bankruptcy filing in 1991. Meanwhile, all but one of the former Carling plants had gradually shut down, leaving only the Baltimore plant in operation. After several more turbulent years, Heileman and its brands were sold in 1996 to the Stroh Brewery Co. of Detroit, the country's fourth-largest brewer. The Baltimore plant was subsequently closed, and just three years later, Stroh exited the brewing business altogether. The Black Label brand, now essentially a historical footnote with no consistent market, was sold to the Pabst Brewing Co., which continues to manufacture the brand today on a minor scale, under contract with the Miller Brewing Co. in Eden, N.C. and Trenton, OH., near Cincinnati. Interestingly, the Stag and Heidelberg brands have survived the roller coaster ride of the past two decades as well, and are also made through Pabst at various Miller breweries.

As a footnote, Red Cap Ale returned to Canada in the mid-1990s, when its rights were purchased by the Brick Brewery of Waterloo, Ontario, which continues to brew it to this day. The Black Label brand was sold to long-time rival Molson Breweries, which continues to brew it in Canada. While E. P. Taylor's Canadian Breweries, Ltd. is history, its greatest legacy is in England and South Africa, where Black Label Beer was introduced in the 1950s and 1960s, and where it remains a best-selling brand (although in England the name was shortened to Carling Beer in 2000).

Meanwhile, back on Quincy Avenue in Cleveland, the Carling plant awaited either a buyer or liquidation through the latter half of 1971. The only serious interest came from the president of the Peoples Brewing Co. of Oshkosh, WI., who visited the plant but determined that it was much larger than what he needed (not to mention that the $7,000,000 asking price would be a huge investment for a relatively small brewery, especially one in questionable financial health—the plant in Oshkosh subsequently closed just one year later). At the end of the year, however, an announcement came that the plant had been purchased for a mere $2.5 million by the C. Schmidt & Sons Brewing Co., the city's only remaining brewer. With headquarters in Philadelphia (and another plant in nearby Norristown, PA.), Schmidt had come to Cleveland in 1964, operating in the old Standard Brewing Co. plant on Train Avenue (see entry #48) across town. With steady growth over the following seven years, Schmidt was the country's twelfth-largest brewer in 1971, with markets throughout the middle Atlantic

Schmidt's logo had replaced Carling's atop the city's largest brewery by 1972

states and into New England, Ohio, and even the deep South. Anticipating further growth in the future, the company needed to seek more brewing capacity. By early 1972, after a million-dollar renovation to the plant, Schmidt had transferred its entire Cleveland operation and more than 200 employees seven miles east, and brewing had begun again on Quincy Avenue, under the supervision of William Hipp, the head brewmaster and Vice-President for Production. Anthony Sapienza, the brewery workers union president, recognized the importance of supporting the city's last remaining brewery, and he launched a campaign by the union to encourage local establishments to carry Schmidt's Beer. He also suggested that the city give the brewery a break on its substantial water and sewer bill, although no break was ever given.

Soon after this, Schmidt announced that it had acquired the rights to brew the brands of the recently closed

COLLECTIBLE BEER CANS

While the collecting of many different types of brewery advertising and memorabilia (known as breweriana) has been popular for many years, it was specifically the hobby of beer can collecting that seemed to draw the greatest interest and greatest number of new collectors to the field.

There were a scant few collectors of metal beer cans in the 1950s and 60s, but around 1970, a group of them in the St. Louis area formed the Beer Can Collectors of America, which today boasts several thousand members around the world. Its greatest growth was in the mid-1970s, when thousands of people, many of them children and teenagers (including the author) who were too young to actually drink beer, became caught up in the fad. Some accumulated more than 10,000 different brand and label designs, and although the hobby's initial wide popularity seemed to fade along with disco music, it still has a loyal following to this day.

While many brewers were happy to give out free samples of their cans to collectors (as good public relations), some breweries saw an opportunity to sell additional product by designing special, limited edition labels to commemorate various celebrations, often of local interest. This was especially true in 1976, as brewers across the country were swept up in Bicentennial fervor, and many special commemorative cans entered the market. Schmidt was no exception, especially with its headquarters in Philadelphia, where much of the Bicentennial was celebrated. Along those lines, a set of five cans was produced throughout 1976, showing scenes of Betsy Ross sewing the first American flag, Signing the Declaration of Independence, Winter at Valley Forge, and the surrender of General Cornwallis at Yorktown. The cans were made at both the Philadelphia and Cleveland plants, in both twelve and sixteen ounce sizes (although at the time, sixteen ounce cans were not permitted for sale in the state of Ohio), and were an immediate hit with collectors. Cans made in Philadelphia had a star dotting the "i" in Philadelphia, while those made in Cleveland used a plain dot. In 1982, just two years before Schmidt closed its Cleveland plant, it released one commemorative can for the city, although by then the interest in the hobby had decreased significantly.

Numerous other brands appeared in the 1980s, most made at the Philadelphia plant, and some specifically aimed at collectors, such as "Rock & Roll Beer", which featured pictures of Chuck Berry and others. However, the original "spirit of '76" for can collecting was never quite recaptured. Although the hobby is still enjoyed by thousands of collectors, sadly, some things just aren't quite the same when one grows up.

Duquesne Brewing Co. of Pittsburgh. Duquesne had always maintained a healthy following in Ohio, such that its Duke Beer was Cleveland's third best-selling brand. In addition, Duquesne had continued to brew the local favorite P.O.C. brand since the closing of Cleveland's Pilsener Brewing Co. (see entry #41) in 1962. Since most of the Duquesne brands were marketed in Western Pennsylvania and Ohio, they were primarily brewed at the Cleveland facility, allowing a homecoming of sorts for P.O.C. As was often the case with Schmidt, these brands were packaged under the name of the original company, so P.O.C. labels still stated "Pilsener Brewing Co.", and Duke labels stated "Duquesne Brewing Co.", albeit with two cities. Through the years, the Cleveland facility under Schmidt went by numerous other names for packaging purposes, including Rheingold Brewing Co., Bergheim Brewery, Erie Brewery, and Ivy League Brewing Co., leading to some degree of confusion among historians.

Success came quickly, although fleetingly, for the brewery's new owners. The plant was operating at capacity, with more than 300 employees keeping the brewing process going twenty-four hours a day, by 1973. Overall, the company was producing three million barrels annually, making it one of the ten largest regional brewers in the country, and the Cleveland plant alone was responsible for as much as $40 million in sales annually. Despite this, some of the same competitive pressures and economic instabilities that were hurting Carling in the mid-1970s began to take their toll on Schmidt. By this time, the Schmidt plant was one of only four remaining operating breweries in the state of Ohio, meaning Schmidt would need to compete primarily with large remaining regional and national breweries. Unlike Carling, Schmidt had multiple brands to rely on, and it was attempting only to maintain regional, not national, success. The Schmidt, Duke, and P.O.C. brands were well-established in their respective regional markets, helping the company to compete locally with the likes of Anheuser-Busch, Pabst, and Miller. Sales dropped in 1974, leading to a loss of four million dollars, and the Norristown, PA. plant, the smallest of the three in the company, was closed. The Schmidt family descendants who still managed the company began looking for a buyer, and after a potential sale to the G. Heileman Brewing Co. fell through, they found a buyer in April 1976, when William H. Pflaumer, owner of the largest Schmidt's wholesale distributorship, purchased the company. With aggressive new marketing, sales improved almost immediately and business was stabilized for a time.

The company acquired the brands of the defunct Reading (PA.) Brewing Co. in 1976, with production of those taking place at the Philadelphia plant. In 1977, the company acquired the Rheingold Breweries, Inc., of NY. and NJ., including New York City favorites Knickerbocker Natural Beer, made for years in Manhattan by the Jacob Ruppert Brewery, and Rheingold Beer, whose larger distribution brought some of its production to Cleveland. Further shakeups in the brewing industry led to the closing of the 123-year-old Erie (PA.) Brewing Co. in early 1978, after which its popular Koehler, Light Lager, Yacht Club, and Olde Pub brands were acquired by Schmidt, and their production continued in Cleveland. In 1981, the century-old Henry Ortlieb Brewing Co. of Philadelphia closed, and again Schmidt was there to keep its brands alive for a few more years.

In 1981, the company renamed itself as the Christian Schmidt Brewing Co. By this time, however, the company had again begun to see dwindling sales, as competition from the larger national companies continued to take a toll and the costs of operation continued to grow. This trend only worsened over the next three years, and in June 1984, the decision was made to close the Cleveland plant for good. The news did not sit well with employees, who tried to understand why their jobs were about to disappear. Union boss Anthony Sapienza stated, "The public just doesn't accept local products. They think if it's made out of the country, or even out of town, it's better." The company had sponsored numerous civic promotions, such as 1983's Days of the Ships Festival, but local sales weren't enough to keep the local plant open. William Hipp stated his frustration as well: "Maybe these were pale in comparison to, say, what Budweiser does out at the airport (the Budweiser Cleveland Grand Prix at Burke Lakefront Airport), but I think ours were more charitable activities than just a race," [both quotes taken from the Cleveland *Plain Dealer*, June 21, 1984]. In any case, the grand, historic brewery on the city's east side,

Cleveland's largest and last, stood quiet and empty at year's end.

In Philadelphia, business was not much better, and the main plant there closed in 1987. Many of the Schmidt brands were purchased by the G. Heileman Brewing Co., thus joining Carling Black Label Beer, still in active production. The Koehler brand (first brewed in 1883), Duke (shortened from Duquesne, it first appeared in 1899), and P.O.C. (first brewed around 1907), were not part of the Heileman purchase, however, and their respective histories came to an end. This saddened the few remaining P.O.C. devotees in Cleveland, although their numbers had dwindled over the years, reflecting a loss of interest in local brands; while 75,000 cases of P.O.C. were being sold each month in Cuyahoga County in the mid-1970s, that number had dropped to between 5,000 and 10,000 cases per month a decade later. Those who were old enough to remember P.O.C.'s glory days happily took note when the brand made a brief comeback in 1999, made by the Local Brewing Co. in nearby Westlake.

Schmidt's Beer was merged with a separate Schmidt Beer, originally made by the Jacob Schmidt Brewing Co. of St. Paul, MN., and made for many years by Heileman. The new Schmidt's Beer received an entirely new label, retaining only the old Schmidt's of Philadelphia logo, and was marketed mainly in the Midwest. Even after Heileman's bankruptcies in 1991 and 1996 and subsequent purchase by the Stroh Brewing Co. (and Stroh's subsequent purchase by the Pabst Brewing Company), Schmidt's continues to be brewed and sold in the Midwest, contract brewed at Miller Brewing Co. plants, to this day. Meanwhile, the Rheingold brand was purchased by a new New York City-based microbrewery, the Rheingold Brewing Co., which currently markets it in its original New York and New Jersey territories.

Back on Quincy Avenue, the huge brewery remained empty for a year, before being purchased by Stern Enterprises of Pittsburgh, with the intention to produce industrial alcohol at the plant, although the plan never took shape. Instead, the plant slowly decayed and was vandalized over the next decade into one of the city's worst eyesores, with the huge smokestack at the rear still stating "Carling Ale" as the only indication of the plant's history. Like many older industrial structures, the plant also turned out to be filled with asbestos, strewn around the property by vandals and those that ventured inside to steal copper pipes and anything else that was salvageable. Demolition was delayed by the high cost of removing the asbestos, and neighbors and city officials complained for years until the owners were fined over $200,000 by the Ohio EPA to have the asbestos removed. Late in 1994, the plant was finally demolished, although after the rubble was gone, the property was found to contain a substantial amount of PCBs (polychlorinated biphenyls, a type of toxic liquid used as an electrical insulator), which still needed to be removed. The EPA continued to be involved with further litigation through 1998, when the cleanup was completed. In total, the Stern estate claimed to have spent $2.5 million on the plant's demolition and cleanup (approximately the same amount that C. Schmidt & Sons had paid Carling for the plant and its equipment in 1971).

Today, the huge 11-acre site remains vacant, surrounded by a high fence. It was a sad end to a site filled with eighty years of industrial history. Nevertheless, Peerless automobiles still exist in museums and collectors' garages, and many Clevelanders fondly remember hearing "Mabel, Black Label" in their younger days, while enjoying a cold brew on a hot afternoon after work or at a ball game. It is those memories which form the true legacy of the city's largest brewery, the one that made a decent run at the big boys, but ultimately fell just shy.

50. Real Brewery, Inc.

Cleveland's only other brewery to begin operations in the post-Prohibition era was considerably less successful than Carling. The Real Distributing Company was formed to take advantage of the return of beer in 1933. Located at 1109 Central Avenue (on a section later renamed as part of Carnegie Avenue), the company was headed by president Thomas W. Centanni, with Peter M. Ciotta as vice-president, Mike Mosa as treasurer, Arthur H. Ganger as secretary, and Walter E. Cook as general manager. In early 1935, the company was reported to be spending $75,000 to establish a small brewing operation in conjunction with the distributorship. Henry Mitenzwey was hired from the Home Brewing Co. of Richmond, VA. to be master brewer, although it appears that the beer produced was sold only in barrels, not bottles. While it is unclear how long brewing operations lasted, there was never any significant degree of success for its Sovereign brand of beer, and both the brewery and distributorship had closed by the end of 1935, leaving no remains.

51. Great Lakes Brewing Company

After the closing of the Schmidt brewery on the city's east side in 1984, Cleveland (and all of northeast Ohio) went for four years with no brewing operation whatsoever. This would change in 1988, with the founding of the city's first and longest-lasting brewpub and microbrewery.

A revolution of sorts had begun in 1977, with the founding of the New Albion Brewery in Sonoma, CA., the country's first "microbrewery", or "craft brewery". Its purpose was not to make as much beer and money as possible, as had been the industry standard for many years. It was, in fact, an attempt to bring back some of the beer styles that had been popular for ages in Europe, but which had been long-lost in America, as consumers had become accustomed to drinking mass-produced, and often fairly bland, beers, most of relatively light body and taste. While the New Albion Brewery had closed by 1982, it sparked an interest in opening similar establishments elsewhere in the country, each of which would tend to cater to a relatively small geographic area. Soon after this came the appearance of the "brewpub", in which the beers made on-site could be consumed along with a meal. Brewpubs, in which the beer that was brewed was generally just sold in that establishment or possibly a few other local spots, tended to be smaller than microbreweries, which made larger amounts of beer for packaging and distribution, either throughout a city or possibly a larger geographic area. As the 1980s progressed, both microbreweries and brewpubs gradually appeared across the country, some seeing tremendous success and others eventually falling by the wayside.

Ohio's first brewpub; in the summer, diners can eat at tables outside, in front of and beside the building

It wasn't until 1988, however, that Ohio finally joined the growing trend, when, on September 6th, the state's first brewpub opened its doors. The Great Lakes Brewing Company was established at 2516 Market Avenue, in the Ohio City district on the near west side of town. The new venture occupied structures originally built in 1864, and which had previously housed the Market Tavern and McClean's Feed & Seed. Its centerpiece is a huge mahogany bar, thought to be the city's oldest. Eliot Ness, the real-life leader of "The Untouchables", had frequented the same bar many years earlier, when he had become the city's safety director, years after taking down Al Capone and his gang. A young John D. Rockefeller worked in a law office upstairs (now banquet rooms) prior to founding the huge Standard Oil Co. In addition, the building stands across the street from Cleveland's famed West Side Market, which operates to this day. Historically, the site was ideal for a Cleveland-oriented brewing establishment.

The brewpub was the brainchild of brothers Patrick and Daniel Conway. Previously a Chicago high school teacher, Patrick had recently spent time in Europe, visiting some of the many small breweries that dot the landscape in Germany, where craft brewing is still appreciated as an art. Many European beer drinkers are conoisseurs of the art and view beer like they do wine, enjoying its many variations. Conway appreciated these robust, flavorful brews and saw the potential for this art to return in America, as it had been a century earlier, when most brewers were still first-generation German immigrants. Cleveland's new brewpub would incorporate a very European approach to brewing from the beginning, as Conway explained, "We were determined to use only the freshest ingredients, no preservatives and chemicals. We also refused to succumb to pasteurization and sterile filtering, both of which ultimately compromise flavor."

Upon his return to America, Conway enlisted the partnership of his younger brother Daniel, a local banker, and the two began putting together a new company and brewing facility. Symbolic of the devotion to producing only a top quality brew, Conway hired Thaine Johnson as his first Master Brewer. Johnson had been the final master brewer at the Schmidt brewery when it closed four years earlier, and he was well versed in the technical aspects of brewing, and the new venture allowed him to formulate new recipes and produce some of the brands that remain popular today. Other head brewers have followed, including Andy Tveekrem (who left in 1998 to join Crooked River's Frederick Brewing Co. division in Maryland), Tim Rastetter (who left to join Akron's Liberty Street Brewing Company and others), and currently Brian Lottig, and they have continued the high standards of brewing established at the company's beginning.

In addition to the brewing of craft beers, the brewpub would quickly develop a favorable repuation for the food served there. A wide variety of soups, salads, sandwiches, steaks, chicken, pizza, seafood, and desserts are available to whet the appetite, and the restaurant has received many stellar reviews in magazines through the years, both locally and nationally. The restaurant occupies several rooms in the old building, including a quaint, stone-lined cellar in which patrons can view the pub's aging tanks, and an adjacent outdoor beer garden when the weather is agreeable.

Upon opening for business, the first brew was named The Heismann, in honor of the player after whom the college football award is named, who lived nearby. This soon was renamed as Dortmunder Gold, and it remains the company's most popular brand to this day. Approximately 1,000 barrels were brewed in the first year, all sold in the pub. Within the first year, however, a small amount of the beer was bottled for distribution to a handful of local retailers, delivered by the Conways themselves.

Other brands include Burning River Pale Ale (named for an infamous incident in 1969 when the heavily polluted Cuyahoga River caught fire from an oil slick on the surface), The Eliot Ness (Vienna Style Lager), The Edmund Fitzgerald Porter (named after the huge cargo ship that sank in 1975 and was made famous in a song by Gordon Lightfoot), Conway's Irish Ale (named after Patrick Conway, the brothers' grandfather, an Irish immigrant who became a local policeman for many years), The Holy Moses (a Belgian wheat beer, named after Moses Cleaveland, the city's founder), Commodore Perry India Pale Ale, Moondog Ale (traditional bitter, named after the Moondog Coronation Ball, thought to be the first rock 'n roll event, staged in Cleveland in 1952 by disc jockey Alan Freed), Barrel Select Pils (introduced at the company's ten-year anniversary celebration, and the label of which shows an actual worker at the old Schlather brewery carrying a barrel), Mather Lager (named after the William G. Mather, a 1925 Great Lakes ore freighter that became a permanent museum along the city's lakeshore), Cleveland Brown Ale (named for the return of the expansion Cleveland Browns football team in 1999), and a newer brand, Locktender Lager (golden Munich Helles lager, named for the nearby Ohio Canal, the locktenders of which also served as tavern owners during the early 1800s; a portion of the proceeds from sales of this brand were to be donated to the Ohio Canal Corridor, a non-profit group involved in developing and promoting the Ohio & Erie Canal National Heritage Corridor, a 110-mile stretch from Cleveland south to Zoar in Tuscarawas County).

Several brands are available on a seasonal basis, such as Rockefeller Bock in the spring, Oktoberfest, and Christmas Ale. In addition, there is a variable array of craft brews on tap in the pub, some unavailable anywhere else and often for only a lim-

The brewery's 1998 expansion into part of the former Schlather brewery complex was topped by a modern, two-story brewhouse with large glass windows showing the public the large brew kettles. Tours of the plant are available to the public on a regular basis.

ited time, such as Cellar Dweller Kolsch Style Ale, Ohio City Oatmeal Stout, Valentine's Day Honey Ale, Emmett's Imperial Stout, Aloha Ale, California Common Beer, CBA Classic Brown Ale, CBC Symposium Beer (a spiced Belgian Ale specially brewed for a craft brewers' conference), Glockenspiel dark wheat beer, Highlander and Loch Erie Scottish Ales, Nosferatu Stock Ale, Mclean's Golden Ale (named after the building's original tenant, McClean's Feed & Seed), Independence American Red Ale, Grand Cru Belgian Ale, Wolfhound Irish Dry Stout, Schwarzbier, York Street Bitter, Peerless Pilsner, Pilot Alt Beer, and Market Street Wheat (hefeweizen). Several of these variations contained alcohol between seven and eight percent, taking advantage of a state law passed in 2002, which changed the definition of beer in Ohio to include brews up to 12% alcohol by volume, instead of the traditional six percent definition of the past. Great Lakes was one of the proponents of the law change, and the change allowed for a wider variety of craft brews similar to those brewed in Europe. These higher-alcohol brews often incur a higher price, and are primarily served only in the pub, as opposed to being packaged for mass distribution. One exception, however, was 2003's bottled Anniversary Ale, which had 9.5% alcohol by volume.

Within three years, Great Lakes beers were being sold by thirty different retailers. The brewery's first expansion, costing $250,000, was completed in 1993, and consisted of new fermentation tanks and a new bottling machine which increased daily output seven-fold. By the end of that year, total production had increased to 5,000 barrels. The next expansion, costing over one million dollars, was completed in early 1995 and extended the 15-barrel brewhouse into an adjacent building, increasing the annual capacity to 12,000 barrels. Another, more dramatic expansion began around 1997 and moved the main brewing facility into a nearby building that had originally served as the Schlather Brewing Company's stables and bottling works (and where what was left of the Cleveland-Sandusky Co. operated during Prohibition). Costing in the neighborhood of $7 million, this expansion included a 75-barrel brewing system and elevated the plant's annual capacity to 70,000 barrels. At this point, the company officially moved into the "microbrewery" category, although the original brewpub across the street continued to flourish.

In 2002, the brewery sold over 21,000 barrels (an impressive seventeen percent increase over 2001), making it the country's 52nd largest brewer, and this number continued to rise in the following years as the Great Lakes brands were being distributed throughout the Great Lakes region, as far west as Chicago, and as far east as Washington, D.C. Allowing this wide geographic distribution is the constant refrigeration of the beer from the time it is bottled, throughout its storage, distribution, and time on store shelves. All bottles have a "consumer friendly" date, which is ninety days from the time of bottling (a relatively brief period for a craft beer). A team of observers monitor Great Lakes beers in stores throughout the region, making sure that the beer is stored properly and rotated on the shelves

Through the years, Great Lakes has won a long and impressive list of awards for most of its beers, beginning in 1990, when Dortmunder Gold won a gold medal at the Great American Beer Festival. The following year, Edmund Fitzgerald Porter won a gold medal, a feat which was repeated in 1993. Great Lakes took two awards in 1992, a gold for Moondog Ale and a bronze for Commodore Perry IPA. 1993 also saw a silver medal given to Burning River Pale Ale. Peerless Pilsner then received a silver medal in 1995. At the 1999 GABF, a bronze medal was given to Ohio City Oatmeal Stout, which was followed in 2001 by a silver medal for Glockenspiel Weizenbock, and in 2002 a third gold medal for Edmund Fitzgerald Porter. In 1994, Great Lakes was named as "Microbrewery of the Year" by Chicago's Beverage Testing Institute. Edmund Fitzgerald Porter won a bronze award at the 1997 World Beer Cup, and a silver the following year. At the World Beer Championships (held by the Beverage Testing Institute), Dortmunder Gold was noted as the world champion in its category for eight straight years from 1994 to 2001, the only beer to achieve such a feat, and also received a gold medal in 2004. In addition, The Eliot Ness Lager won a silver medal at the WBC in 1995, followed by gold medals in 1996-97 and again in 2000-01 and 2003; Burning River and Moondog Ales both won gold medals for three straight years in 1994-96, after which Burning River added silver medals in 2001 and 2002; Edmund Fitzgerald Porter won gold medals in 1994, 1996, 1997, 2001, and 2002; Holy Moses won gold and

silver medals in 1995-96 and again in 2000-01; Conway's Irish Ale won gold medals in 1995 and 2001, and a silver medal in 2002; Munich Dunkel Lager won a silver medal in 1996; Wit's End Belgian White won a silver medal in 1995; Peerless Pilsner won a gold medal in 1995; Emmet's Imperial Stout won a silver medal in 1996 and a gold medal in 2002; Market House Wheat won a silver medal in 1996 and a bronze medal in 2001; Commodore Perry IPA won a gold medal in 1996; Ohio City Oatmeal Stout won a gold medal in 1996 and silver medals in 1999 and 2002; Loch Erie Scotch Ale won silver medals in 1995 and 2002; Locktender Lager won a silver medal in 2002 and a bronze medal in 2003; Barrel Select Pils won a silver medal in 2002; and Christmas Ale won a silver medal in 2001. Undoubtedly more awards will follow in the future.

In 2001, Great Lakes launched a "zero waste initiative", aimed at operating the brewery in the most environmentally-friendly way possible, minimizing use of energy and resources while maximizing re-use of resources. The company has encouraged any ideas which may help to keep waste to a bare minimum, and in many cases increase profits as well. Spent grains are utilized as a medium to grow gourmet mushrooms, as well as various organically-grown vegetables and fruits. They are also used in the making of bread and pretzels, and are being utilized as feed for cattle (and therefore minimizing the use of hormones, antibiotics, and other chemicals that are increasingly thought to be harmful to both the animals and humans). Spent yeast and hops are also mixed in for use in feeding local cattle. Most of these spent grains were, a century earlier, dumped into local sewer systems or just into the street (as was known to happen at the Schlather brewery, and numerous others in the area), where they would create a powerful stench on a hot day, until rains came to wash them away. Recycling of cardboard, glass, and paper also take place in the brewery, and water in the bottle rinsing process is recycled as well. New ideas are always being examined, such as the possible use of solar and wind energy in the future.

The Conway brothers carefully cultivated their product name, and grew slowly over their first fifteen years in business, being careful not to overextend themselves financially. The result was arguably the most successful brewpub/microbrewery entity in the Midwest. Great Lakes watched as more than forty other brewpubs and microbreweries opened in eastern Ohio alone in the 1990s, most of which were unable to survive for more than a few years. As Great Lakes is likely to see continued increases in sales, it is poised for long-term success, all the more impressive considering the instability of the brewing industry and the troubled economy of the early part of the new millenium. A tremendous amount of information about the brewery's history, beers, brewing process, pub menu, trivia, and an online gift shop are available through the company's website, www.greatlakesbrewing.com, and the brewery produces a regular newsletter for the public, appropriately titled *Much Abrew*. Great Lakes also operates a branch pub in the concourse at Cleveland Hopkins Airport, and although no beer is brewed at the site, it gives first-time visitors to Cleveland a quick peek at one of the city's most successful enterprises.

52. Crooked River Brewing Company

The first brewing operation in the historic Flats district in nearly a century, the Crooked River Brewing Company opened its doors June 15, 1994 as the city's first true microbrewery. Operating in the former Scottish Tool and Die Building at 1101 Center Street, just a block from the site of John M. Hughes' nineteenth century ale brewery on West Street, and across the street from the Center Street bridge across the Cuyahoga River (the only operating swing bridge in the country), the brewery incorporated its location into its image and marketing from the beginning. In fact, the brewery's name was most fitting, as "Cuyahoga" is the Mohawk tribe name for "crooked river".

Crooked River brewery standing in the shadow of the Detroit-Superior bridge in 1999

As a microbrewery, the company met the definition by brewing less than one million barrels annually, yet still packaging all of its beer for distribution elsewhere, as compared to a brewpub, which may package some of its beer but still sells most of it on-site in a restaurant or bar setting. While Crooked River did maintain a small bar, it was more of a "tasting room".

The new company was the brainchild of brewmaster Stephan Danckers and partner Stuart Sheridan. Danckers was one of the most experienced brewers in the state, beginning with a Master's Degree in Brewing Science from the University of California at Davis. After additional studies at the University of Munich Brewing and Science School, he returned to America to work for the Stroh Brewery Company. In 1989, he came to Cleveland to take the brewmaster's position at Melbourne's Brewing Co., one of the first brewpubs in the area. Three years later, he and Sheridan were making plans to put together their all-new brewing venture, and after investors were found, work started on the project.

Costing $1.5 million to construct, the Crooked River brewery began operation with an annual capacity of 6,000 barrels, although within three years, additional improvements had doubled this number. Danckers created the recipes for all of the beers produced by the company, and there were many: Black Forest Lager (taking the name from the popular brand made until the 1950s by the Cleveland Home Brewing Co.), Settlers Ale, Lighthouse Gold, Bicentennial Beer (for the city's bicentennial in 1996), Island Hops, Erie Nights Pumpkin Brew, Cool Mule Porter, Irish Style Red, Yuletide Ale (spiced with ginger, cinnamon, cloves, and orange peel), and Doppelbock, just to name a few. Several other seasonal varieties appeared through the following years, as well as Ballpark Draft, sold only at Cleveland Indians baseball games at Jacobs Field, and Arena Draft, sold only at Cavaliers basketball games at Gund Arena.

One feature of Danckers' brewing process was a cold-filtering system which allowed the beer to be sold without pasteurization. Pasteurization gives beer a longer shelf-life, but tends to damage the beer's flavor. While most smaller brewers prefer to avoid pasteurization, it makes their beers harder to sell through retailers due to their need to stay refrigerated. The cold-filtering process allowed Crooked River beers to be kept at room temperature for a longer time without spoiling (120 days from the time of bottling), and this gave the company a great advantage against other craft brewers, all of whom were competing for space on store shelves. Aggressive marketing in the company's early years had Crooked River Beer available at over 1,000 outlets in Northeast Ohio by 1997. In the summer of that year, the brewery was one of the primary sponsors of the Cleveland Grand Prix at Burke Lakefront Airport downtown. Sales grew from 3,300 barrels in 1995 (the first full year in business) to around 9,000 barrels in 1998.

In addition to aggressive marketing came an aggressive approach to growth of the physical plant. Additional expansion of the brewing facility was expensive, but by 1999, Crooked River was utilizing state-of-the-art equipment in every facet of its production. While Danckers was the brewmaster, overseeing all operations, he was assisted by several brewers who came and went over the years, including Mark Ward, Jim Barker, Jay Braun, and Steve Miller.

The brewery's web site, www.crookedriver.com (no longer available), gave a virtual tour of the facility on-line, showed the entire brewing process, and provided the following tidbits: Between 1,700 and 2,100 pounds of malt were used for each thirty-barrel batch of beer brewed. The brewery used city water, which originally came from Lake Erie. The brewery then purified it further to remove chlorine and other impurities. After the beer was brewed, it was transferred to one of ten 60-barrel fermentation tanks. Four 30-barrel tanks were used for the longer lagering process. After each brew, all equipment was cleaned and sanitized (Danckers stated that sixty percent of a brewer's time is spent cleaning equipment). Ales were fermented at 65 degrees over three weeks, while lagers took two weeks at 52 degrees and another three weeks at 32 degrees. The cold-filtering process took place in bright tanks, where the beer was finished. The bottling line cost nearly $250,000 and filled eighty bottles per

minute, or 200 cases per hour. For draft beer, forty kegs could be filled per hour. One of the key elements to the bottling process was the removal of all but one percent of the air in the bottle, which helped to keep the beer fresher longer.

During the company's first several years, it found a high degree of critical success for its various brands and styles of beer. At the Great American Beer Festival, it first won a Silver Medal in 1995 for Irish Red Ale. This was followed by a Gold Medal in 1997 for Cool Mule Porter and Silver Medals in 1999 for Pumpkin Brew and Settler's Ale. At the 1998 World Beer Championships, three Silver Medals were won for Yuletide Ale, Lighthouse Gold Ale, and Settler's Ale. At the 2000 World Beer Cup, another Silver Medal was won for Settler's Ale (by that time renamed as Original ESB).

Expansion of the plant and intense marketing sold a lot of beer, but this came at a heavy price. As the company was growing very rapidly, it required significant investment from outside sources to pay for new equipment and expensive marketing agreements. By early 1998, Sheridan had left the company and a new management team came in to handle the brewery's finances. However, new president Mitch Frankel announced in May that the company would file for Chapter 11 reorganization (allowing the company to be shielded from its creditors while working out plans to repay debts). With debts of $900,000 and assets of $450,000, a large infusion of capital was required to keep the company alive. The future began to look bleak by late summer, when the company went up for sale through U. S. Bankruptcy Court.

Salvation for Crooked River came at the end of August, however, when the company was purchased for $540,000 by 46-year-old local entrepreneur C. David Snyder. Snyder had just recently sold his technology consulting firm, Realogic, reportedly worth $42 million, and was looking to switch gears when he heard of the brewery's financial troubles. Fortunately, he was a fan of Crooked River beers and was willing to bring the needed capital and his keen business acumen to keep the brewery going. He and new partner Chris Livingston eventually formed a new holding company, the Snyder International Brewing Group, LLC (SIBG), to manage Crooked River and other companies yet to come.

Taking a more concrete path toward growth than in the past, Snyder established a definitive short and long-term business plan which involved heavy marketing in the Northeast Ohio area and a gradual expansion into a larger geographic area. Part of this local marketing included the addition of two new brands: Expansion Draft, a kolsch-style ale which was made to celebrate the return of the new expansion Cleveland Browns football team to the NFL in 1999. As soon as the team began playing in its new lakefront stadium, Crooked River also began making Stadium Lager to sell during Browns games. In an unusual twist in the microbrewery industry, the brand was packaged in sixteen-ounce aluminum cans. Since the Cleveland brewery had no canning line, the brand was contract brewed by the 92-year-old Jones Brewing Company of Smithton, PA. Jones had specialized in contract brewing for a number of years, and it had a canning line.

Around this time, Crooked River's four most popular brands were renamed and repackaged with almost generic labels, removing much of the Cleveland connection to the brand as it sought a wider geographic market. In the process, Black Forest became Crooked River Select Lager; Settler's Ale became Crooked River Original ESB (Extra Special Bitter); Cool Mule became Crooked River Robust Porter; and Lighthouse Gold became Crooked River Kolsch Ale. In 2002 came the addition of Crooked River Light Lager as well.

As soon as Crooked River was on sound financial footing, Snyder soon found himself purchasing another financially troubled company. In June 1999, it was announced that SIBG had purchased the rights to brew all of the Hudepohl-Schoenling Brewing Co. brands of Cincinnati. Hudepohl-Schoenling came with a century's worth of history in that city, dating to when Ludwig Hudepohl first began brewing beer at a plant on McMicken Avenue. Hudepohl continued in business after Prohibition, absorbing the nearby Burger Brewing Co. in 1973, and operating as an individual company (best-known for its Hudy Delight and Christian Moerlein brands) until 1986, when it merged with the city's other survivor, the Schoenling Brewing Co. Schoenling had opened in 1934 and was best-known for its Little Kings Ale and Mount Everest Malt Liquor brands, which were sold through much of the midwest. Since 1986, Hudepohl-Schoenling had operated out of the Schoenling plant on Central Parkway.

In 1997, however, that plant with its annual capacity of nearly 400,000 barrels was sold to the Boston Beer

Co., maker of the nationally distributed Samuel Adams brands of beer. The Hudepohl-Schoenling brands were still made under contract at the plant, but their market share had been in gradual decline over the past few years, and the Lichtendahl family which owned the rights to the brands was losing interest in the brewing industry, in favor of their TradeWinds brands of bottled tea. The time was right for SIBG to purchase the aging company and infuse new life and marketing into it. The acquisition added twelve total brands and approximately 65,000 barrels to SIBG's annual output, suddenly putting it on the list of the top twenty brewing groups in the country. Annual sales of the combined companies was $8 million, up from $1.8 million for Crooked River alone. [For a full history of the Hudepohl and Schoenling breweries, I would recommend reading *Over The Barrel, Volumes One and Two*, by Timothy J. Holian, covering the entire history of the brewing industry in the Cincinnati region.]

Two months after the Hudepohl-Schoenling acquisition, SIBG was at it again, on a larger scale. By late August 1999, it had acquired a controlling interest in the Frederick Brewing Co. of Frederick, MD. Frederick was a microbrewer with a history similar to Crooked River, only larger. Formed in 1992, it was the largest craft brewer in the Mid-Atlantic region and had recently occupied a new facility with an annual capacity of 170,000 barrels. Actual output in 1998, however, was only 31,500 barrels, giving it $5.5 million in sales but a net loss of $4.7 million. Its stock was publicly traded on the NASDAQ market, although its value was plummeting. SIBG paid $2 million in cash for 4.4 million shares of Frederick common stock (at roughly 45 cents per share), giving it a 51 percent voting majority. It also paid $422,000 to purchase the brewery's five-acre facility. In the process, it absorbed the company's debt of $2.6 million ($1.2 million of which was forgiven by Frederick's creditors). Chris Livingston became president of Frederick, replacing co-founders Marjorie McGinnis and Kevin Brannon.

The addition of Frederick boosted SIBG's annual output to nearly 110,000 barrels and gave it fifty total brands, including Frederick's four families of beer: Nine varieties of Blue Ridge American-style ales and lagers (six of which had won awards in national competitions), seven varieties of Wild Goose English-style beers, five varieties of Brimstone specialty beers, and two varieties of Hempen Ale, made with actual hemp seeds.

The merger also gave SIBG a tremendous increase in capacity for the production of all of its subsidiary brands. With the relatively small Crooked River facility in Cleveland operating at its maximum capacity of 12,000 barrels annually, economics had dictated by 2000 that the company's birthplace be closed, with all Crooked River brand production being moved to the much larger facility in Maryland by the end of the year. The final products were then shipped back to Ohio and surrounding areas for distribution. Similarly, in 2001, Hudepohl-Schoenling's packaging contract with the Boston Beer Co. expired, with production of the Little Kings and Christian Moerlein brands transferred to Frederick. The Hudepohl and Burger brands, which were sold in cans, were contract brewed and packaged at the City Brewing Co. (formerly the G. Heileman plant) in LaCrosse, WI., and then sent to Cincinnati for distribution. Through all of these changes, Crooked River maintained a distribution facility in Cleveland, and the SIBG headquarters remained downtown at 1940 E. 6th Street.

Despite the reorganization under Snyder, Frederick's operating losses continued; the Snyder group's overall 2002 sales of 34,000 barrels made it the country's 43rd largest brewer, but that represented a decline of more than 22% from 2001. With more than $3.1 million in debts, the company appointed Mark Dottore as receiver in Cuyahoga County Common Pleas Court in January 2003. Over the following year, a reorganization was planned in which the Frederick Brewing Co. would be sold to pay off debts (although the Snyder group was attempting to repurchase the plant), and some of the brands (such as Christian Moerlein) were sold off to a new buyer who intended to continue their production. The Crooked River and Hudepohl-Schoenling brands were seen only sporadically in Ohio through this period. By 2004, there was still no word on the company's long-term financial situation or the future of the various brands.

If one compares Crooked River to the Great Lakes Brewing Co., one sees a dramatic difference in approaches to company growth. Great Lakes grew slowly, first establishing a name and a reputation as a brewpub before undertaking a large-scale expansion to achieve microbrewery status. Crooked River's history is similar to many other microbreweries which opened in the 1990s, growing quickly, then sliding into financial difficulties when expansion was undertaken during difficult times of industry competition. To be sure, if Dave Snyder had not come forward, Crooked River may well have closed its doors like so many other craft brewers did around the same time. As one will see in the following entries, as of 2003 only two other brewpubs remained open in the city of Cleveland, both owned and operated by the same national company. The American brewing industry continues to be a difficult place in which to thrive.

53. Rock Bottom Restaurant and Brewery

The Powerhouse is well-known to most Clevelanders as a giant century-old structure, that for years provided power to Cleveland's electric railway and streetcar system. A city landmark, on the west side of the Flats district at 2000 Sycamore Street, the building is best known for its huge smokestacks. Since the close of the streetcar era, however, it had been empty and awaiting the wrecker's ball. When the Flats district was revived as a social gathering place in the 1990s, the entire structure was renovated and now contains four levels of shops and restaurants, one of which is the Rock Bottom Restaurant and Brewery. When this opened on September 15, 1995, it became the 21st in the Denver-based chain of restaurants across the country. The company also owns a subsidiary chain that includes the Cleveland Chophouse and Brewery.

The Powerhouse and Rock Bottom Brewery with the Cleveland skyline in the background

The original brewer was Steven Miller, and he has had several successors through the years, including Josh Breckle, Tom Gray, Pete Crowley, and most recently Toby Parsons. The 12-barrel J. V. Northwest brewhouse has an annual capacity of 2,500 barrels (with actual output about half of that), with six standard brews available: Cleveland American Light Beer, Terminal Stout, Walleye Wheat, Powerhouse Pale Ale, River Bend Red, and Dawg Pound Brown Ale (named for the Cleveland Browns football team, this replaced Buzzard Brown Ale.) Seasonal and specialty brews have been offered as well, including Blitzen Christmas Ale and Christmas Scotch Ale, Strawberry Blonde Ale, Abbey Dubbel Trappist Ale, Hefe-Weizen, Oktobyfest Lager, Big Ben English Pale Ale, Fire Chief India Pale Ale, Honey Raspberry Wheat, Black Cherry Porter, Catcher In The Rye, Irish and Milk Stouts, Irish Amber, and Devil's Thumb Bock. *Northern Ohio Live* magazine readers voted Rock Bottom as Cleveland's Best Brew Pub of 2000. More information is available on the company web site at www.rockbottom.com.

54. Diamondback Brewery & Pub/Barons of Cleveland

The renovation of Cleveland's "Gateway District" began in 1994 with the opening of Jacobs Field, the home of the Cleveland Indians, and Gund Arena (named, of course, after the Gund brewery family descendants who owned the NBA Cleveland Cavaliers basketball team), home of both the Cavaliers and the minor league Lumberjacks and Barons hockey teams. The area around these buildings quickly developed into a social gathering place, with several restaurants and bars opening for sports fans and workers in nearby office buildings.

The Diamondback Brewery & Pub opened June 12, 1996 at 724 Prospect Avenue, and offered three levels of dining and entertainment. Co-owners David Hill and Jim Harris saw rapid success, especially on days when the Indians or Cavaliers were playing, and their new venture was voted as the "Best New Restaurant for 1997" by *Cleveland Magazine*. Brewmaster Bill Morgan and assistant Dan Maerzluft had a 15-barrel brewhouse installed for the production of five standard brews: Black Diamond pale ale, Bonfire porter, Pennant pilsener beer, Whole Wheat Hefe-Weizen, and Rattler Red. In addition, several seasonal brews appeared, including Harvest Moon multi-grain beer, Dunkel Weizen, 90 Shilling Scotch Ale, Maibock, Abbey Road Dubbel beer, Cherry Bomb beer, Ruby Tuesday raspberry ale, Half Wit white ale, James Brown Ale, Honey Pumpkin Ale, Catcher In the Rye, and Schwarzwald German style black beer.

At the 1996 World Beer Championships, Diamondback's brewers received a silver medal for Oktoberfest lager, and bronze medals for Bonfire smoked porter and Steelcut oatmeal stout. At the Great American Beer Festival in 1997, they received a gold medal for Gueuze Lambic Belgian Style Ale; in 1998 received a gold medal for Russian Imperial Stout and silver medal for Framboise Lambic Belgian Style Ale; and in 1999 received a gold medal for Hempen-Roggen in the "experimental beer" category. In 1997, the brewhouse was expanded to allow an annual capacity of 2,000 barrels, and a kegging line was added to sell beer on draft elsewhere in the region. In early 1999, however, Morgan and Maerzluft left for other brewing positions, and were replaced by Marc Anievas.

Despite the popularity of Diamondback, its success still depended largely on sporting events. While the Indians had tremendous success in the late 1990s, which led to hundreds of sold-out games a half-mile from the brewpub, this only represented six months of the year. The relatively dismal performance of the Cavaliers during this same period led to decreasing attendance at Gund Arena, which worsened after a disastrous 1998 NBA players strike. The arena, which has a capacity of over 20,000, was often only 60% full, while Lumberjacks games only drew a few thousand fans at best.

Several different menus and styles of cuisine were tried in attempts to increase business. In January 2000, however, Hill announced that the popular spot was closing, stating "We're losing money...we used to do $5,000 to $8,000 with the Cavs. Now we barely do $1,800 (in tabs on game nights)."

By the summer of that year, however, the site had been converted into Barons Brewpub, with a new owner in Brett Babick. Anievas remained as the brewer, although Barons had closed its doors after just three months of business.

55. Western Reserve Brewing Company

Cleveland's third microbrewery, the Western Reserve Brewing Co. opened on July 18, 1997 in a former armored car warehouse at 4130 Commerce Avenue, on the city's east side. Andrew Craze was the head brewer, with assistance from Jeff Ogden, and Gavin Smith was the company's CEO. Craze was a native of Cleveland Heights who began home brewing in Seattle while working as an engineer for Microsoft, and he later graduated from the Siebel Institute of brewing. He and Smith, a native of Toledo, found a common interest in brewing while out West and decided to make a career of it.

Their 20-barrel, J. V. Northwest brewing system allowed an annual capacity of 4,500 barrels. Three styles were available year-round: Western Reserve American Wheat Beer, Amber Ale, and Nut Brown Ale. Seasonal brands included Twist & Stout, Cloud Nine Belgian Style White Beer, Lake Effect Winter Ale, McDamon's Irish Ale, and Bockzilla Bock Beer. In a nod to historical tradition, the brewery held a ceremony in April 2000 in which religious leaders of eight different faiths blessed the entire facility. This tradition goes back to the medieval era in Europe, when the local breweries were frequently blessed. The event was covered widely by the local press.

Craze and Smith's philosophy was to make the highest quality beer possible for the greater Cleveland area only, not to grow into a huge company. To quote their web site (www.westernreservebrewing.com), "When people ask us, 'Oh, do you guys plan to be the next Sam Adams?' The answer is, 'No.' The thing that makes the industrial beers so ordinary is the fact that the breweries are so big. The larger a brewery becomes, the more mass-market its beer has to be, to appeal to the greatest number of people. The beer becomes like McDonald's® hamburgers—consistently the same everywhere you go, but not exactly a fine dining experience...All the beer we sell is available within a short afternoon's drive of the brewery, so we can keep an eye on it—we can make sure it's being kept cold and that stock is rotated so that the beer is always fresh." (They also quoted a German proverb: "A happy brewer can stand on the roof of his brewery and see the homes of all of his customers.")

Their goal of quality beer was realized quickly, as Western Reserve's American Wheat Beer won a bronze medal at the 1997 Great American Beer Festival, just months after opening for business. Success continued at the 1998 World Beer Cup, where Amber Ale won a gold medal, and Nut Brown and Lake Effect Ales won silver medals in their respective categories, while Cloud Nine won a silver medal at the 1999 Great American Beer Festival. The company's commitment to Cleveland was highlighted when it won the Medical Mutual Pillar Award in 2000 for community service, based on the involvement of most of the brewery's staff in local charities, as well as the thousands of dollars given by the company to various area organizations.

The critical success of having award-winning beers did not translate into a profitable operation, however. The company continued to accumulate debt with each attempt to expand production and marketing, leaving the company forever in the red (a painfully common problem with many of the region's microbreweries). Early on, Craze and Smith had chosen not to join a large distribution network in lieu of delivering beer themselves to various outlets in Northeast Ohio. While this had increased their profit margin on beer sold, it left consumers with an erratic supply of Western Reserve products. By early 2001, available funds were becoming depleted, although one last chance for the brewery to survive appeared that summer, when Craze and Smith hooked up with a local investor. However, this relationship soon went bad and checks began to bounce, and in November of that year the company declared bankruptcy, closing for good in early 2002. Craze and Smith recognized that the market for craft beers was not the same in Cleveland as it had been in Seattle, and they felt that most beer drinkers in the area who wanted to try a unique brew would automatically try the Great Lakes brand, as it had already established a good reputation and brand recognition, leaving newcomers like Western Reserve out in the cold. And in the end, the beer connoisseurs of Ohio had one less source of quality beer.

56. John Harvard's Brewhouse/House of Brews

Located in the old Customs House at 1087 Old River Road, on the east side of the Flats district, John Harvard's Brewhouse opened September 23, 1997. This was the thirteenth in the chain of John Harvard's restaurants, based in Boston, MA. Brian O'Reilly and Dave Sutula were the brewers, utilizing a 15-barrel system, and their standard brews were John Harvard's Pale Ale, Pilgrim's Porter, Customs House Bitter, Brewhouse Alt, Mid Winter's Old Ale, Raspberry Red Ale, Old Willy India Pale Ale, and Newtown Nut Brown Ale. An extensive number of seasonal brews were available as well, including Munich Helles Lager, Presidential India Pale Ale, Dubbel Wit Bier, Lusty Gnome Scotch Ale, Iron Gate Porter, Harvest Spiced Ale, Bavarian Stock Ale, Milk Stout, Old River Pils, Dunkel Bock, Edgewater Mai Bock, Killarney Irish Stout, and Celtic Strong Ale.

By early 1999, however, the restaurant had closed, only to reopen early that fall under new, local management as the House of Brews. An entirely new lineup of beer followed, under the guidance of brewer Joe Marunowski: Downtown Brown, Standard Pils Lager, Hamilton's American Ale, Biere de Cassis, Cleveland's Cream Ale, Porter of Cleveland, Oxbow Oyster Stout (using ten pounds of fresh oysters added to the brew kettle), Incubus Belgian Tripel, Goat's Breath Double Bock, and Whiskey Island Scotch Ale. After less than a year, however, the House of Brews closed for good on May 1, 2000.

57. Cleveland Chophouse and Brewery

Occupying the ground floor of an office building at 824 West St. Clair Avenue in the city's Warehouse District, the Cleveland Chophouse and Brewery opened May 4, 1998. Owned by Rock Bottom Restaurants, Inc. (who own the nearby Rock Bottom Brewery as well), this is one of three Chophouse restaurants in the United States (others are in Denver and Washington, D.C.) Decorated in a 1940s style, with swing and big band music playing, the Chophouse restaurant features a variety of American dishes.

The original brewer was Brian Vandegrift, although he had left by 2000 and was replaced by Jason Schrider, and later by Toby Parsons (who is also the brewer for the nearby Rock Bottom Brewery). The 8-barrel J. V. Northwest brewing system produces around 500 barrels per year, with five standard brews: New World American Pale Ale, Chophouse Light Ale, Nut Brown Ale, Bohemian Pilsener Beer (which won gold medals at the 2001 and 2002 Great American Beer Festivals), and Irish Stout. Various seasonal brews, such as Oktoberfest Beer, British Bitter, and Belgian Ale, are available through the year as well.

58. Alyce On The East Bank

Located in a renovated warehouse at 1115 West Tenth Street, in the city's Flats District, Alyce On The East Bank opened in the summer of 1998 as the area's third "brewed on premises" brewery (BOP). It was operated by Alyce Derethik, a graduate of the Siebel Institute of Technology (a prominent school for brewers in Chicago), and her brother Gary Derethik.

While much of the company's operation centered around client brewing, there was a tasting bar on the second floor for numerous craft beers made there, such as Crystal Maddness India Pale Ale, Hop Head Red Ale, Honey Cream Ale, Pumpkin Brew, and Chamomile Wheat, Belgian Wheat, and Apricot Wheat Beers. Dustin Derethik, Alyce's nephew, was the brewmaster, having previously worked in a microbrewery in Oregon. Despite a promising start, the brewery had closed by early 2000 and had vacated the site.

59. Wallaby's Grille and Brewpub

The second brewpub franchise in the Wallaby's chain (originating in Westlake) opened September 14, 1998, and was located at 503 Prospect Avenue, on the ground floor of a Marriott hotel, in the Gateway District of downtown (see #54/Diamondback Brewery, above). The pub's head brewer was Rick Kennedy, and using a 10-barrel Newlands brewing system, he produced the three standard Wallaby's brews: Big Red Roo Ale, Great White Wheat Ale, and Ayers Rock Australian Pale Ale. In addition, he added several seasonal and specialty brews, including Prospect Porter, Cleveland's Brown Ale, Oatmeal Stout, Brewer's Bitter, Olde 38 Barley Wine, Vanderbilt's Spring Stout, Roasted Roo, Raspberry Ice, Spring Specialty Maibock, and Gateway India Pale Ale.

Kennedy had been succeeded by Tom Gray (formerly with the Rock Bottom Brewery) by 2000. However, due in part to the same factors that had previously led to the demise of the Diamondback Brewery down the street, the downtown Wallaby's closed its doors on September 1, 2000, just two short years after opening. The remaining Wallaby's franchises in the area closed soon thereafter.

Cleveland Heights

1. The Firehouse Brewery & Restaurant

Located at 3216 Silsby Road, the Firehouse Brewery got its name from its location in a renovated 70-year-old fire station. Opening for business on December 6, 1995, its first brews were released in early 1996. Henryk Orlik was the pub's native German brewmaster, having previously worked at a brewery in Cologne, Germany, and his imported European 15-barrel brewing system had an annual capacity of 2,800 barrels.

One of his first offerings was a true German style Kolsch Lager (which would later win a silver medal from the Beverage Testing Institute). This was followed by Backdraft Stout and 1796 American Ale, which was the official beer of Cleveland's bicentennial celebration in 1996. All three brews became available in local stores the next year when a small bottling line was installed at the site. A "three alarm sampler" included two bottles of each style in a 6-pack. In addition to these standards, a few seasonal brews were available, such as Cinnamon Nut Brown Lager.

Rapid growth of the brewery took its toll on the company's finances, however, and by the end of 1997, Firehouse had closed its doors for good. Orlik later moved to the New Orleans area to continue his craft at the Abita Brewing Co.

Rocky River

1. Rocky River Brewing Company

Located at 21290 Center Ridge Road, approximately eight miles west of downtown Cleveland, the Rocky River Brewing Co. opened as a brewpub on July 27, 1998. Furnished with luxurious oak fixtures and an enormous bar, the brewpub is owned by brothers Bob and Gary Cintron. Matt Cole has been the brewmaster since the beginning, assisted initially by Dan Madden (formerly of Ashtabula's Lift Bridge Brewing Co.) Cole began as a home brewer, then graduated from Chicago's Siebel Brewing Institute before training additionally with several brewers in Germany. Upon his return to America, he was a brewer for the Great Lakes Brewing Co. before coming to Rocky River. He considers his specialty to be alt beers, and his style of brewing is modeled after German brewers he trained with instead of the more common English style of brewing that is seen in most brewpubs in Ohio.

Utilizing a 7-barrel Century brewing system, Cole produces one standard, popular brew: Coopers Gold Kolsch. The remainder of his lineup of beers rotates out of a total of 46 that he chooses from, including Wit's Doctor (also known as Liquid Sunshine) Belgian White, Merlin's Black Magic coffee stout (which won a silver medal at the 2003 Great American Beer Festival), Northern Lights German altbier, Sub Chaser Hefe-Weizen, and Dry Dock Amber Alt. In addition, Cole won a silver medal at the 2000 Great American Beer Festival in the Herb and Spice Beer category for his Santa's Lil' Helper Christmas Ale. At the 2002 Real Ale Festival, he won a silver medal for Oompa Loompa Cream Stout, and a bronze medal for Artisan Saison Belgian Style Ale (which also won a bronze medal at the 2001 Great American Beer Festival, a silver medal at the 2002 and 2003 GABF, and a gold medal at the 2002 World Beer Cup). All beer brewed (approximately 600 barrels per year) is sold on-site, and more information is available at the pub's web site, www.rockyriverbrewco.com.

Strongsville

1. Melbourne's Brewing Co./Mad Crab restaurant & brewery

The Cleveland area's second brewpub opened May 25, 1989 as Melbourne's Brewing Co. Located at 12492 Prospect Avenue, the restaurant was owned by William Ilersich and had an Australian theme, with a brewing operation that also went by the name of Strongsville Brewing Co. Original brewer Stephan Danckers had an extensive background in brewing science, and later left to co-found the new Crooked River Brewing Co. He was replaced by Sorin Petrescu-Boboc, a native of Brasov, Romania, who has an extensive background in engineering, brewery construction, and chemistry, and who trained under several German brewmasters while living in Europe. Among the brands he produced were Down Under Beer, Brewmaster's Special, Bondi Beach Blonde, and Wombat Wheat Beer. Melbourne's closed in June 1995.

The Mad Crab opened in its place in November 1996, under new management and with a menu specializing in seafood. Boboc remained the brewer, using a 7-barrel Continental brewing system to brew Pirate's Pilsner, Rowdy Riptide, Hurricane Honey Lager, and Sturgeon Stout. Mad Crab also had the contract to make Buzz Beer, made famous on television's Drew Carey Show, as a lightly hopped honey cream ale. Seasonal and specialty beers appeared as well, such as India Pale Ale, Blue Whale Wheat Beer, and Oktoberfest Beer. In 2003, however, brewing operations ceased when the restaurant closed.

2. Ringneck Brewing Company/The Brew Kettle

Ohio's first BOP (brewed-on-premises facility), The Brew Kettle opened for business on December 14, 1995. Originally located at 15143 Pearl Road (U. S. Route 42), it operated in conjunction with a small microbrewery at the site, the Ringneck Brewing Co. Amateur brewers can choose from sixty different recipes to brew batches (just over twelve gallons) of nearly any type of beer, with all the ingredients, equipment, and instruction provided by the staff. After several weeks (depending on the brew), the batch is packaged into six cases of bottles, with customized labels for the customer.

The microbrewery initially had a 3-barrel Price Schonstrom brewing system. This was used by brewer Chris McKim to produce several "flagship" beers: Ringneck Black Bear Porter, and Ringneck Golden, Amber, Pale, and Chestnut Brown Ales. Numerous variations and specialty brews have been produced through the years, such as Hazelnut Brown Ale, Imperial Stout, Winter Warmer, Dunkel Weizen, Irish Stout, Big Woody Munich Helles Lager, Pumpkin Patch Weizen Bock, and Pale Rye Ale, as well as contract beers such as Mustang Pale Ale for local restaurants and bars. Ringneck beers are both kegged and bottled for distribution at numerous sites in the region.

At the 1998 Real Ale Festival in Chicago, McKim won two gold medals for Czech Pilsner and Hefe-Weizen, and two silver medals for Imperial Stout and Freedom Pale Ale. At the 1999 National BOP Competition, he won gold medals for Imperial Stout, Winter Warmer, and Dunkel Weizen, a silver medal for Ringneck Chestnut Brown Ale, and a bronze medal for Irish Stout. In late Fall 2002, the company moved further north in Strongsville, to 8377 Pearl Road. New equipment (a 10-barrel system) was purchased from the defunct Bunky's Brewpub in Newark (see Licking County), and a new restaurant and taproom were incorporated into the facility. More information can be found at the company's web site: www.thebrewkettle.com.

Westlake

1. Wallaby's Grille & Brewpub

The first of three Wallaby's Grille & Brewpub franchises in the region opened on May 10, 1995. Located at 30005 Clemens Road, adjacent to Interstate 90, all of its beers, food, and décor had an Australian theme. A 10-barrel Bohemian brewing system was used to produce what became the three standard Wallaby's brands: Great White Wheat Beer, Ayers Rock Pale Ale, and Big Red Roo Strong Ale, with an annual output of approximately 1000 barrels. Joe Marunowski was the pub's original brewer, although after one year he left to oversee the development of the affiliated full-scale brewery (see the next listing), and later worked at Akron's Liberty Street Brewing Co., and the House of Brews in Cleveland.

Marunowski was succeeded by Californian Brad Unruh, who had previously worked at the Crooked River Brewing Co. in Cleveland. He continued to produce the three standards as well as numerous specialty brews such as Matilda Bay Common Beer, Cherry Porter, Billabong Brown, Oatmeal Stout, Raspberry Ice, Croco-Pale Ale, Cranberra Cream Ale, Pumpkin Pie Spiced Ale, Southern Cross Apple & Cinnamon Beer, Aukland Ale, Wallaby's Cask Conditioned Ale, Alexander's Apricot Ale, Gold Cup Lager, and Maori Milk Stout. Unruh won silver medals at the 1996 World Beer Championships for Oatmeal Stout and Maori Milk Stout.

By the end of 1998, Unruh had left to operate the Four Fellows Brewpub in Hudson, and was replaced by Bill Bryson, formerly with John Harvard's in Cleveland. Bryson continued brewing operations as before, adding new specialty brews such as Black Opal Porter, Olde Adelaide, Crocodile Bock, Old Sol, Kakadu Rye Bock, Kalgoorlie Gold, Doppelbock, Amber Cream Ale, Wallaby's Winter Warmer Ale, and Honey Blossom Ale. Two years later, the brewpub trend in the region was in decline, and Wallaby's was among the casualties. This site closed at the end of 2000.

2. Local Brewing Company/Wallaby's Brewing Company

Serving as the headquarters for the Wallaby's group of brewpubs, the Local Brewing Company opened August 8, 1997, at 24400 Sperry Drive. Its opening was heralded by advertisements for a public stock offering to Ohio residents, with 200,000 shares available at $5.00 per share. The facility brewed and packaged all bottled beer for sales of the three "flagship" brands, Great White Wheat Beer, Ayers Rock Pale Ale, and Big Red Roo Strong Ale, at all franchises in the company and in selected stores in the region. When these brands were being produced, the company did business as Wallaby's Brewing Company, to distinguish this from its other operations.

While the company's owner and president was Nick Alexakos, director of brewing operations was Joe Marunowski, and the brewmaster was Thomas Cizauskas, a Siebel Institute graduate and former brewer at microbreweries in Maryland and Philadelphia. Several assistant brewers worked there as well, including Chris Alltmont, Brian Hoyle, and Matthew Hahn. The three vessel, 50-barrel brewhouse, with five 150-barrel fermenters, yielded an annual capacity around 14,000 barrels. By 1998, its second year of operation, Local Brewing Co. was the state's fourth largest brewery.

Local also performed contract brewing for outside distributors, doing business as the Asian Star Brewing Co., with its Asian Moon Golden Lager, and as the Pilsener Brewing Co. The latter began as the brainchild of Stuart Sheridan, one of the founders of the Crooked River Brewing Co. He resurrected the Pilsener Brewing name in early 1999, along with its popular old brand, P.O.C. However, he marketed the new brew as an equivalent of the old P.O.C. of the 1950s, when it was a premium pilsener beer, not the "cheaper, watered-down" version of the 1970s and 80s. Initial interest and media coverage for the new beer seemed to focus on nostalgia as much as anything, and sales (at $4.99 per six-pack) were good that year. However, this interest was not sustained for long, as the brand and distribution company had disappeared without a trace by the end of 2000. The Local Brewing Company itself closed soon after this, along with the entire Wallaby's restaurant chain.

Also Note:

1. Non-brewing "brewers" of the late 1800s

If one looks through the Cleveland City Directory from the period between 1861 and 1890, there are numerous listings for brewers in addition to the establishments previously covered (some of these names have also appeared in *American Breweries II*). Upon further research, it appears that these "brewers" were either small, short-lived home brewing operations, manufacturers of small beer, ginger beer, or cronk beer (soft drinks), or employees of larger breweries elsewhere. In 1865, a well-known distiller (Louis Umbstaetter) was mistakenly listed as a brewer as well. For the sake of completeness, all of these "brewers" are listed here (this list is certainly not complete, as there were many other home-brewers who were never listed as such in the city directories, not to mention actual, substantial brewing establishments that existed prior to the first city directory and which have never appeared in any other local historical literature):

—P. S. Bosworth, brewer for the Forest City Brewery (see entry #8), in 1861 directory only.
—Daniel Fletcher (Pletcher) was a home brewer at 130 Monroe, listed intermittently from 1861 to 1868, as well as his widow Mary after 1865.
—J. B. Smith & Co. was a maltster on Spring Street, in 1861 directory only.
—Francis and James Marlow, listed in the city directory as brewers at 433 W. River St. (later Riverbed) between 1862 and 1867.
—John Laux & Co. in Brooklyn Township, in 1863 directory only.
—Benjamin & George Shutts, in 1863/64 directories; brewers for Thomas Newman (see entry #8).
—Thomas Stacy made spruce and ginger beer at 70 Hamilton St., listed in 1863 directory only.
—John Hardin in Royalton Township (now North Royalton), in 1863 directory only.
—Glendon & (Thomas) Collins, at 103 Detroit, listed in 1866/67 only.
—Frederick Maurer at 130 York, in 1867 directory only.
—Andrew Steinmetz, owner of a livery stable at 235 Lorain, also made small beer in 1866/67.
—Peter Wertz (Wirtz) operated a saloon and brewery at 190 Pearl in 1867/69.
—Nathan and John Brown, brothers who worked at the Stoppel brewery (see entry #21) in 1868.
—F. Hemmerdinger, in 1868 directory, was a brewer for August Burckhardt (see entry #31).
—G. Reubensaal at 60 Bridge St. was a cooper and brewer in 1868 directory only.
—John Prosek at 146 Croton, in 1871 directory only.

—Michael Basel, home brewer from 1871 to 1875 at 14 Beaver Street, producing around ten barrels annually.
—Rudolf Guentzler lived on Vega Avenue, near the Leisy brewery; listed as a cooper and a brewer in 1871/73.
—Baver & Leisgang, brewers for the Star Brewery (later the Diebolt Brewing Co.—see entry #14) on Broadway in 1873.
—Francis (Frank) Geib, listed in *American Breweries II* around 1874, but not in any city directories or census records as a brewer.
—John Miller, listed in 1880, was a brewer for John A. Bishop (see entry #9).
—Michael Mueller, listed in early 1880s, was an early partner of Joseph Beltz on Outhwaite Avenue (see entry #35).
—George Doubert at 357 Pearl, listed in 1884, likely worked at the Baehr brewery (see entry #25).

2. "Phantom" breweries

In addition to the 71 brewing operations listed in this chapter that actually created beer, there have been many companies in Cuyahoga County that existed on paper, but that never actually operated as functional breweries. Most of these "phantom breweries" existed in three distinct eras: the turn of the century (1900-1906), when stock companies appeared all over the country for the creation of local brewing concerns; the immediate post-Prohibition era (1933-36), when the market for the newly available beer was huge, but the Great Depression made the initiation of any company rocky; and the modern era (1990-present), when craft beers were popular, but the economics of operating a brewpub or microbrewery were tricky.

In the first era, the following companies are known to have existed, but never actually brewed beer: Cleveland Co-Operative Brewing Co. (1901), Greater Cleveland Brewing Co. (1902), Cuyahoga Brewing Co. (1905), and the National Brewing & Distributing Co. (1917).

In the second era, the following companies existed: Kloster Brewing Co. (1933), Lauber Bock Beer Co. of Cleveland (1934), Old Tavern Brewing Co. (1934), Old Holland Brewing Co. (1936), Bedford Brewing Co., which was to operate in the former Mason Tire & Rubber Co. factory in suburban Bedford (1933), and Schuster Brewing Co. in suburban Lakewood (1934).

In the modern era, it can be difficult to discern between "rumored breweries", where a restaurant or tavern owner is merely considering the addition of a brewing facility, and actual companies formed for this purpose. The following list is of companies that were actually created, but as of the publication of this book, had never begun brewing commercially: Dark Horse Brewing Co. (whose president, Steve Megay, advertised $1,000,000 worth of company stock for sale to the public in 1998, as well as two proposed brands, Munich Helles Beer and Brown Ale); Rust Belt Brewing Co., which had assembled equipment at 4406 Perkins Avenue but never began brewing; Bingham Smokehouse, Brewery, and Cidery; Bolivar Brewing Co., at 737 Bolivar Road; and Red Brick Brewery in suburban Solon.

3. National brewers

While local brewers dominated the Cleveland beer market in the 1800s, improvements in rail transportation by the end of that century saw an increased presence of five large out-of-town brewers: Pabst, Stroh, Schlitz, Miller, and Anheuser-Busch. By the 1890s, each had established bottling houses in the city for packaging and distribution of its brands.

The Pabst Brewing Company of Milwaukee had a bottling house on Briggs (East 22nd) Street (next door to the Gavagan Ale Brewery), although this was later moved to St. Clair Avenue. The Jos. Schlitz Brewing Company, also of Milwaukee, established its first bottling works in Cleveland around 1883 at 20 Merwin Street in the Flats, although bottling was later moved to a larger facility on East 55th Street near Chester Avenue. Anheuser-Busch of St. Louis had its world-famous Budweiser Beer bottled in Cleveland, initially by local bottler Frank E. Diemer, although the contract was later sold to the William Edwards Company, a wholesale grocer. The Stroh Brewing Company of Detroit established a bottling depot, capable of filling 1,200 bottles daily, at the corner of Bond (East 6th) Street and Theresa Court in 1892. This later moved to 396 Case Avenue (East 40th Street).

The Frederick Miller Brewing Co. of Milwaukee had a bottling depot in Cleveland at 1973 Gordon (W. 65th) St. beginning in 1904, managed by the firm of Michel, McDonough, & Switzer. Each of these brewers maintained bottling facilities in Cleveland until the onset of Prohibition, although none of the brands was ever actually brewed in the city.

In addition to the national brewers, there were bottling houses for other regional brands in the 1800s, the earliest of which was Sands' Ale from New York, bottled by Patrick O'Marah as early as 1865. Later came distributors for the Bartholomay Brewing Co. of Rochester, N.Y. (by the Sylla Bottling Co. at 76 Michigan St.), the Finlay Brewing Co. of Toledo, the Cincinnati Brewing Co. of Hamilton, OH. (by Peter C. Schneider at 315 Superior Ave., and later at 124 Woodland Ave.), the Peter Schoenhofen Brewing Co. of Chicago (originally on Union St. and later by Charles E. Baltes at 3843 Superior Ave.), and the Lion/Windisch-Muhlhauser Brewing Co. of Cincinnati (by Theodore Hymans at 460 Union St.)

4. Philip Meniken's Brewery

Recently, the presence of a bottle label for export beer from Philip Meniken's Brewery in Cleveland came to light (thanks to Bob Bickford). The brewery does not appear in any of the Cleveland directories between 1870 and 1919, nor does it appear in *American Breweries II*, and its appearance leaves more questions than answers. The label appears to be a "stock" label, with a standard design that could be used by any brewer, and Meniken's name is printed on it. It appears to be from the period between 1900 and 1915. Certainly Meniken could have been a small-time home brewer, or he might have intended to have a larger plant but was unable to stay in business for more than a few months. Either way, he did not do his own bottling, as there is a notation of the beer being bottled by John Dater. More information may surface in the future.

5. Cleveland Brewing Company

In 1988, the same year that the Great Lakes Brewing Co. opened, paving the way for the dozens of brewpubs and microbreweries that followed in eastern Ohio, another group began business as the Cleveland Brewing Co. Opening several months before Great Lakes, this was a marketing and distribution company only, and co-founders Craig Chaitoff and David Lowman resurrected an old Cleveland favorite, Erin Brew, to be their flagship brand. The company's office on Lakeside Avenue contained no brewing equipment, as all beer was brewed and packaged under contract with the Pittsburgh Brewing Co. in Pennsylvania and the West End Brewing Co. in Utica, NY. The brand met with a great deal of success initially, as it won a silver medal at the 1989 Great American Beer Festival. The company faced an uphill battle, however, in attempting to educate the public about craft beers at a time when brewpubs were still a novelty in the region. Sales eventually slumped as the market soon became flooded with other craft beers. As a result, the company had closed by 1994, after which the Erin Brew name disappeared into Cleveland history once again.

6. The Drew Carey Show

No, this isn't a real brewery. However, as one of the most visible symbols of Cleveland in the past decade (as well as its biggest cheerleader), Drew Carey has become a household name. In the spring of 1996, at the end of the first season of his hit show on ABC television, which takes place in Cleveland, Drew and his friends decided to begin a microbrewery in his garage. Many episodes over the next five years mentioned their "Buzz Beer" (even a fictional web site, buybuzzbeer.com), and their adventures in attempting to make and sell it.

Back in the real world, the rights to the name were purchased in 2000 by the Mad Crab brewpub in Strongsville, which brewed Buzz Beer for several years before exiting the brewing business.

ERIE COUNTY

Huron

1. Morrison & Wheeler brewery & distillery

By the outbreak of the War of 1812, there were a few fledgling communities in north central Ohio, and a few pioneer industries as well. The small village of Huron was one of these early communities, and it was just south of the village, along the River Road (which had recently been opened on the east side of the Huron River), that the area's first trading post was established around 1810. This was operated by John B. Fleming, a French Canadian who bought furs and sold numerous goods he acquired in trading with Indians. It was adjacent to this post that the region's first brewery was established in the spring of 1812.

Operated by Esquire William Morrison (who later became the village's Justice of the Peace) and John Wheeler, the brewery was combined with a distillery, as was common in the era. Common beer or ale was brewed for the inhabitants of the village, as well as for settlers who were traveling through the area on their way inland to new territories.

When the war broke out, Morrison and Wheeler became army contractors, supplying provisions to United States army troops. The Battle of Lake Erie took place one year later, when Commodore Oliver Hazard Perry defeated a squadron of British navy ships near Put-In-Bay, northwest of Sandusky. While the war continued for more than another year after this, Lake Erie saw no further military action and the region continued to develop uneventfully. While there is no indication of how long the brewery/distillery operated after this, it does not appear that it continued past 1820. There are no remains of any of these pioneer settlements today.

Kelleys Island

1. Island Café and Brewpub/Kelleys Island Brewery

Opening in the spring of 1999, the Island Café was the first and only brewpub on Kelley's Island, a quiet 2,800-acre island of state parks and residences, approximately ten miles north of Sandusky. Owned by Patti Johnson, it is located at 504 W. Lakeshore Drive, across the street from Neuman's Ferry, on the southwest corner of the island.

The Island Café had operated previously for breakfast and lunch service, although expansion and the addition of the 3.5-barrel brewing system led to the addition of a dinner menu as well. The head brewer is Michael Byrd, an area home brewer and graduate of the Siebel Institute, while his wife Dolly is the manager. Four main brews were produced initially: Anglers Ale, a light summer ale, Watersnake Wheat Beer, Pilot House Pilsener Beer, and Dawgbizkit Brown Ale. Pumpkin Ale was brewed in the Fall, and Limestone Lager Beer was also available in 2001. Due to the area's seasonal nature, the brewpub is only open from May 1 to the end of October.

By 2003, the cafe had been renamed as the Kelleys Island Brewery, and currently its primary brews are Island Devil Belgian Ale, Kelleys Gold Beer, Kelleys Gold Light Beer, and Dawg Bizkit Brown.

Milan

1. John Scholl/Joseph Herb/Milan Brewing Corporation

John Scholl was a German immigrant, born in 1817, who in 1850 began brewing beer in a simple wooden structure located just south of the intersection of Lockwood Road and Huron Street on the south side of the village (later taking the address of 42 Lockwood Road). The site had a crystal spring which produced 500 barrels of pure water each day, and Scholl also operated a small distillery at the site. This early brewing establishment was sold in 1863 to Francis and Gottlieb Humbel, although it appears that Scholl continued to operate the distillery for some years after this. In December 1869, financial problems for the Humbels forced the sale of the brewery to 44-year-old Anton Herb, another German native, who came to Milan by way of Dubuque, Iowa.

At this time, the brewery was producing only around 100 barrels of beer annually. Herb had the brewery rebuilt several hundred feet to the north, as a three-story wooden frame structure, although annual production increased very little over the next twenty years. A bottling works had been added by the 1890s, and in addition, Herb built a small dam in the ravine south of the brewery, which created an ice pond from the spring water which ran through the ravine. Herb died in 1892, although his family (wife Mary, and later his sons Joseph and Charles) would continue to operate the plant until Prohibition.

Beer from the brewery won a prestigious award at the 1893 Chicago World's Fair, leading to the slogan "The beer that made Milwaukee jealous", which was used for many years. In addition, the following claim appeared in advertising around 1900: "We do not claim to be the largest brewery in the country, but we do claim that it is impossible to produce a better and purer quality than Milan Pure Beer.....As an appetizing tonic or social beverage it is without an equal. A case, three dozen bottles costs you $3.75 but when you return case and empty bottles we allow you a rebate of $1.65 so you see it only costs you $2.10 to buy a case of the best quality beer in all the world."

In 1904 came the incorporation of the Joseph Herb Brewing Co., with capital stock of $25,000 (later increased to $100,000). A new four-story brick brewhouse was built just after this, and its official opening on April 23, 1906 was a gala affair attended by many townspeople. While Joseph Herb remained as the brewmaster, Robert Streck was the president of this company, with George W. Luckey as vice-president and Charles L. Blatz as secretary. Streck was replaced in 1908 by local businessman John F. Ging. Ging and Herb would continue to run the brewery until the onset of Prohibition in 1919 (brother Charles Herb also had remained with the brewery until his death in 1914). After this, the brewing equipment was dismantled, and for several years the storage cellars were used for growing mushrooms. Herb continued in the ice business, cutting ice from the old pond and delivering it through the area on his own.

After Prohibition's end, a new company was formed in early 1934, to be known as the Milan Brewing Corporation. This consisted of three men from Toledo, Jake Kelly, Edward Kirschner, and Mike Cohen. Joseph Herb was rehired to help

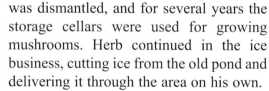

Herb Brewery in the early days: The ice house stands at the far right, with a conveyor visible to raise ice out of the pond during the winter. [provided by Bill Carlisle]

with brewing, and his ice business was abandoned. The mushrooms disappeared, and the plant was completely renovated with new equipment, increasing its annual capacity to 30,000 barrels (but still leaving it as one of the state's smallest breweries). The grand reopening was on June 14, but producing only 100 barrels per day while distributing over a six county area, the brewery was barely able to keep up with local demand.

After just one year, economic difficulties forced the company into receivership, after which it was sold to William Nash of Cleveland, who continued to operate the brewery with the same personnel for the next three years. During this time, the company became known for its Milan Springs Beer and Ale, as well as Old '93 Beer (thought to be a tribute to the award won in Chicago in that year).

By February 1938, however, Nash found operation of the brewery to be uneconomical, citing improved transportation which allowed breweries from the state's larger cities to dominate the market. The plant then closed for several months until new buyers, Thomas Daly and H. Reisner, appeared from Youngstown (the company had six different owners and managers during its seventeen years of existence). By 1940, another change left Frank Razinger as president, master brewer, and plant manager, with Joseph Chovjan as vice-president. By 1945, the company was being operated by Harry and Edward Koppelman. Management changed again in 1948, at which time the president was Oscar Lanzi, with LeRoy J. Contie as vice-president, and Charles Grotenfend as the new master brewer.

Milan brewery as it appears today

By this time, annual capacity had been increased to 50,000 barrels, with several brands being added, including Sholtz, Bingo, Old American Style, and Milan Old German and Old Bohemian Style Beers. Despite distribution of these brands throughout north central Ohio, competition from the larger regional and national brewers was too much to overcome (William Nash's earlier comments about competition from Ohio's larger cities had been just the tip of the iceberg). A century of brewing at the site ended in 1951, when the brewery closed its doors for good.

The building stood vacant until 1955, when it was purchased by the Growers Chemical Corp., which operates in the plant to this day. The main brewhouse and much of the ice pond have remained intact.

Sandusky

1. J. Lea (and other early home brewers)

Sandusky's first known brewery began operations around 1844 or 1845, according to *Sandusky of To-Day*, by G. G. Nichols, from 1888. Begun by John or Joseph Lea, the brewery produced common beer "in a very small way". It was located along Mills' Creek, near Tiffin Avenue. Lea does not appear in the 1850 census, suggesting that his brewing concern was no longer operating by that time.

Lea would appear to have been just one of several practitioners in the business of home brewing in the city around this time. As mentioned in the introduction, "home brewing" in this context refers to a brewer producing less than 100 barrels annually, but producing it for commercial sales, as opposed to the more modern sense of the term. Also mentioned in *Sandusky of To-Day* is an ale brewery operated by a man named Wood, formerly of Cleveland. This supposedly sat at the foot of Putnam Street, but appears in neither the census nor deed records. Interestingly, all but one of Sandusky's known breweries were located within a fairly small area on the city's far west side.

A look through the 1850 census, however, does reveal at least five other men in Sandusky listed as either a "brewer" or "beer maker": John Hammond, Charles Shupe, John Bernard, Robert Huffman, and Sebastian Lea. Bernard was a native of Maryland, while the other four were native Germans. While it is possible that any of these men may have been employed by another brewer in the city, there were no large scale breweries yet existing in the city in 1850. A census for 1870 or 1880, for example, might list a number of men as being "brewers", but most of them would have worked either for the large Kuebeler or Stang breweries. Therefore, the most likely assumption in 1850 would be that each of these men operated their own home breweries, selling their products to any of the multitude of saloons in the town.

As late as 1867, there is a mention of a C. Tomlinson in the city directory, as being a brewer of beer and ale, located at the western city limits. In the same year, Tomlinson's brewery appears on a listing of insured buildings in the city, though it is noted that he had no malt house. However, there is no mention of Tomlinson in any other city directories or census records, and it would therefore appear that he may have run another short-lived home brewing operation.

As Sandusky was a major port for the fishing industry, many thirsty sailors provided a ready market for a wide variety of alcoholic beverages. Numerous distilleries were operating in the area around this time, and the wine industry of the "Firelands", as this region was called, was rapidly developing as well. The wine industry continues to this day along the south shore of Lake Erie and on the nearby islands, as the region's climate is excellent for the growing of grapes.

2. Phoenix Brewery

Established in 1848 by Charles S. Higgins, the Phoenix Brewery was the only known brewing operation to be located in the city's downtown area. Located on the south side of East Water Street, between Hancock and Franklin Streets, it began operation as an ale brewery. Higgins was an Englishman, born in 1821, who appears to have operated a grocery at the site, while brewing operations were performed by Jefferson Jefferin, another English immigrant.

The brewery was still operating as late as 1860, although it appears that brewing operations ceased shortly thereafter. The structure was later converted into a wine cellar by J. P. Dorn, a merchant whose operation at the site continued well into the twentieth century. The Harborview Retirement Community stands at the site today.

3. Dauch/Stang/Cleveland-Sandusky Brewing Company

Sandusky's longest lived brewing establishment appears to have begun operations as the City Brewery in 1852. Located on the east side of the north end of King Street (although in later years the plant had the address of 2207 W. Madison St.), the brewery was situated along the Cleveland, Cincinnati, Chicago, & St. Louis Railroad (also known as the Big Four RR.), just south of the Lake Erie shoreline. Phillip Dauch and Andrew Fischer were the original proprietors, although Dauch operated it alone after Fischer died in 1853. Dauch was a German immigrant who had landed in New York in 1847, and came to Sandusky by way of Cincinnati and Springfield, Ohio. By 1862, he had encountered financial troubles and retired to a nearby farm, selling the brewery to John Bright, Lawrence Cable, & James Alder. They operated the plant until June 1868, when it was sold for $10,000 to George Windisch and Vincenz (Winsen) Fox, who had previously operated the nearby Ilg brewery.

Fox sold an interest in the brewery to Frank Stang and John Homegardner in 1870, and two years later Windisch left the partnership. In 1875, Fox declared bankruptcy, and the plant was sold at public auction to Stang and John Bender, a 55-year-old native of Baden, Germany. Bender began expanding the brewery's annual output, doubling it from 3,000 to 6,000 barrels by 1878, the year in which he died. After this it remained in the name of his wife Magdalena ("Lena") Bender for two more years. At that time, she sold the plant to Stang, who had been running the brewery after Bender's death, for $30,000. Frank Stang had been born in Monroeville, Ohio in 1851, and entered into the brewing industry after moving to Sandusky with his younger brother John. John was the traveling agent for the brewery, spending much of his time on the road until Frank withdrew from the company in 1890, after which John became the new president.

Stang Brewery in the 1880s; the tall limestone building is the malt house, while the dark building is the brewhouse. The small buildings in the rear were ice houses. [photos courtesy of the Sandusky Library Archives]

Stang continued to increase the plant's output, and by the late 1880s, the plant employed twenty men or more, including brewmaster Fred J. Beier, in producing between 15,000 and 20,000 barrels of beer annually. Seven teams of horses would deliver the beer in wagons throughout the city, with a great deal of additional brew being sent to surrounding counties. The stone brewery building was three stories in height, 225 by 250 feet in size, with a large attached ice house, capable of holding 10,000 tons of ice, which was cut from a nearby ice pond.

A disastrous fire in July 1891 destroyed virtually everything at the plant, including the office, malt house, ice house, ice machine, and most of the stored beer on hand, with a loss of over $100,000. Thought to be caused by a spark from the engine of a passing train, this exemplified one of the primary dangers of operating a brewery near a railroad, despite the obvious transportation advantage (a spark from another train five years later caused the destruction of another, newly built ice house at the site). While the nearby Kuebeler brewery agreed to temporarily fill all of Stang's orders, the plant was completely rebuilt from the ground up over the next year. An extremely detailed account of the opening of the new brewery appeared in the Sandusky *Register* on April 13, 1893:

"On the fifteenth day of July, 1891, Mr. Frank Stang's brewery in the west end was completely demolished by fire, and as the spectators viewed the wreck which the devastating flames left they predicted that the business of the firm was ruined and that by the time another brewery was erected the trade would have left entirely. Their prognostications proved false however. Mr. Frank Stang is not the man to be daunted by such a thing as a fire, destructive though it might be, and he rose to the occasion and set about to secure a continuance of his trade while his brewery was rebuilding. The connection was a valuable one and Mr. Stang did the best he could under the circumstances. He called in the aid of the leading brewers in Milwaukee, Cincinnati, Toledo, and Detroit and made contracts for the supply of beer in sufficient quantities to supply his customers. Then he began to devise plans for the re-erection of the brewery and formed a stock company with a capital of $150,000, styled the Stang Brewing Company, under whose auspices has been erected the handsome new structure which Phoenix-like has risen from the ashes of the old building.

Yesterday the new brewery was opened with great rejoicing. Thousands of invitations were issued to the people of Sandusky and surrounding towns to inspect the place and partake of the firm's hospitality and in the afternoon there was a constant stream of visitors. They came in cabs and buggies and crowded street cars, many of which vehicles were gaily adorned with flags, and came prepared to have a good time. The Great Western band was engaged for the occasion and under the leadership of Mr. Fred Bauman they rendered selections of popular airs. The brewery was opened for work on the first of January last, but as beer requires to undergo certain processes of maturing before it is fit for consumption none has yet been sold. It was tapped yesterday for the benefit of the visitors and scores of barrels were used. One long bar, with half a dozen waiters, was rigged up, and needless to say was most consistently patronized; while Charlie Cramer, of the English kitchen, with a staff of assistants, was kept busily engaged in serving lunch to all comers. In another part of the room was erected a platform for the band. Externally the building was decorated with flags and indoors all the rooms were gaily bedecked with flags and star spangled bunting. The festivities were kept up until late at night and if the first brew of the Stang Brewery was not thoroughly well tested it was not the fault of the company, whose hospitality was unbounded.

The contract for the erection of the new brewery was awarded to the firm of Messrs. A. Feick & Brother, of this city. The plans were those of Mr. George Feick, who had the whole of the work under his supervision, receiving valuable assistance from Mr. Fred J. Beier, the foreman of the brewery.

Externally the building presents a commanding appearance. It is situated on King Street, being bounded on the north side by the tracks of the Big Four railroad and Sandusky Bay, and also adjoining the site upon which will be erected the warehouses of the Sandusky & Columbus Short Line railroad. The building is a substantial fireproof structure of brick relieved with stone dressings. It is five stories high surmounted with a tower. The system adopted is that known as the gravity system.

The brewhouse proper covers an area of 44 x 35 feet. On the first floor is the hop jack, where the hops are boiled under pressure. The second floor contains a copper brewing kettle, holding 200 barrels and steam heated, and a mash tub with Kaestner's hydraulic lowering and raising machine. A portion of this floor is partitioned off for the brewmaster's office and laboratory. On the third floor is one of Frisch's high-pressure filters where the malt is mashed under pressure, hot and cold water tanks and a meal scale hopper. The fourth floor contains a Kaestner non-explosive malt mill and affords room for storage; a screening reel for separating the sprouts from the malt and a storage bin for malt. The firm does not carry on the malting process, but purchases the best malt obtainable. They expect, however, soon to erect a malting house.

Adjoining the brewhouse is the mill house, containing the elevators, storage bins and shaftings. An improved bucket elevator is used for the malt, and a platform elevator, provided with safety doors on each floor, is used for other purposes. All the malt undergoes a screening process immediately after it arrives and is then run into bins ready for use.

The engine room is a spacious, well lighted apartment 45 by 48 feet. It contains a 100 horse power engine built by Messrs. Klotz & Kromer, of this city, and an electric lighting engine built by the same firm. There are also a 50 ton Linde ice machine, erected by the Fred W. Wolf Company, of Chicago, and a 35 ton ice machine which went through the fire and was rebuilt by the Hospital Supply Company of Sandusky. It is intended to use one machine in the day time and the other at night, and in case of either one breaking down the other would be sufficient for all purposes. The system adopted is that of forcing ammonia through coils of pipes contained in a huge tank for the purpose of cooling brine which is then run through an elaborate system of pipes in the cellars. An 150 light Eddy dynamo supplies electric light for the whole building, this being constructed by the Electrical Construction Company of Cincinnati. The engine room also contains a duplex air pump for forcing beer from the cellars to the racking room, and a brine pump. The room over the engine house is occupied by open air condensers for both ice machines and a Bendelot beer cooler, shut off by a glazed partition.

Frank and John Stang pose with their employees in the 1880s [courtesy of the Sandusky Library Archives]

The boiler house, which is 45 feet square, adjoins the engine room and contains two boilers each with a capacity of 125 horse power, built by the Sandusky Steam Boiler Company (Fred Kranz & Co.). Space is left for the erection of two more boilers when required.

North of the boiler house is the wash-house, 48 by 65 feet, containing a patent keg scrubber. A brine tank with a capacity of 15,000 gallons is also placed in this room. Below is the pitching and keg storage room, the kegs being pitched by one of Schmidt's patent keg pitching machines. After the kegs are pitched they are sent to the wash room where they are thoroughly cleansed and thence taken to the racking room where they are filled ready for market.

The stock house is on the northwest side of the building and occupies an area of 65 by 95 feet, being four stories in height. The settling room is on the fourth floor and contains three tanks each holding 200 barrels, or one brew. The beer is brought to these huge vats from the cooler, and here the yeast is given. Fermenting is the next process and this takes place on the third floor where there is room for 60 fermenting tanks of 120 barrels each. Thence the beer goes to the stock or storage cellar on the second floor which has space sufficient for 50 storage tanks of from 200 to 250 barrels each. The first floor is divided into four compartments, in one of which are twelve of the largest casks in Northern Ohio, these containing 135 barrels each. They are made by Michel Brothers of this city. The total capacity of the stock house is 30,000 barrels, and the brewery is capable of producing 100,000 barrels a year. In all the cellars the windows are so arranged that the passages are well lighted. The racking of the beer ready for delivery is the last process, this being done in a conveniently fitted room 32 by 48 feet.

A short distance from the brewery is a commodious brick barn, accommodating some 16 horses. The firm have a number of bright painted wagons for delivering beer and these will be seen on the streets today delivering the product of one of the most compact and complete breweries in the state of Ohio. A wagon shed will soon be erected. At the rear of the main pile stands a frame ice house containing about 8,000 tons of ice.

Arrangements have been made by which the Stang company have secured from the Mustcash Mineral Water company a contract for the supply of water from their Crystal Rock springs near Castalia. The water will be brought to the brewery by means of a six and one-fourth inch pipe, and the company has the sole right of the use of the water for brewing.

The arrangements made by the company for the shipment of their beer are very complete, the barrels being placed in cars on the Big Four railroad, the tracks of which run alongside the racking room. A side track from the Short Line will run along the south side, enabling coal cars and grain cars to discharge their cargoes into the boiler house and elevator respectively.

The brewery does a big trade with Elyria, Lorain, Shelby, Crestline, Chicago Junction, Plymouth, Oak Harbor, Clyde, Marion, Grafton, and the islands of Lake Erie in addition to the city trade which is an important one. Mr. John Stang is the travelling agent of the firm. At the opening festivities yesterday customers from all the towns mentioned were present and expressed themselves highly pleased with the equipment of the brewery, everything that scientific skill based upon practical experience can suggest being brought into operation for the production of a class of beer the quality of which it is hoped will give the Stang Brewing Company an enviable reputation in the markets of Ohio.

The brewery is under the management of Mr. Frank Stang, president. Mr. Charles L. Wagner is vice president of the company, and the other directors are Messrs. Cornelius Nielson, Henry Pfeil, Geo. Feick, John Homegardner, and Jacob A. Biehl."

This passage illustrates the great pride which local writers and residents took in describing new industries in their cities. Despite the gradual rise of the temperance movement through this era, modern breweries were admired for their architectural beauty and mechanical technology, as well as respected for providing employment for local men and markets for the grains of local farmers.

The pipeline supplying water from the Crystal Rock spring was five miles in length, and was also used by the Crystal Rock Water Company, which sold water in the city of Sandusky. Soon after the turn of the century, however, the water was found to be less uniform in quality than desired, especially when pumped from greater

New Stang brewery, circa 1900 [courtesy of the Sandusky Library Archives]

depths. After 1904, the spring water was no longer used for brewing beer, and in fact was replaced by water from nearby Sandusky Bay. The pipeline was taken up a few years later, although the Crystal Rock name continued to be well known in the area for many years, due in part to the continuation by the brewery of using the name for its flagship beer.

On March 8, 1896, the Stang Brewing Co. merged with the Kuebeler Brewing and Malting Co. one mile away, forming the Kuebeler-Stang Brewing & Malting Co. Stang became the vice-president of this combine (Jacob Kuebeler was president), which had $700,000 in capital stock, and a collective annual capacity of 350,000 barrels. This entity lasted for less than two years before becoming a part of the Cleveland & Sandusky Brewing Co. conglomerate (which would eventually consist of eleven breweries in three cities) on January 1, 1898.

Stang continued to manage the plant, and eventually became vice-president of the parent company after Kuebeler's death in 1904. The plant continued to operate very successfully as a division of Cleveland & Sandusky until 1919 (It should be noted that the two Sandusky plants continued to use the name Kuebeler-Stang for a number of years in their advertising, even after the formation of the Cleveland & Sandusky Co.) See the section on Cuyahoga County for the operation of the parent company.

Upon the enactment of statewide Prohibition in 1919, the Kuebeler plant was closed, leaving the Stang plant as the city's only surviving brewery. It continued to operate throughout the next fourteen years, capitalizing on the name recognition of its flagship product by renaming itself as the Crystal Rock Products Co. (still a subsidiary of the Cleveland & Sandusky Co.) Crystal Rock Cereal Beverage, Deerfield Ginger Ale, and other soft drinks were produced through the end of Prohibition with a moderate degree of success. Stang had left the company by 1923 to manage a local wine company, after which the plant was managed by Roy Homegardner, who had been with the company since 1902.

With the repeal of Prohibition, the old Stang plant was refurbished as one of only two surviving branches of the Cleveland-Sandusky Brewing Co. (the other being the Fishel plant in Cleveland). In July 1933 it became the first of the two breweries to release beer to the public, when Gold Bond Beer was shipped east for sale in the Cleveland market, followed soon by Crystal Rock Beer, and three new brands, Old Timers and Buccaneer Ales and New York Special Beer.

Brewing operations continued successfully for two years until all of the plant's eighty workers went on strike in April 1935, in connection with a massive brewery worker strike in Cleveland (see the section on Cuyahoga County for more on the strike). The conflict was the culmination of a long standing battle for jurisdiction over brewery truck drivers, who had previously been members of the brewery work-

ers' union, but who had recently switched allegiance to the teamsters' union. While the brewery owners were essentially neutral in this conflict, they ultimately paid the greatest price, as the breweries operated at a reduced capacity with replacement workers for several months.

The old Stang plant was particularly hard-hit, as clashes between strikers and replacement workers turned violent, with several people being injured in early May when a tear gas bomb was thrown. Rocks and stones thrown at the brewery broke windows and lights, and the plant shut down completely for two weeks. By the end of that month, manager Roy Homegardner announced that the plant would close permanently and the equipment would immediately be dismantled and moved to the main Cleveland plant (the only one remaining in the company). By the time the strike finally ended in November, Sandusky's brewing history had come to a sad end.

The brewery stood empty for two years until the buildings and remaining equipment were purchased by local businessman Elliott M. Bender for $100,000. His plan was to sell $300,000 worth of stock in order to make the brewery operable again by the following summer. This plan never took shape, however, and as late as 1938, it was announced that the Sandusky Chamber of Commerce was still looking for a way to get the brewery back in operation. Instead, the plant remained empty for nearly a decade before the entire complex was razed in 1947, leaving no remains today. The Crystal Rock, Old Timers, and Gold Bond brands continued to be produced in Cleveland until the main plant closed in 1962, after which they were produced by the International Breweries Co. in Findlay, OH. and Buffalo, NY. until 1966. The brands were then produced by both the Meister-Brau/Buckeye Brewing Co. in Toledo and the Cumberland Brewing Co. in Cumberland, MD., each of which had rights to the Cleveland-Sandusky name, until approximately 1969. Following a gap of thirty years, the Crystal Rock name resurfaced in 1999 as a brand of Dopple Bock Lager Beer, brewed by the Frontwaters microbrewery in nearby Marblehead (see the section on Ottawa County). The name also lives on at the Crystal Rock campground, near the old spring several miles southwest of Sandusky, which uses the familiar logo to this day.

4. Sandusky City Brewery/Ilg & Co.

Located on the east side of the north end of Harrison Street, along the shore of Lake Erie, the Sandusky Brewery appears to have been established around 1854, although different sources vary on the year. Originally known as the Fox Brewery, the plant was established by Vincenz (also spelled Vincent or Winsen) Fox, a native of Baden, Germany, who was born in 1831. It was sold to George Soergel, Philip Dorn, & Paul Raible, three German immigrants, in September 1866, for $65,000. Dorn & Raible sold their shares in 1871 to John G. Strobel & Anthony Ilg. Strobel was a Bavarian immigrant, born in 1837, who had previously worked in the brewing industry in Cincinnati before coming to Sandusky. Ilg was a native of Wurtemburg, Germany, born in 1820, who also had previously worked in Cincinnati. By this time, annual production of beer ranged between 5,000 and 7,000 barrels.

Soergel, the senior partner in the group, sold his share in 1874. Five years later, Strobel sold his share of the brewery in order to operate a substantial winery in the city. The company was renamed A. Ilg & Co., and it was at this time that the name of the plant became the Sandusky City Brewery, although that title had earlier been used for the Dauch/Stang brewery one mile away, leading to some confusion among historians. Ilg's son Otto had begun working in the brewery when he came of age, and became a full partner in 1885.

The brewery itself was built of limestone and covered five acres. By this time, fifteen employees, including brewmaster R. J. Koch, had increased annu-

Lithograph, circa late 1860s; this is one of the earliest known advertising signs from any Ohio brewery [from the Sandusky Library Archives].

al production to 12,000 barrels, the most popular brand being "Milt and Gold Lager Beer". This was sold throughout the city and the north central portion of the state. In 1890, the company incorporated as the Sandusky Brewing Company, with capital stock of $50,000. This incorporation may have been an attempt to raise cash to keep the brewery alive, but ultimately it proved unsuccessful, as brewing operations ceased later that year. The plant was then sold for $22,150 at a sheriff's sale to Jacob Kuebeler and Frank Stang (this was several years prior to the merger of their respective breweries). After the equipment was removed, the plant was converted into a champagne cellar for both the Diamond Wine Co. and the Lake Erie Wine Co. In 1944, it was purchased by the Peerless Stove Co., which continues to operate in the plant to this day.

5. Bavarian Brewery, George Baier & Charles Pusch

Remains of malt house as it appears today

Located at the southeast corner of Jefferson and Putnam Streets, this small brewery was three stories in height, and like many structures in the Sandusky area, was built of limestone, of which there was a natural abundance in the region. George Baier (also spelled Beier, Bier) was a Bavarian immigrant, born in 1821, who appears to have started brewing operations (and a small adjacent cooper shop) there in 1857. Two years later he formed a partnership with Prussian immigrant Charles T. Pusch (also spelled Bush). Although Pusch sold his interest to Baier after a fire damaged the brewery in 1866, it appears that Pusch continued to work in the rebuilt brewery for several years afterward.

In 1873, brewing operations were taken over by Nicholas Wagner, who then closed the plant for good one year later. The plant was later converted into a pickle factory, then a dairy, and more recently has been used for storage. The malt house of the plant remains standing to this day, and was entered into the National Register of Historic Places in 1982.

6. Bay City Brewery

Edmund G. P. Mittleberger was a native Canadian, born in 1825, who came to Sandusky by way of Cleveland (where he was briefly a partner in Michael Lucas's lager brewery). In 1859, he established this small ale brewery across from the Dauch Brewery, at the far west end of Water Street. The plant stood along a main railroad line, employed six men, and produced mainly "present use" ale.

Mittleberger had sold the plant by 1867 to a group known as Alder & Co., consisting of James Alder, George Windisch, and John Bright. This group converted the plant to production of the more popular lager beer, and continued to operate the brewery for approximately one year until the plant burned down, never to operate again. There are no remains of it today. Mittleberger continued to live in the city for a number of years, operating a saloon and billiard parlor.

7. Jacob Kuebeler/Cleveland & Sandusky Brewing Company

The last and largest of Sandusky's nineteenth century breweries began operation in 1867. Jacob Kuebeler was a native of Heringen, Hesse, Germany, born in 1838, who came to the United States in 1860. After working for a short time in the Oberholtz brewery in Akron, he moved to Sandusky and worked for several years in the Anthony Ilg brewery. In 1867, however, he formed a partnership with his younger brother August, and they subsequently established a new plant on the south side of Tiffin Avenue (today U. S. Route 6 & state route 101).

This plant grew over the years to consist of several buildings. The main brewhouse (four stories in height and constructed of stone) was built in 1873 and contained the city's largest copper brew kettle, allowing 100 barrels of beer to be brewed at a time. The brothers employed two men to assist them in the first year, when 1,500 barrels of beer were brewed and distributed through the city by one horse and wagon. Hard work and aggressive distribution by the Kuebelers over the next twenty years led to an increase in annual output from 7,000 barrels in 1874 to 40,000 barrels in 1892, when thirty men and nine teams of horses were employed by the company.

Some of those barrels were sent across Sandusky Bay to a small fledgling resort on a peninsula known as Cedar Point. Founded in 1870 as a series of bathhouses along a strip of beach, Cedar Point had grown into a popular summer getaway for local residents when, in 1888, a "Grand Pavilion" was built, complete with a dance floor, bowling alleys, an auditorium, and a large beer garden. As one of the founders of the pavilion, Jacob Kuebeler supplied vacationers with fresh brewed beer for a number of years. After the turn of the century, this beer garden was replaced by the Crystal Rock castle (see next page), which continued to provide locally made beer to counter the summer sun. The pavilion is long gone now, but Cedar Point has evolved into one of the world's most popular and well-known amusement parks.

In 1892, the original plant was heavily damaged by fire, after which plans were drawn up for the construction of a much larger, modern, and ornate brewery complex which would allow for more dramatic growth in the future. To raise capital for the construction of this new plant, a stock company was created, to be known as the Jacob Kuebeler Brewing & Malting Company.

After the new brewery was completed in 1893, a thorough description can be found in the following brewery tour by a local reporter:

"Huge bales of hops can be seen stored away in suitable rooms, dry and well ventilated. The barley is at once taken into the elevator and conveyed through what is termed a separator. This apparatus thoroughly cleans it, removing all dust and foreign matter, and from the separator the barley is conveyed by means of a mechanical contrivance to the storage elevator ready for use. This elevator has a capacity of 80,000 bushels.

The next process which the barley undergoes is that of steeping, five immense tanks being used for that purpose. These tanks are fed direct from the bins, and when the steeping process is completed the barley is shot into five drums below. The system by which the barley is converted into malt is that known as the Galland and Henning process, and is the only one in use in this county. In fact it was the first one in the state. By this process fresh air is continually circulating through the drums. The cold air is drawn through an air tower and passes through another chamber filled with coke sprinkled with water. As the air passes through the coke it is purified and thence it is carried through the heating drums and drawn out by means of quickly revolving fans. The barley as it sprouts is thus kept perfectly sweet and fresh, and as the drums revolve slowly—making one revolution in 48 minutes—the whole of the contents are subject to the same temperature.

When it is sufficiently sprouted the barley is conveyed into the malting kilns. There are two of these, one above the other. The sprouted barley is placed first in the upper kiln and next into the lower one. They are styled dumping kilns and by the turn of a lever the floor opens and shoots the malt into the floor below. From the lower kiln the malt drops into the storage bins and is ready for use by the brewer. The greater portion of the malting house is fire proof. From its entry into the elevator to its conversion into malt and storage the barley is never touched by hand, its entire manipulation being carried on by one of the most perfect systems of automatic action ever devised.

Coming to the brew house one is struck by the same perfectness of detail in the mechanical arrangements as is found in the malting department. There is a huge copper boiler, steam heated, which has a capacity of 200 barrels; a rice mash tank and a tank for mashing malt, while in an adjoining room is a fire heated boiler with a capacity of 125 barrels, ready for use in case of emergency. There are eight brews a week. Passing from the kettles the beer is taken through a cooler and thence conveyed to the fermenting department. This place has three floors and contains forty-two tanks varying in capacity from 70 to 125 barrels. After fermenting the beer is run by means of pipes into the storage cellars.

A trip through the cellars alone is interesting. Far below the level of the ground are two floors with innumerable cellars connected by pas-

(above) Jacob Kuebeler [taken from *One Hundred Years of Brewing*]; (left) Kuebeler Brewery lithograph, circa 1880s [from the collection of George Mylander, a great-grandson of Jacob Kuebeler; Mylander is one of several Kuebeler family descendents in the Sandusky area, and he served as the city's mayor for a number of years in the 1980s].

sages which to the uninitiated seem labyrinthine. They are dark and cold but dry and well ventilated. There is an entire absence of those earthy odors peculiar to subterranean vaults, and the floors are laid with solid concrete graded so as to allow of the most efficient drainage. In these cellars are tanks varying in capacity from 40 to 275 barrels each, the aggregate being in the neighborhood of 170,000 barrels or nearly 4,500,000 gallons. The cellars are fire proof and are cooled by means of an elaborate system of cold air pipes supplied from a refrigerating plant on the premises. The tanks are tapped when their contents are ready for consumption and the beer is conveyed in flexible pipes to the room where the barrels are filled.

Another department of equal interest and importance is the washing room. As the wagons arrive at the brewery, bringing in their loads of empties, the barrels are immediately placed in a big tank and thoroughly cleansed with hot water, a small engine operating brushes used in this work. They are afterwards placed on stands and are cooled by means of a current of cold water which passes through them, after which they are ready for use again. The number of barrels which the brewery has in use is astounding.

When they are refilled the barrels are run out on to a sliding arrangement and placed either in the wagons for delivery in the city or into railroad cars on the side track adjoining the brewery for shipment to other towns. The J. Kuebeler Brewing & Malting Co. controls the bulk of the city trade and in addition has a number of cars on the railroad which are used exclusively for the shipment of beer to Findlay, Lorain, Elyria, Chicago Junction, Oak Harbor, Bellevue, Monroeville, Clyde, Vermillion, Huron, and numerous other places.

Adjoining the brewery is a large pond which makes capital ice in the winter, sufficient for all requirements. The ice is stored away into an ice house and is used in packing beer in railroad cars. From the time the beer leaves the brewing room until it reaches the consumer it has to be kept cool, and only those who are familiar with the operations of a great brewery can have any conception of the trouble and expense to that end.

The boiler house is a separate building and contains a couple of large boilers. Another house is being erected to which these boilers will beremoved and a third one will be laid down so as to give increased power. The engine which operates the ventilators and the refrigerator apparatus is kept going day and night. A new refrigerating apparatus is being erected and already a large tank is erected containing no less than 14,000 feet of piping. The plant when complete will be capable of producing 100 tons of ice daily.

Altogether the Kuebeler brewery is one of the finest in the state; there are larger breweries, but none with better facilities. The plant is capable of producing 100,000 barrels a year and is so arranged that its capacity can be doubled in a very short time with the addition of more

The Crystal Rock Castle

In 1904, Jacob Kuebeler's beer garden at Cedar Point was replaced with a new and impressive structure, to be named after his company's most popular brand of beer. The Crystal Rock Castle was built to resemble a medieval European palace, complete with turrets and grey stucco walls. Large quantities of draft beer and locally made wines were served here over the next fifteen years to "lovers of Bohemian life", as the resort continued to grow larger and more popular, drawing patrons from Cleveland and Detroit as well as the local area. In fact, beer was the most popular beverage at the park in the years before Prohibition, with a large authentic German Rathskeller located nearby, adjacent to the large dancing pavilion. Not surprisingly, much of the beer sold was Crystal Rock, and these sales provided a large portion of the revenue that Cedar Point generated. The peninsula's lagoons were dredged several years later, and a boat landing was installed behind the Crystal Rock Castle for patrons to rent a rowboat for an afternoon, before returning to quench their thirst from the afternoon sun.

With the onset of Prohibition, the building was converted into Ye Old Castle Grill, a restaurant serving a wide variety of food. Despite the loss of revenue from alcohol sales, the park continued to flourish in the 1920s. A portion of the huge Crystal Rock Castle was converted into the park's fire house and first aid station. By the onset of the Depression, however, the park had hit hard times financially. The building was converted into the Castle Sandwich Shop, but still remained unprofitable. By the 1950s, the building was only being used to house the park's maintenance department, and in the 1960s, it burned to the ground, bringing an end to a large slice of the park's history. The park would rebound in the 1970s and eventually grow into a world-class attraction, but few who go there today know the history of the Crystal Rock Castle and its importance in the park's early years. [Much of this information is taken from *Cedar Point: The Queen of American Watering Places*, by David W. Francis and Diane DeMali Francis.]

(right) The new brewery at the turn of the century; (below) Large lithograph, circa 1896, showing the two breweries, which were about a mile apart, in an artificial but impressive view [Glenn Kuebeler collection]

malting drums. The popularity of the amber export, pilsener and lager beer brewed here is deservedly great and one of the best testimonies of its high quality is the fact that Kuebeler's amber export and pilsener beer will be sold at the Vienna Café, in the midway plaisance, Columbian Exposition, Chicago."

On March 8, 1896, the Kuebeler and Stang breweries merged, forming the short-lived Kuebeler-Stang Brewing & Malting Co. The new company, of which Jacob Kuebeler became president, had capital stock of $700,000 and a collective annual capacity of 350,000 barrels. This would be absorbed on June 1, 1898 by the Cleveland & Sandusky Brewing Corporation (which would eventually consist of eleven breweries in three cities), under which name the plant would continue to operate until the onset of Prohibition (although, as stated earlier, the two Sandusky plants continued to use the name Kuebeler-Stang in their advertising for some years after the merger.)

Jacob Kuebeler, who became the 1st vice-president of the new combine, died of stomach cancer in 1904 (after which his obituary described him as Sandusky's wealthiest man, a "millionaire brewer"). After this, John Stang managed both Sandusky breweries until Prohibition, producing Bohemian Lager, Amber Export, and Perry Brew (commemorating Admiral Oliver Hazard Perry's victory over the British in the Battle of Lake Erie, just northwest of the city, in the War of 1812), in addition to the region's favorite, Crystal Rock. A more detailed account of the operation of the Cleveland & Sandusky Co. is given in the section on Cleveland breweries.

After passage of the statewide Prohibition bill in late 1918, the Kuebeler plant was closed and vacated, with all brewing in the city shifted to the Stang plant (mainly due to the fact that the Stang plant had a bottling facility, while the Kuebeler plant did not). The buildings remained vacant until 1929, when the ornate Kuebeler brewery fell prey to the wrecking ball, leaving no remains whatsoever at the site. The Kuebeler name continued during Prohibition in the form of a malt tonic produced at the Cleveland plant of the Cleveland-Sandusky Co. August Kuebeler had retired from the business by the time the family brewery closed, and he continued to live in his mansion (which still stands today) across the street until his death in 1927.

Also Note:

The Wallaby's chain of brewpubs, headquartered in Westlake, Ohio, opened a Wallaby's Grille restaurant in 1999 on Milan Road (U.S. Route 250) south of Sandusky. While the Wallaby's beer brands were sold in the restaurant, no beer was brewed at the site, which had closed its doors by the end of 2000.

Lancaster

1. Justus Younghans brewery

Few details are known about Lancaster's first brewing establishment. Justus Younghans was a native of Hesse-Darmstadt, Germany, born in 1813, who had come to America in the late 1830s. Around 1840 he purchased land between the Hocking River and the Hocking Canal in central Lancaster, near the site where present-day Main Street crosses the river. Soon after this he established a small brewing operation there. Most of what is known about the brewery comes from a small historical note in the Lancaster *Eagle-Gazette* from June 1950:

"Zink & Younghans was a brewery of national note. In May, 1848, however, Lancaster was aroused by an alarm of fire before daybreak. Word soon spread that the Younghans Brewery was on fire, and, with the brewery, the flames consumed five or six adjoining buildings. The fire jeopardized the whole of Lancaster.

The catastrophe took place on May 4, 1848 at 4 a.m. when fire broke out in the brewery's dry house, spreading to other parts of the building and soon developed the whole in flames as well as some five or six frame and brick dwellings and shops, measurably consuming most and ruining all of them.

The brewery contained about 3,000 bushels of rye, barley, and wheat, owned by different persons, all of which was lost.

The upper story of a shop in Phillipp & Co., tan-yard was burnt off.

The morning was very calm and the property, being situated on the bank of the canal, gave a plentiful water supply. The engines kept well-supplied and well-managed, or much greater damage would have resulted."

Younghans had been joined in the late 1840s by William Zink, a recent immigrant from Germany who was born in 1810. After the fire, the men quickly rebuilt the brewery, although Zink left the partnership several years later. By 1860, Younghans was being assisted by his 22-year-old son George, as well as five other men, all recent German immigrants. Operations continued into the late 1860s, after which the plant shut down. By 1870, Younghans was listed in the census as a cooper, while his son was working for the nearby Becker brewery. Nothing remains of the Younghans brewery today.

2. Becker/Lancaster Brewing Company

Fairfield County's longest-lasting brewery was located along the east bank of the Hocking Canal, at the southwest corner of the intersection of Union Street and Forest Rose Avenue (originally called Canal Street). Later, the brewery's address would become 302 Union Street. It was established by Frederick, George, and Christian Ochs, all Bavarian natives. According to local literature, brewing operations began in 1867, although other records vaguely suggest that brewing at the site may have begun as much as a decade earlier.

In 1868, the company was joined by Ernest Becker and Theodore Mithoff (Becker's brother-in-law). Becker was born in 1822 in Hanover, Germany. From the age of fifteen he was employed in the local mercantile trade, until 1846 when he embarked on a two-month journey to America, coming to Lancaster, Ohio soon after that. He worked in the mercantile, grocery, and distillery businesses at different times, until he entered the brewing trade in 1868 and became the company's new president.

(right) Becker Brewing Co. plant around the turn of the century; (bottom) Bottle label (Bob Kay collection).

After this, the company was known as Becker, Ochs, & Company. It was joined in 1873 by Charles P. Noll, who became the new brewmaster. Noll was a native of Cincinnati, born in May 1850, who had previously worked in two of that city's largest breweries before moving east to Lancaster. Ernest Becker's son, Harry E. Becker, would later join the company as a director. The brewery thrived and grew over the next decade, producing between 2,000 and 4,000 barrels of beer annually through 1878. The Ochses sold their share of the company that year, after which it was known as Becker & Co. It was then incorporated as the E. Becker Brewing Company in 1884, with a capital stock of $75,000. At that time, the brewery consisted of a three-story brewhouse and office building, with a two-story adjacent ice house. The plant would change very little over the next sixty years; a description of the brewery from The Ohio *Eagle* in June 1888 included the following:

> ...Under the building are two commodius cellars 54 x 45 feet, filled with about 400 large tanks which are used in the preparation of beer and malt. There are also two other cellars, 18 x 62 feet, and one fermenting cellar, the dimensions of which are 40 x 40. The machinery of this brewery is all of the most modern and approved kind, and the total cost of the same runs away up into the thousands. The ice machine now in use cost originally $25,000, and several expensive improvements have been recently made thereon. The capacity is between 15,000 and 20,000 barrels a year, equal to from 600,000 to 800,000 gallons. The new Lightning bottle washer cleanses 100 dozen bottles per hour. About 50,000 bushels of barley are used yearly. None but first quality is purchased, for which this firm is always ready to pay top prices. The bottling machine has a capacity of a gallon per minute. In a single year 100 large bales of hops are used, which cost from $100 to $150 per bale. All the machinery is now run by natural gas. Twenty-five to thirty men are constantly employed at an average salary of forty-five dollars per month...In addition to the many tons of ice manufactured by the chemical process, several large ice houses are filled each year from the reservoir.

One near-disaster occurred on June 23, 1890, when the ammonia still in the ice machine exploded. This blew off a portion of the roof of the ice house, and the resulting leakage of ammonia into the air nearly suffocated several nearby residents. One employee of the brewery was badly injured, but there were no fatalities, and the damage was quickly repaired.

After Becker died of a stomach hemorrhage on July 14, 1892, Theodore Mithoff became the company's president. Mithoff was involved in numerous other business ventures in the city at the same time, helping to start the Hocking Valley National Bank, and also owning one of the state's largest natural gas wells, known as "The Old Man Himself".

Mithoff died just two years later, after which Harry Becker became the company's president, with Noll as vice-president, and Mithoff's son Edward as secretary. A bottling house had been added to the plant by this time, for the packaging of both Export and "Budweiser" Lager Beers. After the turn of the century came the introduction of "Bismarck" and "Noll's Ideal" Beers as well. Additional improvements had increased the plant's annual capaci-

ty to 15,000 barrels. Noll assumed the company's presidency in 1897, a position he maintained until his death in March 1912. Harry Becker then continued to manage the plant for the next four years, until brewing operations came to an end in 1916.

The plant was purchased by the Crystal Ice and Coal Company in 1918. Founded locally by John Kilburger in 1910, this new company would utilize the brewery's ice-making equipment and also supply coal and salt to local customers. After the end of Prohibition in 1933, however, Kilburger saw the potential of expanding into the newly rejuvenated brewing industry. The new Lancaster Brewing Company was subsequently incorporated in 1934, with capital stock of $300,000, to operate in the same facility as the original brewery, except with modernized equipment. The first brew was made available to the public on July 21 of that year.

John Kilburger was the company's president and plant manager, with his son Charles as secretary and treasurer, Leona Stine as vice-president, Albert Kempe as the brewmaster, and Philip Laessle as the chief engineer. The brewery's primary brands of beer were Silver Label and Forest Rose Lager, both of which were distributed throughout central and southern Ohio. The Forest Rose name came from a popular novel with that title, written by Emerson Bennett in 1848. It chronicled an Ohio pioneer family and their adopted daughter who went by the nickname Forest Rose.

In the late 1930s, the company entered the relatively new frozen food industry. A large addition to the icehouse was used for the storage of a wide variety of foods at zero degree temperatures.

Realizing that the future would be more profitable there than in the increasingly competitive brewing industry, Kilburger decided to cease all brewing operations by 1942, spelling the end for the Lancaster Brewing Co.

Kilburger died in 1944, but his son Charles continued to operate the company until 1969. The plant was then vacated and the main brewhouse was razed soon thereafter. The adjacent icehouse remains standing today, remodeled extensively, and is used as a warehouse. The nearby Hocking Canal was eventually filled in, and today U. S. Route 33 follows its course.

GALLIA COUNTY

Gallipolis

1. Brandstetter/Henkel brewery

Xavier F. Brandstetter was born in Renchen, Baden, Germany in 1809. Coming to America in the 1860s, he had made the Ohio River town of Gallipolis his home by 1865. In August of that year he purchased land on the east side of Chillicothe Road, approximately one mile west of downtown, atop a steep hill. Soon after this, he established Gallia County's only brewery at the site. It appears that he operated the brewery with Theodore Augustine, a younger German immigrant (born in 1843), while farming at the same time. The brewery consisted of two one-story buildings; one was a combination brewhouse and residence, the other was an icehouse. The water for brewing came from two on-site wells, and between 300 and 500 barrels of lager beer were produced there annually.

Brandstetter died in August 1876, after which the land was sold to satisfy his debts, and it was subsequently annexed to the city of Gallipolis as Brandstetter's Addition. During this time, it appears that the small brewery was being operated by Frederick Henkel, Brandstetter's nephew. By 1879, Henkel had amassed enough cash to purchase the brewery and property himself. Brewing continued until approximately 1888, after which Henkel continued to operate the plant for beer bottling only. By 1900, the brewery building had been converted into a residence, but within a few years, the entire complex was gone. Today this residential district is known as Brandstetter Heights, with Henkle Avenue running through the area as a reminder of the past.

Cambridge

1. Herman Berns Brewery

Herman(n) Berns (also spelled Berne, Bernes) was a Prussian immigrant, born in 1824, who came from Maryland to the town of Cambridge in 1870. In January of that year, he purchased land along the west side of what is now Dewey Avenue (U. S. Routes 22 and 40), south of Wills Creek. Soon after this he established Guernsey County's first brewery, though it was essentially a home brewing operation, producing less than 100 barrels of beer annually. In the 1870 census, his eight-year-old daughter Frances and his six-year-old son William were both listed as "helping father" for an occupation.

It would appear that brewing operations had ceased by 1877, as the brewery appears on neither Schade's 1878 directory nor Tovey's 1882 directory. However, when Berns sold the property in November 1884, the deed mentions transfer of the entire premises *except* the copper boiler, copper pump, tubs and barrels belonging to the brewery. There is no evidence that the brewery operated after this time, however, so Berns may have either sold the equipment separately or taken it with him to a new location. Nothing remains of the small brewery today.

2. Cambridge Brewing Company

Cambridge area businessmen formed a stock company in early 1901, with a capital of $100,000. Known as the Cambridge Brewing Co., it had a brief and tumultuous history, lasting only eight years altogether. Located at 135-145 Steubenville Ave., at the northwest corner of the intersection of North 2nd St., the plant consisted of a primary four-story brewhouse and several surrounding buildings.

The initial president of the new company was Herbert R. Gill, who had been one of the founders of the Consumers Brewing Co. in Newark, Ohio just four years earlier. Gustave Varrelmann was the new plant's vice-president, superintendent, and brewmaster, and John Lloyd was the secretary. Other directors included Richard Minto and L. E. Carlisle. After the plant's construction, the first brew was started on February 6, 1902. When it was ready several weeks later, "Tip Top" beer hit the local market with slogans such as "Special Brew For Family Consumption", "Specially Brewed For A Mild Tonic", and "Your Doctor Prescribes It".

After only three years of operation, the company was reorganized in 1905 for financial reasons as The Brewery Company, with its capital stock reduced to $25,000. Herbert Gill and John Lloyd remained involved, along with several new investors. This newly formed company would only survive for a few months, however, before being unable to pay its creditors.

Because of this, the entire plant was sold at a sheriff's auction on March 10, 1906, for $38,400 to a Columbus bank, which would in turn sell it to a new group of investors from Bellaire, Ohio, headed by Sebastian Wimmer and D. E. Brown. A new company (again called the Cambridge Brewing Company) was formed with a capital stock of $100,000. The new president was Julius A. Kremer, who had also been one of the original founders of the Consumers Brewing Co. in Newark. Paul M. Cain was now secretary and Herbert J. Kremer was plant superintendent. Other men involved with the new company were J. H. Graves, and Leo and Otis Kremer. Soon after this reorganization, a new ice plant was built at the brewery site, costing $50,000.

The brewing of a new brand, "Bingo" Beer, began at this time, and continued until passage of the Rose "local option" Law in 1908. In a previous special election, the city of Cambridge had become the second city in Ohio to vote itself dry, hurting

(above) Cambridge brewery as seen on the company's letterhead [Bill Carlisle collection]; **(left)** Cambridge City Directory, 1908.

the brewery's sales somewhat. As a direct result of the Rose Law, however, all of Guernsey County and several surrounding counties went dry in 1909, crippling the company's business and causing it to cease operations almost immediately.

By 1910, the plant was occupied by a new, unrelated company, the Cambridge Ice & Storage Co., and later by the Guernsey Creamery Co. as well. Guernsey County voted itself wet again in 1912, although it was not until two more years had passed that another group was formed with the hope of renovating the brewery and restarting operations. These plans never materialized, however, and Cambridge's brewing history had come to an end. Eventually, most of the plant was vacated, and later was razed. The icehouse and wagon building remain standing today on the north side of the complex.

Also Note

In the December 15, 1878 edition of *The Western Brewer*, a mention is made of a new brewery having begun in Cambridge, Ohio, operated by J. H. Bernhard. After much research, I have not been able to find any other mention of this brewery. There was a Joseph S. Bernhard in Guernsey County at the time, and he had purchased three separate properties in the 1870s, but all were in a distant, rural part of the county.

Whether this notice is a mistaken referral to Herman Berns (accuracy was more difficult to ensure in those days), or a possible home brewing operation by Bernhard, one may never know. Based on the information available, however, one can assume this is a referral to Berns.

HOCKING COUNTY

Hide-A-Way Hills

1. Blueberry Hill/The Lodge at Hide-A-Way Hills brewpub

Located in a remote and hilly area several miles southeast of Lancaster, Hide-A-Way Hills is a private resort of nearly 600 homes, originally laid out in 1961. Located in a dry territory, however, the restaurant in the main lodge was unable to obtain a full liquor license unless it took advantage of a loophole in Ohio law (which has since been changed). This law allowed such establishments a "pub license" if they brewed beer on-site. Therefore, the decision was made to invest in a 10-barrel all grain brewing system, made by the Century Manufacturing Co. With that, Hocking County's only brewing venture began operation on June 24, 1993. The restaurant was known as "Blueberry Hill" when the brewery was established; it then adopted its current name of "Lodge at Hide-A-Way Hills" in 1998, after a change in management. The brewing operation itself is known as the Rush Creek Brewery.

The brewpub is managed by Jim Palmer, and the brewer is Scott Francis, who also was involved with the formation of similar brewing operations at private clubs near Columbus and at Atwood Lake in Carroll County. Francis had been a home brewer for many years and had operated The Winemaker's Shop in Columbus before becoming involved with the Columbus Brewing Co., one of Ohio's earliest brewpubs. He currently is the brewer for the two Barley's Brewing Company sites in the Columbus area.

Francis brews Rush Creek Pale Ale and Rush Creek Lager Beer for sale only in the clubhouse, with batches brewed as needed. While the beer is primarily for members of the resort, the public can come to the pub if reservations are made in advance.

HOLMES COUNTY

Millersburg

1. Millersburg Brewery

Pierre Mailleard (also spelled Mailliard, Maillard) was born in France in 1835, and came to America at the age of thirteen. After living in Massillon for several years, he moved to Holmes County and in 1865 purchased eleven acres of land north of the town of Millersburg, where he would soon establish the county's first brewery. It was located on the east side of Wooster Road, now state route 83, approximately one mile north of town.

During its brief life, the brewery produced 400-500 barrels of lager beer per year. Production appears to have ceased by 1877, and the property was sold at a sheriff's auction two years later to help satisfy several of Mailleard's debts. Appraised at $1,800 at that time, the property was sold for $1,200, and the brewery was subsequently dismantled. There is no trace of it today. Confusing the research on Mailleard is the fact that he Americanized his name at various times, using the name Peter Moyers. In his obituary from October 1908, he is referred to as Peter C. Myers, although his tombstone retains his original French name.

Winesburg

1. Leo Weigand Brewery

Leopold ("Leo") Weigand was a German immigrant, born in 1824 in Eppingen, Baden, Germany. He settled in the village of Weinsberg (which was Anglicized to "Winesburg" after the turn of the century) in 1868, and established this small brewery soon after. It was located on a hillside at the southern edge of the village, just south of the intersection of Vintage and Chestnut Streets. He operated both a vineyard and lager beer brewery at the site, where "the best quality of Beer and Wine can be bought cheap for cash", according to the 1875 Holmes County Atlas. The water source was from any one of several springs in the area, and it appears that Weigand stored and aged his beer in a natural underground cave in a ravine about a half-mile away. This cave had a spring inside of it as well.

Production of beer was less than 200 barrels per year, and most of it was likely distributed to the seven taverns in the small village. The brewery business was gone by the mid-1880s, although Weigand stayed in the area and died in 1894. Today, a house which may have been Weigand's residence remains at the site, while the brewery building has disappeared without a trace. The underground cave and spring remain untouched by time, and can be accessed by a pleasant walk through the countryside.

2. Godfrey Schmidt

There appears to have been a small home brewing operation at another site in Winesburg in the 1880s. Godfrey Schmidt, born locally in 1844 to German immigrants, purchased land and buildings on the south end of the village in the 1870s and initially operated a tavern. By the mid-1880s, however, he had established a small home brewing operation at the site. There was also a beer garden or beer hall behind the brewery for the enjoyment of local residents and travelers, and it appears that most, if not all, of the beer produced was sold there.

It appears very possible that Schmidt had some affiliation with Leo Weigand's brewery down the street in the 1870s, and that some equipment for his brewing operation may have been transferred from Weigand's brewery, which ended production around the same time this one began. The time frame of Schmidt's brewing operation is unknown, but it is likely that it had ended by 1900. The beer garden may have continued for some time after that, but it was gone by the onset of Prohibition. Part of the building remains as a residence at what is now 2172 Main Street (U.S. Route 62), and it still contains the stone beer cellar with vaulted ceiling in the basement.

Huron County

Monroeville

1. Monroeville Brewery

John S. Roby was a native of Detroit, who came to Monroeville and in 1848 established the village's only brewery with 38-year-old Englishman Isaac Harper. Roby's brothers Henry and Ruel later came to town and joined in the partnership. The brewery, which was located at the southwest corner of Monroe and Ridge Streets, was part of a larger complex which included a malt house half a mile to the east along Monroe Street, and two ice houses along the bank of the west

Trade card, circa 1875 [Ken Bryson collection]

branch of the Huron River. Below the icehouses was a large underground cellar, 100 feet in length, which could store several hundred barrels of ale and lager.

Foreman for the brewery for many years was recent immigrant Anthony Lais, who worked with his brothers Joseph and Charles until 1870, when he moved to nearby Norwalk and purchased the Star Brewery. In 1866, the Robys transferred operation of the brewery to Charles P. Prentiss, a native Ohioan who was born in 1821. However, it was not until October 1872 that he actually purchased the property, for $15,000.

By 1877, Prentiss had become financially insolvent, and the brewery was sold to a group of four German immigrants calling themselves Urlau, Rupp, & Co. This consisted of Robert Urlau, who assumed most of the brewing operations, Nicholas Rupp, Caroline Lais, and Blasius Smith. Rupp and Smith were primarily farmers, although they retained a financial interest in the brewery. Brewing operations continued until approximately 1884, after which Urlau operated a saloon and grocery in town. The Robys continued to operate the nearby malt house until several years later. That building later housed the Yingling Brothers Handle Works, which continued to operate into the 1940s. The entire complex, including the old brewery, was later razed, with no remains today.

Norwalk

1. Star Brewery

Pickett Latimer was a native of Connecticut, who moved west along with many others in the 1820s, when the region of Northern Ohio known as the Western Reserve was first settled. He became a prominent Norwalk merchant and owned numerous tracts of land throughout Huron County. Around 1827 he established a distillery on one of these tracts at the southeast corner of South Pleasant and West Elm Streets (later 30 South Pleasant Street), at the top of the bank of Norwalk Creek.

Until the 1850s, South Pleasant Street was a dirt alley known as Distillery Street, and it led past a schoolyard to the distillery on the south edge of town. A local resident, wanting to improve the image of the area, renamed the alley as Pleasant Street at that time. According to *"Just Like Old Times", Book V*, a collection of local historical information, by Henry Timman, one of the curious attractions in the area was the droves of hogs that were kept near the distillery by Latimer and later owners. The hogs were fattened by feeding on the residual mash from the distilling process. Although they may have been an attraction, the general unsanitary conditions around the hogs may have been at least partly responsible for local cholera epidemics in 1849 and 1854.

The distillery was operated by several different parties until it was sold by Latimer in 1848 to Richard, Augustus, and John Joslin, three brothers from New York. Around 1859, they converted the distillery to a brewery, which was operated mainly by John Joslin and Norman Moulton. They continued to operate until March 1862, when the property was surrendered by foreclosure to the Norwalk Bank.

The plant was then purchased by Frank Humbel (who was also a part owner of the brewery in nearby Milan) in April 1864, and he operated it until February 1866, when his debts led to the property being sold again at a sheriff's sale to John Beardsley. Beardsley & Joseph Farr, who was also the owner of a tannery across the road, then sold the brewery property to Irish immigrants Patrick & James Brady in January 1869. The Bradys operated the brewery until September 1870, when they sold it to Anthony Lais for $2,500. Patrick Brady would continue to work in the brewery with Lais for an additional two years or so.

Henry Lais

Lais was a native of Baden, Germany, born in 1826. Emigrating to America in 1849, he worked for two decades as the plant superintendent at the nearby Monroeville Brewery before moving to Norwalk. At the time of his purchase, the Star Brewery was still fairly small and produced only ale, but it slowly expanded over the next decade, with between 1,000 and 2,000 barrels of ale and lager beer being produced annually. He also developed an ice pond south of the brewery, which became a popular recreational spot for youngsters, both as a skating pond in the winter and a swimming hole in the summer. The pond was stocked with German carp, which supposedly would all congregate at the edge for feeding when Lais would whistle. He continued to run the brewery with his sons Henry, John, Charles, and William, until his death in 1886.

At that time, Henry took over brewing operations. Henry had been born in Monroeville in 1853, and had worked for his father since finishing school. He continued to expand the plant, adding a new malt house and bottling house and increasing the annual capacity to approximately 6,000 barrels by the turn of the century. Between six and eight men were employed by the brewery, depending on the season, and seven horses were kept for the delivery of beer throughout the town.

Lager beer and ale produced by Lais was sold mostly in saloons in Huron and Erie Counties. One such saloon was owned by Peter Troendle, a German immigrant who by 1893 had built up considerable debt to Henry Lais, presumably for beer sold in his tavern. In the ensuing legal action, Troendle's house was sold at a sheriff's auction to pay off the debt, and he left town with his family, moving

Star Brewery, circa 1904, as shown in *Norwalk Illustrated*, which was published by the *Evening Herald* in that year. (Thanks to Henry Timman)

north to Detroit. His son George remained in Detroit, where, in 1929, he purchased radio station WXYZ. Four years later, he created the original Lone Ranger series, and in 1936 the Green Hornet series, to draw a larger children's audience.

In April 1906, Lais purchased the nearby City Brewery for $15,000 from Theresa Ott, after which the City Brewery was permanently closed. A new stock company, known as the Lais Brewing Company, was then formed, with capital of $50,000. Henry Lais was the new company's president, with local saloon owner George Gfell as vice-president and local banker Frank M. Roth as secretary and treasurer.

Operations continued until 1912, when the plant closed. The buildings were subsequently used for storage, until all remaining buildings were razed in the 1920s. There are no remains of the Star Brewery today, although the basin of the ice pond remains, just south of the old brewery site, and Lais Avenue runs just east of the site, on land originally owned by the family. Lais remained in Norwalk, becoming the vice-president and director of the Huron County Banking Co., until his death in 1925.

2. Norwalk Brewery

George A. Merkle established this brewery in early 1837, and was advertising his common strong beer and porter for sale by that summer. Located on the east side of Benedict Avenue (U. S. Route 250), near the intersection of Norwood Avenue and overlooking Norwalk Creek, his small wooden frame establishment gave rise to the name "Brewery Hill" for this area of town for many years, long after brewing had ceased. It appears that the "Brewery Lot" property was owned during this time by a man named John Adams, but it does not appear that he was involved with the brewing process.

Despite a destructive fire in 1838, Merkle rebuilt and continued brewing until early 1841, when the brewery was purchased by James Pearse. The sale may not have been particularly amicable, however, as a subsequent message from Pearse was placed in the Norwalk *Reflector* that read, "Whereas, an advertisement appeared in the last week's *Experiment* (the other newspaper in town), that J. Pearse was indebted to a G. A. Merkle $1000, I wish to inform that gentleman that he has received in full of all demands against me. J. Pearse wisheth Merkle to call at the Brewery and pay for Beer, delivered last summer, immediately." It is not known what the source of this conflict was, nor how it was resolved.

It appears that brewing operations ended around 1844, after which the Brewery Lot was divided into smaller parcels for sale. The building was dismantled and moved north into town, where it was rebuilt at the corner of Railroad Avenue and Monroe Street, where it housed a small vehicle manufacturing company. Nothing remains of the Norwalk Brewery at either site today.

3. Zechariah Standish brewery

Zechariah Miles Standish was born near Syracuse, N. Y. in 1811. A direct descendent of the Pilgrim Miles Standish, he moved to Huron County at the age of twenty, and in 1849 moved into Norwalk and purchased land on Railroad Avenue. He began a small home brewing operation at his residence there soon after this. It appears, however, that brewing only lasted into the mid-1850s. Standish remained in Norwalk until his death in 1891.

4. Norwalk City Brewery

Augustus Ott was a native of Norwalk, born in 1833, who in May 1859 purchased property on Brewery Hill, south of downtown Norwalk, a few hundred yards west of where the old Merkle brewery had previously stood. His partners in this transaction were his younger brother Peter, born in 1836, and Feit (also spelled Veith) Bishop, a 31-year-old native of Baden, Germany, and the three men soon established a new brewing operation at the site. In later years, this site would take the address of 8-16 Oak Street.

The new brewery stood atop the steep bank of Norwalk Creek, which allowed the construction of two underground storage cellars into the bank and beneath the brewery. In addition, part of the creek was diverted to

Skaters on the Ott Brewery ice pond on a winter afternoon in the 1890s. The icehouse is at the far left and the other brewery buildings are on the hill. (Photo originally taken by Henry C. Morrison, a local merchant and amateur photographer. It was provided to me by Henry Timman.)

create a large ice pond, and two icehouses were built on the shore at the base of the hill. The creek also helped supply water for brewing in the early days, when the water was still fairly pure. In later years, pollution forced the digging of wells for a new water supply.

Bishop sold his share of the brewery in 1860 to the Ott brothers, although he continued to work there until 1866, when he left the area. Over the next decade, the Otts built the City Brewery into the largest one in town, with a 50-barrel brewkettle that produced between 2,000 and 3,000 barrels of ale and lager beer annually. However, by late 1876 the brothers had become insolvent, and the brewery was subsequently sold at a public auction to satisfy their debts. The new owners, Levi Fletcher and Joseph Miller, operated the brewery for the next two years. In 1878, Peter Ott had recovered financially to the extent that he was able to purchase a half interest in the brewery, which was placed in the name of his 38-year-old wife Theresa. By 1881, the Otts were able to purchase the remaining half of the brewery. However, Augustus Ott was no longer involved in brewing operations after this time.

Peter Ott died in 1890, after which his son Edward became the brewmaster. Theresa continued to oversee operations at the plant until 1906, when she sold it to Henry Lais, of the nearby Star Brewery, for $15,000. The City Brewery was subsequently closed, and within a few years had been torn down. Edward J. Ott became the plant manager of the Herb Brewery in Milan, a few miles away. Theresa Ott remained in Norwalk until her death in 1935, at the age of 96. There are no visible remains of the brewery today, although the cellars remain underground. Several sections of these have collapsed through the years, however.

Peru

1. Peru Brewery

In *History of Huron County, Ohio*, from 1909, there is a description of the small village of Peru, also known as Macksville, several miles south of Norwalk. In this description is the following passage: "At one time there were four stores, two distilleries, three breweries, two asheries, and a hotel which frequently kept twenty to twenty-five teams and teamsters overnight. This was before the time of railroads and when the wagon trade was something immense."

The existence of the distilleries is well documented, going back to at least 1817, when the area was first being settled and the buildings were made of logs. The only known mention of a brewery is an advertisement in the Norwalk *Reporter* on January 12, 1828, mentioning strong beer sold at the Peru Brewery, which was operated by William Taggart. It does not appear that this was a long-lived establishment, however.

(Thanks again to Henry Timman for his extensive help in finding photos and assisting me with his vast knowledge of the history of Huron County.)

Wellston

1. Wellston Brewing and Ice Company

The history of Jackson County's only brewery began eleven years prior to the company's first brew. In 1894, The Wellston Ice and Cold Storage Company was organized by A. B. Leach, to operate in conjunction with his existing store and planing mill. An adjacent ice house with a daily capacity of 17 fi tons of ice was built, along with four cold storage rooms. The plant, located between South Ohio and Pennsylvania Avenues, just south of East 12th Street, operated as such until 1901, when it was sold to Jasper Corn.

In 1905, Corn and his partner Louis Quasser organized the Wellston Brewing and Ice Company, with a capital of $45,000, to build a new associated brewery with an annual capacity of 15,000 barrels. Other investors at the time included Mary Corn, and Rosa and Anton Zix, the latter party also being the company's brewmaster. A four-story brewhouse was built, as well as a new bottling house nearby, and the brewing of beer soon began. Initial sales were good, and the plant was expanded the next year, with the capital stock being increased to $75,000. In 1908, however, the passage of the Rose Law led to Jackson County going dry at the beginning of 1909, along with most other southern Ohio counties. With the closure of all local saloons, and the company's reliance on local sales, the brewing of beer lasted only one more year before coming to an end in 1910.

Ice production continued as before, but profits were not sufficient to cover the heavy investment in the nearly new brewing plant. By 1912, the company was bankrupt, and the plant was sold several months later to Clarence Wolf of Dayton, Ohio. In 1913, he sold the plant to a new group from Chillicothe, Ohio, which would be known as the Wellston Ice Company. By 1921, the plant had been sold again, this time to Henry Holzapfel.

Holzapfel was born near Ironton, Ohio in 1866. He had previously worked as a miner, grocer, and ice cream manufacturer before the purchase of the old brewery with his twin sons, Leonard and Andrew. In 1928, the plant was expanded again and modernized for increased ice production. With Prohibition's repeal in 1933, the company, now known as Holzapfel Brothers, also became a local distributor for beer, and an effort was made to raise capital to restart brewing operations. This never occurred, however, and the company remained only a distribution center. Ice production continued through 1953, when it was no longer felt to be profitable in competition with mechanical refrigeration. After that, the plant was used for the storage of produce, and it remained nearly completely intact until 2001, when it was razed to make way for a Super 8 motel.

Remains of Wellston brewery in 1999 (Thanks to Karen Davis of the Wellston Public Library for photographic assistance)

JEFFERSON COUNTY

Steubenville

1. Steubenville Brewery

Steubenville is one of Ohio's oldest communities, having been laid out around 1797. Situated along the Ohio River, immediately west of Pittsburgh, it quickly became an important site for both industry and commerce. The small town's first known brewing establishment, located on the east side of North Third Street, near the intersection of Ross St., began operations in 1815. Unlike many of Ohio's pioneer breweries, its history is fairly well documented by various sources, and these sources give one a good idea of how this and other similar breweries of the era operated.

Although the brewery site was originally owned by James Ross, a Pittsburgh lawyer who was one of Steubenville's founders, the brewery was erected and operated by Andrew Dunlap, an Irish immigrant. A number of different brews were produced by the new plant, as outlined in the following newspaper excerpt from March 7, 1817 (this and the following excerpts are all from the *Western Herald and Steubenville Gazette*):

Western Herald and Steubenville Gazette, August 23, 1816

Steubenville Brewery

"The proprietor of the Steubenville Brewery has now on hand a quantity of Strong Beer, Ale, and Porter, brewed during the winter, which he will warrant equal to any brewed on this or the other side of the mountains.

Prices as follows:

Strong Beer	7 dolls. per bbl.	including cask 8
Common Beer	6 dolls. per bbl.	including cask 7
Strong Ale	7 dolls. per bbl.	including cask 8
Fine Pale Ale	7 dolls. per bbl.	including cask 8
Porter	8 dolls. per bbl.	including cask 9
Table beer	3 fi dolls. per bbl.	including cask 4 fi

Terms of Sale.

After this date, CASH will be required on delivery.

The success of his establishment, as well as every other manufactory, will depend in these critical times on prompt payment, particularly where the capital is limited, and bank accommodations cannot be had—It requires the constant attention of the proprietor to superintend the operations of his brewery, he has no time to collect debts, and it is at all times a disagreeable business which may be avoided by the above regulations.

The encouragement already given to this establishment by the public is very flattering and gratefully acknowledged, and no exertions shall be wanting to ensure its continuance. Twenty years experience enables the proprietor to promise with some confidence, a uniformity in the taste and flavor of his malt liquor.

DELINQUENTS

Those who are delinquent in payment up to this date, will be so good as to pay up their arrearges—and it is hoped that all who wish well to a new and useful manufacture, which will *keep our money at home*, will promptly pay up and readily accede to the above necessary regulations, as to the terms on which malt liquor will be delivered.

For sale SEED BARLEY & HOPS at the brewery.

Dunlap and subsequent proprietors frequently advertised for barley, hops, and other grains to be bought and sold by the brewery. In addition, as was common at the time, a malt distillery was also operated in conjunction with the brewery. The following two excerpts give some idea of the products of the distillery:

Irish Whiskey, made in Steubenville [February 17, 1818]

"The Malt Distillery, connected with the Steubenville Brewery, is in operation, where *Malt Whiskey* can now be had (of a very superior quality) by the barrel or gallon. It has been manufactured and distilled on the most approved methods practiced in *Ireland*—carefully rectified, and entirely freed from the *grosser* parts (retaining the finest particles) of the *essential oil*, and such a spirit as is generally made into *Lemon Punch*, the favorite drink among the sons of Hibernia.

To those who are in the habit of drinking spirits, the Steubenville Malt Whiskey will be found a *mild* and *wholesome* beverage, (use it in moderation) it is preferable to any imported spirits, and as different from the spirits generally made in the western country, as coarse *cider brandy* is, compared with *Cogniac*—this is saying much in its favor—it is all true, and when it is stated that the proprietor of the Steubenville brewery has distilled more than a million of gallons of whiskey in Ireland, before he came to this country, and has devoted 25 years' attention to the process of distilling, and freeing spirits from its *faetid oil*, and all its obnoxious qualities, he may be permitted to speak with confidence. He is not afraid to submit his malt whiskey to the test of public opinion, and the first rate connoisseurs. Orders may be sent to the brewery where the spirits will be delivered for *Cash only*."

Brewery and Malt Distillery CASH STORE [May 2, 1818]

"For the convenience of the public, and the advantage of all, Mr. DUNLAP will, on Monday next, open a store opposite Mr. Jenkinson's tavern, for the sale of the products of his brewery and malt distillery, where may be had, by the gallon or quart,

Malt Whiskey of a superior quality	$1 per gallon
Gin	1 per gallon
Brandy	1.25
Patent Bitters	1.12 fi

Strong beer and ale by the gallon.
Yeast will be kept at the store for sale, as well as at the brewery.
The spirits being made entirely from malt are of a superior quality.
Those who wish to have at home a fine good whiskey, will call at the brewery and malt distillery store.
Gentlemen who wish to have a cask of *fine spirit* put away for *age* and improvement have now a good opportunity."

BOTTLED PORTER/NEW PORTER CELLAR

Mr. Dunlap having relinquished bottling at his brewery, JOHN HAMILTON, near the court house, has commenced bottling Porter from the Steubenville brewery, and is now fit for using. Tavern keepers and others in town will be supplied, during the summer, with Bottled Porter of the first quality, and delivered at their houses; he will also keep constantly on hand, during the summer, strong beer on draught of the best quality.

Orders left at the Porter Cellar near the court house will be immediately attended to.

Despite his plant's early success, Dunlap wished to establish another brewery in Louisville, KY., and therefore put the Steubenville Brewery up for sale in July 1818. The following excerpt from July 11, 1818 gives an extensive description of the brewery, as well as the town. Its intention was to draw potential owners from the east, as the advertisement was also run for three weeks in newspapers in New York and Philadelphia.

Profitable Investment In Capital

"For sale, an extensive Brick Brewery, Malt house, Malt Distillery, and Dwelling House, situated in the town of Steubenville, on the bank of the Ohio river—capable, at present, of brewing 50 barrels per week, and may be extended to 100 or 150 barrels per week, with a very trifling additional expence. Attached to the brewery, is a deep vault, capable of storing 500 barrels—the temperature of the vault is now, at this season, (10th July) 62 degrees on the thermometer, and peculiarly situated for preserving malt liquor in the summer months. The situation of the brewery for a current of air for cooling, is very favorable for summer brewing. This is the third season which this brewery has been in operation, and continued to brew fresh beer and ale the two preceding summers, and *now in operation*. Attached to the brewery, is also an extensive fermenting cellar, capable of storing 500 barrels.

The consumption of the town of Steubenville is very considerable, and increasing rapidly; besides that of the neighboring towns, with the whole range of the river, as an outlet to the Falls of Ohio or New Orleans, for the sale of any surplus that may be occasioned by the extension of the works.

Grain (barley) can be had in great abundance, at from 62 fi to 75 cents per bushel—and Hops from 20 to 25 cents per pound: while strong beer sells for 7 dollars, and porter for 8 dollars per barrel.

A hop yard is also in progress, which, in another year, will be fully adequate to the supply of the brewery.

The lot of land on which the brewery is built, contains nearly three acres; and bounds 360 feet on the best street in Steubenville—which at no distant period will be wanted for town lots, when, it is probable, the front lots alone, may sell for more than the whole of the purchase, money buildings and all.

The whole of the above property, together with all the Brewery Utensils, Stills, Worms, Tubs, etc. will be sold for $12,000—the terms of payment will be one half *Cash*—For the other half, a long credit will be given if required.

Or one half the above concern will be sold to any suitable person who will carry on the business on joint account—In case of only half the property being sold, there will be a difference in the proportion of the *Cash* payment.

As respects the situation for business, there are few towns in the western country so distinguished for its rapid extension of manufacturing establishments. At present, Steubenville possesses one of the best conducted Woolen Factories in the United States—Also, a Steam Flour Mill, and Cotton Factory, a Foundry for castings, and an extensive Steam Paper Mill, together with the Brewery and Distillery above mentioned.

Steubenville was first founded by Bazaleel Wells, Esq. The scite of the town, when viewed from the surrounding hills, presents a most beautiful and extensive prospect along the line of the river. The banks are high, and never inundated in that part where the town is built.

One peculiar advantage which Steubenville possesses as a manufacturing town, is, the extensive and inexhaustible *Coal Banks* of an excellent quality in the rear of the town—from which they are supplied with coal at from 6 to 8 cents per bushel.

If the above property is not sold at private sale, previous to the first of October next, it will, on that day, be sold at public auction. Application by letter, addressed to the *"Proprietor of the Brewery, Steubenville, Ohio,"* will meet due attention."

The property was eventually purchased April 1819 by Bazaleel Wells and John C. Wright. Wright was a local lawyer, while Wells was a former surveyor for the government, who had received for his services a large tract of land along the Ohio River. Wells and James Ross laid out a small town on this land, and named it Steubenville after the Prussian Baron Frederick William Augustus von Steuben, who had assisted the colonists in the recent Revolutionary War (interestingly, Wells was also one of the founders of the city of Canton, and originally owned the land on which that city's first brewery was built).

Operation of the small brewery was taken over by Robert Thompson and William Shiras, Jr. at that time, although operation was later transferred to Charles F. Laiblin. Laiblin leased the plant for several years, although it was not until June 1833 that he finally purchased the property himself. In July 1840, he leased the property to Joseph Basler and Francis Zimmerman, two recent immigrants from Germany. They operated it for five years before leasing the nearby Armstrong Brewery. In 1846, Laiblin sold the property to Thompson Hanna, owner of the adjacent Hartje paper mill. Hanna then converted the old brewery into tenement houses. Nothing remains of the city's first brewery today.

2. James & John Fife brewery

James and John Fife were brothers from Philadelphia, where they had worked for several years in a large brewery. Upon coming to Steubenville, they had established themselves by 1816 as bottlers of porter, ale and other liquors at their establishment on Third Street. In December of that year, they purchased a site near the corner of Market and Third Streets, where they set about establishing their own brewery, which was opened by the following autumn. A prominent advertisement in the *Western Herald and Steubenville Gazette* indicated that they would be brewing beer, ale, and porter, to be sold at their bottling works and store on Third St. Their optimism was short-lived, however, as brewing operations appear to have ceased by late 1818, when the property was sold.

3. Alexander Armstrong/Joseph Basler brewery

Alexander Armstrong opened the city's third brewery, located on North Water St., just south of the intersection with Washington St., in 1820. However, it appears that he did not actively operate the brewery for long. According to *History of Jefferson County*, it was soon rented by an Englishman named Woods. A man named Rolly then operated the brewery, until it was leased in 1834 by Frederick Beter and George Shipler. They operated the brewery for ten years, paying $200 each year for its use. By this time, the actual ownership of the property, including "all the hogsheads, barrels, half barrels, vats, & malt house", and an adjacent tavern and cooper shop, had been transferred to Alexander Armstrong, Jr.

Around 1845, the brewery was leased by Joseph Basler, a 34-year-old native of Baden, Germany, who had previously leased the Laiblin brewery upon first coming to Steubenville. Basler continued brewing at the site until 1852, when the operation was moved to a new facility on High St. The original brewery sat idle for several years until it was purchased by Francis Zimmerman, Basler's original brewing partner, who established a residence at the site. There are no remains of the brewery today, as much of the city's riverfront area has been rebuilt with light industry and the State Route 7 freeway.

4. Joseph Basler/Basler & Brother brewery

After brewing beer in the old brewery on North Water St. for several years, Joseph Basler moved his operation in 1852 to a new four-story brick facility at 130 South High St., between Market and Adams Sts. His three teenage sons, William, Maximillian, and Joseph, Jr., gradually entered the business as they came of age. Brewing only ale, they gradually increased their production to nearly 2,000 barrels annually by the early 1870s. At this point, they were utilizing 4,000 bushels of barley and 4,500 pounds of hops each year in the brewing process, and the plant was valued at $35,000.

An affiliated business of wholesale liquor sales had developed by this time, known as Basler & Brother, operated by Max and Joseph, Jr. (Joseph, Sr. had retired by this time, and William had died in 1856). Over the next few years, the production of ale gradually dwindled to several hundred barrels annually by the late 1870s, at which time the brewing of lager beer began. Production continued until approximately 1883, when the brewery was partially destroyed by fire. Brewing operations permanently ceased at that point, and the structure was then sold to John McClave, who rebuilt the ruins into a residence. None of this remains today. Joseph, Jr. later became a prominent local real estate broker and remained in the area until his death in 1906, at the age of 62.

5. Ernhart H. Schaffer brewery

Ernhart Henry Shaffer (also spelled Shafer, Schaefer) was a native of Wurtemburg, Germany, born in 1830. After coming to Steubenville, he established a small lager beer brewery on Third Street in 1859 (exact location uncertain). It appears, however, that he moved his operation in 1862 to a new location near the southeast corner of the intersection of Third and Washington Streets (later taking the address of 144 N. Third). While producing around 1,000 barrels annually, operations appear to have come to a close around 1877, after which Shaffer ran a saloon nearby, and later he became a dealer for Cincinnati's Windisch-Muhlhauser brewery. There are no remains of his brewery today, as a post office parking lot covers the site.

6. Butte/City Brewery/Buehler/Steuben Brewing Company
(by Carl Miller; edited from an article originally published in the Steubenville *Herald-Star* newspaper, February 28, 1996)

Although Steubenville did not boast particularly large numbers of Germans during the 19th century, it was a lager beer brewery that ultimately prospered far more than any other in town. John C. Butte was a native of Ahlen, Kassel, Germany, born in 1823, who came to the United States in 1841, originally living in Pittsburgh. He later moved to Steubenville, working initially at the Beatty glass works. However, in 1860 he erected a small lager beer brewery at the base of the Adams Street hill, which had previously been the site of a small distillery as early as 1798. Known simply as the City Brewery, Butte's operation would provide beer to Steubenville residents for nearly sixty years.

In order to achieve the cold temperatures necessary for aging lager beer, Butte excavated cellars 100 feet deep into the solid rock hillside adjacent to his brewery. The beer was kept cold with large blocks of ice harvested during the winter, while the cool underground temperatures helped preserve the ice well into the warm season. In their day, Butte's aging cellars, which could hold as much as 2,500 barrels, were called "the finest and most complete" in Ohio.

Although that characterization may have been a bit exaggerated, the City Brewery was enjoying a healthy trade by 1872. Its beer was not just consumed locally, but was shipped in both directions along the Ohio River. Six men were employed at the brewery, and production amounted to about 100 barrels of beer per month. Plans for expansion were under way, and it was predicted that the brewery's output would climb immediately to 150 barrels per month as soon as additions were completed. By 1880, the plant's annual capacity was nearly 10,000 barrels.

Butte remained at the City Brewery for more than 20 years, although he briefly relinquished ownership to business partner Bernhard "Benj" Miller between 1873 and 1876. In 1882, he transferred operation of the plant to Charles L. Rall and Sophia Klein, possibly leasing the property to the pair, before selling the works to them in 1886 and retiring. He died five years later.

The new proprietor, Charles L. Rall, was a native of Pittsburgh who had spent his early manhood learning the brewing trade in Milwaukee. He became the full owner of the brewery by purchasing Klein's share in 1887. In 1895, however, Rall died unexpectedly at the age of 38. The coroner ruled that death was caused by "softening of the brain," a typical diagnosis of the day.

Rall's widow, Lucie Rall, sold the City Brewery the following year to John Buehler, a recent arrival from Pennsylvania. Born in 1861 in Germany, Buehler had studied the art of brewing in his home province of Wurttemburg before emigrating to America in 1887. He immediately began a major overhaul of the City Brewery. Artificial refrigeration, perhaps the single most important development in the brewing industry during the 19th century, was added to the plant in 1898, rendering the underground aging cellars obsolete. And in 1901, an entirely new brewhouse and stockhouse were erected, complete with their own electric power plant. The rebuilt plant now had the address of 904 Adams Street.

Indeed, those brewers who entered the new century without modern, efficient operations were ill-equipped to contend with what would prove to be competitive times ahead. Names like Budweiser, Schlitz, and Pabst, with aggressive promotion and distribution behind them, were quickly becoming a serious threat to small regional brewers everywhere.

In Steubenville, one observer estimated that as many as fifteen outside brewing companies were represented locally by independent agents or brewery-owned distribution depots. Saloons, where the vast majority of beer was sold in the early days, were aggressively targeted by outside brewers. A popular sales tactic was to push bottled beer rather than kegs, so that saloonkeepers didn't have to add extra tapping equipment in order to sell a new brand side-by-side with the local brands.

Many regional brewers sought to protect their local trade by purchasing large numbers of saloon properties, thereby locking out competition. But John Buehler refused to engage in this rather expensive and troublesome strategy, maintaining that he was in the beer-making business, not the "retail thirst" business.

However, Buehler recognized that ever-increasing competition would require special measures. A new bottling plant was erected adjacent to the brewery, and, in 1906, Buehler introduced a bottled beer called Steuben Brew for the

(above right) Advertising tray, circa 1906; (right) John Butte's brewery, circa 1861 (taken from *100 Years of Brewing*); The tall building in the background is the icehouse, while the brewery is the dark building at the right.

expressed purpose of competing with outside brands. Advertised to be "wholesome and nutritious", "possessing great tonic qualities", "essentially pure", and "attractive in appearance and aroma", the new Steuben Brew became the featured product among the brewery's other brands—City Brew, Pale American, and Select Beers, as well as ale and porter. These brews were distributed in three states, within a radius of 100 miles.

More threatening to the industry's well-being than competition, the temperance movement began making inroads in legislative circles by the turn of the century. In 1908, state-wide passage of the Rose Law allowed voters to render their districts dry on a county-by-county basis, by making saloon operation illegal. The voters of Jefferson County elected by a wide margin to abolish their 141 saloons (about 80 of which were inside Steubenville proper) at the beginning of 1909.

The manufacture of beer was still legal under the new law, allowing the City Brewery to continue selling beer to saloons in wet counties, as well as to local households. But the bulk of the brewery's trade had been with the area saloons, and survival under the new conditions was difficult.

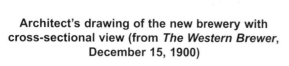

John Buehler

In the absence of legal saloons, "speakeasies" were soon rampant throughout the county. Local authorities, in their battle to gain control of the situation, targeted John Buehler as a primary source of the trouble. It was charged that the great majority of beer consumed at the illicit drinking spots came from the City Brewery. Buehler soon found himself facing a handful of criminal convictions for illegal sales of beer. Buehler, of course, vehemently denied any wrongdoing. But, in the end, he was forced to close the City Brewery in order to avoid further prosecution. In March 1910, production stopped and it was announced that the brewery would remain idle as long as the anti-saloon law was in effect.

Illegal drinking establishments continued in abundance regardless of the brewery's closing. Realizing that anti-saloon enforcement was failing miserably, the citizens of Jefferson County voted to re-legalize saloons effective January 2, 1912. By January 5th, plans had already been put in place to reopen the City Brewery. The Steuben Brewing Co. was incorporated at this time by Buehler and several local businessmen, with capital stock of $250,000. President of the new company was Wilbert A. Meyer, with John L. Hellstern as vice-president, Buehler's son Charles as secretary and treasurer, and Buehler himself as the plant's general manager. Also involved in the venture was Steubenville mayor Thomas W. Porter, who ultimately served as the company's vice-president. The production of Steuben Brew was resumed as before, and the brewery eventually regained sound footing.

The efforts of the Prohibitionist forces did not slow however, and it was only a short time before Ohio's brewers were again facing disaster. In a 1918 referendum, the entire state was voted dry, to take effect in May 1919. Passage of the 18th Amendment to the Constitution soon followed, thus enacting National Prohibition.

By September 1919, the Steuben Brewing Co. had been dissolved and the brewery was producing soft drinks and near beer as the Steuben Beverage Works. As with many other brewers who sought survival with similar products, the Steuben Beverage Works soon failed.

In 1920, the Buehlers leased the old brewery to the Premier Malt Products Co., an Illinois-based manufacturer of malt syrup. Charles T. Buehler, who had spent several years working with his father in the brewery, was hired

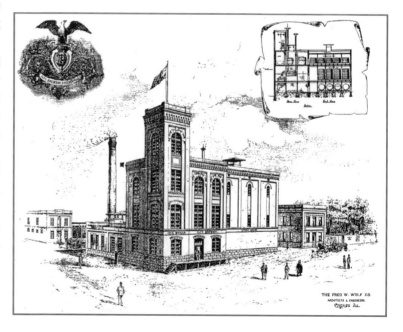

Architect's drawing of the new brewery with cross-sectional view (from *The Western Brewer*, December 15, 1900)

as manager of the Premier operation.

However, the production of malt syrup was halted in 1924, and the plant was closed. Charles T. Buehler, on a fast track within Premier's management, moved to Peoria, IL., where Premier later merged with the Pabst Brewing Co. of Milwaukee. Buehler ultimately held a position as one of Pabst's highest ranking officials. John Buehler, incidentally, also made the move to Peoria, where he spent many of his remaining years in retirement. He died in 1934 while vacationing in Florida. Charles Buehler remained in Peoria until his death in 1957, at the age of 67.

Remains of brewhouse in 1999

The brewery plant later housed the Steubenville Pure Milk Co., and still later the brewhouse was converted into a cold storage warehouse. Upon the repeal of Prohibition in 1933, efforts were made to reopen the old brewery. The Fort Steuben Brewing Co. was organized by a group of local men, among them August W. Koch, the proprietor of the Pure Milk Co. Operating briefly as a beer distributorship, this venture never fully materialized as a brewing concern, and Steubenville has never since been home to its own brewery.

In 1960, the plant was occupied by the Famous Supply Co., which continues to operate there to this day. The entire complex of well-preserved buildings, with arched windows and staid brickwork so characteristic of early breweries, and even the underground cellars from 1860, remain intact at the base of the Adams Street hill.

7. John Scofield

John Scofield (also spelled Schofield) was a native of England, born in 1804, who briefly operated a home brewing facility out of his residence at 416 N. Fifth St. It appears that this operation only took place between approximately 1869 and 1873, and that brewing took place primarily during the winter season, with sales most likely being to nearby saloons. His home is no longer standing.

Also Note:

Three other names appeared while researching Steubenville's brewing industry:

1. Joseph Eckenberger (or Egansberger) was a German immigrant, born in 1812, who appeared in the 1850 census as a brewer, and also in the 1850 city directory, living on Water Street, above Market. He appears in no other directories, census records, nor was he recorded as being involved in any property transfers. I would view him as either a small-time home brewer or as an employee of another brewery in town, and therefore I have not given him a separate listing.

2. John Stadden was also listed in the 1850 census as a brewer, although he did not appear in any city directories nor deed transfers. He most likely was employed elsewhere in town.

3. Michael Weishaar appears in the 1874-75 brewery listings as a brewer, although he was shown as producing no beer during those years. He was listed as a brewer in *American Breweries II*, but due to the fact that he appears in no city directories, census, nor deed transfer records, I would not give him a separate listing.

Knox County

Mount Vernon

1. Arentrue/Keller brewery

John Arentrue was a native of Ireland, born in 1809. After emigrating to the United States, he came to Mount Vernon, where in March 1837 he purchased land on the south side of town, at the northeast corner of the intersection of McKenzie St. and Howard St., at the railroad tracks. Soon after this he established Knox County's third brewery, and one of very few in the state to be operated by an Irish native. Primarily an ale brewery, it was able to produce between 200 and 400 barrels per year. Assisting Arentrue was Frederick Soulter, a German immigrant, born in 1817.

Drawing of brewery as seen in the 1870 lithographic map of Mount Vernon [taken from the Library of Congress web site]

Arentrue died in 1858, after which production was continued by his wife Anne, who was also born in Ireland, in 1815. By 1860 she was being assisted by their eighteen-year-old son John, as well as another Irishman, 28-year-old William Darmany. Anne Arentrue continued to oversee brewing operations until 1871, when she sold the small plant, now valued at $4,600, to three local men, Joseph Miller, Young H. Rowley, and George Keller. The latter, at 33 years of age the oldest of the three, appears to have been in charge of brewing operations, having previously worked with John Bechtel at his brewery just two miles or so to the east. Since then he had also served as a corporal for the Union Army in the Civil War. Also working with the three young men was Swiss native Peter Bowers.

Operations continued until 1875, when the three men sold their brewery to John Younger of Cleveland. His attempt to operate the brewery was not met with much success, as it closed for good just one year later. This was most likely due to the strength of the local temperance forces, which had caused the demise of John Bechtel's brewery around the same time. George Keller died of pneumonia just five years after that. The plant was later occupied by the Mt. Vernon Plow Works, and still later by the Black Furnace Co. The entire plant was razed in the 1920s, and nothing remains of it today.

Pleasant Township

1. Frederick Rohrer tavern and brewery

Knox County's earliest known brewing establishment appears to have begun operations around 1825, according to *History of Knox County*, from 1881. Frederick Rohrer (also spelled Rhorer) owned a tavern south of

Mount Vernon, along the Martinsburgh Road (today state route 586), just south of the intersection with Hopewell Rd. Apparently he also brewed beer at the site, although it was most likely a home brewing operation for tavern sales. Little is known about Rohrer, except that he was born in 1784, and died in May 1832, after which the brewing of beer ceased. There are no remains of the tavern today.

2. John Bechtel brewery

134-year-old Bechtel brewery structure, as it appeared in 1969, sitting alone in a large field. Five years later, it was gone, to be replaced by the First Baptist Church. The small structure at the right appears to have been an entrance to an underground cellar. [photo from the Knox County Historical Society, with special thanks to the Reverand Neal Koch of the First Baptist Church.]

This longstanding rural brewery was located just east of the Mount Vernon city limits along the Gambier Road (now Ohio Route 229), at the southwest corner of Edgewood Rd. At one time, the village in which it stood was known as Fleaville City. The one-story brick brewery building was constructed around 1835 by Jacob Kurtz, and sold two years later to George Pfeifer (also spelled Phifer), a French native, born in 1782. The two men operated the brewery together until 1850 when they were joined by John Bechtel (also spelled Bechtol), another native of France, who was born in 1817. Kurtz soon left the area, and Pfeifer died in 1853, after which Bechtel assumed sole ownership. Some years later he was briefly joined by George F. Keller, a young local man who would later move into town to operate the small brewery there. Still later, Bechtel was joined in the business by another young local man, John Medscure, born in 1843.

The brewery was relatively small, producing around 300 barrels of beer per year, and it appears that it also functioned as a distillery as well. Operations continued through the late 1870s. According to *History of Knox County*, the "Crusaders" (temperance advocates) depreciated Bechtel's business, causing him to abandon the brewery. The farm remained in the Bechtel family for another century, however, and the brewery building remained standing until the 1970s, when it was razed for the construction of the First Baptist Church building, which stands at the site today.

LAKE COUNTY

Painesville

1. Painesville Brewery
(by Carl Miller, with thanks to Carl Thomas Engel for tremendous help on research)

The making of alcoholic beverages was undertaken in Painesville at an early date. The production of beer, however, seems to have been confined exclusively to households during the village's early days. Articles periodically appeared in the local newspaper offering helpful hints to the home brewer. One such article in 1823 insisted that, with a little practice, any household was capable of making ale and table beer "better than any that can be purchased in London, and for which purpose a tea kettle and two pan mugs are sufficient apparatus."

However, not long after the conclusion of the Civil War, the town's growing population and expanding industrial activity sparked demand for more and more commercially produced goods, malt beverages among them. The "Painesville Brewery" was thus established in February 1866 by Schram, Garfield & Company. The works was housed in a converted tannery at the base of the Main Street hill, near the Grand River. The products of the brewery included pale ale, amber ale, scotch ale, cream ale, porter, and lager beer, the qualities of which led the Painesville *Telegraph* to predict a bright future for the brewers: "We have no doubt they will be liberally patronized, as the article they manufacture is so much purer and better than that brought from abroad." And, indeed, expansion of the brewery was underway already in July 1866, when $4,000 was spent to erect a three-story stone malt house adjoining the brewery.

In 1867, the firm of Schram, Garfield & Co. ceased when S. S. Schram withdrew his interest and left co-founder Alexander H. Garfield as the sole proprietor. Garfield–a cousin of President James A. Garfield, whose summer estate was situated in nearby Mentor–had been a respected businessman in Painesville for a number of years, operating livery stables and a carriage service for guests of the Parmly House, a local hotel.

Once involved in the Painesville Brewery, Garfield continually attempted to develop and expand the enterprise. In 1868, a new four-story cider mill was built next to the brewery, and apple cider and vinegar were added to the list of products. The cider mill, however, apparently did not bring the expected profits and its operation ceased in 1871. A few years later, a ravaging fire not only destroyed the cider mill, but threatened to consume the brewery as well. Flaming debris repeatedly ignited the rear portions of the brewery, which was reportedly saved only through the tremendous efforts of the firemen on hand.

Local merchant Daniel Warner, who described himself as a "dealer in everything that can be bought or sold," had been taken on as a partner in the brewery in 1868, the firm thereafter doing business as Garfield & Warner. The brewery's level of output seems to have peaked in 1875, during which year over 1,400 barrels of beer and ale were sold. By 1878, however, production had dwindled to just 560 barrels, and business was soon suspended. In January 1880, it was announced that local resident Harmon Carroll had purchased the brewery and was prepared to begin the manufacture of lager beer in the plant. Carroll conducted the business with apparently moderate success throughout much of the 1880s.

By February 1889, however, the production of beer had been halted and the old brewery buildings were sold for storage space to a nearby milling operation. A fire that occurred later that year destroyed a portion of the plant, although the remaining buildings later housed the Painesville Steam Laundry for many years. Eventually those buildings were razed, and Painesville was never again home to its own brewery. The Painesville Plaza Hotel stands at the site today.

Willoughby

1. Oscar White brewery

Oscar F. White was a native of New York State, born in 1819. Moving to Willoughby in the 1850s, it was not until 1878 that he purchased land on the east side of Euclid Avenue (today U. S. route 20), between Wilson and Wright Avenues. It was here that he established a small brewing operation in a long one-story wooden building that stood behind his residence. While primarily an ale brewer, White produced some lager beer as well. Essentially a home-brewing operation, White's backyard brewery never turned out more than 100 barrels in a year, and appears to have operated only between 1879 and 1884. After ceasing operations, the building remained vacant for more than thirty years before being razed around the time of World War I.

2. Willoughby Brewing Company

Located at 4057 Erie Street in downtown Willoughby, the Willoughby Brewing Co. had its grand opening on February 9, 1998. The brewery and associated restaurant are situated in a building constructed in 1897 to house the repair shop for the Cleveland, Painesville, & Eastern Railroad Co. Established by owner T. J. Reagan and a group of local investors, the brewing operation consists of a 15-barrel J. V. Northwest system, which cost approximately $1.3 million. The original brewer was Chris Alltmont, although he was later succeeded by Dave Sutula and Erik Gruetzmacher, and later by Bill Bryson, Jack Kephart, and Jason Sims.

Several regular brews are produced: Northern Trail Nut Brown Ale, Willoughby Wheat Beer, Last Stop Stout, Railway Razz (which won bronze medals at the 1998 World Beer Championships in Chicago and the 1999-2001 Great American Beer Festivals), Shore Line Light Lager, RG Lager, and Lost Nation Pale Ale. Specialty brews appear as well, such as Wild Irish Red, Helles Bock, Spring Bok lager, 80 Rupee India Pale Ale, Erie Street Pumpkin Brew (later evolving into PumpkinHead Ale, made with sixty pumpkins carved, baked, and added to the mash), Saison L'Ete (French for "Summer Season", it won a silver medal at the 2000 Great American Beer Festival in the Belgian and French Style Specialty Ales category), Saison L'Hiver winter ale, Victoria Imperial IPA (with 10.5% alcohol by volume), Abbey Road Belgian Trippel (with 10% alcohol by volume, both made after the change in the Ohio law regarding the allowable alcohol content in beer made in the state), Red Barrel Porter, Black Douglas Scottish-style export ale, KaiserHof Kolsch golden ale, Wenceslas spiced ale, Limerick Irish Export Stout, Legislation Barleywine (Ale), Hazy Days Hefe Weizen, Abbot's Mill English mild ale, Mad Cow Milk Stout, London Porter, and Lake County Lager, a 20 percent corn, pre-Prohibition style lager beer. A limited amount of the beer is kegged and bottled for distribution at bars across a three-county area. The company web site, at www.willoughbybrewing.com, provides more information.

Also Note:

1. *American Breweries II* featured a mysterious mention of the Northern Breweries Company in Fairport (today known as Fairport Harbor), a small town along the Lake Erie coast near Painesville. This was based on a listing in *The American Brewing Trade List and Internal Revenue Guide For Brewers* from 1906, which shows the company as a brewer of lager beer. In addition, a stock certificate for the Northern Breweries Co., dated July 15, 1911, surfaced in recent years. It stated that the company was incorporated in the state of Ohio, and had a total capital stock of $275,000, with shares being $500 apiece.

However, there is no listing for a "Northern Breweries" in the local directories of the era, and no record of property being either bought or sold by the company in Lake County. In addition, there is no mention of the company in any other trade literature from the era. It would most likely appear to be a stock company in name only, which never gained the necessary capital to proceed to the brewing phase, and eventually disappeared into history. (Thanks to Dale Van Wieren for sharing his information on this one!)

2. The Wallaby's brewpub chain of Westlake, Ohio opened a Wallaby's Grille Restaurant on Station Street in Mentor in August 2000. While the Wallaby's beer brands were sold at the restaurant, no beer was brewed on-site, and the restaurant had closed by 2003.

Ironton

1. Joseph Hochgesang/East Ironton Brewery

Joseph Hochgesang (also spelled Hochesang, Hockesang) was a native of Baden, Germany, born in 1830. In November 1858, he purchased property on the south side of 2nd St., between Spruce and Pine Streets in East Ironton (later incorporated into the city of Ironton), and within a few months had established a small brewery, producing as much as 500 barrels of common and lager beer annually. For much of the next fifteen years, brewing operations were assumed by Jacob Blessig, a French native born in 1821, although Hochgesang himself worked in the small plant, with Conrad Fronterol, a Swiss native. The only exception was a brief period in the early 1870s, when the plant was leased by "Geiger, Loeb, & Co.," which consisted of Peter Geiger and Loeb Loeb, two young German immigrants.

By late 1875, the brewery was being operated by Meyer & Rothenberg, although by the following spring, Jacob Meyer, a 36-year-old native of Wurtemburg, Germany, was operating it alone. He would continue to brew for an additional four years, before closing the brewery in 1880. Hochgesang remained in the area and operated a saloon and a small distillery in town for several years. Meyer became a local agent for Cincinnati's Moerlein brewery, and later the Windisch-Muhlhauser brewery, as well as operating his own saloon. Nothing remains of the East Ironton Brewery today.

2. Leo Ebert brewery

Shortly after coming to Ironton from Cincinnati in late 1861, Leo Ebert (for a more complete biography, see the following listing) briefly leased property on a hillside near the Iron Railway bridge over Storms Creek, just north of the city limits. With only twenty dollars to his name at the time, he established a small brewery at this site (looking at various biographies of Ebert, it appears possible that brewing had previously taken place at this site, although based on local records, there is no real evidence of this). The site was chosen because of its proximity to a spring which produced pure water for brewing.

Ebert brewed common beer, often selling it when only three days old. In a 1949 interview, Ebert's daughter, Fannie Geiger (then 90 years old), stated that kegs of beer which were produced there were delivered by handcar along the Iron Railway and into town for sale. The owner of the railroad had given Ebert special permission to operate the handcar during certain hours when no trains would be coming, and he would take four kegs at a time two miles into town. The kegs would be unloaded at Second Street and rolled to various saloons. Empty beer kegs were washed out with water from Storms Creek instead of the pure spring water, and this water was brought up the hill by a windlass, operated by an old white mule.

Ebert made enough money with this early brewery that in 1863 he was able to purchase land in town, where he soon moved his brewing operation. The Iron Railway later became part of the Detroit, Toledo, and Ironton Railroad Company, and was an important transportation link for many years. Its rails have since been taken up, although the old rickety wooden railroad bridge over Storms Creek remained standing as of 2000. It served as the only marker of Ebert's first brewery, which is long gone.

3. Eagle Brewery/Leo Ebert Brewing Company

Leo Ebert was born into a family of brewers in Klingenberg-on-the-Main, Germany, in June 1837. Leaving school at the age of twelve, he worked in his father's brewery for five years before taking various jobs in breweries in other cities, including a Master Brewer position at a brewery in Lohr, Bavaria. In 1859, he and his new wife Matilda left from Bremerhaven aboard the *Nord Amerika* sailing ship, and after a 56-day journey, landed in New York. Leo soon began working at breweries there and later in Cincinnati before coming to Ironton in late 1861. He initially operated the small brewery listed previously for approximately eighteen months. In March 1863, he purchased land at the northeast corner of North 7th Street and Railroad Avenue, where he then established the much larger Eagle Brewery, which opened later that spring.

Ebert's new brewery grew rapidly, and was producing nearly 6,000 barrels of beer and ale annually by 1875, although by 1879 that number had dipped to 2,700 barrels. In 1881, Ebert formed a business partnership with Joseph Fisher, which continued until the latter's death some years later. After a devastating fire in 1891 which caused $10,000 in damages, the brewery was rebuilt with a new four-story malthouse and brewhouse, and annual production had rebounded to nearly 7,000 barrels within three years. The brewery was operated as Leo Ebert & Co. until 1897, when the firm was incorporated as the Leo Ebert Brewing Co., with a capital stock of $50,000. By this time, Herman Strobel had been hired as the plant's brewmaster. In 1902, new ice machinery was installed, producing up to 25 tons of pure ice each day.

Ebert was very active socially and politically, running for United States Congress twice as the Democratic nominee in 1884 and 1886. He had begun his political career as a Republican, but switched in 1872 to the Democratic party. Due to a large majority of Republicans in the district, however, he never made it to Washington. He also ran for the office of county commissioner, but was again defeated, although he did serve on both the Ironton city council and school board. He served as the president of the Ohio State Brewers Association for eight years and was president of the United States Brewers Association from 1895 to 1897. At the 36th annual convention for that organization, held in Philadelphia in June 1896, Ebert made a forceful address to the audience, an excerpt of which follows (as originally printed in *One Hundred Years of Brewing*):

"Memory carries me back to another notable brewers convention assembled in this city. It was held in the centennial year, when every American brewer came to Philadelphia filled with just pride at the unprecedented success of the brewers exhibit, placed in a magnificent hall, erected by our association.

Some of you undoubtedly recollect the profound impression made upon the public mind by this exhibit and our printed statements concerning the wholesomeness of our product and its inestimable value as a temperance agent.

The people were with us then, and they are with us now. What we hoped for then has been amply realized. Our product has indeed become the popular beverage of the American people. Two simple figures tell the tale—ten million barrels in 1876, thirty-four million barrels in 1896! On the surface it would seem that such an enormous progress must have been easily accomplished, aided by favorable circumstances. But we know, gentlemen, that it is progress effected by incessant struggle and contention, by a never-ending combat against absurd prejudices, unprovoked enmity and unreasonable opposition; progress consummated in the face of legal restrictions bordering on prohibition and of prohibition itself; progress made

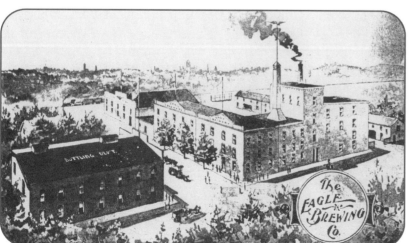

(above) Leo Ebert; (left) Artist's rendition of the Eagle Brewery plant in 1897

in spite of unfounded accusations concerning the purity of our product. Your committees' reports will again remind you of this very forcibly. I need not, therefore, enter into details. But there are one or two things I would like to dwell on for a few moments.

The very fact that our product is now the drink of the great masses of the people imposes on us the duty to make a more aggressive stand against the accusations I have referred to. This association has frequently declared its willingness to abide by any conclusion which, after duly studying the question, any properly constituted authority may reach in regard to the raw materials that may legitimately be used in brewing. We have solicited official analyses of our product and aided legislative measures tending in this direction. In this we have often been successful, and whenever official analyses have been instituted, all the charges brought against us as to the alleged adulterations have been utterly refuted. Yet, in spite of these gratifying results, the work of defamation goes on, and the professional "strikers", combining with greedy manufacturers of certain materials, continue to harass us by legislative propositions which no sane man, knowing anything about brewing, could possibly sanction. Let it be known to all the world that, far from fearing the most scrutinizing investigations, we challenge them, and really wish for no better opportunity to demonstrate the correctness of our position. I know that political considerations militate against the course proposed, but that is a matter for Congress to consider. Adulteration bills have been passed and others are introduced at every session. Nobody can prevent this. What we can do, however, is to ask that before any such measure be applied to our trade, the lawmakers should first ascertain, by competent and impartial inquiry, what constitutes an adulteration, considered both from a hygienic and a commercial point of view. We have a right to ask this, at least, especially in view of the predicament in which we are placed by the conflict of opinions between the legislative and executive branches of the Federal Government. While the Department of Agriculture endorses and urgently recommends the use by brewers of cereals other than barley, Congress compels us to prove that the use of such cereals is neither an adulteration nor a menace to public health.

There is another matter to which I wish to call your attention. In our efforts to produce an absolutely healthful beverage we have availed ourselves of all mechanical improvements and the results of scientific research, and we now succeed in manufacturing a drink quite as wholesome as, but far more effervescent than, the beers of old. The percentage of alcohol in American beers is growing less from year to year, and this fact ought to exempt our product entirely from any of the restrictions now applied to intoxicants. There was a time when the lawmakers of several states of our Union classed beers having less than a fixed maximum of alcoholic percentage (usually three per cent) as non-intoxicants, and it is my conviction that, in the interest of public morals and public health, we ought now to inaugurate a vigorous movement in favor of such exemption of malt liquors and light domestic wines."

Leo Ebert died of natural causes in February 1908. His passing was a significant event in the city, as he had established himself as one of its leading and most charitable citizens. In his obituary, for example, it was noted that during a flood in 1884, he had donated a great deal of money and converted the brewery into a soup kitchen for refugees, at his own expense. His funeral was one of the largest in the city's history. His son Otto, born in Ironton in 1870, had been working in the brewery since the age of seventeen, and Otto now assumed management of the company. The timing of this transition in management was ironic, as passage of the controversial Rose Law at this same time allowed Lawrence County citizens to vote their territory dry through local option between 1908 and 1911. With all Lawrence County saloons outlawed for three years, Ebert attempted to continue brewing operations and distribute beer into nearby Kentucky during this time. However, this operation proved unprofitable, and thus the brewery went into receivership (the receiver was Fred W. Geiger,

(above) Bottle label, circa 1910 [John Phillips collection];
(below) Ebert brewery from the rear, with the ice pond [empty at the time of the photo] in the foreground. The mechanism at the right would take the ice into the icehouse during the winter, when the pond was filled with water and frozen. As much as 300 tons of ice could be harvested in the winter, although the ice was not pure and was used only for keeping the beer cool during the rest of the year, not for consumption. The brewhouse is left center, and the Ebert family residence is at the far left. The basin of the ice pond remains behind the brewery site to this day. (photo courtesy of Hale and Todd Milano)

Ebert's brother-in-law.) All brewing operations ceased on July 1, 1909, after which the brewery sat idle and was used only for cold storage. During this time Otto Ebert operated a saloon and liquor distributorship in Catlettsburg, KY, several miles up the Ohio River at the junction of Ohio, Kentucky, and West Virginia. In early 1912, after voters had reversed their decision and allowed alcohol back into the county, the brewery reopened with a reorganized company, known as The Ebert Brewing Co., which had a capital stock of $75,000. Otto Ebert was the new concern's president and plant manager, with W. C. Miller as vice-president, Fred W. Geiger as secretary and treasurer, and Leo Geiger as the brewmaster. The old plant was remodeled and new machinery installed to modernized operations at this time.

In 1917, the company reorganized again as the Ironton Brewing Co., with John W. Truby as president, Ebert as vice-president, and Edward P. Newman as secretary and treasurer. Otto Wagner had joined the company in 1915 as brewmaster. Formerly brewmaster of the West Virginia Brewing Co. in Huntington, just a few miles up the Ohio River, Wagner was out of a job when that state went dry in 1914. With statewide Prohibition in Ohio rapidly approaching in early 1918, brewing operations in Ironton again ceased, this time for good.

Later that year, a new and unrelated company, known as Court Products Co., leased the plant in order to convert it to the production of vinegar. However, within a few months the new company had declared bankruptcy without any vinegar ever having been made. The plant, still valued at $50,000, was then converted again, this time for the canning of produce, cold storage, and ice production. However, the majority of the plant was destroyed by a fire (thought to have been caused by faulty wiring) in August 1919. One building, used as a beer cellar, remained standing into the 1990s, while a small storage building at the rear of the plant remains standing to this day. Much of the block where the brewery stood is residential today.

Otto Ebert later moved to Indianapolis, where he worked in an ice factory until retiring around 1940. Due to the manpower shortage during World War II, he temporarily returned to work in the factory. In 1946, however, he died when overcome by ammonia fumes from a leak in the same factory.

LICKING COUNTY

Newark

1. Michael Morath brewery

Michael Morath was a native of Loffingen, Baden, Germany, born in 1807. After coming to America in the 1830s and working in a Columbus brewery for three years, he moved to Newark in the early 1840s, where he purchased numerous parcels of land over the following decade. One of these parcels was on the south side of Walnut St., along the main railroad lines through the city, and near the intersection of First St., and it was here that he established his (and the city's) first brewery in 1844. Employing eight men, this brewery appears to have continued operations until 1858, when he built a new, larger plant on the western edge of town. Nothing more is known about Morath's first brewery, and nothing remains of it today.

2. John Kneule/Korzenborn Brewing Company

John Kneule was a native of Wurttemberg, Germany, born in 1822. After coming to America, he established a small brewery at 42 E. Walnut Street, facing the main railroad lines through town. Operations appear to have begun in the late 1840s, and Kneule was assisted by a succession of young German immigrants through the years. In October 1865, he sold the operation to William Hager & Henry Knosman, and they continued brewing operations until April 1869, when they sold the plant to Charles Korzenborn and Otto Bingmann.

Korzenborn and Bingmann were both Prussian immigrants, born in 1823 and 1840, respectively. Upon purchasing the plant, now known as the Newark Brewery, Bingmann assumed most of the brewing operations, while Korzenborn operated an adjacent saloon. Annual production of ale, lager and common beer during this period usually ranged between 1,000 and 1,700 barrels. Bingmann sold his share of the plant to Korzenborn in 1875, although he continued to work there for a number of years. By 1891, brewing operations had been assumed by Bingmann's son Charles. Korzenborn died one year later.

In 1897, the brewery was renamed as the Charles Korzenborn Brewing Company, although Charles Bingmann continued to operate both the brewery and the saloon (with assistance from Jacob Reichert) until his death in 1914. It was during this period that the brewery was referred to by some local residents as the "Case House", due to the fact that a case of beer could be had for a dime. Supposedly, the saloon became a favorite local spot for underworld characters as well. After Bingmann's death, a brief attempt was made by new owner Daniel Dietrich to operate the small plant as the Home Brewery, but this had failed by 1917, and the plant was vacated. Nothing remains of the brewery today.

Bottle label, circa 1916

3. Jacob Graff/William Rickrich brewery

Jacob Graff (also spelled Greff) was a native of Darmstadt, Germany, born in 1817. After coming to the United States, he established a small brewery on the west side of Second Street, just south of the main railroad tracks through the city, in the late 1840s. Operating the brewery alone for the first decade, he was joined around 1859 by Wilhelm (William) Rickrich, also a native of Darmstadt, born in 1821. Rickrich purchased the brewery at that time and continued to operate it with Graff until purchasing land south of the town in 1865, with his brothers Philip and Charles, after which a new brewery was established there. It appears, however, that they continued to operate the small brewery on Second St. with Graff until approximately 1870 before closing it for good. The small, one-story plant was later occupied by an egg packing company before being razed, leaving no remnants today.

4. Michael Morath, City Brewery

After operating his small brewery on Walnut Street for a number of years, Morath expanded his operation in 1858 by moving to the west side of Newark, just north of Main Street and between Sixth and Seventh Streets, where he owned a large tract of land. His new, modern, three-story brewery building was built into a hillside on which he had planted grape vines and fruit trees. Adjacent to the brewery and among the trees was a beer garden, where many of the local German immigrant families could come and enjoy their lager beer with friends in the atmosphere of the old country. Supposedly, a sparkling spring in the brewery's basement provided water for brewing.

1866 Licking County Atlas

Morath's son Augustus worked in the brewery during his teenage years, until moving to the south side of town to operate his own small brewery (see the next entry). The City Brewery, which produced cream and stock ales, lager and common beer, and porter, remained a popular place for several years, although Michael Morath had retired by 1870. The brewery continued to operate, presumably under his supervision, for another year or two, run by several young German immigrants. By 1871, brewing had ceased, and the large tract of land was annexed by the city. It was briefly used by the city as a fairground, but eventually was sold off in individual lots. There are no remains of the brewery today. Morath continued to live in Newark until his death in 1884.

5. Augustus Morath, Rock Hill Brewery

This small brewing establishment was operated by Augustus H. Morath, the eldest son of local brewer Michael Morath, born in 1838. It was located approximately one-half mile south of Newark along the Jacksontown pike (now state route 13), just south of the intersection of Linnville Road. Supposedly the brewery was located in a hollow somewhat below the level of the road. While local records give minimal information, it appears that August worked for several years in his father's brewery before establishing his own operation in the early 1860s. Production of lager beer and ale only continued until approximately 1869, when August sold the property and left the area. Little else is known about the brewery, although nothing remains of it today.

6. Rickrich Brothers, Spring Hill Brewery

Philip Rickrich (also spelled Rickrick) was a native of Hesse, Germany, born in 1837. After emigrating to America in the mid-1850s, he worked at Jacob Graff's brewery on Second Street for several years, with his brothers William and Charles. However, in late 1865 he purchased land several blocks south of this, on the outskirts of town. It was here that he erected a new plant, opening in 1866, to be known as the Spring Hill Brewery. The location was just east of Linnville Road (South Second Street) and just south of the Licking River. A small access road to the brewery was later known as Spring Street. The brewery itself was on a hillside, from which a small spring flowed, providing water for brewing.

The brothers' operation was known variously as Rickrich & Co., Rickrich and Brother, and Rickrich and Senger at different times (Mr. Senger was affiliated with the brewery only in its later years). Production never was greater than 1,000 barrels per year, and in some years was as low as 200 barrels. It appears that brewing ended after approximately 1884, although the spring would later provide water for the Spring Hill Bottling Works at the same site. Nothing remains of the brewery today.

7. Benner, Bentlich & Eichhorn, White Top Brewery

Although concrete evidence about the White Top Brewery's origin is scarce, it appears to have been established around 1864. In that year, Adolph Bentlich (also spelled Beutlick, Bentligh, or Boutley) purchased a site on the north side of Walnut St., between 5th and 6th Streets, facing the main railroad lines through the city. Soon after this he opened a saloon with a small brewery on the property. Bentlich was a native Prussian, born in 1820, and supposedly his brewery was so named due to the white cork used to seal its bottles of ale.

By 1870, Bentlich had become incapacitated and sold the property to his son William (born in 1840), Ernest Benner (born in Prussia in 1834), and Peter Eichhorn (also spelled Elkhorn, and born in Prussia in 1843). Annual production of ale, lager, and common beer was generally between 200 and 400 barrels, most of which was consumed in the adjacent saloon. Brewing operations appear to have ceased around 1884, although the saloon continued to operate for a number of years. The buildings stood until some years after the turn of the century, although by 1920 the land on which they stood had been purchased by the railroad company, and the entire block had been leveled.

8. Consumers Brewing Company

Consumers Brewing Co. was an unusual entity in Ohio: a brewery beginning operations in the 1890s. It began as one of the state's earliest stock company breweries, incorporated on April 8, 1897, with a capital stock of $20,000, which was later raised to $75,000. The company chose an old factory building at First and Locust Streets to establish its brewing operation (the official address was 75 E. Locust Street). This had previously been occupied by the Blandy Machine Works, and the structure dated back to the mid-1860s. It was purchased by the new company for $8,100, and was soon renovated into a brewery with modern equipment and cellars capable of storing 18,000 barrels. The first batch of "Newark Beer" was for sale on the local market by May, 1898.

Charles Andre was the company's first president and plant manager. Born in Hesse-Cassel, Germany, in 1846, Andre had already worked as a brewer's apprentice before emigrating to the United States in 1862. He served in the Union army during the Civil War, then worked in numerous breweries over the years, including eighteen years with the large Born & Company brewery in Columbus, Ohio. Herbert R. Gill was the new company's secretary. Other initial directors included Julius A. Kremer, E. Kremer, and A. W. Gill.

Herbert Gill left the company in 1901 and moved fifty miles east to form the short-lived Cambridge Brewing Co. His place as secretary was taken by Julius Kremer, a native of Dinslaken, Rheinpreussen, Germany, who also was born in 1846. His education and training were in architecture, which he undertook upon coming to America in 1869. He supervised the construction of the Born & Co. brewery in Columbus, where he worked with Andre, and it was here that they first planned the formation of their own brewing concern.

The company initially used city water for the brewing process, although deep wells were drilled in 1900 for a new and presumably purer water source. Upon opening, the brewery had an annual capacity of 30,000 barrels, entirely of lager beer. Their goal was to sell 10,000 barrels in their first year, a goal that was nearly realized, and business steadily grew from there. The company's sales increased significantly in 1903 due to a strike by brewery workers in Columbus, which temporarily shut down all of that city's brewing operations. By 1905, Consumers was selling 23,000 barrels annually.

Natural ice was fairly scarce in the region at this time, and most ice had to be shipped in from Zanesville. To eliminate this cost, Consumers built its own ice house on the premises in 1901. Sales of distilled "crystal ice", at $2.00 per ton, were very successful, and the company increased its capital stock to $150,000 in 1907. Soon after this, the company purchased two delivery trucks for home sales of both beer and ice. These were thought to be the first delivery trucks in use in the city.

Andre and Kremer continued to oversee the company throughout this era. Harry W. Rossel, who had joined the company at its beginning as a sales agent, had risen to the position of vice-president and general manager by 1914, when he died of blood poisoning following a leg injury. Henry J. Schneidt was hired as plant superintendent soon after this. Production of Consumers Special and Extra Pale Lagers, which had been introduced primarily as bottled beers for home sales, continued successfully over the next decade. A new addition to the focus on home sales by this time was an attempt to target women as potential customers. One advertisement from 1918 stated: " 'Everywhere I go my friends serve Consumers Beer. If I look into their ice boxes I find a row of shining bottles; when I make an afternoon call, they welcome me with appetizing sandwiches and Consumers. If I am invited out to dinner I am quite apt to find this popular beer served with the meal. Many of my friends consider that their day is not happily completed until after a late supper, a steaming rarebit or a cheese and cracker luncheon, and a bottle of their favorite brew.' The experience of this one woman simply shows the ever-growing popularity of Consumers Beer."

At the close of 1918, statewide Prohibition had forced beer production to cease, and the uncertainty of the times was reflected in the brewery's 1919 advertising calendar, which stated, "Accept this calendar as a token of our appreciation of your past good will and patronage. What the future will bring to us is uncertain. Our investment is too large to lie idle, so we bespeak, as far as is consistently possible, a continuation of this good will and patronage." When all alcohol sales stopped the following May, the company reorganized as the Consumers Products Co., as producers of Consumers New Special Cereal Beverage, as well as

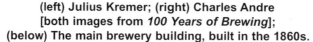

**(left) Julius Kremer; (right) Charles Andre
[both images from *100 Years of Brewing*];
(below) The main brewery building, built in the 1860s.**

Lemon and Lime, Grape, Cherry, Strawberry, and Raspberry Sodas, Glee Club Ginger Ale, Whistle Orange Soda, and Dr. Swett's Root Beer. Andre and Kremer retired soon after this, and Schneidt became president of the new company, with Harry W. Rossel, Jr. as secretary. Production of non-alcoholic beverages continued until approximately 1930, after which the old brewery closed its doors and the remaining equipment was liquidated.

With the repeal of Prohibition three years later, a new company was organized to return the brewing of beer to Newark. The new firm was led by Master Brewer Joseph Weiss, who had previously been the brewer for the August Wagner & Sons Brewing Company in Columbus. The plant was completely refurbished with modern equipment, which increased its annual capacity to 85,000 barrels. The new company was joined in early 1935 by John C. Bruckmann, who was also an officer of Cincinnati's Bruckmann brewery, who became the plant manager. New brands were introduced at this time with some old names from the past: Consumers Special Beer, Newark Old Town Beer and Ale, Old Master Brew, Blue Grass Winner Beer, Elk's Brew Beer, and Winter Stout were all produced in the 1930s and 40s.

The plant's output grew steadily, and the number of employees had doubled from 41 to 85 by 1936. Despite good sales, the company was unable to operate at a profit during the depths of the Great Depression, and had filed for bankruptcy by January 1939 with debts of more than $400,000. Reorganization took nearly a year, but was successful in allowing the brewery to continue operation under new management. By 1940, Roy R. Smith had become the company's president, with Walter J. Conlon as vice-president and general manager, and C. G. Murphey as secretary and treasurer. Weiss was retained as the master brewer.

(above) Consumers Brewing Company used 24 trucks like this one [pictured by the Cincinnati Union Terminal in 1936] to deliver beer to central and southern Ohio; (above right) Metal plate, 1940s.

As was not uncommon during the era, the company still suffered from financial instability, and would reorganize twice more in the next decade. By the end of World War II, the company was being run by Frank Holters as president, with Ray Hoffman as vice-president and treasurer, Carl Tangeman as secretary, and Ray Bowers as master brewer.

In May 1946, the company was sold to another group, led by Ulreh Vogt, the head of the Peerless Distributing Company, a beer and wine distribution business in Chicago. The plant became a family-run operation, with Daisy Vogt as vice-president and Ulreh Vogt, Jr. as treasurer. Harry W. Rossel, Jr., son of the company's vice-president years earlier, was now the plant manager, and Edward Heller was brought in as the new master brewer. By 1951, however, Rossel and Heller had been replaced by Reinhold Asbeck, who had previously run the ill-fated Hocking Valley Brewery in Nelsonville, Ohio.

Throughout all of these changes, the production of beer had

continued, with the same popular brands being distributed throughout the state. In September 1953, brewing operations came to a halt, as the company became yet another victim of national and regional competition. The plant was liquidated over the next year, and remained vacant until it was razed in 1970. The main Newark branch of the United States Post Office occupies the site today.

9. Bunky's Brewpub/Legends Brewing Company

Newark's first brewing operation in more than forty years opened in May 1998. Located in a former A & P supermarket building at 1650 West Church St., on the far west side of town, it consisted of a restaurant (Bunky's) and the brewing operation contained within it (Legends Brewing Company). Both were owned by Robert "Bunky" Allen (a childhood nickname) and his wife Theresa "Tess" Allen. Their brewmaster was Angelo Signorino, formerly of both Hoster's and Barley's Brewing Companies in Columbus.

Using a 10-barrel brewing system, several brands were produced: Legends Light Ale, Tess' Red Ale, Woody English Porter, Wild Welshman Ale, Cherry Valley Wheat Beer, Patriot Pale Ale, Bunky's Fest-Bier, Nerk Nut Brown Ale, Jingle Bell Brew (during the Christmas season), and Big 10-Malt Oatmeal Stout. Despite the brewpub's local popularity, it had ceased operation by the spring of 2001. Once dismantled, the company's equipment was moved to Strongsville (see Cuyahoga County section), where it was incorporated into the Ringneck Brewing Company's new facility.

Also Note:

Two other names appeared while researching Newark's brewing industry:

1. Alfred Willoughby, a 56-year-old native of New York, was listed as a brewer in the 1850 census, and also listed with him is 24-year-old A. P. Willoughby. Neither men appear in any other census records or directories, and would therefore appear to have been either small-time home brewers or employed by another brewer in the city.

2. Talbot and Henry Chapman, natives of Vermont, also appear in the 1850 census as brewers, but similarly, they are listed nowhere else. The same assumption can be made regarding them.

LORAIN COUNTY

Amherst

1. William Braun Brewery

William Braun was a native of Kassel, Germany, born in 1834, who had come to America in the 1850s, eventually settling in the small village of Amherst (formerly known as both North Amherst and Amherstville). In October 1868, he purchased a plot of land on the south side of Milan Avenue, along the east bank of Beaver Creek, just west of the town square, and just north of a main line of railroad tracks. The site was chosen due to its proximity to the village spring, which had a reputation as being one of the purest in the region. Soon after this, he established a small brewery at the site, leasing the use of the spring from Fred Beesing, the property owner. The water was piped from the spring to the brewery for Braun's use.

The brewery's foundation was of stone blocks, and according to local literature, it was originally used as the foundation for a grist mill, possibly as far back as the 1820s, when the area was first settled. Later, the site was home to a tannery, wagon shop, distillery, and furniture manufacturer at different times. Around 1869, Braun built a new one-story frame building at the site for the purpose of brewing beer.

The brewery produced nearly 1,500 barrels of ale and lager annually in its early days, although by the late 1870s annual production had dropped to only 400 to 500 barrels. Braun continued production until approximately 1884, at which time he sold the property to the railroad company. He remained in the area until his death in 1904.

The brewery building was later torn down, although the underground stone beer cellars remained. They were sealed over during the Great Depression as part of a government-funded program, which established a park around the natural spring. The cellars remain underground to this day. The park around the spring remains, as do the stone blocks which comprised the brewery foundation, built into the hillside. Interestingly, as one walks around the site, one can see what appears to be a large millstone lying nearby, most likely from the original gristmill.

Avon

1. Creekside Brewhouse and Tavern

Lorain county's first post-Prohibition brewery began operation in late July 2000. Ray Rider had been the operator of the Blue Chip Beverage carryout store for some time, when he decided to add a half-barrel brewing system in an adjacent space that had previously housed the French Creek Tavern. This new pub would be known as the Creekside Brewhouse and Tavern.

The building, at the northwest corner of the intersection of Ohio routes 611 and 254, has stood at the site in the center of the village since the early 1800's, when the area was first settled. At the grand opening on September 9, 2000, the beer was tapped for the first time. Rider's signature brand was Crawfish Dark Ale, a cask-conditioned brown ale, with all that was brewed being sold on-site. By early 2003, however, brewing operations at the site had ceased.

Elyria

1. John Bishop Brewery

John Bishop was a native Bavarian, born in 1822, who had come to the United States in the early 1850s (after which his native name of Bishoff was Anglicized.). In 1864 he purchased a two-acre parcel of land on the south side of Elyria, along the west side of East River Road, and along the bank of the East Branch of the Black River. Soon after this, he established a very small brewery in which he was assisted by George Becker, a young German immigrant, born in 1849. Essentially a glorified home brewer, Bishop produced around 100 barrels of lager beer annually through 1877.

By 1877, Bishop had incurred over $1,100 in debts. As part of a settlement with his creditors, his land and brewery were auctioned off by the sheriff in October of that year. John Savage purchased the property for $3,340, but it appears that the small brewery was then operated by Andrew Plocher for two more years before being shut down in 1879. There are no remains of the brewery in this quiet residential neighborhood today.

Lorain

1. Cleveland and Sandusky Brewing Company, Lorain Branch
(by Carl Miller and Robert Musson)

During the days before Prohibition, the city of Lorain often attracted the attention of brewery interests. Around the turn of the century, beer distribution depots were maintained in Lorain by many of the nation's major brewers. In 1899, entrepreneurs from Cleveland and Lorain sought to establish the city's first brewery, but the plans never fully materialized. The following year, it was reported that other parties had organized the Lorain Brewing & Ice Manufacturing Company with the intention of converting the "old brass works" into a modern brewery and ice plant. But, again, nothing concrete ever developed.

By 1904, however, Lorain was able to count a brewery among its manufacturing enterprises. The Cleveland & Sandusky Brewing Company—a consolidation of eleven breweries in those cities—decided that establishing a brewery in Lorain would better enable the company to sell its beer in the region between its two constituent cities. The company had already been operating a distribution depot on 5th Avenue (which later became 12th Street) between Park and Reid (and adjacent to the Nickel Plate Railroad), and it was at this location that the Lorain Brewery began operation in 1904. Although wholly owned by the Cleveland & Sandusky Brewing Company, the new brewery was independently incorporated as "The Lorain Brewing Company" with a capitalization of $10,000.

The formal opening of the plant was held on October 27, 1904 when 300 guests—including a number of city officials—were invited to a grand celebration inside the brewery. In true German style, the guests were treated to entertainment by the Lorain City Band, which performed such German favorites as "Down where the Wurtzburger Flows", and "Ach Du Lieber Augustine". Amidst decorations which included side-by-side American and German flags, as well as large portraits of both President Roosevelt and German Emperor Wilhelm II, the visitors enjoyed a large banquet while listening to guest speakers extoll the virtues of brewing and drinking beer. The brewery's product—called simply "Home Brewed Beer"—was undoubtedly sampled in great abundance. The festivities concluded with an obligatory tour of the plant. In honor of this "great" event, nearly all of the city's saloons closed down for the night so that patrons could enjoy the fun.

Costing $200,000 to build, the new Lorain Brewery was capable of producing 50,000 barrels of beer annually. This was calculated at the time to be equivalent to 140,160,000 glasses of beer. At its peak, the works

(left) Lorain Brewing Co. plant;
(below left) William Seher.

employed about 30 men, all under the supervision of German-trained brewmaster Alfred Graaf. He would later be succeeded by Charles Kraatz, who would in turn be succeeded in 1912 by G. K. Mayer. The plant's chief engineer was E. D. Dornbusch.

At the head of the business, however, was the brewery's director, William B. Seher. He had come to Lorain in 1895 at age 27 to establish a beer distribution depot for the Kuebeler-Stang Brewing & Malting Co. of Sandusky. When that firm joined the Cleveland & Sandusky Brewing Co. in 1898, Seher remained in charge of the beer depot which then distributed the products of several Cleveland breweries as well as the Kuebeler-Stang brewery. When the Lorain Brewery was established, Seher was put in charge of the new operation, a position he held throughout the duration of its existence.

Initially, the plant's output was packaged exclusively in kegs for tavern consumption, although a bottling works was added later to facilitate home sales of beer. The plant enjoyed much success from the outset, as a large majority of the city's 150 saloons handled Cleveland & Sandusky beers, which were supplied by the Lorain Brewery. Soon after opening, the Lorain Brewery purchased an additional eighty saloons in the county, including thirty in the city of Lorain alone, which gave it an even larger share of the local market.

After passage of the Aiken Bill in 1907 and the Rose Law in 1908, local option became a threat to the success of all breweries. The Lorain Brewery was in a fortunate location, however, because Lorain County remained wet throughout the era, although the brewery began producing dry (non-alcoholic) beer to be shipped into nearby dry counties.

The next decade would pass relatively uneventfully, although late in 1909, a spark from a passing train ignited a fire which destroyed the plant's storage house at the rear of the facility. This would quickly be rebuilt, however, and business continued as before.

With statewide Prohibition rapidly approaching by the Fall of 1918, beer production at the plant ceased, as it did at several of the remaining branches of the Cleveland & Sandusky Brewing Co. The parent company then sold off the Lorain branch entirely. The buildings were later home to numerous "men of the road", or "hobos", who road the rails nearby, before the facility was eventually razed.

During Prohibition, Seher utilized the plant's bottling works next to the main brewhouse to create his own bottling company, where he manufactured a wide variety of soft drinks. This operated with apparent success for a number of years before Seher died in 1935 at age 67.

Wellington

1. John M. Crabtree Brewery

John Crabtree was a 43-year-old recent immigrant from England when, in 1871, he purchased a five-acre plot of land on the east side of what is now State Route 58, approximately one-half mile north of the center of the village of Wellington. Soon after this, he established a very small brewing operation, producing between 100 and 400 barrels of beer annually. Production continued only through approximately 1876, after which Crabtree worked in the village as a butcher. Nothing remains of the brewery today.

Also Note:

1.	The Steel City Brewing Company was organized in Lorain in 1907, with backers from both Lorain and Cleveland. A site was chosen on Tenth Avenue to construct a new brewery, but due to local option laws and the chance that Lorain County could go dry (although it never did), plans never materialized. One year later, plans were briefly revived, and it was thought for a time that the new brewery might now be built in Elyria. Once again, the plans fell through, likely due to uncertainty about the growing Prohibition movement.

2.	After Prohibition ended, vague plans were reported in *Brewery Age* regarding the construction of a new brewery in Elyria in early 1935. However, protests from the city council prevented this project from ever taking place.

MAHONING COUNTY

Austintown

1. Meander Brewing Company

The Mahoning Valley's first brewpub was located at 5011 Mahoning Avenue, in a renovated Dutch Pantry restaurant. Owned and operated by Glenn L. Wright, the Meander Brewing Co. opened in the spring of 1991 and offered three primary brews: Meander Gold, a light bodied English ale; Smoky Hollow Amber, a reddish ale; and Idora Dark, a dark German styled beer named after Youngstown's Idora Park amusement park. These brews were all sold on-site, with no bottling taking place. Despite a promising start, the brewpub had closed by 1993. The building is currently occupied by the Moss Brothers supply company.

New Albany

1. William Moff brewery

William Moff was a German immigrant who had come to the United States in the early 1850s with his parents (his father, George Moff, operated a small brewery in North Georgetown, in northern Columbiana County). Within a few years he had established a small home brewing operation on the east side of Main Street in the village of New Albany, in Green Township, just north of the town of Salem. Brewing operations ceased when he sold the property in 1862 and moved into Salem, where he then established a far more substantial brewery, which continued to operate until 1890.

New Springfield

1. John Seeger hotel and brewery

John Seeger (also spelled Sager) was a native of Wurtemburg, Germany, born in 1838, who came to America in the 1860s. Around 1870 he became the proprietor of a small hotel and saloon in the village of New Springfield. He operated a small brewery and distillery at the site, located on the south side of Woodworth Road (now state route 165). Seeger was listed in an 1874 business directory as "manufacturer of and dealer in pure wines, liquors, ale, and beer; pure rye whiskey for medical use". Brewing was only known to operate until 1879, with less than 100 barrels of ale and lager brewed annually. Seeger continued to sell liquor for a number of years after this, and he remained in New Springfield until his death in 1904. There are no remains of the brewery or hotel today.

Youngstown

1. John Smith/Youngstown Brewery/Smith Brewing Company

John Smith was a native of Staffordshire, England, born in 1813, who emigrated to the United States with his family in 1842. Working initially as the manager of a steel rolling mill in Pittsburgh, Smith moved to Youngstown in 1846. Purchasing an old tannery on the city's west side, he converted the building into the city's first brewery, at 507-523 Federal Street. The site was along three main lines of railroad tracks through the city, and was adjacent to the Mahoning River. When brewing operations officially began in July 1846, Smith was producing only two barrels of ale per week, but he gradually increased the size of his operation until the daily capacity reached 125 barrels. In the traditional English style, Smith brewed XX and XXX Cream and Kennett Ale, Porter, and Brown Stout.

In order to increase output further, work began in the summer of 1867 on a completely new brewing facility to replace the old frame one. In November of that year, a news article described the new plant:

John Smith, circa 1860

"…the main building fronts on the street and is 40 x 136 feet, three stories high. It presents as a building for manufacturing purposes one of the neatest fronts we have ever seen. Everything is tasty and nothing is out of place. The windows and the doors are all arched which together with the extreme length of the building gives quite an imposing appearance. Inside, everything is well planned. The arrangement of the malt rooms, malt kilns, and large storerooms for barley and malt, the large brewing room, the barreling and other rooms, could not have been better made. Beneath the entire building extend the vaults, two of which are arched and so built as to secure an even temperature, winter and summer. These vaults are intended for stocking ale. Adjoining and to the rear of the brewery is the engine and boiler house, likewise of brick."

Smith died in 1870, after which the brewery, now referred to at times as the "Youngstown Brewery", was operated by his sons John, Jr. (born in 1842) and Alfred (born in 1845). Annual production during this time ranged from 3,000 to over 7,000 barrels. A new addition to the plant was erected in 1878, at which time the production of lager beer began. With additional improvements, the plant's annual capacity had reached 12,000 barrels by the early 1890s.

John Smith, Jr. died in 1894, after which all of the company's holdings were appraised. In addition to five saloons in the city owned by the Smith brothers, the following list gives one an idea of the extensive amount of equipment and supplies used by a typical medium-sized brewery of the era (courtesy of the Mahoning Valley Historical Society):

Lager Beer Department: Beer on hand, 4230 barrels (@ $3.50), ~1000 half barrels, ~2000 quarter barrels, ~2500 eighth barrels; total value of beer on hand: $21,130.

Ale Cellar: 204 barrels of ale (present use and stock), 64 barrels of porter, 336 half barrels, 376 quarter barrels, 1 hand pump; total value of ale on hand: $2,080.

Malt House: 8500 bushels of malt, 3 lots of tools, 100 elevators cups,

Smith brewery photo from 1896 (The Mahoning Valley Historical Society, Youngstown, Ohio)

stock, 1 10-ft. conveyor, 321 bags of grit, 5 bags of corn meal, 11 bags of porter malt, 63 bales of hops, 2 tons of hard coal, 1 lot of charcoal.
Brewer's Office: 1 jug of alcohol, 1 dozen thermometers, 1 letter press, 2 desks, 3 chairs, 1 table, 1 wash stand, 18 lbs. of salicylic acid, 3 lbs. of benzulic acid
Bottling Department: 1 3-horsepower boiler, 1 bottle corker, 1 automatic bottler, 1 clock, 2 bottle washing tubs, 4 bottle racks, 1 lot of beer boxes and cases, 1 stove, 1 bottle washer, 1 lot of miscellaneous tools, 1 cooler, 1 lot of rubber corks, 2 gasoline stoves, 1 bag of bottle covers.
Attic, 3rd floor of brewery: 1 scale, 1 lot of pipe covering and lot miscellaneous supplies and scrap, 1 lot of brewer's instruments and measures, 1 section of 1-inch hose—50 feet, 1 lot of ammonia fittings.
Ice House: 4 ice saws, 1 ice plow, 1 branding machine, 4 bob sleds, 1 farm wagon, 2 trucks, 1 lot of bottles, 5 old puncheons, 4 old vats.
Contents of barn: 28 tons of baled and loose hay, 3 tons of straw, 800 bushels of oats, 1 feed cutter, 1 dump cart, 18 horses (@ $70 each), 9 sets double and 2 sets single harnesses, 1 set cart harness, 1 mirror, 1 clock, 6 chairs, 1 table, 8 blankets, 1 lot of barn tools, 1 grain wagon, 1 carriage, 4 beer trucks (@ $75 each), 6 spring wagons, 1 suction hose.
Tool House: 60 lbs. Isinglass, 31 advertising clocks (@$1.00 each), 1 counter scale, 20 boxes preserving powder, 12 lbs. cream tartar, 100 patent washers, 8 gross small corks, 4 beer pumps, complete, 1 carbonater, complete, 1 lot of brass/iron cocks and fillings, 2 gallons Linseed oil, 8 gallons stamp paste, 180 advertising signs, 1 lot of ammonia fittings, 1 lot of brass and iron scrap, 2 hand pipe cutters, 3 thread cutters, 1 bench pipe vice, 8 pipe tongs, 1 extra lot of tools, 8 shovels, 4 picks, 1 bale of wood plugs, 1 brace and extension bit, 1 bung auger, 2 hand saws, 1 set of taps, 4 patent bung pulleys, 1 differential pulley, 1 ratchet drill, 50 gross of corks, 14 barrels of bungs, 1000 high bungs, 3 barrels of chip, 21 scrub brooms, 2 dozen corn brooms, 4 dozen corn scrubs, 10 dozen root scrubs, 18 brushes for taps and glasses, 1000 paving bricks.
Miscellaneous Items: 1 lot of cooper's tools and stock, 1 2-way cock and lot of strainers, 2 stoves, 2 sections of 1-inch hose—50 feet, 1 desk, 1 old malt mill, 1 set of belt stretchers, 4 drums of ammonia, 12 empty drums, 1 step ladder, 1 wheel barrow, 3 oil tanks, 1 small steam pump, 1 portable forge, 30 beer pumps used by patrons, 4 chip boxes, 3 tons of scrap in yard, 1 box of Braddish Protectors, 8 gallons varnish, 20 gallons sulphate lime, 5 barrels pitch, 1 barrel glucose, 300 ft. of 1 inch hose, 50 feet of 1 fi inch hose, 175 feet of 1/ inch hose, 7 brass racking cocks, 1 2-way racking cock, 6 heavy buckets, 2 heavy cans, 1 chip washer, 75 lbs. filter material.
Total Value of All Personal Goods: $13,200.

Alfred Smith retired in 1900, selling the plant to a group of investors who incorporated in January 1901 as John Smith's Sons Brewing Co., with a capital stock of $250,000. This new group was led by John J. O'Reilly (who was also vice-president of the Crockery City Brewing Co. in East Liverpool, 40 miles to the south), who became president, with Edward A. Nisbet as secretary, and J. J. Hamilton as treasurer. Around the same time, brewmaster Henry Kuntz was replaced by Ernst Langbehn, who would remain until the onset of Prohibition.

Financial instability prevented the brewery from thriving during this time. A proposed sale to a new group, which had incorporated as both the Mahoning and Youngstown Brewing Companies in May 1903, never took place (the new corporation[s] were subsequently dissolved). The company was reorganized again in 1904 and renamed as the Smith Brewing Co., with new officers: Samuel Wainwright (who was also president of the Crockery City Brewing Co.) as president, John Hynes as vice-president, and Hamilton as secretary and treasurer. This newly reorganized company was involved in an attempt in early 1906 by Cleveland investors to form a large syndicate of breweries in the region, to include the Renner, Crockery City, Alliance, and Consumer's (Ashtabula) breweries in Ohio, as well as plants in Sharon, Meadville and New Castle, PA. In the end, the investors were unable to raise the needed funds and the proposed syndicate never materialized.

Stock serving tray, circa 1915

While the company's variety of ales and its new flagship brands, known as Standard Gold, Jewel Export, and Tip Top Beers, remained popular, the company began placing greater emphasis on ice production over the next fifteen years, gradually converting much of the original plant to ice storage. A new modern brewhouse was built on the south side of the plant in 1912, four stories in height and built of fireproof brick, steel, and concrete. This would contain all new equipment, including a 300-barrel brew kettle, which increased the company's annual capacity to 80,000 barrels.

Wainwright was later succeeded as president by J. H. McGraw. Despite the death of vice-president John Hynes in 1914 and McGraw in 1915, the brewery continued to operate until the onset of Prohibition in 1919, when it reorganized again as the Smith Products Co. Under new president W. D. Murray and technical chemist George Hartung, the company continued to produce ice, as well as Tip Top soft drinks and extracts. This company had some short-term success, but 79 years of business at the site came to an end in 1925, when the plant closed for good.

It was later utilized by The Ice & Fuel Co. and several other small businesses before being razed in January 1933. Demolition workers at that time came across a cornerstone from 1878, when the lager beer addition was built. Inside were newspapers, two silver dollars, testimonials from local merchants, photos, family history, a Lake Erie cruise advertisement, and a curious letter signed by brewery employee Sam Cornell. This asserted that George Booth, another brewery employee, was the biggest liar on Earth, and promised to furnish twenty barrels of lager beer free to any who should find a bigger liar in 100 years! A Pennsylvania Railroad depot was later built on the site, and as of 2000 this housed a fireworks store. There are no remnants of the Smith Brewery today.

2. American Brewery, Enoch Smith

The American House hotel was one of Youngstown's first when it was built in 1825. A simple two-story frame building, it was purchased by Enoch Smith in the early 1850s. Smith was a native of England, born in 1816, who had recently emigrated to America. It appears that soon after this, Smith established a small brewery in the rear of the property, at what later became 240 West Federal Street, near the Atlantic & Great Western Railroad depot. Ale, porter, and lager beer were brewed here for sale in the hotel, and probably other local saloons.

By the end of the Civil War, Youngstown was beginning to grow larger, and Smith had plans to expand as well, as mentioned in the following news item from August 30, 1865: "We are glad to announce that Mr. Enoch Smith, proprietor of the American Hotel in this place, proposed removing the frame building and also the brewery now in the rear of the premises and erect thereon a substantial four-story brick hotel, sixty feet front. The estimated cost is $30,000. This will give a much better appearance to the center of town, besides add materially to the pleasure and comfort of transient business visitors. The brewery will be removed over the river, a place certainly more befitting for it." Smith planned to build a large brick brewery on Mahoning Avenue on the west side of town. However, neither of these plans ever came to pass.

Smith retired and ceased brewing operations around 1873. The American Bottling Works, operated by his son George Smith, had also operated out of the same location behind the hotel, and this continued for a number of years after brewing ceased. The American House remained in business (still as the original frame building) until 1907, when it burned down. The George Voinovich Government Center stands at the site today.

3. Matthias Seeger/City Brewery/Renner Brewing Company

Youngstown's longest operating brewery was founded in early 1865 by Philip Schuh (also spelled Schub, Schule) and John Bayer, two German immigrants. Bayer had sold his share to Schuh by the end of the year, however, and continued to run his nearby saloon. Matthias Seeger (also known as Martin Sager, Segur, and Seiger in various listings), a native of Wurtemburg, Germany, born in 1835, assumed brewing operations in 1869, assisted by Englishman Daniel Perkins, after which time the plant was known as the City Brewery. Also owning a part of the brewery at this time was Christian Genkinger (also spelled Cenkaner), who owned a brewery in New Castle, PA., twenty miles to the east. He sold his interest to Seeger in 1874.

The plant was located at 203-209 Pike Street, on a hillside facing a main line of railroad tracks and the Mahoning River. Water for brewing was taken from on-site artesian wells (not from the river, as was often rumored, although by the 1930s the water was being taken from Meander Lake, west of town). By the early 1870s, the brewery was producing around 1,500 barrels annually, although Seeger had nearly doubled this number by 1879. He died in May 1880, after which brewing operations were briefly assumed by his son Christian. The brewery (which was appraised at over $16,000) was purchased again at auction for $9,000 in 1881 by John Bayer, who now was 55 years old. While operating the brewery, Bayer attempted to sell the property for two years, although he defaulted on his loans in 1883, and the property was sold to John Smith's Sons Co. (the other major brewers in town). The plant sat idle until September 1885, when it was sold for $4,800 to George Jacob Renner, Jr.

Renner was born in 1856 in Cincinnati, where he had received his training in the Moerlein and Schaller & Gerke breweries, beginning at the age of 15. He later moved to Wooster, where he became a part owner of the local brewery with his father, George J. Renner, Sr. After the elder Renner moved to Mansfield (and later to Akron) to operate breweries there, the son considered moving to Harrisburg, PA. to purchase a brewery of his own. On the advice of a tramp (or as Renner later described the man, "an aristocratic train hiker") that he met, who knew of the unused brewery, Renner moved to Youngstown instead to become the sole proprietor of his own plant.

Renner remodeled the old brewery and quickly developed a thriving trade in the area. A big man, standing six-foot-three, Renner could lift a full barrel of beer into a wagon himself, and he had no problem with the physical labor required of a Nineteenth Century brewer. Once (as told in his obituary in 1935), while collecting money at a saloon called "Smoky Hollow", he was challenged by a professional wrestler who wanted to tussle right there, the loser to pay for everyone's drinks. Since the custom at the time was for the collector to pay for the drinks of everyone present anyway, Renner politely refused. The wrestler persisted, however, much to Renner's annoyance. Renner then spread his arms, invited the wrestler to get a hold, and when the challenger was ready, Renner caught hold of him, tossed him over his head, and walked out. In later years, he had both a billiard room and a gymnasium installed in the brewery to help satisfy his love of sport.

1889 City Directory; the brewery burned down later that year.

On the night of January 24, 1889, an exploding boiler led to a fire which destroyed the entire plant (valued at $75,000 by this time). The explosion was powerful enough to kill George Richter, the plant engineer, and injure three others. Renner's seven-year old son Emil was in the brewery at the time and was knocked against the wall, but escaped injury. He later recalled that the force of the explosion blew Richter's head off at the shoulders, killing him instantly. Parts of the exploded boiler flew across the river, several hundred feet away, and remained there for many years. The ensuing fire threatened the family home next door, but Mrs. Renner handed out all of the family belongings to neighbors in order to save them from the fire. By some miracle, the house did not burn, and within three weeks every last item had been returned to the Renners, giving them faith in the people of Youngstown and a desire to stay there and rebuild.

George J. Renner, Jr., taken from *100 Years of Brewing*

Renner's insurance covered only $18,000 of the loss, putting him in danger of losing his business entirely. Fortunately, he was able to secure loans from a local bank and a Pittsburgh malt dealer for the remaining money to replace the brewery. While beer was brought in from other cities to supply Youngstown's saloons, work began immediately on rebuilding the plant from the ground up. By the fall of 1890, the new facility was open for business. The impressive new plant was built solidly, with 36-inch-thick walls, and its interior was described in some detail by the Western Brewer in October 1890, highlights of which follow:

"To the right of the driveway is the brewhouse, three stories in height. Beginning with the main entrance for teams opening on the driveway on the left of the brewhouse, a broad wagon way runs through the rear of the ground floor of the brew house into the wash house and out through front of same upon Pike Street. It connects immediately with the washing and racking off departments, affording unequaled facilities for the loading and the shipping of the product.

Upon the ground floor is located the hop jack…The second floor contains the 200 bbl. brew kettle, mash tub, and Baudelot cooler…On the third floor is located the 350 bbl. hot water tank, a beer tank which is used instead of the usual surface cooler, and rice tank…The stock hoppers in the rear of the mill house have a storage capacity of 15,000 bushels.

Renner brewery after being rebuilt in 1890, as shown in the *Western Brewer.*

Next to and immediately adjoining the brewhouse on the right is the mill house, which is a model of mechanical construction and arrangement, containing five floors. The first floor is given up to office purposes, and is handsomely furnished. The second is used for hop storage. The third contains the grinding machinery, which is fitted with an automatic fire extinguisher…The entire milling machinery is controlled from this floor by a device which will stop or start the same instantly. The fourth floor contains a Morgan malt scourer…and the scale hopper of 350 bushels capacity. On the fifth floor is the scale hopper, which debouches upon the fourth. A feature of machinery on this floor is the screens, which make three screenings of the grain before delivering it to the hopper. Two of S. Howes' Silver Creek automatic magnetic separators and a nail separator of 200 to 250 bushels' capacity per hour are located on the sixth floor.

In the rear of the brewhouse is the stockhouse and cellars, five stories in height. The ground floor is occupied by the racking room and chip casks. There are twenty chip casks in all. On the second floor are twenty storage casks…and the third floor contains twenty more. The fermenting rooms are on the fourth floor, containing twenty casks. Two large water tanks and three settling tubs occupy the fifth floor.

Every department of the brewery is fitted up with the most approved modern appliances for the rapid and economical manufacture and handling of the product. No pains or expense have been spared by its enterprising and energetic proprietor to make this establishment a model in its class."

The new plant had an annual capacity of 18,000 barrels. A two-story bottling house was built on the east side of the plant in 1895, and this would be further enlarged in 1913, while additions to the stock house came in 1911. The plant's stables held as many as 52 horses for pulling delivery wagons throughout the city. The entire operation was incorporated in 1914 as the Renner Brewing Co., with capital stock of $200,000. Renner became the vice-president of the new company, while his son Emil became the president. Secretary and treasurer was Gustave Weaver, with Harry Weaver, Renner's brother-in-law, as brewmaster, a position he had held since 1890. Grossvater Beer (German for "grandfather", it replaced "Yellow Band" Beer in 1912) and Eagle Brew became the company's most popular brands, as they were also at the Renner breweries in Akron and Mansfield (after Prohibition, most ties were loosened with these other Renner plants, which took on the roles of "friendly competitors").

With the onset of Prohibition in 1919, the Renner Co. plant converted to the production of RENO non-alcoholic beer, ice, and other soft drinks, as well as managing the Renner Realty Co., originally established as a real estate holding company for the numerous saloons and other property owned by the brewery. RENO, oddly advertised with the slogan, "Divorced from beer", was brewed as normal beer, with the alcohol subsequently boiled away. Unfortunately, this occasionally left the brew with a burnt taste, and needless to say, sales never approached those of the real thing. Production of RENO ended in 1921, after which much of the brewery plant stood dormant, save for the management office, ice machines, and the bottling department for production of soft drinks. Thanks to the extensive real estate holdings, however, the Renner family business was able to survive the next twelve years intact.

Serving tray, circa 1915; the only indications that it is from Youngstown (and not Akron or Mansfield) are "Both Phones 92" at the side, and the label on the bottles

After the repeal of Prohibition in April 1933, the company's capital stock was raised to $600,000, and $250,000 of that was spent refurbishing the brewery. This had a significant impact on the local economy even prior to the first beer being brewed, as 200 otherwise unemployed men were hired to bring the old plant up to date. Among the items to be updated at the time were the following: all new brewing equipment, bringing the annual capacity up to 100,000 barrels (it would later be further increased to 175,000 barrels); new bottling machinery (costing $44,000); a new ice machine of 50 ton capacity; 50,000 bushels of malt; 75,000 lbs. of hops; 20,000 gross of bottles; 15-20 new delivery trucks; new water towers; 75,000 beer cases (while some of these were wooden, Renner was one of few brewers in Ohio to utilize steel crates, largely due to the plentiful steel mills throughout the area); in addition, $10,000 was spent rehabilitating the old buildings, with new wiring, plumbing, painting, etc.

Harry Weaver started brewing operations immediately, and by the early summer of 1933, Renner's Beer and Ale were on the market again. Other brands to enter the market soon after this included Old Vet, Old Oxford and Old Dublin Ales, Old Bavarian Beer, Clipper Beer, Old German Beer, and Prize Cup Beer. Weaver, who by this time had been brewmaster for more than forty years, was encouraged to return to a brewing institute in Chicago to learn all of the recent advances in the field, in order to modernize his technique. His unwillingness to do so led to his dismissal in 1934, after which he became one of the driving forces in the formation of the rival Youngstown Brewing Co. elsewhere in town (ironically, this new venture started with used equipment that Renner sold him).

Replacing Weaver as director of brewing in 1934 was Dr. Arnold Wahl, of the Wahl College of Brewing in Chicago. A noted international authority on the scientific aspects of beer brewing, Wahl's name was used in much of the company's advertising in the next few years. His view of the American brewing industry at the time was very positive (as quoted in an advertisement in the Akron *Beacon Journal* in October 1934):

"The American brewery can make better beers than the Europeans who originated them, due to better equipment, more accurate measuring, and scientific control of every step. We take the original recipes and give the beers we brew more delicious flavor, a finer bouquet, and build in better digestive qualities—that is, if we are one of those breweries that has broken away from tradition and are actually brewing along scientific lines as we are doing at the Renner Brewery. For instance, we are making a Bavarian or German style beer here at Renner's that has a distinctive malt taste all its own. With our scientific control of every step we have been able to give it a better taste than the original Bavarians ever thought possible. We have made the collar creamier, have added a sparkle and clearness, and have given it more beneficial health qualities besides making it uniform—every glass and bottle the same. Beer is a delicious drink. It is an extremely healthful beverage and when made correctly, every glass should call for another."

Wahl's words were prophetic of the future, at least in Ohio: within twenty years, the only breweries which would survive were those which had gone to a streamlined, mechanical, and purely scientific approach to the brewing of beer. Those that used older, more traditional techniques were unable to compete. Another twenty years after that, nearly all of Ohio's original brewing companies were out of business, unable to compete with the national giants and their entirely "industrial" approach to brewing.

A major change in brewing philosophy after Prohibition, as described recently by Bob Renner, was the concept of "Süffigkeit", the mysterious word which appears on much of the brewery's advertising in the 1930s. Prior to Prohibition, most beers were fairly heavy, with a high malt content. As a result, they were very filling, and one or two bottles were enough to satisfy the average saloon patron. After Prohibition, there was a dramatic move toward lighter, pilsener style beers, with a lower malt content. These were far less filling, and allowed the average beer drinker to consume a much larger amount at one time. Because the allowable alcohol content in beer was much lower than in the pre-Prohibition era, the amount of alcohol consumed was not necessarily more, but more beer could be sold by the breweries. This philosophy was represented by the German term "Süffigkeit", meaning "one leads to another".

One modern innovation which helped in marketing these new brands was the steel can for packaging beer. Renner began to utilize conetop cans made by the Continental Can Co. in 1938, for the marketing of Clipper and Old Bavaria Beers and Old Oxford Ale. The conetop cans had a major advantage over cans with flat tops: they could be filled using the existing bottling equipment, since they were sealed with a cap, and therefore the company would not need to purchase a separate (and very expensive) canning line.

After George J. Renner, Jr.'s death in December 1935, his son Emil "Spitz" Renner became Chairman of the Board for the remainder of the brewery's history, with Emil's son Robert ("Bob"), a graduate of the University of Michigan, as vice-president and later president (after serving in the United States Navy during WWII), and

Renner beers were packaged in cone-topped cans between 1938 and 1961

R. E. Bedeaux as master brewer (later replaced by Albert Kempe and then George Guehring). Grover Meyer became the company's president in 1940, but Robert Renner replaced him in 1948 after the company showed a significant drop in sales ($1.16 million for 1947, down from $1.5 million in 1946). C. Gilbert James, Emil's nephew, was the company's secretary and later vice-president.

Bob Renner took control of the company and its 75 employees at a critical time. Recognizing the need to modernize marketing and advertising methods, he hired numerous consultants in an effort to stay competitive with larger national breweries. When surveys indicated that local drinkers found Renner beers to be too bitter and strong, and not well-accepted with younger people, brands were reformulated and marketing was shifted, utilizing more radio and putting less emphasis on ale and more on beer. Focusing on what was felt to be the majority of the beer-drinking market, the light-to-moderate drinkers, Renner introduced Golden Amber Beer in March 1952, with its slogan, "The Light Beer For Your Lighter Moments". This quickly rebounded the company to one of its best years ever, with Golden Amber becoming the top selling brand in Youngstown. This success, however, would be in peril by the end of the decade.

Golden Amber became the company's flagship brand, replacing Renner Premium Beer and a number of other lesser brands which disappeared from the market. For the next decade, the company's efforts were focused on sales of Golden Amber, Old Oxford Ale, Old German Beer, and a new brand, King's Brew. A new logo, known as "Sneaky Pete", was unveiled around this time, consisting of a young man in a traditional Bavarian outfit. The favored story in town was that Golden Amber Beer had a tendency to "sneak up" on its consumers, making them inebriated very quickly. While some thought that the brewery was producing beer with a higher alcohol content than the law allowed, this rumor was never substantiated. In fact, the highest alcohol content was found in Renner Premium Ale, a true top-fermented ale which approached 6% alcohol, as opposed to most of the other brands which generally ranged from 3.2% to 4.0% alcohol. Old Oxford Ale, one of the longstanding favorites in Youngstown, was a blend of Renner Premium Ale and Golden Amber Beer.

Intense competition from national brewers through the late 1950s brought new brands of beer into Youngstown. Due to the depressed financial state of the region, Renner found it increasingly difficult to compete with these national companies' huge advertising budgets. This was in spite of the fact that the brewery only widely distributed its brands in three counties: Mahoning, Trumbull, and Columbiana (their beers were sold to a lesser extent in Akron and western Pennsylvania as well). A million-dollar investment was made in the company in 1960 in an attempt to stay in business. In addition to increased advertising, the company purchased a new canning line in late 1961, for packaging beer in flat-topped cans (Renner was one of very few breweries still using the cone-topped cans by this time). The flat-topped cans were easier to carry and to display in stores.

In addition to Renner's financial struggles at the time, a lawsuit was filed by the company in 1962 against the state of Ohio, when work was being complet-

Sneaky Pete made his debut in the early 1950s [courtesy of Don Augenstein]

ed on a section of freeway (which would later become part of Interstate 680) on the hillside just south of the brewery. During construction, which had inadvertently overlapped onto the brewery's property, large amounts of dirt were piled against the walls of the company's truck garage, damaging the building and leaving it largely unusable. In the end, the state was forced to pay $82,000 in damages.

At the same time that the company was making a large investment in its future, several cost cutting measures were also made (for example, all distribution and sales staff were let go in 1961 when distribution was turned over to other local companies, due to the damaged garage and an inability to house the delivery trucks). Despite all of these efforts, the company was posting as much as $50,000 in annual losses, and brewing operations were eventually shut down in November 1962, after which all equipment was liquidated. The company's remaining brands (Old Oxford Ale, Golden Amber Beer, and Old German Beer) were then purchased by the Old Crown Brewing Co. of Fort Wayne, IN., which continued to brew all three and distribute them in eastern Ohio until that brewery closed in 1973.

Bob Renner in the 1950s [photo courtesy of Jim Nicholson and Mary Ann Renner]

The Renner Co. continued to operate, purchasing the Miller Spreader Co., a local manufacturer of paving equipment, in 1963. In later years, there was a merger of the remaining Renner Co. with Forge Industries, the real estate division of the George J. Renner Brewing Co. of Akron. This continues to operate successfully as a holding company in Boardman, Ohio to this day. Overseen by Carl James, a great-great-grandson of George Renner, Jr., the company still owns Miller Spreader, as well as the Akron Gear Co., and Bearing Distributors, Inc., of Cleveland. Emil Renner remained in Youngstown until his death in 1976. Bob Renner left the family business and worked in sales and management for other companies in town, and later moved to the San Diego, CA. area. He died there in 2004, at the age of 92.

That Bob Renner was able to keep the brewery going as late as 1962 in an extraordinarily competitive industry, and in a relatively small market, is a testament to his ability to adjust and adapt to the changing times (although Bob recently stated that he was probably just lucky!) It was also a testament to the loyalty that Youngstown beer drinkers had for their local brand. By the time the brewery closed, only ten other breweries remained in Ohio, and in another twelve years, that number would be down to four (Hudepohl, Schoenling, Anheuser-Busch, and C. Schmidt).

The entire plant was purchased for $35,000 by a group of investors in 1963, with an intention to convert it into a warehouse or light manufacturing plant. These plans never came to pass, and the plant remained vacant for the next fifteen years. Much of it burned on October 14, 1978, as firefighters were unable to reach the site due to trash and logs strewn along Pike Street, which by then had also been abandoned. Most buildings in the complex were later razed and the area was backfilled, although the bottling house at the far east end still remained standing as of 2000.

4. Christian Haid/Jacob Knott brewery

Located at 16 Henrietta Street (later renumbered as 239; Henrietta Street later became North Avenue), this small brewery appears to have begun operation in the late 1860s. Christian Haid (also spelled Hiet, Hyde, Hait), a Prussian native born in 1835, was the original brewer, although he died around 1873, after which brewing was continued by his wife Mary. Around 1876, brewing operations were assumed by Jacob Knott, a native Bavarian, born in 1840. Knott, who briefly had a partnership with J. Klahs in 1879, increased the small plant's annual output from 200 barrels to over 1,000 by 1879. The brewery ran in connection with the City Bottling Works, operated by Samuel Kline, which was one block away on Henrietta St. In late 1890, Knott retired, and brewing operations ceased for good. There are no remains of the brewery today.

5. Youngstown Brewing Company

After Prohibition's repeal, there was only one brewery (Renner) remaining in Youngstown, as the Smith

Brewing Co. had never reopened. Recognizing the potential for another brewery to enter the regional beer market, a group of local investors incorporated the Youngstown Brewing Co. on December 26, 1934. Located at 305 North Avenue, at the northeast corner of the intersection with Rayen Avenue, the plant occupied the old Youngstown Sanitary Laundry buildings, originally built at the turn of the century. The old three-story brick plant required a great deal of rebuilding by the well-known DeBartolo Construction Co. in order to support the heavy brewing equipment, and fifteen months later the plant was ready for operations.

The grand opening, on May 1, 1936, gave the public an opportunity to view the new plant and its modern features: a 140-barrel brew kettle, which could produce up to 50,000 barrels annually (later additions increased this number to 80,000 barrels); huge tanks in the three aging and fermenting cellars capable of holding over 8,000 barrels of beer until mature; two large ice machines; a racking room capable of filling 250 barrels per hour; a bottling works capable of filling 2,500 cases of bottles per day; artesian wells capable of producing 25,000 gallons of pure water every day for both beer and ice making; an on-site cooperage shop for repair and manufacture of barrels; and a large hospitality room in the office building which could be rented out for any private function, free of charge.

The company's original officers included Harry Weaver (the former brewmaster of the Renner brewery from 1890 to 1934) as president; Joseph Barber, a former distributor of Sunrise Beer in Cleveland, as vice-president; A. H. Weitzman, formerly superintendent of a brewery in Wyandotte, MI., as general superintendent, overseeing the plant's 40 employees; and E. L. Moran, a local salesman, as secretary and treasurer. Frank Razinger was in charge of brewing operations, under Weaver's supervision. Initial sales were reasonably good, and the plant's beer was marketed under several different brand names: Bismarck and Wolf's Head Ales, Steel City, Old German, Old Bohemian, Silver Bond, Moerlein, and Crystal Top Beers were all sold in Youngstown and western Pennsylvania. Financial difficulties had set in by late 1938, however, and after the company declared bankruptcy and reorganized in 1939, Barber acquired the company and became its president, with Weitzman becoming vice-president and treasurer, and Frank Freundl becoming the new master brewer.

At the end of World War II, however, sales were in decline, and new management attempted to revive the company. By 1945, David Friedman, the president of the Youngstown Cartage Co., a local trucking company, had become the brewery's president. Two years later came a change in the company name to the Crystal Top Brewery, Inc., with new officers (all associated with the Youngstown Cartage Co.): Louis J. Bellos as president, Arrel Friedman as vice-president, Evelyn Bender as secretary, Frances Bellos as treasurer, and Frank Razinger returning from a stint at Cleveland's recently closed Tip Top brewery to be brewmaster. Crystal Top became the company's flagship brand and was sold in eastern Ohio as a low-budget beer, costing $2.75 per case and undercutting every other brand in the region. The company also invested in a canning line for the first time in an attempt to increase its market share with this new and increasingly popular type of packaging. Flat-topped cans of Crystal Top appeared in the area in small numbers over the next few months, but sales were not affected in any significant way.

After one year, despite the company's

(above) Steel can from 1947; (right) Youngstown's newest brewery, as shown in the Youngstown *Vindicator*, May 1, 1936; the office building is on the left, with the brewhouse on the right

best efforts, it became obvious that Crystal Top Beer would never establish a significant market share against the national brands with large advertising budgets. Even in Youngstown alone, the company had difficulty competing with the larger Renner Co. The brewery thus closed for good in late 1948. Much of the plant remains standing as of 2004 and is used as a warehouse for the Tartan Textiles Company. The small office building has been razed, and the top floor of the main brewhouse has been removed, leaving an unmarked two-story building, with the smaller bottling building next door.

6. Ohio Brewing Company/B & O Station Brewery & Restaurant

The Ohio Brewing Company had operated in Niles, Ohio for five years (see Trumbull County), when in June 2002 operations were moved to a century-old Baltimore & Ohio railroad station on the west side of Youngstown, at 530 Mahoning Avenue. After more than $300,000 was spent on improving the site, the brewing facility would operate briefly as the Ohio Brewing Co., and then as the B & O Station Brewery & Restaurant. Brothers Michael and Chris Verich were the original owners, with Chris as the brewmaster, although the move to Youngstown saw new partners Joe Pedaline and Robert Arroyo entering the picture. Eric Watson, and later Doug Beedy from Cleveland, were also hired to be the head brewers. The Verich brothers had sold their interest in the company by the end of 2002, however, and later made plans to reopen the Ohio Brewing Co. in Akron (see Summit County). After this, Arroyo and Pedaline purchased the building from the city of Youngstown for $50,000.

Upon opening, Verich Gold was the first brew offered by the brewery. Once established, other brands appeared such as Railcar Rye (a honey rye ale), Light Rail Lager (one cask-conditioned version of which contained honey and was known as "Lightly Buzzed"), Youngstown Brown Ale (which came in several versions, one of which being a maple nut brown ale), Summer Sensation Belgian light ale, Gandydancer Imperial Stout, Deralement (made with juniper berries and orange peel, along with one cask-conditioned variation using blueberries, known as "Shakin' The Blues", and another using Chai spices, known as "Chai Ching"), Arroyo Amber and Arroyo Berry Ales, Fruition (a light ale flavored with raspberries), Semaphore Stout, Imperial IPA, Porter (made with chocolate, and coming in at least two cask-conditioned varieties, one with vanilla added, and one with coffee), MVP (Mahoning Valley Pale Ale), Hearth Ale, and Pedaline's Pale Ale (which came in several varieties, including a standard India Pale Ale with English and Belgian malts plus four English varieties of hops, "Hopanero", with hot peppers added to the cask, and "Bark of the Angry Tree", with Angostura Bitters added).

After Pedaline and Arroyo were arrested and imprisoned in the summer of 2004 for operating an "indoor marijuana factory" (as reported in the Youngstown *Vindicator*), the brewery's days were numbered. Arroyo's daughter Laura then operated the brewpub, while Beedy left to operate the Cornerstone Brewery in Berea. The B & O Station Brewery closed after a final party on October 30, 2004.

Also Note:

1. Golden Age Beverage Company

The Golden Age Beverage Co., located at 134 E. Woodland Ave., began operation as the Chero-Cola Bottling Co. during Prohibition. By the time of Repeal, it had been renamed as Golden Age, for the bottling of Ginger Ale and other soft drinks. With Repeal came a move into the distribution of beer as well. The company was a local distributor of Schlitz and Kingsbury Beers from Wisconsin, and also began distributing beer and ale under its own name in 1933-34. The beer and ale were actually brewed by the Christian Diehl Brewing Co. of Defiance, OH., the Roth Brewing Co. of Monongahela, PA., and the Yough Brewing Co. of Connellsville, PA. While there was an intention for the company to develop its own brewing operation, this never came to pass. It would later gain the local contract to bottle Pepsi-Cola, and was eventually purchased by the American Beverage Corporation. The building still stands today.

2. Youngstown Temperance Beer Company

This appears to have been a distributorship, although it does not appear in any of the Youngstown city directories from the time. Its sole product was known as Bishop's Beer, a non-alcoholic beverage which had a brief but interesting history. It was invented in 1895 by Charles Ogren, a brewing scientist, at the request of the Rt. Reverend Samuel Fallows, A. M., LL. D., D. D., a bishop of the Reformed Episcopal Church in Chicago. Fallows established a number of temperance saloons in which Bishop's Beer was served. As stated in a brochure for the beverage, from around the turn of the century, "It is recognized by the more progessive element that man is a social being and must have places to congregate. The saloon furnishes this place. This social feature of the saloon is not objected to by progressive, broad-minded men and women. It is the evil wrought by intoxicating liquor." Supposedly recognized as "The Twentieth Century Beverage", Bishop's Beer (which was also distributed out of Dayton) was claimed to have become the leading beverage in Ohio, sold in nearly every dry town in the state, in just one year of existence. Despite these claims, an article in the *Western Brewer* in 1904 mentions the company filing for receivership due to a lack of demand for its product, Bishop's Beer.

3. Banner Brewing Company

Despite the fact that there is no information on this company in any local literature or official records, a blob top bottle is known to exist with this name, suggesting that its existence might have been prior to 1900. While it is possible that it represents a bottling company, no further information has yet surfaced.

4. Pabst Brewing Company

A large branch of the Pabst Brewing Co. of Milwaukee existed for many years in Youngstown, although it was for bottling and distribution only, with no beer brewed there. It had begun operation in the late 1880s at 324-326 W. Federal Street, managed by E. O. Jones, who was a dealer of Gehring's Cleveland Beer and Phillip Best's Milwaukee Lager Beer (the latter later evolved into the Pabst Brewing Co.) This operation later moved to 906-912 W. Rayen Avenue, where it continued to operate until the onset of Prohibition. Smaller bottling and distribution houses existed in Youngstown for the Cleveland & Sandusky, Herancourt (Cincinnati), Wiedemann (Newport, KY.), Miller (Milwaukee), Independent (Pittsburgh), and Schoenhofen (Chicago) breweries.

5. Ronneburg Brewery-Youngstown

In January 1984 came the announcement of a proposed new brewery, the area's first completely new one in fifty years. It would be a joint venture between area investors (led by the Cafaro Company, a prominent Youngstown family business of real estate and shopping mall development) and Kosmos Export GmbH of Hamburg, West Germany. The new plant would cost over $30,000,000, employ 132 people, produce over 200,000 barrels of beer annually from Meander Lake water, and was to be built in the Youngstown Commerce Park in North Jackson, approximately ten miles west of the city. The site would have access to both Interstates 76 and 80, allowing distribution of beer in a 200-mile radius.

The brewery was to produce Ronneburg Super Premium Beer and Ronneburg Classic, both of which would be made in accordance with German brewing standards, which are somewhat different than in the United States. Therefore, they would be fermented at a slower rate than American beers, and would have no artificial ingredients or preservatives. At that time, the American beer market was fairly flat, while the market for export beers was booming. Ronneburg was hoping to compete in the latter market, which in retrospect is similar to what many microbreweries and brewpubs were able to do a decade later. The brewery was to also produce sparkling mineral water.

Negotiations to begin construction continued for more than a year, but in the end, despite a great deal of optimism on the part of all potential investors, none of the plans ever came to pass, and the plant was never built.

Medina County

Medina Township

1. The Burkhardt Brewing Company

January 1999 marked the opening of Medina County's first-ever brewing establishment. Located at 3571 Medina Road (state route 18), this brewpub was an expansion of the Burkhardt Brewing Co. in Green, Summit County. Operated by Tom Burkhardt, of the well-known brewing family, this new site emphasized the nostalgic aspects of the Burkhardt brewing saga. Chuck Dahlgren remained the head brewer, and a steam powered 3 1/2-barrel brewing system was used. The beer was not bottled, but was sold in half-gallon growlers for take-out.

In keeping with the theme, Mug Ale was the specialty, still made by the same recipe used since 1902. Burkhardt's Select Export Beer, a light, medium bodied malt lager, was revived as well. Wolf Creek Pale Ale (named for the original source of water for the family brewery in downtown Akron) was introduced later, and along with Eclipse Dark Ale, these four brews were available at all times. Seasonal brews were made as well, including peach, raspberry, and honey ales, Irish Red, Oktoberfest, wheat and bock beers, and stout. Burkhardt's entire brewing operation was consolidated at this site when the original location in Green closed in 2000. However, by late 2001, the Medina location had closed its doors as well, bringing an end to another chapter in the family's long brewing saga.

2. Wallaby's Grille & Brewpub/Brown Derby Roadhouse

Opening in April 1999, Wallaby's first franchise south of Cleveland was located in a converted Shoney's restaurant at 5051 Eastpointe Drive. The site was adjacent to Interstate 71 and state route 18, one mile east of Burkhardt's. Wallaby's Australian theme continued with its three standard brews, Great White Wheat Ale, Ayers Rock Pale Ale, and Big Red Roo Red Ale. These were made in the 5-barrel Newlands brewhouse, along with several other seasonal and specialty brews, such as Spiced Pumpkin Ale, Strawberry Wheat and Blueberry Wheat Beers, Dr. Evil's India Pale Ale, Blackbeard Stout, and Maori Milk Stout.

Tom Gray was the initial brewer, and was succeeded by Daniel Maerzluft (formerly of the Crooked River and Diamondback Breweries in Cleveland) after several months. Maerzluft won a Silver Medal for Blackbeard Stout at the 2000 World Beer Cup, although he left the company soon after this. He was briefly succeded by Chris Alltmont before the restaurant closed, along with most of the Wallaby's chain, at the end of 2000.

By 2001, however, the site had been purchased and reopened as a part of the local chain of Brown Derby Roadhouse restaurants, specializing in steak with a country theme. Alltmont remained as the brewer, and continued production of Blackbeard Stout, along with Wild Wild Wheat and Road House Red. By early 2004, Alltmont was gone and had been replaced by Jack Kephart.

Meigs County

Pomeroy

1. Gottlieb Wildermuth Brewing Company

Frederick Schaffer was a native of Wurttemburg, Germany, born in 1824. Coming to the United States in the mid-1840s, he had moved to Pomeroy by 1849, when he purchased land along 2nd Street (later Condor Street), on the north side of town. Soon after this, he established Meigs County's only brewery at the site, which later had the address of 517-535 Condor St. Located at the base of a steep cliff and only one block from the Ohio River, Schaffer's brewery grew slowly over the years, until his death in 1865.

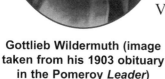

Due to outstanding debts by Schaffer, the brewery was sold at a public auction in January 1866 for $8,200. The buyer was Gottlieb Wildermuth, who had been Schaffer's assistant brewer from the beginning until 1861. Wildermuth was born in the town of Rielinghausen, Wurttemburg in May 1828. He had also come to America in the 1840s, with his parents David and Magdalena. After working at various jobs in Pittsburgh, Chillicothe, OH., and Cincinnati, he came to Pomeroy around the same time as Schaffer. Initially, David Wildermuth was a part owner of the brewery as well, but he was primarily a farmer and apparently did not take part in the brewing operation. He had sold his share of the brewery to Schaffer by 1856. At the outset of the Civil War, Gottlieb enlisted in the Union Army at Mason, WV., just across the river, in Company M of the First West Virginia Cavalry. He returned to the area at the war's end, in time to purchase the brewery.

Gottlieb Wildermuth (image taken from his 1903 obituary in the Pomeroy *Leader*)

Wildermuth continued brewing operations as before, and was assisted during this time by two young German immigrants, Jacob Anther and John Bloomaschine. Within a few years, however, Wildermuth's primary assistant was his son Charles, who had been born in 1859. Producing around 1,300 barrels of lager in 1874, the brewery enlarged over the next several years, such that production had doubled by 1878. It was around this time that a new three-story brewhouse was built, with stables and an icehouse across the street. In 1883, a bottling works was added to the plant. By the mid-1890s, annual production had increased to over 5,000 barrels. During this period, the plant was known as the Roller Mill Brewery until it was incorporated as the Gottlieb Wildermuth Brewing Company in 1899, with a capital stock of $100,000. Wildermuth also operated a tavern on the premises during this era, for drinking the beer at its freshest.

Wildermuth died of pneumonia in August 1903, after which Charles Wildermuth succeeded him as company president, while another son, Max W. Wildermuth, born in 1870, became the secretary and treasurer. In addition, Carl Schwope was hired as the new brewmaster, producing Wildermuth's Special Lager as well as Wildermuth's Extra Pale Beer.

After passage of the Rose Law of 1908, the voters of Meigs County and much of southern Ohio exer-

Malt house of the Wildermuth brewery as it appeared in the 1950s. The storage cellars were under this building [photo taken by the late Ernie Oest and provided by the American Breweriana Association].

cised their local option and went dry beginning in 1909. However, the brewery continued production for sales into West Virginia and areas in Ohio which remained wet. In addition, it placed a low alcohol temperance beer on the market for sales in dry counties. By early 1912, Meigs County and most of the surrounding areas were wet again, and production continued as before.

The brewery continued as a family operation until the onset of Prohibition in early 1919, when all beer production at the plant ceased. Ice production continued briefly, as the plant had been a major supplier of ice in the area for many years. However, by the end of 1919 the plant had shut down for good and was vacated. Charles Wildermuth remained in the area until his death in 1926. After Prohibition, a brief attempt was made to restart brewing operations one last time. A new group of investors, retaining the Wildermuth Brewing Co. name and including Max Wildermuth, purchased the brewery in early 1935 with the goal of renovating the old plant, but these plans never materialized. By the end of the year, the company had reorganized, but new investors Vincent and Leo O'Donnell, and Joseph Seidenstricker, of Columbus, and William Seyfferle of Cincinnati, fared no better, and brewing would not return to Pomeroy (Leo O'Donnell was later involved with the Canton Brewing Co. when it closed in 1941).

Bottle label, circa 1915
(John Phillips collection)

The plant remained vacant for many years, until most of it was razed in the late 1970s, with the exception of half of the ice house and bottling works, across the street from the main brewhouse. The eastern half of this building has remained standing, albeit in a sad state of decay, for many years since then. In addition, a stone arch which stood at the entrance to the wagon shed remained intact as of 1999, although it was just a gateway to an empty lot.

Monroe County

Miltonsburg

1. Frederick Stauzel brewery

Frederick Stauzel (also spelled Stenzel, Stencil, Stansle) was born in France in 1812 and came to America in the early 1840s. In 1842 he purchased land on the south side of the tiny village of Miltonsburg(h), in northern Monroe County, an area heavily populated with German and French immigrants, most of whom were farmers. Located on the west side of Main Street (today state route 145), the site was soon home to the county's first brewery. There it appears that he was assisted by Gottlieb Blocker (born in 1824 in Wittemburg) and George Coonrad (born in 1827 in Prussia). The brewery is listed in the 1853 Ohio Business Directory as being operated by Walters & Stencil, but it remains unknown who Walters was, as there were numerous people in the area at that time with the surname of either Walters or Walter. While it is likely that this was a very small operation, the exact size and output of the brewery remain unknown.

Production continued into the mid-1860s, then came to an end. Stauzel was listed in the 1870 census as being a cooper, and Blocker had died by that time. While the brewery building itself has long since disappeared, a man-made underground storage cave, likely used by Stauzel for aging his beer, remains in the village.

Woodsfield

1. Michael Lang brewery

Michael Lang was born in 1818 in the town of Canton Neterbron, in Alsace-Lorraine. He came to America in the late 1830s, residing initially in Pittsburgh, PA. In April 1848 he and his family moved to Woodsfield, where he worked for several years as a cooper, and later as a cattle farmer. In the mid-1860s he founded a small brewery on his property, located on the west side of Walnut Street (today Sycamore Street), just south of Court Street (today state route 78.)

The small brewery produced only between 100 and 200 barrels of lager beer annually, and continued to operate through 1882. After this, Lang's 39-year-old son John took over operations for another two years. It appears that all brewing ceased after 1884, although the family remained in the area and continued farming for a number of years, until Michael Lang died in 1896. There is no trace of the brewery today.

MORGAN COUNTY

McConnelsville

1. T. D. Young brewery

Theabold David Young was a native Bavarian, born in 1812, who had come to the United States around 1850. In March 1862 he came to the Muskingum River Valley, purchasing land in the town of McConnelsville, at the southeast corner of Jefferson and Elm (today Second St.) Soon after this he established Morgan County's only brewing establishment at the site of his residence. Located just two blocks from the river and its busy wharf, Young had a ready-made customer base with river workers who now had locally-made beer that didn't need to be shipped in from Zanesville or Marietta.

Although he was producing just under 200 barrels of beer annually, Young continued to operate his small plant until 1875. At that time the brewery came into the hands of Christian Burckholter, and while the details are unclear, it appears that the transaction may have helped to settle Young's debts. Burckholter was a native Ohioan, born in 1836, who had recently inherited a large candy factory and grocery nearby. While this remained the primary focus of his work, he did operate the brewery intermittently over the next four years before closing it for good around 1880 (Schade's directory of 1879 indicates operation by "Burckholter & Reed", although it remains unknown who Mr. Reed was). The brewery soon disappeared into history, and a residence is at the site today.

Muskingum County

Zanesville

1. George Painter/Jacob Young brewery

Certainly one of the first, if not THE first known brewery in the eastern half of Ohio was established around 1808 (Cincinnati's first brewery is thought to have begun between 1805 and 1811, and therefore MAY have been the state's first). Zanesville was a logical site for this early establishment, situated along the National Road, midway between Columbus and the Ohio River. With no railroads or canals yet built in the region, the National Road (later U. S. Route 40) and some of the larger rivers were virtually the only routes of transportation through Ohio. Begun in 1806, the National Road initially was built from Cumberland, Maryland to Vandalia, Illinois in order to allow settlers to migrate westward through and beyond the Appalachian Mountains.

Situated along the Muskingum River, the town of Zanesville was settled between 1800 and 1810. By the latter year it was the third largest town in the state, and its importance was demonstrated when it became the new state capital in that year. This only lasted for two years, however, before the capital returned to Chillicothe (briefly), before moving to Columbus in 1816.

Numerous small industries and businesses began to form in the town after 1800, as the population slowly grew. Three breweries and several distilleries had been established by 1820 (although two of the breweries were very short-lived), partly due to the fact that many of the local wells were not considered pure for drinking water. Alcoholic beverages were considered relatively pure due to the boiling involved in the process, as well as the presence of the alcohol.

The exact time of the first brewery's origin is uncertain, as it is only mentioned in Everhart's *History of Muskingum County, Ohio* from 1882. The brewery was started "…by a Philadelphian, whose name has not found a record or lodgment in anybody's memory, but was purchased by one George Painter in 1807. It was located on the site now the northwest corner of South and Fifth Streets. Painter continued to brew there until 1811, when he sold to Jacob Young, who continued the business until 1815, when he abandoned the business."

However, deed transfer records indicate that Painter purchased the land for $500 in September 1808 from Jonathan Zane and John McIntire, who were two of the founders and initial leaders of the town. They had previously purchased the land in 1802, and although it is possible that they (or someone else) had established a brewery at the site, there is no real evidence that they did so. There is no evidence of Jacob Young purchasing the brewery, although it is possible that he may have rented it for brewing purposes. It appears that Painter died in 1814, and that the brewery ceased to function after that time.

2. William Marshall brewery

Also mentioned in *History of Muskingum County, Ohio* is this brewery, located in a frame building on the north side of town, near the end of what is today known as Warwick Avenue. It was at the top of a hill which later was the site of a city reservoir and water works power house No. 3. Founded by William Marshall in November 1813, the brewery produced around thirty barrels of beer per week. James Boyd was the brewer. Barton &

McGowan purchased the brewery in 1815, and subsequently converted it into a distillery. None of this information, however, is supported by local deed transfer records.

3. Lattimore/Ballentine/Wainwright/Muskingum Steam Brewery

1866 Muskingum County Atlas

According to *History of Muskingum County, Ohio*, this brewery was established in 1816 by Joseph Lattimore, with brewing operations performed by Caleb Johnson. The plant was located along the Muskingum River, on the west side of Glass House Street (later River Road, and today known as Wayne Avenue, or State Route 60). The property was purchased in 1829 by David Ballentine, who continued brewing operations for an additional six years. In 1835, the brewery was converted into a flour mill, and it appears that it had varying functions over the next twenty years.

Ballentine sold the property to his son John, and Adam Clark, in 1836. They in turn sold the property in 1840 to the Bank of Zanesville. It appears that the plant continued to operate as a mill until 1849, when it was purchased by Robert Hazlett and his son, William. Robert Hazlett, born in Pennsylvania in 1797, was a dealer in dry goods in the town, but upon the purchase of the old brewery lot, he began to manufacture white lead (lead carbonate, a powder used in making paint and other materials) there.

In July 1859, Hazlett sold the factory for $2,000 to Jarvis Wainwright. Naming the plant the Muskingum Steam Brewery, Wainwright refitted it for brewing operations and began producing Wainwright's Pale Ale, while living across the street. By 1871, however, he had accumulated over $5,000 in debts, and the brewery was sold at a sheriff's auction on October 30th to pay his creditors. The property was appraised at $11,000, and was sold for $7,725, or just over two-thirds the value. It appears that brewing operations ceased at that time.

The brewery building later housed a meat packing plant, and still later became a vegetable and fruit canning factory, owned by Ungemach & Stern, for several years. It was later razed, and nothing remains of it today.

4. America House Tavern and Brewery/Market Brewery

Founded in 1835 by Christian F. Haas, this establishment was originally known as the America House Tavern. Located on the north side of Market Street, between 4th and 5th Streets, the tavern had a small attached brewing establishment as well. Haas operated both over the next few years, until his death in the 1840s. After this, the property was sold by his widow to John Clossman in 1848 for $5,250.

Clossman was a native of Germany, born in 1800, who took over operation of the tavern and what was now known as the "Market Brewery", producing both ale and lager beer. He was assisted by his sons John Jr. (born 1824) and David (born 1828), as well as William Cline, another young German immigrant, born in 1824. Clossman sold the property in December 1868, and it appears that brewing operations ceased at that time. The Zanesville city municipal building stands at the site today.

5. C. F. Achauer/Washingon Brewery/Simon Linser

Muskingum County's largest and longest-lasting brewery began operations in the 1840s, although exactly when Christian Frederick Achauer built the Washington Brewery remains unclear. Achauer was born in 1804 in Wurtemburg, Bavaria. He embarked on a nine-week voyage to America in 1835, landing in New York. He came to Zanesville soon after this, and initially worked in the American House Brewery of Christian Haas. In September 1841 he purchased the property on which the brewery would stand, at 350 E. Main Street, on the top of a hill overlooking the city. He and his family then moved to Dresden, in northern Muskingum County, for several years. Whether the brewery had been built by that time or not is unknown.

In any case, Achauer returned to Zanesville around 1848, and after that time he is known to have operated the Washington Brewery. Consisting of a main three-story stone brewhouse and a nearby malting house, the plant had two stone-lined underground caves built into the hillside for storing beer. The steep hill forced the horse-drawn beer wagons to stop to rest on their way to the brewery. This might have been a problem for a larger establishment, but this one was producing under 500 barrels of ale and common beer annually through the 1870s. By that time, the city had gradually worked on reducing the hill's steep grade, so that horses could climb it much more easily without having to rest.

(inset) Simon Linser, Sr. [from *One Hundred Years of Brewing*]; (above) 1866 Muskingum County Atlas.

In May 1881, Achauer was killed when he fell from a gangway in the brewery. A storm was moving through the area, and was blowing open windows and doors in the brewhouse. When he went out to try to close them, he accidentally fell through a trap door and died soon afterward. His son, Herman Achauer, was an attorney who lived across the street. He continued operation of the brewery for three years before selling it to Simon Linser, Sr. and Henry Zinsmeister in 1884.

Linser was born in Baden, Germany in 1852 and came to America in 1873. After working in New York and Cincinnati, he came to Zanesville in 1880, where he first worked for the Brenner & Co.'s City Brewery before purchasing the Washington Brewery. In 1891, he bought out Zinsmeister's share to become the sole owner. By this time, the plant's annual capacity had increased to 10,000 barrels and employed ten to twelve men.

The brewery was incorporated as the Simon Linser Brewing Company on January 1, 1901, with a capital stock of $200,000. By this time, the company had purchased the Star and Riverside (renamed as the

Two stock trays for American Maid Beer, circa 1915

(left) Original century-old Linser brewhouse, circa 1949, after its conversion to a beverage distribution warehouse; (below) Simon Linser, Jr., in later years.

Bavarian Brewing Co.) breweries elsewhere in town, and it continued to operate each for several years. Linser was the president and general manager of the new corporation, with his son Simon, Jr. as secretary and treasurer, and another son, Charles, as the brewmaster. David Schmid (Smith), who also owned a large roofing company in town, was the vice-president. Linser lived next door in the former Achauer home with his wife and twelve children (from two marriages).

Linser began a process of expansion of the brewery in 1895 with the addition of a modern refrigerating plant. New brewing equipment was added after the turn of the century, expanding production dramatically to over 40,000 barrels annually by 1903. A decade later came the addition of a 30-ton ice plant and a modern bottling house. With the renumbering of streets at this time, the plant's address became 976 East Main Street.

Around this time came the introduction of Hill Top Beer, which became the company's anchor brand for several years. Typical advertising slogans at the time included "They cry from the house top, Give Us Linser's Hill Top"; "A glass of Linser's Hill Top makes your lunch palatable"; "Linser's hobby: pure beer or no beer"; and "If your system's out of gear, try a glass of Linser's beer". Some years later, the Hill Top name was replaced by a new anchor brand, "American Maid" Beer, which was advertised in a similar fashion. Linser retired from active brewing in 1915, at which time William Weisman was hired to be the brewmaster. Remaining plant operations were turned over to Simon Linser Jr. and another son, Herman. Their father remained in Zanesville, however, until his death in 1941.

Beer production came to a halt on November 18, 1918 due to the immediate post-war Prohibition act. The remaining beer on hand was sold off over the next few months, at which time the company converted production to near beer and soft drinks, known as Hill Top Beverages, while continuing ice production. The capital stock was lowered to $100,000 at this time. Production continued until 1928, when it was no longer felt to be profitable, and the plant shut down completely.

After Repeal in 1933, Linser Jr. reorganized the Simon Linser Company, with the hope of starting brewing operations again. The plan involved a complete modernization of the plant, costing between $50,000 and $75,000. Due mostly to economic factors of the Great Depression, it never became a reality, and brewing operations never took place again. The company became a distributorship for beer and wine, including the local contracts for Leisy Beer (of Cleveland), Gambrinus Beer (of Columbus), and Burkhardt Beer (of Akron).

Linser retired around 1958, but continued to live in the century-old house next door to the brewery until his death in 1963. The plant was then rented to the Gambrinus ("Gam") Distributing Co., which operated it until 1965. For the next ten years, the plant sat vacant until vandals set fire to one of the buildings. It was condemned by the city after that, and partly razed in 1975. The remaining buildings, including the original one from the 1840s, were razed in 1982, and the underground beer cellars were filled in with dirt. An empty lot is all that remains today, although a few feet of brick foundation from one of the buildings remains on the hillside.

6. City Brewery/Brenner & Company

Located at the northwest corner of Spring & High Streets, the City Brewery & Malt House was established in 1854 by Rev. George F. Goebel & Conrad Fisher (also spelled Fischer). A small establishment, it only produced around 250 barrels of beer per year. After only two years, Fisher left the partnership to establish his own brewery around the corner, and Goebel operated the brewery himself (with help from Sebastian Bohn for several years) until approximately 1861. He then sold the property to Frank Kirsner & Adolph Horn.

Horn & Kirsner operated the plant until 1865, when they established a new brewery south of town and sold the City Brewery to John A. Brenner & Company (Brenner and Frederick Horn). Brenner operated the plant until 1885, producing between 1,000 and 1,700 barrels of beer annually. At that point, he purchased the larger Red Star Brewery around the corner, and converted the City Brewery into his malting plant. At this point, the plant consisted of one primary two-story building with an adjacent ice house.

Within several years, the plant was being used as a pop bottling works, still owned by Brenner, although by 1893 it was called the Zanesville Star Bottling Works, operated by Joseph X. Laube. It appears that the plant was then purchased by Frank L. Normann in 1898, and he brewed beer there for only two years, producing less than 500 barrels of lager beer annually before operations shut down for good in 1900. The building later housed a machine shop, but had been razed entirely by the 1940s. Today, a Hampton Inn stands at the site of the brewery, just north of Interstate 70.

7. Conrad Fisher/Star/Armbruster & Schmitt Brewery

Conrad Fisher left the brewing partnership with George Goebel in 1856 in order to establish his own brewery and malt house just around the corner. Located at 29 Monroe St. (also spelled Munroe, and previously known as Main St.), this was known as the Red Star Brewery, and it continued to operate even after Fisher's death, being run by his family until 1885 (after 1875, it was known as Fisher Bros. Brewery). It was one of the city's largest breweries of the era, producing more than 2,000 barrels of beer annually by the late 1870s.

In July 1885, the Fisher family sold the brewery for $8,000 to John A. Brenner & Co. (see section on the City Brewery). Brenner enlarged the plant and operated it until early 1893, when a new group calling itself the Star Brewing Co. leased the plant to continue operations. Managed by William F. Reilly, a nearby saloon owner, this new company did not survive for long, and had accepted assignment by the end of that year. Brenner himself was in a position of financial insolvency at that time, as he was unable to pay bills amounting to over $10,000, reportedly "owing to slack times".

In March 1894, the plant was sold at a public auction for $16,000 to Albert & Fabian Armbruster, and Alois Schmitt, who continued brewing operations. Also working for the new company were Albert & William Schmitt. By now, annual production was just over 5,000 barrels, although the new owners were able to nearly double that capacity by 1898. With the renumbering of streets around this time, the plant's new address was 727 Monroe St. The company merged with the larger Simon Linser Brewing Co. in late 1900, although Armbruster & Schmitt continued to operate the brewery as Plant No. 2 of the Linser Co. (with Charles Linser as foreman) until 1905, when it was closed.

Remains of the Star Brewery in the 1950s (photo courtesy of the late Ernie Oest). The billboard at the bottom of the wall advertises Gambrinus Beer from Columbus. The building is no longer standing.

After this, Albert Armbruster operated a saloon in town and was the local agent for the Nicholas

Schlee brewery of Columbus. The brewery plant was later utilized by the West Jefferson Creamery Co. as a dairy, then as a garage for the state highway department, and still later as a trucking company. It was razed in the early 1970s. By the late 1990s, the neighborhood had been leveled completely and rebuilt as a commercial district with access to Interstate 70. During the construction of the Tumbleweed Restaurant, which stands on the site of the Star brewery today, workers encountered the original underground cellars, which still remained.

8. Marietta Street Brewery (Sebastian/August Bohn)

Sebastian Bohn was a native of Baden, Germany, born in 1821. After taking part in the German rebellion of 1848, he left for Switzerland, and in 1854 came to the United States. Within several years he came to Zanesville, where he worked at George Goebel's City Brewery for a time, before deciding to establish his own plant on the south side of town. This new brewery was to be located at 144 Marietta St., at the southwest corner of Spurck St. (this later became 1016 Marietta St. when streets were renumbered after the turn of the century).

Local literature states that this brewery was established in 1860, although records indicate that Bohn purchased the property in November 1865 (it is possible that he rented at the site prior to purchasing it). In any case, the brewery was relatively small, producing only a few hundred barrels of beer each year while Sebastian was alive. The plant itself consisted only of a two-story brick brewhouse and malt house, as well as a small ice house and stable, while Bohn lived in an attached dwelling next door.

Bohn died in March 1892, and operations were taken over by his son August, who had been born in Somerset, Ohio in 1858. He began working in the brewery at the age of fifteen, and continued to work there for the remainder of his life. He made numerous improvements to the thirty-year-old plant after taking ownership, and production steadily increased over the next decade. An addition built in 1905 increased the plant's annual capacity to 10,000 barrels, although actual production never approached that level. Bohn's lager beer was sold mainly in the town of Zanesville, and most of his advertising was by word of mouth.

Remains of the Bohn brewery in 1999, facing Marietta Street. The main buildings, built in the 1860s, now house apartments. It is the only one of the nine breweries in Zanesville still standing.

In later years, Bohn was joined by John Homola, who became the brewmaster of the small plant. Brewing continued until November 18, 1918, when all beer production ceased due to statewide Prohibition. Although Bohn was reportedly going to start producing a cereal beverage at the facility, there is no evidence that he ever did so. The remaining beer on hand was sold off over the next few months, at which point Bohn essentially retired. Having never married, he continued to live alone in the house next to the brewery for the remainder of his years. Interestingly, he was still listed as a brewer in the city directory until his death in September 1926.

After this, the brewery building housed a beer distributorship for a time before being converted into apartments. Some of the smaller back buildings have been razed through the years, but the main original building facing Marietta Street remains intact to this day, still housing apartments.

9. Horn & Kirsner/Merkle/Riverside/Bavarian Brewing Company

Located across the street from the Muskingum Steam Brewery on Glass House Street (now Wayne Avenue), this brewery was established around 1865 for the production of both ale and lager beer. It was originally operated by Horn & Co., consisting of Adolph H. Horn, Frank K. Kirsner, and Adolph and Edmund Merkle. The first two men had previously operated the City Brewery in town. The latter two were brothers and natives of Alsace-Lorraine, who had just come to Zanesville in 1864. They operated a saloon in town prior to their involve-

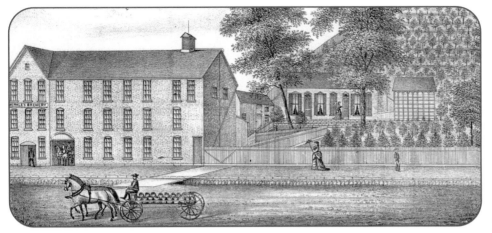

Muskingum County Atlas, 1875

ment with the brewery.

Horn & Kirsner sold their interest in the plant to the Merkle Brothers for $8,000 in November 1869. The brothers built it into the city's largest brewery of the era, with a three-story main brewhouse capable of producing just under 3,000 barrels of beer annually through the 1870s. After 1880, it was operated by Adolph Merkle alone, and he expanded production to between 4,000 and 5,000 barrels over the next decade. Production continued until the summer of 1890, when debts forced Merkle to accept assignment to pay his creditors.

The brewery was then sold in 1891 to a new group of local men who had formed a stock company worth $50,000. Known as The Riverside Brewing Co., the group was headed by president Henry C. Lindsay, who was a local architect. Vice-president was John C. Stevens, who was proprietor of the Zane House hotel in town. Charles J. Oshe was secretary and treasurer, and also owned a saloon at 162 Main St., where the brewery's main office was. August V. Kuehn was the plant manager, although he would later move south to Marietta, where he would become one of the principals of the Marietta Brewing Co. Also involved with the new company was Wilhelm (William) Feller, who would later be a driving force behind the development of both the Marietta and Bellaire Brewing Companies. Producing both lager and export beer, the company continued to operate until 1897, when it was taken over by Joseph Hoffer. Hoffer continued brewing operations through early 1900, when the brewery went into receivership.

At that time it came into the hands of David Schmid (Smith), the vice-president of the Linser Brewing Co. Over the next few months, the entire brewery was modernized with new equipment. It then reopened as the Bavarian Brewing Co. (also known as Plant No. 3 of the Linser Brewing Co.) when it was incorporated in 1901. Fred Fisch was hired as the brewmaster for the plant at this time, although he had been replaced by Andrew Buck (formerly with August Bohn's brewery just a mile away) by 1906.

Brewing at the plant continued until 1914, when the parent Linser Co. consolidated all operations at the original brewery on Main St., after which the Bavarian brewery was vacated for good. The building was razed some years later, and there are no remains of it today.

Also Note:

1. In *History of Muskingum County, Ohio*, there is a mention of a man named Edward Didas, who in 1855 "…began to brew in a small way." This was most likely a home brewing operation, although Didas does not appear in any census or deed records or city directories from the era. Without additional information, I would not consider this to be an actual brewing establishment.

2. A second attempt was made after Prohibition's Repeal in 1933 to form a new brewing establishment in the city of Zanesville. A group of Zanesville and Newark, Ohio capitalists intended to purchase the old Star Ice & Storage Co. (not connected with the Star brewery branch of the Linser Co., however), and convert it into a brewery. The men were affiliated with a parent company which owned the Consumers Brewing Co. in Newark. However, as with so many other fledgling companies of the era, the plans never materialized.

Ottawa County

Marblehead

1. Frontwaters Restaurant and Brewing Company

Ottawa County's first ever brewing operation began in May 1996, when Frontwaters Restaurant opened at 8620 East Bayshore Road. Established and operated by brothers Chris and Jeff Kolar, the brewery and restaurant operated out of a restored 1830s winery mansion. Due to the seasonal nature of the region, being a prime summer vacation spot, Frontwaters was open only between April and October, and was closed during the winter.

A 10-barrel brewing system was employed, and numerous brews comprised the 1500 barrel annual output, with four being on tap in the pub: Summerfest seasonal wheat beer, Lake Erie's Gale Warning Ale, Marblehead Red Pale Ale, and Russian Imperial Stout. Also brewed for bottling were Port Clinton Porter, Crystal Rock Dopple Bock Lager (resurrecting a favorite area name), Coriander Amber Lambic Ale, Belgian Abbey Ale, and Lightkeeper's Ale. The latter was a tribute to the nearby Marblehead Lighthouse, built in 1822, which remains the oldest operating lighthouse in all of the Great Lakes region. Four of these varieties won awards (two silver medals and two bronze medals) at the 1997 World Beer Championships. Most of the brands were bottled on site for sale in the area. Other seasonal beers were available through the years, including Blueberry Ale, Pumpkin Ale, Hefe-Weizen, S.O.S. oatmeal rye stout, and Honey Brown Ale.

In later years, the brewpub became part of the South Beach Resort complex, including a large hotel, with cottages, swimming pools, and a marina, aimed primarily at the area's summer vacation crowd. However, by the 2003 season, the cost of brewing operations had become prohibitive; by the opening of the 2004 season, the brewery had been dismantled, although the restaurant continued to operate.

Middle Bass Island

1. J. F. Walleyes Eatery and Brewery

Middle Bass is a primarily residential island, known mainly for its century-old Lonz Winery, which closed in 2000. Opening in June 1998, J. F. Walleyes was the island's first brewing establishment, located at 1810 Fox Road, just around the corner from the winery and adjacent ferry dock. In a situation similar to some of the other small brewpubs in the state, the establishment of an on-site brewing operation enabled the pub to obtain a license to sell liquor, due to a loophole in Ohio liquor laws. The brewpub was open most of the year, although it would close for several weeks during the winter.

While the restaurant was owned by William Gross, Matt Allen of Detroit was the original brewer, setting up the equipment and establishing the recipes for the beer brewed. He remained a consultant, while Jim Millinger was the regular brewer and manager. Using DME equipment, two brews were made per summer, with Walleyes Porter and Walleyes Light Beer being the primary brands, all sold in the restaurant. While the brewpub's popularity continued to grow, disaster struck on October 19, 2002, during a large turkey roast. A turkey fryer overheated and caught fire, and aided by strong winds, the fire consumed the entire restaurant. In less than an hour, the establishment had burned to the ground, with a loss of $700,000. Despite the setback, rebuilding began soon after, and the restaurant was open for business by the 2003 season, with brewing operations continuing as well. Taking advantage of new state laws, some of the beers now had a much higher alcohol content than in the past.

2. Hazards Microbrewery and Restaurant

Opening in 1999, this brewpub is the most recent addition to the St. Hazards Village On The Beach, a resort with a distinct Caribbean theme, located at 1233 Fox Road. The name and logo are another reference to Oliver Hazard Perry, who defeated the British in the Battle of Lake Erie, a major turning point in the War of 1812. As the island area tends to be seasonal, the resort operates mainly between April and October.

Similar to Walleyes (above), the establishment of a brewing operation enabled the pub to have a liquor license due to a peculiarity of Ohio law. Its brewer is Matt Cole from the Rocky River Brewing Co. in Cuyahoga County. Cole uses a small 2 1/2-barrel brewing system to brew one primary beer, a Hefe-Weizen wheat beer, although at other times he has also made a raspberry ale. He estimated a total of ten barrels being brewed per summer. One particular challenge for Cole was the use of the local well water for brewing, which significantly altered the beer's taste. A water filtration system was added in later years to solve this problem.

Put-In-Bay/South Bass Island

1. Put-In-Bay Brewing Company, aka Brewery At The Bay

The island area's first brewing operation began in May 1996 in a building which formerly housed Put-In-Bay's fire department at 441 Catawba Avenue. The Brewery At The Bay is operated by Chris and Carl Krueger (Carl is in charge of brewing), and like many island establishments, it is open only between May and October. Several brews have been made through the years, such as Summer Brew mild wheat beer, Fat Man's Friend nut brown ale, PIB Blonde pilsner, and Ole Cotton Top Irish Red. In general, one or two home-brewed beers are available at any given time, in addition to a number of bottled brands.

In a village where golf carts far outnumber cars as the way to get around and a party atmosphere is always in the air, the brewpub operates adjacent to a large gift shop and is across the street from the Beer Barrel Saloon, which has the world's longest continuous bar, at 405 feet in length.

Also Note

1. The Bay Brewing Company appeared in 1991, when 21-year-old local entrepreneur Eric Booker announced that he would be releasing Island Gold Beer. Tired of mass-marketed national beers, Booker was attempting to create a unique brew along the lines of what was appearing in the region's brewpubs. At the same time, he wanted a beer with a style unique to the island area, which was already known for its native wines. While the exact figure was not released, Booker invested between $20,000 and $50,000 of his own money in the venture, and contracted with the Frankenmuth Brewing Co. of Michigan to brew and bottle the beer (none was ever produced at Put-In-Bay). After Booker met with Frankenmuth's Brewmaster Fred Scheer, the beer was formulated as a pilsner type of lager, with a malty taste and 3.5% alcohol, somewhat less than the average national beers. This was specifically for tourists who were in the area and wanted to drink while sightseeing, yet not get drunk.

Appearing in bottles only, the beer was initially sold at taverns and stores in the island area before its distribution began to slowly widen. Priced at around $20 per case, the beer was set to compete with premium beers like Anheuser-Busch's venerable Michelob. Island Gold Light Beer was added later that year, but production of the brands continued only for a few years before they disappeared into history.

2. The Beer Barrel Saloon, mentioned previously as having the world's longest bar, is one of the central points of Put-In-Bay's society. In the mid-1990s, the saloon contracted with the G. Heileman Brewing Co. of LaCrosse, WI. to produce its own house brand of beer. Packaged in 16-ounce cans, the brand was sold only at Put-In-Bay and was short-lived.

Portage County

Brimfield Township

1. Blimp City Brewery

The greater Akron area's first true microbrewery was established in the summer of 1998. At that time, Tim Kuss, his wife Nancy, and his brother Mark (previously the head brewer for the Ohio Brewing Co. in Niles) invested $200,000 into the equipment needed to begin brewing operations, for the specific purpose of selling beer to local area bars, as opposed to operating a brewpub themselves. Located in a small industrial park at 330 Tallmadge Road (building "F"), the Blimp City Brewery had a 10-barrel brewhouse and initially began with an annual capacity of just under 500 barrels.

Kuss's venture into the world of brewing beer was a dramatic career change, as he had previously been a freelance television producer, while his wife was a radio host and producer at nearby Kent State University. Growing up in Suffield Township, near the Goodyear Tire and Rubber Company's Wingfoot Lake blimp hangar, Kuss was inspired from an early age by the frequent sight of blimps flying through the sky. A graduate of Chicago's Siebel Institute for brewing, he had originally hoped to establish a blimp museum and associated brewpub, but eventually decided to focus just on the beer itself. The Kusses' initial goal for the company was to remain small while establishing a presence and reputation in the area.

Once the brewery was established, four primary brews were produced: All-American Blonde Pale Ale, K-Ship Kolsch (named after a type of blimp produced by Goodyear during WWII to patrol America's coasts against submarines), Blimp City Black Ale (German style schwarzbier), and Akron/Macon German Style Alt Bier (named after two of Goodyear's giant airships, both built in Akron in the 1930s, both of which later crashed.) Beer was sold in kegs and in 22-ounce bottles, and all brands were available at a number of restaurants and stores in the Akron area. Ray's Classic Ale was bottled for sale at Ray's Place, a restaurant in Kent, and Blue Devil Blonde Beer was made for Delanie's Grille in nearby Tallmadge. One other limited brand, Aeros' Ale, was produced in 2000 for the minor league Akron Aeros baseball team, and was sold during games at Canal Park stadium. Sales gradually increased throughout the greater Akron area, sparking speculation that the company might open an affiliated brewpub at the end of 2002. However, the high cost of installing a bottling line had prevented the brewery from operating at a profit, especially with the downturn of the economy around the same time. By February 2003 the brewery had closed its doors for good, and once again the only blimps from the Akron area said "Goodyear" on their sides.

Garrettsville

1. Garretts Mill Brewing Company

Portage County's first post-Prohibition brewery came to life in June 1995. The Garretts Mill Brewing Co. was a brewpub which operated within Alessi's Restaurant at 8148 Main Street (state route 82) in downtown Garrettsville. The pub was located in a grain mill, with an operating water wheel, which was originally constructed by pioneer John Garrett along Eagle Creek in 1804, when the area was first settled. The three-barrel brewing system yielded approximately 300 barrels per year, with several different brews being produced by brewmaster Tom Divis through the years: Uncle Eric's Pale Ale, Hazelnut Brown Ale, Mocha Brown Ale, Farmer's Daughter Light Ale, John Garrett's Ghost, golden ale, stout, and honey porter. By late summer of 2002, however, both the brewpub and the restaurant had closed.

Kent

1. Mugs Brew Pub

Located at 211 Franklin Avenue, across from the old railroad depot in downtown Kent, Mugs opened in 1998 as a tavern, with the plan to eventually add an on-site brewing operation. After a number of delays in getting a brewing license, the first brew was started in the summer of 2000, utilizing a 5-barrel extract system, and was tapped in September. Two brews were available at that time: Black Squirrel dark beer and the aptly named Overdue Brew light beer. Located just off the campus of Kent State University, the tavern quickly became a popular spot in town, although license problems continued to persist, and the limited brewing operation had been discontinued by the end of 2003.

Ravenna Township

1. Philip Balser

Soon after the end of the Civil War came the beginning of Portage County's only pre-Prohibition brewery. It was located in an area known today as Black Horse, at the northeast corner of the intersection of what is now Brady Lake Road and West Main Street (state route 59), just west of the city of Ravenna. It appears to have been founded by Adam Grohe, soon after he purchased the land in September 1865.

One year later, however, he sold the land and brewery to Philip Balser, a German immigrant who came to Ravenna by way of Warren, Ohio, and Anthony Wolf, for the sum of $1,925. Wolf then sold his share to Balser just one month later. In 1868, the brewery was sold again, to Nicholas Englehart, who appears to have operated it until it was sold back to Balser in 1872. Balser then continued to operate it until 1876, when brewing ceased for good. It appears that mounting local temperance forces of the era may have played more than a small role in the closing, although with an annual production of less than 200 barrels of lager, the small brewery could not have posed a huge threat to the local population. Nothing remains of the brewery today.

RICHLAND COUNTY

Mansfield

1. Leuthner and Schmutzler/Mansfield City Brewery

Richland County's earliest known brewing establishment appears to have begun operations in 1844. The property at the site was purchased in June of that year by George Lord, who began brewing beer soon afterward. Located on the west side of North Diamond Street, between Temple Court and Bloom Avenue (now East 5th St.), the brewery later took the address of 119 N. Diamond, prior to renumbering of streets.

While operating the brewery, Lord had incurred over $1,200 of debt by April 1847, at which time the brewery was sold at a sheriff's auction to Joseph Lindley. He in turn sold it to John Long, a native German born in 1817, and John Kraft for $800 in July 1849. Kraft sold his share to Long in 1853 and moved west to Galion, Ohio, where he established a new brewery. Later that year, Long sold the plant to Joseph Leuthner (also spelled Lithner, Leitener), another native German born in 1825, and Frederick Eiler (also spelled Eahler) for $3,700. Long then purchased what would become the Eagle Brewery two blocks away with John Harvey. Eiler sold his share to 32-year-old German immigrant Frederick Schmutzler in March 1856.

After this the brewery expanded slowly over the next decade, as the partners purchased several lots adjacent to the plant. During this time, they were also assisted by George Rikart, another native German born in 1830. Between 1864 and 1866, Henry Weber leased a partial interest in the brewery, before co-founding the Union Brewery across the street. By 1871, the brewery had grown to the extent that when Leuthner sold his interest to Schmutzler that year, his share in the partnership was worth over $10,000. Leuthner died just two years after that.

After 1871, the operation was known as Schmutzler & Co., consisting mainly of Schmutzler and Conrad Cook, a native Bavarian. Between 400 and 500 barrels of lager beer and ale were being produced annually when brewing operations ceased around 1876 (although Schmutzler is still listed in the 1880 census as a brewer). Schmutzler then operated a saloon in town until his death in 1885. Nothing remains of the small brewery today.

2. Eagle Brewery/The Renner & Weber Brewing Company

Founded in 1857 by John Harvey, an Englishman born in 1820, and John Long (see the previous listing), the Eagle Brewery originally consisted of an old grain warehouse which had been remodeled and enlarged. The brewery was established initially for the production of both ale and whiskey, but lager beer was introduced several years later, and underground cellars were blasted out of the underlying sandstone. The distilling of whiskey was abandoned around the same time.

The brewery was located between Temple Court and East 4th St., on a hillside. This site was desirable for the formation of a brewery because of its proximity to the "Big Spring", which was an early source of

Original Renner & Weber Brewery, circa 1870s. The building had originally been used as a grain warehouse [photo taken from *100 Years of Brewing*]; (inset) Henry Weber.

water for locals. In fact, all three of Mansfield's nineteenth-century breweries developed within a half-mile of the spring and each other. As the brewery grew, however, the spring could no longer supply all the water needed, so two on-site wells were dug. The later address of 75 Temple Court corresponded with the plant office, which was across the alley from the main brewhouse.

In 1859, Harvey sold his interest in the brewery to Theodore Aberle, a native of Wurtemburg, Germany, born in 1823. Five years later, Long rented his interest in the brewery to Martin Frank, and then in 1866 he sold his interest to Andrew Reiman. Reiman was a native of the village of Ida, in the state of Hesse, Germany. Born in 1826, he emigrated to the United States as an adult and came to the city of Mansfield in 1857. A well-respected citizen, he was a city councilman for many years while operating the brewery. Reiman and Aberle continued to operate the plant until 1883, when Henry Weber purchased Aberle's interest.

Henry Weber was born in Schillingstadt, Baden, Germany, into a family of brewers. The Weber family brewery was fairly small, producing only ten barrels of beer per day, but its image would later grace the label of the American company's "Grossvater" Lager Beer label. Weber came to the United States in 1859, and worked in the Eberhardt Brewery in Pittsburgh for one year before coming to Mansfield, where he worked in the Eagle Brewery for two years. He then spent time working in breweries in Sandusky and Bucyrus, Ohio, before returning to Mansfield. He then worked at the Leuthner & Schmutzler brewery for two years before helping to found the Union Brewery across the street with Martin Frank in 1866. Seventeen years later, he returned to the Eagle Brewery, this time as a part owner.

One year later, in September 1884, Reiman sold his interest in the brewery to George J. Renner, another native of Germany, for $11,000 (for background information on him, see the George J. Renner Brewing Co. in Akron). Until this time, the brewery had slowly grown, to the extent that annual production was around 2,500 barrels. Both Renner and Weber had capital to infuse into the company, such that it was subsequently enlarged and modernized significantly. In fact, within a decade of the formation of this partnership, the brewery's annual production was nearly 8,000 barrels. In 1888, however, Renner placed his control in the hands of John Weaver, while he moved to Akron to purchase the Horix brewery there. Renner would continue to live in Akron for the rest of his life,

while retaining a business interest in the Mansfield brewery.

In 1895, a large four-story brewhouse was built at a cost of $25,000, with a large building behind that housing the cellars. The company was incorporated on July 1, 1902 as the Renner & Weber Brewing Company, with a capital stock of $40,000. At this time, George Renner was elected president, with Weber as vice-president, and John Weaver as secretary and treasurer. Weber died of a stroke in 1910, to be replaced by his son Julius.

Before the turn of the century, the company's primary brand of lager beer was Red Band. This had been mentioned as early as 1895, in an advertisement urging local residents to patronize their home industry. Also mentioned was that the brewery provided employment to Mansfield residents and gave local farmers a market

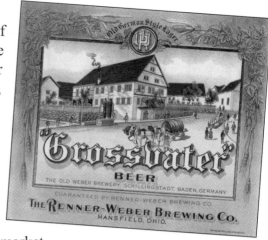

for their barley, stating, "Keep your nickels from building up Milwaukee, Chicago, and Cincinnati." Even in the early days, the brewery's need for barley was so great that farm wagons loaded with it often lined up along Temple Court, waiting to unload the grain into storage bins.

Around 1912 came a new "anchor" brand of beer: Grossvater Lager. This brand was also produced at the Akron brewery and at the Youngstown brewery operated by Renner's son, George J., Jr. Also produced in Mansfield around this time was Eagle Export Beer. Both brands were produced by brewmaster John Scior, who had joined the company just prior to the turn of the century. He remained in charge of brewing operations for nearly twenty years before being replaced by Sherman Weaver, the son of John, who was now the company's secretary and treasurer.

Brewing of beer continued until Prohibition, at which time production briefly was converted to the making of Red Band Cereal Beverage. This did not last for long, however, and the large brewhouse soon shut down all operations. The company continued to function in the production of ice and soft drinks, and was a distribution center for the Renner Products Co. of Akron, which was producing Grossvater and Zepp near beers throughout Prohibition.

After Repeal in 1933, the plant was completely refitted and modernized for beer production, while expanding significantly. The new stain-

Renner & Weber brewery in the late 1890s, after the addition of the new brewhouse [taken from *100 Years of Brewing*]

(left) Brewery workers posing on a delivery truck, circa 1915 [courtesy of John Phillips];
(below) Convex lighted glass sign [Bill Carlisle collection].

less steel aging tanks doubled the plant's annual capacity to over 50,000 barrels. The first brews were made late in the year, and were on the market by March 10, 1934. Their return on that Saturday was advertised by a brass band hired by the brewery from the local German society. The band rode around town on one of the company's delivery trucks playing typical German songs such as "Ach du lieber Augustine".

Red Band Beer briefly returned after Prohibition, but was soon replaced by new brands of beer such as Old German Lager, Lord Mansfield Ale, Lucky Shoe Beer, and Weber's Beer. The Grossvater brand name, however, did not return to Mansfield after Prohibition's end, being produced only in Renner's Akron brewery. A loose association had remained between the Mansfield, Akron, and Youngstown Renner plants after Prohibition, with Renner family members serving as directors of all three companies, although each one ran more or less independently. The Mansfield company was guided throughout the era by three of Henry Weber's children: Julius Weber as president, Adolph Weber as vice-president, and Julia Renner as secretary and treasurer. In addition, John Steinkirchner was the master brewer, and Al Brooker was chief engineer.

Grain rations during World War II curtailed the plant's growth, while allowing some of the national and regional brewers to gain ground in the local market. During this time, the plant's extensive underground storage caves were made available to the public as potential bomb shelters, with a capacity of nearly 1,000 people. After the war, brewing in Mansfield was gradually scaled back, with the majority of beer actually brewed in the Akron Renner plant, for distribution by the Mansfield company.

Ninety-four years of brewing came to an end in 1951, when all remaining operations ceased. Renner & Weber

End of an era: The Renner-Weber brewery came to a fiery end on June 14, 1978, in one of Mansfield's most spectacular fires ever. [Thanks to Linda Johnson and Ellen Smith at the Mansfield *News Journal*]

had become another victim of the regional competition in the industry, which had accelerated after the end of the war. The space was briefly occupied by a beer distributor before being vacated for good. The plant remained standing for many years, and plans were made for it to be renovated into shops and restaurants. It had been entered onto the National Register of Historic Places, and $200,000 of state and federal aid had been approved for the project by 1978, but these plans never came to pass. A fire damaged most of the plant in June of that year, and the remains were later razed. Except for the main office and storage building and a few of the scattered underground storage cellars, nothing remains of it today.

3. M. Frank & Son/Union Brewery

Established in 1866, the Union Brewery began as a collaboration between Henry Weber, who had been involved with both the Eagle Brewery and the City Brewery across the street, and Martin Frank. Both men were natives of the village of Schillingstadt, Baden, Germany. Frank was born there in 1830, then emigrated to America in 1855. He came to Ohio four years later, first to Galion, where he met his wife-to-be, who was the daughter of John Kraft, the brewer who had previously operated the Eagle Brewery in Mansfield. By 1860, Frank had moved to Mansfield himself, first working in the Eagle Brewery before establishing this new plant. Located along Temple Court, between N. Franklin and N. Diamond Streets, it used the address of 110 N. Diamond before Prohibition and 121 N. Franklin after Prohibition.

Production of lager beer grew slowly over the next twenty years, increasing from just over 1,000 barrels annually in the 1870s to nearly 5,000 barrels by 1898 (still leaving it as one of the region's smallest operating breweries). In 1883, Weber sold his share in the brewery to Frank, who operated it alone until 1899, when he was joined by his son, Louis, who was born in Mansfield in 1865. Martin Frank died just two years later. Production then continued under the name M. Frank & Son until the onset of Prohibition in 1919. Louis died in May 1915, after which the brewery's operations were guided by his two young sons Albert and Martin. The only other addition to the

(above) Advertising tray, circa 1934;
(left) Frank Brewery plant as photographed in 1952 by the late Ernie Oest, twelve years after brewing operations had ceased. The brewhouse is at left, and the bottling house is in the center
[courtesy of Bob Kay].

company was in 1906, when a new brewmaster by the name of Conrad Berg was hired.

At the onset of Prohibition, production of Frank's Beverage, a non-alcoholic cereal product, was attempted, but it did not last for long. However, production of soft drinks and ice continued throughout the following fourteen years. The company had remained relatively small, and was able to survive the transition fairly well.

In 1933, $20,000 was spent refitting the plant again for brewing beer, which was available to the public on December 16th of that year. Until its own beer was ready, the company distributed Gambrinus Beer from the August Wagner brewery of Columbus. When brewing resumed, there were three main brands, Frank's Old Fashioned and Tru-Bru Beers, and Shanty Ale. Louis Frank's son Martin was now the president and brewmaster, while his brother Albert G. Frank was the company's vice-president.

By 1940, however, the small plant was no longer able to make a profit from its brewing operation, and this came to a halt. The company continued to produce soft drinks and ice for an additional two years before closing for good at the outset of World War II. The plant was briefly occupied by the Mansfield Bottling Co., and later was used intermittently as a warehouse. Martin Frank left the area after this, while Albert remained in Mansfield, where he died in 1975 at the age of 81. Most of the plant was eventually razed, although portions of the rear cellar building and other portions of the foundation remain to this day. The remaining building has been remodeled with a modern exterior, and bears little resemblance to its days as a brewery.

4. Wooden Pony Brewing Company

Mansfield's first brewing operation in 45 years began operations on February 21, 1996. The Wooden Pony was a brewpub with an annual capacity of 1,000 barrels. Located in a renovated century-old stone office building at 37 W. 4th St., it was just around the corner from the sites of Mansfield's three earlier breweries. The name came from the nearby Richland Carousel Park, a large enclosed carousel with carved horses, located in the heart of downtown.

The brewery utilized a JV Northwest brewing system, which was brought from the Hoster Brewing Co. in Columbus, when the latter expanded. The company was owned by Don Welsh, and the brewmaster was Larry Horwitz, who produced several different brews: Red Band Pale Ale, Reformatory Stout (a reference to the famous nineteenth-century state reformatory on the north side of

town, which was featured in *The Shawshank Redemption*, *Air Force One*, and several other movies), Black Forest Cherry Wheat, Sandstone Special Golden Ale, Big Spring Bitter (a light bodied ale), Pony Pub Light Ale, and the Brewmaster's Special, which was a variable seasonal brew.

Despite the initial success, operations had ceased by November 1998 and the restaurant had closed. Its location, in a relatively non-commercial area of downtown, may have been a factor in its demise. It was sold at a sheriff's auction in the spring of 1999 and the site remained empty for two years. By early 2001, however, new owner and brewer Robb Burgie had resurrected the pub and its brewing operation under the same name. It operated for another year before closing by late 2002.

Alliance

1. Alliance Brewery

The first brewery in the city of Alliance began operation in the mid-1860s in a small building on the south side of Market Street, on the near-west side of the city of Alliance. The original proprietor was Henry Klingler, an immigrant from Wurtemberg, Germany, who was born in 1840. He was assisted by Florian Knam, another German immigrant, born in 1837. Production of lager beer and ale generally ranged between 400 and 1,000 barrels per year throughout the brewery's existence.

Klingler had left the Alliance brewery by the mid-1870s, but continued to operate a saloon and billiard parlor in town until he died in 1879. Knam continued to operate the brewery until his death, also in 1879. His wife Mary continued operations briefly until ceasing production the next year, after which she also ran a saloon in town. Nothing remains of the brewery today.

2. The Alliance Brewing Company

Following the popular brewing industry trend of the early twentieth century, a stock company known as the Alliance Brewing Co., with capital of $150,000, was formed in 1905 by saloonkeepers in the Alliance area, in order to create a new source of beer at a reasonable price. A new plant was to be constructed at 1345 East Summit Street, along a main line of the Cleveland & Pittsburgh Railroad, in the southeast corner of the town. It consisted of one main building for most of the brewing functions, with a six-story brewhouse. Another building housed the office and bottling works, with a smaller building for stables and wagon storage.

The original officers included Herman Mueller as president, Joseph C. Klingler as vice-president and manager, and William Shidler as treasurer. The former two were saloonists, and the latter was the owner of a livery stable, as well as a township trustee. Klingler was the son of Henry Klingler, the German immigrant who had begun the earlier Alliance brewery in the 1860s. There would be a continually changing list of officers and directors over the next 14 years, though Klingler would remain with the company until the late 1930s. Mueller would remain until 1912, when he returned to running his saloon.

The brewery had a capacity of 30,000 barrels per year, with the beer on tap in local saloons as well as bottled for home consumption. The bottled brand was initially known just as A B C Beer, although Gold Crown Export Beer was added in later years. The sales market was primarily Alliance and parts of four surrounding counties of Northeast Ohio. In addition to beer, the plant also went into the ice business in the spring of 1911 with the addition of a new refrigerating and ice-making building, 80 x 40 feet in size, which had a 60-ton daily capacity.

Within the company's first year of existence, it was swept up in rumors of a proposed consolidation of regional breweries, similar to the Cleveland & Sandusky Brewing Co. and the Stark-Tuscarawas Co. Under the proposal, the Alliance Brewing Co. would combine with the Smith and Renner breweries of Youngstown, Standard brewery of New Castle, PA., Union brewery of Sharon, PA., Meadville (PA.) Brewing Co., Consumers Brewing Co. of Ashtabula, and the Crockery City brewery of East Liverpool. In the end, however, arrangements

(left) Illustration of the Alliance Brewing Company from the Alliance *Review and Leader*, July 1906; (below) Bottle label, circa 1912 [Bob Kay collection].

could not be agreed upon, and the merger never took place.

By 1908, there was a new vice-president, Otto Beltz. The son of noted Cleveland brewer Joseph Beltz, Otto continued to reside in Cleveland while an officer of the brewery and of his family's Cleveland Home Brewing Co. (of which he would later be president—see the section on Cuyahoga County). By 1911, the Alliance brewery had a new president, by the name of Peter Samman (also noted as Shamman in various listings), who was also a resident of Cleveland. He would remain with the brewery until the onset of Prohibition, at which time his son, George P. Samman, would become an officer, remaining with the company until the 1950's.

The company's original brewmaster was Fred Keifer of Cleveland. He was later succeeded by Henry Bieberson, who was then succeeded by Max Lechner in 1914. Three years later, another brewmaster & manager briefly joined the company, by the name of Emil Hirzell. His stay would be brief, however, because of Prohibition.

With beer production becoming illegal in December, 1918, the company decided to stake its future in the production of ice. The remaining supply of beer was sold off over the next few months, and when all alcohol sales stopped on May 26, 1919, the company was already out of the beer business. At that point, it reincorporated as the Alliance Beverage Co., for the production of ice, cereal beverages, and carbonated soft drinks. It would also begin to distribute coal over the next few years.

At that time, Joseph Klingler remained as president, with both Peter and George Samman as officers, although the former had left the company by 1922. Edward Eberhard was the plant manager, a post he would retain for the next 15 years. By late 1924, the company had ceased all beverage production, which was no longer profitable. The company merged with the local Alliance Ice & Coal Co. in 1925, and operations continued into the 1940s. George Samman remained as the company's owner throughout this time, still living in Cleveland.

The main brewhouse was torn down in the 1930s, with the remaining buildings being used for ice production and coal storage. In 1951, the remaining plant was purchased by the local Sunnyside Dairy, which moved all of its operations there, while continuing to operate the Alliance Ice and Coal Co. This would continue until 1956, when the dairy company was absorbed by a local competitor. After this, the buildings remained vacant for several years before being torn down in the mid-1960s. Only an empty field remains at the site today.

Canal Fulton (aka Fulton)

1. Fulton/Fountain Brewery

Canal Fulton's only brewery was located on the south side of Brewery Street, in the southwest corner of town. At that time, the town was known only as Fulton, with the "Canal" part added in later years. Also in later years, the street was renamed Wooster Street. The brewery was located on the side of Quality Hill, also known as

Brewery Hill, where a small spring existed, supplying water to the brewery and to local residents for drinking. It was known as both the Fountain Brewery and Fulton Brewery at different times.

The small brewery was founded in the early 1840s by Michael Ruch, a German immigrant who had been born in 1806. He was the owner of a drydock along the Ohio & Erie Canal in town, and was also a builder and farmer. He was a community leader as well, and at one time worked for the creation of the first large public school building in town.

The brewery was later turned over to Ruch's son Christian, who was operating it by the late 1860s. Christian was also a farmer and lived nearby with his wife Mellissa and their thirteen children. By this time, the brewery consisted of an "L"- shaped two-story building of stone foundation and wood frame, with an adjacent two-story icehouse on the west side. This was for storage of ice that was cut out of the canal and local ponds during the winter, then hauled by horse & wagon to be stored for year-round use. A small building was built across the alley in later years for bottling the beer. Ruch had several partners through the years, including a Mr. Kline and a Mr. Moore at different times.

In the mid-1870s, production was temporarily halted for several years, but had resumed by 1878. Production during this period was generally between 600 and 1,000 barrels per year. The beer was distributed primarily in town and along the canal. Ruch continued to operate the brewery until approximately 1885, when operation was briefly taken over by George Maher. Ruch maintained ownership of the brewery during this time, however.

Operation was transferred in 1888 to Ernest Schneider, whose operation was also known as Schneider Bros. Ruch took over operations again in 1891, but according to one local source, it was sold in 1894 to Jacob Babst, who operated the City Hotel. (This latter transaction, however, cannot be confirmed by census or deed transfer records). Brewing operations ceased soon after this, however. The brewery building had been torn down by 1898, but the icehouse survived and was converted to a residence. No evidence of the brewery remains today. Christian Ruch concentrated on farming after leaving the brewing business, and in later years moved into southern Stark County, where he died in 1912.

Canton

1. Canton Brewery

Stark County's first brewery was built in September 1817, with production of common beer and porter beginning one month later. It was located in the small village of Canton, along Market Street near the East Bridge. It was built and owned by Samuel Coulter and Thomas Hartford, but was run by John Cake and Henry Walling. Coulter was an attorney who had come to Canton from Pennsylvania in 1807, at which time he established a tavern. At a later time, he became postmaster of the village as well. Hartford was a medical doctor who had come from New York State. It appears that there was a distillery and a malting house associated with the brewery, as it advertised for other distilleries to bring their rye to be malted there. The brewery's products were supplied to local tavern owners and families. It was still running as late as 1823, when it was put up for sale, although it appears that there were no buyers, as the brewery did not operate after this time. Coulter would later move on to become a state senator.

Ohio *Repository*, October 9, 1818

2. Nighman/Balser City Brewery

This was one of the smallest yet longest-lasting brewing concerns in Stark County. Its origins were around the year of 1830, when it was established by George Nighman (also spelled Neighman), who had been born in Kent, Ohio in 1800. His father (also named George) had been one of the earliest settlers of the Western Reserve.

Young George spent several years in Pennsylvania learning the art of brewing and distilling, before returning to Canton to work with an uncle in a distillery. After several years, he opted to strike out on his own, and with the financial backing of George Dewalt, he purchased a lot at the northwest corner of North Market and Second Streets. On that site he erected a brick building, thirty-three by seventy-five feet in size, for the establishment of a brewery and distillery (the latter lasted only for a short time). An on-site well provided a source of water for brewing.

Nighman's success was brief, however, as he died in March 1833. Operation of the brewery was continued by his widow, Lydia, for several years. By the 1840s, however, the brewery was being rented and operated by Peter Melchior, an immigrant from Alsace-Lorraine and Augustus Bicking (also spelled Bucking), an immigrant from England. In 1847, they were joined by sixteen-year-old Thaddeus C. Nighman, son of George, and nephew of Bicking. Thaddeus had been born in 1831, and was only two years old when his father died. He had already been working in a drugstore in Massillon for two years when he returned to Canton to learn the brewing business. Soon after, Melchior left to build his own brewing establishment in Canton.

At that time, Bicking entered into an interesting agreement with Nighman, who was still a minor and had no brewing experience. The official deed of lease reads as follows:

"It is agreed by and between Annabella Neighman and Thadeus Constantine Neighman by Thomas Bonfield, his guardian of the first part, and Augustus Bucking of the second part as follows, to wit, The Said party of the first part hereby rents and leases to said party of the second part Lot No. Thirteen in the town of Canton, Stark County, Ohio and the Brewing Establishment and buildings, fixtures, and improvements thereon, for the purpose of carrying on the brewing business from the first day of March, A.D. 1847, until the second of February, A.D. 1852, being a period of four years and eleven months, at and for the annual rent of one hundred and twenty-five dollars to be paid quarterly at the end of each quarter of each year.

The party of the second part agrees to keep and use said property himself and not to rent it to any one else. He also agrees to board and supply with good and sufficient necessaries of life and to furnish with good and decent common wearing apparel, the Said Thadeus Constantine for the period of three years from and after the commencement of this lease and also to teach the said Thadeus C. during said period, provided he shall properly serve the said party of the second part as an apprentice to the brewing business, the art and mystery of brewing, so far as said party of the second part knows or can teach the same, and especially to teach and fully instruct said Thadeus C. in the new art or mode of brewing which said party of the second part acquired in the city of London, England.

Said party of the second part also agrees to put to said Brewing Establishment a good new malt kiln with the necessary enclosure or building to protect the same, outside of the present brewing establishment and to leave the same at the expiration of this lease, on said premises without charge.

Said party of the second part also agrees that the said parties of the first part, and also Mrs. Lorenzo Bucking, shall during the period of this lease, have the right to obtain and use so much water from the well in the brewing establishment aforesaid, from time to time as they may need for domestic use. During the period of said lease...it is also agreed that said party of the second part may, should he see fit, abandon said lease at the expiration of any one year thereof by giving three months previous notice to the other party of his intention. It is also agreed that said party of the second part shall build a board fence (similar to that on D. Bonfield's lot in Canton) from the wash house to the southeast corner of said lot No. 13 and deduct the reasonable and fair expense thereof from the rent to be paid aforesaid, next falling due after the making of the same. It is also agreed that said party of the second part may remove the partition of the lower part of said brewing establishment in the front part of the building, he saving the materials thereof for the purpose of replacing the same. It is also agreed by said party of the second part that he will not and is expressly understood that he shall not have the power to sublease said premises, nor assign, or transfer his leasehold right. It is also agreed that in case the said Bucking should die before the said expiration of said period, then this agreement shall cease, and said parties of the first part be entitled to the repossession and control of said property. It is also agreed, by said Bucking, that he will keep said property in good repair during the period he shall occupy the same as aforesaid, and whenever he shall leave the same according to this agreement, or at the expiration of this lease, he agrees to surrender up peaceable possession of the same in as good order and repair as they are when he received the same, ordinary wear, decay, and unavoidable accidents excepted."

After the expiration of this lease agreement, Nighman took over complete ownership of the brewery. It is unclear at which point Bicking left the establishment, however. Operation of the brewery continued through 1860, after which Nighman suspended operation. After this, he was elected city marshal, a position he held through the end of the Civil War. Later, he became involved with the transfer business, owning several teams of horses for transfer and delivery of goods in the city.

It appears that the brewery did not function again until 1865, when it was purchased in November for $4,900 by Kasper (also spelled Casper) Balser, a thirty-year-old immigrant from Hesse-Darmstadt, Germany. After this, it was known as the City Brewery. By that time, there was an adjoining two-story beer hall and beer garden, the address of which was 56 North Market Street (later 80 N. Market). Production at the brewery remained small throughout its existence (usually 300-600 barrels per year), with the products being sold primarily in the beer hall.

Balser's City Brewery in the mid-1880s [courtesy of the Stark County Historical Society]

Illustrating a typical problem for a small city brewery in a residential neighborhood is the following petition, signed by nearby residents in 1870 to present to the city council: "…The front of the premises known as the 'City Brewery' are now, and for some time have been in a most filthy and unhealthy condition. Large pools of beer slops and brewery off'all are constantly kept in front of the said premises which, in their present stagnant condition, emit a most disagreeable stench, which pervades the entire neighborhood, to the great discomfort and disgust of the citizens of the vicinity, and those who are obliged to pass the premises." Although the outcome of this petition is unknown, it is hoped that the Balsers cleaned up their act, at least for a while.

One incident in 1874 gave the small brewery a more infamous place in the city's history. The temperance movement of the era had been building momentum for several months in Canton, fueled by a perceived need to clean up the city's Fourth Ward, in which much of the local German population lived. This was often referred to as the "Bloody Fourth" because of frequent saloon brawls, shootings, and knifings.

The local women's temperance crusade was characteristic of a trend going on in many other cities at the time, in which women of the highest social standing and character would visit saloons and ask their proprietors to close down. Upon refusal, the women would kneel down and pray outside of the saloon. This practice, however, was met with much derision by the city's German population, for whom the saloons were important social meeting places, and for whom the drinking of beer and harder liquor was an ingrained part of their culture.

One day in the summer of 1874, fifteen women crusaders visited the beer hall, and after being refused admission, began to have a meeting on the sidewalk outside. Louisa Balser, irritated by this interference, decided at that moment that the sidewalk needed to be cleaned. She took a mop and bucket and began to clean vigorously. However, in the process, the dirty water went all over several of the women's dresses as they knelt in prayer. Both Henry and Louisa were arrested, and the ensuing trial became somewhat of a public spectacle, drawing large crowds to watch. William McKinley (who would later become the country's 25th President), a local attorney and advocate for the temperance movement, was the prosecutor. However, the jury could not reach a decision, and the charges were eventually dropped.

Kasper Balser died in 1876, but operation of the brewery and saloon was continued by his 40-year-old wife Louisa, and 16-year-old son Henry. In July 1889, however, the small brewery was gutted by fire, bringing nearly sixty years of brewing operations to a close. The family continued to operate the saloon, with the addition of a concert hall on the premises, until after the turn of the century. The building was later torn down to make way for Loew's Theater.

3. John Scholder/Christian Graff brewery

Little is known of this small brewery, which was located on the east side of Canton, near the intersection of what is now Tuscarawas Street and the east bridge over the Nimishillen Creek. It appears to have been established in the early 1830s by Jacob Hahn. By 1835, however, Hahn had amassed enough debts that the brewery was sold at a sheriff's sale to John Scholder for $1,200. After this, it appears that Scholder operated the brewery with his brother Henry until 1852, when it was sold to Christian Graff (also spelled Groeff) for $2,500. After this, Henry Scholder moved south to Waynesburg, where he purchased the local brewery there. It appears that Graff's brewing operation continued only into the late 1850s, however, as his name does not appear in any other histories or census records from the time.

4. Peter Melchior brewery

Peter Melchior was born in Alsace-Lorraine in 1816, the son of Nicholas Melchior, a former soldier under Napoleon Bonaparte. His family had come to America in 1830, and soon after that, Peter became involved in the Canton brewing industry. He rented the Nighman brewery for several years before purchasing land on the south side of town in November 1848. It was at this site, on the west side of South Market Street by Raynolds Street and the railroad depot, that he soon established his own brewery. Production of beer was most likely only several hundred barrels per year, distributed to local taverns.

By the late 1850s, Peter was being assisted by his son George, and production continued until Melchior's sudden death in December 1864. Soon after this, his widow, Elizabeth, sold the brewing equipment and razed the brewery, building a new home on the site. Nothing remains of either the brewery or the home today.

5. Graber/Giessen brewery

This was a short-lived brewing establishment, begun in the late 1860s on land owned by John D. Graber. It was located approximately two miles south of the city limits of Canton, on the west side of South Market Street (although today the site is within the Canton city limits). The brewery itself was a modest two-story frame and brick structure with an attached icehouse. It was built on seven acres of land near a branch of Nimishillen Creek and next to an ice pond. According to *One Hundred Years Of Brewing*, the brewery had been founded by Charles Freeze as an ale brewery, although none of the local literature or records confirm that.

Otto Giessen's first brewery in Canton Township, from the 1875 Stark County Atlas

Graber did not operate the plant for long, as it was vacant by 1873. At that time, it was purchased by Joseph Klopfenstein and Otto Giessen, the latter a Bavarian immigrant, born in 1848, who had come to America in 1865. Giessen first learned bookkeeping in Cleveland, then was an apprentice in the brewery of Schmidt & Hoffman there until 1869. He then became an assistant at the Gaessler brewery in Akron (upon leaving, Giessen was replaced by Wilhelm Burkhardt, whose family would operate that brewery for the next 80 years.) Klopfenstein would soon sell his interest to John Baker, who remained a partner for several years.

Giessen restarted production at the small plant in 1875, brewing more than 2,300 barrels of both ale and lager, making it the largest brewery in Stark County at the time. Production continued to increase each year, with nearly 3,000 barrels being produced in 1879. In 1883, however, the plant was completely destroyed by fire. Giessen would rebuild the brewery, however this time it would be in downtown Canton (see the Canton Brewing Co.). Nothing remains of the original country brewery today.

6. Union Brewery

This brewery was founded in 1874 by Joseph Klopfenstein. It was located on more than five acres of land at the northwest city limits, at the north end of Hazlette Ave., just east of the Westlawn Cemetery. The site had both on-site wells for a water supply as well as a pond for cutting ice during the winter. The plant consisted of two main buildings, two- and three-story brick and stone structures, with beer cellars underneath, and an ice machine in later years. Klopfenstein's production of lager beer reached 652 barrels in its first year, but in October

Stark County Atlas, 1875; today the McKinley monument stands atop the hill at the right.

1875, he sold the plant to Adam Knobloch and George Hermann, for the sum of $16,000. Klopfenstein then continued business as a local saloon owner.

Knobloch had been born in Prussia in 1843, coming to America with his parents at the age of three. He grew up on the family farm near Richville in Stark County, and became a clerk for his father at the age of fourteen. He had no experience in brewing when he purchased the brewery, but he had good business skills. Hermann was also a native German, born in 1844, who came to America in 1862 and learned the brewing trade at several companies in Cincinnati before coming to Canton.

The brewery's products were expanded now to also include porter, cream ale, and stock ale, in addition to "Vis Vitae" lager beer. By 1878, production was just under 2,000 barrels, but had increased to nearly 4,000 by 1881. Hermann left the partnership the following year to become a saloon owner himself, and Knobloch assumed brewing operations alone until 1888, when he sold his interest to George Edel & John Seiferth, two brewers from Pittsburgh, PA. After this, Knobloch became the superintendent of the Canton Buggy & Gear Co.

George Edel had been born in Alsace-Lorraine, in 1840. He came to America in 1862, and was involved with a brewery on the south side of Pittsburgh for more than twenty years before moving west to Canton. Edel and Seiferth operated the plant as the Union Brewing Co. until 1891, when it merged with the Canton Brewing Co., of which Edel then became president. In September of that year, Seiferth was seriously injured when an ammonia drum in the ice plant exploded, releasing the gas into his face. Although he survived, his eyesight and lungs sustained severe damage. He would no longer be an active partner in the business after this time.

All brewing operations at the site subsequently ceased in December of that year, and the plant was vacated. The land was purchased in 1903 by the McKinley Memorial Foundation, which was established to build a memorial to President William McKinley, who had been assassinated in 1901. The McKinley monument was built on a site immediately north of the brewery, which by then had been razed. No indication of the brewery remains today.

7. Canton/Stark-Tuscarawas Brewing Company

Otto Giessen's country brewery, south of town, had been destroyed by fire in 1883. He would rebuild immediately, although this time he would pick a site inside the city limits. The new site was at 34 North Cherry Street, along the Conotton Valley Railroad tracks (in later years the city would renumber addresses and this would become 216-230 North Cherry St).

The new plant was much larger, with a four-story brewhouse, and was equipped with much more modern brewing technology, allowing an annual capacity of 20,000 barrels. The water source

Delivery wagon for Otto Giessen's brewery, most likely circa 1880s [from a tintype, courtesy of Bill Carlisle]

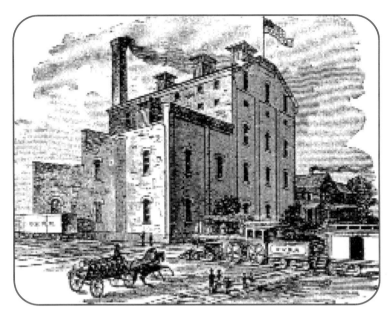

Canton Brewery, circa 1891
[Stark County Historical Society collection]

was from an on-site well, and full production had begun by early 1884.

After only three years at the new site, Giessen opted to sell the plant to William Roemmel (aka Rommel) and John U. Kraft in the spring of 1887. Rommel was a native German who had emigrated to the United States in 1869, living in Dayton and Middletown, Ohio before coming to Canton. They would now do business as the Canton Brewing Co., producing lager and export beer, ale, and porter. Giessen would become a wine importer and saloon owner after this, and was involved with the incorporation of the Canton Buggy & Gear Co. in 1888. Later, he would become an officer of both the Royal Brick Company and the Crystal Springs Ice Company. Giessen died in February 1897, after a case of grippe (influenza), which developed into typhoid fever.

Rommel bought out Kraft's interest in 1888, after which production of beer continued until August 1891, when the Canton Brewing Co. merged with the Union Brewing Co. on the west side of the city. At that time, the Union Brewery's president, George Edel, became president of the Canton Brewing Co., with Rommel becoming secretary, treasurer, and plant manager. George Hermann, a saloon owner who had retained a financial interest in the Union Brewery, became vice-president. Other directors at that time included Charles Raspiller, John Roos, Anton Schwertner, and George Wagner. The new Canton Brewing Co. was incorporated that year with capital of $120,000. The Union brewery was quickly phased out and was vacant by year's end.

Over the next four years, the Canton brewery was completely rebuilt again, at a cost of over $80,000, to dramatically increase the annual capacity to 50,000 barrels. Actual production went from 8,000 barrels in 1891 to over 12,000 barrels in 1894, and nearly 18,000 by 1896. A bottling works was added along with refrigeration machinery, horse stables, boiler house, wash house, office, and a new, five-story brewhouse. The latter was designed by the architecture firm of Beyer & Raufert of Chicago, and cost $50,000 itself.

The company's capital increased to $150,000 in 1894. In that year, Jacob Nikolas, a recent graduate of the Wahl & Henius College in Chicago, joined the plant as the new brewmaster. The two primary brews being produced at the time were Canton Standard Beer and Canton Export Lager, and their distribution was now being aimed at home sales in addition to taverns. Production continued largely unchanged over the next ten years, although Rommel's sons, John and Edward, and Edel's son George J. had joined the company during this time.

Mirroring a trend that was prevalent in many other cities at the time, the decision was made in 1905 to consolidate five of the area's largest breweries into one company in an attempt to dominate the local beer market and reduce overhead. On March 21st, the merger of the Canton Brewing Co., Stark Brewing Co., Schuster Brewing Co. in Massillon, Dover Brewing Co., and New Philadelphia Brewing Co. was completed. The new company was known as the Stark-Tuscarawas Breweries Co., with a capital of $3,000,000, and it paid $750,000 for the Canton Brewing Co. plant, which was by far the largest one in the group. The overall corporation would now have a capacity in excess of 100,000 barrels per year, employing approximately 125 men. In addition, the

Canton City Directory, 1899; This view of the new plant is from the same perspective as the above drawing of the old brewery

Remains of brewhouse and beer cellar building on the east side of the plant, as they appear today.

company owned numerous saloons and other properties in the two-county area, with a value of over $200,000.

The company's initial president was John Schuster of Massillon. William Rommel had retired by this time, but his thirty-year-old son John became president in 1906, and would remain so throughout the company's existence. George Edel, now 65 years old, retired from active business at the time of the merger, although he remained a director until his death in 1916. Production at the Canton Brewery continued much as before, with Canton Export Beer being its primary product, although soon came the introduction of two new brands, Tuscora (in 1908) and Zest (from the Schuster plant in Massillon).

Within one year of incorporation, rumors began to circulate that the Stark-Tuscarawas Co. would soon find itself to be the target of an acquisition by the larger Cleveland & Sandusky Brewing Co., which already dominated brewing along the southern shore of Lake Erie. While merger talks did in fact take place, in the end the two companies would continue to operate separately.

Business was not quite as dominant as planned in the local market, however, due to competition from the large Home Brewing Co. in Canton after 1906. Also a problem was the Rose "local option" law of 1908. After this, Tuscarawas County voted itself dry for three years, necessitating the temporary closing of the company's two breweries there. Despite this, the company's overall production for 1911 was more than 73,000 barrels, yielding a profit of over $52,000. However, in 1912, the company's capital stock was reduced to $1,500,000.

In 1919, as Prohibition arrived, the market for non-alcoholic cereal beverages was dismally small, and production dropped off severely. Because of this, there was no longer a need for two divisions of the company in Canton. At that time, the Canton brewery closed its doors for good, and all operations of the Stark-Tuscarawas Co., including beverage production, would continue several blocks away at the Stark brewery. Over the years, the space in the Canton brewery has been used for cold storage, apartments, and the City News Agency (in the former stables). The plant remains largely intact to this day.

8. Stark/Stark-Tuscarawas Brewing Company

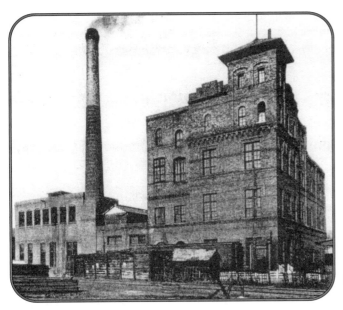

Incorporated in 1902 with a capital stock of $100,000, The Stark Brewing Co. was the first of two breweries formed in Canton primarily by saloon owners. The original officers were John A. Brobst as president, John F. Weiss as vice-president, and William F. Schumacher as treasurer. Other officers included Edward Antony, George L. Schleininger, Henry Bobsean, Oscar A. VonLuebtow, Christian Schauweker, and Joseph Munter, Jr. All were saloonkeepers except Munter, who was a local businessman, previously a director of the local Munter & Williams Coal Co.

The plant itself used typical turn-of-the-century brewery architecture, with a five-story brewhouse, ice

Stark Brewing Company brewhouse, facing the railroad tracks
[Stark County Historical Society collection]

plant, and bottling works, built facing the Conotton Valley Railroad tracks, at 620-632 North Cherry Street. Once production commenced, the company's primary brands were Velvet Brew and Stark Lager, both of which were sold throughout Stark County.

Independent production was brief, however, as in 1905 the company took part in the five-way brewery merger that became the Stark-Tuscarawas Breweries Co. On March 21st of that year, the new company paid $300,000 for the Stark plant, less than half the amount paid for the nearby Canton Brewing Co. Many of the directors of the Stark brewery left at that time to form the Home Brewing Co. Weiss remained, however, and was secretary and treasurer for the new company until Prohibition began, while Brobst became the superintendent of sales and collections. Initially, John Schuster of the Massillon brewery was president, although he was soon succeeded by John G. Rommel from the Canton Brewing Co. He would remain president throughout the company's existence.

Two young men about to enjoy Tuscora Beverage in a postcard dated 1919

Production continued as before, for the next fourteen years, although by 1915, two new brands, Tuscora and Zest, had joined Velvet Brew and other brands produced by the company. Sales continued to improve during that period, increasing from 70,000 barrels in 1910 (for all four plants) to over 100,000 barrels by 1917 (with gross sales of just under $1,000,000 for that year, yielding a net profit of over $56,000).

(above) Delivery truck from the pre-Prohibition era; (below right) Postcard showing Stark-Tuscarawas's two flagship brands [both courtesy of Bill Carlisle]; (below left) Coaster, circa 1915.

After the onset of Prohibition in 1919, the Stark-Tuscarawas Co. would produce only cereal beverages and soft drinks. The company had contracted to be the only local bottler of Coca-Cola, while also producing Whistle, Welchade, Green River, and Cherry Blossom soft drinks. Production of cereal beverages was cut back significantly with the drop in demand, although the main product, Tuscora Cereal Beverage, was the best-selling non-alcoholic beer in the area. There was no need for two breweries in Canton at this time, however, and as the Stark plant was the newer of the two in the group, it remained open while the Canton brewery was shut down. Soon after this, Weiss left the company and was replaced by Lennon A. Bowen. The plant superintendent at this time was A. F. Hieronimus. Rommel remained president through this period, while his brother Edward had moved up through the company to be vice-president by 1928, when the Stark-Tuscarawas Co. officially dissolved. At that time, the Rommels continued in business, reincorporating as the Coca-Cola Bottling Co.

In 1933, with the Repeal of Prohibition, the Rommels attempted to return to the brewing business by incorporating as the Tuscora Brewing Co. This was to be run in conjunction with the Coca-Cola Bottling Co. after $250,000 worth of stock was sold, with the goal of upgrading the entire plant. The latter was now 31 years

old, and most of the brewing facility had been unused for some time. Sufficient funds were never raised, however, and brewing operations never took place again at the site.

John Rommel would remain with the Coca-Cola Bottling Co. until his retirement in approximately 1940. The company remained at the site until 1975, after which the majority of the brewery was razed. One small section of the plant remains as a warehouse today.

9. Home Brewing Company

Formed in 1905, soon after the formation of the Stark-Tuscarawas Breweries Co., this was one of Canton's largest yet shortest-lived breweries. It was the second one begun primarily by saloon owners, many of whom had previously been involved with the Stark Brewing Co., but who had left after its incorporation into the large combine. This new plant was to be located on East Fifth Street at the Pennsylvania Railroad tracks. The streets were later renumbered and the plant's working address became 1205-1215 2nd Street NE. The corporation had an initial capital stock of $250,000.

The building itself was a large structure, with a main six-story brewhouse. Construction of this began in the summer of 1905 and was completed the following April, at a cost of $75,000. It was built to have a capacity of 40,000 barrels per year, and production was up to 75% of capacity after the first four years. The plant was able to fill 16,000 pint bottles every day, and these would be sold to homes in cases of 36. In addition, there were two ice machines, with daily capacities of 45 and 65 tons. The plant was powered by two 150-horsepower boilers, and it employed approximately thirty men.

The first brew was marketed throughout the city on August 13, 1906. The brewery's sales were mainly in Stark County alone, and home delivery in the city of Canton was a primary goal for the plant (nine horse-drawn wagons were used in this process). Initially, there were three primary brands of beer: Home Brew, a mellow, light beer, primarily distributed in barrels; Golden Export, a high grade beer which was pasteurized before being bottled for sale directly to consumers; and Hof Brau, a much heavier beer which was advertised as being for people of low vitality to help them recuperate. In addition to these, there was Solo, a temperance beer with less than one half of one percent alcohol, to be sold in dry areas of the county. This could be sold at any soda fountain, tax-free. These four brews would remain the primary products until 1918, when a new brand called Cascade briefly entered the market before Prohibition.

The company's original president was Edward Antony, who was the co-proprietor of the Antony & Morrow Sample Room. This was a tavern where Kropf Ale (brewed in southern Stark County) had previously been the specialty. Vice-president was William H. Fishel, the proprietor of the Gold Front Sample Room. Secretary was Joseph Munter, Jr., who was a local businessman, and the only non-saloon owner in the group. Treasurer was Henry Bobsean, while the plant manager was William Schumacher. Antony, Munter, Bobsean, and Schumacher

Home Brewery plant in 1995

had previously been officers of the Stark Brewing Company.

By 1908, Fishel would be replaced as VP by John H. Foley, another saloon owner. Bobsean succeeded Antony as president in 1909, and would remain in the position until his death in 1911, from complications of diabetes. Foley then moved into the presidency for the remainder of the brewery's existence. Other officers over the next decade included Alois Seiler, Christian Schauweker, George Laubacher, F. G. Benskin, John Eicher, and Frank Lisch.

With the onset of national Prohibition in the spring of 1919, production switched to soft drinks and cereal beverages. The limited market for these products was not enough, however, especially with competition from the nearby Stark-Tuscarawas Co. By 1923, the Home Brewing Co. was dissolved and the brewing equipment liquidated.

After Prohibition's repeal in 1933, a brief attempt was made to revive the Home Brewing Co. name with a new company, at a new location, but this one never progressed to the production phase. Another attempt was made in 1933 by a group calling itself the Munich Brewery, Inc. This consisted mainly of three men, A. R. Arbaugh, M. F. Berberich, and M. J. Weiss. Their plan was to acquire the old Home plant and refurbish it as a brewery, but again the attempt was unsuccessful.

The giant building remained vacant until 1930, when it was occupied by the new Canton Ice & Fuel Company. This was later renamed as the Canton Ice & Cold Storage Co., and even later renamed as the Canton Cold Storage Co. At the present time, the company continues to occupy the entire plant, which has remained more or less intact.

10. Canton Brewing Company

The repeal of Prohibition in 1933, and the demand for beer that followed, necessitated the creation of a new brewing facility in the city. At that time, four different companies were formed for the development of breweries in Canton. However, in the midst of the Great Depression, the Munich, Tuscora, and Home Brewing Companies never gained enough capital to actually begin brewing operations. The only survivor of the era began as the Graber Brewing Co. for a few months in 1933, but the name had been changed to the Canton Brewing Co., Inc. by December of that year. The site was an old two-story warehouse at 1216 High St., SW. The new brewery's capital was $45,000, and its primary beer was called "Topaz".

The fledgling company would have a very turbulent history, with numerous changes of officers in its brief life, as it tried to stay solvent during the depths of the Depression. Initially, its president was Joseph A. Tucker, a local dentist. Saul Sidlow was vice-president, Howard N. Roshong was secretary and treasurer, and Samuel Graber was brewmaster. The latter had previously been the owner of the Wooster Artificial Ice and Brewing Co., and had been involved with the formation of the Graber Brewing Co. His involvement would not last long, however, as he was soon replaced by John F. Kneisner.

(above) Bottle label from 1934; note the recycled logo from the old Stark-Tuscarawas Co.; (below) Canton Brewing Co. building in the early 1980s [courtesy of Bill Carlisle]

By April 1934, operation of the company was taken over by William A. and Carl T. Schuster, who had previously been involved with the Schuster/Stark-Tuscarawas Brewing Co. in Massillon. Also, Walter Gruner, formerly the master brewer of The Akron Brewing Co. (before Prohibition), now became the new master brewer as well as secretary. At this time, the Schuster,

Zest, and Tuscora brand names were revived from the pre-Prohibition era.

Management soon changed again, however, and by 1936, Carl F. Faller was the new president, with Elliott J. Shaffrank as vice-president. Otto Weber was brewmaster and superintendent by this time. Sales were not sufficient to keep the company going past 1937, however, and the building was vacant by 1938.

One last attempt was made to revive the company, and in October 1939, The Canton Brewing Co. (specifically with the word "The") was incorporated with capital stock of $25,000. Joseph A. Tucker was again behind this effort, this time with Samuel L. Bowlus, the owner of a local automobile service company, as vice-president. Joseph Nebel was the new brewmaster and manager of the forty employees, although within two years he had been replaced by Alex Hostettler. Old English Ale and Stark, Four Star, and Tiny Tusc Beers were new brands being produced by this time, and were placed on the market on December 15th.

Production continued through 1941, at which time the company was being operated by three men from Columbus, Ohio. Leo J. O'Donnell was president, Michael Toole was vice-president, and Robert J. Phelan was secretary when all brewing operations ceased and the equipment was liquidated in that year.

The building later served as an oil well supply warehouse, and later yet as a general contractor's warehouse. It was vacant by 1987, and soon after that it was razed. Nothing remains of it today.

Jackson Township

1. Kropf Brewery

Little is known about this small rural brewery, which was operated by Christian Kropf (a cousin of the Christian Kropf who operated two other breweries in Stark County). Kropf had been born in Germany in 1833, and came to the United States in the early 1850s. Kropf was primarily a farmer, owning land on the north side of what is now Shuffel Drive, just west of the intersection of Pittsburg Avenue. This is in Jackson Township, but is listed in some directories as being in nearby New Berlin, which is now North Canton.

In the late 1860s, he also built a brewery on his farm, with products being sold locally to taverns and other farmers in the area. Production of lager and weiss beer was generally between 500 and 1,000 barrels per year. Kropf's son, Henry C. (who was born on the farm in 1854), was a partner in the business after the mid-1870s. Production appears to have ended in the mid-1880s, although Christian continued to live on the farm until his death in 1903. While the Kropf farmhouse remains standing to this day and is occupied by a small business, there is no trace of the brewery itself.

2. The Brewhouse/New Berlin Brewing Co./Gridiron Brewpub & Grille

Stark County's first brewery in over fifty years, the Brewhouse began operations in November 1996 in a former Rax restaurant building at 4262 Portage Street NW, near Interstate 77. Initially, the head brewer and part owner was Mike Horvath, with Brian Greenwell as the other part owner.

Brewing around 250 barrels annually with its 5-barrel system, The Brewhouse offered several brews in its first four years: Galloping Ghost Amber Ale, Golden Boy Pale Ale, Crazy Legs India Pale Ale, Bulldog Brown Ale, Sammy's Summer Wheat Beer, Daddy Cool Breeze (a raspberry/blackberry wheat beer), Brewhouse Berry Weiss Beer, Night Train Porter, Papa Bear Imperial Stout, Mad Stork Winter Spice, and Old Man Winter. New brands and seasonal variations continued to appear through the year, while a wide variety of other local microbrews were available on tap at the bar.

New ownership in January 2000, however, brought in Mike Mickley as the new brewer, and by the end of the year, the pub's name had changed to the New Berlin Brewing Co., reflecting the original name of nearby North Canton. New brews continued to appear, such as Mother's Milk Oatmeal Stout, Elfin Magic, Sasquatch Smoky Maple Porter, and Pushpin Pale Ale, until the pub changed ownership again in October 2001. New owners David and Darlene Singleton soon renamed the bar as the Gridiron Brewpub and Grille. Mickley remained as the brewer, producing Big Buddha and Brave Sir Robin Ales, but the pub had closed its doors by early 2003.

3. Thirsty Dog Brewing Company

Located at 5419 Dressler Road NW in the Belden Village area, this brewpub began operations in February 1997 in a former Cantina Del Rio restaurant building. Fred Karm, who began home brewing as a hobby, was the founder and head brewer. In the first year, 900 barrels were brewed using a 10-barrel J.V. Northwest system, with Irish Setter Red Beer being one of the best sellers, along with Labrador Lager, Nut Brown Ale, Dierdorfer Gold Pilsner, and Spiced Pumpkin Ale. The following brews were later added: Old Leghumper Porter, Raspberry Ale, Summer Wheat Ale, Airship Light, Goldlings Retriever Pale Ale, Robinson's English Stout, Hoppus Maximus Ale, and an Irish Stout. He also offered a rich Oktoberfest Beer in the fall. The Raspberry Leghumper and Old Leghumper Porter won silver and bronze medals, respectively, at the 2000 World Beer Cup competition, while Raspberry Leghumper won a gold medal at the 2000 Great American Beer Festival.

The restaurant's décor and menu also followed the canine theme (bone shaped tap knobs at the bar, etc). In 1998, the company expanded with new brewpubs in the Dayton/Centerville area and Copley Township, west of Akron (see the section on Summit County), each site carrying the same lineup of beers. In the summer of 2004, however, this original location in Jackson Township closed and the building was razed.

Louisville

1. George Dilger/Louisville Brewing Company

Peter B. Moinet, who was born in France in 1815, established this small brewery around 1865. It was located on the south side of Main Street in Louisville, just west of the Pittsburgh, Ft. Wayne, and Cleveland Railroad tracks. By 1869, Moinet had sold the plant to his thirty-year-old son, Joseph. The latter then sold a part interest in the brewery to John Graber and Jacob Roth for $1,200 in October 1873. By 1875, with various improvements, the plant's annual output had grown from several hundred barrels of lager beer to over 1,600, and this number had increased to over 2,000 by 1878.

In 1876, Moinet and Roth sold their shares of the brewery to George Dilger, a German immigrant born in 1843, with Roth's share costing $7,000. Graber would sell his share in August 1878 to Simon Menegay, a local farmer, also for $7,000. This partnership would only last for three years, however, as Menegay sold his share to Dilger in September 1881, for $6,000.

After this time, the plant was known as the George Dilger Brewery, and would continue to see slow growth, with production varying between 3,000 and 6,000 barrels per year through the 1890s. Beer from the brewery was sold primarily in Louisville, Canton, and elsewhere in northern Stark County. Business was profitable until 1891, when Dilger amassed significant debt due to a shortage of ice during the previous winter (the winter of 1890 was the warmest of the past century, with an average daily temperature of 38 degrees F., around 10 degrees warmer than normal; this was one of the greatest risks of having only an ice pond instead of modern refrigeration equipment). The situation did not improve over the next few years, and by 1894 he had become insolvent. For the next two years, the brewery's assignees were Andrew M. McCarty and William J. Piero. The brewery's final ten years of existence were quite turbulent, with only intermittent periods of production.

After a public auction, the plant was sold in February 1897 for $7,000 to the Kropf Ale Co. The latter was a newly formed stock company, with a capital of $10,000, and which consisted of Henry Kropf, who would be the new plant manager, and Harry R. Rex, as well as several other area investors. It appears that there was some connection between this company and the Kropf Brewery in southern Stark County, which also was primarily producing ale at the same time, although the exact connection is unclear. In fact, Christian Kropf, from the southern Kropf Brewery filed suit against the Kropf Ale Co. for $1,000, citing infringement and damages, although the case was dismissed.

With some improvements, the plant was then sold again in May 1899 to a group of Cleveland investors, for $10,000. The group called itself The Louisville Brewing Company, and was led by two men named Spiezka and Theobold. Their plan was to double the size of the plant, to 12,000 barrels per year, and add a refrigeration unit. These plans did not materialize, however, and over the next two years, they were unable to operate the plant at a profit.

The plant was sold again in May 1901 to another group of Cleveland investors, which would call itself Louisville Brewing Company (no "The"), for $4,678, or two-thirds of its appraised value. This group was led by two men named Weber and A. W. Stadler. It appears that George Dilger returned to run the brewery for the new company during the next four years, although it is unknown exactly when this happened. The brewery appears to have had a low-level production of ale alternating with extended periods of inactivity over that time.

Dilger, however, committed suicide in March 1905, leaving a wife and four children. He was found to have hanged himself in the basement of the brewery. After this, the plant remained idle while the owners attempted to sell the property to another group. The first attempt was with a group of investors from Cleveland and Canton, who formed a stock company worth $30,000, the majority of which was to be used to bring the plant up to modern standards. The plant still consisted of old one- and two-story wooden buildings (in an era when a modern state-of-the-art brewery would have had a four- to six-story brick brewhouse) and obsolete equipment, and the only refrigeration was an ice house, supplied by the small ice pond behind the brewery. Therefore, any realistic attempt to make the plant profitable would require it being rebuilt from the ground up. This requirement did not make it attractive to potential investors, and the plan eventually fell through.

One final attempt to sell the plant was made in the spring of 1906, when another stock company was formed in response to the recent passage of the Aiken Bill. The latter was a law supported by the temperance movement, which would require a $1,000 annual tax on saloons, to take effect in May 1906. Its effect was to put some of the smaller saloons out of business, while other saloon owners would lay off bartenders and work themselves to save money. The new stock company, worth $50,000, consisted of investors from Louisville, Alliance, Canton, and Massillon. The goal was to establish saloons in each of those towns, and sell beer at three cents a glass, a significant discount over the usual five cents a glass. By sheer volume, the investors hoped to make more than enough money to overcome the effect of the new tax, as well as make a profit. As the Louisville *Herald* stated, "Three cent beer would fill lots of old boozers with happiness."

Unfortunately, these plans never materialized either, and the small plant never returned to production. Within several years, the icehouse and brewhouse had been torn down, while the remaining buildings had been converted into John Martig's small cheese factory. These buildings remained standing for many years before eventually being razed. Nothing remains of the brewery today.

Massillon

1. Forest City Brewery

In approximately 1842, Charles J. Bammerlin erected a small brewery in Lawrence Township along the Pittsburgh, Fort Wayne, & Cleveland Railroad tracks, approximately three miles northwest of the city of Massillon. The actual site was approximately one-half mile south of the intersection of Orrville Street and Kenyon Avenue. Bammerlin was a German native, born on November 28, 1793, who had come to the United States

Forest City Malt House in the 1870s
[Massillon Museum collection]

**Inside the Bammerlin Brewery cellars today
[photo courtesy of Emmitt Shaffer]**

in 1834. His son, Leonard, was born in 1832 and learned the brewing business from his father as he grew up. Leonard would take over ownership of the brewery in 1862. By that time, it consisted of one primary brewhouse that was a two-story frame structure with stone foundation, 85 feet by 66 feet in size. A large stone vault with arched ceiling was also built underground for cooling and lagering. The plant, valued at $12,000, had a capacity of 120 barrels per month.

The business had grown somewhat over the years, and by the 1870s, the Forest City Company consisted of two main components: the brewery and the Forest City Malt House. The latter was on South Erie Street in Massillon, at the northwest corner of Tremont. The malt house actually provided the larger proportion of the company's business, with a capacity of 30,000 bushels of barley for malting per year. It consisted of several buildings, the largest one being three stories. Bammerlin's original malt house had been further north on Erie Street, but that was destroyed by fire in January 1878. The new plant was built immediately after that and consisted of the company's main office, the malting plant, and a beer hall for local residents to drink Bammerlin's brews. All of these were produced at the brewery, where they were barreled (the company did no bottling) and shipped into town along the railroad.

During its existence, the brewery produced both ale and lager beer, and production generally was in the range of 1,000 to 1,200 barrels per year. Bammerlin ran the brewery until 1881, when operations ceased. Bammerlin was attempting to sell the small plant when it was destroyed by fire in July 1883. The malt house was subsequently sold to Martin Huss & Co., who ran it only for a brief time before it closed for good. Charles Bammerlin died in 1881, and Leonard died of cancer in 1912. The brewery's stone foundations remain to this day, and the stone cellars underground remain and are accessible to brave explorers. Nothing remains of the Forest City Malt House in Massillon.

2. City/Empire Brewery

Frederick Haag was a native of Wurtemburg, Germany, born in 1821, who in March 1845 purchased a seven-acre lot of land near Massillon's western limits. The site was north of Wooster Street (later the Lincoln Highway, and today state route 172), in a ravine near Little Sippo Creek and an old stone quarry. Soon after this, Haag and his younger brother Conrad established a small brewery, which would come to be known as the City Brewery, at the site.

Haag continued to operate the small plant, producing just under 1,000 barrels of lager beer annually, until approximately 1871. At that time, brewing operations were taken over by John Stoolmiller, who was briefly joined in the business by George Seippel. The small brewery was enlarged over the next few years, such that annual production had increased to between 1,500 and 1,800 barrels per year. The plant was then sold to 22-year-old Emmaline Holbyson in March 1877, for the sum of $26,257. Holbyson's father John was a farmer who had previously been a partial owner of the property prior to his death in 1871.

It does not appear that Emmaline operated the brewery herself, but instead leased it to other parties over the next few years, including an M. Webber by 1879, and Leonard Bammerlin (owner of the nearby Forest City brewery and malt house) in 1881. By 1883, operation of the plant had been taken over by Julius Wittman, a local saloon owner who was also involved with the formation of the Massillon Brewing Co. with James McLain around the same time. At that time it was renamed as the Empire Brewery, and a bottling works was added to the plant.

In July 1884, Wittman accepted assignment on the property due to rising debts, and it appears that brewing operations ceased at that time. The small Empire Brewery was soon dismantled, and there is no trace of it today.

3. McLain/Kopp/Schuster Brewery

James H. McLain was born in Massillon in November 1842, and had become involved with several local business ventures before purchasing an old flour mill in 1876. This mill was located four miles north of Massillon in Millport, now known as Crystal Springs. Millport was little more than a crossroads, but it was located along the Ohio & Erie Canal, which was still an important artery of transportation for the region at that time. Calling his new business James H. McLain & Company, McLain operated the flour mill for seven years before converting the mill into a brewery in 1883. Also involved in the business by then were Christian Schott and Julius Wittman, the latter being a local saloonist who had briefly run the small Empire brewery on the west side of Massillon. By 1885, the plant had been renamed as the Massillon Brewing Co.

The plant itself was built on seventeen acres of land and consisted of six separate buildings: the main brewhouse, 50 x 100 feet in size; an ice machine house, 50 x 40 feet; an ice storage house, 50 x 80 feet; boiler house, 24 x 30 feet; office building, 15 x 20 feet; and a dwelling house, 20 x 30 feet. All buildings were of stone foundation with wood frame or brick construction. Three large steam boilers powered the plant with 500-horsepower capacity. Two ice machines were used, with 25- and 15-ton capacity.

View of the brewery from the mid-1890s, showing the canal boat used to take barrels of beer to the bottling works in town [Massillon Museum collection]

The plant's annual capacity was 25,000 barrels, consisting of two types of lager beer, Standard and Export.

Once the beer was produced in barrels, it was loaded onto a specially constructed canal boat, to be shipped along the canal into Massillon for bottling and sale. The main bottling house, built in 1893, was at the corner of Exchange and Charles Streets, and was four floors high, each having 4,000 square feet of space. Sales of products were throughout the western and southern portions of Stark County, mainly along the canal, and also into Canton and Wayne County as well.

McLain sold the brewery in December 1887 to Carl F. Erhard & Robert Schimke, two Austrian immigrants who had previously worked at the Schmidt & Hoffman brewery in Cleveland. McLain continued to be involved with his other business ventures in Massillon and Canton until his death in 1894.

In December 1888, Erhard sold his share of the brewery to Schimke, although the former remained the brewery's manager for two more years. The entire plant was sold again in May 1894 to Anton Kopp, a Bavarian immigrant, born in September 1840 in Augsburg. He had come to the United States in 1868, and Canton twenty years later. He had previously worked in the Leisy and August Burckhardt breweries in Cleveland and more recently had been the foreman at the Canton Brewing Co. He ran the plant at somewhat below capacity, producing just over 10,000 barrels in the first year, until selling it to John W. Schuster in June 1898, for $45,500. After this, Kopp retired from brewing. He died in February 1903, from complications of diabetes.

Schuster was a native Bavarian, born in the city of Kallstadt in 1852. He came to America in 1870, and worked several jobs before coming to Cleveland four years later, where he became a wholesale wine dealer. He continued in this profession until coming to Massillon in 1898 and purchasing the brewery. He operated it for two years before building an entirely new plant in Massillon and abandoning the old one in July 1901. The original plant burned in 1913, the same year that a flood severely damaged the Ohio & Erie Canal, essentially ending Ohio's canal era. Today, Erie Avenue (formerly U.S. Route 21) runs through the middle of the brewery site, and nothing remains of the original plant.

4. Schuster Brewing Company

John Schuster had formed a stock company, known as the Schuster Brewing Co., for his brewery in Millport on July 1, 1900, with a capital stock of $200,000. At that time, work commenced on a new state-of-the-art plant in the city of Massillon. This would consist of a four-story brick brewhouse and stockhouse, with bottling works and modern mechanical refrigeration. The new plant opened in July 1901, and the old one was abandoned. The plant's address was 33-49 N. West Street, although this later became 209 N. West St. when streets were renumbered, and by 1933, the street name had changed, making the plant's new address 227 3rd St. NW.

(above) Postcard, postmarked in 1913; The sender wrote "This is where I shine" at the top; (below left) Schuster beer wagon, circa 1905; The driver is Ulysses Grant Ruch, son of Christian Ruch, the brewer from Canal Fulton [Massillon Museum collection].

Upon moving into the new plant, the company's president was John W. Schuster, with Fred Kuefer as vice-president and Frank H. Schuster, John's eldest son, as secretary. This arrangement continued until 1905, when the company merged with the Canton, Stark, New Philadelphia, and Canal Dover Breweries to form the Stark-Tuscarawas Breweries Co. The new combine paid $400,000 for the Schuster plant, and John Schuster was its first president, until his retirement the following year. Frank Schuster remained on as a bookkeeper, while his younger brother William A. Schuster became the manager of the plant. William had been born in 1884, schooled in Cleveland, and apprenticed in the brewing trade at the age of eighteen.

Production at the plant continued largely unchanged over the next thirteen years, with the plant's primary product being Schuster's Zest Lager Beer. The Schusters were also officers of the City Ice & Coal Co. in Massillon, which utilized the brewery's ice plant as its own. With the onset of Prohibition in 1919, the Schuster plant withdrew from the Stark-Tuscarawas Co., renaming itself Schuster & Co., bottlers and distributors of carbonated beverages, including Apella, a sparkling apple juice. This would later evolve into the local NeHi and Chero-Cola Bottling Co., after the Schuster family left the business (they would later be briefly involved with the post-Prohibition Zoar Brewery and Canton Brewing Co., however). By 1927, the plant became the Peoples Coal & Beverage Co., and later would gain the local contract for bottling Royal Crown Cola in addition to NeHi.

After Prohibition's end in 1933, a brief attempt was made to begin brewing again at the plant, as the Massillon Brewing Co. Even in the 1933 city directory, the company is listed as producing Green Seal Beer, although there is no evidence that any beer production actually took place. Production of soft drinks continued until approximately 1960, when the company went out of business. The remaining buildings were vacant for several years before being razed in the early 1970s, at a time when much of the nearby Tuscarawas River and local roads were being rerouted as part of a flood-control project. There is no trace of the brewery today.

Navarre

1. Daniel Groff/Edward Hug brewery

Navarre's only brewery proved to be one of the most confusing ones to research, as it changed hands frequently during its thirty-year existence. Located along the south bank of the Ohio & Erie Canal, on the west side of Main Street (today state route 21), the brewery appears to have been established by Daniel Groff around 1850. Groff and his partner Isaac Rudy operated the brewery in conjunction with an adjacent grain mill, with their beer sold in the village of Navarre and along the canal. This continued until 1853, when personal debts forced the sale of the brewery in two halves: one half was sold to a group of men led by Thomas McCullogh of Massillon, while the other half was sold to Jacob Zinsmaster.

The following progression of owners (nearly all German or Swiss immigrants) is included only for the sake of historical completeness: Zinsmaster sold his share of the brewery in 1859 to Peter Grafs (also spelled Grass, Gross), who sold it in 1860 to George Eberhard (also spelled Everhart). Later that year it was sold to Frederick Hess, who then sold it to Barnhard Klein in 1863. The other half of the brewery was sold by McCullogh in 1856 to Jacob & Christian Snyder, who then sold it to Peter Dommy in 1862. Dommy sold the same share to James Leeper in 1864. Leeper and Klein then operated the brewery together until 1865, when they sold both halves to William Hanson. Two months later, Hanson sold the entire brewery to Christian Ruch, the owner of the brewery in Canal Fulton, ten miles north along the canal. One year later, Ruch sold the property for $3,500 to Edward Grossklaus, Alexander Garver, and David Ricksaker. Garver sold his share to Edward J. Hug in 1867, and Ricksaker had left the partnership one year after that.

Hug, born in Switzerland in 1841, was operating the brewery alone by 1874, producing between 300 and 700 barrels per year. Brewing operations ceased around 1876, and the building later housed a saloon. It remained standing well after the turn of the century, although there are no remains of it today. Hug, Grossklaus, Garver, and Ricksaker all remained in Navarre and were involved in various mercantile trades for several years.

Nimishillen Township (aka Rome)

1. Sommer/Kropf Brewery

The Sommer family brewery in Perry Township was well-established by the late 1860s. At that time, they built a second associated brewery, to be operated by Henry Sommer's youngest son, John. It also had an associated distillery, and was located in Nimishillen Township in Stark County. The site was along the East Branch of Nimishillen Creek, on the west side of Paris Avenue at the railroad tracks. This is approximately two miles east of Louisville, and was listed in several directories as having been in the village of Rome, although that name does not appear on any local maps from the time. The brewery burned down soon after being built, but was rebuilt soon after. Sommer sold this plant to Christian Kropf in October 1872, for $12,000. The plant produced between 500 and 1,000 barrels of lager beer per year, and operations continued until approximately 1884, after which the plant appears to have been abandoned. Nothing remains of it today.

Perry Township

1. Sommer/Kropf Brewery

Located on the Sommer family farm in Perry Township, this brewery appears to have begun operating sometime between the late 1840s and 1852. It consisted of two primary wooden buildings, both three stories in height, with stone block foundations. Today this site is on Kropf Road, near the village of Richville, southwest of Canton.

The primary product of this brewery was ale, which was supposedly very high in alcohol content, in the European tradition (having between ten and fifteen percent alcohol, as opposed to most American beers/ales which would have between four and eight percent). Lager beer was produced after the 1890s, in addition to the ale. The products were all distributed in barrels to taverns throughout Stark County, and no bottling was ever done there. The

1875 Stark County Atlas

water source was a series of wells on the property. There also was a pond on the farm from which ice would be cut during the winter, for cooling the ale in the icehouse year round. A large vaulted cellar was adjacent to the brewery, approximately ten feet underground. This led to another cellar, which was at least twenty-five feet underground and lined with sandstone.

Exactly which Sommer family members were involved with the brewing is uncertain. However, Henry Sommer appears to have begun brewing beer soon after purchasing the property in the late 1840s. He was a native of Alsace-Lorraine, born in 1802, who had come to America around 1830. Brewing was later assumed by his sons Christian, born in 1846, and John, born in 1849, and they continued until 1878. Annual production was over 2,000 barrels at this time, making it the largest brewery in Stark County.

In 1878, one year after Henry Sommer died, brewing operations were taken over by Christian Kropf, another Alsacian immigrant, born in 1840, who had married into the Sommer family. In fact, numerous members of the Sommer family married into the Kropf family, making the recording of events somewhat more complicated. In addition, there are several different lines of Sommer and Kropf families in the area, and there is much duplication of names from one generation to the next.

Ale production continued as before, although the plant's annual output dropped into the range of 500 to 1,000 barrels, where it remained for the next thirty years. In the 1880s, the site's mailing address was changed to Canton, although it actually was nowhere near the city limits. Christian Kropf died of cancer in 1902, and two years later, the plant's name was changed to the Kropf Cream Ale Co. However, all brewing operations had ceased by early 1912. The brewing equipment was dismantled at that time, although the farm continued to operate, staying in the Kropf family for many years.

The underground storage cellar was sealed over, filled with dirt, and remained inaccessible for many years. In the spring of 1999, however, a new owner of the property, Robert Miller, began excavating the entire cellar with a backhoe and shovel. Hundreds of bottles of various types were found there, as well as many relics of the brewing era, barrel rings, horseshoes, Model T car parts, parts to the old beer wagons, toys, cowbells and other various items. It appears that the cellars served as a dump for the family for the better part of the 1900s. Miller's goal at the time was to clear out the entire cellar and brewery foundation, and possibly to establish a small museum at the site.

Uniontown

1. Philip Seesdorf brewery

Philip Seesdorf purchased a small plot of land on the west side of what is now Church Street in Uniontown in November 1851. Soon after this he established a small brewing operation at the site. In late 1855, he sold the brewery for $600 to Frederick Housholter, a 42-year-old Alsacian immigrant. Housholter continued brewing operations through October 1860, when he sold the property to Peter Follmer, who in turn sold the property two years later to Jonathan Hubler. Hubler sold the property in 1865 to satisfy debts, and it appears that brewing operations ceased at that time. The brewery was later dismantled, leaving no remains to this day. Seesdorf stayed in the area, however, until his death in 1884, at the age of 82.

Waynesburg(h)

1. Morledge/Gruber Brewery

Waynesburg's only brewery appears to have begun operation around 1840, when it was founded by Roger Morledge, an English native who had come to the United States in 1812. Morledge had purchased the site in 1836, and began brewing sometime later. The site was one-half block north of East Lisbon St., next to the village cemetery.

Morledge died in 1848, at which time the brewery was purchased by Henry Scholder of Canton, who then operated the brewery until 1857. It was then purchased by James Ross, who sold it again five months later to Madison Mays. Mays had been born locally in 1830, and was primarily a farmer and dealer in livestock. He operated the brewery for five years before selling it to Henry Gruber in 1862 for $1,000.

Gruber had been born in 1825 in Wurtemberg, Germany, and left the Fatherland for America in the early 1850s. He would operate the small plant with his young sons Christian and Charles. Annual production of lager beer generally ranged from 500 to 700 barrels, which were distributed to local taverns. By 1877, operations had been turned over to Christian, who was now 26 years old, while Henry would die on June 20th of the following year. Charles Gruber moved on to be a saloonkeeper in the town. Production appears to have ceased around 1888, and there is no trace of the brewery today.

Also Note:

1. The Stark-Tuscarawas Breweries Company was a stock company, formed in 1905 by the combination of five breweries in Stark and Tuscarawas Counties. For specific histories and related breweries, see: Stark Brewing Co.; Graber/Giessen brewery; The Canton Brewing Co.; Union Brewing Co.; McLain/Kopp/Schuster brewery; Schuster Brewing Co.; New Philadelphia Brewing Co.; and Bernhardt/Dover Brewing Co.

2. The Independent Brewing Company was formed in Massillon as a stock company in 1912. The incorporators were C. B. De Bos, Julius Schneider, Emil Sondregger, and Jacob Stuhldreher. Their intention was to construct an entirely new brewery in town to compete with the Stark-Tuscarawas Co. However, for unknown reasons, these plans never came to pass.

3. Stoneware bottles have appeared periodically from the Canton Small Beer Company. Not appearing in any city directories, this would appear to have existed for a few years in the 1850s or 1860s, possibly in conjunction with a bottling works in the city. As mentioned in the introduction, small beer came to refer to a number of different beverages, and based on available information, it appears that in this case it was a non-alcoholic, essentially "soft" drink.

SUMMIT COUNTY

Akron

1. John & Jacob Good brewery

Summit County's first well-documented brewery began operation in 1845, located on the west side of the Ohio & Erie Canal near Lock 11, and near the Aetna Mills on the north side of downtown. At the time, this was a growing hub of industrial activity, located on the edge of the Little Cuyahoga River Valley. As the canal descended into the valley, a series of locks along the canal provided water power for a number of mills and factories. Commercial activity along the canal in this region had led to the formation of the northern half of the town of Akron in the 1820s and 1830s.

This first fledgling brewery was operated by John T. Good, a native of Alsace-Lorraine, near Strasbourg. Born in 1818, he subsequently came to the United States in 1838, and Akron in 1842. Initially, he was in partnership with Michael Bittman (also spelled Bitman), another German immigrant, born in 1829.

Good purchased Bittman's share of the brewery in March 1850 for a total of $500, although Bittman continued to operate the brewery for the remainder of the year while Good left for the gold mines of California with nearly 200 other men from the area. Ill health did not allow him to stay long in the mines, however, and he returned to his brewery in Akron in December of that year. It is uncertain how long Bittman worked at the brewery after that. Income from the brewing operation allowed Good to enter the grocery business in Akron, in which he continued for the next 15 years.

It appears that Good sold a partial interest in the brewery to his cousin, Jacob Good, in 1855. Jacob was also a native Alsacian, who had come to America in 1846, and who had also spent time in the gold mines of California. By 1860, the Goods had outgrown the small brewery along the canal, and they would then move south into the city's commercial district to build a new and larger one (see #4 in this section). The original brewery near Lock 11 soon disappeared into history, leaving no trace to this day.

2. Marshall Viall brewery

The existence of this small brewery has recently surfaced, although little is known about it. Marshall Viall was born in New York State in 1818, and came to Akron in the 1840s. He purchased a lot near the intersection of present day Bank and Williams Streets in March 1846. This was in the village of Middlebury, three miles east of the city of Akron, in the narrow valley of the Little Cuyahoga River.

Viall began what was probably a glorified home brewing operation soon after this, with his younger brother James. Whether the brewing was done at home or at another location is uncertain. There was a beer bottle factory close to Viall's home, but it is unclear whether he had any connection with this or not. The Middlebury area was rich with clay, which led to a burgeoning clay products industry (stoneware, bottles, sewer pipe, etc.) in the village.

Viall's brewing operation was short-lived, and may have been gone by 1855. He is listed in the 1860 census as a farmer, living in southern Summit County. The village of Middlebury was annexed into the city of Akron soon after this.

3. Oberholtz/Horix/George J. Renner Brewing Company

The origin of eastern Ohio's longest-lasting brewery had remained a mystery to this author until recently, when new information was uncovered. In *Brewing Beer In The Rubber City*, I stated that this brewery had been established around 1862, but it now appears that brewing operations began at the site somewhat earlier.

The tract of land on which the brewery sits was purchased in August 1848 for $50 by 45-year-old George Harmann (also spelled Herman) and 38-year-old John Brodt, two German immigrants. Soon after this, they established a small brewery at the site, where they were assisted by two other men, John Stoltz and Samuel Jeckell. The site was ideal for brewing beer: it was in a ravine where a spring flowed to provide pure water (in later years, several wells were dug which could provide up to 5,000 barrels of pure water daily); storage caves could easily be dug into the surrounding hillsides; and the site was immediately south of both the Pennsylvania & Ohio Canal and the Atlantic & Great Western Railway tracks, the latter being a main line through the area.

The site was also on the south side of what was later known as Forge Street, a road that led from Akron to an area known as the "Old Forge" in the nearby Little Cuyahoga River valley. At the time, this area was outside of Akron's city limits, in Portage Township. However, the land was annexed into the city in 1869, at which time the brewery took the address of 313–315 N. Forge St. (still later the streets were renumbered and the brewery took its modern address of 247–275 N. Forge St.)

Harmann and Brodt continued to operate the brewery until August 1855, when they sold it to George Kempel, a German native who had come to America in 1849. After spending three years in the California gold mines, Kempel returned to Akron and established a shoe business before purchasing the brewery. It appears that he operated the latter until April 1866, when he sold it to Christopher Oberholtz. Oberholtz was another German native, born in 1822, who had arrived in Akron in 1842 and subsequently had purchased a large amount of land in the area surrounding the brewery. After owning a cooperage nearby for a number of years, he now entered the business of filling the barrels he had produced.

Oberholtz operated the brewery for only three years before dying of pneumonia in 1869, after which the land and brewery were willed to his wife Susannah and his 26-year-old son Frederick. Business continued to slowly increase until disaster struck. In the early morning hours of June 10, 1873, a fire destroyed much of the plant, less than half of which was insured. Frederick Oberholtz quickly rebuilt the plant with a new three-story brick brewhouse, which was finished early in 1874.

At this point, Oberholtz found himself $30,000 in debt to several parties, and he subsequently lost ownership of the plant. The brewery changed hands twice more while sitting idle, until September 1876, when it was purchased by John A. Kolp. He operated it briefly before defaulting on several loans himself. It was then sold at a sheriff's auction in January 1879 to Fred Horix, for $8,334, or two-thirds of its appraised value. Oberholtz later moved to Kansas City for a time before returning to Akron, where he died of consumption (tuberculosis) in 1888.

Horix had successfully operated a small brewery on East Exchange Street for several years. When he took ownership of this plant, it consisted only of an icehouse, a small storage building, and the main brewhouse with a potential annual capacity of 20,000 barrels. Horix was immediately able to invest a significant amount of money into the plant, and brewing operations had begun again by mid-1879.

Just one year later, in August 1880, a second fire struck the plant. Beginning late at night in the boiler room, it quickly spread through the main building. Horix, who lived in a house next door to the plant, saw the fire and ran up the Forge Street hill in his nightclothes to the nearest firebox a half-mile away. Despite a rapid response by the fire department, the top two floors of the plant were gutted, with a loss of nearly $12,000. This time, however, the plant was fully insured, and was quickly rebuilt.

Within several years, the plant had increased in size to seven buildings, and annual production had increased to nearly 7,000 barrels; the brewery was finally

Fred Horix in later years [courtesy of Frank Fairbanks]

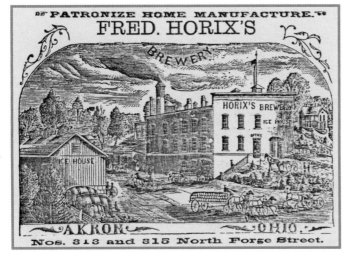

Akron City Directory, 1881

operating at a profit. In 1888, however, Horix chose to sell the plant for $45,000 to George J. Renner. The deed of transfer mentioned that while Renner would take ownership of the entire plant and house, Horix would retain his personal records, family furniture, and "a spotted horse called Dick". Horix then spent a year in Germany before returning to Akron, where he was involved in several different business ventures before opening a delicatessen on South High Street. After the turn of the century, he would return to the brewing business, becoming involved with the newly formed Akron Brewing Company.

George Jacob Renner was a native of Dannstadt, a Bavarian village, where he was born in 1835. Well over six feet tall and nearly 260 pounds, Renner was an imposing figure and would likely have been forced to join the Kaiser's army had he stayed in Germany. Largely to avoid being drafted, he emigrated to America in 1849, after which he lived in Cincinnati for several years, attending brewing school, then working in several breweries in both Cincinnati and Covington, KY. In 1881, however, he moved north to Wooster, Ohio, where he was part owner of the brewery there, with his son George, Jr., for three years. He then purchased a half interest in what became the Renner & Weber Brewing Co. in Mansfield. Four years later he moved to Akron, where he would spend the remainder of his life.

Renner immediately began to invest money into the plant, installing a mechanical ice machine and establishing a side business of ice production. A second machine followed in 1895, giving the plant a daily capacity of 45 tons of ice. Meanwhile, the Renner Brewing Co. was incorporated in 1893 with capital stock of $60,000. George was president; vice-president and plant foreman was his 23-year-old son William; Eleanora, his daughter, was secretary and treasurer; and his son-in-law, Ernest C. Deibel, a Youngstown native, was brewmaster and plant manager.

(above) George J. Renner posing with his employees around 1900; (below left) George J. Renner, circa 1900 [image taken from *One Hundred Years of Brewing*].

Numerous other additions to the plant followed over the next decade, increasing the annual capacity to 50,000 barrels (although actual production was about half of that) and establishing a bottling works for home sales of beer. Several brands were being produced by 1908: Renner's Blue Label Beer, Yellow Band Lager, Renner's Extra Table Beer, Atlas and Eagle Pilsner Export Beers, and Renner's Bock Beer (each spring). In 1912 came the introduction of what would prove to be the company's anchor brand for the next forty years: Grossvater (the German word for grandfather).

After the turn of the century, the company re-incorporated as the George J. Renner Brewing Co., establishing a distinct identity apart from the Renner breweries in Youngstown (operated by George J. Renner, Jr.) and Mansfield. While there re-

mained a loose association between the three breweries (Grossvater and Eagle Beers were made by all three before Prohibition and Old German Lager was made by all three after Prohibition), they would operate after Prohibition as "friendly competitors", individual companies with individual brands, into the 1950s.

As Akron's population exploded over the next twenty years, due to the growth of the numerous rubber factories, annual sales of Renner beers increased to a peak of 65,000 barrels by 1917. The brewery had remained a family operation throughout this period, although in that year, Deibel opted to devote more time to management of the brewery, and Max Illenberger was hired as the new brewmaster. Illenberger had begun his career with Cleveland's Schlather brewery, and more recently had been the brewmaster of the Sioux City Brewing Co. in Iowa. The good times were about to draw to a close, however.

The country's temperance forces, which had been attempting to ban alcohol for more than 40 years, were finally succeeding, with cooperation from the national government. By the end of World War I, rising taxes had doubled the cost of a barrel of Renner beer, to $17.50. The allowable alcohol level in beer had gradually dropped as well, and in May 1919, when statewide Prohibition took effect, this level dropped to 0.5%.

**Prohibition-era bottle label
[courtesy of John Phillips]**

In that year, the brewery renamed itself as the Renner Products Co., and Grossvater de-alcoholized Beer hit the market. Advertisements took great pains to point out that this was not the same as near beer, since it was brewed as beer, with the alcohol subsequently extracted through a special vacuum process. Zepp Brew (named in honor of the giant zeppelins produced at the Goodyear airdock south of Akron during that era) made its appearance five years later, and both would continue to be produced through the end of the Prohibition era. In addition, a nameless "hop flavored malt beverage tonic", Renner's "High Power" Malt Tonic, and Old Grossvater Malt Syrup were briefly sold in the 1920s.

Renner died of pneumonia in 1921, after which Deibel assumed control of the company. Both Renner's son William and daughter Nora would die before the end of Prohibition, and their positions were filled by other Renner or Deibel family members. Sales of cereal beverages over the next decade were only around 20% of the pre-Prohibition numbers, and these alone would not have allowed the company to survive. However, diversification in the form of numerous real estate holdings and oil and gas wells allowed the company to operate successfully until 1933. Because the brewing equipment was still intact at that time and the plant had continued to function, it would be in a tremendous position when beer became legal again.

By the time President Roosevelt legalized the sale of 3.2% beer in April 1933 (full strength beer would not return for eight more months), only three breweries in Ohio were actively producing beer for de-alcoholizing. These breweries and several in Chicago and elsewhere in the Midwest would

Renner Brewery as it appeared in 1914; All buildings remain standing today.

be the only sources of beer in the first few days and weeks after the beverage became legal. Renner was the first brewery in Ohio to obtain a license to sell liquor. However, since no other establishments in the Akron area had licenses yet, sales could only be made directly at the brewery or via shipments to other cities.

Therefore, at 12:01 A.M., on April 7, 1933, in a persistent cold rain, a crowd of 2,000 people waited in line outside the brewery on Forge Street to purchase some of the 5,000 cases of Grossvater Beer that were available at $3.25 per case. By noon the next day, 10,000 cases had been sold at the brewery and through shipments all over northeast Ohio and western Pennsylvania. It was several days before all the back orders were filled.

Along with a return of the name George J. Renner Brewing Co. came a number of changes in how the business of brewing was undertaken. Various improvements in brewing equipment and technique over the next decade would increase the plant's annual capacity to 200,000 barrels, although actual production was generally closer to 125,000 barrels. Improvements in both refrigeration and transportation allowed the brewery to distribute its beers throughout a 200-mile radius around Akron. The company's delivery fleet gradually evolved from a few pick-up trucks and vans to a fleet of tractor-trailer rigs that could haul much larger loads at once.

Grossvater Lager Beer remained the company's flagship brand, although other brands entered the market between 1933 and 1935, including Old Cockney Ale, Old Gross Half and Half, Lucky Shoe Ale and Beer, and Old German Style Beer. Zepp Brew returned for several years, for sales into territories that had remained dry, and for Sunday sales in public places. Weber's Beer was brewed in Akron for distribution in Mansfield after WWII, when the Mansfield Renner brewery scaled back brewing operations and became mainly a distribution center. Souvenir Beer was introduced in the late 1930s, and would become the company's most advertised brand in the years after WWII. In addition, the company briefly brewed and bottled Silver Foam Beer on a contract basis for the Grand Rapids Brewing Co. of Michigan in 1934. Most of these beers could be tasted for free at the plant's hospitality room, known as the München office, which was decorated with scenes of the Rhine River and the German countryside.

Another marketing innovation after Prohibition was the introduction of the steel can in 1935. Four years later, Renner began packaging Grossvater Beer in cap-sealed cans produced by the Crown, Cork, & Seal Co. of Philadelphia. These would soon be replaced by the "crowntainer", a two-piece steel can also referred to as the "silver goblet" (Renner was the only brewery in Eastern Ohio to use the crowntainer). These cans were ideal for the smaller brewers, as they could be filled using existing bottling equipment and not forcing investment in a new, separate canning line. While the majority of Renner beers were bottled, canning of Grossvater, Souvenir, and Old German Beer continued sporadically until the plant closed.

Ernest C. Deibel remained in charge of the com-

(top left) Serving tray, 1935; (left) Three cans filled at Akron's Renner brewery. The can at the far left is known as a "J-spout" cone top, and was used around 1940; the middle is a "crowntainer", used in the 1940s, both before and after World War II; the can at right was used around 1950.

pany until his death in 1950. His cousin, Ernest E. Deibel, had been vice-president for some years and succeeded him as president, although he died just one year later. Robert F. Holland, a Deibel family member who had joined the company in 1936 as a cashier after graduating from high school, gradually worked his way up through the company, despite several years in the U. S. Air Force during WWII. He became the brewery's final president in 1951. Max Illenberger retired in 1948 after thirty years as plant brewmaster, to be replaced by Anton ("Tony") Weiner.

After WWII, the brewing industry continued to change, with an increasing dominance by regional and national brewers with large budgets for advertising and distribution. Sales of Renner beers gradually began slipping in the late 1940s, after which a team of consultants was hired to make recommendations for changes in production and marketing. Souvenir Beer had become the company's dominant brand, although an attempt was made to reformulate and repackage the aging Grossvater brand in 1948.

Despite these changes, the brewing operations became increasingly unprofitable, and at the end of 1952, the decision was made to stop brewing altogether. The final brew was made on December 8th of that year, and when that was finished and packaged six weeks later, the plant closed for good. Most of the plant's 75 employees were laid off as the equipment was liquidated over the next few months.

Despite the cessation of brewing, the company continued to operate successfully as the Renner Akron Realty Co., a branch of the brewery which had originated before Prohibition as a management company for the numerous saloons in Akron that were owned by the brewery. After Prohibition, breweries were no longer legally allowed to operate saloons, but they were allowed to continue to own the property on which the saloons stood. This company operated for a number of years at the plant office on Forge Street, run by Holland, Edward Steinkerchner, and Robert Myers. The company name later changed to Forge Industries, reflecting its shift toward operating as a holding company for small industrial concerns. Its offices then moved to Boardman, Ohio, where it continues today as a family operation, managed by Carl James, the great-great-grandson of George J. Renner. The company owns the Akron Gear Co., the Miller Spreader Co. in Youngstown (which was owned by the Youngstown Renner Co. until it merged with the Akron company some years later), and Bearing Distributors, Inc., of Cleveland, which it purchased in 1966. The latter company is involved in the international distribution of steel bearings made in Cleveland. Robert Holland remains affiliated with the company and divides his time between Port Clinton, OH. and Florida.

The brewery plant remains almost entirely intact, with its 75,000 square feet of floor space rented out to a number of small businesses, including the AccuChrome plating company, and the Russell Products Co., makers of protective coatings for glass, etc. The original brick and stone building from 1873 remains at the center of the plant, with many additions around it. Even the München office remains intact to this day, with its scenes of the Fatherland, and a large mural of five old beer-drinking gentlemen that years earlier appeared in the brewery's logo, with a box of cigars labeled "George".

4. John Good/Jacob Guth brewery

John and Jacob Good had operated their small brewery along the Ohio & Erie Canal since 1845 (see #1 in this section). The brewery continued to operate along with their grocery business until 1860, when increasing business made expansion necessary. Over the next year, a new brewery was constructed approximately one mile south of the original one, on the west side of South Howard Street. This one was three stories tall with a deep vaulted beer cellar in the basement, and would be used as a combination brewery and grocery store.

The brewery's exact timeline of ownership and operation is unclear over the next seven years, although John Good had left the partnership soon after the new facility was built. Jacob eventually followed, while continuing to operate both a grocery and a saloon. By 1868, it is known that the brewery was being run by Jacob R. Guth, another native Alsacian. Between 1871 and 1873, however, he retired from the business, and the small plant ceased to function.

John Good continued in the grocery business until purchasing an oil refinery, which eventually made him a wealthy man, before dying in 1883. His son, J. Edward Good, later founded the Hardware Supply Co. in Akron, and gave a large tract of land to the city, which is now Good Park municipal golf course on the west side of town.

Jacob Good continued to operate both the grocery and saloon until dying in 1893. Guth died in 1876.

The brewery building housed a number of different businesses through the years, until being razed in the late 1960s, during a period of widespread urban renewal. Nothing remains of it or of South Howard Street today.

5. Fink/Lockert/Wirth/South Akron Brewery

At the time when *Brewing Beer In The Rubber City* was written, I had found no evidence to confirm the existence of this brewery. However, new evidence has arisen to show that it was a functioning plant, albeit one that changed hands numerous times in less than a decade of existence. Located on the east side of South Broadway, just south of Cedar Street, it was along the main line of railroad tracks through the city (originally used by both the Atlantic & Great Western and the Cleveland, Mt. Vernon, & Columbus railroad companies).

Conrad Fink was a native of Darmstadt, Hesse, Germany, born in 1816, who came to the United States in 1849. With his brother John (born in 1821) and Frederick Haushalter (who had formerly operated the small brewery in Uniontown, Ohio), he purchased several lots which comprised the brewery site around 1863, and soon after this the group appears to have established the small brewery for production of both ale and common beer. In November 1864 Conrad Fink and Haushalter sold their interest in the new establishment to another brother, William Fink (born in 1819), for $4,500. John and William in turn sold the brewery to Jacques Lockert, a French immigrant, in June 1866 for $7,000. Lockert operated the brewery with German immigrant Theodore Schell for two years before selling his share to Louis Lockert, who then purchased Schell's share the following year. Lockert (also a native of France, born in 1843) operated the brewery for one year before selling it in 1870 for $8,000 to Joseph C. Wirth.

Wirth was a native of Switzerland, born in 1846, who had previously operated a restaurant nearby, but his attempt to operate the brewery left him $1,500 in debt by the end of 1871. As a result, the property was sold at a sheriff's auction in January 1872, after which brewing operations ceased and the small plant was dismantled.

After working in the brewery, Conrad Fink worked as an insurance salesman, John Fink owned a livery, William Fink ran a grocery, Lockert left the area, and Wirth worked in the area as a machinist. In later years, the property was purchased by the railroad companies, and buildings owned by them stand at the site today.

6. Burkhardt Brewing Company

The exact origin of the Burkhardt brewery remains as elusive now as it was when *Brewing Beer In The Rubber City* was written. While *One Hundred Years of Brewing*, from 1903, states that this brewery was started by Jacob Fornecker as early as 1863, there is no real evidence in the local records to support that claim (although Fornecker was known to make barrels for the brewery some years later). The first solid evidence of brewing at the site began in March 1865, when the land was purchased by Frederick Gaessler, a German immigrant, who then established the Wolf Ledge Brewery for the brewing of ale and lager beer. The plant's original address was 152-156 Sherman Street, in a ravine along Wolf Creek in the Wolf Ledges section of Akron. The creek supposedly provided some of the area's purest water for brewing. As the plant grew, it eventually extended to Grant Street, one block over, and in later years, the plant's working address became 509-543 Grant Street.

Gaessler built the brewery into a successful venture, due in part to its location in the heart of the city's German section. By the mid-1870s, annual production was well over 2,000 barrels. German immigrant Otto Giessen was Gaessler's brewing assistant until he left for Canton in 1874, where he operated a small rural brewery south of town, and later founded what would become the Canton Brewing Co. Giessen's replacement in Akron was another German immigrant by the name of Wilhelm Burkhardt.

Born in 1849, Burkhardt had studied brewing prior to his emigration to America at the age of 19. After working as a brewmaster in Cleveland for a short time, he came to Akron to become part owner of the Wolf Ledge Brewery. By 1877, the plant was known as Burkhardt & Co., although annual production had leveled off at just under 2,000 barrels during this period.

In June 1879, the wooden brewhouse was completely destroyed by a fire that had begun in a defective flue, with the loss valued at $4,000. After this, Gaessler left the partnership to operate a nearby saloon, selling his share of the remains to Burkhardt. By early the next year, a completely new and enlarged brick brewery had been built and was ready for operation, with an annual capacity of nearly 4,000 barrels.

Just two years later, however, Burkhardt died of blood poisoning at the age of 32. His wife, Margaretha, was faced with a critical decision: to sell the brewery and her source of income, or operate it herself while raising two young sons, William and Gustav. She chose the latter, and despite considerable adversity, she proved to be remarkably successful at running the company. After 1886, it was to be known as "Burkhardt's Brewery, Mrs. Margaretha Burkhardt, proprietor". Her pride, strong character, and a bit of stubbornness would guide the company through the next forty years. For example, when a tornado went through the area in 1890, causing $3,000 in damage to the brewery, she refused any charity herself and instead insisted on donating to the fund to pay for damaged homes.

(right) Wilhelm Burkhardt; (below left) Margaretha Burkhardt [both courtesy of Tom Burkhardt]; (below) Wolf Ledges Brewery, circa 1875; The two men in the foreground are thought to be Frederick Gaessler and Wilhelm Burkhardt, while the man sitting at the left is Jacob Fornecker, who made barrels for the brewery. He is sitting at a *schnitzelbank* (German for "carving bench"), a device used to make wood shavings for the brewing process [photo courtesy of Enlarging Arts].

Over the next few years, both of her sons began working in the brewery as well. Gus attended the American Brewing Academy in Chicago, and by 1899, he was both brewmaster and plant manager at the age of 25. William, who was three years younger, worked as the company's bill collector and office manager. After the turn of the century, a gradual expansion of the plant was undertaken, and to help finance this, the brewery incorporated as the M. Burkhardt Brewing Company in November 1902, with a capital stock of $50,000. Margaretha was president, with Gus as vice-president, and William as secretary, treasurer, and general manager. A new brewmaster was hired at this time (another recent German immigrant), by the name of Martin Fritch. Burkhardt's Select Export Lager Beer was the company's primary brand by this time, with small amounts of ale and bock beer produced as well.

A new six-story brick brewhouse was built in 1904, and a large icehouse was built around the same time. Over the next

Brewery employees outside the office building, circa 1905

Postcard view of brewery, circa 1910; aside from the bottling house added in the foreground in 1916, the plant remains largely unchanged today.

five years, virtually the entire plant was rebuilt and was operating with modern equipment, turning out as much as 40,000 barrels annually. During that time, a greater emphasis was placed on the bottling of beer for the rapidly growing market of direct home sales, partly as a way to distance the brewery from the undesirable image of the smoky saloons, especially as the temperance movement continued to gain strength in Ohio. The plant's bottling works was continually improved and enlarged, such that in 1908, over two million bottles of beer were sold.

Branching out from the brewing business, the family formed the Burkhardt Realty Company in 1907. This was a land development company which also oversaw the operation of the nearly 100 saloons in the city owned by the brewery. Two years later saw the incorporation of the City Ice & Coal Company, which was run by the Burkhardts but which operated out of a plant at 331 South Broadway. That same year, Margaretha retired from the presidency, although she remained a director until her death in 1925. Gus became the new president, with brother William as vice-president.

Expansion continued during this period, with the construction of a large three-story icehouse and stable building in 1912. Four years later, a large new bottling house was built on the north side of the plant, at a cost of $146,000. This was in response to the continuing growth of the home sale market, despite the growing threat of statewide Prohibition. Burkhardt's Standard Lager was now available in addition to Select Export, and a small amount of Burkhardt's Near Beer was brewed for counties that were already dry. The company's capital stock had increased to $100,000 by this time.

After statewide Prohibition was approved by voters in the election of November 1918, all alcohol production ceased. In May of the following year, the sale of remaining beer came to a halt as well, and marketing was shifted to Burkhardt's Select Beverage, along with Burkhardt's Ginger Ale, Root Beer, Parfay, and Orange Dee-Light. Several years later, the company was awarded the contracts to produce Hires Root Beer, Whiz Grape Drink, Whistle Orange Drink, Our Club Ginger Ale, and Old Tavern Brew Near Beer, and distribute White Rock Mineral Water from Wisconsin (ironically, the White Rock company had recently lost a suit against the former Akron Brewing Co. over the use of the name for its White Rock cereal beverage). During this time, the company was known as the Burkhardt Products Co., but in 1923 came the formation of the Burkhardt Consolidated Co., which, as the name suggests, was a consolidation of the realty company, beverage production in the brewery, and the management of the City Ice & Coal Co. Its diversity was reflected in a capital stock of $1,500,000.

Both Margaretha and William Burkhardt died in 1925, leaving Gus as president, with Jacob Gayer as vice-president. Production of Burkhardt Select Beverage (sales of which were never particularly profitable, especially competing with the more popular Grossvater and Zepp beverages sold by the Renner brewery in Akron) gradually dwindled over the next few years, and by 1930 it had come to a complete halt. The brewery itself was vacated and the offices briefly moved elsewhere. The plant was then occupied by the Akron Malt Products Co., a manufacturer of malt syrup, until the end of Prohibition.

Gustav "Gus" Burkhardt was president of the company when Prohibition ended

With the repeal of Prohibition in April 1933, the company returned to beer production, and therefore the Burkhardt Brewing Co. was incorporated as a division of the Burkhardt Consolidated Co., with capital stock of $500,000. The brewery had not been in use for several years, however, and most of the remaining equipment was outdated by now anyway, so the company was therefore unable to take advantage of the huge demand for 3.2% beer that month.

The plant was completely renovated over the next few months with the most modern equipment available. New glass lined storage tanks were installed in the cellars, automatically keeping the beer at the correct temperature; automatic conveyors helped to speed the movement of kegs, bottles, and other items throughout the plant; new packaging equipment allowed the entire process of sterilizing, pasteurizing, filling, and labeling the bottles to be done at one time. These operations were under the supervision of Brewmaster George Dippel, a recent graduate of the Wahl-Henius Institute in Chicago.

When the plant was ready for production of full strength (5.0% alcohol) beer and ale in November 1933, it had an annual capacity of 150,000 barrels, employed more than 100 men, and was the country's first completely air-conditioned brewery. When the beer first went on sale in January 1934, several new brands were available: Burkhardt's Select Beer was joined by Burkhardt's Special, XX Dark Special, Old German, and Old Scout Beers, as well as Burkhardt's Ale, which soon took on a more enduring name, Mug Ale.

The Burkhardt name retained a tremendous loyalty with Akronites, especially the thousands of workers in the city's numerous rubber factories, many of whom had enjoyed Burkhardt Beer before Prohibition. The company's success continued throughout the period leading up to World War II. Despite grain rationing during the war, Burkhardt continued to lead the city in production and sales of beer.

Gus Burkhardt died in 1944, and was replaced as president by his 30-year-old nephew William L. Burkhardt, who was on duty at the time in the Pacific War Theater as an ensign in the United States Naval Reserve. William had also received a Master Brewer degree after graduating from Notre Dame University, and had already served as the company's vice-president for several years.

(top right) Local delivery truck, circa 1915 [courtesy of Tom Burkhardt and Enlarging Arts]; by the late 1940s, local deliveries were giving way to fleets of tractor-trailer rigs (below, outside the bottling house) for regional delivery; **(left)** William L. Burkhardt.

By this time, the company was distributing its beer throughout northern Ohio as well as in Michigan, West Virginia, western Pennsylvania, and western New York, covering an area with a radius of 175 miles. Most of this was shipped by tractor-trailer rig, with each load consisting of nearly 700 cases. The company also established several distributorships through these territories, assuring strong sales in each area.

Burkhardt beers had only been available in kegs and bottles until 1948, when cap-sealed

(left) Cone-topped cans first appeared in 1949; by 1952 they had been replaced by the flat-topped cans seen at right, in a variety of brands and labels

cans produced by the Continental Can Co. were used for the first time, for the packaging of Burkhardt Special Beer (Mug Ale would also be canned beginning in 1952). While these cap-sealed cans were less expensive to fill, using existing bottling lines, they were not as easy to display as flat-topped cans, which were becoming increasingly popular. While the latter necessitated a separate canning line and equipment, the investment was felt to be worthwhile if it meant that the brewery's brands competed more successfully for limited display space in grocery or beverage stores.

In 1953, Burkhardt made the investment and switched to flat-topped cans. Two additional brands, Tudor Beer and Ale and Banner Beer and Ale, appeared in cans around this time. Produced briefly in Akron as the house brands for large grocery store chains, these were distributed through much of the Midwest and East Coast. Similar contracts with grocery store chains led to the production of the Best and Embassy Club brands of beer and ale, although these were sold only in bottles. All four of these brands were simultaneously brewed by several other regional breweries to allow distribution throughout all stores in the chain, over a large portion of the country, and assuring consistency of the brand name without incurring huge shipping costs.

In 1953, the company's vice-president position was filled by 24-year-old Gus Burkhardt, Jr., William's cousin. A recent graduate of Northwestern University, Gus was not a brewer by profession but was well-trained in business issues. The company's real estate branch continued to operate, although it had become less involved with owning bars and more involved with development of existing properties. It also branched out into the insurance business, purchasing a local existing insurance agency and renaming it as the Burkhardt Insurance Co. Each of these companies, the brewery, and the City Ice & Coal Co. continued to be managed by Burkhardt Consolidated.

Competition from larger regional and national breweries had gradually increased after the end of Prohibition. It accelerated rapidly after WWII, and had become a serious problem to the small and medium-sized brewers by the 1950s. As advertising became increasingly vital to a brewery's survival, Burkhardt hired the agency of Rollman & Peck, of Cincinnati. This led to an increase in point-of-sale advertising (signs, etc.) as well as increased use of radio and television. "Burkhardt's Custom Inn" appeared on Cleveland station WNBK, Channel 4, in 1954. Running nightly at 11:15, the program ran fifteen minutes and was set in a fictional tavern in which local entertainers would appear and talk or sing. Burkhardt also sponsored a weekly feature film at the station.

The brewery celebrated its 75th anniversary (of Burkhardt ownership) in 1955, with a special Diamond Jubilee Beer and a completely redesigned bottle and can label. Lasting for six months, the celebration was heavily advertised, and the public was invited to come to the brewery for tours. The "celebration" masked the reality of rapidly shrinking profits for the company.

By early 1956, competition in the brewing industry had continued to intensify, and the Burkhardt family recognized that despite their best efforts, brewing operations might soon become unprofitable altogether. The search began to find a buyer for the plant, and in June a deal was completed with the Burger Brewing Co. of Cincinnati. All of the Burkhardt stock and equipment was purchased by Burger for just over $2,000,000.

The Burger Brewing Company had incorporated in 1934, and it occupied the mammoth, ornate plant originally known as the Lion Brewery, and later the Windisch-Muhlhauser Brewing Co., on Cincinnati's north side. It was already one of Ohio's larger breweries, employing 475 people, and its brands were distributed throughout the Midwest. Burger had a goal of becoming a major regional brewer, and this was the first step in attempting to conquer the state of Ohio. With the addition of the Burkhardt plant, which had continued to modernize through the past twenty years and now boasted an annual capacity of 300,000 barrels, Burger was able to produce 1.5 million barrels annually. This would allow the company to compete with other regional giants such as Carling in Cleveland.

(left) Test can, circa 1960, that was made entirely of aluminum, but was never used in regular production

W. J. Huster was Burger's president, with J. F. Koons as vice-president, and Frank Sellinger as manager of the Akron plant and its 185 employees. George Dippel remained with the plant as the brewmaster. With this purchase, the production of Burkhardt's Beer came to an end. Mug Ale, which had established itself as an Akron area favorite, continued to be produced for another decade, along with Burger Beer and Ale, which were brewed by the same formula as in Cincinnati. Around 1960, the brewery briefly experimented with all-aluminum cans as a lighter and easier-opening alternative to steel, although these were never filled due to production problems. However, the steel cans had aluminum tops placed on them after this time, making them easier to open by puncturing. Although the self-opening tab top was invented in 1962, it never was used for any cans produced in the Akron brewery.

In 1960, A. J. Hausch was promoted to manager of the Akron plant. Business continued steadily until January 1964, when Burger decided to close the Akron brewery altogether. While the plant itself was running efficiently, the state's tax structure made it much more difficult to make a profit on any beer brewed in Ohio. This tax was just another nail in the coffin of Ohio's brewing industry, giving another advantage to out-of-state brewers and leaving only eight operating breweries in the state. Burger's dreams of becoming a regional power died when the company went bankrupt and closed in 1973, selling its holdings to the nearby Hudepohl Brewing Co. Hudepohl in turn sold out to the Schoenling Brewing Co., also in Cincinnati, in 1987. Hudepohl-Schoenling's brands were purchased in 1999 by Cleveland's Crooked River Brewing Co., and for three more years, Burger Beer continued to be sold in the Cincinnati area, although it was contract brewed by the City Brewery of LaCrosse, WI. Production of the brand became sporadic while Crooked River's parent company was undergoing a financial reorganization in 2004, and at this time, the brand's future remains uncertain.

With the closing of Burger's Akron plant, the rubber city's brewing industry ground to a halt for the first time in 119 years. The brewery complex remains entirely intact as of 2001, although the brewhouse and most attached buildings are badly dilapidated and treacherous to any who enter. The large bottling plant is owned by the Akron Public Schools for offices and storage space. The large stable and garage building was owned for a time by the Best Moving and Storage Co., and later housed a beverage distributor. The main office building is currently occupied by the Buckeye Metal Fabricating Co.

After brewing operations were sold, the Burkhardt family concentrated on realty and insurance, as well as the City Ice & Coal Co., although the latter closed in 1960. Gus Burkhardt was killed in a tragic automobile accident in 1957, at the age of 28. This left cousin William as the only family member in the company until he was joined by sons Thomas and William Jr. in the 1960s. After William Sr. died in 1972, his sons ran the Burkhardt Consolidated Co. themselves, concentrating primarily on real estate development (the insurance company was sold some years later). The family had owned a large tract of land west of the city for many years, where they operated a horse farm for delivery wagons. Having put the first water and sewer lines into the area, they would be instrumental in the development of this land into the commercial district known as Montrose. The site of their horse farm is now occupied by a Lowe's home improvement store. In 1991, Tom Burkhardt brought the family name back to the brewing business with the opening of a brewpub in Green, which is discussed later in this chapter.

7. Fred Horix brewery

Fred Horix was born in Darmstadt, Hesse, Germany on October 3, 1843, and after formal schooling was apprenticed to a maltster. He continued in the business of brewing until emigrating to America in 1868, most likely to avoid military service. A tall man (well over six feet in height), Horix would almost certainly have been drafted into Otto Von Bismarck's army during this turbulent period in Germany.

Horix initially worked in a Cleveland brewery, but soon came to Akron, where in 1870 he established his own brewery on the north side of East Exchange Street, between Fountain and Beaver Streets. The land was owned by John Kirn, who had recently become Horix's father-in-law, and who initially assisted Horix in the brewery, until selling the property to him in 1873. Annual production of ale and lager beer was up to 2,000 barrels by 1875, and it stayed at that level until 1879, when Horix purchased the larger, though vacated, Oberholtz Brewery on the north side of town (see George J. Renner Brewing Co.). He then transferred his operations there and vacated the smaller brewery on Exchange St. It was later razed, and no trace of it remains today.

8. The Akron Brewing Company

At the outset of the twentieth century, the predominant trend in the brewing industry was toward the formation of stock companies, many of which were operated by local saloon owners. The Akron Brewing Company began as one of these, when in October 1902, approximately fifty saloonkeepers from the Akron area banded together to create a new brewery in the city. Many of them had argued for years that the prices they had to pay for beer from the existing breweries were too high, which made it more difficult to realize a profit. Therefore, with the creation of their own company, they would have a guaranteed supply of beer at a reasonable cost. It was also assumed that many of the 250 saloons in Summit County would patronize this new establishment.

(above) Akron Brewing Company plant in 1914, from the book *Akron, City of Opportunity*; the artist exaggerated the stockhouse (to the right of the brewhouse tower), showing three peaks instead of two; (below) Serving tray, circa 1905.

The new company was incorporated in April 1903, with a capital stock of $200,000. The initial president was John Koerber, the owner of the Bank Café in downtown Akron, and who had previously been involved with the formation of other brewery stock companies elsewhere before coming to Akron. Vice-president was Fred Horix, who had previously operated a small brewery on East Exchange Street, as well as what was now known as the Renner brewery on North Forge Street. A native Prussian, he had more experience with the brewing of beer than anyone else in the group, and was currently the operator of a small delicatessen and saloon on South High Street.

The company's treasurer was John Lamparter, a local real estate dealer and owner of the Palace Drug Store. Secretary and general manager was F. Wm. Fuchs, the proprietor of the Buckeye Supply House, who had previously been an Akron agent for the L. Schlather brewery of Cleveland. Other initial directors included John Backe, Ed Kearn, Christian Koch, Jacob Gayer, Adolph Kull, George Good, William Evans, Frank Selzer, William Carter, Sam Woodring, Ed Curran, and brothers Jacob, John, and Louis Dettling, all of whom were local businessmen or saloon owners.

Construction of a new modern brewery building, costing $150,000, began in September. The site was at 841-869 South High St., at the corner of Voris St., although High St. was renamed South Broadway in later years. This new plant, made primarily of steel, was considered to be fireproof and it contained storage cellars that were made of enameled steel. Eliminating wood from the storage vats meant no need for frequent varnishing, and the beer would never taste like wood. The plant's five-story brewhouse initially had an annual capacity of 30,000 barrels, but it could be enlarged to 100,000 barrels if necessary.

The plant's brewmaster was John Hau, and his first brew took place on February 24, 1904. Three months later, White Rock Export Beer made its debut in the Akron market. In addition to sales in many local saloons, the beer was also bottled and marketed heavily for home consumption, the latter being an emerging trend in the industry at the time. A decade later, Wurzburger Beer would make its appearance as an alternative to White Rock.

In 1906, Koerber sold his share in the company and was subsequently replaced by John Backe, another saloon owner. Koerber then moved to Ionia, Michigan, where he purchased and rebuilt a small local brewery that had recently burned. The rebuilding was successful, but when the county voted itself dry by local option in 1909, the business collapsed, and Koerber was ruined. He died of kidney disease just two years later. His family remained in the business, however, later operating the Koerber Brewing Co. in Toledo and two breweries in Michigan after Prohibition ended.

By 1911, Louis Dettling had become president of the brewery. With his brothers Jacob and John, Dettling was the proprietor of The Rathskeller, a prominent restaurant and tavern in downtown Akron. When Louis died in 1917, he was replaced as president by his brother Jacob. Also joining the company during this period was new master brewer Ernst Hafenbrack. He was replaced shortly thereafter by Walter Gruner, who would eventually become the company's president in 1921 upon the death of Jacob Dettling.

In 1913 came the appearance of the Diamond Land and Improvement Co., a real estate development company owned by the brewery's stockholders. It began as a management office for the 82 saloons in Akron that were owned by the brewery, although other non-saloon properties were later acquired by the company.

Despite indications that Prohibition was inevitable, the company undertook a major expansion in late 1916, building a large new four-story brewhouse and expanding the cellars into the original brewhouse. This radically changed the appearance of the plant, as it lost a great deal of the original ornate architecture. Soon after this, the company's capital stock was increased to $400,000.

When statewide Prohibition took effect in May 1919, the company reincorporated as the Akron Beverage and Cold Storage Co., with capital stock of $500,000. This would continue to produce White Rock Cereal Beverage, with less than 0.5% alcohol by volume. In addition, there was another cereal beverage known as Tiro, named for the city's slogan as The Rubber Capital of the World. First appearing in the spring of 1918, it apparently met with disappointing sales, as it did not last for long. In

(above) Serving tray, circa 1906;
(right) Brewery complex as of 1995.

addition, the original bottling house was converted into the new White Rock Dairy, producing a wide range of dairy products. Walter Gruner remained president of the company until 1923, when he was replaced by Fred W. Fuchs, son of F. Wm. Fuchs, one of the company's original officers. Fred had begun working for the brewery in 1914 upon graduating from nearby Buchtel College, later known as the University of Akron.

A long-standing legal feud between the brewery and the White Rock Mineral Water Co. of Wisconsin erupted during this period. The brewery had previously won the right to use the White Rock name for its beer despite a claim of copyright infringement. However, with soft drinks now being produced, the mineral water company (which also produced its own line of soft drinks) returned to court again with a similar claim. In 1924, a federal judge ruled again in favor of the brewery, allowing them the use of the name.

Ironically, that use only continued for another few months, as the dairy business merged with the local People's Dairy Co. in late 1924. With this, the production of cereal beverages came to an end for good, and the entire dairy operation moved to a new plant on Bellows Street. It continues to operate today as the Borden Dairy Co. Fuchs remained with the dairy company for many years before leaving to join the Kramer Clothing Co.

The plant remained vacant for two years until a portion was purchased by the local Sumner Dairy Co., which continues to operate there to this day. The large brewhouse and cellars were utilized for many years by a cold storage company. Some of the smaller buildings on the south side of the plant were razed in the 1950s for construction of Interstate 76/77, which runs a few feet south of the main buildings. The main plant, however, remains a well-known landmark on the south side of Akron.

9. Akron Brewing Company

After the repeal of Prohibition in 1933, the city of Akron had two well-established breweries that resumed full production. The original Akron Brewing Company had completely dissolved, however, leaving a void in the local brewing industry which was soon to be filled by a new company.

Emmanuel Wiener had been in the wholesale produce business for over thirty years, originally with the Wiener Bros. Co., and more recently with his own E. H. Wiener Corporation. This was a successful business, but as an enterprising capitalist, he was looking for other ways to make money in the early days of the Great Depression. With the end of Prohibition becoming more and more likely, Wiener decided to go into the business of brewing beer, and on March 29, 1933, a charter was filed for the formation of The Akron Brewing Company. A new charter was filed in early 1934, however, renaming the firm as "Akron Brewing Company" (no "The"), to avoid confusion with the previous firm. Wiener was the company's initial president, with Walter S. Billman as vice-president, Harry Englehart as treasurer, and A. J. Hammerl as secretary. The company's initial capital was $350,000.

The Wiener Corp. had been operating out of a refitted factory building at 260 S. Forge Street. This had originally been built in the mid-1860s as part of John F. Seiberling's Excelsior Mower & Reaper Works, which was one of early Akron's largest employers. Excelsior (later called Empire) had disappeared by 1905, and the large complex then housed several different businesses before Wiener occupied it in the late 1920s. The three-story building was ideal for the development of a brewery—its solid construction would certainly be able to hold heavy vats and tanks. In addition, the plant was along the city's primary north-south railroad line, which facilitated the transport of products elsewhere. During late 1933 and into 1934, the empty factory space was transformed into the city's newest brewing establishment.

Charles A. Kraatz was chosen to be the company's brewmaster. The son of August Kraatz, one of the

Image from the 1870 lithographic map of Akron [taken from the Library of Congress web site]

(left) Convex lighted glass sign surrounded by neon ring, circa 1934; (below right) Metal sign, circa 1938.

earliest directors of the Belmont Brewing Co. in Martins Ferry, he had over thirty years of experience in the field, much of it with the Lorain Brewing Co. branch of the Cleveland & Sandusky combine before Prohibition. Kraatz would remain as the brewmaster throughout the new company's existence. By April 30, 1934, the first brew was ready for marketing as White Crown Lager Beer. White Crown Ale would follow in October, with both brews showing good sales.

Despite early success in this new field, Wiener soon encountered difficulties with organized labor. In addition, his company had built a three-story warehouse adjoining the brewery building in 1929, but by 1935, he was unable to make payments to the builder, the Carmichael Construction Company. As part of a settlement, the latter company thus took ownership of the brewery in mid-1935. The brewery's new officers were all from Carmichael: Cornelius Mulcahy as Chairman, John J. Mulcahy as President, and Harry Ulrich as Secretary. Harry Englehart remained as the vice-president and treasurer.

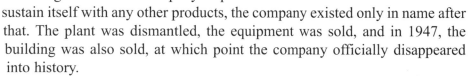

Throughout all of this turmoil, the brewery continued to function, doing a good business both with home sales and in local bars. The plant's annual capacity was 75,000 barrels, which made it the smallest brewery in the city, although it remained a profitable operation. The beer was packaged in bottles and kegs, and while White Crown Beer and Ale remained the flagship brands, Old German Lager also had appeared by 1936.

By 1940, F. Charles Bristol had been hired as the new general manager, and he was assisted by Tom LaRose, who was originally the local sales manager, and his brothers Joe and Peter. Business continued through the onset of World War II, when grain rations took effect, limiting production somewhat. In 1943, the Leisy Brewing Co. of Cleveland purchased the company's grain rations to increase its own production, and this brought the Akron company's operation to an immediate halt. Unable to sustain itself with any other products, the company existed only in name after that. The plant was dismantled, the equipment was sold, and in 1947, the building was also sold, at which point the company officially disappeared into history.

Englehart and Ulrich continued to work for the Carmichael Construction Co., while the LaRose Brothers built their family's beverage distributorship into what is now known as The House of LaRose, which remains one of the nation's largest distributors of Anheuser-Busch products. Joe LaRose continued to run the company into the new millenium.

The factory building and adjoining warehouse later held several other businesses before being purchased in the late 1970s by the University of Akron. The oldest factory section was razed in the early 1980s, while the warehouse was renovated into the Olsen Research Laboratory building, which is still standing. None of the area has even a slight resemblance to its industrial nature of the 1800s.

10. Liberty Street Brewing Company

Opening late in 1994, the Liberty Brewing Company was the first brewing operation within Akron's city limits in thirty years. Located at 1238 Weathervane Lane, in the Liberty Commons condominium & office park on the city's northwest side, it took the place of the defunct Carnaby Street restaurant, and quickly gained a reputation for its cuisine as well as for its beers. The brewpub began as a joint business venture by three Akronites, Rory O'Neil, Chuck Graybill, and David Russo, who came from diverse backgrounds to form the partnership. Russo, who had studied cooking in New Orleans at Emeril's, Commander's Palace, and K-Paul's (under Chef Paul Prudhomme), was the chef and designed the menu, which had a decidedly Cajun flair.

Tim Rastetter, originally from Cleveland's Great Lakes Brewing Co., was the original brewmaster, and he was placed in charge of building the 7-barrel brewhouse and installing the equipment, as well as establishing the original lineup of beers and ales. Two brews (14 barrels) were made at a time, with an annual output around 1000 barrels. No stranger to success, Rastetter's beers had already won several gold medals in national competitions, in a variety of categories, while he was with Great Lakes. Liberty's most popular brand from the beginning was Dragonslayer Scottish Export Ale, to go along with a standard lineup of American golden ale, English pale ale, American steam beer, porter, and imperial stout. Numerous variations followed, with colorful names such as Nutsy Fagin, Old Man Winter, Fat Cat, Zeppelin, Pride of Akron, Benedict Arnold, Inventure Ale, Cascade Locks Ale, and Mad Cow Stout. Many seasonal varieties appeared throughout the year as well. Several silver and gold medals were won by various brands in the brewery's first year at both the Great American Beer Festival and the Beverage Testing Institute's beer competition. Many more awards followed through the years.

The rights to the brewpub's name came into question in late 1995, when Fritz Maytag (of the washing machine family), who owns and operates San Francisco's popular Anchor Steam Brewery, claimed all rights to the name "Liberty" based on one of his brewery's brands. The Akron operation's name was voluntarily changed to "Liberty Street" at that time to avoid further conflict.

Rastetter left to work in a new microbrewery in Covington, KY. in 1996, and was succeeded by Joe Marunowski, formerly of Wallaby's brewpub in Westlake, OH. One year later, he was succeeded by Randy Mellon, who was later followed by Doug Beedy. Rastetter returned in 1999 as a consultant. With a largely young and professional clientele, the brewpub remained popular until the stock market slide in early 2001. "This economic downturn is definitely affecting us," said O'Neil in June of that year. "We've been struggling for a while and I don't see a bright light ahead." The pub closed on June 16th, idling its forty employees, and although a buyer was sought to maintain the restaurant as a brewpub, none was found and the brewhouse was dismantled. Beedy later became head brewer for Youngstown's B & O Station Brewery & Restaurant.

Barberton

1. Specht Brewery

Charles W. Specht and his wife, Christina, had emigrated from Germany in 1881, eventually settling in southwest Summit County. By 1894, Specht had begun operation of this small brewery on the south side of Hopocan Avenue, near Wolf Creek. This was in Norton Township, in an area that was later annexed into the city of Barberton. Less than 500 barrels of lager and weiss beer (of relatively low alcohol content) were produced annually, suggesting that this was just an expanded home brewing operation. However, there is evidence that the beer was sold commercially in Barberton.

Specht died in 1898, and brewing operations were taken over by Christina. She continued until approximately 1902, after which operations ceased. No trace of the brewery remains today.

Boston Township

1. Boston Mills Brewery

Little is known of this early pioneer brewery, which was likely the first one in Summit County. It was located approximately two miles west of the village of Boston Mills, along Brewery Road. The village was settled in the 1810s, and it appears that the brewery probably operated some time soon after that. A series of springs in the hills on the edge of the Cuyahoga River Valley provided pure water for brewing. This water runs downstream over Blue Hen Falls, which today is one of the most popular sites in the Cuyahoga Valley National Park. The stream continues downhill, travels through the Boston Mills ski resort, and eventually empties into the Cuyahoga River. It appears that brewing operations only lasted for a few years, and had likely ceased by 1830. The name Brewery Road lasted throughout much of the nineteenth century, however, before the road was renamed as Boston Mills Road. Nothing remains of this small pioneer brewery today.

Copley Township

1. Thirsty Dog Brewing Company

In the fall of 1998 came the expansion of the Thirsty Dog chain into Summit County. Occupying a building which formerly housed a Fuddruckers hamburger restaurant, the brewpub is located at 37 Montrose Avenue West, near the intersection of Intersection of Interstate 77 and state route 18, in the thriving commercial district known as Montrose.

Brewmaster and manager is Fred Karm, who had previously guided the Canton location since its inception. Beers produced in the 10-barrel J. V. Northwest brewhouse are the same as those originally brewed at the North Canton location, and include: Airship Light Ale, Man's Best Friend Draft Lager, Mixed Breed Black & Tan, Labrador Lager, Raspberry Ale, Irish Setter Red, Nut Brown Ale, Goldling's Retriever Pale Ale, Dog Drool Stout, Robinson's English India Pale Ale, Stud Service Stout, Hoppus Maximus Ale, Siberian Night Russian Imperial Stout, Twisted Kilt Scotch Ale, and Old Leghumper Porter. Several seasonal brews appear through the year as well, including Wheatweiler wheat beer, 'Bout Time Barley Wine, Karminator Dopplebock, Old Cerberus ale, California Crisp golden ale, Summer Wheat and Spiced Pumpkin Ales. At the World Beer Cup competition in 2000, the Raspberry Leghumper variety won a silver medal, while Old Leghumper took home a bronze. Raspberry Leghumper came back to win a gold medal, however, at the 2000 Great American Beer Festival. The following year, Hoppus Maximus won a silver medal at the GABF, and in 2002, a silver medal was taken by McDoogin's Irish Stout, while Old Leghumper won a gold medal at that year's World Beer Cup. At the 2003 GABF, California Crisp won a gold medal in the specialty beer category, while Hoppus Maximus and Siberian Night each won bronze medals.

By 2003, Thirsty Dog had entered into a contract with the Frederick Brewing Company of Frederick, MD. (owned by Crooked River of Cleveland) to bottle Hoppus Maximus (noting its GABF silver medal), Old Leghumper, Siberian Night, and Balto Heroic Golden Lager. These four brands began showing up in six-packs at selected area stores that spring. In February 2005, however, the Copley location closed its doors, leaving the company with only one brewpub in Centerville, OH., near Dayton.

Cuyahoga Falls

1. Cuyahoga Falls Brewery

Joseph Clarkson was a 32-year-old recent immigrant from England when he started this small brewing operation in 1856. It was located on the north side of Broad Street, at the intersection of Water Street and the Pennsylvania & Ohio Canal. This would be at the northwest corner of Broad and Main Streets today.

According to *One Hundred Years of Brewing*, "He first commenced brewing with a small iron kettle having a capacity not to exceed two barrels. Afterward he put in a copper kettle with a capacity of about five barrels. The output never exceeded twenty-five barrels per week. All operations were performed by hand, there being no machinery or power used. Both ale and lager were manufactured. Joseph Clarkson died June 22, 1873, and the business was then permanently discontinued." Nothing remains of the brewery today.

Green

1. Burkhardt's Brewpub/Brewing Company/Mugsy's Brewpub

The fourth and fifth generations of the Burkhardt family brought brewing back to the Akron area for the first time in 27 years. Tom Burkhardt, son of William, the last president of Akron's Burkhardt Brewing Co. in the 1950s, had worked for the family's real estate company for many years and had been brewing beer at home as a hobby for some time. In late 1990, he purchased the former Tavern On The Green restaurant at 3700 Massillon Road (state route 241), near the intersection of Interstate 77.

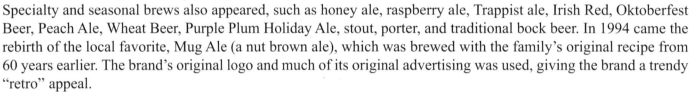

A 7-barrel brewing system, consisting of Grundy tanks from England, was constructed in an empty storeroom across the hall from the restaurant. Brewing operations were overseen by Tom Burkhardt, Jr., with the first brew being made in April 1991. Known initially as Burkhardt's Brewpub, the name had changed to the more traditional Burkhardt Brewing Co. by 1995. Water from several area wells was used for the brewing process. The quality of this water was similar to that found in Burton-On-Trent, England, one of the world's best known areas for the production of ale, and therefore Burkhardt chose to focus primarily on ale production at the brewpub.

Initially, the three primary brews produced were Northstar, a golden light ale, White Cliff, an English style pale ale, and Eclipse, a medium bodied dark Scottish ale. Specialty and seasonal brews also appeared, such as honey ale, raspberry ale, Trappist ale, Irish Red, Oktoberfest Beer, Peach Ale, Wheat Beer, Purple Plum Holiday Ale, stout, porter, and traditional bock beer. In 1994 came the rebirth of the local favorite, Mug Ale (a nut brown ale), which was brewed with the family's original recipe from 60 years earlier. The brand's original logo and much of its original advertising was used, giving the brand a trendy "retro" appeal.

Expansion of the brewhouse in 1996 allowed two brews to be made each week, with an annual output around 700 barrels. These were overseen by head brewer Chuck Dahlgren, who joined the company that year when Tom Burkhardt, Jr. left. Looking to expand production again, Burkhardt opened a second brewpub in Medina County in 1999. As his focus shifted more to brewing operations by 2000, the restaurant portion of the brewpub in Green was sold off and renamed as Mugsy's Brewpub (a reference to the bulldog that was used in advertising for Mug Ale in the 1940s). By the end of that year, however, brewing operations at the site had ceased for good, although Burkhardt's Medina operation would continue for one more year.

Hudson

1. The Four Fellows Pub & Eatery

Opening in January 1999, Hudson's first brewpub was constructed within the existing Hudson Crossings restaurant (formerly known as the Pub In Hudson), located at 5416 Darrow Road (state route 91). It was operated by Brad Unruh, a brewmaster who had previously been associated with both the Crooked River and Wallaby's Brewing Companies of Cleveland. Originally hailing from San Francisco, where America's brewpub trend began, Unruh began his brewing career in San Diego before moving to the Cleveland area. An avid home brewer for many years, Unruh came to the Akron area to manage and operate this new establishment.

Brewing was performed using a 10-barrel Century system with five fermenters and two keg lines, for a maximum of seven beers on tap at any given time. Five flagship brews made were Parmalee Pale Ale, Crossings Cream Ale, Norton Nut Brown Ale, Brandywine Lager (a light pilsner style beer), and Oviatt Porter, with other craft brews added on occasion. Being within a four-star restaurant gave a unique atmosphere to this small brewpub, but it did not necessarily spell success, as the pub and its brewing operation had closed by the end of 2000.

Northfield

1. Northfield Park Microbrewery

On June 6, 1998 came the newest addition to the world of harness racing: the grand opening of an onsite microbrewery. Located at 10705 Northfield Road (state route 8), directly on the line between Summit and Cuyahoga Counties, Northfield Park was built in 1957 on the site of an earlier greyhound track built in 1934 by mobster Al Capone. A $10,000,000 renovation in 1997 included the addition of the brewery and the hiring of David Gunn, formerly of Ogden, Utah, as the brewmaster.

Four standard beers are currently brewed in Gunn's 20-barrel brewhouse: Crimson Colt Ale (a rich red ale with a crisp and slightly bitter taste), Silks Cream Ale (a bright, mild golden ale), Winners Wheat (a lager beer with light body and fruity aroma), and 40-1 Stout (a dark beer with a rich and robust malt flavor). These are on tap in each of the on-site bars and concession stands, and a small amount is bottled for sale in the clubhouse dining room. Other brands, such as Loch Erie Scotch Ale, Peruvian Hanover German-style pale ale, Brew 102 dark beer, Juni Bock, Winter Moon Ale, White Winter Ale, Vienna Perle Ale, Tasmanian Lager, Mild Stallion Ale, Prestige Porter and New Albion Brown Ale, have been brewed on an occasional or seasonal basis.

Also Note:

1. After the repeal of Prohibition in April 1933, the O'Neill Brewing Company was quickly incorporated in Barberton. With $12,500 of capital stock, this was to be a division of the Tawney Dairy Products Co., located at 529 Brady Avenue, whose president was Joseph O'Neill. Already a distributor of beer, his intention was to build a new brewing facility either in Barberton or Akron. Presumably due to economic difficulties in the Great Depression, these plans never came to fruition. The new corporation, whose other directors were Lewis A. Seikel and George Hargreaves, was dissolved in 1934.

2. The White Rock Brewing Company was formed in April 1933 by Walter Gruner, who had previously been master brewer and president of the pre-Prohibition Akron Brewing Company. After leaving that company, he had formed the Akron Malt Products Co., operating out of the unused Burkhardt brewery on Grant Street. His plan was to build an entirely new brewing operation with an annual capacity of 30,000 barrels. Like many similar plans, however, this one never came to pass.

3. Akron had several beer bottlers prior to 1890, the most prominent of which were Philip and Charles Austgen, who were the local agents for the huge Hoster Brewing Co. in Columbus. The Schlather brewery of Cleveland also had a branch in Akron, operated by F. Wm. Fuchs, who later was involved with The Akron Brewing Company. None of these bottlers brewed beer on-site.

4. In late 2003 came the announcement that brewing might return to the Rubber City after a nearly three-year absence (and to *downtown* Akron, after a forty-year absence). Brothers Michael and Chris Verich, who had operated their Ohio Brewing Company in Niles from 1997 to 2001, and in Youngstown in 2002, signed a letter of understanding to buy 12,000 square feet of space in the former O'Neil's department store at 222 South Main Street. Built in the late 1920s, the O'Neil's building was a major landmark in the city, even after the store closed in the 1980s. Its later renovation coincided with the construction across the street of Canal Park, the stadium for the Akron Aeros minor league baseball team, which brought several thousand fans downtown on many nights each summer. Initial plans were to spend approximately $850,000 for the space, equipment (a Bohemian brewing system from the Czech republic), and furnishing the restaurant. While plans called for the brewpub (along with a specialty coffee shop and a banquet area) to open in time for the Aeros' season opener in April 2004, there was still no visible activity at the site as of one year later.

Trumbull County

Niles

1. The Ohio Brewing Company

Located in a refurbished Shoney's restaurant at 5790 Youngstown-Warren Road (U. S. Route 422), the Ohio Brewing Co. began operations as a brewpub/restaurant in May 1997. Owned by brothers Michael and Chris Verich, the facility's brewing operation was overseen by Chris and head brewer Mark Kuss, and among the brews produced in the 10-barrel system were: Steel Valley Stout (a full-bodied dry Irish stout), Fest Ale (a malty, full-bodied amber ale), Verich Ale (a light Kolsch-style ale), lightly hopped Cardinal Ale, medium bodied English style Buckeye Brown Ale, Alt-Ernative Amber Ale, Cherry Wheat Ale, Presidential Pale Ale, Maple Porter, Mai Bock, and Pumpkin Spice Ale in the Fall. In 1999, Niles was awarded a Class A minor league baseball team, the Mahoning Valley Scrappers, and Scrappers Ale (an Irish Red Ale) was produced to sell at the new stadium near the brewery.

Within the first year of operation, Verich won three awards at the World Beer Championship in Chicago, taking a gold medal for Cardinal Ale, and silver medals for his Ohio Fest and Stout. Various brews, especially Verich Ale, were being kegged and distributed to bars and restaurants throughout Northeast Ohio and into western Pennsylvania.

Michael Verich, a Warren attorney, had been an elected state representative for sixteen years, when in 1998 he was appointed to a permanent state government position. His position in the Ohio state legislature was filled for the next two years by brother Chris. By early 1999, the restaurant had closed, as Verich chose to devote more time to his political position; it was later replaced by a Max & Erma's franchise. Brewing operations, however, continued in a microbrewery format at the same location, and a small bottling operation was later added for distribution of bottled beer in regional stores. In early 2002, the operation in Niles was closed and moved to downtown Youngstown (see Mahoning County).

Warren

1. Augustus Graeter/Jacob Waldeck brewery

Augustus Graeter was a German immigrant, born in 1803, who came to Warren in 1836, working initially as a dealer in dry goods. Around 1838 he established the city's first brewery just east of the intersection of South and Chestnut Streets, on Warren's east side. It was situated along Red Run, a small creek which ran just east of the brewery, but which has since been covered over. This creek was the original source of brewing water.

Graeter operated the brewery along with a farm he owned west of Warren for nearly twenty years. By the

Image of brewery from the 1870 lithographic map of Warren (taken from the Library of Congress web site).

time his son Herman came of age in the late 1850s, Graeter decided to concentrate on farming, and he transferred brewing operations to Herman, assisted by Robert Kraetenbrick, a teenage brewer's apprentice. The elder Graeter died in 1863, and his widow Sarah sold the brewery in September 1867 for $5,000 to Jacob Waldeck and William Mack. One year later, Mack sold his share to Waldeck and left the area.

Jacob Waldeck was a recent immigrant from Hesse-Darmstadt, Germany, born in 1835. Upon purchasing the brewery, he established an adjacent saloon as well. By this time, the brewery was of average size, producing between 1,000 and 2,000 barrels of ale and lager beer annually. Brewing operations appear to have ceased around 1877, although Waldeck continued to operate the small plant as a bottling works for several years. It was later razed, leaving no trace today.

2. George Clements Brewery

George Clements was a native of Wurtemburg, Germany, born in 1801, who came to Warren in 1857. Soon after this he established the city's second brewery, located on the east side of Pine Street, near the intersection of Canal Street, and along the north bank of the Pennsylvania & Ohio Canal. While retaining ownership of the small plant, he rented it to Daniel Bishop and Kasper Balser, two recent German immigrants, for a brief time in the mid-1860s. In 1865, however, Balser left the area and moved to Canton, where he purchased the old City Brewery with his wife Louisa.

Clements was brewing just under 2,000 barrels of lager beer annually through the mid-1870s, by which time brewing operations had been taken over by his son, George, Jr., who had been born in 1837. Production dropped to around 700 barrels by the end of the decade, and early in 1880 Clements had become insolvent due to rising debt. The brewery was subsequently sold for $1,334 (2/3 of its appraised value) at a sheriff's auction in May of that year. Brewing operations appear to have ceased at that time. The elder Clements died just one year later, although his son remained in the area until his death in 1902.

Image of brewery from the 1870 lithographic map of Warren, showing the Pennsylvania and Ohio Canal to the right (taken from the Library of Congress web site).

Also Note:

After the repeal of Prohibition in 1933, a group of Warren businessmen formed a new corporation known as the Western Reserve Brewing Co., with an intention to erect a new facility for the brewing of beer in the city. Peter J. Corll was the group's initial president, although he was succeeded after a few months by Harry S. Braman. Vice-president was C. H. Heist, with J. K. Anderson as secretary, and William Raub as the master brewer. However, as with many similar fledgling companies of the era, no beer was ever brewed, most likely due to an inability to raise sufficient capital in difficult economic times.

Tuscarawas County

Canal Dover (aka Dover)

1. Dover Steam Brewery

This small brewing operation along the north bank of the Ohio & Erie Canal was likely the first commercial brewery in the county. Frederick Crater purchased the site in 1848, and began brewing operations soon after that. Crater had been born in 1814 on a sailing ship, as his parents were making the Atlantic crossing from Germany to begin a new life in America.

Crater continued operations until selling the plant to George Diehl and Basil Downey in March 1862. The plant was again sold in May 1869, to Jacob Zahler, Louis Geib, and Philip Miller. It is uncertain, however, whether the brewery was in continuous operation through this entire period. By 1870, the company was known as Miller & Co., operating both the Dover Steam Brewery and the nearby malting house. Here, barley was malted for local brewers as well as ones as far away as Cleveland. The brewery was producing pale, amber, spring, and stock ales, and apparently did not brew lager beer at any time.

The malting business appears to have been more profitable for Miller, as brewing operations had ceased by 1873. Miller was joined in 1876 by Jacob Horn, a young man who would later become a prominent citizen, and be a major investor in the ill-fated Tuscarawas Valley Brewing Co. Within several years, however, the malting business had closed and the plant was abandoned.

The small brewery was gone by the turn of the century, although one building from the complex, at the foot of Crater Ave., survives to this day. It appears to have been part of the malting house, although its basement housed a beer cellar, which has the characteristic stone and arched ceiling construction. It is on a residential lot and is used for storage.

2. Bernhardt/Dover/Stark-Tuscarawas Breweries Company

Dover's longest-lasting brewery began as a very small operation on a two-acre site, at 222-230 E. Front Street, which was within several hundred feet of both the Ohio & Erie Canal and the Tuscarawas River. It also was less than one half-mile west of the Dover Steam Brewery. The exact date of origin of this plant remains uncertain. Nicholas Montag purchased land at the site in late 1856, and started brewing operations some time later with his brother, Valentine. Montag had been born in October 1826 in the small town of Bibles in Germany. He came to the United States in 1845, and to Canal Dover soon after that. Initial production was only 50 barrels of lager beer per year, with water for brewing supplied by Artesian wells dug at the site.

Andy Dangleisen appears to have been the next owner of the brewery, purchasing the property in 1865. In September 1870, however, he was unable to make a mortgage payment to Montag, and ownership returned to the latter at a sheriff's sale. Dangleisen later moved to Massillon to operate a saloon and restaurant. The plant sat vacant until December 1872, when Frederick Bernhardt purchased the plant for $2,700.

Bernhardt (also spelled Bernhard and Barnhardt) was a recent immigrant, born at Bisterschied, Germany in 1845. He had come to America in 1866 and had worked in a number of different breweries, including Michael Berger's in nearby New Philadelphia, before coming to Canal Dover. When he restarted brewing operations in 1873, the brewery was still very small, with a capacity of under 500 barrels per year. That number had increased to nearly 1,000, however, by 1878, and the plant continued to grow over the next twenty years.

Bottle label, circa 1905

Around 1890, much of the plant was rebuilt to increase the capacity significantly. A new, four-story brewhouse was built along with a bottling works, malt house, and an ice plant capable of producing twenty tons of ice per day. By this time, the water for brewing was being piped in from the city water works. By 1894, the plant was producing nearly 7,000 barrels per year, and within ten years, the annual capacity had grown to 10,000 barrels of "Dover Beer". In 1896, the plant was renamed The Dover Brewing Co., although it was sometimes referred to as the Lion brewery. Bernhardt retired from active brewing in 1899, turning operations over to his son, Christian. The latter had been born in 1873, and had been brewmaster of the plant since 1893, when he graduated from the Wahl & Henius College in Chicago. Another son, Fred, Jr., born in 1869, had also been involved with the plant's business operations since 1893.

After the turn of the century, as consolidation had become a growing trend in the brewing industry, the Stark-Tuscarawas Breweries Co. was created on March 21, 1905. The Dover Brewing Co. joined ranks with the New Philadelphia Brewing Co., Schuster Brewing Co. in Massillon, and the Canton and Stark Brewing Companies in Canton. The new company had a capital stock of $3,000,000, and it spent $90,000 to purchase the Dover brewery. This was less than one-eighth of the cost of the larger Canton brewery, as the Dover plant was the smallest in the group. At that time, the management of the plant was taken over by A. J. Snavely, although Fred Bernhardt, Sr., continued to be business manager, as well as a director of the Stark-Tuscarawas Co.

The primary brands produced after the merger were Canton Export and Stark Velvet Beers, both originally from Canton. Their production would not last long at the plant after the merger, however. The Rose local option law of 1908 allowed Tuscarawas County to vote itself dry beginning the next year, and foreseeing this, the Stark-Tuscarawas Co. suspended brewing operations at the plant in mid-1908. Snavely then became a local bottler and distributor for Budweiser Beer.

The plant continued to produce ice, however, and had been renamed by 1918 as the City Ice and Coal Co., operated by Henry Seibold (of the New Philadelphia brewery) and Henry Patterson. This continued until 1933, when the Seibold family got out of the industry entirely.

Fred Bernhardt continued to live in Dover until his death at age 76, in 1921. His sons, Christian and Fred, Jr. eventually moved to Idaho to seek their fortunes. Nicholas Montag, the brewery's original owner, later was both county treasurer and a Justice of the Peace at different times. He died in 1901.

This drawing is from local advertising in the 1890s and uses a fair amount of artistic license; for example, the bottling house shown at left never existed. The Tuscarawas River and the Ohio and Erie Canal are seen in the background. No photographs of the brewery at the time of operation are known to exist.

The brewery stood empty for one year before it was occupied by the Dover Auto Wrecking Co., and later by an auto body shop. At some point, the building suffered the same fate as the Tuscarawas Valley brewery down the river, as the top two floors were removed from the brewhouse. Much of the plant remains standing today and has been converted into a residence.

3. The Tuscarawas Valley Brewing Company

A group of local businessman from the Canal Dover area formed a stock company in 1903, to be known as the Tuscarawas Valley Brewing Co., for the creation of a new state-of-the-art brewing facility. The plant was to be located along the Tuscarawas River at 115 W. Broadway, on the south side of the town. It also was built along a main line of the C. & P. Railroad, giving it excellent access for distribution of products. The company's initial capital stock was $200,000.

The brewery itself cost $135,000 to build, and consisted of a six-story brewhouse, bottling house, and fully modern ice plant, the latter having a capacity of 50 tons of ice per day. The plant was entirely fireproof, its construction using only steel, stone, concrete, and brick, and no lumber. Construction began soon after incorporation, and the first brew was made on October 14, 1906, with the first product being sold on February 7, 1907. The plant had an annual capacity of 50,000 barrels, making it much larger than the nearby New Philadelphia Brewing Co. However, once in business, actual production never even approached that number. The company's brews were sold throughout Tuscarawas County and the surrounding rural areas.

The company's president was William Martin, who had been born in Ireland in 1865. He left for America on Christmas Day, 1882, coming to Ohio soon after. He spent time in Canal Dover, then Homestead, PA., where he worked in the steel industry. He became a liquor dealer in 1899, and soon after that he returned to Canal Dover to found the brewery.

Vice-president was Jacob Horn, a prominent local hotel and restaurant owner. He had been born in Canal Dover in 1849, and had previously been involved in the local brewing & malting business with Philip Miller. John Stahl was the company's treasurer; he was also president of the Homestead, PA. National Bank, and was a trustee of the Independent Brewing Co. of Pittsburgh. (The latter would become the Duquesne Brewing Co. after Prohibition.) John D. Bold was secretary, and was also a prominent attorney and former mayor of Canal Dover. The plant's general manager was Walter H. Scheu. Also on the board of directors were George E. Fertig and Dr. F. H. Waldron, a local dentist.

Less than two years after brewing operations began, Tuscarawas County voted itself dry in accordance with the Rose Law. This law took effect on January 1, 1909, but the brewery found itself testing the law within the first week by avoiding the recently outlawed saloons and selling beer directly to consumers. However, the company was indicted and fined for this and no further sales were made in Tuscarawas County. With no local saloon trade, and relying only on sales to other areas, the company was unable to make a profit, and had gone bankrupt by late 1911. The Colonial Trust Co. of Pittsburg(h), which held the mortgage, foreclosed at that time. The plant, which was valued at $98,000, was put up for sale, and after five attempts, it was finally sold at a sheriff's auction for $35,000. Representing the bank as purchasers were David Newell of Greensburg, PA. and William Heath of Buffalo.

Several months later, the brewery was purchased again by William Martin and his wife Nina for $75,000. By then, Tuscarawas County had voted itself wet again, and there was room for a second brewery in the county. Martin organized a new company, with new investors and a capital stock of $100,000, to run the plant in early 1912, first as The Martin Brewery, and several months later renamed as the Consumers Brewing & Ice Co. However, by 1914, brewing operations were no longer profitable and were shut down. The brewery's history had been brief but disastrous for its investors, including Jacob Horn, who went bankrupt and died in 1916.

The remaining operation then became the Dover Ice & Cold Storage Co., and later the Dover Ice & Coal Co., owned by Edward Horn, Jacob's son. In 1933, Jack Harris of Cleveland came to Tuscarawas County, looking to enter the brewing business. He nearly purchased the old Tuscarawas Valley brewery, but eventually decided to go further south into New Philadelphia. No other attempt was made to restart brewing operations at the plant after Prohibition.

Tuscarawas Valley Brewing Company, circa 1906 [courtesy of the Tuscarawas County Historical Society]

Soon after World War II, ice production came to an abrupt end when the plant's smokestack came crashing down on the ammonia tanks during a storm. After that, the top four floors of the plant, which were in bad disrepair, were removed. They had been largely unusable for some time; when the large brew kettles had been removed, large holes had been cut in most of the building's floors. Some of the upper walls were dynamited away, leaving a nondescript yellow brick building which remains to this day.

Since ice production ceased, the building has been occupied by the Wills Machine Shop, owned by Bud Wills, Jacob Horn's great-grandson. He states that the only remaining relic of the brewing era is in a small building on the property, built in 1920. Its wooden floor is made of oak from the brewery's vats.

New Philadelphia (aka Blackfield, Lockport)

1. The New Philadelphia Brewing Company

New Philadelphia's only brewery had a relatively long lifespan as compared to other breweries in the region, its origins having been in 1864. In that year, Michael Berger, a German immigrant, founded the small brewery along the banks of the Ohio & Erie Canal, at 430 South Broadway. At various times, the area where the brewery was located was known as Blake's Mills, Blakesfield, Blackfield, and Lockport (a reference to the canal), although it officially became part of the town of New Philadelphia around the turn of the century. This area was somewhat south of the town, but at that time, the canal was the primary route of transportation in the region, and the brewery's products could easily be transported along the canal in either direction. Local residents often referred to the plant as the "South Side Brewery", even into the 1940s. The brewery's original water source was a pair of on-site artesian wells.

The plant had an annual capacity of 100 barrels when it was first built, and it grew very slightly over the next ten years. Berger died in 1871, and the plant was then sold at a public auction the following May to Rudolph Kapizky for $3,510. He enlarged the plant slightly, such that its production was around 500 barrels of lager annually by 1875. On May 1, 1876, however, the brewery was purchased by Michael Seibold and Adolph Hafenbrak, for $5,000. The deed of property transfer included mentions of the property, buildings, and equipment, as well as two thirteen-year-old bay horses named Jim and Sam, six chickens, one rooster, and two ducks.

Seibold was a German immigrant, born in Wurtemberg, Germany, in May 1849. He had come to the United States at the age of eighteen and initially worked at a brewery in Cincinnati. Nine years and five different cities later, he found himself in Cleveland, where he saw an advertisement for this small brewery in the *Beobachter* newspaper. At that time, he moved south to New Philadelphia with his wife Anna and their five children. Hafenbrak was born in Ludwigsburg, Germany in 1846, and came to America in 1871.

Over the next eight years, Seibold and Hafenbrak rebuilt and enlarged the brewery significantly, extending sales in town and along the canal. Their first expansion was the construction of a malthouse in 1876, followed

Michael Seibold (left) and son Henry (below left)
[courtesy of the Tuscarawas County Historical Society]

by a bottling works in 1880. By then, annual production was between 1,500 and 2,000 barrels. Hafenbrak retired from the partnership in 1884, at which time Seibold renamed the company as The New Philadelphia Brewing Co., a name which it would retain for the next twenty years. Hafenbrak remained in the area until his death in 1901, due to "stomach trouble". Seibold's brother Anton came from Germany in 1882 and assisted at the brewery as well, until his death in 1903.

Michael would continue to travel throughout his life, returning to Germany several times, as well as going into the western United States. He was financially involved with a rubber plantation in Mexico, a mining company in Montana, and was the president of The Great Republic Gold and Copper Co. in Arizona. At home, he was the president of both the Peoples Bank & Savings Co. and the Valley Transit, Light, & Power Co.; he was one of the founders of the Tuscarawas County Telephone Co., and was a director of the Tuscarawas Valley Finance Co. He also was on the school board and was a city councilman.

In 1884, a new two-story brewhouse was built. It would remain a prominent portion of the plant throughout its remaining 65 years of business. Production continued to increase as the plant was further enlarged over the next decade, and by 1894, over 8,000 barrels were being produced annually. Three types of beer were produced: Lager, Export, and Bohemian. In 1903, a new four-story addition was built behind the original brewhouse. This was for fermentation and cooling tanks, and enabled the plant's capacity to increase to 11,000 barrels per year. At the same time, the company was incorporated with a capital stock of $100,000. The incorporators were Seibold, John C. Kelly, F. G. Kuenzil, John Russer, John Benson, and A. W. Reiser.

By 1905, the business of selling beer had begun to change, and many breweries in the country were beginning to consolidate to expand their markets and limit the remaining competition. On March 21st of that year, the New Philadelphia Brewing Co. became part of that trend when it joined into a partnership with the Schuster Brewing Co. in Massillon, the Canton Brewing Co. and Stark Brewing Co. of Canton, and the Dover Brewing Co. in nearby Canal Dover. The new combine was known as the Stark-Tuscarawas Breweries Co., with capital stock of $3,000,000. The company paid $180,000 for the New Philadelphia plant, which would operate within the combine for the next twenty-two years.

During this time, Seibold's son Henry became the plant's manager. Henry had been born in 1876, and after graduating from the Wahl &

Brewery scene from across the canal in the 1890s. Michael Seibold is wearing a suit and tie.
(courtesy of the Tuscarawas County Historical Society)

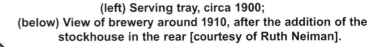

(left) Serving tray, circa 1900; (below) View of brewery around 1910, after the addition of the stockhouse in the rear [courtesy of Ruth Neiman].

Henius College in Chicago in 1896, he became the brewmaster. Another son, John (also spelled Jno) began to work in the brewery office. Born in 1879, he was primarily involved with the business side of the brewery, as well as managing the bottling department. Michael had largely retired from the actual business of brewing, although he remained an officer of the Stark-Tuscarawas Co. throughout its existence.

New refrigeration equipment costing $25,000 was installed in 1908, and business at the plant continued at roughly the same level during the era. The temperance forces were gaining strength during this time, however, and the first blow was the passage of the Aiken Bill in 1907, which raised saloon license fees to $1000 per year, an amount that many small tavern owners could not afford. The next year, the Rose Law was passed. Following this, Tuscarawas County voted itself dry beginning on January 1, 1909, leading to the closing of the approximately 100 saloons in the county. The Stark-Tuscarawas Co., which had recently suspended brewing operations at the nearby Dover plant, subsequently suspended operations at the New Philadelphia plant until 1912, when the county voted itself wet again.

With several renovations, the brewery restarted production that summer. Production was temporarily halted again in March 1913 after torrential rains caused a tremendous flood which hit much of Ohio. The land around the brewery was flooded, as it lay between the canal and the Tuscarawas River, but the brewery escaped without any damage, and it continued to operate after the floodwaters receded. However, damage done to the canal during this flood effectively ended the canal era in Ohio.

After Ohio voted itself dry in November 1918, beer production at the plant came to a halt on December 1st. The 5,000 barrels of unfinished beer which were in the process of brewing and aging were allowed to be completed, although the remaining grains which had not yet been used represented a loss of $20,000 to the company. The beer on hand was sold off until May 26, 1919, when statewide Prohibition actually took effect, causing the cessation of all alcohol sales.

The plant's twenty employees were not yet out of work, however, as the combine was reorganized as the Stark-Tuscarawas Products Co. Its primary products at that time were Tuscora Near Beer, Whistle, Cherry Blossom, and other soft drinks. The market for cereal beverages in Tucarawas County was just as weak as it was elsewhere in the state, however, and by 1927, the company had dissolved. Three of the other four plants in the group had closed, but the New Philadelphia branch continued production as the Seibold Products Co., still being run by Michael, Henry and John Seibold. With the renumbering of street addresses in the city around this time, the plant's address had become 640-646 South Broadway.

The Seibold Products Co. continued to function as before, as bottlers and distributors of soft drinks, as well as distributors of both Tuscora and Blatz near beers (the latter being produced in Milwaukee). Soon after this came the introduction of its own brand of liquid malt syrup, known as "Seipro", which retained a small but loyal following on the south side. The company sponsored a local basketball team, and also held a series of boxing matches in 1931, one of which featured a young athlete named Woody Hayes, from nearby Newcomerstown. Hayes would later go on to much greater things with The Ohio State University football team. Production of Seipro continued through the end of Prohibition in 1933.

After the repeal of Prohibition, beer production started up within the next few months. However, the Seibold family was not involved this time around. Michael was now eighty-four years old and retired from active business. He died at home in January 1934, of old age. Henry later became president of both the local Peoples Bank & Savings Co., as well as the Buckeye Machine & Supply Co., and was a director of several other local firms. He was also a well-known beagle dog owner, breeder, and trainer for many years. He died at the family home in 1955. John became an officer with the Tuscarawas Valley Finance Co., and died in 1951.

In May 1933, the brewery was purchased by Jack H. Harris, a businessman from Cleveland who already had an interest in the Forest City Brewery there. He had also previously run a printing business and had been Cuyahoga County commissioner for several years. He and his partner, Carl F. Lang, formed a new company known as The New Philadelphia Brewery, Inc., with James W. Bevyl as the initial manager and superintendent. Other officers during the next seven years included Odon Guttman, who later became the general manager, and James F. Carl, who later became superintendent.

When the old plant was purchased from the Seibolds, approximately $25,000 was invested in upgrading the brewing equipment, and nearly $150,000 was spent on the plant as a whole (modernizing the bottling house, purchasing new delivery vans, etc.). In the process, the capacity was increased to 60,000 barrels per year (this number would increase to 75,000 barrels after World War II). Thirteen trucks and four salesmen now allowed the plant's beers to be distributed throughout most parts of the state.

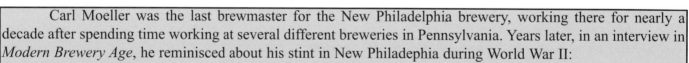

Limiting the plant's success, however, was its relatively small number of distribution agents in the region, making it more difficult to compete with the larger regional breweries. Prior to Prohibition, this was not a major issue, since a brewery could survive just on local sales. However, the competition intensified rapidly in the 1930s, as advances in refrigeration and distribution techniques and mechanization of the brewing process had allowed other regional brewers to have a strong national presence.

Another large difference for the brewery in the post-Prohibition era was a large number of new beer brands. The most widely advertised new brew was Old

---

Carl Moeller was the last brewmaster for the New Philadelphia brewery, working there for nearly a decade after spending time working at several different breweries in Pennsylvania. Years later, in an interview in *Modern Brewery Age*, he reminisced about his stint in New Philadephia during World War II:

"The brewhouse equipment, undersized, obsolete and worn out, was designed for a normal annual output of 40,000 barrels. Wartime restrictions and priorities made it almost impossible to get new equipment, replacement parts, or even enough metal to accomplish makeshift repairs. Our president, Mr. J. H. Harris, told me one day that we just have to get more production. So I went to work. It was practically a hand-made job in rehabilitating all the equipment and working it around the clock. I practically lived in the brewery during those days to keep the equipment producing. It was a tremendous experience. How we did it I'll never know, but we did produce 78,000 barrels of bottled goods that year without losing anything from the high quality of our product."

There was in those years a serious shortage of bottle caps. Harris and Moeller designed and built a complete set of machinery to reprocess used bottle crowns, sterilizing, restamping, and coating them. New caps were also stamped from scrap metal such as lard cans, and surplus caps were sold to other breweries.

After the New Philadephia brewery closed, Moeller moved to Cleveland where he served as the brewmaster for the Standard Brewing Co. for more than a decade.

Lockport Lager Beer. Other brands to begin production during this time included Scotch Highland Ale, Old Bohemia Lager and Pilsner, "World's Best" Beer, Royal Canadian Style Beer, Schoenbrunn Pale and Muenchner Style Beers, Red Label Beer, Old German or "O G" Beer, John Bull Beer, Olde Vat Beer, Black Jack Lager, Cafe Society Beer and Ale, and Lord Derby Beer and Ale. A completely modernized bottling department allowed the brewery to fill up to 58,000 packages of beer each day.

It was only in the post-Prohibition era that the brewery's advertising capitalized on the region's Schoenbrunn spring water, which supposedly provided the water source for brewing. "Schoenbrunn" was a term used by the earliest settlers in the area (in the mid-1700s), most of whom were Moravian, and it meant "beautiful spring". Due to the impurity of many wells in the region, the success of any settlement depended on finding a source of pure water, and in this particular area, the water was relatively consumable.

BEER SHAMPOO

As the brewing industry became increasingly competitive after World War II, many smaller brewers found themselves unable to continue operating at a profit. In New Philadelphia in the late 1940s, owner Max Swartz found himself in this position as well, and began looking for alternative uses for his brewery. By April 1949, he had found the answer: Beer Shampoo.

Developed and patented by Swartz and Chicago businessman and engineer Frank A. Weaner, the shampoo was "brewed" with the existing equipment. As Swartz explained, "Beer Shampoo is a three-in-one product which cleans, rinses, and sets the hair in one operation. It contains less than one per cent of alcohol, is completely odorless when dry, and leaves no trace of beer smell. No soap is used in the formula, but the shampoo contains a detergent which has been scientifically blended with the brewed beer. It not only cleans the hair thoroughly but it rinses it as well and gives it a high sheen. It is non-alkaline and non-acid and therefore is not irritating to the most sensitive scalp."

The shampoo was sold in department stores, drug stores, beauty salons, and barber shops. It was packaged in seven-ounce beer bottles which sold for 89 cents. Its "world premier", at the Lazarus Department Store in Columbus that April, was described by local newspapers as being met with "phenomenal success". A nationwide advertising campaign followed, and the brewery's bottling house found itself running around the clock that summer to keep up with the demand.

Columbus *Citizen* columnist Ben Hayes interviewed Swartz at the time in a column entitled "Here's Suds In Your Ear": "There was the day when they put the head on the beer; now they are going to put the beer on the head...It will make you pretty as pilsener...If you are in the habit of drinking shampoo, you can drink Beer Shampoo. It will do nothing but put a gentle wave in your ulcers...It's all in one bottle; no chaser—I mean, no rinse is needed."

With the new product's popularity, the New Philadephia brewery suddenly was busier than it had been in years. The company's four remaining brands of real beer were phased out by early summer, as Beer Shampoo was outselling all of them. The outdated plant, however, was unable to keep up with the demand, and Swartz closed it for good that November. After this, production continued in Columbus (Swartz's home town) and Chicago.

Max Swartz looking at his aging bottling equipment, suddenly made busier than ever with the production of beer shampoo. At left is Frank A. Weaner, a Chicago industrial engineer who was a former Wisconsin brewery owner himself, and who had invented the formula for beer shampoo [images from Modern Brewery Age, July 1949].

Canned beer produced in New Philadelphia

Most of the brands were packaged only in bottles, but in 1938, the brewery began to use cap-sealed cans from the Continental Can Co. to package beer, mainly for export. Many of the cans were shipped to the Buffalo, NY. area, where the brewery had a distribution agent. Also, based on the finding of a fairly large number of the brewery's cans in the Kansas City area in recent years, it appears that some were exported as far west as Missouri. Old Bohemia and John Bull cans were produced from 1938 to 1941, after which all canning stopped due to metal usage in World War II. Canning of beer would briefly return in 1947-48 for the Old Bohemia, Olde Vat, and Scotch Highland Ale brands. Joining the company around this time was new vice-president and general manager Philip M. Kunzi, who had previously been general manager of Harris's Forest City Brewery in Cleveland. Frank C. Lohmann was the plant's Master Brewer, although by 1945 he had been succeeded by Carl F. Moeller, with Hugh C. Barrett as his assistant.

After a reorganization in 1940 to improve the company's financial status, the brewery's success peaked in 1941. Looking at records from April of that year, the brewery had $51,000 of sales, with 4,900 barrels of ale and beer produced by the 65 employees. This translated into nearly 260,000 bottles and 135,000 cans sold. This success would be short-lived, however, as grain rations during World War II reduced production for several years, during which time many of the country's larger brewers were able to enlarge their plants even further. This would ultimately overwhelm most of Ohio's small local brewers.

Harris retired in May 1947, selling his interest in the brewery to 65-year-old Max Swartz, a Columbus businessman, and Albert Lange, who had previously been with the Wooden Shoe Brewing Co. in Minster, OH. By the late 1940s, however, the small plant was finding itself unable to compete with other breweries in the state. The local sales were no longer enough to make a profit, and in fact the brewery operated at a loss after late 1947.

One final effort to survive resulted in a short-lived beer shampoo (see prior page). This began in early 1949, and quickly became so popular that the remaining beer brands were discontinued by early summer. However, it was only a passing fad, and on November 11, 1949, the plant closed its doors forever, bringing 85 years of brewing history to an end. The following April, former employees of the plant made an attempt to purchase the brewery from Swartz, in order to continue brewing operations themselves. Swartz offered to sell the plant and equipment for $50,000, with the funds to be raised by selling stock in the proposed new company to residents of the area. In the end, the funds never materialized, and the proposal fell through.

All equipment was auctioned off in June 1951 (the copper brew kettle sold for $3,800), and the plant remained vacant until it was razed in 1963. Today, the U. S. Route 250 bypass runs directly through the site, and there are no remnants of the brewery.

Strasburg

1. Strasburg Brewery

Jacob Seikel was born in March 1804 in Somborn, Hesse, Germany, and came to the United States in 1851 with his wife, Anna, and their eight children. After landing in Baltimore, they later moved to Canal Dover, and in 1873 purchased land in Strasburg, which would soon be the site of this small brewing operation. It was located at the northwest corner of the main road in Strasburg, today known as Wooster Road, or U.S. Route 250, and what is now 2nd Street. Interestingly, it was the only one of the six breweries in the county not to be situated along the banks of either the Tuscarawas River or the Ohio & Erie Canal.

Production of lager began around 1875, although it appears that operation of the plant at the time was by Harberdier and Klopfenstein (according to Schade's directory). Seikel apparently operated it himself after 1877. The beer was stored in a sandstone-lined cellar built into a hillside approximately one mile south of town, presumably for lagering, and was then distributed to the seven saloons in town. The cellar had a natural spring inside, which may have provided a source of pure water for brewing.

It also appears that Rudolph Kapizky, a prominent local landowner and hotel owner, may have had some involvement with the brewery, although the connection is not clear. Kapizky had previously owned the New Philadelphia brewery for five years before moving north to Strasburg. His hotel was actually a large farmhouse on the north side of town, with an icehouse in the rear. It is likely that Seikel's beer was served there.

During fifteen years of operation, the brewery's annual output was usually in the range of 200-300 barrels. The brewery continued operation until around 1890, when production ceased. Seikel died in 1896. It appears that the brewery building may have stood for a number of years, being used as a garage, before burning to the ground. A gas station stands at the site today, although the stone-lined cave remains in the hillside outside of town, on the north side of Cherry Run Road. Its entrance has been nearly covered over by erosion, and the spring inside has created a small underground lake.

Zoar

1. Zoar Society Brewery

One of the most historically significant breweries in Ohio, the Zoar Society brewery operated under conditions different from any other in the state. No description of the brewery would be complete, however, without a description of the unique society itself. The Zoar Society originated around 1817, when approximately 350 German immigrants, mostly poor, came to eastern Ohio and settled on a tract of 5,000 acres of land, along the banks of the Tuscarawas River. They were comprised of both Lutherans and Roman Catholics, who were coming to America to escape persecution. Joseph Bimeler was a teacher who became their political and religious leader. The village was named after the biblical city to which Lot fled from Sodom and Gomorrah.

Under the community's Articles of Association, the earnings of every individual were to be turned over to a common treasury. While some families remained intact, there were some families which were broken up due to poverty, so that some homes were comprised only of men, while others were comprised only of women. The primary occupation in the community was farming, producing food for the community and for sale.

It is likely that beer was brewed in the village at a very early point, possibly in either a home brewing setting, or possibly in a small village structure. However, it appears that it was not until the mid-1820s, after the completion of the Ohio and Erie Canal through the village, that a large wooden barn-like building was built at the west end of what is now known as 5th Street, to house the village's brewing operation. It is unclear what the output was in the early days, but by the 1870s the brewery was producing between 200 and 400 barrels of lager beer per year. The barley and hops used for brewing were grown in town, and were often picked by children. The brewery was operated for profit in later years, with much of the beer sold to guests at the bar of the Zoar Hotel in town, as well as the one other tavern in the village. The hotel, which was run in later years by Christian Ruof, the son of one of the Society's founders, was a very busy place after the mid-to-late 1800s. Wealthy people from all over Ohio came to Zoar as a peaceful retreat from the city. Native German industrialists in particular came to the village for vacations, as life in the village reminded many of them of their childhood in the Fatherland, and most conversations there were spoken in German. Leonhard Schlather, owner of a large brewery in Cleveland, owned a house in Zoar, where he and his family frequently stayed. In fact, two concrete plaques from the Cleveland brewery sit near his old home in Zoar to this day.

The Zoar Brewery, as it looked when it was still operated by the Society. Note the workers and barrels near the lower entrance. [Photo courtesy of Whitemyer Advertising, Zoar, Ohio]

In the latter part of the nineteenth century, it appears that a small amount of beer was sold to nearby farmers, and some was shipped via canal boats to other towns. All of the beer was barreled, however, as the plant never had a bottling works. Over the years, the Zoar Brewery's beer developed a reputation as being some of the best in the state.

According to *The Zoar Story,* by Hilda Morhart, "in the summertime a pint of beer was sent to each man working in the fields daily, at lunch time. On very hot Monday mornings, a medium-sized glass of beer was given to the women while they were doing their laundry work." Even though the brewery's beer was supplied generously to the society's families, it was rare for anyone to become intoxicated in the village. Beer was used as a standard daily beverage, like milk and cider, due to the questionable purity of water supplies in the area. Between the boiling of the water in the brewing process and the alcohol contained within, beer could generally be counted upon to be free of dangerous bacteria.

It is uncertain how many people worked in the brewery, but it is known that the master brewer in 1860 was Johanus Grotzinger. By 1870, he had been succeeded by John Shaffer, and by 1880 Shaffer had been succeeded by Anton Burkhart.

The Society's time had passed by the end of the nineteenth century, and for a variety of reasons its members decided to disband in 1898, and sell all of the commonly owned property, including the brewery. At this time, ownership of the brewery fell into the hands of John Relker and O. J. Kappel, two Society members. They sold the structure and a five-acre plot of land on which it stood to Alexander Gunn, a wealthy Cleveland industrialist. He had vacationed in Zoar for many years, and developed a taste for life in the village, as well as its favorite beverage. Although it is difficult to confirm, it is possible that he continued operation of the brewery, although at a minimal level of production, for an additional three years, before his death in 1901. During that time, he converted some of the upper floors of the old brewhouse building into a clubhouse for friends, complete with oak trim and a large fireplace, where a good portion of the beloved brew was enjoyed. This no doubt caused some consternation among the local residents, many of whom were former Society members who had stayed in the village after the dissolution. After Gunn's death, it appears that the brewery closed for good. The old building was later used as a tavern, operated by a man named Keller. It was converted into a dance hall in the 1930s, and was still hosting weekly dances when the complex burned to the ground in 1959. The foundations of the buildings still remain visible today, although a residence stands at the site. In recent years, there have been discussions of rebuilding the brewery in some form, as it was a large part of the village's history, or even opening a brewpub in the village, although no concrete plans have yet formed.

A brief attempt was made to form a new Zoar Brewery after Prohibition in late 1933. At that time, the buildings of the former community were still being used as a vacation spot for many of the wealthy people of Northeast Ohio, particularly Clevelanders. A company was formed by William Schuster, formerly of the Schuster Brewing Co. of Massillon, and A. V. Weitz of Cleveland, with the intention of building a new plant with a five-story brewhouse in the village.

Located on the east side of the village, along Goose Run, the new plant had some preliminary construction performed before the project was abandoned. Today, many of the buildings of the community have been preserved as remnants of another time and remain a popular tourist attraction.

WASHINGTON COUNTY

Marietta

1. Stockade Brewery

Driving through a quiet residential neighborhood on the north side of the town of Marietta, one can clearly see a remnant of the town's brewing history. A brick-lined arch in a backyard hillside at the southeast corner of 6th and Montgomery Streets invites one to a small room inside. Pitch blackness and a foot or more of water prevent most from entering, however. This was the cave used as a beer cellar for the Stockade brewery, and it appears that it was originally a natural cave. An underground spring, which was once used to supply water for brewing, has flooded the cave, although it is said that the cave continues well beyond the area used for beer storage more than a century ago.

Often considered to be Ohio's oldest city, Marietta was founded in 1788 and was the first capital of the Northwest Territory, prior to Ohio's statehood in 1803. One might therefore expect that it would have held the state's first brewery, but this is not the case. While there may have been some small scattered home brewing establishments in Marietta's early days, the Stockade Brewery does not appear to have begun operation for the production of common beer until the mid- to late 1840s.

Its original owner was John Smith (formerly Schmidt), a German immigrant born in 1819. On November 4, 1850, however, he sold the land and brewery to Jacob Gaddel (aka Grittle, Gadden, Gaddle, and Goeddle) for the sum of $1,075. Gaddel was also a German immigrant, born in 1818. He died several years later, however, and operations were then continued by his wife, Caroline. By this time, the brewery consisted only of a single one-story wooden building, 20 by 50 feet in size, with a 20-barrel copper boiler, as well as the underground cave.

The cave may have taken on another use by this time. Marietta was a prominent city in the network known as the Underground Railroad, bringing runaway slaves from the south to safety in Canada. Local legend suggests that the beer cave was one of the sites in which slaves were hidden for a period of time along the way north.

In November, 1860, Gaddel leased the brewery to 21-year-old Bernhard E. Stoehr and Jacob Hennemann, two recent immigrants from Germany, for a five year period. This appears to be when the small brewery began producing lager beer. Under the terms of the lease, Stoehr and Hennemann paid $300 the first year, and $350 every other year until 1865. At that time, the property was retaken by Gaddel. Stoehr would later work at the Union brewery elsewhere in town, and even later would become an agent for the Moerlein brewery of Cincinnati.

Around 1865, a new company was formed, known as Gaddel, Maser, & Co., consisting of Charles Gaddel (Caroline's son), William Maser, & Jacob Weber. Brewing operations continued until ceasing around 1873. Nothing remains of the brewery itself, although the underground cave is likely to remain for many years.

2. Frederick Grohs (aka Gross)

Frederick Grohs was a native German, born in 1828, who came to America in the late 1840s. By 1850, and for several years after, he was living in Marietta and working at the Stockade Brewery. By the latter part of that decade, however, he had purchased a small site on Muskingum Street between Ohio & Butler Streets.

Although the street no longer exists, it would have directly faced the Muskingum River. At this site he established his own small brewing operation, where he was assisted by Peter Shener, a French immigrant who had been born in 1838. Brewing operations on Muskingum Street appear to have ceased in the early 1860s, however, and there is no evidence that brewing took place there after that period. Nothing remains of the small brewery today.

3. Union Brewery/Marietta Brewing Company

Marietta's longest-lasting brewing establishment was located at 613 2nd Street, at the northwest corner of St. Clair Street. Originally known as the Union brewery, it was built in 1866 by Christian Held. In May 1868, however, the plant was sold for $2,500 to Martin Seamon (aka Seeman), who then sold it seven months later to George M. Kestel for the sum of $5,600. Kestel continued production of lager beer through 1876 despite having accepted assignment in 1875 to protect himself from his creditors. The brewery was then sold at auction in January 1876, to brothers Fidel and William Rapp, for $6,000. One year later, they sold the plant to John Schneider. Brewing operations appear to have continued throughout this period, with annual production as high as 2,000 barrels. Success was brief, however, as Schneider had died by 1884, with management being assumed by his wife, Elizabeth, and sons Charles & Martin. Production at the small plant continued through 1890, when brewing operations ceased. The Schneider brothers became saloon owners after this, while the brewery stood idle.

In November 1898, the empty Union brewery was purchased by a three-man group, William Feller & Co., which consisted of Feller, August V. Kuehn (both formerly involved with the Riverside Brewing Co. of Zanesville), and Jacob Epple, all three German immigrants. They invested a great deal of money into the plant to bring it up to the standards of the day, including the addition of an ice plant, bottling house, and other machinery.

Renamed as the Marietta Brewery, the plant was employing 20 men, as its capacity had been greatly increased to 15,000 barrels per year, although generally its production was only half to two-thirds of that. The icehouse could

Brewery employees, circa 1900; this photo and the one on the following page appear to have been taken on the same day (courtesy of the Washington County Historical Society)

produce up to 15 tons a day, while the bottling equipment could fill up to 500 dozen bottles of export beer per day. All of this machinery was powered by an 80 horsepower engine. The plant itself (somewhat outdated by the standards of the time) consisted of a series of two-story buildings, mostly of wooden frame.

By 1903, Feller had sold his interest to the other two men and moved north to Bellaire, Ohio, where he became a driving force behind the creation of the new Bellaire Brewing Co. Incorporated as the Marietta Brewing Co. in that year, with a capital stock of $60,000, the plant was then led by Kuehn as president, with Epple as vice-president, and Kuehn's son George as secretary and treasurer. The brewery's products were sold primarily in town and in the surrounding rural areas, as well as along the Ohio River, as

Marietta remained a primary port for steamboats well into the 1900s.

After the Rose Law was passed in 1908, Washington County went dry the following year, forcing the company to shut down and temporarily sell its facility to the Crystal Ice Co. However, despite the county remaining dry, beer production resumed in 1911 with products shipped to Parkersburg, WV., thirteen miles down the Ohio River, for distribution. By the next year, Washington County was once again wet and production resumed at its previous level. George Kuehn succeeded his father as company president when the latter died in 1913 at the age of 64, due to "rheumatism and gout", according to local reports.

Production continued until Prohibition arrived in 1919, after which a brief attempt was made to brew cereal beverages. The company had closed by 1924, however, after which the plant operated as the local Whistle soft drink bottling plant. This continued through the end of Prohibition.

In 1933, after Repeal, a brief attempt was made to revive the Marietta Brewing Co., but no production ever took place. However, another attempt was made, with the name American Brewery Co., which lasted through 1935. It was located in one of the smaller buildings in the brewery complex, with Elmer Epple, Jacob's son, as brewmaster, and T. L. Archer as manager. It appears that no actual beer production took place, however. By 1937, this same location was occupied by the Covert Baking Co., which, oddly enough, was listed in the city directory as a beer distributor, not a bakery. This company was gone by the onset of World War II.

The main brewhouse was razed in the 1940s, and the site was occupied by a service station. That building was later removed, and a medical office building now stands at the site. Two of the smaller buildings in the complex, including the bottling plant, remained standing until 1999, when they were razed for an addition to the office building.

4. Marietta Brewing Company

The shiny copper kettles in the window at 167 Front Street indicate that the brewing of beer has returned to Marietta after a 78-year interval. In September 1997, the new Marietta Brewing Co. opened for business as a brewpub and restaurant. Brewing operations began under the supervision of Terry Hawbaker, although by early 1998, he had been succeeded by Kelly Sauber.

Using a 7-barrel J. V. Northwest brewing system, Sauber brews approximately 300 barrels annually, all sold on-site. Among the brews that have been available in the first three years are True Meridian Golden Lager, Auld Starfire Irish Ale, McLaren's Scotch Ale, George's First Inaugural Light Lager, Weepin Willie's Oatmeal Stout, Marietta Mild Beer, Marie's Last Chopping Block Nut Brown Lager, Schwartzenwald Oktoberfest Style Lager, Putnam's Porter, Red Ochre Moundbuilder's Brew (American style red ale), and Mudcat Hefe Weizen German Style Wheat Beer. At any given time, there are generally five standard beers and one specialty brew available. The brewpub quickly became a popular spot in the city's historic downtown area.

Also Note:

Prior to Prohibition, Marietta had a number of bottling plants for other Ohio breweries, including Moerlein, Gerke (Cincinnati), Hoster (Columbus), Finlay (Toledo), and Bellaire. No beer was brewed at any of these sites, however.

Smithville

1. Smithville Brewery

This was most likely the first full-scale brewery to exist in Wayne County, although it is possible that some of the other early settlers of the area may have done some home brewing. It is thought that for some of the early farmers in the area, it was more profitable to use their grains to brew beer than to attempt to take the grains to market. In the early 1800s, prior to the development of the railroads, farmers in the area were forced to travel on hilly back roads to Canal Fulton in order to have access to the Ohio & Erie Canal, which would take their products to larger towns to sell. It was easier for some to brew the grain into beer, then sell it locally or haul it to Akron or Wooster for sale.

In any event, the Smithville Brewery appears to have begun around 1830, on the farm of John Burkholder. This was on the south side of Smucker Road, approximately one mile south of Smithville in Green Township. Burkholder had been born in Bern, Switzerland in 1801, and had come to the United States in 1817, via a 14-week voyage. He came to Smithville in 1823 and began working on his uncle's farm. Around 1830 he began brewing beer on the farm, a tradition which would last more than 50 years. The operation grew very little over the years, as the brewery was only producing 500 barrels of beer per year by the 1870s. The beer was sold locally and to a small extent in surrounding towns. Beer was produced only in barrels, as there was no bottling works present. John Burkholder's son Jonathon was born in 1826, and continued the farming and brewing trade, even after his father's death in 1875.

According to *Creative Congregationalism* (a history of the nearby Oak Grove Mennonite Church), by James O. Lehman, there developed a strong movement within the Mennonite church around this time to distance itself from alcoholic beverages, or at least the production and sale thereof. Despite the fact that many of the church members were of German descent, the leaders of the church had been strongly influenced by the American temperance movement and incorporated this philosophy into their own. Although this was a devisive issue, especially among the recent immigrants who were unfamiliar with the idea of temperance, the congregation gradually came

The Smithville Brewery, located on the Burkholder family farm, operated in the simple two-story building on the right side of this photo, taken in 1875. The building was razed in the 1950s. (photo courtesy of Charles Hostetler)

to agree with the leaders, even though three of the members were brewers (see the following sections).

Burkholder was the first member of his congregation to voluntarily stop his brewing operation, in approximately 1882. With his farm well-established to provide income, he could afford to leave the brewing business. The brewery building remained standing until being dismantled in the 1950s. The farm has continued to operate and still remains in the family to this day, 180 years after its original purchase.

Sterling

1. Peter Rich brewery

Located one mile east of the present-day village of Sterling in northern Wayne County, this rural brewery was situated in a triangle of land bounded by Sterling, Rittman, and Shorle Roads. At that time, the village of Sterling did not yet exist, and the nearest locality was the Amwell post office stop along the Lakeshore and Tuscarawas Valley Railroad. Some early directories just list the brewery as being in Milton Township.

The brewery was on the farm of Peter Rich, an Alsacian immigrant who was born in 1833, although it appears that he did not actively take part in the brewing process. Census records indicate that Nicklaus Kraft, a young German man, born in 1852, was originally in charge of brewing operations, with four men working under him, including Christian and John Rich, who appear to have been nephews of Peter. Christian, born in 1859, would later take over operation of the brewery. The exact time of the brewery's origin is uncertain, but it appears to have been around 1871, soon after Rich came to the United States with his brother Martin (who was a part owner of the Apple Creek Brewery in Wooster at the same time). Production of lager beer was generally between 1,000 and 1,500 barrels per year, with products being sold both locally and in surrounding towns.

According to *Creative Congregationalism* (see the above section on Smithville), Rich came under pressure during the 1870s from his Mennonite church to leave the brewing business. Unlike his brother Martin and Jonathon Burkholder, he disagreed with the church's stance and refused to close his brewery. Because of this, he was subsequently excommunicated from the church. He later joined a congregation near Cincinnati, to which he could only travel once a month or so, claiming that every trip to church cost him $50!

Apparently bad luck plagued him after this, as the brewery burned to the ground just one year after leaving the church. He quickly rebuilt it, yet it burned a second time. Once it was rebuilt again, brewing continued through approximately 1888, after which production ceased for good. Rich gradually moved into the business of tobacco farming, although he eventually died a poor man. Nothing remains of the brewery today, and in fact, Amwell itself is just a distant memory.

Wooster

1. Wooster Brewing Company

Around 1860, Joseph J. Ramseyer built Wooster's first brewery for the production of both ale and lager beer. It was known at that time as the Apple Creek Brewery, standing just a half-mile from the creek. The brewery's actual location was at the intersection of Dalton Road, Apple Creek Road, and Pittsburg Avenue, just outside of the city limits in an area known as Soaptown. Today, the site is between East Lincoln Way (U. S. Route 30) and Sylvan Rd.

The brewery started as a small enterprise in the 1860s, producing several hundred barrels per year, but was enlarged in the mid-1870s to a size which it would retain for the next 40 years, producing between 2,000 and 2,500 barrels per year. It had a simple three-story wooden frame brewhouse, with an attached icehouse and beer cellar. A large pond was behind the plant and was used for cutting ice in winter. Another smaller icehouse was beyond the pond. In later years, however, mechanical refrigeration was introduced, and the plant produced large quantities of ice. A bottling house was added in the early 1890s as well. While the creek provided the brewery's original water supply, a large well was dug on the property in 1904, providing a much purer source of water at a rate sufficient to supply the growing plant's needs.

Local records indicate that the property changed ownership numerous times during the 1860s and 1870s, but Ramseyer appears to have operated the plant until 1870, when it was sold to Martin L. Rich (a recent immigrant from Alsace, whose brother Peter operated a brewery in nearby Amwell) and Jacob Roth. The latter sold his interest in 1874 to Jacob Mougey (also spelled Mongey), the son of French immigrants. Rich soon found himself under pressure from his Mennonite church to leave this profession which produced alcoholic beverages. However, since Rich had no other income source, he spent several years attempting to sell his share of the brewery, while investing in his own farm. He would finally sell his brewery interest in 1879 to John Graber, who was Mougey's brother-in-law.

Mougey sold his interest in 1882 to George J. Renner, Sr., a prominent German brewer who had recently come north from Cincinnati. Renner and his son, George, Jr., were both involved with the plant for two years. George, Sr. would move on to Mansfield in 1884, operating the Renner & Weber brewery until 1888, when he moved to Akron to operate his own brewery there until his death. George, Jr. would move to Youngstown to establish his own brewery there.

Between 1884 and 1888, Graber operated the brewery alone, until selling it to Frederick Weis. The latter operated it until 1890, when he defaulted on his mortgage with Graber (the plant was valued at $15,000 by this time, and Weis still owed $11,000). This was due to an

Wooster Brewery, circa 1880 (courtesy of the Wooster Public Library)

inability to secure an adequate supply of ice during the previous winter, the warmest of the past century, with a subsequent loss of 500 barrels of stored beer. Operations were thus suspended until Graber retook control of the plant late in the year, after which it was renamed as the Wooster Brewing Co.

In 1895, Graber again sold the brewery, this time to Robert Weisman of Chicago, and F. Runge, formerly superintendent of a brewery in Monterey, Mexico. As before, the change was brief, as the pair had sold the company back to Graber one year later. Also in 1895, the dam of the brewery's ice pond broke during a late summer storm, flooding the immediate area and damaging several buildings, although they were quickly rebuilt.

In late 1903, a stock company was formed by a group that included John Koerber, who was also the principal force behind the founding of The Akron Brewing Co. at the same time. This new company called itself the Wooster Artificial Ice & Brewing Co., and had a capital stock of $50,000. A new group of investors, all local restaurant and saloon owners, became officers of the company, including Henry Howard as president, Isiah Fisher as vice-president, Fred Faber as secretary, and Frank Naftzger as treasurer. Other directors included Henry Schuch, James Schliner, and W. J. Noggle. All of them served "Wooster Lager" in their establishments, where a quart bottle could be had for a nickel. Graber's son, Samuel E. Graber, also remained with the company, and within several years became its new president.

In 1908, the Rose "local option" Law was passed, allowing largely rural Wayne County to vote itself dry between 1909 and early 1912. This seriously hurt the company's brewing operations, although the increasing emphasis on ice production would allow the plant to stay functional during this period.

In 1913, the Mougey Ice Co. was formed in Wooster, with its main warehouse at 545 Pittsburg Ave., although it appears that this was just a distribution company for ice produced by the brewery. Its founder, Jacob Mougey, had remained loosely tied to the brewery as a family member, although after selling his share of the brewery many years earlier, he had been the county sheriff for a brief time, a saloonkeeper, and more recently a horse trader. The ice company was managed by Andrew M. Smith, a younger family member.

In 1916, brewing operations ceased, and Graber sold his interest to the Mougey Co. (Graber would later become a lumber dealer, and was briefly involved with the Canton Brewing Co. in 1933 and 1934 as its brewmaster). The plant continued to produce ice, however, until 1927, when the Mougey Co. closed. For a brief time before closing, the company was renamed the Mougey Beverage Co., bottling cola in addition to making ice. The company also sold coal during the 1920s. Andrew Smith's son, James, was the company's secretary during this time. The property stayed in the Smith family for many years after that, and it appears that the brewery building stood until the early 1960s, when it was razed for the construction of the U.S. Route 30 bypass. There are no remains of it today.

2. Wendell Young brewery

This short-lived brewery was in the city of Wooster, located at the southeast corner of Beaver & Larwill Streets. In later years, Beaver became Bever St., and the site's address became 77 N. Bever (the address was later renumbered again, to 245 N. Bever.) It was operated by Wendell Young, a German immigrant born July 12, 1820. He came to America in 1846, coming to Wooster soon after that. Initially working odd jobs, he eventually had enough capital by 1864 to build a substantial brewery, producing just under 2,000 barrels of lager beer per year. In 1878, however, the brewery burned to the ground, bringing an end to his beer production.

Young soon rebuilt his plant, but this time it would only be a bottling works for beer and mineral water. This company was later run by Young's son, Edward, and it continued until approximately the turn of the century. Nothing remains of it today.

Also Note:

In 1997, plans were made to bring the brewing of beer back to Wayne County for the first time in eighty years. The site chosen for this venture was the old city jail, built in 1865, but not in use since 1977. The plan was to establish an upscale brewpub, to be known as the Olde Jaol Brewing Co. However, due to restrictions brought on by the old building's original construction, brewing equipment was never installed, and no brewing ever took place at the site. The restaurant remains open as of this time, however.

APPENDIX: OHIO U-PERMIT NUMBERS

With the end of Prohibition in 1933, the United States Government issued individual licenses to each operating brewery, on a state-by-state basis. Along with each license came a permit number, uniquely indentifying the brewery. These numbers, known as U-permit numbers, were required to be present on all labels (and later, cans) that were produced by the breweries (a similar system was used during Prohibition, when breweries that produced cereal beverages were all issued L-permit numbers). While the permit numbers were required only between April 1933 and September 1935, they are also seen on many labels that were produced as late as mid-1936. Despite their brief usage, they are often used as a reliable way to date early labels. The following is a list of all known U-permit numbers for Ohio breweries (originally compiled by Jody Farra and taken with permission from Gary Bauer's Michigan brewery history web site www.mi-brew.com.)

OHIO-U-600 The Bruckmann Co. (Ludlow Ave.), Cincinnati
OHIO-U-600 Grand Pop Bottling Co., Cincinnati
OHIO-U-600 The Royal Bottling Co., Cincinnati
OHIO-U-604 August Wagner & Sons Brewing Co., Inc., Columbus
OHIO-U-605 The Geo. J. Renner Brewing Co., Inc., Akron
OHIO-U-606 The Star Beverage Co., Minster
OHIO-U-607 The Buckeye Brewing Co., Toledo
OHIO-U-608 The Bruckmann Co., Inc. (Spring Grove Ave.), Cincinnati
OHIO-U-609 Cleveland & Sandusky Brewing Co., Sandusky
OHIO-U-610 Belmont Brewing Co., Martins Ferry
OHIO-U-611 Christ. Diehl Brewing Co., Inc., Defiance
OHIO-U-612 Eilert Brewing Co., Cleveland
OHIO-U-613 Miami Valley Brewing Co., Inc., Dayton
OHIO-U-614 The Koch Beverage & Ice Co., Inc., Wapakoneta
OHIO-U-615 Pilsener Ice, Fuel, & Beverage Co., Inc., Cleveland
OHIO-U-615 The Pilsener Brewing Co., Cleveland
OHIO-U-616 The Cleveland Home Brewing Co., Inc., Cleveland
OHIO-U-618 Crockery City Ice & Products Co., East Liverpool
OHIO-U-619 Dostal Products Co., Bucyrus
OHIO-U-619 Bucyrus Products Co., Bucyrus
OHIO-U-620 Hollenkamp Products Co., Inc., Dayton
OHIO-U-621 The Cleveland & Sandusky Co., Inc., Cleveland
OHIO-U-622 The Renner Co., Inc., Youngstown
OHIO-U-623 The Standard Food Products Co., Inc., Cleveland
OHIO-U-623 The Standard Brewing Co., Cleveland
OHIO-U-624 The Hudepohl Brewing Co. Inc., Cincinnati
OHIO-U-625 Red Top Brewing Co., Inc., Cincinnati
OHIO-U-626 Freimann's Beverage & Ice Co., Upper Sandusky
OHIO-U-629 Forest City Brewery, Inc., Cleveland
OHIO-U-631 The Consumers Brewing Co., Inc., Newark
OHIO-U-637 The Olt Bros. Brewing Co., Dayton

OHIO-U-638 The Foss-Schneider Co., Inc., Cincinnati
OHIO-U-640 Koerber Brewing Co., Inc., Toledo
OHIO-U-643 The Krantz Brewing Co., Inc., Findlay
OHIO-U-646 Lange Products Co., Inc., Piqua
OHIO-U-647 Washington Breweries, Inc., Columbus
OHIO-U-650 New Philadelphia Brewery, Inc., New Philadelphia
OHIO-U-653 Vienna Brewing Co., Cincinnati
OHIO-U-655 Lubeck Brewing Co., Toledo
OHIO-U-658 The Old Munich Brewing Co., Inc., Cincinnati
OHIO-U-662 Sunrise Brewing Co., Inc., Cleveland
OHIO-U-667 Lion Brewery, Inc., Cincinnati
OHIO-U-669 Riverside Brewing Co., Columbus
OHIO-U-673 The Squibb-Pattison Breweries, Inc., Cincinnati
OHIO-U-676 Graber Brewing Co., Canton
OHIO-U-676 Canton Brewing Co., Canton
OHIO-U-678 M. Frank & Son, Mansfield
OHIO-U-679 Burkhardt Brewing Co., Akron
OHIO-U-682 The Hamilton Brewing Co., Inc., Hamilton
OHIO-U-686 The Renner & Weber Brewing Co., Mansfield
OHIO-U-687 The Clyffside Brewing Co., Cincinnati
OHIO-U-689 The Franklin Brewing Co., Columbus
OHIO-U-691 The Leisy Brewing Co., Inc., Cleveland
OHIO-U-692 Akron Brewing Co., Akron
OHIO-U-693 The Schoenling Brewing and Ice Co., Cincinnati
OHIO-U-694 Brewing Corporation of America, Cleveland
OHIO-U-695 The Milan Brewing Corp., Milan
OHIO-U-697 The Burger Brewing Co., Inc., Cincinnati
OHIO-U-698 The Lancaster Brewing Co., Inc., Lancaster
OHIO-U-701 The Delatron Brewing Co., Cincinnati
OHIO-U-705 The Hudepohl Brewing Co (Plant 2), Cincinnati
OHIO-U-706 Old Capitol Brewery, Inc., Chillicothe

BIBLIOGRAPHY

Books and miscellaneous sources

Aldrich, Lewis Cass. History of Erie County, Ohio, with Illustrations and Biographical Sketches of Some of its Prominent Men and Pioneers. Syracuse: D. Mason & Co., 1889.

Baron, Stanley Wade. Brewed in America: A History of Beer and Ale in the United States. Boston: Little, Brown, & Co., 1962.

Baughman, A. J. History of Huron County, Ohio, its Progress and Development. Chicago: S. J. Clarke Pub. Co., 1909.

Beer Can Collectors of America. United States Beer Cans: The Standard Reference of Flat Tops and Cone Tops. Topeka, KS.: Jostens Inc., 2001.

Behr, Edward. Prohibition: Thirteen Years That Changed America. New York: Arcade Publishing, Inc., 1996.

Caldwell, J. A. History of Belmont and Jefferson Counties, Ohio. Wheeling, W. Va.: Historical Pub. Co., 1880.

Cleveland und Sein Deutschthum, 1897. Cleveland: Deutsch-Amerikanische Historisch-Biographische Gesellschaft, 1897.

Cleveland und Sein Deutschthum, 1907. Cleveland: Deutsch-Amerikanische Historisch-Biographische Gesellschaft, 1907.

Commemorative Biographical Record of Wayne County, Ohio, Containing Biographical Sketches of Prominent and Representative Citizens, and of Many of the Early Settled Families. Chicago: J. H. Beers, 1889.

Danner, John. Old Landmarks of Canton and Stark County, Ohio. Logansport, IN.: B. F. Bowen, 1904.

Doyle, Joseph B. 20th Century History of Steubenville and Jefferson County, Ohio and Representative Citizens. Chicago: Richmond-Arnold Pub. Co., 1910.

Doyle, William B. Centennial History of Summit County, Ohio and Representative Citizens. Chicago: Biographical Pub. Co., 1908.

Everhart, J. F. History of Muskingum County, Ohio. Columbus, OH.: J.F. Everhart, 1882.

Firelands Pioneer. Norwalk, OH.: Firelands Historical Society (magazine), 1863 and 1918.

Francis, David W. and Diane DeMali. Cedar Point, The Queen of American Watering Places. Fairview Park, OH.: Amusement Park Books, Inc., 1995.

Frohman, Charles E. Milan and the Milan Canal. Milan, OH.: Charles E. Frohman, 1976.

Frohman, Charles E. Sandusky's Potpourri. Ohio Historical Society, 1974.

Gates, William C. The City of Hills and Kilns: Life and Work in East Liverpool, Ohio. East Liverpool, OH.: East Liverpool Historical Society, 1984.

General Business Review Fairfield County, Ohio for 1888. Newark, OH.: Lyon & Ickes, 1888.

Graham, A. A. History of Fairfield and Perry Counties, Ohio: their Past and Present, Containing a Comprehensive History of Ohio. Chicago: W.H. Beers, 1883.

Hill, N. N., Jr. History of Coshocton County, Ohio: Its Past and Present, 1740-1881. Newark, OH.: A. A. Graham, 1881.

Hill, N. N., Jr. History of Knox County. Mt. Vernon, OH.: A. A. Graham & Co., 1881.

History of Richland County, Ohio, its past and present. Mansfield, OH.: A. A. Graham & Co., 1880.

History of the Fire Lands, Comprising Huron and Erie Counties, Ohio, with Illustrations and Biographical Sketches of Some of the Prominent Men and Pioneers. Cleveland: Press of Leader Print. Co., 1879.

History of Trumbull and Mahoning Counties. Cleveland: M. Z. Williams and Brothers, 1882.

The History of Tuscarawas County, Ohio. Chicago: Warner, Beers, 1884.

Holian, Timothy J. Over the Barrel: The Brewing History and Beer Culture of Cincinnati, Volume I. St. Joseph, MO.: Sudhaus Press, 2000.

Holian, Timothy J. Over the Barrel: The Brewing History and Beer Culture of Cincinnati, Volume II. St. Joseph, MO.: Sudhaus Press, 2001.

Illustrated Review of Zanesville, Ohio. 1887.

Jackson County, Ohio: History and Families. Wellston, OH.: Jackson County Genealogical Society, 1991.

Lane, Samuel A. Fifty Years and Over of Akron and Summit County. Akron, OH.: Beacon Job Department, 1892.

Lehman, James O. Creative Congregationalism: A History of the Oak Grove Mennonite Church in Wayne County, Ohio. Smithville, OH.: Oak Grove Mennonite Church, 1978.

Lorey, Frederick N. History of Knox County, Ohio: 1876-1976. Mount Vernon, OH.: Knox County Historical Society, 1992.

Maccombs, Gary. History of Hocking Valley Brewery, Inc. Term paper, 1975.

McCord, William B. History of Columbiana County, Ohio, and Representative Citizens. Chicago: Biographical Pub. Co., 1905.

Miller, Carl. Breweries of Cleveland. Cleveland, OH.: Schnitzelbank Press, 1998.

Morhart, Hilda Dischinger. The Zoar Story. Dover, Ohio: Seibert Printing, 1969.

Morrow, Frank C. A History of Industry in Jackson County, Ohio. Wellston, OH., 1956.

Nichols, George G. Sandusky of To-Day. 1888.

Norwalk Illustrated. Norwalk, OH.: The Evening Herald, 1904.

One Hundred Years of Brewing. Chicago & New York: H. S. Rich & Co., 1903.

Phillips, Glen C. On Tap: The Odyssey of Beer and Brewing in Victorian London-Middlesex. Sarnia, Ontario, Canada: Cheshire Cat Press, 2000.

Shaffer, Dale E. Salem As It Was—A Collection of Historical Articles and Photographs. Salem, OH.: Shaffer, Dale E., 1989.

Sutor, J. Hope. Past and Present of the City of Zanesville and Muskingum County, Ohio. Chicago: S.J. Clarke Pub. Co., 1905.

The Tallow Light, Magazine of the Washington County Historical Society, Marietta, OH. Volume 28, Number 2, Fall 1997.

Timman, Henry. Just Like Old Times, Book I (As published originally in the Norwalk Reflector). Norwalk, OH.: Larry's Printing, 1982.

Timman, Henry. Just Like Old Times, Book V (As published originally in the Norwalk Reflector). Norwalk, OH.: Laser Images, Inc., 1989.

Van Wieren, Dale P. American Breweries II. West Point, PA.: Eastern Coast Breweriana Association, 1995.

von Schulenburg, Ernst. Sandusky Then and Now. Cleveland: The Western Reserve Historical Society, 1959.

W.W. Reilly & Co.'s Ohio state business directory for 1853. Cincinnati: Morgan & Overend, Printers, 1853.

White, Wallace B. Milan Township and Village, One Hundred and Fifty Years. Milan, OH.: Ledger Publishing Co., 1959.

Willard, Eugene B. (general supervising editor) A Standard History of The Hanging Rock Iron Region of Ohio, Volume II. Chicago: The Lewis Publishing Co., 1916.

Wimberg, Robert J. Cincinnati Breweries. Cincinnati: Ohio Book Store, 1997.

Wingerter, Charles A. History of Greater Wheeling and Vicinity. Chicago: Lewis Publishing, 1912.

Wiseman, C. M. L. Centennial History of Lancaster, Ohio, and Lancaster People, 1898, the 100th Anniversary of the Settlement of the Spot Where Lancaster Stands. Lancaster, Ohio: C.M.L. Wiseman, 1898.

Wright, G. Frederick. A Standard History of Lorain County, Ohio. Chicago: The Lewis Publishing Co., 1916.

Schade's brewery directory of 1878-79

United States Census records

Miscellaneous pamphlets, brochures, and other advertising pieces produced by various brewers

Records of deed transfers from the county recorder's office in each county researched

Trade Journals

The Beverage Journal
Brewer and Maltster
The Brewers Digest
The Brewers Journal
Brewers News
Brewery Age
Buckeye Tavern
Great Lakes Brewing News
Modern Brewer/Modern Brewery
Modern Brewery Age
The Western Brewer

City Directories

Akron, Alliance, Ashtabula, Bellaire, Cambridge, Canal Dover, Canal Fulton, Canton, Cleveland, East Liverpool, Gallipolis, Ironton, Lancaster, Leetonia, Lorain, Louisville, Mansfield, Marietta, Martins Ferry, Massillon, McConnelsville, Milan, Monroeville, Mount Vernon, Nelsonville, New Philadelphia, Newark, Niles, Norwalk, Painesville, Pomeroy, Salem, Sandusky, Steubenville, Warren, Willoughby, Woodsfield, Wooster, Youngstown, Zanesville.

County Atlases

Ashland, Belmont, Columbiana, Coshocton, Cuyahoga, Erie, Fairfield, Gallia, Holmes, Huron, Jefferson, Knox, Lake, Lawrence, Licking, Lorain, Mahoning, Meigs, Monroe, Morgan, Muskingum, Portage, Richland, Stark, Summit, Trumbull, Tuscarawas, Washington, Wayne.

Newspapers

Akron *Beacon Journal* and *Germania*
Alliance *Review and Leader*
Bellaire *Daily Leader*
Canton *Repository*
Cleveland *Herald*, *Plain Dealer*, and *Press*
Columbus *Citizen*
East Liverpool *Review*
Grindstone City Advertiser
Ironton *Register* and *Journal*
Lancaster *Daily Gazette*, *Daily Eagle*, and *Eagle-Gazette*
Lorain *Daily News* and *The Journal*
Louisville *Herald*
Mansfield *Daily Shield*, *News*, and *News Journal*
Martins Ferry *The Daily Times*
Massillon *Independent*
Milan *Advertiser* and *Ledger*
Nelsonville *Tribune*
New Philadelphia *The Daily Times* and *Times Reporter*
Newark *Leader* and *Advocate and American Tribune*

Norwalk *Evening Herald, Experiment, Reflector* and *Reporter*
Ohio *Repository*
Painesville *Telegraph*
Pomeroy *Leader*
Sandusky *Register, Daily Register* and *Daily Commercial Register*
Steubenville *Herald-Star* and *Weekly Herald*
Tuscarawas Advocate
Wachter Und Anzeiger
Wellston *Telegram*
Western Herald and Steubenville Gazette
Youngstown *Vindicator*
Zanesville *Times Recorder*

INDEX

'84 Pilsener Beer	59
A-1 Beer	146
Aberle, Theodore	250
Abita Brewing Co.	163
Achauer, Christian Frederick	13,239,240
Achauer, Herman	240
Aenis, William brewery	114
Aiken Bill	25,219,269,303
Airship Light Ale	293
Akron Aeros baseball team	247,295
Akron Beverage and Cold Storage Co.	289
Akron Brewing Co. (postPro)	100,290-291
Akron Brewing Co., The (prePro)	17,18,266,278, 284,288-290,295,315
Akron Gear Co.	229,281
Akron Malt Products Co.	284,295
Akron/Macon German Style Alt Bier	247
Alban, Edward	57
Albl, Frank E.	131
Albl, Michael	17,130
Alder & Co.	177
Alder, James	172,177
Alessi's Restaurant	248
Alexakos, Nick	165
All-American Blonde Pale Ale	247
Allen, Matt	245
Allen, Robert "Bunky"	216
Allen, Theresa "Tess"	216
Alliance Beverage Co.	256
Alliance Brewery	255
Alliance Brewing Co.	53,69,113,223, 255
Alliance Ice & Coal Co.	256
Alltmont, Chris	166,205,233
aluminum cans	287
Alyce on the East Bank	162
Ambrose, Harry F.	56
America House Tavern & Brewery	239,240
American Beverage Corp.	231
American Bottling Works	224
American Brewery Co. (Marietta)	311
American Brewery (Youngstown)	224
American Brewing Academy	283
American Brewing Co.	117
American Can Co.	132
American House hotel	224
American Maid Beer	241
Amwell Brewery	313
Anchor Steam Brewery	292
Anders, Carl	116,117
Anders, Fred J.	117
Anderson, J. K.	297
Anderton, J. & Co. brewery	71
Anderton, Jonathan	71
Andre, Charles	213-215
Angel, Mrs. Mary	114
Anhaeusser Co-Operative Bottling Co.	109
Anhaeusser Malt Tonic	109
Anhaeusser, Herman	109
Anheuser-Busch, Inc.	13,16,20,21,120, 122,140-142,147,148,151,167,229,246,291
Anievas, Marc	161
Anther, Jacob	234
Anti-Saloon League	25-28,69
Antony, Edward	263,265
Apella apple juice	272
Apple Creek Brewery	313,314
Arbaugh, A. R.	266
Archer, T. L.	311
Arentrue, Anne	202
Arentrue, John	202
Arentrue, John, Jr.	202
Arizona Brewing Co.	146
Armbruster, Albert	242
Armbruster, Fabian	242
Armstrong, Alexander brewery	50,197
Armstrong, Alexander, Jr.	197
Arnold, William	72
Arroyo, Laura	231
Arroyo, Robert	231
Asbeck, Reinhold J.	57,215
Ashtabula Brewing & Cold Storage Co.	55
Asian Moon Golden Lager Beer	166
Asian Star Brewing Co.	166
Atlantic Brewing Co.	103
Atwood Yacht Club Brewpub	66,187
Aubele, John, Jr.	127
Augustine, Theodore	184
Austgen, Charles	295
Austgen, Philip	295
Ayers Rock Pale Ale	163,165,233
B & O Station Brewery and Restaurant	231,292
Babick, Brett	161
Babst, Jacob	257
Bachmann, George	70
Backdraft Stout	163
Backe, John	288,289
Baehr brewery	106,107,110,123, 167
Baehr, Emil	107
Baehr, Herman C.	107
Baehr, Jacob	96,106,107
Baehr, Magdalena	107
Baehr-Phoenix Brewery	107,110,125
Baier, George	177
Baker, John	260
Ballantine, P. & Sons, Inc.	142
Ballentine, David	239
Ballentine, John	239
Balser, Henry	259
Balser, Kasper	258,259,297
Balser, Louisa	259,297
Balser, Philip brewery	248
Baltes, Charles E.	168
Balto Heroic Golden Lager Beer	293
Bamer, William	70
Bammerlin, Charles J.	269,270
Bammerlin, Leonard	270

323

Banner Beer and Ale	286	Bender, Magdalena	172
Banner Brewing Co.	232	Bender, Rudolph A.	63
Barber, Joseph	230	Benner, Ernest	213
Barker, Jim	157	Bennett, Emerson	183
Barley's Brewing Co.	187,216	Bennett, Robert	79
Barons Brewpub	161	Benskin, F. G.	266
Barrett & Barrett	80,115	Benson, John	302
Barrett Brewing Co.	114,115,123,139	Bentlich, Adolph	213
Barrett, Charles	115	Bentlich, William	213
Barrett, Hugh C.	305	Berberich, M. F.	266
Barrett, William	115	Berea Brewery	77
Barrett/Bohemian brewery	125,126,128	Berg, Conrad	254
Bartholomay Brewing Co.	168	Berger, Michael	299,301
Barton & McGowan	238,239	Bernard, John	172
Basel, Michael	166	Bernhardt, Christian	299
Basler, Joseph	197,198	Bernhardt, Fred, Jr.	299
Basler, Joseph, Jr.	198	Bernhardt, Frederick	298,299,308
Basler, Maximillian	198	Berns, Frances	185
Basler, William	198	Berns, Herman brewery	185,186
Baumaister, Matthias	12	Berns, William	185
Baumann, Fred	10	Best Beer and Ale	286
Bavarian Brewery (Sandusky)	177	Beter, Frederick	197
Bavarian Brewing Co. (Zanesville)	241,244	Bevera beverage	99
Baver & Leisgang	167	Beverwyck Brewing Co.	138
Bay Brewing Co.	246	Bevyl, James W.	304
Bay City Brewery	177	Bicking, Augustus	258
Bayer, John	224	Bieber, Lewis	74
Beardsley, John	191	Bieberson, Henry	61,256
Bearing Distributors, Inc.	229,281	Bieberson, Henry, Jr.	61
Beaver Falls Brewing Co.	67	Biehl, Jacob A.	174
Bechtel, John brewery	24,202,203	Biery, Samuel	72
Becker, E. Brewing Co. (Lancaster)	12,181-183	Big Red Roo Ale	163,165,233
Becker, Ernest	181,182	Billman, Walter S.	290
Becker, George	218	Bilsky, Marvin	129,130
Becker, Harry E.	182,183	Bimeler, Joseph	307
Becker, Ochs, & Co.	182	Bingham Smokehouse, Brewery, & Cidery	167
Bedeaux, R. E.	228	Bingmann, Charles	211
Bedford Brewing Co.	167	Bingmann, Otto	211
Beedy, Doug	78,231,292	Bingo Beer (Cambridge)	186
Beer Barrel Saloon	246	Bingo Beer (Milan)	171
Beer Can Collectors of America (BCCA)	150	Bishop, Daniel	297
Beer Shampoo	305,306	Bishop, Feit	192,193
Beggs, Robert	80	Bishop, John A. brewery	82,167
Beier, Fred J.	173	Bishop, John brewery (Elyria)	218
Bel-Brew	62,64	Bishop's Beer	232
Bellaire Beverage Co.	59	Bismarck Beer	182
Bellaire Brewing Co. (I)	58,59,62,244, 310,311	Bittman, Michael	276
		Black Dallas Malt Liquor	102,103
Bellaire Brewing Co. (II)	65	Black Forest Beer	113,114,157,158
Bellos, Frances	230	Black Jack Beer	304
Bellos, Louis J.	230	Black Label Beer 140-149,152	71,87,133,138,
Belmont Ale Brewery Corp.	64	Black Label Malt Liquor	147
Belmont Beer	61,63	Black, George M., Jr.	145
Belmont Brewing Co.	59-65,291	Blackbeard Stout	233
Belmont Products Co.	19,59,62,63	Blackstone, Ira	57
Beltz Brewing Co.	125	Blackwell, Lloyd, & Co.	81
Beltz, Carl E. Weiss Beer Brewery	133	Blaett, Jugend	89
Beltz, Carl	112	Blatz Near Beer	304
Beltz, John J.	112	Blatz, Charles L.	170
Beltz, Joseph 256	112,113,133,167,	Blessig, Jacob	207
		Blimp City Brewery	247
Beltz, Lawrence C.	112	Block, Adrian	14
Beltz, Otto W.	113,256	Blocker, Gottlieb	236
Ben Brew Beer	119	Bloomaschine, John	234
Ben Franklin Department Stores	120	Blueberry Hill brewpub	187
Bender, Elliott M.	176	Bobsean, Henry	263,265
Bender, Evelyn	230	Bockzilla Bock Beer	161
Bender, John	172		

Boehmke, Henry	109	Buckeye Brewing Co. (Bedford Heights)	76
Boes, Charles	74	Buckeye Brewing Co. (Toledo)	130,176
Bohannon, Benton P.	137	Buckeye Weiss Beer Brewing Co.	120
Bohannon, James A.	137,140-145	Bucyrus Brewery	12
Bohemian Brewing Co.	90,114-116,121, 123,124,139	Budweiser Beer	101,120,122,142, 146,167,199,299
Bohn, August	243,244	Buehler, Charles T.	200,201
Bohn, Frederick	75	Buehler, John	25,199-201
Bohn, Sebastian	242,243	Bula Beer	54
Bola Beverage	95,126	Bull Dog Ale	70
Bola Products Co.	126	Bullinger, Frederick	77
Bold, John D.	300	Bunky's Brewpub	165,216
Bolivar Brewing Co.	167	Burckhardt, August brewery	110,166,271
Bond, Alan	149	Burckholter, Christian	237
Booker, Eric	246	Burger Beer and Ale	287
Booth, George	224	Burger Brewing Co.	131,158,286,287
Borger, Jacob	114	Burgerer, Samuel	72
Born Brewing Co.	213	Burgie, Robb	254
Bossert, Henry	70	Burkhardt Brewing Co. (Green)	233,287,294
Boston Beer Co.	20,158,159	Burkhardt Brewing Co. (Medina)	233
Boston Mills Brewery	292	Burkhardt Brewing Co. (Akron)	13,18-20,50,241, 282-287,294,295
Bosworth, P. S.	166		
Bowen, Lennon A.	264	Burkhardt Consolidated Co.	284-287
Bower, P. A.	59	Burkhardt Insurance Co.	286
Bowers, Peter	202	Burkhardt Products Co.	284
Bowers, Ray	215	Burkhardt Realty Co.	284
Bowlsby, Cornelia A.	96	Burkhardt, Gus, Jr.	286,287
Bowlus, Samuel L.	267	Burkhardt, Gustav	283-285
Boyd, James	238	Burkhardt, Margaretha	283,284
Brading Breweries	141	Burkhardt, Thomas	233,287,294
Brady, James	191	Burkhardt, Tom, Jr.	294
Brady, Patrick	191	Burkhardt, Wilhelm	260,282,283
Braman, Harry S.	297	Burkhardt, William L.	285,287,294
Brandstetter, Xavier F. brewery	184	Burkhardt, William	283,284
Brannon, Kevin	159	Burkhardt, William, Jr.	287
Braun, Frank	110	Burkhardt's Custom Inn	286
Braun, Jay	157	Burkhardt's Diamond Jubilee Beer	286
Braun, William brewery	217	Burkhardt's Select Export Beer	233,283-285
Breckle, Josh	160	Burkhart, Anton	308
Brenner & Co.	240,242	Burkholder, John	312
Brenner, John A.	242	Burkholder, Jonathon	24,312,313
Brew Keeper, The	76	Burning River Pale Ale	154,155
Brew Kettle, The	164	Butte, John C.	198,199
brewed on premises brewery (BOP)	76,162,164	Buzz Beer	164,168
Brewer, John C.	79	Byrd, Dolly	169
Brewery At The Bay	246	Byrd, Michael	169
Brewery Company, The	185	Cable, Lawrence	172
Brewhouse, The	267	Cafaro Co.	232
Brewing Corp. of America	19,50,87,115, 127,132,137,139-145	Cain, Paul M.	185
		Cake, John	257
Brewing Corp. of Canada	139-141	Cambridge Brewing Co.	18,185,213
Brewmaster's Special Beer	127,128	Cambridge Ice & Storage Co.	186
Brick Brewery	149	Canadian Ace Brewing Co.	103
Briggs Street Brewery	106,107	Canadian Breweries, Ltd.	139,141,145, 147-149
Bright, John	172,177		
Bristol, F. Charles	291	Canal Park stadium	247,295
Brobst, John A.	263,264	Canton Brewery	50,257
Brodt, John	277	Canton Brewing Co. (prePro)	235,260-264, 271,272,282,299,302
Brooker, Al	252		
Brooks, Doug	56	Canton Brewing Co. (postPro)	27,266,267,272, 315
Brown Derby Roadhouse	233		
Brown, D. E.	185	Canton Ice & Cold Storage Co.	266
Brown, John	166	Canton Small Beer Co.	275
Brown, Nathan	166	Canton Standard/Export Beer	262,299
Bruckmann, John C.	215	Captain Tony's Pizza and Pasta Emporium	76
Bruh, Michael	74	Cardinal Ale	296
Bryson, Bill	165,205	Carey, Drew	164,168
Buck, Andrew	244	Carl, James F.	304

Carling & Co.	80,96,114	Cleveland Brown Ale	154
Carling Ale, Porter, & Stout	80,114,115,126	Cleveland Browns NFL team	128,129,138,158, 160
Carling Amber Crème Ale	143		
Carling Brewing Co.	138,146-149	Cleveland Cavaliers NBA team	85,157,160,161
Carling Malt Liquor	147	Cleveland Chophouse and Brewery	21,160,162
Carling National Brewing Co.	149	Cleveland City Brewery	81,105,106
Carling O'Keefe Breweries	149	Cleveland Co-Operative Brewing Co.	167
Carling, Sir John	80,139	Cleveland Grand Prix	151,157
Carling, Thomas	80,139	Cleveland Home Brewing Co.	50,88,112-114, 125,142,157,256
Carling, W. & J.'s City Brewery	139		
Carling, William	139	Cleveland Hygeia Ice Co.	90
Carling's Inc.	143	Cleveland Indians baseball team	101,136,148,157, 160,161
Carlisle, L. E.	185		
Carmichael Construction Co.	291	Cleveland Lumberjacks hockey team	160,161
Carroll, Harmon	204	Cleveland Metroparks Zoo	104
Carter, George S.	103,119,120	Cleveland Rams NFL team	128
Carter, William	288	Cleveland Trust Co.	85,107,137
Cascade Beer	265	Clevelander Beer	113
Cedar Point	178,179	Cleveland-Sandusky Brewing Corp.	95,127-130,142, 175,176
Centanni, Thomas W.	152		
Chagrin Falls Brewery	78	Cleveland-Sandusky Co.	126,155,180
Chaitoff, Craig	168	Clicco-Brew Beer	126
Chapek, Joseph V.	131	Cline, William	239
Chapman, Henry	216	Clipper Beer	227
Chapman, Talbot	216	Clossman, David	239
Chapman, William	124	Clossman, John	239
Charters, Alexander	107	Clossman, John, Jr.	239
Cheerio Ale	87	Cloud Nine Belgian Style White Beer	161
Chero-Cola	231,272	Coca-Cola	18,70,71,149, 264,265
Childs, Herrick	79		
Chormann, Louis	90	Cohen, Mike	170
Chovjan, Joseph	171	Cole, Matt	163,246
Christian Moerlein Beer	158,159	Coliseum in Richfield	85
Christiansen, Hans	14	Collins, Thomas	166
Church Street Brewery	78	Colt 45 Malt Liquor	149
Cincinnati Brewing Co.	168	Columbia Brewing Co.	105,111,123,126
Cintron, Bob	163	Columbus Brewing Co.	187
Cintron, Gary	163	Columbus-Associated Breweries Co.	18
Ciotta, Peter M.	152	Commodore Perry India Pale Ale	154,155
City Bottling Works (Youngstown)	229	Conlon, Walter J.	215
City Brewery (Canton)	257-260,297	Consumers Beer	214
City Brewery (Cleveland)	80,105	Consumers Brewing & Ice Co. (Dover)	300
City Brewery (LaCrosse, WI.)	159,287	Consumers Brewing Co. (Ashtabula)	18,52-55,69,223, 255
City Brewery (Massillon)	270		
City Brewery (Newark)	74,212	Consumers Brewing Co. (Newark)	17,57,185,213-216,244
City Brewery (Norwalk)	192,193		
City Brewery (Sandusky)	172	Consumers Products Co. (Newark)	214
City Brewery (Steubenville)	198-200	Contie, LeRoy J.	171
City Brewery (Youngstown)	224,225	Continental Can Co.	71,227,286,304
City Brewery (Zanesville)	240,242,243	Continuous Brewing Process	148
City Brewing Co. (Tiffin)	13	Conway, Daniel	153,155,156
City Ice and Coal Co. (Akron)	284,286,287	Conway, Patrick	153,155,156
City Ice and Coal Co. (Canal Dover)	299	Conway's Irish Ale	154,155
City Ice and Fuel Co.	117	Cook, Conrad	249
City Products Co.	119	Cook, Walter E.	152
Cizauskas, Thomas	165	Cooke, John Hawley	79
Clark, Adam	239	Cool Mule Porter	157,158
Clarkson, Joseph	293	Coonrad, George	236
Clements, George brewery	297	Coopers Gold Kolsch Beer	163
Clements, George, Jr.	297	Coors Brewing Co.	20
Cleveland & Sandusky Brewing Co.	18,50,52,88,89, 93,95,98,105,107-115,123-130,134,139,175,180,218,219,232,263,291	Corlett, Amanda	99
		Corll, Peter J.	297
Cleveland American Light Beer	160	Corn, Jasper	194
Cleveland Arena	118	Corn, Mary	194
Cleveland Barons hockey team	118	Cornell, Sam	224
Cleveland Brewers' Board of Trade	124	Cornerstone Brewing Co.	78,231
Cleveland Brewery	79,105	Coulter, Samuel	257
Cleveland Brewing Co.	88,113,123,124, 126,168	Court Products Co.	210

Covert Baking Co.	311	Derethik, Gary	162
Crabtree, John M. brewery	219,220	Dertinger, William	92
Crater, Frederick	298	Dettling, Jacob	288,289
Craze, Andrew	161	Dettling, John	288,289
Creadon, Stephen S.	121,133,135	Dettling, Louis	288,289
Creadon, George E.	135,137	Dew, James	56
Creadon's Ginger Ale	135	Dewalt, George	258
Creekside Brewhouse and Tavern	217	DeWitt Beer and Ale	132
Creighton, Paul L.	143	DeWitt, J. I.	55
Creighton, S. Taylor	143	Diamond Land and Improvement Co.	289
Crimson Colt Ale	295	Diamondback Brewery & Pub	21,160,161,163, 233
Crockery City Brewing & Ice Co.	17,18,53,68-70, 72,94,223,256	Didas, Edward	244
Crockery City Farms	70	Diebolt Brewing Co.	89-91,121,123, 167
Crockery City Ice & Products Co.	70	Diebolt, Anthony J.	90,91,124
Crooked River Brewing Co.	78,114,156-159, 164,166,233,287,293,294	Diebolt, Frank	90
Crooked River Select Lager Beer	158	Diebolt, Joseph	90,91
Cropper, Marshall	62	Diebolt, Mathias	90,91
Crowley, Pete	160	Diebolt's White Seal Beer	90
Crown, Cork, & Seal Co.	280	Diehl, Christian Brewing Co.	231
Crowntainer beer can	280	Diehl, George	298
Crump, Porter, & Brother	107	Diemer, Frank E.	168
Crystal Ice and Coal Co.	183	Dietrich, Daniel	211
Crystal Rock Beer	126-129,175, 176,179,180	Dietz, George	110
		Dilger, George brewery	268,269
Crystal Rock Castle	178,179	Dilger, George	13
Crystal Rock Cereal Beverage	126,175	Dillon, Thomas A.	52
Crystal Rock Dopple Bock Lager Beer	245	Dillonvale Brewing Co.	65
Crystal Rock Products Co.	19,126,175	Dippel, George	285,287
Crystal Rock spring	174,175	Distillers & Brewers Corp. of America	63
Crystal Top Beer	230,231	Ditton, John	78
Crystal Top Brewery, Inc.	230,231	Divis, Tom	248
Cumberland Brewing Co.	176	Dommy, Peter	273
Curran, Ed	288	Donnenwirth, George, Jr.	12
Cuyahoga Brewing Co.	167	Dorn, J. P.	172
Cuyahoga Falls Brewery	293	Dorn, Philip	176
Dahlgren, Chuck	233,294	Dornbusch, E. D.	219
Dalin, Andrew	55	Dortmunder Gold Beer	154,155
Daly, Thomas	171	Dottore, Mark	159
Danckers, Stephen	157,164	Doubert, George	167
Dangeleisen, John brewery	89	Dover Beer	299
Dangerfield, James	82	Dover Brewing Co.	262,272,298-300,302
Dangleisen, Andy	298	Dover Ice & Cold Storage Co.	300
Dark Horse Brewing Co.	167	Dover Steam Brewery	298
Darmany, William	202	Dover, James	14
Dater, John	168	Dowie, Ian R.	145,147
Dauch, Phillip	172	Downer, Truman	81,91,95
Daugherty, Oral	57	Downey, Basil	298
Davies, John	106	Downs, William	55
Davis, Edward	77	Dragonslayer Scottish Export Ale	292
Davis, Edward, Jr.	77	Drybrough, F. W.	132
Dawg Pound Brown Ale	160	Duke Beer	151,152
Dayton Breweries Co.	18	Dunkle, Harry W.	118
DeBartolo Construction Co.	230	Dunlap, Andrew	195,196
DeBos, C. B.	275	Duquesne Beer	120
Dee Light Beer	114	Duquesne Brewing Co.	120,150,151,300
Deerfield Ginger Ale	126,175	Eagle Beer	278,279
Degnan, James	72	Eagle Brewery (Cleveland)	81,91,104
Deibel, Ernest C.	278-280	Eagle Brewery (Ironton)	208-210
Deibel, Ernest E.	281	Eagle Brewery (Mansfield)	249-253
DeLuca, Anthony C.	70	Eagle Export Beer	251
DeLuca, George A.	70	East Ironton Brewery	207
DeMaioribus, Alessandro "Sonny"	113,114	East Liverpool Ice & Coal Co.	68
DeMaioribus, Dr. Anthony D.	113	East Liverpool Spring Water Brewery	67
Denbert, George	114	Eberhard, Edward	256
Derethik, Alyce	162	Eberhard, George	273
Derethik, Dustin	162		

Eberhardt Brewing Co. (Pittsburgh)	250	Fink, John	282
Ebert Brewing Co.	210	Fink, William	282
Ebert, Leo brewery	207,208	Finlay Brewing Co.	52,168,311
Ebert, Leo Brewing Co.	208-210	Firehouse Brewery & Restaurant	163
Ebert, Leo	207-209	Fisch, Fred	244
Ebert, Otto	209,210	Fischer, Andrew	172
Eckenberger, Joseph	201	Fishel $500 Bond Beer	125
Eckert, Glenn	63,65	Fishel Brewing Co.	95,123,125,126
Eclipse Dark Scottish Ale	233,294	Fishel, Oscar J.	126,127
Edel, George J.	262	Fishel, Simon	114,124-126
Edel, George	261-263	Fishel, Theodore	126
Edmund Fitzgerald Porter	154,155	Fishel, William H.	265
Edwards, Richard	137	Fisher Bros. Brewery	242
Edwards, William Co.	106,168	Fisher, Conrad	242
Ehle, Frederick	120	Fisher, Isiah	315
Ehrlich, Joseph G.	132	Fisher, Joseph	208
Eicher, John	266	Fisher, Lewis	51
Eichhorn, Peter	213	Fix, Karlos brewery	103
Eick, Albert W.	59,60,62,63	Fleming, John B.	169
Eick, Ferdinand H.	60-62	Fletcher, Daniel	166
Eiler, Frederick	249	Fletcher, Levi	193
Eilert Beverage Co.	122	Fletcher, Mary	166
Eilert Brewing Co.	122-123,140,142	Foley, John H.	266
Eilert, Henry F.	105,122,123	Follmer, Peter	275
Eilert's Clev-Ale	122	Ford, Daniel	99
Eilert's Supreme Lager	122	Forest City Brewery (I)	80,128,139
Eisele, Albert	53	Forest City Brewery (II)	82,166
Elk's Brew Beer	215	Forest City Brewery (Massillon)	269,270
Embassy Club Beer and Ale	286	Forest City Brewery of Cincinnati	131
Embree, Davis	14	Forest City Brewery, Inc.	131
Emish, Frank	56	Forest City Brewing Co.	17,50,87,130,
Empire Brewery	270,271	131,142,143,304,305	
Englehart, Harry	290,291	Forest City Malt House	269,270
Englehart, Nicholas	248	Forest City New Process Co.	131
Epple, Elmer	311	Forest Rose Beer and Ale	57,183
Epple, Jacob	310	Forge Industries	229,281
Epple, Minnie	311	Formula Ten-O-Two	137
Erhard, Carl F.	271	Fornecker, Jacob	282,283
Erie Brewing Co.	52,55,151	Fort Steuben Brewing Co.	201
Erie Sales Co.	85	Fountain Brewery (Canal Fulton)	256,257
Erin Brew/Ehren Brau Beer	20,134-137,168	Fountain City Brewing Co.	12
Erlanger, Joseph	105	Four Fellows Pub & Eatery	165,294
Evans, William	288	Fovargue, Creasey, Jr.	82
Excelsior Brewing Co.	121	Fovargue, Daniel	82
Excelsior Mower & Reaper Works	290	Fox, John	107
Excelsior Success Beer	121	Fox, Vincenz	172,176
Expansion Draft Beer	158	Francis, Scott	187
Extra Pilsener Beer	116	Frank, Albert G.	254
Faber, Fred	315	Frank, Louis	253
Fahle, Franz	107	Frank, Martin & Son brewery	253,254
Faller, Carl F.	267	Frank, Martin (I)	250,253
Faller, Carl	99,101	Frank, Martin (II)	254
Fallows, Reverend Samuel	232	Frank's Beverage	254
Falstaff Brewing Corp.	142,145,147	Frankel, David	86
Famous Supply Co.	201	Frankel, Harry	86
Farr, Joseph	191	Frankel, Mitch	158
Feick, George	173	Frankenmuth Brewing Co.	146,246
Feighan, Francis	137	Franklin Brewing Co.	119
Feighan, John T.	133,135,137	Frederick Brewing Co.	154,159,293
Feighan, John T., Jr.	137	Freeze, Charles	260
Feller, William/Wilhelm	58,59,244,310	Freundl, Frank	230
Fertig, George E.	300	Friedman, Arrel	230
Fetterman, John	118	Friedman, David	230
Fickel, Jacob	83	Frisbie, Ken	55
Fife, James brewery	50,197	Fritch, Martin	283
Fife, John	50,197	Froehlich, John F.	114
Fifty-Fifty Beverage	126	Fromm, Carl	103,118
Fink, Conrad	282	Fronterol, Conrad	207

Frontwaters Restaurant and Brewing Co.	176,245	Good, J. Edward	281
Fuchs, F. Wm.	288,295	Good, Jacob	276,281,282
Fuchs, Fred W.	290	Goodspeed, Jeanne	146
Full Weight Tonic	134	Goodwin, Albert A.	78
Fulton Brewery	256,257,273	Goodyear blimp	247
Gaddel, Caroline	309	Goodyear Tire & Rubber Co.	279
Gaddel, Charles	309	Graaf, Alfred	218
Gaddel, Jacob	309	Graber Brewing Co.	266
Gaennsler, Philip	110	Graber, John D. brewery	260
Gaessler brewery	260	Graber, John	268,314
Gaessler, Frederick	282,283	Graber, Samuel E.	266,315
Gambrinus Beer	241,254	Graeter, Augustus brewery	296,297
Ganger, Arthur H.	152	Graeter, Herman	297
Garfield, Alexander H.	204	Graeter, Sarah	297
Garlach, Jacob	72	Graf, John	51
Garretts Mill Brewing Co.	248	Graff, Christian	259
Garver, Alexander	273	Graff, Jacob	212,213
Gavagan Ale Brewery	167	Grafs, Peter	273
Gavagan, Patrick	106	Grand Rapids Brewing Co.	280
Gayer, Jacob	284,288	Graves, J. H.	186
GB Beer	129	Gray, Tom	160,163,233
Gehring Beer	232	Graybill, Chuck	292
Gehring, Albert	92	Great American Beer Festival	155,158,160-162,164,168,205,268,292,293
Gehring, C. E. Brewing Co.	91-93,123,124,126		
		Great Lakes Brewing Co.	21,95,153-156,159,163,168,292
Gehring, C. E., Jr.	92		
Gehring, Carl Ernst	81,91,95	Great White Wheat Ale	163,165,233
Gehring, Frederick W.	92,93,124	Greater Cleveland Brewing Co.	167
Gehring, John A.	92	Green Dragon	139
Geib, Francis	167	Green Hornet	192
Geib, Louis	298	Green, Stephen S.	121
Geiger, Fannie	207	Greenwell, Brian	267
Geiger, Fred W.	209,210	Greenwood Brothers Brewery	67
Geiger, Leo	210	Greenwood, Henry	67
Geiger, Loeb, & Co.	207	Greenwood, Joseph	67
Geiger, Peter	207	Greenwood, Martha	68
General Foods	85	Greenwood, Thomas	67,68
Genkinger, Christian	224	Gridiron Brewpub & Grille	267
Genuine 51 Flavor	119	Griebel, Philip	110
Gerke Brewing Co.	311	Griesedieck-Western Brewing Co.	146
Gerke, William A.	65	Groff, Daniel	273
Gfell, George	192	Grohe, Adam	248
Giessen, Otto	260-262,282	Grohs, Frederick brewery	309,310
Gill, A. W.	213	Gromlich, J.	89
Gill, Herbert R.	185,213	Gross, William	245
Ging, John F.	170	Grossklaus, Edward	273
Gintz, Slat, & Car brewery	308	Grossvater Beer	226,250-252,278-281,284
GlaCo Products Co.	65		
Glantz, Harry A.	128	Grossvater Brew	251
Glaser, John P.	65	Grotenfend, Charles	171
Glaser, Joseph	65	Grotzinger, Johanus	308
Glunz, William C.	121	Grouche, R.	65
Goebel, Rev. George F.	242,243	Growers Chemical Corp.	171
Gold Bond Beer	125-129,175,176	Gruber, Charles	275
Gold Bond Beverage Co.	126	Gruber, Christian	275
Gold Bond Beverage	95	Gruber, Henry brewery	275
Gold Bond Polka Party	129	Gruetzmacher, Erik	205
Gold Crown Export Beer	255,256	Gruner, Walter	266,289,290,295
Golden Age Beverage Co.	231	Guehring, George	228
Golden Dawn Beer and Ale	85,86	Guentzler, Rudolf	166
Golden Export Beer	265	Guggenheim, Arthur L.	131
Golden Seal Beer	121	Guinness Stout	15
Goldling's Retriever Pale Ale	268,293	Gund Arena	85,157,160,161
Gollwitzer, Frank	127	Gund Brewing Co.	50,84,113,123
Good Park golf course	281	Gund Realty Co.	84,87
Good, John T. brewery (I)	276	Gund, George F. II	19,84,124
Good, John T. brewery (II)	281	Gund, George F.	83
Good, George	288	Gund, George Foundation	85

Gund, George III	85	Heath, William	300
Gund, Gordon	85	Hecht, Joseph	85
Gund, John Brewing Co.	83	Heidelberg Beer	146,147,149
Gund's Clevelander Beer	84	Heidelberg Brewing Co.	146
Gund's Crystal Beer	84	Heileman, G. Brewing Co.	149,151,152,159, 246
Gunn, Alexander	308	Heilman, Howard J.	65
Gunn, David	295	Heintel, Charles	121
Guth, Jacob R.	281,282	Heismann, The Beer	154
Guttman, Odon	304	Heist, C. H.	297
Haag, Conrad	270	Held, Christian	310
Haag, Frederick	270	Helfenbein, William H.	61
Haas, Christian F.	239,240	Heller, Edward	215
Hafenbrack, Ernst	289	Hellstern, John L.	200
Hafenbrak, Adolph	301,302	Hemmerdinger, F.	166
Hager, William	211	Henkel, Frederick	184
Hahn, Jacob	259	Hennemann, Jacob	309
Hahn, Matthew	166	Henninger, George brewery	78
Haid, Christian brewery	229	Herancourt Brewing Co.	232
Haid, J. V.	62	Herb, Anton	170
Haid, Mary	229	Herb, Charles	170
Haley, John P.	80	Herb, Joseph Brewing Co.	50,170,193
Half and Half Beer	118	Herb, Joseph	170
Halle, Moses	114	Herb, Mary	170
Haller, Benjamin	72	Hermann, George	261,262
Haller, Jacob F.	121,122	Hess, Frederick	273
Haller, Martin	114	Hieronimus, A. F.	264
Halm, Jacob	12	Higgins, Charles S.	172
Haltnorth, Frederick	96-98,103,109	Hill Top Beer	241
Hamilton, George W.	81,104	Hill Top Beverages	241
Hamilton, J. J.	223	Hill, David	160,161
Hamilton, John	196	Hipp, William	150,151
Hammer, John J.	120	Hirsch, Howard R.	122
Hammerl, A. J.	290	Hirzell, Emil	256
Hammond, John	172	Ho Ho Ho Magic Tincture	76
Hammond, Venewel	106	Hoag, Bernard C.	119
Hankey, Charles brewery	58	Hochgesang, Joseph	207
Hanna, Thompson	197	Hochwald estate	103
Hansky, Max	131,132	Hock Hocking Beer	56-57
Hanson, William	273	Hocking Canal	181,183
Happy, William	61	Hocking Valley Brewery, Inc.	57
Hardin, John	166	Hocking Valley Brewing Co.	56-57,215
Harding, Warren	26	Hocking Valley Cereal Beverage Co.	57
Hargreaves, George	295	Hock-Ola	57
Hariot, Thomas	14	Hodge, Clark R.	106
Harmann, George	277	Hoffer, Joseph	244
Harper, Isaac	190	Hoffman, Louis	88
Harr, Henry P.	54	Hoffman, Ray	215
Harris, Jack H.	131,132,300,304, 306	Hoffman, Robert	88
		Hoffmann, Henry brewery	111
Harris, Jim	160	Hoffmann, William	111
Harry, J. H.	305	Hohenadel, Eugene	56
Hartford, Thomas	257	Hohman, Paul	90
Hartung, George A.	122,224	Holbyson, Emmaline	270
Harvey, John	249,250	Holbyson, John	270
Hardware Supply Co.	281	Holland, Robert F.	281
Hau, John	289	Holters, Frank	215
Hausch, A. J.	287	Holy Moses, The Beer	154,155
Haushalter, Frederick	282	Holzapfel, Andrew	194
Hawbaker, Terry	56,311	Holzapfel, Henry	194
Hawley, Joseph	79	Holzapfel, Leonard	194
Hawley, Richard	79	Home Brewery (Newark)	211
Hawley, Thomas	79	Home Brewing Co. (Canton)	17,263-266
Hayes, Rutherford B.	24	Home Brewing Co. (Richmond, VA.)	152
Hayes, Woody	304	Homegardner, John	172,174
Haynes, Plummer G.	65	Homegardner, Roy	175,176
Hazard's Microbrewery and Restaurant	246	Homola, John	243
Hazlett, Robert	239	Hoover, Herbert	27
Hazlett, William	239		

Hoppus Maximus Ale	268,293	Ives, Levi F.	95,96
Horix, Fred brewery (I)	287	Ives, Samuel C.	79,81
Horix, Fred	277,278,287,288	Jacobs Field	157,160
Horn & Co. brewery	243	Jahreis, John C.	143
Horn, Adolph H.	242-244	James, C. Gilbert	228
Horn, Edward	300	James, Carl	229,281
Horn, Frederick	242	Jeckell, Samuel	277
Horn, Jacob	298,300,301	Jefferin, Jefferson	172
Horvath, Mike	267	Jewel Export Beer	223
Horwitz, Larry	254	John Bull Beer	304-306
Hoster Brewing Co. (brewpub)	216,254	John Harvard's Brewhouse	162,165
Hoster Brewing Co.	12,295,311	John L. Ale	63
Hostettler, Alex	267	Johnson, Caleb	239
House of Brews	162,165	Johnson, Earle	99
House of LaRose	291	Johnson, Patti	169
Housholter, Frederick	275	Johnson, Thaine	153
Howard, Henry	315	Jones Brewing Co.	158
Hoyle, Brian	56,166	Jones, E. O.	232
Huber, Joseph	78	Jones, Jno H.	89
Hubler, Jonathan	275	Joseph, Emil	105,111
Hudepohl Beer	128	Joseph, Isaac	105
Hudepohl Brewing Co.	229,287	Joslin, Augustus	191
Hudepohl, Ludwig	158	Joslin, John	191
Hudepohl-Schoenling Brewing Co.	20,21,158,159	Joslin, Richard	191
Hudson Crossings Restaurant	294	Jung, J. C.	62
Hudy Delight Beer	158,159	Kaenzig, Christian	82
Huebner brewery	131	Kaenzig, Elizabeth	82
Huebner-Toledo Breweries Co.	18	Kaercher, Gustav	83
Huetteman & Cramer Co.	56	Kaffee Hag Corp.	85
Huffman, Robert	172	Kalsen, Otto	103,130
Hug, Edward J.	273	Kapizky, Rudolph	301,307
Hughes Brewing Co.	96	Kappel, O. J.	308
Hughes, Arthur	96	Karm, Fred	268,293
Hughes, Eliza	95	Keane, Thomas J.	70
Hughes, Hazen	80	Kearn, Ed	288
Hughes, John M. brewery	13,81,91-93,95, 96,156	Keenan, Robert	89
		Keg Bottle	148
Hughes, Michael	72	Keifer, Fred	84,256
Humbel, Francis (Frank)	170,191	Keller, George F.	202,203
Humbel, Gottlieb	170	Kellersaft Beer	126
Humel, Adolph	117	Kelley, James F.	135
Humel, Vaclav	116,130	Kelleys Island Brewery	169
Huss, Martin & Co.	270	Kellogg Co.	85
Huster, W. J.	287	Kelly, Jake	170
Hymans, Theodore	168	Kelly, John C.	302
Hynes, John	223	Kempe, Albert	183,228
Ice & Fuel Co., The	224	Kempel, George	277
Ilersich, William	164	Kennedy, Rick	163
Ilg, A. & Co.	176	Kephart, Jack	205,233
Ilg, Anthony	176,177	Kern, Jacob	61
Ilg, Otto	176	Kestel, George M.	310
Illenberger, Max	279,281	Keys, Daniel H.	105,106
Imbery, Hermann	115	Kilburger, Charles	183
Independent Brewing Co. (Ashtabula)	55	Kilburger, John	183
Independent Brewing Co. (Massillon)	275	Kindsvater, Paul	83
Independent Brewing Co. (Pittsburgh)	120,123,232,300	King Kole Beer	122
International Breweries, Inc.	130,146,176	King's Brewery	122
International Harvester Co.	100	Kingsbury Beer	231
Iron Railway	207	Kirkwood, John H.	96
Ironton Brewing Co.	210	Kirn, John	288
Iroquois Beverage Corp.	130	Kirschner, Edward	170
Irr, Joseph	90	Kirsner, Frank K.	242-244
Island Café & Brewpub	169	Klahs, J.	229
Island Gold Beer	246	Klein, Barnhard	273
Island Hops Beer	157	Klein, J. J.	305
Italian Swiss Colony Wine	130	Klein, Joseph L.	131
Ives Brewery	13	Klein, Sophia	199
Ives, Eliza	79	Kline, Samuel	229

Klingler, Henry	255	Kuebler, Gotthold	135
Klingler, Joseph C.	255,256	Kuebler, Gottlieb	109
Klopfenstein, Joseph	260,261	Kuefer, Fred	272
Kloster Brewing Co.	167	Kuehn, August V.	244,310
Knam, Florian	255	Kuehn, George	310,311
Knam, Mary	255	Kuenzil, F. G.	302
Kneisner, John F.	266	Kull, Adolph	288
Kneule, John	211	Kunkle, W. W.	55
Knickerbocker Natural Beer	151	Kuntz, Henry	223
Knobloch, Adam	261	Kunzi, Philip M.	305
Knopp, Frank	116-118	Kupetz, Nicholas	160
Knosman, Henry	211	Kurtz, Jacob	203
Knott, Jacob	229	Kurzenberger, Louis	121
Koch, August W.	201	Kuss, Mark	247
Koch, Christian	288	Kuss, Nancy	247
Koch, R. J.	177	Kuss, Tim	247
Koehler Beer	151,152	Laessle, Philip	183
Koehler, Jackson	52	Laiblin, Charles F.	197
Koenig, Valentine	112	Lais Brewing Co.	192
Koerber Brewing Co.	289	Lais, Anthony	190,191
Koerber, John	288,289,314	Lais, Caroline	190
Koestle, Elizabeth	108	Lais, Charles	190,191
Koestle, Joseph	106-108	Lais, Henry	191-193
Kolar, Chris	245	Lais, John	191
Kolar, Jeff	245	Lais, Joseph	190
Kolp, John A.	277	Lais, William	191
Kolsch Ale	158	Lake City Ice Co.	135
Koons, J. F.	287	Lake Effect Winter Ale	161
Kopp, Anton	110,271	Lamparter, John	288
Koppelman, Edward	171	Lancaster Brewing Co.	183
Koppelman, Harry	171	Lang, Carl F.	131,132,304
Korzenborn, Charles Brewing Co.	211	Lang, Gerhard brewery	90
Korzenborn, Charles	211	Lang, Hascall C.	126,127
Kosmos Export GmbH	232	Lang, John	236
Kraatz, August	61,290	Lang, Michael brewery	236
Kraatz, Charles A.	219,290	Langbehn, Ernst	223
Kraetenbrick, Robert	297	Lange, Albert	306
Kraft, John U.	262	Lanzi, Oscar	171
Kraft, John	249,253	LaRose, Joe	291
Kraft, Nicklaus	313	LaRose, Peter	291
Krantz Brewing Co.	130	LaRose, Tom	291
Kratochvil, Frank	116,117	Last Stop Stout	205
Kraus, J. & Co.	104	Latimer, Pickett	190
Krause, Fred W.	51	Lattimore, Joseph brewery	50,239
Kremer, E.	213	Laubacher, George	266
Kremer, Herbert J.	185	Laube, Joseph X.	242
Kremer, Julius A.	185,213-215	Lauber Bock Beer Co. of Cleveland	167
Kremer, Leo	186	Laux, John & Co.	166
Kremer, Otis	186	Lea, J.	171
Kress Weiss Beer Co.	121	Lea, Sebastian	172
Kress, Andrew	121	Leach, A. B.	194
Kresser, Herbert J.	141	Lechner, Max	256
Kropf Ale Co.	268	Leeper, James	273
Kropf Ale	265	Leetonia Brewing Co.	69,72
Kropf Cream Ale Co.	274	Legends Brewing Co.	216
Kropf, Christian brewery (Jackson Twp.)	267	Leicht, John M.	108,124
Kropf, Christian brewery (Perry Twp.)	268,274	Leisy & Bros. Union Brewery	96,106
Kropf, Christian brewery (Rome)	273	Leisy Beer	55,97-104,241
Kropf, Henry C.	267,268	Leisy blimp	102
Krueger, Carl	246	Leisy, Isaac Brewing Co.	13,19,20,50,52,
Krueger, Chris	246	94,96-104,119,120, 130,142,166,271,291	
Kuebeler Brewing Co.	13,123,126	Leisy Growler	100
Kuebeler, August	177,180	Leisy Pilsner Beer	103
Kuebeler, J. Brewing & Malting Co.	173,177-180	Leisy Premier Theatre	101
Kuebeler, Jacob	124,175,177-180	Leisy Schooner	100
Kuebeler-Stang Brewing & Malting Co.	18,175,180,219	Leisy Sports Review	101
Kuebler Malt Tonic	126	Leisy, August	96,97
Kuebler, Gothold	56	Leisy, Henry	96,97

Leisy, Herbert F.	99,103,104	Ludwig, Joseph A.	121
Leisy, Hugo	99,103	Luehman, Arvid	101
Leisy, Isaac	96-98	"Mabel.....Black Label"	146,152
Leisy, John	96	MacBeth, John S.	80,114,115
Leisy, Otto	16,55,98,124	Mack Brothers Brewery	87
Leisy, Rudolph	96	Mack, Charles	112
Leisy's Dortmunder Beer	100,101	Mack, John M. brewery	87,111,112
Leisy's Mellow-Gold Beer	102	Mack, Matilda	112
Lepper, Gerhart brewery	51	Mack, Matthias	87
Leuthner, Joseph	249	Mack, Morris	112
Lezius, George	113	Mack, William	297
Lezius, Louis	82,90	Mad Crab, The	164,168
Liberty Brewing Co.	291,292	Madden, Dan	55,163
Liberty Street Brewing Co.	21,78,154,165, 292	Maerzluft, Dan	160,161,233
		Maher, George	257
Lift Bridge Brewing Co.	55,163	Mahoning Brewing Co.	223
Lighthouse Gold Beer	157,158	Mahoning Valley Scrappers baseball team	296
Lightkeeper's Ale	245	Mailleard, Pierre	188
Lindley, Joseph	249	Main Sail Ale	66
Lindsay, Henry C.	244	Mall, Jacob Brewing Co.	50,83
Linser, Charles	241,242	Mall, Jacob	83
Linser, Herman	241	Manning, M. I.	55
Linser, Simon Brewing Co.	18,240-242,244	Mansfield Bottling Co.	254
Linser, Simon, Jr.	241	Mansfield City Brewery	249,250,253
Linser, Simon, Sr.	240,241	Marblehead Lighthouse	245
Lion Brewery (Canal Dover)	299	Marblehead Red Pale Ale	245
Lion Brewery (Cincinnati)	168,286	Marietta Brewery	310
Lion Brewery (Cleveland)	83	Marietta Brewing Co. (brewpub)	311
Lion Brewery, Inc. (Cincinnati)	131	Marietta Brewing Co.	58,244,310,311
Lipphardt, Albert	61	Marietta Street Brewery	243
Lipphardt, William	60,61	Market Brewery (Zanesville)	239
Lisch, Frank	266	Marks, Rich	66
Liska, Joseph	116	Marlow, Francis	166
Little Kings Ale	158,159	Marlow, James	166
Livingston, Chris	158,159	Marshall & Boyd brewery	50,238
Lloyd, Henry	81,105,106	Marshall, William	238
Lloyd, James	89	Marshman, Homer	128,129
Lloyd, John	185	Martig, John	269
Lloyd, William	106	Martin Brewery	300
Local Brewing Co.	120,152,165,166	Martin, Nina	300
Lockert, Jacques	282	Martin, William	300
Lockert, Louis	282	Marunowski, Joe	162,165,292
Locktender Lager Beer	154,156	Maser, William	309
Lodge at Hide-A-Way Hills	187	Masino, John	54,55
Loeb, Loeb	207	Massillon Brewing Co.	270,271
Lohmann, Frank C.	305	Matz Brewing Co.	19,59,60
London Brewery	80	Matz Olden Time Beer	59
Lone Ranger	192	Matz, William	59-61,63,65
Long, John	249	Maurer, Frederick	166
Lonz Winery	245	Mayer, Conrad	75
Lopeman, Charles	65	Mayer, Frederick	74
Lorain Brewing & Ice Manufacturing Co.	218	Mayer, G. K.	219
Lorain Brewing Co.	13,124,126,218, 219,291	Mayer, Leo	114
		Mays, Madison	275
Lord Derby Beer and Ale	304	Maytag, Fritz	292
Lord Mansfield Beer	252,253	McCarty, Andrew M.	268
Lord, George	249	McCullogh, Thomas	273
Lottig, Brian	154	McGinnis, Marjorie	159
Louisville Brewing Co.	268,269	McGraw, J. H.	223
Lowe, George J.	53,69	McIntire, John	238
Lowman, David	168	McKechnie, J. & A. Brewing Co.	96
Lowrie, William	104	McKim, Chris	164,165
Lubeck Brewing Co.	87	McKinley, William	259,261
Lucas, H. G. & Co.	79	McLain, James H.	270,271
Lucas, Henry G.	79	Meadville Brewing Co.	53,69,223,255
Lucas, Michael brewery	104,177	Meander Brewing Co.	221
Luckey, George W.	170	Medlin, Wenzl	90,114,116,121,124
Lucky Shoe Beer and Ale	252,280	Medlin, Wenzl's International Weiss Beer Brewery	121

Medscure, John	203	Morley, Philip	68
Megay, Steve	167	Morrison & Wheeler brewery & distillery	50,169
Meister Brau Beer	113	Morrison, Esquire William	169
Meister-Brau Brewing Co.	176	Mosa, Mike	152
Melbourne's Brewing Co.	157,164	Mougey Beverage Co.	315
Melchior, Elizabeth	260	Mougey Ice Co.	315
Melchior, George	260	Mougey, Jacob	314,315
Melchior, Peter brewery	258,260	Moulton, Norman	191
Mellon, Randy	292	Moyers, Peter	188
Menegay, Simon	268	Mueller, Alfred A.	70
Meniken, Philip brewery	168	Mueller, Dr. O.	52
Meredith, George W.	17,68,70,94	Mueller, Ernst W.	88,113,124,125
Merkle, Adolph	243,244	Mueller, Herman	255
Merkle, Edmund	243,244	Mueller, Hermann	88
Merkle, George A.	192	Mueller, Jacob	96
Metzger, Charles	114	Mueller, Julius	88
Meyer, Eugene J.	132	Mueller, Michael	112,167
Meyer, Grover	228	Mueller, Omar E.	113
Meyer, Jacob	207	Mueller, Rudolph	88,110,113
Meyer, Wilbert A.	200	Mug Ale	233,285-287,294
Michel, Charles J.	65	Mugs Brew Pub	248
Michel, McDonough, & Switzer	168	Mugsy's Brewpub	294
Michelob Beer	21,246	Mulcahy, Cornelius	291
Mickley, Mike	267	Mulcahy, John J.	291
Milan Brewing Corp.	50,170	Munich Brewery, Inc.	266
Milan Springs Beer and Ale	171	Munter, Joseph, Jr.	263,265
Miller High Life Beer	146	Murphey, C. G.	215
Miller Spreader Co.	229,281	Murray, W. D.	224
Miller, Abraham	85,86	Muskingum Steam Brewery	239,243
Miller, Bernhard	199	Muth, George V.	108,110
Miller, Frederick Brewing Co. (Milwaukee)	13,20,138,148, 149,151,152,168,232	Muth, George	108
		Muth, Matthias	108
Miller, Frederick	51	Myers, George	111
Miller, John	167	Myers, Robert	281
Miller, Joseph (Mt. Vernon)	202	Naftzger, Frank	315
Miller, Joseph (Huron)	193	Nash, William	171
Miller, Philip	298,300	Nation, Carry	23
Miller, Steven	157,160	National Bohemian Beer	149
Miller, W. C.	210	National Brewing & Distributing Co.	167
Millersburg Brewery	188	National Brewing Co.	148,149
Millinger, Jim	245	National Register of Historic Places	133,177,253
Milt and Gold Lager Beer	177	Nebel, Joseph	267
Minto, Richard	185	Neel, George C.	65
Mitenzwey, Henry	152	Neel, R. Shively	65
Mitermiler, Andrew	94,97,116	NeHi soda	272
Mithoff, Edward	182	Neidmayer, George J.	72
Mithoff, Theodore	181,182	Ness, Eliot	153
Mitseff, Boris	70	Neubrand, George	77
Mittleberger, Edmund G. P.	177	Neugart, Charles F.	59
Moeller, Carl F.	137,305	Neumann, Charles	127
Moerlein Brewing Co.	12,16,207,225, 309,311	New Albion Brewery	153
		New Berlin Brewing Co.	267
Moff, George	72,73,221	New Philadelphia Brewery, Inc.	304-306
Moff, John	72	New Philadelphia Brewing Co.	12,50,131,262, 272,299-303,307
Moff, William	73,221		
Moinet, Joseph	268	New York Special Beer	175,176
Moinet, Peter B.	268	New York Special Brew	126,129
Molson Breweries	149	Newark Beer	213
Monroeville Brewery	190,191	Newark Brewery	211
Montag, Nicholas	298-300	Newarth, Daniel	73
Montag, Valentine	298	Newarth, Kasper	73
Moondog Ale	154,155	Newell, David	300
Moran, E. L.	230	Newman, Edward P.	210
Morath, Augustus	212	Newman, George	79
Morath, Michael	74,211,212	Newman, Thomas	82,166
Morgan, Bill	160,161	Newman, Thomas, Jr.	82
Morgan, John V.	56	Nichols, Louis H.	70
Morledge, Roger	275	Nielson, Cornelius	174

Nighman, George	257,258	Original ESB Beer	158
Nighman, Lydia	258	Orlik, Henryk	163
Nighman, Thaddeus C.	258	Ortlieb, Henry Brewing Co.	151
Nikolas, Jacob	262	Oshe, Charles J.	244
Nisbet, Edward A.	223	Ott, Augustus	192,193
Noggle, W. J.	315	Ott, Edward J.	193
Noll, Charles P.	182,183	Ott, Peter	192,193
Noll, Herbert	101	Ott, Theresa	192,193
Normann, Frank L.	242	P. O. C. Beer	20,116-120,137, 151,152,166,342
Norment, R. T.	63		
North Shore Export Brewing Co.	77	Paas, Edward	57
Northern Breweries Co.	206	Pabst Beer	87,199
Northern Trail Nut Brown Ale	205	Pabst Brewing Co.	20,106,140,141, 148,149,151,152,167,201,232
Northfield Park Microbrewery	295		
Northstar Golden Light Ale	294	Pabst Old Tankard Ale	142
Norwalk Brewery	192	Packaging Corp. of America	103
O'Donnell, John M.	135	Paczek, Henry	70
O'Donnell, Leo J.	235,267	Painesville Brewery	204,205
O'Donnell, Vincent	235	Painter, George brewery	50,238
O'Hooley's Pub and Brewery	56	Painter, George	14
O'Marah, Patrick	168	Palmer, Jim	187
O'Neil, Rory	292	Panck, Albert	131
O'Neill Brewing Co.	295	Pannonia Brewing Co.	77
O'Neill, Joseph	295	Parkhurst, Ross W.	65
O'Reilly, Brian	162	Parsons, Toby	160,162
O'Reilly, John J.	68,223	Paschen, William	111
Oberholtz, Christopher	277	Patterson, Henry	299
Oberholtz, Frederick brewery	177,277,288	Patton, Frank	56
Oberholtz, Susannah	277	Pavlik, Jaro	85-87,116,128, 134,135
Obert, William F.	70		
Ochs, Christian	181	Payer, Frank	89
Ochs, Frederick	181	Pearse, James	192
Ochs, George	181	Pedaline, Joe	231
Ogden, Jeff	161	Peerless Motor Company	19,139,140
Ogren, Charles	232	Peerless Stove Co.	177
Ohio and Erie Canal	75,79,80,95,96, 154,257,271,273,276,281,298,301,303,306,308,312	Pennsylvania & Ohio Canal	277,293,297
		Peoples Brewing Co.	149
Ohio Brewers Association	84	Peoples Coal & Beverage Co. (Massillon)	272
Ohio Brewing Co. (Columbus)	118	Pepsi-Cola	231
Ohio Brewing Co. (Youngstown)	231	Perkins, Daniel	224
Ohio Brewing Co. (Niles)	295,296	Perlex Beverage	91
Ohio Gang	26	Perry Brew	180
Ohio State Brewers Association	126,208	Perry, Oliver Hazard	169,180,246
Ohio Union Brewing Co.	53	Persch, John P.	123
Ohio Wine Co.	60	Peru Brewery	193
Old '93 Beer	171	Petrescu-Boboc, Sorin	164
Old Beeswing Ale	79	Pfeifer, George	203
Old Bohemia Lager Beer	304-306	Pfeiffer, John	68
Old Cockney Ale	280	Pfeil, Henry	174
Old Crown Brewing Co.	229	Pflaumer, William H.	151
Old Holland Brewing Co.	167	Phelan, Robert J.	267
Old Leghumper Porter	268,293	Phoenix Brewery (Sandusky)	172
Old Lockport Lager Beer	304	Phoenix Brewing Co. (Cleveland)	107,110,123,124
Old Mammoth Stout	76	Piel Bros. Brewing Co.	71
Old Oxford Ale	227-229	Piero, William J.	268
Old South Brewing Co., Inc.	64	Pilsener Brewing Co.	20,50,84,85,102, 103,116-121,123,131,137,142,151,166
Old Tavern Brew	65		
Old Tavern Brewing Co.	167	Pilsener Cellars	118
Old Timers Ale	127,129,175,176	Pilsener Ice, Fuel, & Beverage Co.	117
Old Town Beer and Ale	215	Pilsener Square	117
Olde Jaol Brewing Co.	315	Pink Elephant Ale	63,64
Olde Vat Beer	304-306	Pittsburgh Brewing Co.	68,123,168
Oldfield, Barney	139	Plocher, Andrew	218
Olivo, Dominic	70	Polizzi, Alfred "Big Al"	87
Oompa Loompa Cream Stout	164	Pollner, W. C.	105
Oppman Brewing Co.	13,90,109	Pontiac Improvement Co.	99,103
Oppmann, Andrew	106	Porter, A. & Co.	107
Oppmann, Andrew W.	108-110	Porter, Thomas W.	200

Portsmouth Brewing & Ice Co.	59	Renner, George J.	225,250,251,278,279,281,314
Powell, Charles R.	58	Renner, George J., Jr.	224-227,251,278,314
Powerhouse Pale Ale	160	Renner, Julia	252
Premier Malt Products Co.	200,201	Renner, Robert "Bob"	227-229
Prentiss, Charles P.	190	Renner, William	278,279
Prize Cup Beer	227	RENO non-alcoholic beer	226
Progress Beer	70	Renz, Charles	135
Prohibition Party	24	Reubensaal, G.	166
Prosek, John	166	Rex, Harry R.	268
Prouty, Jim	56	Reynolds, H. M.	55
Pusch, Charles T.	177	Reynolds, J. P.	56
Put-In-Bay Brewing Co.	246	Rheingold Beer	151
Quarry Ridge Brewpub	78	Rheingold Breweries, Inc.	151
Quarryman Taverne	78	Rheingold Brewing Co.	152
Quasser, Louis	194	Rich, Christian	313
Queen City Brewing Co.	130	Rich, John	313
Quinn, John	81	Rich, Martin L.	313,314
Raible, Paul	176	Rich, Peter brewery	13,313
Railway Razz Beer	205	Richter, George	225
Rall, Charles L.	199	Rickrich Brothers Brewery	213
Rall, Lucie	199	Rickrich, Charles	212,213
Ramseyer, Joseph J.	313,314	Rickrich, Philip	212,213
Ranft, Joseph	83	Rickrich, Wilhelm	212,213
Rapp, Fidel	310	Ricksaker, David	273
Rapp, William	310	Ridenour, G. D.	56
Raspberry Leghumper	268,293	Rider, Ray	217
Raspiller, Charles	262	Rikart, George	249
Rastetter, Tim	154,292	Rindelhardt, Otto P.	141,143
Rathbone, Basil	101	Ringneck Brewing Co.	164,216
Rattler Red Ale	160	Riverbend Red Ale	160
Raub, William	297	Riverside Brewing Co. (Zanesville)	240,244,310
Razinger, Frank	171,230	Riverside Brewing Co. (Columbus)	119
Rea, Dr. Joseph L.	143	Robust Porter	158
Reading Brewing Co.	151	Roby, Henry	190
Reagan, T. J.	205	Roby, John S.	190
Real Ale Festival	164,165	Roby, Ruel	190
Real Brewery, Inc.	152	Rochotte, Henry	89
Red Band Beer	251,252	Rock Bottom Restaurant and Brewery	21,160,162,163
Red Band Pale Ale	254	Rock Hill Brewery	212
Red Brick Brewery	167	Rockefeller Bock Beer	154
Red Cap Ale	87,133,139,140,142-149	Rockefeller, John D.	153
Red Label Beer	137,138	Rockwood Brewing Corp.	64
Red Star Brewery	242,243	Rocky River Brewing Co.	163,246
Red Top Brewing Co.	20	Rodewig, Charles W.	58
Red Velvet Ale	137,138	Rogers, Charles C.	80,82,128
Regal Lager Beer	118	Rogers, William H.	80,82
Reichert, Jacob	211	Rohrer, Frederick tavern and brewery	50,202,203
Reilly, William F.	242	Roller Mill Brewery	234
Reiman, Andrew	250	Rommel, Edward	262,264
Reindl, Gottfried	108	Rommel, John G.	262-265
Reiser, A. W.	302	Rommel, William	262,263
Reisner, H.	171	Ronneburg Brewery-Youngstown	232
Relker, John	308	Roos, John	262
Renner & Weber Brewing Co.	50,249-253,278,280,314	Roosevelt, Franklin D.	27,279
Renner Akron Realty Co.	281	Rose Law	18,25,54,57,67,69,72,186,194,200,209,219,234,263,299,300,303,311,315
Renner Brewing Co. (Youngstown)	13,20,50,53,69,223,226,231,255,281	Roshong, Howard N.	266
Renner Golden Amber Beer	228,229	Ross, James	195,197,275
Renner Premium Beer and Ale	227,228	Rossel, Harry W.	214
Renner Products Co.	19,251,279	Rossel, Harry W., Jr.	215
Renner Realty Co.	226	Rosser, E. J.	56
Renner Yellow Band Lager Beer	278	Roth Brewing Co.	231
Renner, Eleanora	278,279	Roth, Charles	51
Renner, Emil	225-229	Roth, Frank M.	192
Renner, George J. Brewing Co.	12,27,50,229,250,252,277-281,284,288,314	Roth, Jacob	268,314
		Rothman's Pall Mall, Ltd.	141,148

Rowe, Francis	79	Schmidt, C. W.	88
Rowe, G. M.	65	Schmidt, Carl	88
Rowley, Young H.	202	Schmidt, Charles	88
Royal Crown Cola	272	Schmidt, Christian Brewing Co.	21,151
Ruble, Edward A.	90	Schmidt, Emil	58
Ruch, Christian	257,273	Schmidt, Godfrey brewery	188,189
Ruch, Michael	257	Schmidt, Herman	113
Rudy, Isaac	273	Schmidt, Jacob Brewing Co.	152
Rumbach, Conrad	58,59	Schmitt, Albert	242
Runge, F.	314	Schmitt, Alois	242
Ruof, Christian	307	Schmitt, William	242
Rupp, Nicholas	190	Schmutzler, Frederick	249
Rush Creek Brewery	187	Schneible, Joseph Co.	52
Russell, Henry E.	147,148	Schneider, Charles	310
Russer, John	302	Schneider, Christian	110,111
Russo, David	292	Schneider, Elizabeth	310
Rust Belt Brewing Co.	167	Schneider, Ernest	257
Salem Brewery	73,94	Schneider, John (Union Brewery-Cleveland)	111
Samman, George P.	256	Schneider, John (Marietta Brewery)	310
Samman, Peter	256	Schneider, John (Schlather Brewery-Cleveland)	94
Samuel Adams Beers	158,161	Schneider, Julius	275
San Jose Sharks NHL team	85	Schneider, Martin	310
Sanders, E. B.	122	Schneider, Peter C.	168
Sands' Ale	168	Schneider, William & Co.	110
Sandusky Brewing Co.	177	Schneider, William	59
Sandusky City Brewery	176,177	Schneidt, Henry J.	214,215
Sanka	19,85	Schoenbrunn spring water	304
Santa's Lil' Helper Christmas Ale	164	Schoenhofen, Peter Brewing Co.	168,232
Sapienza, Anthony C.	148,150,151	Schoenling Brewing Co.	19,158,229,287
Sarstedt, F. A.	105	Scholder, Henry	259,275
Sasquatch Pale Ale	76	Scholder, John brewery	259
Sauber, Kelly	56,311	Scholl, John brewery	170
Saules, L. A.	55	Schott, Christian	271
Savage, John	218	Schram, Garfield, & Co.	204
Schaefer Brewing Co. of Ohio, Inc.	138	Schram, S. S.	204
Schaefer, F. & M. Brewing Co.	138	Schram, Simon	72
Schaefer, Frederick	138	Schrider, Jason	162
Schaefer, Maximilian	138	Schroeder, Carl F.	113
Schaefer, Rudolph J. III	138	Schuch, Henry	315
Schaefer, Rudolph J.	138	Schuh, Philip	224
Schaffer, Ernhart H. brewery	198	Schumacher, William F.	263,266
Schaffer, Frederick	234	Schumann, Adam	108
Schaller & Gerke Brewing Co.	225	Schuster & Co.	272
Schauweker, Christian	263,266	Schuster Beer	267
Scheer, Fred	246	Schuster Brewing Co.	167,262,272,299, 302
Scheidt, Adam Brewing Co.	138	Schuster, Carl T.	266
Schell, Theodore	282	Schuster, Frank H.	272
Scheu, Walter H.	300	Schuster, John W.	263,264,271,272
Schillp, John	72	Schuster, William A.	266,272,308
Schimke, Robert	271	Schwertner, Anton	262
Schimkola, Joseph	77	Schwope, Carl	234
Schlather Pilsener Beer	126	Scior, John	251
Schlather, Frederick	93	Scofield, John brewery	201
Schlather, L. Brewing Co.	17,52,68,73,93-95,124,126,155,279,288,295	Scotch Highland Ale	304-306
Schlather, Leonhard	16,81,91-95,98,307	Seamon, Martin	310
		Seattle Brewing & Malting Co.	83
Schlee, Nicholas Brewing Co.	243	Seeger, Christian	224
Schleininger, George L.	263	Seeger, John hotel and brewery	221
Schliner, James	315	Seeger, Matthias	224
Schlitz Beer	101,142,199,231	Seesdorf, Philip brewery	275
Schlitz, Joseph Brewing Co.	20,140-142,147,167	Segal, Joseph	106
		Seher, William B.	219
Schmid, David	241,244	Seiberling, John F.	290
Schmid, W. A.	118	Seibold Products Co.	19,303
Schmidt & Hoffman Brewery	83,88,260,271	Seibold, Anton	302
Schmidt, C. & Sons Brewing Co.	120,138,149-153,229	Seibold, Henry	299,302-304
		Seibold, John	12,303,304

Seibold, Michael	12,301-304
Seidenstricker, Joseph	235
Seiferth, John	261
Seikel, Jacob	306,307
Seikel, Lewis A.	295
Seiler, Alois	266
Seippel, George	270
Seipro Liquid Malt Syrup	304
Sellinger, Frank	287
Selzer, Frank	288
Settlers Ale	157,158
Seyfferle, William	235
Seyler, Carl	89
Shaffer, John	308
Shaffrank, Elliott J.	267
Shanty Ale	254
Sheffield, Emory	78
Shener, Peter	310
Sheridan, Stuart	157,158,166
Shidler, William	255
Shipler, George	197
Shiras, William, Jr.	197
Sholtz Beer	171
Shupe, Charles	172
Shutts, Benjamin	166
Shutts, George	166
Siberian Night Russian Imperial Stout	293
Sidlow, Saul	266
Siebel Institute of Brewing	161-163,165, 169,247
Siegle, Louis T.	72
Signorino, Angelo	216
Silhavy, John	131
Silver Bond Beer	230
Silver Label Beer	183
Sims, Jason	205
Singer, W. D.	63
Singleton, Darlene	267
Singleton, David	267
Sioux City Brewing Co.	279
Sleigh, George	74
Sleigh, George, Jr.	74
Smith Brewing Co.	50,53,69,223,255
Smith Products Co.	223
Smith, Alfred	222,223
Smith, Andrew M.	315
Smith, Blasius	190
Smith, C. S.	55
Smith, Enoch	224
Smith, Gavin	161
Smith, George	224
Smith, J. B. & Co.	166
Smith, James	315
Smith, John (Marietta)	309
Smith, John (Youngstown)	222
Smith, John B. (Cleveland)	81
Smith, John, Jr.	222
Smith, John's Sons Brewing Co.	223,224
Smith, Roy R.	215
Smithville Brewery	312,313
Snajdr, Vaclav	116
Snavely, A. J.	299
Sneaky Pete	228
Snyder International Brewing Group, LLC	158,159
Snyder, C. David	158,159
Snyder, Christian	273
Snyder, Jacob	273
Sobotka, Zdenek	116
Soergel, George	176
Solo Temperance Beverage	265
Sommer Bros. brewery (Perry Twp.)	274
Sommer, Christian	274
Sommer, Henry	273,274
Sommer, John	273,274
Sondregger, Emil	275
Soulter, Frederick	202
South Akron Brewery	282
South Side Brewery (New Philadelphia)	301
Souvenir Beer	280,281
Spark-Lin-Ale Co.	63
Spear, Hannibal E.	81
Specht, Charles W. brewery	292
Specht, Christina	292
Spencer Brewing Co.	96
Spencer, Hugh	80,96
Spietschka, Vinzenz	116
Spring Hill Brewery	213
Spring Street Brewery (Cleveland)	81,91,95
Squire, Andrew	105
St. Hazards Village on the Beach	246
Stacy, Thomas	166
Stadden, John	201
Stadium Lager Beer	158
Stadler, A. W.	269
Stag Beer	146,149
Stahl, John	300
Stamberger, Henry	128
Standard Brewing Co. (New Castle, PA.)	53,69,223,255
Standard Brewing Co. (Cleveland)	17,19,20,50,85, 102,121,123,125,133-138,142,149
Standard Food Products Co.	135
Standard Gold Beer	223
Standard Premium Beer	137,138
Standish, Zechariah Miles brewery	192
Stang Brewing Co.	13,50,123,126, 127,172-175
Stang, Frank	172-174,177
Stang, John	172-175,180
Star Brewery (Cleveland)	89,108,167
Star Brewery (Norwalk)	190-193
Star Brewing Co. (Cleveland)	108,123-125
Star Brewing Co. (Minster)	18
Star Brewing Co. (Zanesville)	240,242
Star Ice & Storage Co. (Zanesville)	244
Stark Brewing Co.	17,18,262-264, 266,272,299,302
Stark Lager Beer	264
Stark Velvet Beer	299
Stark-Tuscarawas Breweries Co.	18,262-266,272, 275,299,302,303
Stark-Tuscarawas Products Co.	264,303
Starlight Beer	95,126
Star-Peerless Brewing Co.	130
Stauzel, Frederick brewery	236
Steel City Beer	230
Steel City Brewing Co.	220
Steideman, O. F.	143
Stein, George F. Brewing Co.	102
Steinkerchner, Edward	281
Steinkirchner, John	252
Steinmetz, Andrew	166
Sterling, John	106
Stern Enterprises	152
Steuben Beverage Works	200
Steuben Brew	199,200
Steuben Brewing Co.	200

Steubenville Brewery	50,195-197	Troendle, Peter	191
Steubenville Pure Milk Co.	201	Trommer, John F. Brewing Co.	71
Stevens, John C.	244	Troyan, Joseph F.	17,130
Stine, Leona	183	Tru-Bru Beer	254
Stockade Brewery (Marietta)	309	Truby, John W.	210
Stoehr, Bernhard E.	309	Tuborg Beer	149
Stoffel, William	70	Tucker, Joseph A.	266,267
Stoltz, John	277	Tudor Beer and Ale	286
Stone, Frank D.	80	Turnbull, Joseph	68,69
Stoolmiller, John	270	Tuscarawas Valley Brewing Co.	18,131,298,300, 301
Stoppel Co-Operative Brewing Co.	105		
Stoppel, Alphonso	105	Tuscora Beer	263,264,267
Stoppel, J. & Co.'s Belle View Brewery	104,166	Tuscora Brewing Co.	264
Stoppel, Joseph	104	Tuscora Near Beer	303,304
Stoppel, Omar	105	Tutbury, John	81
Stoppel's Actien Brewery	104	Tveekrem, Andy	154
Stoppel's Sons & Co.	105	Twist & Stout	161
Storer, James	111	Uehlein, August	90
Strangmann, Carl A.	108	Ulrich, Harry	291
Strasburg Brewery	306,307	Umbstaetter malt house & distillery	114
Streck, Robert	170	Umbstaetter, Louis	166
Strickland, Lawrence J.	143	Ungerleider, Samuel	63,65
Strobel, Herman	208	Union Brewery (Loudonville)	51
Strobel, John G.	176	Union Brewery (Mansfield)	249,250,253
Stroh Brewery Co.	138,149,152,157, 167,168	Union Brewery (Marietta)	309,310
		Union Brewing Co. (Canton)	12,13,260-262
Strongsville Brewing Co.	164	Union Brewing Co. (Sharon, PA.)	53,69,223,255
Stuhldreher, Jacob	275	Union Brewing Co. (Cleveland)	111,123
Stumpf, Louis	81	United States Brewers Association	24,84,126,208
Stumpf, Martin	81,83,106	Unruh, Brad	165,294
Stumpf, Michael	81,83	Urlau, Robert	190
Stumpf, William	81	Urlau, Rupp, & Co.	190
Sub Chaser Hefe-Weizen Beer	164	vacuum aging process	102
Suffigkeit	20,227	vacuum fermentation technology	105
Suhr, Robert C.	118	van de Westelaken, Frank P.	127,128
Sullivan, Frank	118	Van Sweringen, Mantis	91
Sumner Dairy Co.	290	Van Sweringen, Oris	91
Sunrise Beer and Ale	85,86,230	Vandegrift, Brian	162
Sunrise Brewing Co.	50,85,140,142	Varrelmann, Gustave	185
Sutula, Dave	78,162,205	Velvet Brew Beer	264
Swartz, Max	305,306	Verich Ale	296
Sykes, William H. brewery	78	Verich Gold Beer	231
Sylla Bottling Co.	168	Verich, Chris	231,295,296
Taggart, William	193	Verich, Michael	231,295,296
Tangeman, Carl	215	Viall, James	276
Tankard Can	148	Viall, Marshall brewery	276
Tawney Dairy Products Co.	295	Vigne, Jean	14
Taylor, E. P.	140,141,143,145, 148	Vis Vitae Lager Beer	261
		Voelker, Catherine brewery	115
Taylor, H. Mendel	65	Voelker, Jacob	115
Terminal Stout	160	Voelker, Jacob, Jr.	115
Thirsty Dog Brewing Co. (Copley)	293	Vogel, John E.	58
Thirsty Dog Brewing Co. (Jackson Twp.)	268	Vogt, Daisy	215
Thompson, "Mother" Elizabeth	24	Vogt, Ulreh	215
Thompson, Robert	197	Vogt, Ulreh, Jr.	215
Tip Top Beer (Cambridge)	185	Volkopf, Conrad	111
Tip Top Beer (Youngstown)	223	Volstead Act	26,27,126
Tip Top Beer (Cleveland)	87	Volstead, Andrew	26
Tip Top Brewing Co.	87,143,230	VonLuebtow, Oscar A.	263
Tip Top Distributing Co.	87	Wagner Brewing Co. (Granite City, IL.)	117
Tiro Cereal Beverage	289	Wagner, August & Sons Brewing Co.	215,254
Toby Ale	118,142	Wagner, Charles L.	174
Tomlinson, C. brewery	172	Wagner, George J.	143
Tonawanda Brewing Co.	54	Wagner, George	262
Toole, Michael	267	Wagner, Jacob brewery	106
Topaz Beer	266	Wagner, John C.	60,61
Topper, John C.	53,54	Wagner, Nicholas	177
Troendle, George	192	Wagner, Otto	210

Wahl & Henius College/Institute	54,262,285,299,302
Wahl College of Brewing	227
Wahl, Dr. Arnold	227
Wainwright, Jarvis	239
Wainwright, Samuel J.	68,70,223
Waldeck, Jacob	297
Waldorf Beer and Ale	132
Waldron, Dr. F. H.	300
Wallaby's Brewing Co.	165
Wallaby's Grille & Brewpub (Cleveland)	162,163
Wallaby's Grille & Brewpub (Medina)	233
Wallaby's Grille & Brewpub (Westlake)	165,292,294
Wallaby's Grille (Mentor)	206
Wallaby's Grille (Salem)	73
Wallaby's Grille (Sandusky)	180
Walleye Wheat Beer	160
Walleye's, J. F. Eatery & Brewery	245,246
Walling, Henry	257
Wal-Mart stores	120
Walter Brewing Co.	103
Walton, Sam	120
Ward, Mark	78,157
Warner, Daniel	204
Washington Brewery (Zanesville)	13,239,240
Watson, Eric	231
Watt, John B.	58
Weaner, Frank A.	305
Weaver, Gustave	226
Weaver, Harry	226,227,230
Weaver, John	250,251
Weaver, Sherman	251
Webb Corporation	70
Webber, Ambrose E.	70
Webber, Leonard C.	70,71
Webber, M.	270
Webber's Old Lager Beer	70
Weber Brewing Co. (Cincinnati)	13
Weber, Adolph	252
Weber, Henry	249-251,253
Weber, Jacob	309
Weber, Julius	251,252
Weber, Otto	27,267
Weber, William	107
Weber's Beer	252,280
Weideman, J. C.	114
Weidenkopf, Frederick	104
Weigand, Leo brewery	188,189
Weiner, Anton "Tony"	281
Weis, Frederick	13,314
Weisgerber, Ernst	106
Weishaar, Michael	201
Weisman, Robert	314
weiss beer	112,115,120,121,133,292
Weiss, John F.	263,264
Weiss, Joseph	215
Weiss, M. J.	266
Weitz, A. V.	308
Weitzman, A. H.	230
Weldon, Dr. Samuel J.	79
Wells, Bazaleel	197
Wellston Brewing & Ice Co.	70,194
Wellston Ice and Cold Storage Co.	194
Wellston Ice Co.	194
Welsh, Don	254
Wertheimer, Al	104
Wertz, Peter	166
West End Brewing Co.	168
West Virginia Brewing Co.	210
Western Reserve Brewing Co. (Warren)	297
Western Reserve Brewing Co. (Cleveland)	161
Wheeler, John	169
Wheeler, Wayne	25-27
Wheeling Terminal Railway	61
Whistle Orange Drink	18,126,264,284,303,311
White Cliff Pale Ale	294
White Crown Beer and Ale	291
White Label Pilsener Beer	71
White Rock Beer	289
White Rock Brewing Co.	295
White Rock Dairy	290
White Rock Mineral Water Co.	284,290
White Top Brewery	213
White, Oscar F. brewery	205
White, Paul A.	119
Whitlock, John	104
Wiedemann Brewing Co.	232
Wiener, E. H. Corp.	290
Wiener, Emmanuel H.	290
Wildermuth Brewing Co. (postPro)	235
Wildermuth, Charles	234,235
Wildermuth, David	234
Wildermuth, Gottlieb Brewing Co. (prePro)	234,235
Wildermuth, Gottlieb	234
Wildermuth, Max W.	234,235
Wilkinson, Lysander B.	78
Willard, Frances	24
Willey, Elijah F. brewery	80
Willoughby Brewing Co.	78,205
Willoughby Wheat Beer	205
Willoughby, Alfred	216
Wills, Bud	301
Wimmer, Sebastian	58,59,185
Windisch, George	172,177
Windisch-Muhlhauser Brewing Co.	52,131,168,198,207,286
Winefordner, Joe B.	56
Wirth, Joseph C.	282
Wittlinger, George	107
Wittman, Julius	270,271
WKYC-TV	87
Wolf Ledge Brewery	282
Wolf, Anthony	248
Wolf, James C.	116,117
Women's Christian Temperance Union	24,28
Wooden Pony Brewing Co.	254
Wooden Shoe Brewery	306
Woodring, Sam	288
Wooster Artificial Ice & Brewing Co.	266,315
Wooster Brewing Co.	13,314,315
Wooster Lager Beer	315
World Beer Championships	155,158,160,165,205,245,296
World Beer Cup	155,158,161,164,233,268,293
Wright, Garin	76
Wright, Glenn L.	221
Wright, John C.	197
Wyman, Thomas F.	81
X-L-N-T De-Alcoholized Beer	131
Yahraus, Charles	89
Yako beverage	113
Ye Old Lager Beer	84
Yellow Band Beer	226

Yough Brewing Co.	231
Young, Edward	315
Young, Jacob	238
Young, Theabold David brewery	237
Young, Wendell brewery	315
Younger, John	202
Younghans, George	181
Younghans, Justus brewery	13,181
Youngstown Brewery	222
Youngstown Brewing Co. (postPro)	227,229-230
Youngstown Brewing Co. (prePro)	223
Youngstown Cartage Co.	230
Youngstown Temperance Beer Co.	232
Zahler, Jacob	298
Zane, Jonathan	238
Zanesville Star Bottling Works	242
Zanini, Dominick	72
Zeile, Charles	53
Zelle, Gustav	73,94
Zepp Brew	251,279,280,284
Zest Beer	263,264,267,272
Zika, Joseph	110
Zimmerman, Francis	197,198
Zink, William	181
Zinsmaster, Jacob	273
Zinsmeister, Henry	240
Zix, Anton	70,194
Zix, Rosa	194
Zoar Society Brewery	15,50,272,307, 308
Zunt Heit Beer	116

DEDICATION

As a personal note, I thought I'd add one last page to dedicate this book to my mother, who died six months before the book was finished. While going through old family photos, I came across this one, showing my parents Frances and Irv (at the right) relaxing with friends on a beach at Lake Erie around 1950 (more than a decade before I was born). Although my parents were never heavy drinkers, there is no mistaking the carton of P.O.C. Beer from Cleveland in the background. At least when they did drink, they supported the local brewing industry! As I mentioned in the acknowledgements section, my parents have always been amazingly supportive of my hobby, and Mom will be missed forever......